Lecture Notes in Computer Science 11368

More information about this series at http://www.springer.com/series/7410

Tanja Lange · Orr Dunkelman (Eds.)

Progress in Cryptology – LATINCRYPT 2017

5th International Conference on Cryptology
and Information Security in Latin America
Havana, Cuba, September 20–22, 2017
Revised Selected Papers

 Springer

Editors
Tanja Lange
Technische Universiteit Eindhoven
Eindhoven, The Netherlands

Orr Dunkelman ⓘ
University of Haifa
Haifa, Israel

ISSN 0302-9743   ISSN 1611-3349   (electronic)
Lecture Notes in Computer Science
ISBN 978-3-030-25282-3   ISBN 978-3-030-25283-0   (eBook)
https://doi.org/10.1007/978-3-030-25283-0

LNCS Sublibrary: SL4 – Security and Cryptology

This Springer imprint is published by the registered company Springer Nature Switzerland AG
The registered company address is: Gewerbestrasse 11, 6330 Cham, Switzerland

Preface

This book constitutes the proceedings of the 5th International Conference on Cryptology and Information Security in Latin America, LATINCRYPT 2017, held in La Habana, Cuba, in September 2017.

LATINCRYPT 2017 used a double-blind review process applied to the 64 submissions from 25 countries all over the world. After a careful review process (where submissions received at least three reviews, and committee member submissions received at least five reviews), which included more than 300 comments, the Program Committee selected 20 papers for presentation and publication.

Along with the 20 presentations of the selected contributions, attendees of LATINCRYPT 2017 enjoyed three invited talks: by Nadia Heninger, who discussed "Adventures in RSA Key Recovery," Phil Rogaway, who publicly admitted he has "An Obsession with Definitions," and Adi Shamir, who talked about "Towards Quantitative Analysis of Cyber Security." We are grateful for the contributed paper by Phil Rogaway that captures his invited talk.

We would like to express our sincere gratitude to all the members of the Program Committee, as well as all the additional reviewers who helped in the challenging reviewing process, composed of close to 210 reviews. The submission and review processes were done using the iChair software package, and we wish to express our sincere gratitude to Thomas Baignères and Matthieu Finiasz for the iChair software, which facilitated a smooth and easy submission and review process.

We would like to thank the general chair, Prof. Luis Ramiro Piñeiro Díaz, and the local organizing team. In addition, we would like to thank the LATINCRYPT Steering Committee, and especially Francisco Rodríguez-Henríquez for making this conference possible.

April 2019

Tanja Lange
Orr Dunkelman

Organization

Progress in Cryptology – LATINCRYPT 2017

La Habana, Cuba, September 20–22, 2017

General Chair

Luis Ramiro Piñeiro Díaz	Universidad de La Habana, Cuba

Program Chairs

Orr Dunkelman	University of Haifa, Israel
Tanja Lange	Technische Universiteit Eindhoven, The Netherlands

Steering Committee

Michel Abdalla	École Normale Supérieure, France
Diego Aranha	University of Campinas, Brazil
Paulo S. L. M. Barreto	University of Washington Tacoma, USA and Universidad São Paulo, Brazil
Ricardo Dahab	University of Campinas, Brazil
Alejandro Hevia	Universidad de Chile, Chile
Julio López	University of Campinas, Brazil
Daniel Panario	Carleton University, Canada
Francisco Rodríguez-Henríquez	CINVESTAV-IPN, Mexico
Alfredo Viola	Universidad de la República, Uruguay

Program Committee

Diego Aranha	University of Campinas, Brazil
Roberto Avanzi	ARM, Germany
Shi Bai	Florida Atlantic University, USA
Paulo S. L. M. Barreto	University of Washington Tacoma, USA and Universidad São Paulo, Brazil
Lejla Batina	Radboud University, The Netherlands
Iddo Bentov	Cornell University, USA
Daniel J. Bernstein	University of Illinois at Chicago, USA and Technische Universiteit Eindhoven, The Netherlands
Joppe W. Bos	NXP Semiconductors, Belgium

Additional Reviewers

Akash Shah
Alex Davidson
Alfred Menezes
Alfredo Viola
Andrew Klapper
Bart Mennink
Benedikt Gierlichs
Berkant Ustaoglu
Boris Skoric
Carles Padro
Carmit Hazay
Chitchanok Chuengsatiansup
Emmanuelle Anceaume
Felix Günther
Frank Blom
Gregory Neven
Gunnar Hartung
Harry Halpin
Jens Groth
Joan Daemen
John Sheekey
Joost Renes
Junqing Gong

Luca Allodi
Marcel Keller
Meilof Veeningen
Miroslav Knezevic
Nabil Alkeilani Alkadri
Niels de Vreede
Patrick Longa
Philippe Gaborit
Po-Chun Kuo
Ralph Ankele
Ratna Dutta
R. Kabaleeshwaran
Sanjay Deshpande
Sayantan Mukherjee
Sebastien Duval
Shai Halevi
Steve Lu
Stjepan Picek
Tapas Pandit
Thomas Peters
Wei-Kai Lin
Weiqiang Wen
Yosuke Todo

Contents

Theory of Symmetric-Key Cryptography

Multiparty Computation and Privacy

New Constructions

Adversarial Cryptography

Invited Talk

An Obsession with Definitions

Phillip Rogaway$^{(\boxtimes)}$

Department of Computer Science, University of California, Davis, USA
rogaway@cs.ucdavis.edu

Abstract. Many people seem to think that cryptography is all about creating and analyzing cryptographic schemes. This view ignores the centrality of *definitions* in shaping the character of the field. More than schemes or their analysis, it is definitions that most occupy my thoughts. In this paper, written to accompany an invited talk at Latincrypt 2017, I try to explain my own fascination with definitions. I outline a few of the definitions I've recently worked on—garbling schemes, online AE, and onion encryption—and provide some general advice and comments about the definitional enterprise.

Keywords: Cryptographic definitions · Garbling schemes ·
Onion encryption · Online authenticated-encryption · Provable security

1 Introduction

Cryptography is about more than creating and analyzing cryptographic schemes. While these two activities are central cryptographic tasks, cryptography is also, and importantly, about definitions.

Cryptographic definitions emerged within the provable-security framework, which largely begins with Goldwasser and Micali [18]. The basic steps are to *define* a cryptographic problem, to devise a *protocol* for it, and to *prove* that the protocol satisfies its definition, assuming that some other cryptographic scheme satisfies *its* definition. This type of proof is known as a *reduction*.

It seems little discussed that cryptographic definitions can be significant beyond the provable security framework. (a) Definitions can have a profound role in what we *see* in our field—what is rendered visible—and how we approach working on problems [23]. (b) Definitions can enable clear communication and clear thinking. When you encounter confusion in cryptography—which is often— the root cause is often a lack of agreement as to what you're trying to accomplish, and what the words even mean. (c) Definitions can be useful in breaking schemes. I remember breaking the NSA's Dual Counter Mode encryption scheme [10] in minutes, as I read the spec. The NSA claimed this authenticated encryption (AE) scheme to be the product of a 1.5 year effort. It's not that I'm a skilled cryptanalyst—I am not. What I had that the NSA authors obviously didn't was an understanding of a definition for AE. (d) Definitions can give rise to schemes with improved efficiency. When I started off, I anticipated that there would be a

T. Lange and O. Dunkelman (Eds.): LATINCRYPT 2017, LNCS 11368, pp. 3–20, 2019.
https://doi.org/10.1007/978-3-030-25283-0_1

cost, in running time, to doing things with definitions and proofs. And sometimes there is. But, just as often, the exact opposite happens. By having definitions and proofs you are sometimes able to develop mechanisms that let you "cut to the bone," but no deeper, thereby improving efficiency.(e) Finally, there are definitional models that fall outside of the provable security paradigm, such as work done purely in the random-oracle model, the random-permutation model, or the ideal-cipher model; or things in Dolev-Yao style models.Such work absolutely *is* cryptography, begins with definitions, and shouldn't be denigrated because it doesn't fall within the reduction-based tradition.

My plan for this paper is to provide examples of definitions in three different domains. I've chosen definitions that are relatively recent, and that have something to do with encryption. I'll discuss *garbling schemes* (or *garbled circuits*), *online AE*, and *onion AE* (or simply *onion encryption*). The hope is that by giving multiple examples I'll manage to communicate something about the character of definitional work that I wouldn't manage to communicate if I spoke more abstractly, or if focused on a single example. My conclusions, supported by the three examples, are in Sect. 5.

I first wrote about the value of cryptographic definitions more than a decade ago [22]. The current paper is from a different perspective and uses different examples. The examples are from papers with Mihir Bellare, Viet Tung Hoang, Reza Reyhanitabar, Damian Vizár, and Yusi Zhang [4,19,25,26].

2 Garbling Schemes

In a conventional boolean circuit, a *label*, zero or one, is associated to each wire. These represent truth values, the 0-label corresponding to false and the 1-label corresponding to true. The labels propagate up the circuit, moving from the input wires toward a designated output wire. If you possess the labels for the inputs to some gate then you possess the label for its output, which you compute according to the functionality of the gate. An or-gate with input labels of 0 and 1 gives you an output label of 1; an and-gate with input labels of 0 and 1 gives you an output label of 0; and so on.

A *garbled circuit* is similar, but instead of propagating labels with known semantics you propagate *tokens* with unknown semantics. There are two tokens associated to each wire. They are strings, maybe 128 bits each. You can think of them as random 128-bit strings. Possession of one token doesn't imply what the other one is. To be sure, there is a semantics, a truth values, associated to each token; if a wire has tokens of A and B, either A represents true and B represents false, or else it's the other way around. But you can't just look at a token and know what its semantics is.

If you happen to possess an A token (of A and B) for the left-hand wire of an and gate, and you have the C token (of C and D) for the right-hand, and if the output wire has tokens of E and F, then *if* A has hidden semantics of false and C of true, then you need to be able to compute the output token, whether E or F, that has hidden semantics of false. In general, each gate, which you can call a *garbled gate*, is a little algorithm, a recipe, that tells you how to propagate tokens from the input wires to the output wire, doing this in a way that respects the hidden semantics. You evaluate the garbled circuit in this manner until you acquire a token for the final output, and usually the semantics associated to that particular token is made manifest from the token itself. This is how evaluating a garbled circuit works.

Garbled circuits were first described in oral presentations given by Andy Yao in the early or mid 1980s, and it become customary to cite a certain 1986 paper of Yao's for the garbled-circuit idea [30]. But if you read the paper, you won't find there any hint of garbled circuits. I'm actually not sure if the conventional citation is even the paper corresponding to Yao's talks; a 1982 paper of Yao's looks to be more relevant [31], although there's nothing described there like garbled circuits, either. Perhaps the informal and oral culture surrounding this area is part of what launched garbled circuits on a trajectory in which definitions weren't seen as essential. This became characteristic of multiparty computation (MPC) more broadly, despite it being embraced by the theoretical computer science, STOC/FOCS, community.

You might guess that in the intervening 25 years, *someone* would have gone back and defined just what a garbled circuit was intended to do. Strangely, this didn't happen. I think the reason for this is that an entire community had come to view garbled circuits as a *technique*. Being seen as a *method* for solving other problems, it wasn't conceptualized as something in need of a definition.

Originally, garbled circuits had been seen as a tool to solve two-party secure-function evaluation. One party, call it B, presents to the other party, call it A, a garbled circuit specialized to his own (that is, B's) input. The sending party B also helps the receiving party A to acquire exactly one of the two tokens for each input wire held by A—in particular, to acquire the token with the *correct* semantics for that wire, as per A's input. Party A then evaluates the garbled circuit on its own, pushing tokens up the circuit until it has the garbled output, which, as I said before, was supposed to be interpretable as an actual output.

So my coauthors and I wanted to identify the problem that garbled circuits are implicitly intended to solve [4]. I think that one of the key realizations was that garbled circuits really have nothing to do with circuits. In fact, there were already examples in the literature in which people were garbling other things—arithmetic circuits, for example, or branching programs, or DFAs. More recently, people have been wanting to garble Random Access Machine (RAM) computations, or Turing Machine computations. The part of garbling that one really needed to focus on wasn't the garbled *thing*, but the garbling *scheme* that produces it—the process that takes in a function and turns it into a garbled version of that function. This should be done in a way that's representation-independent. That was our first goal for a definition in this domain. A second goal was to make sure that we would encompass as many applications as possible. There are already over a thousand papers that used garbling and we weren't going to be able to have an abstraction that would work for all of them. But we wanted something that would work for most.

So here is an overview for our definition of a garbling scheme. First, and quite importantly, we have to lay down the *syntax* for what a garbling scheme does. When I speak here of syntax, I mean the types of algorithms one must specify for a scheme—the signature (the domain and range) for each. By way of example, if you are defining a blockcipher, the syntax is that of a map $E: \mathcal{K} \times \{0,1\}^n \to \{0,1\}^n$ such that $E(K, \cdot)$ is always a permutation. It seems really useful to separate the syntax of the object you're defining from the measure of security for it. Yet it's common for people to try to define cryptographic goals without attending much to the desired syntax. This is a mistake.

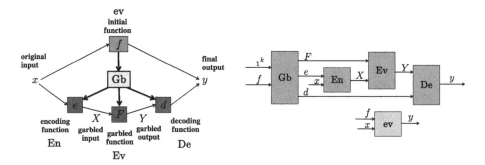

Fig. 1. Garbling schemes. Left: Informally, a function f is probabilistically factored into a triple of functions $d \circ F \circ e$. In actuality, all of these are strings. They represent functions using the maps ev, En, Ev, and De. **Right:** Formally, a garbling scheme consists of functions (Gb, En, De, Ev, ev) satisfying the indicated relationship. The function Gb is probabilistic; the remaining functions are deterministic.

So here's the basic idea for a garbling scheme's syntax. See the left-hand side of Fig. 1. You're given some function f—think of it as the *initial* function— and *garbling* it is a way of "factoring" f, probabilistically, into three pieces: $f = d \circ F \circ e$ (with composition written right-to-left). We're going to feed f (maybe a circuit you want to garble) into a *garbling scheme* that will produce those three pieces: an *encoding function* e, which will take in the *initial inputs* and produce the *garbled inputs*; the *garbled function* F itself; and the *decoding function* d, which will take in the *garbled output* and produce the *final output*. We intend that if f maps x to y, then you will get the same result by feeding x into e to get the garbled input X, then feeding X into the garbled function F to get the garbled output Y, then feeding Y into decoding function d to get y.

A problem with what I've just described is that I am treating f, e, F, and d as both functions and as strings that are either fed into algorithms or spat out by them. That doesn't work in this setting, because the whole point of garbling is to deal with matters of how things are represented. We therefore need to be quite explicit about how we interpret strings as functions. In many contexts in cryptography we don't need to bother with that; we treat strings as describing functions with very little fuss. But here we're going to regard f, F, e, and d as strings that describe functions under the auspices of maps named ev, En, Ev, and De, respectively. See the right-hand side of Fig. 1, where a garbling scheme is shown to be a 5-tuple of algorithms $\mathcal{G} = (\mathsf{Gb}, \mathsf{En}, \mathsf{De}, \mathsf{Ev}, \mathsf{ev})$. The main algorithm, the "business end" of things, is the probabilistic garbling algorithm Gb. It maps a string representing a function to a string representing a garbled function. Then there are four more functions. These encode the initial input, decode the garbled output, evaluate the string representing the garbled function, and evaluate the string representing the initial function. We intend first a *correctness condition*, as illustrated on the left side of Fig. 1. You always get the same thing when you go through the route on the top and the route on the bottom. There's also a *nondegeneracy* condition that makes sure that the main work is done in the garbling function itself; we don't want you to factor f in such a way that the real work is happening in the encoding or decoding step.

What I've described so far is the syntax of a garbling scheme; I haven't described security. In our paper [4], we define notions we call *privacy, authenticity*, and *obliviousness*. I'll only describe the first. The basic intuition for privacy is that learning (F, X, d)—the garbled function, the garbled input, and the decoding function—shouldn't reveal anything except the final output y. But the basic intuition isn't quite right, because real garbling schemes always leak something beyond the output y. A garbled circuit typically leaks the topology of the underlying circuit—the pattern of how gates are connected up—if not the circuit itself. You could hide these things, but you would still leak the circuit's size. In order to capture what is understood to be leaked, we provide a *side-information function*, denoted Φ. Given an initial function f, it indicates the information $\Phi(f)$ that we expect to leak by revealing F. For circuit garbling, side-information functions $\Phi_{\mathrm{circ}}(f)$, $\Phi_{\mathrm{topo}}(f)$, and $\Phi_{\mathrm{size}}(f)$ return all of f, the topology of f, and the size of f, respectively. We always assume that we leak at least the *signature* of the function f, meaning the values n and m where $f\colon \{0,1\}^n \to \{0,1\}^m$.

Now ready to define privacy for a garbling scheme, we imagine that an adversary is presented one of two types of oracles—a left-handed oracle or a right-handed oracle. Which type of oracle the adversary gets is determined by a coin flip $b \leftarrow \{0,1\}$: if $b = 0$ the adversary gets a left-handed oracle; if $b = 1$ it gets a right-handed oracle. Our adversary presents to its oracle a pair of pairs (f_0, x_0), (f_1, x_1). If the oracle is left-handed then it properly garbles the left-hand pair: it computes $(F, e, d) \leftarrow \mathsf{Gb}(1^k, f_0)$ and then sets $X \leftarrow \mathsf{En}(e, x_0)$. If the oracle is right-handed then it garbles the right-hand pair: it computes $(F, e, d) \leftarrow \mathsf{Gb}(1^k, f_1)$ and then sets $X \leftarrow \mathsf{En}(e, x_1)$. Either way, the oracle now returns (F, X, d): the garbled function, the garbled input, and the decoding function. The adversary's job is to guess the bit b. We do have to ensure that $f_0(x_0) = f_1(x_1)$; otherwise, it would be easy for the adversary to compute the value b. We also have to ensure that the side-information doesn't allow a trivial distinguishing attack. Formalizing these requirements, regardless of b, the oracle begins by testing if $\Phi(f_0) \neq \Phi(f_1)$ or $\mathsf{ev}(f_0, x_0) \neq \mathsf{ev}(f_1, x_1)$. If so, the oracle just returns a distinguished symbol $\bot$. The adversary's advantage $\mathbf{Adv}_{\mathcal{G}, \Phi}^{\mathrm{prv.ind}}(\mathcal{A}, k) = 2\Pr[b' = b] - 1$ is the probability that $\mathcal{A}$ correctly identifies b, renormalized, as usual, to the interval $[-1, 1]$.

There is also a simulation-based notion for garbling privacy. Here the adversary presents to its oracle a single pair (f, x). The oracle will behave in one of two ways, based on a coin flip $b \twoheadleftarrow \{0, 1\}$. If it's a "real" oracle, $b = 1$, then it garbles the function f and its input x, computing $(F, e, d) \twoheadleftarrow \mathsf{Gb}(1^k, f)$ and $X \leftarrow \mathsf{En}(e, x)$. It returns (F, X, d). When the oracle is a "fake" oracle, $b = 0$, a simulator must provide (F, X, d) without benefit of seeing f and x. What it is given instead is $\Phi(f)$ and $f(x)$. This definition of privacy also seems like a relatively direct way to capture the idea that the garbled input, the garbled function, and the decoding function don't leak anything that shouldn't be leaked. Adversarial advantage is defined as before, $\mathbf{Adv}^{\mathrm{prv.sim}}_{\mathcal{G}, \Phi, S}(\mathcal{A}, k) = 2\Pr[b' = b] - 1$.

How do these two notions relate? They're quite close. The simulation definition implies the indistinguishability version, and the indistinguishability version implies the simulatability version if you add in some modest side-condition.

Where does this go from here? By having definitions for what a garbling scheme is supposed to do we are able to achieve much improved efficiency [2]: we can do garbled circuit evaluation, in the ideal-permutation model, where the work associated to evaluating a gate is, say, a single AES computation employing a fixed key. In practice, something like 25 clock cycles, or 7.5 ns, per gate. Much of this efficiency improvement, however, isn't due to any cryptographic advance, but to a different definitional aspect: formalizing circuits in a particularly clean way, then implementing directly to that formalization. In another direction, we look at *dynamic* adversaries (they corrupt parties as-they-go) [3]. We find that garbled circuits, as conventionally realized, don't work for dynamic adversaries. When papers implicitly assumed that conventional circuit garbling works even in the case of dynamic adversaries, they made claims that were not correct.

3   Online AE

I will next describe online authenticated-encryption (online AE), sketching joint work with Hoang, Reyhanitabar, and Vizár from 2015 [19].

I hope that readers have seen the "basic" notion of AE, what I'll call nonce-based AE (NAE). Under NAE, encryption is a deterministic way to make a key K, associated data A, and a message M to a ciphertext C; formally, an NAE scheme is a function $\mathcal{E}: \mathcal{K} \times \mathcal{N} \times \mathcal{A} \times \mathcal{M} \rightarrow \mathcal{C}$ where $\mathcal{E}(K, N, A, \cdot)$ is an injection, where $x \in \mathcal{M}$ implies $\{0, 1\}^{|x|} \subseteq \mathcal{M}$, and where $|\mathcal{E}(K, A, M)| = |M| + \tau$ for some constant τ. We can then define the decryption function from the encryption function, letting $\mathcal{D}(K, N, A, C) = M$ if there is an M for which $\mathcal{E}(K, N, A, M) = C$, and letting $\mathcal{D}(K, N, A, C) = \bot$ otherwise. Since we have defined the behavior of $\mathcal{D}$ from $\mathcal{E}$, we can omit the usual correctness condition, which would mandate that they appropriately compose.

For NAE security, we ask for the following indistinguishability condition [24]. In the "real" game, an adversary is given an oracle that encrypts according to $\mathcal{E}_K$: for a K chosen uniformly from $\mathcal{K}$ at the beginning of the game, it responds to a query (N, A, M) with $\mathcal{E}_K(N, A, M)$. It also has a second oracle that decrypts according to $\mathcal{D}_K$: given (N, A, C), it returns the plaintext $M = \mathcal{D}_K(N, A, C)$.

We ask the adversary to distinguish this pair of oracles from an "ideal" pair of oracles—the first of which spits out $|M| + \tau$ random bits and the second of which always answers $\perp$, an indication of invalidity.

When you make a definition like this, you need to add in provisos to outlaw trivial wins. The adversary could always encrypt some (N, A, M) to get C, then decrypt (N, A, C) to get back either M or $\perp$, thereby identifying the operative game. Similarly it could repeat a nonce value N in an encryption query, violating the intent of a nonce. So we must either forbid these activities, or give the adversary no credit if it engages in them. The advantage is defined as $\mathbf{Adv}_{\Pi}^{\text{nae}}(\mathcal{A}) = \Pr[\mathcal{A}^{\mathcal{E}_K, \mathcal{D}_k} \rightarrow 1] - \Pr[\mathcal{A}^{\$, \perp} \rightarrow 1]$. This NAE notion has been quite influential. For example, the CAESAR competition going on right now [7] has resulted in dozens of submissions designed to meet it.

Now one of the often-heard complaints about NAE is that a conforming scheme can fail completely if nonces are reused. And we know from experience that nonces *do* get reused with alarming regularity. A recent example is the KRACK attack on WPA2 [29]. Nonce reuse is usually a result of error, but there are also settings in which it is difficult or impossible to ensure that nonces don't get reused. So a nice strengthening of the NAE notion is the notion of *misuse-resistant* AE, or MRAE [24]. It's not a great name, as the misuse we are considering here is only one form of misuse, namely, nonce reuse.

The definition of MRAE looks just like the definition of NAE except that we allow the adversary to repeat N-values on encryption queries, as long as it doesn't repeat an entire (N, A, M) triple. That's it. Yet the notion becomes quite different to achieve. One of the key differences between NAE and MRAE is that, for the latter, you've got to read the entire plaintext before you can output even the first bit of ciphertext: online encryption is impossible. This is easy to see because if the first bit of ciphertext didn't depend on the last bit of plaintext then you'd have an easy way to win the MRAE game.

There are situations where the can't-be-online restriction is a problem. You might have a long input an no ability to buffer it all. You might need to act on the prefix of a message before hearing the suffix. There has therefore been a perceived need to achieve something *like* MRAE, but where online encryption would be possible. When I say that online encryption is possible, I mean that you should be able to read in a plaintext left-to-right, and, using a constant amount of memory, spit out bits until you extrude the entire ciphertext.

In order to answer this need, Fleischmann, Forler, and Lucks (FFL) proposed a security notion for online authenticated-encryption [15] that I'll call OAE1. It was said to imply security against nonce reuse, yet to be achievable by online schemes. The notion quickly caught on. Among the round-1 CAESAR submissions (2014), fully a dozen claimed OAE1 security. Additional schemes were said to achieve something closely related to OAE1 security. This is an extraordinary degree of influence for a 2012 definition.

But there are problems with OAE1. To define the notion, I must go back to an earlier definition from Bellare, Boldyreva, Knudsen, and Namprempre for an *online cipher* [1]. They start by fixing a block length n and assuming that we're going to be enciphering strings that are a multiple of n bits. They imagine an ideal object in which the i-th n-bit block of plaintext gets enciphered to the i-th n-bit block of ciphertext. This block may depend only on blocks 1 to i. A good online cipher must approximate this ideal object. More formally, let $\mathsf{B}_n = \{0,1\}^n$ and define a *multiple-of-n cipher* as a map $\mathcal{E}\colon \mathcal{K} \times \mathsf{B}_n^* \to \mathsf{B}_n^*$ where $\mathcal{E}(K, \cdot)$ is a length-preserving injection for each K. Let $\mathrm{OPerm}[n]$ be all multiple-of-n ciphers π where the i-th block of $\pi(X)$ depends only on the first i blocks of X. A good online cipher is a multiple-of-n cipher $\mathcal{E}$ where $\mathcal{E}(K, \cdot)$ is indistinguishable from a random permutation $\pi \twoheadleftarrow \mathrm{OPerm}[n]$.

FFL's definition for OAE1 modifies the online-cipher notion in a simple way. FFL again assume that n is fixed and that the plaintext is a multiple of n bits. They assume that the output is going to look like a ciphertext piece that is exactly as long as the original plaintext, followed by a τ-bit authentication tag T. The ciphertext piece must be given by an online cipher, although tweaked by a header that encodes the nonce N and associated data A. The tag T should be pseudorandom: it should look like τ random bits. This is the privacy notion. There is also a standard notion of authenticity that goes with it, capturing unforgeability under an adaptive chosen-message attack.

Unfortunately, the OAE1 definition doesn't make a whole lot of sense. Its problems include:

1. *Admits unexpected attacks.* OAE1 doesn't guarantee the anticipated degree of privacy in the face of nonce reuse. With an OAE1-secure scheme, if you're given an oracle that takes in a message-prefix, appends a secret suffix, and then encrypts the whole thing, then you can play with that oracle to recover that secret suffix, in its entirety, with a small number of queries. Attacks like this can be damaging, as seen in the BEAST attack on SSL/TLS [14]. Still, this is not the worst problem for OAE1. Maybe it's just incorrect intuition about what online AE can be expected to achieve; maybe any online-AE scheme must fall to this sort of attack.

2. *The blocksize should be user-selectable, not a scheme-dependent constant.* Why were we trying to make an online-AE scheme in the first place? It is due to some memory or latency restriction. Maybe the encryption is realized by an ASIC or FPGA, and we can only give over so much memory for the task. Maybe a video file is being streamed to a user, and there is only so long the user should wait. Whatever the restriction is, it has nothing to do with the blocksize of some implementing blockcipher. That value, which is likely to be quite small (like or 64 or 128 bits), has nothing to do with the extent to which a scheme can buffer things or wait. Since we can't realistically know what the user's actual constraint is, it is best if this is left unspecified—a user-selectable value, not a scheme-dependent constant.

3. *Decryption also needs to be online.* It's very strange to demand that encryption be online but make no analogous requirement for decryption. In fact, it's hard to even think of a context in which it would be OK for decryption to require buffering the whole message, and yet there was a constraint that this not be done at encryption time. The OAE1 notion effectively demands

that decryption *not* be online, as the authenticity formalization effectively demands that no information be released until the ciphertext, in its entirety, is checked for validity.

4. *Security needs to be defined for strings of all lengths.* The OAE1 definition inherits from the definition of an online cipher the peculiar characteristic that the length of the input *must* be a multiple of n. When you actually describe a general-purpose scheme you're going to want to ensure that it works on all bit strings, or at least all byte strings. So we need a security definition that is applicable to all bit strings or all byte strings. And saying that you achieve a rich domain through padding begs the question: what exactly is it that you are achieving through the use of padding?

5. *The reference object is not ideal.* Finally, the reference object that OAE1 measures a scheme against is not ideal: one can do better than something that looks like an ideal online cipher with a small n followed by a bunch of random-looking bits. We should not be taking such an object as our yardstick.

In order to address these concerns we need to change not only the OAE1 security notion, but to completely revise the basic syntax.

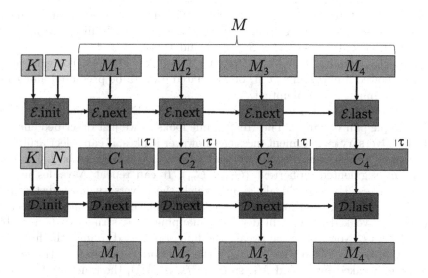

Fig. 2. Operation of an OAE2-secure AE scheme. The plaintext is broken into segments $M = M_1 M_2 \cdots M_m$ of arbitrary and possibly varying lengths. Each M_i is encrypted to a ciphertext segment C_i of length $|M_i| + \tau$. The key K and nonce N initialize the process. Decryption reverses the process. If an authenticity error should arise, it continues for all subsequent blocks. The figure omits associated data.

Refer to Fig. 2. Messages to be encrypted or decrypted will be *segmented*. We think of the encryption scheme's user as selecting the segmentation. To be fully general, we allow the segments to have varying lengths (although we expect that, typically, all segments but the last will have the same length). Segmenting the plaintext amounts to supporting an API that says: here's the first piece of message I'd like to encrypt; and here's the next piece; and so on, until one presents the final message chunk. We would normally expect that each ciphertext segment C_i has a length $|M_i| + \tau$ that is a fixed amount greater than the corresponding plaintext segment. We expect that each plaintext M_i will fit in memory, but the concatenation of all plaintext segments might not. After processing a plaintext segment, the encryption algorithm can remember what it wants by updating its constant-size internal state. The initial state is determined by the key K and the nonce N.

Decrypting the segmented ciphertext $(C_1, C_2, \ldots, C_m)$ that arose from encrypting $(M_1, M_2, \ldots, M_m)$ should result in the original segmentation, while changing the segmentation in any way should result in an authentication failure from that point on. If a ciphertext segment gets corrupted, this should result in an authentication failureon trying to decrypt that segment, and decryption of all future segments should also fail.

Here now is the syntax for what we want. We say that a *segmented-AE scheme* is a triple $\Pi = (\mathcal{K}, \mathcal{E}, \mathcal{D})$ where $\mathcal{K}$ is a distribution on strings (or the algorithm that induces it), and $\mathcal{E} = (\mathcal{E}.\text{init}, \mathcal{E}.\text{next}, \mathcal{E}.\text{last})$ and $\mathcal{D} = (\mathcal{D}.\text{init}, \mathcal{D}.\text{next}, \mathcal{D}.\text{last})$ are triples of deterministic algorithms where $\mathcal{E}.\text{init}: \mathcal{K} \times \mathcal{N} \to \mathcal{S}$ and $\mathcal{E}.\text{next}: \mathcal{S} \times \mathcal{A} \times \mathcal{M} \to \mathcal{C} \times \mathcal{S}$ and $\mathcal{E}.\text{last}: \mathcal{S} \times \mathcal{A} \times \mathcal{M} \to \mathcal{C}$ and $\mathcal{D}.\text{init}: \mathcal{K} \times \mathcal{N} \to \mathcal{S}$ and $\mathcal{D}.\text{next}: \mathcal{S} \times \mathcal{A} \times \mathcal{C} \to (\mathcal{M} \times \mathcal{S}) \cup \{\bot\}$ and $\mathcal{D}.\text{last}: \mathcal{S} \times \mathcal{A} \times \mathcal{C} \to \mathcal{M} \cup \{\bot\}$. For simplicity, assume $\mathcal{A} = \mathcal{M} = \mathcal{C} = \{0,1\}^*$ and $\mathcal{N} \subseteq \{0,1\}^*$. For generality, we have allowed a new segment A_i of associated data to be presented alongside each new segment M_i of plaintext.

How do we define security? The notion we call OAE2 can again be described with a simple pair of games. The "real" game looks as we just described encryption: the adversary can segment messages however it likes, it can select arbitrary nonces, and for each such nonce N and $(M_1, \ldots, M_m)$ it gets back the corresponding segmented ciphertext $(C_1, \ldots C_m)$. It can repeat N-values in any manner it likes. For the "ideal" game, which the adversary must distinguish from the "real" one, the $\mathcal{E}.\text{next}$ functionality is replaced by a random injective function f, tweaked as we will describe, mapping ℓ-bit strings to $(\ell + \tau)$-bit strings for all ℓ. Now as for the tweaks:the function f used to map the first segment is tweaked by N, so $C_1 = f_N(M_1)$; the function f used to map the second segment is tweaked by N and M_1, so $C_2 = f_{N,M_1}(M_2)$; the function f used to map the third segment is tweaked by N, M_1, and M_2, so $C_3 = f_{N,M_1,M_2}(M_3)$; and so on. The last block is different. It is important to distinguish the last block from prior ones, as the *end* of a message is a distinguished status. For the last block, then, for the ideal functionality corresponding to what is processed in the "real" scheme using $\mathcal{E}.\text{last}$, we set $C_m = f_{N,M_1,M_2,\ldots,M_{m-1},*}(M_m)$, the $*$ denoting another variant tweak. Throughout, distinct tweaks correspond to independent random injections. For simplicity, our description has omitted the associated data.

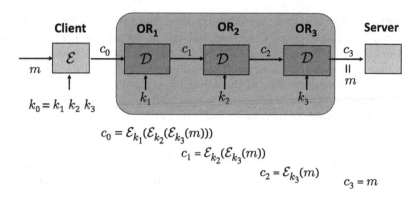

Fig. 3. The nested-encryption approach for onion routing. The client shares a key k_i with each onion router OR_i. To send a message m to a server, the client iteratively encrypts it. Each OR will "peel off" (decrypt) a single layer of encryption. The nested-encryption idea, for the public-key setting, is from Chaum [11].

The development of OAE2 would now continue by exploring definitional variants, then investigating schemes that meet the notions. I don't think it particularly desirable to create schemes for a task like this from scratch; better to start with an NAE or MRAE scheme.

In describing where OAE2 came from, I told it as a story of wanting to fix the OAE1 definition from FFL. But I could have arrived at the same definition from other directions. The kind of online AE goal we are after has been known for a long time. Prior work by Tsang, Solomakhin, Smith [28] and by Bertoni, Daemen, Peeters, Van Assche [8] gives related notions and schemes. Netflix has posted a protocol description for an object that does virtually the same thing as we do [20]. In general, for questions of practical importance in cryptography, practitioners will often have noticed the problem and posed solutions long before it gets on the radar of any theory-minded cryptographer.

4   Onion Encryption

The last definitional problem I'd like to describe is that of *onion encryption*, or *onion-AE*. This is recent work with Yusi Zhang [25, 26].

The task we address is another type of AE. See Fig. 3. A *client* (or *user*) wants to send a message to a *server* (or *destination*), transmitting it over an *onion-routing network*, which is a collection of cooperating servers (onion routers). In the usual solution, the client will iteratively encrypt the message m it wants to send, once for each intermediate OR (onion router). So, in the figure, the plaintext m is turned into a ciphertext $c = E_{k_1}(E_{k_2}(E_{k_3}(m)))$. The ORs will each decrypt the ciphertext they receive, so that, at the end, the plaintext m will be recovered. The idea goes back to the early development of Tor [13, 16, 17, 27] and, reaching back further still, to the idea of mixnets, from David Chaum [11].

As with garbling schemes, nested encryption has been understood as technique, not a solution to some clearly articulated problem. The question Zhang and I asked is: just what goal is it that nested encryption aims to solve?

Of course it is easy to answer such questions in vague English. The client is trying to get some message over to the server in such a way that individual ORs won't know the association between the sender and the receiver. They shouldn't even know who is the client (except for the initial OR) and who is the destination (except for the final OR). We want to make it hard for an adversary that has less than a total view of the network to know who is communicating with whom. We hope that bogus ciphertexts inserted into the network will not emerge from the exit node. One can go on in such a vein, and it is not useless, but there is a large gap between this level of discourse and a cryptographic definition.

We begin, as always, by formalizing the syntax for the object we are after. We say that an *onion-encryption scheme* is a triple of algorithms $\Pi = (\mathcal{K}, \mathcal{E}, \mathcal{D})$ as follows. (a) The key-generation algorithm $\mathcal{K}$ is a probabilistic algorithm that maps a number n (the number of ORs) to a vector of $n + 1$ strings: $(k_0, k_1, \ldots, k_n) \twoheadleftarrow \mathcal{K}(n)$. The first key in the vector is intended for the client; the next n keys are intended specific the ORs, key k_i for router OR_i. (b) The encryption algorithm $\mathcal{E}$ is a deterministic algorithm that maps a key k_0, a message m, and the user's state u to a ciphertext c_0 and an updated state u'. It specifies what the client must do to encrypt a message. It is important that $\mathcal{E}$ is stateful: each time the client encrypts a message, its internal state gets updated. The initial state is the empty string. (c) The decryption algorithm $\mathcal{D}$ is a deterministic algorithm that maps a key k_i, a ciphertext c, and an OR's current state s_i to something that is either a plaintext m', a ciphertext c', or the symbol $\Diamond$, an indication of failure. Decryption also produces an updated state s_i'. The decryption algorithm specifies what an OR must do on receipt of a ciphertext c. Only ciphertext outputs (or $\Diamond$) can be produced using keys from $k_1, \ldots, k_{n-1}$, and only plaintext outputs (or $\Diamond$) can be produced using the key k_n. Throughout, plaintexts and ciphertexts are recognizably distinct, the former coming from a message space of $\{0, 1\}^{l_1}$ and the latter coming from a ciphertext space of $\{0, 1\}^{l_2}$ with $l_2 > l_1$.

After defining a scheme's syntax one typically specifies a *correctness condition*. It captures the fact that, in the absence of an adversary, everything works as you expect. Formally, we assert that for every number n and every vector of strings $m \in \{0, 1\}^{**}$, if $k \twoheadleftarrow \mathcal{K}(n)$ is a vector of keys then the following predicate $\text{Correct}_\Pi(k, m)$ is true:

---

procedure $\text{Correct}_\Pi(k, m)$
$(k_0, k_1, \ldots, k_n) \leftarrow k; \quad (m_1, \ldots, m_\ell) \leftarrow m; \quad u, s_1, \ldots, s_n \leftarrow \varepsilon$
for $i \leftarrow 1$ **to** ℓ **do**
$\quad (c_0^i, u) \leftarrow \mathcal{E}(k_0, m_i, u)$
$\quad$ **for** $j \leftarrow 1$ **to** n **do** $(c_j^i, s_j) \leftarrow \mathcal{D}(k_j, c_{j-1}^i, s_j)$
return $\bigwedge_{1 \leq i \leq \ell} (m_i = c_n^i)$

The goal we aim to formalize looks like stateful AE [6,9], but with the decryption done by the OR network itself. Privacy will be formalized in the tradition of indistinguishability from random bits. This will make for an easy way to get the desired anonymity property. The authenticity property we aim for is authenticity checked at time of exit. One can, alternatively, check authenticity earlier and repeatedly, at each OR. This notion might be more desirable, but it's not how Tor's relay protocol does things [12,13], so it's not the approach we take, either.

One can write a pair of games that directly corresponds to what we've sketched. They would look something like this. The "real" game would run an Initialize routine that, given the number n of ORs, would initialize keys $(k_0, k_1, \ldots, k_n) \leftarrow \mathcal{K}(n)$. The game would support oracle calls of $\mathrm{Enc}(m)$ and $\mathrm{Dec}(i, c)$. A call to $\mathrm{Enc}(m)$ would compute $(c, u) \leftarrow \mathcal{E}(k_0, m, u)$ then return c. A call to $\mathrm{Dec}(i, c)$ would compute $(m, s_i) \leftarrow \mathcal{D}(k_i, c, s_i)$ then return m. In contrast, in the "ideal" game a call to $\mathrm{Enc}(m)$ would return the appropriate number of random bits, while a call to $\mathrm{Dec}(i, c)$ would return the appropriate number of random bits if $i < n$, and an indication of invalidity $\Diamond$ if $i = n$.

So far, nothing I've said is unexpected or complex. But, left as is, it is also wrong. If an adversary were to first encrypt a message m for a sequence of $n = 3$ ORs, getting back a ciphertext $c_0 \leftarrow \mathrm{Enc}(m)$, and if it were to next perform the sequence of decryption calls $c_1 \leftarrow \mathrm{Dec}(1, c_0)$, $c_2 \leftarrow \mathrm{Dec}(2, c_1)$, $c_3 \leftarrow \mathrm{Dec}(3, c_2)$, then the adversary would have a trivial way to win: by returning 1 if and only if $c_3 = m$. Intuitively, this sort of win shouldn't count, for all the adversary did was to use the OR network to decrypt a plaintext it knew the decryption of. But how, precisely, do we forbid the adversary from scoring this sort of win? What does *this sort of win* actually mean? Formalizing it is rather complex. The code gets complicated enough that it's hard to verify if it's right—and none to easy to use, either. Perhaps this is emblematic of a wider problem we face in dealing with complex cryptographic definitions. We're pretty good with "simple" definitions, but as you move up to harder tasks, formalizing things can get unconvincing and obscure.

Might there be a better way? I'd like to describe the approach that Zhang and I have been working on [25, 26]. It is offered as a general framework for doing indistinguishability definitions in settings where an adversary must distinguish a "real" and an "ideal" world. This isn't much of a constraint, as success-style games, where the adversary wants to induce some event to happen, can be rewritten in the real/ideal format. We will think of the real and ideal worlds as being described by pieces of pseudocode.

In our onion-encryption example, and in other examples of this paper, the simple indistinguishability-based definition you would *like* to write down is not achievable; there exists some simple adversarial attack which *would* distinguish between the two worlds. Usually we use our intuition to inform us as to what restrictions are necessary so as to not credit these trivial attacks. You can either say "the adversary's not allowed to do *this*"—you pose it as a restriction on the class of acceptable adversaries—or, alternatively, you let the adversary do what it wants, but, at the end of the game, you have a "finalization procedure" look

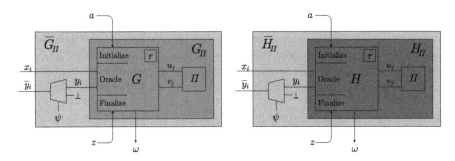

Fig. 4. Oracle silencing. Game G captures the *real* environment; game H, the *ideal* one. Both depend on some scheme Π. An adversary (not shown) makes a sequence of *oracle calls*. In the *silenced* games $(\overline{G}, \overline{H}) = \text{Silence}_C(G, H)$, responses are suppressed according to predicate $\Psi = \text{Fixed}_{C,G}(x_1, y_1, \dots, x_k, y_k, x)$, which is true if there exists a unique y such that $\text{Valid}_{C,G}(x_1, y_1, \dots, x_k, y_k, x, y)$. The *Valid* predicate asserts that there is some $\Pi \in C$ that can give rise to the indicated partial transcript.

back at what transpired and *if* the adversary misbehaved, you penalize it—you deny it credit for the win. Bellare, Hofheinz, and Kiltz call these two approaches *exclusion-style* definitions and *penalty-style* definitions [5]. They carefully investigate two versions of each for the problem of IND-CCA secure public-key encryption (PKE).

I'd like to suggest a third possibility. We put a little bit of smarts in the oracle itself, so that the oracle recognizes that it's about to provide the caller an answer that would give away the show. When this happens, the oracle shuts up. It returns a distinguished value $\bot$. This happens in both the real and the ideal game. We call this style of game modification *oracle silencing*. In our early work, the oracle would shut up just for the one query. Now we've been doing things so that the oracle, once silenced, stays so.

This doesn't sound like much progress, for you ought to be able to rewrite an oracle-silencing definition as an exclusion-style or penalty-style one. Maybe it's just a matter of personal taste. But we introduce another idea that seems to combine most naturally with oracle silencing. It is this: that *when* an oracle is silenced is *not* directly specified by the cryptographer creating a definition, but, instead, it is determined *automatically* by the *correctness* requirement.

Usually what's going on is that the oracle should be silenced if the adversary has asked a question where the correctness constraint dictates the response. In the real setting, that is, there's only one answer possible, as mandated by the correctness condition. The answer doesn't depend on the particular protocol Π that underlies the game, nor does it depend on any coins. It only depends on the query history and the fact that the underlying protocol *is* correct. In such a case, we want to silence the response. See Fig. 4.

A bit more formally, one begins by defining a pair of *utopian* games G and H. They are called "utopian" because we expect that an adversary *can* distinguish between them, just by exploiting some simple test that ought not be permitted.

The cryptographer also defines a *correctness condition* C, which is just the class of correct schemes. Now we automatically and generically modify G and H, using C, to get a new pair of games $\overline{G}$, $\overline{H}$. The modification is to add in a little "gadget" that takes in the value that is about to be returned to the adversary and sometimes replaces it by some distinguished symbol $\perp$. The *silencing function*, which depends on G and C, takes in the transcript that describes the interaction between the adversary and its oracles. It silences exactly when the transcript fixes the oracle's response in the real game. The silencing function (or something close to it) needs to be efficiently computable: only in this way do we know that the adversary knows that its query is inappropriate. The adversary's ability to distinguish between the silenced games is what we call the INDC measure of security: indistinguishability up to correctness.

When we carry out the paradigm described for onion encryption, the utopian games are very simple: they look like the naïve games sketched before. Each game can be described with about six lines of code. But it is not this pair of games that the adversary must distinguish. It is the silenced pair of games obtained by "compiling" the utopian games using the correctness condition earlier described.

One use of INDC security is to justify complicated games: if distinguishing them is equivalent to distinguishing the pair of games one gets from silencing utopian games using correctness, this is a demonstration that the games are in some sense right. Alternatively, INDC security can be used to conveniently define games described in no other way.

5   Conclusions

I want to wrap up now, making some final comments.

- First, as already mentioned, I strongly advise, when writing definitions, to completely separate the syntax from the security notion, and to pay much more attention to the former than people routinely do. Syntax guides security, and has a profound impact on what security properties we can even express.
- Another point concerns where to find problems in need of definitional work. An often overlooked source is cryptographic practice itself—cryptographic practice that hasn't met up with theory. Often things can be well established in cryptographic practice without any theoretically minded person noticing, or perhaps caring, that there is an important problem to address. Both our second and third examples, online encryption and onion encryption, are cases of theory seriously lagging practice.
- Relatedly, things that are in need of defining may be sitting in plain view, seemingly without anyone taking notice. I mentioned that there were more than a thousand papers using garbled circuits without anyone attending to the fact that what garbled circuits accomplished, on their own, hadn't been defined.
- Definitions can be wrong. When you hear somebody say "it can't be wrong, it's a *definition*", challenge this sophistry. Definitions can be wrong for a

variety of reasons, but the most important is that they fail to model what you are really wanting or needing to model. When you encounter definitions you believe to be wrong, develop your arguments and speak out, even though this can be difficult to do. It can be difficult because lots of people may be invested in the downstream work that springs from a definition, and calling a definition into question impugns everything that uses it.

- In the examples given today, and in all of the definitional work I've done over my career, I get the overwhelming sense that I am *constructing* a definition, not *discovering* it. But you hear people speak in the opposite terms, as though there are these cryptographic definitions *out there*, waiting to be discovered, and that our job as cryptographers is to find them. I don't think the world works this way. I think we create definitions in order to satisfy the needs of some particular community, and the value of a definition is the extent to which it does. The idea is explored in a separate essay [23].
- Definitional work can be practical. Many people assume the opposite. Perhaps they think that definitional work is impractical because it's slow, and practice can't wait. Definitions usually needs lots of refinement, and frequent backtracking. Nonetheless, spending the time to hammer out the definitions and make them beautiful can come to have a large practical payoff.
- Definitional work is dialectical. You might think that by working out the definitions thoughtfully enough, you will manage to arrive at the *right* definition. Being *right*, it won't *need* to evolve. It *shouldn't* evolve. But I don't buy it. My experience has been that definitional notions evolve much more than people imagine, and that the definitional process does not really terminate.
- Definitions are fundamentally fictions. We attend to the things that we want to attend to, and we ignore the rest. The rest hasn't gone away, and we do well to remember that. That definitions are fictions does not mean that we shouldn't take them seriously. We absolutely should take our definitions seriously, in the sense of wanting to fully understand their consequences, relationships, and limitations. But we should not take our definitions seriously in the sense that we delude ourselves into believing the definition is a genuine surrogate for the thing we are interested in. They are abstractions—platonic models of some aim.
- Finally, I'll comment that part of why I like working on cryptographic definitions is that it seems to involve a unique style of modelling. The creation of a definition integrates social, technical, and philosophical concerns. The last figures into the process more than outsiders might imagine; in developing a definition, philosophical discourse may even dominate discussions. Perhaps there are other disciplines where modelling has this same character, but I have yet to encounter them. In most scientific, engineering, and even social-science disciplines, empiricism plays a major role. Does the rod bend in the manner predicated by the PDE? Does the economy evolve in the way the equations predict? In making cryptographic definitions, there is rarely any experimental or observational aspect; instead, the technical work is entwined with social, philosophical, and aesthetic considerations. Ultimately, this may be the aspect of the definitional enterprise that I like most.

Acknowledgments. Thanks first to the coauthors of papers whose definitions I have summarized: Mihir Bellare, Viet Tung Hoang, Reza Reyhanitabar, Damian Vizár, and Yusi Zhang [4,19,25,26]. Good definitions require good coauthors. Further thanks to Tung and Yusi for helpful proofreading.

Many thanks to the NSF for their support under grants CNS 1314885 and CNS 1717542. Of course all views expressed in this paper are entirely my own.

This paper was prepared to accompany an invited talk at Latincrypt 2017, which was held in Havana, Cuba. My kind thanks to all of those involved in organizing Latincrypt and inviting my participation, particularly Program Chairs Orr Dunkelman and Tanja Lange, General Chair Luis Ramiro Piñeiro Díaz, and Steering Committee member Francisco Rodríguez-Henríquez.

Latincrypt 2017 was my first time in Cuba, a place so close to the U.S. that a woman has managed to swim that gap [21]. Yet for decades the U.S. has maintained bizarre policies towards this neighbor, causing much suffering. I myself was born in 1962, during the brief interval between the Bay of Pigs Invasion and the Cuban Missile Crisis. One might have assumed that, 55 years later, relations would surely have normalized. It is very sad that this is still not the case.

References

1. Bellare, M., Boldyreva, A., Knudsen, L., Namprempre, C.: Online ciphers and the hash-CBC construction. In: Kilian, J. (ed.) CRYPTO 2001. LNCS, vol. 2139, pp. 292–309. Springer, Heidelberg (2001). https://doi.org/10.1007/3-540-44647-8_18
2. Bellare, M., Hoang, V. T., Keelveedhi, S., Rogaway, P.: Efficient garbling from a fixed-key blockcipher. In: IEEE Symposium on Security and Privacy, pp. 478–492 (2013)
3. Bellare, M., Hoang, V.T., Rogaway, P.: Adaptively secure garbling with applications to one-time programs and secure outsourcing. In: Wang, X., Sako, K. (eds.) ASIACRYPT 2012. LNCS, vol. 7658, pp. 134–153. Springer, Heidelberg (2012). https://doi.org/10.1007/978-3-642-34961-4_10
4. Bellare, M., Hoang, V. T., Rogaway, P.: Foundations of garbled circuits. In: ACM Conference on Computer and Communications Security (CCS 2012), pp. 784–796 (2012). Full version is Cryptology ePrint Archive, Report 2012/265 (2012)
5. Bellare, M., Hofheinz, D., Kiltz, E.: Subtleties in the definition of IND-CCA: when and how should challenge decryption be disallowed? J. Cryptol. **28**(1), 29–48 (2015)
6. Bellare, M., Kohno, Y., Namprempre, C.: Breaking and provably repairing the SSH authenticated encryption scheme: a case study of the encode-then-Encrypt-and-MAC paradigm. ACM Trans. Inf. Syst. Secur. **7**(2), 206–241 (2004)
7. Bernstein, D.: Cryptographic competitions. competitions.cr.yp.to. Accessed 1 Feb 2018
8. Bertoni, G., Daemen, J., Peeters, M., Van Assche, G.: Duplexing the sponge: single-pass authenticated encryption and other applications. In: Miri, A., Vaudenay, S. (eds.) SAC 2011. LNCS, vol. 7118, pp. 320–337. Springer, Heidelberg (2012). https://doi.org/10.1007/978-3-642-28496-0_19
9. Boyd, C., Hale, B., Mjølsnes, S.F., Stebila, D.: From stateless to stateful: generic authentication and authenticated encryption constructions with application to TLS. In: Sako, K. (ed.) CT-RSA 2016. LNCS, vol. 9610, pp. 55–71. Springer, Cham (2016). https://doi.org/10.1007/978-3-319-29485-8_4
10. Boyle, M., Salter, C.: Dual Counter Mode (2001). Unpublished manuscript. gitweb.tinyurl.com/dual-counter-mode

11. Chaum, D.: Untraceable electronic mail, return addresses, and digital pseudonyms. Commun. ACM **24**(2), 84–90 (1981)
12. Dingledine, R., Mathewson, N.: Tor protocol specification. The Tor Project. gitweb.torproject.org/torspec.git/tree/tor-spec.txt (2018)
13. Dingledine, R., Mathewson, N., Syverson, P.: Tor: the second-generation onion router. Naval Research Lab, Technical report (2004)
14. Duong, T., Rizzo, J.: Practical padding oracle attacks. USENIX Workshop on Offensive Technologies (WOOT) (2010)
15. Fleischmann, E., Forler, C., Lucks, S.: McOE: a family of almost foolproof online authenticated encryption schemes. In: Canteaut, A. (ed.) FSE 2012. LNCS, vol. 7549, pp. 196–215. Springer, Heidelberg (2012). https://doi.org/10.1007/978-3-642-34047-5_12
16. Goldschlag, D.M., Reed, M.G., Syverson, P.F.: Hiding routing information. In: Anderson, R. (ed.) IH 1996. LNCS, vol. 1174, pp. 137–150. Springer, Heidelberg (1996). https://doi.org/10.1007/3-540-61996-8_37
17. Goldschlag, D., Reed, M., Syverson, P.: Onion routing. Commun. ACM **42**(2), 39–41 (1999)
18. Goldwasser, G., Micali, S.: Probabilistic encryption. J. Comput. Syst. Sci. **28**(2), 270–299 (1984)
19. Hoang, V.T., Reyhanitabar, R., Rogaway, P., Vizár, D.: Online authenticated-encryption and its nonce-reuse misuse-resistance. In: Gennaro, R., Robshaw, M. (eds.) CRYPTO 2015. LNCS, vol. 9215, pp. 493–517. Springer, Heidelberg (2015). https://doi.org/10.1007/978-3-662-47989-6_24
20. Netflix: Netflix/msl. github.com/Netflix/msl/wiki. Accessed 6 April 2016
21. Nyad, D.: Never, ever give up. Talk at TEDWomen 2013 event (2013)
22. Rogaway, P.: On the role of definitions in and beyond cryptography. Manuscript. web.cs.ucdavis.edu/ rogaway/papers/def.pdf
23. Rogaway, P.: Practice-oriented provable security and the social construction of cryptography. IEEE Secur. Priv. **14**(6), 10–17 (2016)
24. Rogaway, P., Shrimpton, T.: A provable-security treatment of the key-wrap problem. In: Vaudenay, S. (ed.) EUROCRYPT 2006. LNCS, vol. 4004, pp. 373–390. Springer, Heidelberg (2006). https://doi.org/10.1007/11761679_23
25. Rogaway, P., Zhang, Y.: Onion-AE: foundations of nested encryption. In: Proceedings on Privacy Enhancing Technologies (PETS 2018), issue 2. De Gruyter Open (2018, to appear)
26. Rogaway, P., Zhang, Y.: Simplifying game-based definitions: indistinguishability up to correctness and its application to stateful AE. Manuscript (2018)
27. Syverson, P., Goldschlag, D., Reed, M.: Anonymous connections and onion routing. In: 1997 IEEE Symposium on Security and Privacy, pp. 44–54. IEEE Computer Society Press (1997)
28. Tsang, P., Solomakhin, R., Smith, S.: Authenticated Streamwise On-line Encryption. Dartmouth Computer Science Technical Report TR2009-640 (2009)
29. Vanhoef, M., Piessens, F.: Key reinstallation attacks: forcing nonce reuse in WPA2. In: ACM Conference on Computer and Communications Security (CCS 2017), pp. 1313–1328 (2017)
30. Yao, A.: How to generate and exchange secrets. In: FOCS 1986 (27th Annual Symposium on the Foundations of Computer Science), pp. 162–167. IEEE Computer Society Press (1986)
31. Yao, A.: Protocols for secure computations. In: FOCS 1982, 23rd Annual Symposium on the Foundations of Computer Science, pp. 160–164. IEEE Computer Society Press (1982)

Security Protocols

Anonymous Single-Round
Server-Aided Verification

Elena Pagnin[1]([✉]), Aikaterini Mitrokotsa[1], and Keisuke Tanaka[2]

[1] Chalmers University of Technology, Gothenburg, Sweden
{elenap,aikmitr}@chalmers.se
[2] Tokyo Institute of Technology, Tokyo, Japan
keisuke@is.titech.ac.jp

Abstract. Server-Aided Verification (SAV) is a method that can be employed to speed up the process of verifying signatures by letting the verifier outsource part of its computation load to a third party. Achieving fast and reliable verification under the presence of an untrusted server is an attractive goal in cloud computing and internet of things scenarios. In this paper, we describe a simple framework for SAV where the interaction between a verifier and an untrusted server happens via a single-round protocol. We propose a security model for SAV that refines existing ones and includes the new notions of SAV-*anonymity* and *extended unforgeability*. In addition, we apply our definitional framework to provide the first generic transformation from any signature scheme to a single-round SAV scheme that incorporates verifiable computation. Our compiler identifies two independent ways to achieve SAV-anonymity: *computationally*, through the privacy of the verifiable computation scheme, or *unconditionally*, through the adaptibility of the signature scheme.

Finally, we define three novel instantiations of SAV schemes obtained through our compiler. Compared to previous works, our proposals are the only ones which simultaneously achieve existential unforgeability and soundness against collusion.

Keywords: Server-aided verification · Digital signatures · Anonymity · Verifiable computation

1 Introduction

The design of new efficient and secure signature schemes is often a challenging task, especially when the target devices on which the scheme should run have *limited resources*, as it happens in the Internet of Things (IoT). Nowadays many IoT devices can perform quite *expensive* computations. For instance, smartphones have gained significant computational power. Carrying out several expensive tasks, however, leads to undesirable consequences as, *e.g.*, draining the battery of the device [11]. We consider signed auctions as a motivating example in an IoT setting. In signed auctions, bidders sign their offers to guarantee that

© Springer Nature Switzerland AG 2019
T. Lange and O. Dunkelman (Eds.): LATINCRYPT 2017, LNCS 11368, pp. 23–43, 2019.
https://doi.org/10.1007/978-3-030-25283-0_2

the amount is correct and that the offer belongs to them. The auctioneer considers a bid valid only if its signature is verified. Imagine that the auctioneer checks the validity of the bids using a resource-limited device. In this case, running the signature verification algorithm several times drastically affects the device's performance. In this setting one may wonder:

> Can an auctioneer *efficiently*, *securely* and *privately* check the authenticity of signed bids using a *resource-limited* device?

This paper addresses the above question in case the auctioneer has access to a computationally powerful, yet untrusted, server. This is indeed the setting of server-aided verification.

1.1 Previous Work

The concept of Server-Aided Verification (SAV) was introduced in the nineties in two independent works [1,18], and refined for the case of signature and authentication schemes by Girault and Lefranc [15].The aim of SAV is to guarantee security and reliability of the outcome of a verification procedure when part of the computation is offloaded from a trusted device, called the verifier, to an untrusted one, the server.

All existing security models for SAV consider existential forgery attacks, where the adversary, *i.e.*, the malicious server, tries to convince the verifier that an invalid signature is valid [8,15,21,23,25,26]. Despite the fundamental theoretical contributions, [15] did not consider attack scenarios in which the malicious signer colludes with the server, *e.g.*, by getting control over the server, in order to tamper with the outcome of the server-aided verification of a signature. The so-called collusion attack was defined by Wu *et al.* in [25,26] together with two SAV schemes claimed to be collusion-resistant. Subsequent works revisited the notion of signer-server collusion [8,22,23]. The most complete and rigorous definition of collusion attack is due to Chow *et al.* [8], who also showed that the protocols in [26] are no longer collusion resistant under the new definition [7,8]. Recently, Cao *et al.* [7] rose new concerns about the artificiality and the expensive communication costs of the SAV in [25].

Chow *et al.* [8] showed that the enabler of many attacks against SAV is the absence of an integrity check on the results returned by the server. Integrity however, is not the only concern when outsourcing computations. In this paper, we address for the first time privacy concerns and we introduce the notion of anonymity in the context of SAV of signatures.

1.2 Contributions

The main motivation of this work is the need for formal and realistic definitions in the area of server-aided verification. To this purpose we:

- Introduce a formalism which allows for an intuitive description of *single-round* SAV signature schemes (Sect. 3);

- Define a security model that includes three new security notions: SAV-*anonymity* (Sect. 4.3), *extended* existential unforgeability and extended *strong* unforgeability (Sect. 4.1);
- Describe the *first compiler* to a SAV signature scheme from any signature and a verifiable computation scheme (Sect. 5). Besides its simplicity, our generic composition identifies *sufficient requirements* on the underlying primitives to achieve security. In particular, we prove that under mild assumptions our compiler provides: extended (existential/strong) unforgeability (Theorem 1); soundness against collusion (Theorem 2); and SAV-anonymity when either the employed verifiable computation is private (Theorem 3) or the signature scheme is adaptive (Theorem 4).
- Apply our generic composition to obtain *new* SAV schemes for the BLS signature [3] (Sect. 6.1), Waters' signature Wat [24] (Sect. 6.2) and the *first* SAV for the CL signature by Camenisch and Lysyanskaya [5] (Sect. 6.3). While preserving efficiency, our proposals achieve better security than previous works (Table 1).

2 Preliminaries

Throughout the paper, $x \leftarrow A(y)$ denotes the output x of an algorithm A run with input y. If X is a finite set, by $x \xleftarrow{R} X$ we mean x is sampled from the uniform distribution over the set X. The expression $cost(A)$ refers to the computational cost of running algorithm A. For any positive integer n, $[n] = \{1, \ldots, n\}$ and $\mathbb{G}_n$ is a group of order n. A function $f : \mathbb{N} \to \mathbb{R}$ is said to be *negligible* if $f(n) < 1/poly(n)$ for any polynomial $poly(\cdot)$ and any $n > n_0$, for suitable $n_0 \in \mathbb{N}$. Finally, ε denotes a negligible function.

2.1 Signature Schemes

Signature schemes [4,5,13] enable one to sign a message in such a way that anyone can verify the signature and be convinced that the message was created by the signer. Formally,

Definition 1 (Signature scheme). *A signature scheme* $\Sigma = $ (SetUp, KeyGen, Sign, Verify) *consists of four, possibly randomized, polynomial time algorithms where:*

SetUp(1^λ): *on input the security parameter* $\lambda \in \mathbb{N}$, *the setup algorithm returns the global parameters* gp *of the scheme, which include a description of the message and the signature spaces* $\mathcal{M}$, $\mathcal{S}$. *The* gp *are input to all the following algorithms, even when not specified.*
KeyGen(): *the key generation outputs public-secret key pairs* (pk, sk).
  Sign(sk, m):
  on input a secret key sk *and a message* $m \in \mathcal{M}$, *the sign algorithm outputs a signature* $\sigma \in \mathcal{S}$ *for* m.
Verify(pk, m, σ): *The verification algorithm is a deterministic algorithm that given a public key* pk, *a message* $m \in \mathcal{M}$ *and a signature* $\sigma \in \mathcal{S}$, *outputs* b = 1 *for acceptance, or* b = 0 *for rejection.*

Definition 2 ((In)Valid signatures). *Let Σ be a signature scheme. We say that a signature $\sigma \in \mathcal{S}$ is valid for a message $m \in \mathcal{M}$ under the key* pk *if* Verify(pk, m, σ) = 1. *Otherwise, we say that σ is invalid.*

In this paper, we refer to (in)valid *signatures* also as (in)valid message-signature *pairs*.

2.2   Verifiable Computation

Verifiable computation schemes enable a client to delegate computations to one or more untrusted servers, in such a way that one can efficiently verify the correctness of the result returned by the server [2,12]. Gennaro *et al.* [14] formalised private verification of outsourced computations as:

Definition 3 (Verifiable Computation scheme[14]). *A verifiable computation scheme $\Gamma = ($KeyGen, ProbGen, Comp, Verify$)$ consists of four possibly randomized algorithms where:*

KeyGen(λ, f): *given the security parameter λ and a function f, the key generation algorithm produces a public key* pk, *that encodes the target function f, and a secret key* sk.
ProbGen(sk, x): *given the secret key* sk *and the input data x, the problem generation algorithm outputs a public value ω_x and a private value τ_x.*
Comp(pk, ω_x): *given the public key* pk *and the encoded input ω_x, this algorithm computes ω_y, which is an encoding of $y = f(x)$.*
Verify(sk, τ_x, ω_y): *given* sk, *τ_x and the encoded result ω_y, the verification algorithm returns y if ω_y is a valid encoding of $f(x)$, and $\perp$ otherwise.*

A verifiable scheme is efficient if verifying the outsourced computation requires less computational effort than computing the function f on the data x, *i.e.*, $cost(\mathsf{ProbGen}) + cost(\mathsf{Verify}) < cost(f(x))$.

In the remainder of the paper, we often drop the indexes and write $\tau_x = \tau$, $\omega_x = \omega$, $\omega_y = \rho$ and denote by y the output of Verify(sk, τ, ρ).

3   Single-Round Server-Aided Verification

In the context of signatures, server-aided verification is a method to improve the efficiency of a resource-limited verifier by outsourcing part of the computation load required in the signature verification to a computationally powerful server. Intuitively SAV equips a signature scheme with:

- An additional SAV.VSetup algorithm that sets up the server-aided verification and outputs a public component pb (given to the server) and a private one pr (held by the verifier only).[1]

---

[1] In [8,26] the output of SAV.VSetup is called **Vstring**.

- An interactive protocol AidedVerify executed between the verifier and the server that outputs: 0 if the input signature is invalid; 1 if the input signature is valid; and $\perp$ otherwise, *e.g.*, when the server returns values that do not match the expected output of the outsourced computation.

In this work, we want to reduce the communication cost of AidedVerify and restrict this to a single-round (two-message) interactive protocol. This choice enables us to describe the AidedVerify protocol as a sequence of three algorithms: SAV.ProbGen (run by the verifier), SAV.Comp (run by the server) and SAV.Verify (run by the verifier). This limitation is less restrictive than it may appear: all the instantiations of SAV signature schemes in [15, 17, 21, 23, 25, 26, 28] are actually single-round SAV.

We define single-round server-aided verification signature schemes as:

Definition 4 (SAV). *A single-round server-aided verification signature scheme is defined by the following possible randomized algorithms:*

SAV.Init(1^λ): *on input the security parameter $\lambda \in \mathbb{N}$, the initialisation algorithm returns the global parameters* gp *of the scheme, which are input to all the following algorithms, even when not specified.*

SAV.KeyGen(): *the key generation algorithm outputs a secret key* sk *(used to sign messages) and the corresponding public key* pk.

SAV.VSetup(): *the server-aided verification setup algorithm outputs a public verification-key* pb *and a private one* pr.

SAV.Sign(sk, m): *given a secret key* sk *and a message m the sign algorithm produces a signature σ.*

SAV.ProbGen(pr, pk, m, σ) : *on input the private verification key* pr, *the public key* pk, *a message m and a signature σ, this algorithm outputs a public-private data pair (ω, τ) for the server-aided verification.*

SAV.Comp(pb, ω): *on input the public verification key* pb *and ω the outsourced-computation algorithm returns ρ.*

SAV.Verify(pr, pk, m, σ, ρ, τ): *the verification algorithm takes as input the private verification-key* pr, *the public key* pk, *m, σ, ρ and τ. The output is $\Delta \in \{0, 1, \perp\}$.*

Intuitively, the output Δ of SAV.Verify has the following meanings:

- $\Delta = 1$: the pair (m, σ) is considered valid and we say that (m, σ) *verifies in the server-aided sense*;
- $\Delta = 0$: the pair (m, σ) is considered invalid and we say that (m, σ) does *not verify in the server-aided sense*;
- $\Delta = \perp$: the server-aided verification has failed, ρ is rejected (not σ), and nothing is inferred about the validity of (m, σ).

Unless stated otherwise, from now on SAV refers to a single-round server-aided signature verification scheme as in Definition 4. Definition 4 implicitly allows to delegate the computation of several inputs, as long as all inputs can be sent in a single round, as a vector ω.

Completeness and efficiency of SAV are defined as follows.

Definition 5 (SAV completeness). *A* SAV *is said to be complete if for all* $\lambda \in \mathbb{N}$, gp←SAV.Init(1^λ), *for any pair of keys* (pk, sk) ← SAV.KeyGen(), (pb, pr) ← SAV.VSetup() *and message* $m \xleftarrow{R} \mathcal{M}$; *given* σ ← SAV.Sign(sk, m), (ω, τ) ← SAV.ProbGen(pr, pk, m, σ) *and* ρ ← SAV.Comp(pb, ω), *it holds:*

$$\text{Prob}\left[\text{SAV.Verify}(\text{pr}, \text{pk}, m, \sigma, \rho, \tau) = 1\right] > 1 - \varepsilon$$

where the probability is taken over the coin tosses of SAV.Sign, SAV.ProbGen.

Definition 6 (SAV efficiency). *A* SAV *for a signature scheme* $\Sigma = (\text{SetUp}_\Sigma,$ KeyGen$_\Sigma$, Sign$_\Sigma$, Verify$_\Sigma$) *is said to be efficient if the computational cost of the whole server-aided verification is less than the cost of running the standard signature verification, i.e.,*

$$\big(cost(\text{SAV.ProbGen}) + cost(\text{SAV.Verify})\big) < cost(\text{Verify}_\Sigma).$$

4   Security Model

In server-aided verification there are two kinds of adversaries to be considered: the one that solely controls the server used for the aided-verification, and the one that additionally knows the secret key for signing (signer-server collusion). In the first case, we are mostly concerned about forgeries against the signature scheme, while in the second scenario we want to avoid some kind of repudiation [7]. Existing security models for SAV consider existential unforgeability (EUF) and soundness against collusion (SAC) [8,26]. In this section, we extend the notion of EUF to capture new realistic attack scenarios and we consider for the first time signer anonymity in server-aided verification.

In what follows, the adversary $\mathcal{A}$ is a probabilistic polynomial time algorithm. We denote by q_s (*resp.* q_v) the upper bound on the number of signature (*resp.* verification) queries in each query phase.

4.1   Unforgeability

Intuitively, a SAV signature scheme is unforgeable if a malicious server, taking part to the server-aided verification process, is not able to tamper with the output of the protocol. All the unforgeability notions presented in this section are based on the unforgeability under chosen message and verification attack (UF-ACMV) experiment:

Definition 7. *The unforgeability under chosen message and verification experiment* ($\mathbf{Exp}_\mathcal{A}^{\text{UF-ACMV}}[\lambda]$) *goes as follows:*

Setup. The challenger $\mathcal{C}$ runs the algorithms SAV.Init, SAV.KeyGen *and* SAV.-VSetup *to obtain the system parameters* gp, *the key pair* (pk, sk), *and the public-private verification keys* (pb, pr). *The adversary $\mathcal{A}$ is given* pk, pb, *while* sk *and* pr *are withheld from $\mathcal{A}$.*

Query Phase I. *The adversary can make a series of queries which may be of the following two kinds:*

- <u>sign</u>: $\mathcal{A}$ chooses a message m and sends it to $\mathcal{C}$. The challenger behaves as a signing oracle: it returns the value $\sigma \leftarrow$ SAV.Sign(sk, m) and stores the pair (m, σ) in an initially empty list $L \subset \mathcal{M} \times \mathcal{S}$.

- <u>verify</u>: $\mathcal{A}$ begins the interactive (single-round) protocol for server-aided verification by supplying a message-signature pair (m, σ) to its challenger. $\mathcal{C}$ simulates a verification oracle: it runs SAV.ProbGen(pr, pk, $m, \sigma) \rightarrow (\omega, \tau)$, returns ω to $\mathcal{A}$, and waits for a second input. Upon receiving an answer ρ from the adversary, the challenger returns $\Delta \leftarrow$ SAV.Verify(pr, pk, $m, \sigma, \rho, \tau)$.

The adversary can choose its queries adaptively based on the responses to previous queries, and can interact with both oracles at the same time.

Challenge. *$\mathcal{A}$ chooses a message-signature pair (m^*, σ^*) and sends it to $\mathcal{C}$. The challenger computes $(\hat{\omega}, \hat{\tau}) \leftarrow$ SAV.ProbGen(pr, pk, $m^*, \sigma^*)$. The value $\hat{\tau}$ is stored and withheld from $\mathcal{A}$, while $\hat{\omega}$ is sent to the adversary.*

Query Phase II. *In the second query phase the sign queries are as before, while the verify queries are answered using the same $\hat{\tau}$ generated for the challenge, i.e., $\mathcal{A}$ submits only ρ and $\mathcal{C}$ replies with $\Delta \leftarrow$ SAV.Verify(pr, pk, $m^*, \sigma^*, \rho, \hat{\tau})$.*

Forgery. *$\mathcal{A}$ outputs the tuple (m^*, σ^*, ρ^*).*
The experiment outputs 1 if (m^*, σ^*, ρ^*) is a forgery (see Definition 8), and 0 otherwise.

Unlike unforgeability for digital signatures, in SAV the adversary can influence the outcome of the signature verification through the value ρ^*. Moreover, $\mathcal{A}$ can perform verification queries. This is a crucial requirement as the adversary cannot run SAV.Verify on its own, since pr and τ are withheld from $\mathcal{A}$. In practice, whenever the output of the server-aided verification is $\perp$ the verifier could abort and stop interacting with the malicious server. In this work, we ignore this case and follow the approach used in [8] and in verifiable computation [14] where the adversary 'keeps on querying' independently of the outcome of the verification queries.

Definition 8 (Forgery). *Consider an execution of the UF-ACMV experiment where (m^*, σ^*, ρ^*) is the tuple output by the adversary. We define three types of forgery:*

type-1a forgery: *$(m^*, \cdot) \notin L$ and $1 \leftarrow$ SAV.Verify(pr, pk, $m^*, \sigma^*, \rho^*, \hat{\tau})$.*
type-1b forgery: *$(m^*, \sigma^*) \notin L$ and $1 \leftarrow$ SAV.Verify(pr, pk, $m^*, \sigma^*, \rho^*, \hat{\tau})$.*
type-2 forgery: *$(m^*, \sigma^*) \in L$ and $0 \leftarrow$ SAV.Verify(pr, pk, $m^*, \sigma^*, \rho^*, \hat{\tau})$,*

Existential unforgeability for SAV signature schemes is defined for a quite weak adversary: the second query phase is skipped and only type-1a forgeries are considered:

Definition 9 (Existential Unforgeability (EUF) [8]). *A SAV scheme is (ε, q_s, q_v)-existentially unforgeable under adaptive chosen message and verification attacks if* Prob $\left[\mathbf{Exp}_{\mathcal{A}}^{\mathsf{UF\text{-}ACMV}}[\lambda] = 1 \right] < \varepsilon$ *and the experiment* $\mathbf{Exp}_{\mathcal{A}}^{\mathsf{UF\text{-}ACMV}}[\lambda]$

*outputs 1 only on **type-1a forgeries**, and no query is performed in the **Query Phase II**.*

This notion of unforgeability fails to capture some realistic attack scenarios. For instance, consider the case of signed auctions. The adversary is a bidder and wants to keep the price of the goods he is bidding on under a certain threshold. A simple way to achieve this goal is to get control over the server used for the SAV and prevent signatures of higher bids from verifying correctly. This motivates us to *extend* the notion of EUF in [8,26] to also account for malicious servers tampering with the verification outcome of honestly generated message-signature pairs:

Definition 10 (Extended Existential Unforgeability (ExEUF)). *A SAV scheme is (ε, q_s, q_v)-extended existentially unforgeable under adaptive chosen message and verification attacks if* $\mathsf{Prob}\left[\mathbf{Exp}_{\mathcal{A}}^{\mathsf{UF\text{-}ACMV}}[\lambda] = 1\right] < \varepsilon$ *and the experiment* $\mathbf{Exp}_{\mathcal{A}}^{\mathsf{UF\text{-}ACMV}}[\lambda]$ *outputs 1 on **type-1a** and **type-2 forgeries**.*

Extended existential unforgeablility deals with a stronger adversary than the one considered in EUF: in ExEUF the adversary can perform two different types of forgeries and has access to an additional query phase (after setting the challenge). Resembling the notion of the strongly unforgeable signatures [4], we introduce *extended strong* unforgeability for SAV:

Definition 11 (Extended Strong Unforgeability (ExSUF)). *A SAV scheme is (ε, q_s, q_v)-extended strong unforgeable under adaptive chosen message and verification attacks if* $\mathsf{Prob}\left[\mathbf{Exp}_{\mathcal{A}}^{\mathsf{UF\text{-}ACMV}}[\lambda] = 1\right] < \varepsilon$ *and* $\mathbf{Exp}_{\mathcal{A}}^{\mathsf{UF\text{-}ACMV}}[\lambda]$ *outputs 1 on **type-1a, type-1b** and **type-2 forgeries**.*

In ExSUF there is no restriction on the pair (m^*, σ^*) chosen by the adversary: it can be a new message (type-1a), a new signature on a previously-queried message (type-1b) or an honestly generated pair obtained in the first Query Phase (type-2).

4.2 Soundness Against Collusion

In collusion attacks, the adversary controls the server used for the aided verification and holds the signer's secret key. This may happen when a malicious signer hacks the server and wants to tamper with the outcome of a signature verification. As a motivating example consider signed auctions. The owner of a good could take part to the auction (as the malicious signer) and influence its price. For instance, in order to increase the cost of the good, the malicious signer can produce an invalid signature for a high bid (message) and make other bidders overpay for it. To tamper with the verification of the invalid signature, the malicious signer can use the server and make his (invalid) signature verify when the bid is stated. However, in case no one outbids him, the malicious signer can repudiate the signature as it is actually invalid.

We define collusion as in [8], with two minor adaptations: (i) we use our single-round framework, that allows us to clearly state the information flow between $\mathcal{A}$ and $\mathcal{C}$; and (ii) we introduce a second query phase, after the challenge phase (to strengthen the adversary).

Definition 12 (Soundness Against Collusion (SAC)). *Define the experiment* $\mathbf{Exp}_{\mathcal{A}}^{\mathsf{ACVAuC}}[\lambda]$ *to be* $\mathbf{Exp}_{\mathcal{A}}^{\mathsf{UF\text{-}ACMV}}[\lambda]$ *where:*

- *in the Setup phase, $\mathcal{C}$ gives to $\mathcal{A}$ all keys except* pr, *and*
- *no sign query is performed, and*
- *the tuple (m^*, σ^*, ρ^*) output by $\mathcal{A}$ at the end of the experiment is considered forgery if $\Delta \leftarrow$ SAV.Verify$(\mathsf{pr}, \mathsf{pk}, m^*, \sigma^*, \rho^*, \hat{\tau})$ is such that $\Delta \neq \perp$ and $\Delta \neq$ SAV.Verify$(\mathsf{pr}, \mathsf{pk}, m^*, \sigma^*, \rho, \hat{\tau})$, where $\rho \leftarrow$ SAV.Comp$(\mathsf{pb}, \hat{\omega})$ is generated honestly. A SAV signature scheme is (ε, q_v)-sound against adaptive chosen verification attacks under collusion if* $\mathrm{Prob}\left[\mathbf{Exp}_{\mathcal{A}}^{\mathsf{ACVAuC}}[\lambda] = 1\right] < \varepsilon$.

Definition 12 highlights connections between the notions of extended existential unforgeability and soundness against collusion. In particular, it is possible to think of collusion attacks as unforgeability attacks where $\mathcal{A}$ possesses the signing secret key sk (and thus no *sign* query is needed), and a forgery is a tuple for which the output of the server-aided verification does not coincide with the correct one, *e.g.*, if $\sigma^* \leftarrow$ SAV.Sign(sk, m^*) then SAV.Verify$(\mathsf{pr}, \mathsf{pk}, m^*, \sigma^*, \rho^*, \hat{\tau})$ returns 0.

4.3 Anonymity

We initiate the study of anonymity in the context of server-aided verification of signatures and provide the first definition of SAV-anonymity.

Consider the running setting of signed auctions. If a malicious server can distinguish whose signature it is performing the aided-verification of, it can easily 'keep out' target bidders from the auction by preventing their signatures from verifying (in the server aided sense). To prevent such an attack, bidders may want to hide their identity from the untrusted server. SAV-anonymity guarantees precisely this: the auctioneer (trusted verifier) learns the identities of the bidders (signers), while the untrusted server is not able to determine whose signature was involved in the SAV.

Definition 13 (SAV-anonymity). *A SAV scheme is (ε, q_v)-SAV-anonymous if* $\mathrm{Prob}\left[\mathbf{Exp}_{\mathcal{A}}^{\mathsf{SAV\text{-}anon}}[\lambda] = 1\right] < \frac{1}{2} + \varepsilon$ *and* $\mathbf{Exp}_{\mathcal{A}}^{\mathsf{SAV\text{-}anon}}[\lambda]$ *is:*

Setup. The challenger runs the algorithms SAV.Init, SAV.VSetup to obtain the system parameters and the verification keys $(\mathsf{pb}, \mathsf{pr})$. Then it runs SAV.KeyGen twice to generate $(\mathsf{sk}_0, \mathsf{pk}_0), (\mathsf{sk}_1, \mathsf{pk}_1)$ and draws $b \xleftarrow{R} \{0,1\}$. $\mathcal{C}$ gives $\mathsf{pb}, \mathsf{pk}_0, \mathsf{pk}_1$ to $\mathcal{A}$ and retains the secret values $\mathsf{pr}, \mathsf{sk}_0, \mathsf{sk}_1$.

Query I. $\mathcal{A}$ can adaptively perform up to q_v partial-verification queries as follows. The adversary sends a pair (m, i), $i \in \{0,1\}$ to $\mathcal{C}$. The challenger computes

$\sigma \leftarrow$ SAV.Sign(sk_i, m), *runs* SAV.ProbGen$(\mathsf{pr}, \mathsf{pk}_i, m, \sigma) \rightarrow (\omega, \tau)$ *and returns* ω *to* $\mathcal{A}$.

Challenge. *The adversary chooses a message* m^* *to be challenged on, and sends it to* $\mathcal{C}$. *The challenger computes* $\sigma \leftarrow$ SAV.Sign(sk_b, m^*) *and* $(\omega, \tau) \leftarrow$ SAV.ProbGen$(\mathsf{pr}, \mathsf{pk}_b, m^*, \sigma)$; *and sends* ω *to the adversary.*

Query II. $\mathcal{A}$ *can perform another query phase, as in Query I.*

Output. *The adversary outputs a guess* $b^* \in \{0, 1\}$ *for the identity* b *chosen by* $\mathcal{C}$. *The experiment outputs 1 if* $b^* = b$ *and 0 otherwise.*

The fundamental difference between anonymity for signatures schemes [13,27] and SAV-anonymity lies in the choice of the challenge message m^*. In the former case, it is chosen by the challenger at random, while in SAV we let the adversary select it. This change increases the adversary's power and reflects several application scenarios where $\mathcal{A}$ learns the messages (*e.g.*, bids in signed auctions). We remark that in SAV-anonymity the adversary does not have access to the verification outcome Δ, as this would correspond to having a verification oracle, which is not allowed in the anonymity game for signature schemes [13,27].

5   A Compiler for SAV

We present here the first generic compiler for server-aided verification of signatures. Our generic composition method allows to combine any signature scheme Σ with an efficient verifiable computation scheme Γ for a function f involved in the signature verification algorithm, and outputs SAV$_\Sigma^\Gamma$, a single-round server-aided verification scheme for Σ.

The idea to employ verifiable computation in SAV comes from the following observation. All the attacks presented in [8] succeed because in the target SAV schemes the verifier never checks the validity of the values returned by the server. We leverage the efficiency and security properties of verifiable computation to mitigate such attacks.

5.1   Description of Our Compiler

Let $\Sigma = ($SetUp$_\Sigma$, KeyGen$_\Sigma$, Sign$_\Sigma$, Verify$_\Sigma)$ be a signature scheme and $\Gamma = ($KeyGen$^\Gamma$, ProbGen$^\Gamma$, Comp$^\Gamma$, Verify$^\Gamma)$ be a verifiable computation scheme.[2] In our generic composition, we identify a computationally-expensive sub-routine of Verify$_\Sigma$ that we refer to as Ver$_\mathsf{H}$ (the *heavy* part of the signature verification); and we outsource $f =$ Ver$_\mathsf{H}$ using the verifiable computation scheme Γ. To ease the presentation, we introduce:

ProbGen$^\mathsf{PRE}$: This algorithm prepares the input to ProbGen$^\Gamma$.

---

[2] To improve readability, we put the subscript Σ (*resp.* superscript Γ) to each algorithm related to the signature (*resp.* verifiable computation) scheme.

$\mathsf{Ver_L}$: This algorithm is the computationally *light* part of the signature verification. More precisely, $\mathsf{Ver_L}$ is Verify_Σ where $\mathsf{Ver_H}$ is replaced by the output y of Verify^Γ. It satisfies: $cost(\mathsf{Ver_L}) < cost(\mathsf{Verify}_\Sigma)$ and $\mathsf{Ver_L}(\mathsf{pk}_\Sigma, m, \sigma, y) = \mathsf{Verify}_\Sigma(\mathsf{pk}, m, \sigma)$ whenever $y \neq \bot$.

Definition 14 ($\mathsf{SAV}_\Sigma^\Gamma$). *Let Σ, Γ and f be as above. Our generic composition method for single-round server-aided verification signature scheme $\mathsf{SAV}_\Sigma^\Gamma$ is defined by the following possibly randomized algorithms:*

$\mathsf{SAV.Init}(1^\lambda)$: *the initialisation algorithm outputs the global parameters* $\mathsf{gp} \leftarrow \mathsf{SetUp}_\Sigma(1^\lambda)$, *which are implicitly input to all the algorithms.*
$\mathsf{SAV.KeyGen}()$: *this algorithm outputs* $(\mathsf{pk}_\Sigma, \mathsf{sk}_\Sigma) \leftarrow \mathsf{KeyGen}_\Sigma()$.
$\mathsf{SAV.Sign}(\mathsf{sk}_\Sigma, m)$: *the sign algorithm outputs* $\sigma \leftarrow \mathsf{Sign}_\Sigma(\mathsf{sk}_\Sigma, m)$.
$\mathsf{SAV.VSetup}()$: *the verification setup algorithm outputs a pair of verification keys* $(\mathsf{pk}^\Gamma, \mathsf{sk}^\Gamma) \leftarrow \mathsf{KeyGen}^\Gamma(\lambda, f)$, *where the function f is described in* gp.
$\mathsf{SAV.ProbGen}(\mathsf{sk}^\Gamma, \mathsf{pk}_\Sigma, m, \sigma)$: *this algorithm first runs* $\mathsf{ProbGen}^{\mathsf{PRE}}(\mathsf{pk}_\Sigma, m, \sigma) \to x$ *to produce an encoding of* pk_Σ, m, σ. *Then x is used to compute the output* $(\omega, \tau) \leftarrow \mathsf{ProbGen}^\Gamma(\mathsf{sk}^\Gamma, x)$.
$\mathsf{SAV.Comp}(\mathsf{pk}^\Gamma, \omega)$: *this algorithm returns* $\rho \leftarrow \mathsf{Comp}^\Gamma(\mathsf{pk}^\Gamma, \omega)$.
$\mathsf{SAV.Verify}(\mathsf{sk}^\Gamma, \mathsf{pk}_\Sigma, m, \sigma, \rho, \tau)$: *the verification algorithm executes* $\mathsf{Verify}^\Gamma (\mathsf{sk}^\Gamma, \rho, \tau) \to y$; *if $y = \bot$, it sets $\Delta = \bot$ and returns. Otherwise, it returns the output of* $\mathsf{Ver_L}(\mathsf{pk}_\Sigma, m, \sigma, y) \to \Delta \in \{0, 1\}$.

Intuitively, the $\mathsf{SAV.ProbGen}$ algorithm prepares the inputs for the delegated computations (ω) and the private values for the verification of computations (τ). The $\mathsf{SAV.Comp}$ algorithm performs the verifiable delegation of the bilinear pairing computation, and returns ρ, which includes the encoding of the bilinear pairing and some additional values to prove the correctness of the performed operations. Finally, $\mathsf{SAV.Verify}$ checks the correctness of the values received by the server, and proceed with the (light-weight) verification of the signature, only if the server has behaved according to the protocol.

Completeness of $\mathsf{SAV}_\Sigma^\Gamma$. The correctness of $\mathsf{SAV}_\Sigma^\Gamma$ is a straight-forward computation assuming that Σ is complete and Γ is correct (see the extended version of this paper [19] for a detailed proof).

Efficiency of $\mathsf{SAV}_\Sigma^\Gamma$. It is immediate to check that $cost(\mathsf{Verify}_\Sigma) = cost(\mathsf{Ver_L}) + cost(\mathsf{Ver_H})$. The $\mathsf{ProbGen}^{\mathsf{PRE}}$ algorithm is just performing encodings of its inputs (usually projections), and does not involve computationally expensive operations.[3] By the efficiency of verifiable computation schemes we have: $cost(\mathsf{Ver_H}) > cost(\mathsf{ProbGen}^\Gamma) + cost(\mathsf{Verify}^\Gamma)$ and thus $cost(\mathsf{Verify}_\Sigma) > cost(\mathsf{ProbGen}^{\mathsf{PRE}}) + cost(\mathsf{ProbGen}^\Gamma) + cost(\mathsf{Verify}^\Gamma) + cost(\mathsf{Ver_L})$, which proves the last claim.

Our generic composition enjoys two additional features: it applies to *any* signature scheme and it allows to reduce the security of $\mathsf{SAV}_\Sigma^\Gamma$ to the security of its building blocks, Σ and Γ. To demonstrate the first claim, let us set $f = \mathsf{Ver_H} = \mathsf{Verify}_\Sigma$ and $\mathsf{ProbGen}^{\mathsf{PRE}}(\mathsf{pk}_\Sigma, m, \sigma) \to x = (\mathsf{pk}_\Sigma, m, \sigma)$. The correctness of Γ

---

[3] This claim will become clear after seeing examples of SAV signature schemes.

implies that $y = \mathsf{Ver}_\mathsf{H}(x) = \mathsf{Verify}_\Sigma(\mathsf{pk}_\Sigma, m, \sigma)$. In this case, $\mathsf{Ver}_\mathsf{L}(\mathsf{pk}_\Sigma, m, \sigma, y)$ is the function that returns 1 if $y = 1$ and 0 otherwise. We defer the proof of the second claim to the following section.

5.2 Security of Our Generic Composition

The following theorems state the security of the compiler presented in Definition 14. Our approach is to identify sufficient requirements on Σ and Γ to guarantee specific security properties in the resulting $\mathsf{SAV}_\Sigma^\Gamma$ scheme. All the proofs can be found in the extended version of this paper [19]. We highlight that the results below apply to all our instantiations of the SAV signature schemes presented in Sect. 6, since these are obtained via our generic composition method.

Theorem 1 (Extended Unforgeability of $\mathsf{SAV}_\Sigma^\Gamma$). *Let Σ be an $(\varepsilon_\Sigma, q_s)$-existentially (resp. strongly) unforgeable signature scheme, and Γ an $(\varepsilon^\Gamma, q_v)$-secure verifiable computation scheme. Then $\mathsf{SAV}_\Sigma^\Gamma$ is $(\frac{\varepsilon_\Sigma + \varepsilon^\Gamma}{2}, q_s, q_v)$-extended existentially (resp. strongly) unforgeable.*

The proof proceeds by reduction transforming type-1a (*resp.* type-1b) forgeries into existential (*resp.* strong) forgeries against Σ; and type-2 forgeries, into forgeries against the security of Γ.

Theorem 2 Soundness Against Collusion of $\mathsf{SAV}_\Sigma^\Gamma$). *Let Σ be a correct signature scheme and Γ an $(\varepsilon^\Gamma, q_v)$-secure verifiable computation scheme. Then $\mathsf{SAV}_\Sigma^\Gamma$ is $(\varepsilon^\Gamma, q_v)$-sound against collusion.*

The intuition behind the proof of Theorem 2 is the same as in Theorem 1 for the case of type-2 forgeries.

We present now two independent ways to achieve SAV-anonymity for schemes obtained with our compiler: leveraging either the privacy of the verifiable computation scheme or the adaptibility of the signature scheme.

Theorem 3 (Anonymity of $\mathsf{SAV}_\Sigma^\Gamma$ from Private Verification). *Let Σ be a correct signature scheme and Γ an $(\varepsilon^\Gamma, q_v)$-private verifiable computation scheme. Then $\mathsf{SAV}_\Sigma^\Gamma$ is $(\varepsilon^\Gamma, q_v)$-$\mathsf{SAV}$-anonymous.*

Theorem 3 does not require Σ to be anonymous and SAV-anonymity comes directly from the privacy of the verifiable computation scheme.

Key-homomorphic signatures have been recently introduced by Derler and Slamanig [10]. In a nutshell, a signature scheme provides *adaptibility* of signatures [10] if given a signature σ for a message m under a public key pk, it is possible to publicly create a valid σ' for the same message m under a new public key pk'. In particular, there exists an algorithm Adapt that, given pk, m, σ and a shift amount h, returns a pair (pk', σ') for which $\mathsf{Verify}(\mathsf{pk}', m, \sigma') = 1$ (cf. Definition 16 in [10] for a formal statement).[4]

---

[4] To provide an example, consider the BLS signature scheme [3]. Given $\mathsf{pk} = g^{\mathsf{sk}}$, $m \in \{0,1\}^*$, $\sigma \in \mathbb{G}_p$ and $\mathsf{h} \in \mathbb{Z}_p$, the output of Adapt can be defined as: $\mathsf{pk}' = \mathsf{pk} \cdot g^\mathsf{h}$ and $\sigma' = \sigma \cdot H(m)^\mathsf{h}$. It is immediate to check that (σ', m) is a valid pair under pk'.

Theorem 4 (Anonymity of $\mathsf{SAV}_\Sigma^\Gamma$ from Perfect Adaption). *Let Σ be a signature scheme with perfect adaption and Γ a correct verifiable computation scheme. If the output of $\mathsf{ProbGen}^{\mathsf{PRE}}$ depends only on the adapted values, i.e., for all $\mathsf{pr}, \mathsf{pk}, m, \sigma$ there is a function G such that:*

$$\mathsf{ProbGen}^{\mathsf{PRE}}(\mathsf{pr}, \mathsf{pk}, m, \sigma) = \mathsf{G}(\mathsf{Adapt}(\mathsf{pk}, m, \sigma, \mathsf{h}), m)$$

for a randomly chosen shift amount h, then $\mathsf{SAV}_\Sigma^\Gamma$ is unconditionally SAV-anonymous.

Theorem 4 provides a new application of key-homomorphic signatures to anonymity. The proof is inspired to the tricks used in [10], intuitively SAV-anonymity follows from the indistinguishability of the output of Adapt from $(\mathsf{pk}'', \sigma'' \leftarrow \mathsf{Sign}(\mathsf{sk}'', m))$ for a freshly generated key pair $(\mathsf{pk}'', \mathsf{sk}'')$. Many signatures based on the discrete logarithm problem enjoy this property, *e.g.*, BLS [3] and Wat [24].

6 New Instantiations of SAV Schemes

Our generic composition requires the existence of a verifiable computation scheme for a function $f = \mathsf{Ver}_\mathsf{H}$ used in the signature verification algorithm. To the best of the authors' knowledge, there are verifiable computation schemes for arithmetic circuits [9,20] and bilinear pairings [6], but no result is yet known for simpler computations such as hash functions and group exponentiations. Following previous works' approach, we consider only SAV for pairing-based signatures [8,21,26,28], since bilinear pairings are bottle-neck computations for resource-limited devices.[5]

All our instantiations of SAV schemes are obtained using the compiler in Definition 14. Their security therefore follows from the results of Sect. 5.2, once shown that that the chosen schemes satisfy the hypothesis of the theorems. For conciseness, we only define the two algorithms $\mathsf{ProbGen}^{\mathsf{PRE}}$ and Ver_L. Appendix A contains thorough descriptions.

6.1 A Secure SAV for BLS ($\mathsf{SAV}_{\mathsf{BLS}}^{\mathsf{CDS_1}}$)

The BLS signature by Boneh *et al.* [3] has been widely used for constructing server-aided verification schemes, *e.g.*, Protocols I and II in [26]. Cao *et al.* [7] and Chow *et al.* [8] have shown that all the existing SAV for BLS are neither existentially unforgeable, nor sound against collusion. This motivates us to propose $\mathsf{SAV}_{\mathsf{BLS}}^{\mathsf{CDS_1}}$ (described in Fig. 1). As a verifiable scheme for the pairing computation, we employ '*a protocol for public variable A and B*' by Canard *et al.* [6], which we refer to as $\mathsf{CDS_1}$.

---

[5] To give benchmarks, let M_p denote the computational cost of a base field multiplication in $\mathbb{F}_p$ with $\log p = 256$, then computing z^a for any $z \in \mathbb{F}_p$ and $a \in [p]$ costs about $256 M_p$, while computing the Optimal Ate pairing on the BN curve requires about $16000 M_p$ (results extrapolated from Table 1 in [16]).

$\mathsf{ProbGen}^{\mathsf{PRE}}(\mathsf{pk}_\Sigma, m, \sigma)$: on input $\mathsf{pk}_\Sigma \in \mathbb{G}_1$, $m \in \{0,1\}^*$ and $\sigma \in \mathbb{G}_1$, the algorithm returns $x = \big((\mathsf{pk}_\Sigma, H(m)), (\sigma, g)\big)$.

$\mathsf{Ver}_{\mathsf{L}}(\mathsf{pk}_\Sigma, m, \sigma, y)$: this algorithm is $\mathsf{Verify}_{\mathsf{BLS}}$ where the computation of the two pairings is replaced with the output $y = (y_1, y_2)$ of $\mathsf{Verify}^{\mathsf{CDS}_2}$. Formally, $\mathsf{Ver}_{\mathsf{L}}$ checks whether $y_1 = y_2$, in which case it outputs $\Delta = 1$, otherwise it returns $\Delta = 0$.

Fig. 1. The core algorithms of $\mathsf{SAV}_{\mathsf{BLS}}^{\mathsf{CDS}_1}$.

By the correctness of the CDS_1 scheme $y_2 = e(\mathsf{pk}_\Sigma, H(m))$ and $y_2 = e(\sigma, g)$, thus $\mathsf{Ver}_{\mathsf{L}}$ has the same output as $\mathsf{Verify}_{\mathsf{BLS}}$. Given that BLS is strongly unforgeable in the random oracle model [3] and that CDS_1 is secure in the generic group model [6], $\mathsf{SAV}_{\mathsf{BLS}}^{\mathsf{CDS}_1}$ is extended strongly unforgeable and sound against collusion. Our SAV scheme for the BLS is not SAV-anonymous: the signer's public key is given to the server for the aided verification. However, SAV-anonymity can be simply gained via the adaptability of BLS [10].

In $\mathsf{SAV}_{\mathsf{BLS}}^{\mathsf{CDS}_1}$ the verifier does not need to perform *any* pairing computation. This is a very essential feature, especially if the verifying device has very limited computational power, *e.g.*, an RFID tag.

6.2   A Secure SAV for Wat ($\mathsf{SAV}_{\mathsf{Wat}}^{\mathsf{CDS}_1}$)

Wu *et al.* [26] proposed a SAV for Waters' signature Wat [24], which is neither existentially unforgeable nor sound against collusion. Here we propose $\mathsf{SAV}_{\mathsf{Wat}}^{\mathsf{CDS}_1}$ (described in Fig. 2), which is similar to Protocol III in [26], but has strong security guarantees thanks to the verifiable computation scheme for *'public A and B'* CDS_1 [6].

$\mathsf{ProbGen}^{\mathsf{PRE}}(\mathsf{pk}_\Sigma, m, \sigma)$: given $\mathsf{pk}_\Sigma \in \mathbb{G}_1$, $m \in \{0,1\}^*$ and $\sigma \in \mathbb{G}_1$, select $\mathsf{h} \xleftarrow{R} \mathbb{Z}_p$, compute $(\mathsf{pk}'_\Sigma, \sigma') \leftarrow \mathsf{Adapt}(\mathsf{pk}_\Sigma, m, \sigma, \mathsf{h})$, return $x = (\mathsf{pk}'_\Sigma, m, \sigma')$.

$\mathsf{Ver}_{\mathsf{L}}(\mathsf{pk}'_\Sigma, m, \sigma, y)$: this is $\mathsf{Verify}_{\mathsf{Wat}}$ where the computation of the two pairings is replaced with the outputs y_1, y_2 of $\mathsf{Verify}^{\mathsf{CDS}_1}$. Formally, $\mathsf{Ver}_{\mathsf{L}}$ checks if $y_1 = \mathsf{pk}'_\Sigma \cdot y_2$, in which case it outputs $\Delta = 1$, otherwise it returns $\Delta = 0$.

Fig. 2. The core algorithms of $\mathsf{SAV}_{\mathsf{Wat}}^{\mathsf{CDS}_1}$.

By the correctness of the CDS_1 scheme $y_1 = e(\sigma_1, g)$, and $y_2 = e(H(m), \sigma_2)$. Thus, $\mathsf{Ver}_{\mathsf{L}}$ has the same output as $\mathsf{Verify}_{\mathsf{Wat}}$. Given that CDS_1 is secure in the generic group model [6], and that Wat is existentially unforgeable in the standard model [24] our $\mathsf{SAV}_{\mathsf{Wat}}^{\mathsf{CDS}_1}$ is extended existential unforgeable and sound against collusion. Similarly to Protocol III in [26], $\mathsf{SAV}_{\mathsf{Wat}}^{\mathsf{CDS}_1}$ achieves SAV-anonymity thanks to the perfect adaption of Wat [10].

6.3   The First SAV for CL ($\mathsf{SAV}_{\mathsf{CL}}^{\mathsf{CDS_2}}$)

The verification of the BLS and the Wat signatures only requires the computation of two bilinear pairings. We want to move the focus to more complex signature schemes that would benefit more of server-aided verification. To this end, we consider scheme A by Camenish and Lysyanskaya [5], which we refer to as CL, where Verify$_{\mathsf{CL}}$ involves the computation of five bilinear pairings. For verifiability we employ CDS$_2$, 'a protocol with public constant B and variable secret A' by Canard et al. [6]. Our $\mathsf{SAV}_{\mathsf{CL}}^{\mathsf{CDS_2}}$ scheme is reported in Fig. 3.

ProbGen^{PRE}($\mathsf{pk}_\Sigma, m, \sigma$) : this algorithm simply returns the first two entries of the signature $\sigma = (\sigma_1, \sigma_2, \sigma_3)$, i.e., $x = (\sigma_1, \sigma_2)$.

Ver$_{\mathsf{L}}$($\mathsf{pk}_\Sigma, m, \sigma, y$) : this algorithm is Verify$_{\mathsf{CL}}$, except for two pairing computations which are replaced with the outcome $y = (\beta_1, \beta_2)$ of Verify$^{\mathsf{CDS_2}}$. More precisely, the Ver$_{\mathsf{L}}$ algorithm computes $\alpha_1 = e(\sigma_1, Y)$, $\alpha_2 = e(X, \sigma_1)$ and $\alpha_3 = e(X, \sigma_2)^m$. It then checks whether $\alpha_1 = \beta_1$ and $\alpha_2 \cdot \alpha_3 = \beta_2$. If both of the conditions hold, the algorithm returns $\Delta = 1$, otherwise $\Delta = 0$.

Fig. 3. The core algorithms of $\mathsf{SAV}_{\mathsf{CL}}^{\mathsf{CDS_2}}$.

By the correctness of CDS$_2$ we have: $y_1 = \beta_1 = e(\sigma, g)$, and $y_2 = \beta_2 = e(H(m), \mathsf{pk}_\Sigma)$. Therefore Ver$_{\mathsf{L}}$ performs the same checks as Verify$_{\mathsf{CL}}$ and the two algorithms have the same output. Given that CL is existential unforgeable in the standard model [5] and CDS$_2$ is secure and private in the generic group model [6], $\mathsf{SAV}_{\mathsf{CL}}^{\mathsf{CDS_2}}$ is extended-existential unforgeable, sound against collusion and SAV-anonymous. Therefore $\mathsf{SAV}_{\mathsf{CL}}^{\mathsf{CDS_2}}$ is an example of a scheme which is SAV-anonymous although the base signature scheme is not anonymous.

6.4   Comparison with Previous Work

Table 1 gives a compact overview of how our SAV schemes compare to previous proposals in terms of unforgeability, soundness under collusion and SAV-anonymity. We report only the highest level of unforgeability that the scheme provides. A yes (resp. no) in the table states that the scheme does (resp. does not) achieve the property written at the beginning of the row, e.g., Protocol III does not employ a verifiable computation scheme and provides SAV-anonymity. Every scheme or property is followed by a reference paper or the section where the claim is proven.

Regarding efficiency, the computational cost of pairing-based algorithms is influenced by three main parameters: (i) the elliptic curve, (ii) the field size, and (iii) the bilinear pairing. As a result, it is impossible to state that a given algorithm is efficient for all pairings and for all curves, since even the computational cost of the most basic operations (e.g., point addition) variates significantly with

Table 1. Comparison among our SAV schemes and previous works: Protocol I (Fig. 3 in [26]), Protocol II (Fig. 5 in [26]), Protocol III (Fig. 4 in [26]), SAV-ZSS [15] (depicted in Fig. 1 in [26]).

	Protocol I [26]	Protocol II [26]	$SAV_{BLS}^{CDS_1}$	Protocol III [26]	$SAV_{Wat}^{CDS_1}$	SAV-ZSS [15]	$SAV_{CL}^{CDS_2}$
Signature	BLS [3]	BLS [3]	BLS [3]	Wat [24]	Wat [24]	ZSS [28]	CL [5]
Verifiability	no	no	CDS_1 [6]	no	CDS_1 [6]	no	CDS_2 [6]
Unforgeability	EUF [26]	no [8]	ExSUF (Sect. 6.1)	no [19]	ExEUF (Sect. 6.2)	EUF [15]	ExEUF (Sect. 6.3)
Collusion resistance	no [8]	no [19]	yes (Sect. 6.1)	no [19]	yes (Sect. 6.1)	no [19]	yes (Sect. 6.2)
Anonymity	no [19]	no [19]	no (Sect. 6.3)	yes [19]	yes (Sect. 6.3)	no [19]	yes (Sect. 6.3)

the above parameters. For example, CDS_2 provides a 70% efficiency gain[6] for the delegator (verifier) when the employed pairing is the Optimal Ate pairing on the KSS-18 curve [6], but is nearly inefficient when computed on the BN curve [16].

7 Conclusions

In this paper, we provided a framework for single-round server-aided verification signature schemes and introduced a security model which extends previous proposals towards more realistic attack scenarios and stronger adversaries. In addition, we defined the first generic composition method to obtain a SAV for any signature scheme using an appropriate verifiable computation scheme. Our compiler identifies for the first time sufficient requirements on the underlying primitives to ensure the security and anonymity of the resulting SAV scheme. In particular, we showed sufficient conditions to achieve both computational and unconditional SAV-anonymity. Finally, we introduced three new SAV signature schemes obtained via our generic composition method, that simultaneously achieve existential unforgeability and soundness against collusion.

Currently, Canard *et al.*'s is the only verifiable computation scheme for pairings available in the literature. Considering the wide applicability of bilinear pairings in cryptography, a more efficient verifiable computation scheme for these functions would render pairings a server-aided accessible computation to a large variety of resource-limited devices, such as the ones involved in IoT and cloud computing settings.

Acknowledgements. We thank Dario Fiore (Assistant Research Professor) for providing useful comments on the contributions of this paper. This work was partially supported by the Japanese Society for the Promotion of Science (JSPS), summer program, the SNSF project SwissSenseSynergy and the STINT project IB 2015-6001.

---

[6] Efficiency gain is the ratio $\big(cost(\mathsf{SAV.ProbGen}) + cost(\mathsf{SAV.Verify})\big)/cost(\mathsf{Verify}_\Sigma)$.

A Detailed Descriptions of Our SAV Schemes

In this Appendix we present thorough descriptions of the new SAV scheme proposed in this paper (Sect. 6). The complete explanations of the algorithms in $\mathsf{SAV}_{\mathsf{BLS}}^{\mathsf{CDS_1}}$, $\mathsf{SAV}_{\mathsf{Wat}}^{\mathsf{CDS_1}}$ and $\mathsf{SAV}_{\mathsf{CL}}^{\mathsf{CDS_2}}$ are presented in Figs. 4, 5 and 6 respectively. For consistency, we adopt the multiplicative notation for describing the operation elliptic curve groups.

$\mathsf{SAV.Init}(1^\lambda) = \mathsf{SetUp}_{\mathsf{BLS}}(1^\lambda)$. This algorithm generates the global parameters of the scheme, that include: a Gap Diffie-Hellman bilinear group $(p, g, \mathbb{G}, \mathbb{G}_T, e)$ according to the security parameter λ; and a hash function $H : \{0,1\}^* \to \mathbb{G}$ that maps messages $m \in \mathcal{M} = \{0,1\}^*$ to group elements in $\mathbb{G}$. The output is $\mathsf{gp} = (p, g, H, \mathbb{G}, \mathbb{G}_T, e)$.

$\mathsf{SAV.KeyGen}() = \mathsf{KeyGen}_{\mathsf{BLS}}()$. The key generation algorithm draws a random $s \xleftarrow{R} \mathbb{Z}_p^*$ and outputs $(\mathsf{pk}, \mathsf{sk}) = (g^s, s)$.

$\mathsf{SAV.VSetup}() = \mathsf{KeyGen}^{\mathsf{CDS_1}}()$. This algorithm outputs $\mathsf{pr} = \mathsf{void}$ and $\mathsf{pb} = (p, \mathbb{G}, \mathbb{G}_T, e, g, \hat{\beta})$, where $\hat{\beta} = e(g,g)$.

$\mathsf{SAV.Sign}(\mathsf{sk}, m) = \mathsf{Sign}_{\mathsf{BLS}}(\mathsf{sk}, m)$. The signing algorithm outputs $\sigma = H(m)^s \in \mathbb{G}$.

$\mathsf{SAV.ProbGen}(\mathsf{void}, \mathsf{pk}, m, \sigma)$. This algorithm runs $\mathsf{ProbGen}^{\mathsf{PRE}}(\mathsf{pk}, m, \sigma) \to ((\mathsf{pk}, H(m)), (\sigma, g))$ and returns the outputs of $\mathsf{ProbGen}^{\mathsf{CDS_1}}$ on the two pairs $(\mathsf{pk}, H(m))$ and (σ, g). In details, for $(\mathsf{pk}, H(m))$ the problem generator algorithm selects two random values $r_1, r_2 \xleftarrow{R} \mathbb{Z}_p$, computes the points $R_1 = \mathsf{pk}^{r_2^{-1}} g^{r_1}$, $R_2 = H(m)^{r_1^{-1}} g^{r_2}$ and $\hat{U} = \hat{\beta}^{r_1 r_2}$. This process (with fresh randomness) is applied to the pair (σ, g) as well. The final outputs are $\omega = ((\mathsf{pk}, H(m), R_1^{(1)}, R_2^{(1)}), (\sigma, g, R_1^{(2)}, R_2^{(2)}))$ and $\tau = ((\hat{U}^{(1)}, r_1^{(1)}, r_2^{(1)}), (\hat{U}^{(2)} r_1^{(2)}, r_2^{(2)}))$.

$\mathsf{SAV.Comp}(\mathsf{pb}, \omega)$. The algorithm computes the following bilinear pairings: $\alpha_1^{(1)} = e(\mathsf{pk}, H(m))$, $\alpha_2^{(1)} = e(R_1^{(1)}, R_2^{(1)})(e(\mathsf{pk}, g)e(g, H(m)))^{-1}$, $\alpha_1^{(2)} = e(\sigma, g)$, $\alpha_2^{(2)} = e(R_1^{(2)}, R_2^{(2)})(e(\sigma, g)e(g, g))^{-1}$. It returns $\rho = (\rho_1, \rho_2) = ((\alpha_1^{(1)}, \alpha_2^{(1)}), (\alpha_1^{(2)}, \alpha_2^{(2)}))$.

$\mathsf{SAV.Verify}(\mathsf{void}, \mathsf{pk}, m, \sigma, \rho, \tau)$. The verification algorithm first runs $\mathsf{Verify}^{\mathsf{CDS_1}}(\rho_i, \tau_i)$ for $i \in [2]$, i.e., checks whether $\alpha_2^{(i)} = \hat{U}^{(i)}(\alpha_1^{(i)})^{(r_1^{(i)} r_2^{(i)})^{-1}}$ and $\alpha_1 \in \mathbb{G}_T$. If any of the previous checks fails, the verification algorithm returns $\Delta = \bot$ and halts. Otherwise, it sets $y_i = \alpha_1^{(i)}$, for $i \in [2]$ and runs $\mathsf{Ver}_{\mathsf{L}}(\mathsf{pk}, m, \sigma, y)$, which returns $\Delta = 1$ if $y_1 = y_2$, and $\Delta = 0$ otherwise.

Fig. 4. $\mathsf{SAV}_{\mathsf{BLS}}^{\mathsf{CDS_1}}$: Our SAV for the BLS Signature in [3].

SAV.Init$(1^\lambda) = $ SetUp$_{\text{Wat}}(1^\lambda)$. This algorithm generates a bilinear group $(p, g, \mathbb{G}, \mathbb{G}_T, e)$ according to the security parameter λ; selects $n+1$ group elements $V_0, V_1, \ldots V_n \xleftarrow{R} \mathbb{G}$ and defines a function $H : \{0,1\}^n \to \mathbb{G}$ as $H(m) = V_0(\prod_{i=1}^n V_i^{m_i})$. The output is gp $= (p, g, H, \mathbb{G}, \mathbb{G}_T, e)$.

SAV.KeyGen$() = $ KeyGen$_{\text{Wat}}()$. The key generation algorithm draws a random $s \xleftarrow{R} \mathbb{Z}_p^*$ and outputs $(\text{pk}, \text{sk}) = (e(g,g)^s, s)$.

SAV.VSetup$() = $ KeyGen$^{\text{CDS}_1}()$. This algorithm outputs pr $= $ void and pb $= (p, \mathbb{G}, \mathbb{G}_T, e, g, \hat{\beta})$, where $\hat{\beta} = e(g,g)$.

SAV.Sign$(\text{sk}, m) = $ Sign$_{\text{Wat}}(\text{sk}, m)$. The signing algorithm picks a random $a \xleftarrow{R} \mathbb{Z}_p$ and outputs $\sigma = (\sigma_1, \sigma_2) = (g^s(H(m))^a, g^a) \in \mathbb{G}^2$.

SAV.ProbGen(void, pk, m, σ). This algorithm runs ProbGen$^{\text{PRE}}(\text{pk}, m, \sigma) \to (\text{pk}', \sigma')$ to create a signature for a new public key, i.e., it picks two random values h, $b \xleftarrow{R} \mathbb{Z}_p$ and sets pk$' = $ pk$\hat{\beta}^{\text{h}}$, $\sigma' = (g^{\text{h}}\sigma_1 H(m)^b, \sigma_2 g^b)$. (By the adaptivity of Wat if σ is a valid signature for m under sk with randomness a, then σ' is a valid signature for m under sk$' + $ h with randomness $a + b$.)
Secondly, the problem generation algorithm runs ProbGen$^{\text{CDS}_1}$ on (σ_1', g) and $(H(m), \sigma_2')$. In details, for each pair (A, B), the algorithm selects two random values $r_1, r_2 \xleftarrow{R} \mathbb{Z}_p$, computes the points $R_1 = A^{r_2^{-1}}g^{r_1}$, $R_2 = B^{r_1^{-1}}g^{r_2}$ and $\hat{U} = \hat{\beta}^{r_1 r_2}$. The final outputs are $\omega = (R_1^{(1)}, R_2^{(1)}, R_1^{(2)}, R_2^{(2)})$ and $\tau = (\text{pk}'\hat{U}^{(1)}, r_1^{(1)}, r_2^{(1)}, \hat{U}^{(2)} r_1^{(2)}, r_2^{(2)})$.

SAV.Comp(pb, ω). The algorithm parses ω as $((R_1^{(1)}, R_2^{(1)}), (R_1^{(2)}, R_2^{(2)}))$; for each pair (A, B) it computes $\alpha_1 = e(A, B)$ and $\alpha_2 = e(R_1, R_2)(e(g, B), e(A, g))^{-1}$. It returns $\rho = (\alpha_1^{(1)}, \alpha_2^{(1)}, \alpha_1^{(2)}, \alpha_2^{(2)})$.

SAV.Verify(void, pk, m, σ, ρ, τ). The verification algorithm parses $\rho = (\rho^{(1)}, \rho^{(2)}) = ((\alpha_1^{(1)}, \alpha_2^{(1)}), (\alpha_1^{(2)}, \alpha_2^{(2)}))$ and $\tau = (\text{pk}', \tau^{(1)}, \tau^{(2)}) = ((\hat{U}^{(1)}, r_1^{(1)}, r_2^{(1)}), (\hat{U}^{(2)} r_1^{(2)}, r_2^{(2)}))$. For $i \in [2]$ it runs Verify$^{\text{CDS}_2}(\rho^{(i)}, \tau^{(i)})$, i.e., it checks if $\alpha_2^{(i)} = \hat{U}^{(i)}(\alpha_1^{(i)})^{(r_1^{(i)} r_2^{(i)})^{-1}}$ and $\alpha_1 \in \mathbb{G}_T$. If any of the previous checks fails, the verification algorithm returns $\Delta = \perp$ and halts. Otherwise, it returns $y^{(i)} = \alpha_1^{(i)}$ and runs Ver$_L(\text{pk}, m, \sigma, y)$, which returns $\Delta = 1$ if $y^{(1)} = \text{pk}' y^{(2)}$, and $\Delta = 0$ otherwise.

Fig. 5. SAV$_{\text{Wat}}^{\text{CDS}_1}$: Our SAV for the Wat Signature in [24].

SAV.Init(1^λ) = SetUp$_{\text{CL}}(1^\lambda)$. The setup algorithm generates the global parameters of the scheme, that include a bilinear group $(q, \mathbb{G}, g, \mathbb{G}_T, \hat{g}, e)$.

SAV.KeyGen() = KeyGen$_{\text{CL}}$(). The key generation algorithm draws two random values $x, y \xleftarrow{R} \mathbb{Z}_q$, computes $g^x = X$, $g^y = Y$ and returns pk $= (X, Y)$ and sk $= (x, y)$.

SAV.VSetup() = KeyGen$^{\text{CDS}_2}$(). This algorithm outputs pr $=$ void and pb $=$ $(p, \mathbb{G}, \mathbb{G}_T, e, G, B, \hat{\beta})$, where $G \xleftarrow{R} \mathbb{G}$, $B = g$ and $\hat{\beta} = e(G, B)$.

SAV.Sign(sk, m) = Sign$_{\text{CL}}$(sk, m). The sign algorithm picks a random $a \xleftarrow{R} \mathbb{G}$ and outputs the signature $\sigma = (\sigma_1, \sigma_2, \sigma_3) = (a, a^y, a^{x+mxy}) \in \mathbb{G}^3$.

SAV.ProbGen(void, pk, m, σ). This algorithm first runs ProbGen^{PRE}(pk, m, σ) $\rightarrow$ (σ_2, σ_3). Then it runs ProbGen$^{\text{CDS}_2}$ on σ_2 and σ_3. In more details, for $i \in \{2, 3\}$ it selects three random values $r_1^{(i)}, r_2^{(i)}, u^{(i)} \xleftarrow{R} \mathbb{Z}_q$, computes the points $R_1^{(i)} = \sigma_i \cdot G^{r_1^{(i)}}$ and $R_2^{(i)} = \sigma_i^{u^{(i)}} \cdot G^{r_2^{(i)}}$, and calculates $\hat{X}_1^{(i)} = (\hat{\beta})^{r_1^{(i)}}$, $\hat{X}_2^{(i)} = (\hat{\beta})^{r_2^{(i)}}$. The final outputs are $\omega = (R_1^{(2)}, R_2^{(2)}, R_1^{(3)}, R_2^{(3)})$ and $\tau = (u^{(2)}, \hat{X}_1^{(2)}, \hat{X}_2^{(2)}, u^{(3)}, \hat{X}_1^{(3)}, \hat{X}_2^{(3)})$.

SAV.Comp(pb, ω). The algorithm parses $\omega = (R_1^{(2)}, R_2^{(2)}, R_1^{(3)}, R_2^{(3)})$ and returns $\rho = (e(R_1^{(2)}, g), e(R_2^{(2)}, g), e(R_1^{(3)}, g), e(R_2^{(2)}, g))$.

SAV.Verify(void, pk, m, σ, ρ, τ). The verification algorithm first runs Verify$^{\text{CDS}_2}(\rho, \tau)$, i.e., for $i \in \{2, 3\}$ it checks if $\alpha_2^{(i)} = \hat{X}_2^{(i)}(\alpha_1(\hat{X}_1^{(i)})^{-1})^u$ and $\alpha_1^{(i)} \in \mathbb{G}_T$. If any of the previous checks fails, the verification algorithm returns $\Delta = \bot$ and halts. Otherwise, the values $y^{(i)} = \beta_1^{(i)}(\hat{X}_1^{(i)})^{-1}$, for $i \in \{2, 3\}$ are used as input for Ver$_\text{L}$. In details, Ver$_\text{L}$(pk, m, σ, $y = (y^{(2)}, y^{(3)})$), computes: $\beta_1 = e(\sigma_1, Y)$, $\beta_2 = e(X, \sigma_1\sigma_2^m)$. If both $\beta_1 = y(1)$ and $\beta_2 = y^{(2)}$, the algorithm returns $\Delta = 1$; otherwise it returns $\Delta = 0$.

Fig. 6. SAV$_{\text{CL}}^{\text{CDS}_2}$: Our SAV for the CL Signature in [5].

References

1. Béguin, P., Quisquater, J.-J.: Fast server-aided RSA Signatures secure against active attacks. In: Coppersmith, D. (ed.) CRYPTO 1995. LNCS, vol. 963, pp. 57–69. Springer, Heidelberg (1995). https://doi.org/10.1007/3-540-44750-4_5

2. Benabbas, S., Gennaro, R., Vahlis, Y.: Verifiable delegation of computation over large datasets. In: Rogaway, P. (ed.) CRYPTO 2011. LNCS, vol. 6841, pp. 111–131. Springer, Heidelberg (2011). https://doi.org/10.1007/978-3-642-22792-9_7

3. Boneh, D., Lynn, B., Shacham, H.: Short signatures from the weil pairing. J. Cryptol. **17**(4), 297–319 (2004)

4. Boneh, D., Shen, E., Waters, B.: Strongly unforgeable signatures based on computational diffie-hellman. In: Yung, M., Dodis, Y., Kiayias, A., Malkin, T. (eds.) PKC 2006. LNCS, vol. 3958, pp. 229–240. Springer, Heidelberg (2006). https://doi.org/10.1007/11745853_15

5. Camenisch, J., Lysyanskaya, A.: Signature schemes and anonymous credentials from bilinear maps. In: Franklin, M. (ed.) CRYPTO 2004. LNCS, vol. 3152, pp. 56–72. Springer, Heidelberg (2004). https://doi.org/10.1007/978-3-540-28628-8_4

6. Canard, S., Devigne, J., Sanders, O.: Delegating a pairing can be both secure and efficient. In: Boureanu, I., Owesarski, P., Vaudenay, S. (eds.) ACNS 2014. LNCS, vol. 8479, pp. 549–565. Springer, Cham (2014). https://doi.org/10.1007/978-3-319-07536-5_32

7. Cao, Z., Liu, L., Markowitch, O.: On two kinds of flaws in some server-aided verification schemes. Int. J. Netw. Secur. **18**(6), 1054–1059 (2016)
8. Chow, S.S., Au, M.H., Susilo, W.: Server-aided signatures verification secure against collusion attack. Inf. Secur. Tech. Rep. **17**(3), 46–57 (2013)
9. Costello, C., et al.: Geppetto: versatile verifiable computation. In: 2015 IEEE Symposium on Security and Privacy (SP), pp. 253–270. IEEE (2015)
10. Derler, D., Slamanig, D.: Key-homomorphic signatures and applications to multiparty signatures. Technical report, IACR Cryptology ePrint Archive **2016**, 792 (2016)
11. Ding, X., Mazzocchi, D., Tsudik, G.: Experimenting with server-aided signatures. In: NDSS (2002)
12. Fiore, D., Gennaro, R., Pastro, V.: Efficiently verifiable computation on encrypted data. In: Proceedings of the 2014 ACM SIGSAC Conference on Computer and Communications Security, pp. 844–855. ACM (2014)
13. Fischlin, M.: Anonymous signatures made easy. In: Okamoto, T., Wang, X. (eds.) PKC 2007. LNCS, vol. 4450, pp. 31–42. Springer, Heidelberg (2007). https://doi.org/10.1007/978-3-540-71677-8_3
14. Gennaro, R., Gentry, C., Parno, B.: Non-interactive verifiable computing: outsourcing computation to untrusted workers. In: Rabin, T. (ed.) CRYPTO 2010. LNCS, vol. 6223, pp. 465–482. Springer, Heidelberg (2010). https://doi.org/10.1007/978-3-642-14623-7_25
15. Girault, M., Lefranc, D.: Server-aided verification: theory and practice. In: Roy, B. (ed.) ASIACRYPT 2005. LNCS, vol. 3788, pp. 605–623. Springer, Heidelberg (2005). https://doi.org/10.1007/11593447_33
16. Guillevic, A., Vergnaud, D.: Algorithms for outsourcing pairing computation. In: Joye, M., Moradi, A. (eds.) CARDIS 2014. LNCS, vol. 8968, pp. 193–211. Springer, Cham (2015). https://doi.org/10.1007/978-3-319-16763-3_12
17. Guo, F., Mu, Y., Susilo, W., Varadharajan,V.: Server-aided signature verification for lightweight devices. Comput. J. bxt003 (2013)
18. Lim, C.H., Lee, P.J.: Server(Prover/Signer)-aided verification of identity proofs and signatures. In: Guillou, L.C., Quisquater, J.-J. (eds.) EUROCRYPT 1995. LNCS, vol. 921, pp. 64–78. Springer, Heidelberg (1995). https://doi.org/10.1007/3-540-49264-X_6
19. Pagnin, E., Mitrokotsa, A., Tanaka, K.: Anonymous single-round server-aided verification (2017). http://eprint.iacr.org/2017/794
20. Parno, B., Howell, J., Gentry, C., Raykova, M.: Pinocchio: nearly practical verifiable computation. In: 2013 IEEE Symposium on Security and Privacy (SP), pp. 238–252. IEEE (2013)
21. Wang, B.: A server-aided verification signature scheme without random oracles. Int. Rev. Comput. Softw. **7**, 3446 (2012)
22. Wang, Z.: A new construction of the server-aided verification signature scheme. Math. Comput. Model. **55**(1), 97–101 (2012)
23. Wang, Z., Wang, L., Yang, Y., Hu, Z.: Comment on Wu et al's server-aided verification signature schemes. IJ Netw. Secur. **10**(2), 158–160 (2010)
24. Waters, B.: Efficient identity-based encryption without random oracles. In: Cramer, R. (ed.) EUROCRYPT 2005. LNCS, vol. 3494, pp. 114–127. Springer, Heidelberg (2005). https://doi.org/10.1007/11426639_7
25. Wu, W., Mu, Y., Susilo, W., Huang, X.: Server-aided verification signatures: definitions and new constructions. In: Baek, J., Bao, F., Chen, K., Lai, X. (eds.) ProvSec 2008. LNCS, vol. 5324, pp. 141–155. Springer, Heidelberg (2008). https://doi.org/10.1007/978-3-540-88733-1_10

26. Wu, W., Mu, Y., Susilo, W., Huang, X.: Provably secure server-aided verification signatures. Comput. Math. Appl. **61**(7), 1705–1723 (2011)
27. Yang, G., Wong, D.S., Deng, X., Wang, H.: Anonymous signature schemes. In: Yung, M., Dodis, Y., Kiayias, A., Malkin, T. (eds.) PKC 2006. LNCS, vol. 3958, pp. 347–363. Springer, Heidelberg (2006). https://doi.org/10.1007/11745853_23
28. Zhang, F., Safavi-Naini, R., Susilo, W.: An efficient signature scheme from bilinear pairings and its applications. In: Bao, F., Deng, R., Zhou, J. (eds.) PKC 2004. LNCS, vol. 2947, pp. 277–290. Springer, Heidelberg (2004). https://doi.org/10.1007/978-3-540-24632-9_20

Secure Channels and Termination: The Last Word on TLS

Colin Boyd and Britta Hale[(✉)]

NTNU, Norwegian University of Science and Technology, Trondheim, Norway
{colin.boyd,britta.hale}@ntnu.no

Abstract. Secure channels are one of the most pivotal building blocks of cryptography today. Internet connections, secure messaging, protected IoT data, etc., all rely upon the security of the underlying channel. In this work we define channel protocols, as well as security for channels constructed from stateful length-hiding authenticated encryption (stL-HAE) schemes. Furthermore, we initiate the concept of *secure termination* where, upon receipt of a signifying message, a receiver is guaranteed to have received every message that has been sent, and will ever be sent, on the channel. We apply our results to real-world protocols, linking the channel environment to previous analyses of TLS 1.2, and demonstrating that TLS 1.2 achieves secure termination via fatal alerts and `close_notify` messages, per the specification of the Alert Protocol.

Keywords: Secure channels ·
Stateful length-hiding authenticated encryption (stLHAE) ·
Authenticated encryption with associated data (AEAD) ·
Secure termination · Controllable channel protocol ·
Transport Layer Security (TLS)

1 Introduction

Communication security is built on a fundamental cornerstone commonly referred to as a *secure channel*. Creation of secure channels is the essential goal of secure email, end-to-end encrypted messaging applications, end-to-end encrypted VOIP, HTTPS internet connections and TLS in general, WPA2 WiFi protection, SSH, IPSec, Bluetooth, etc. Examples are innumerable. Additionally, many constructs rely on the existence of secure channels once established, e.g. key transport. Despite this, a general understanding of what *secure channels* are and how they are constructed is lacking. Research relating to secure channels has spiraled concentrically around the topic with frequently contradicting goals, particularly in the analysis of real-world protocols.

Authenticated encryption with associated data (AEAD), or even simply authenticated encryption (AE), has been argued as the foundational secure channel building block. Extensive work has been done on both AEAD [32], and AE in their various forms [3,16,17,21,33,34]. Stateful length-hiding AE (stLHAE) is

© Springer Nature Switzerland AG 2019
T. Lange and O. Dunkelman (Eds.): LATINCRYPT 2017, LNCS 11368, pp. 44–65, 2019.
https://doi.org/10.1007/978-3-030-25283-0_3

often the apparent goal of real-world protocols and has consequently been used frequently in their analysis [20, 23, 29]. Work has also been undertaken for building secure channels explicitly from AE schemes [28]. However, the view of secure channels as simply AEAD or AE is incomplete. In real-world protocols, multiple instances of a protocol may be run, session resumption/renegotiation may be performed, and message authentication (MAC), encryption, and even exporter keys may be derived from a single master session key output of a key exchange protocol. Essentially, the real-world is not simple. Cross protocol attacks, renegotiation attacks [13], and triple handshake attacks [5] are just some attack examples that cannot be captured when considering secure channels as AEAD or AE under a single communication flow.

Expanding on the modeling of channels, authenticated and secure channel establishment (ACCE) was proposed, which considers both key exchange and channels established under the derived key in the context of stLHAE [20]. Furthermore, ACCE considers parallel sessions – an improvement over the basic, low-level view of secure channels as the stLHAE primitive. Work analyzing the TLS protocol [20, 23] has employed ACCE as the foundational secure channel building block, as TLS does not achieve key indistinguishability. However, not all protocols suffer from a lack of key indistinguishability (e.g. the current TLS 1.3 draft [30]), thus rendering the ACCE pre-accept/post-accept phase combination unnecessary. Similarly to ACCE, Augmented Secure Channels (ASC) have been proposed as a means of capturing more of the channel context than an AEAD primitive allows [2]. ASC is developed in the vein of constructive cryptography, but still suffers from the same underlying drawbacks as ACCE; namely the inability to model communication flows, under potentially different security demands, which are protected by keying material derived from the same master secret. Neither ACCE nor ASC model session resumption – despite its importance in TLS 1.2 (analyzed in the ACCE model) and TLS 1.3 (analyzed in the ASC model for draft 8). Work has also been done on multi-key channels [14], focusing on the evolution of a master key over time, and requirements on it (e.g. forward secrecy), but lacking formal definitions for the channel context. It also uses a single, fixed AEAD construction, lacking flexibility in scheme selection, and does not address termination in the channel environment.

In response to these issues, we define keyed two-party controllable channel protocols which capture parallel and consecutive sessions, with security controlled via the underlying primitives. Each session at a principal is initiated via the generation of a master session key – as would be the case at the conclusion of a key exchange protocol. In turn, the session is modeled by a collection of read and write connections, with connection keys derived from the master session key. Channels are defined by a shared key between a pair of read and write connections. This captures the behavior of real-world protocols: for example, a master session key may be used to derive a MAC key as well as an encryption key, which would result in parallel connections under the different channel keys. Simultaneously, this higher-level view of the channel environment provides a framework for analysis of session resumption; connections can be closed, and channel keys destroyed, with new connections instantiated and channel keys derived from the original session keying material. Compared to the ACCE model, our model permits separate consideration of session and connection keys and even consideration of connection closure.

Security for keyed two-party controllable channel protocols is realized via the cryptographic schemes and key derivation functions (KDF) used for connections. In real-world correlations, TLS 1.2 uses cipher suites – for example, the partial suite AES_128_GCM_SHA256, which defines both a scheme for securing the channel (AES_128_GCM) and pseudo-random function for key derivation of the channel key (HMAC using SHA256). Our model captures such real-world protocols by considering channel security under both a scheme (e.g. stLHAE) goal and a KDF goal. Considering secure channels in the context of stLHAE allows certain analysis benefits; statefulness gives assurance that the i-th packet processed on the receiving end of a channel is the same as i-th packet output on the sending end. However, the stLHAE framework is again incomplete. How does a receiver know that all sent packets have been received? If an adversary drops the last n packets on a channel, the receiver could convinced that the transmission is shorter than in reality. When final messages contain critical information, warnings, etc., this scenario should undoubtedly be considered as an attack. Classically, this is referred to as a *truncation* attack. In order to capture this attack in our secure channel environment, we define secure termination.

Truncation attacks have been shown to be a very real problem [35], including effects on voting. Usually these attacks follow from a failure of the implementation to check for the closure alert (if TLS), or from a misinterpretation of what constitutes a "terminate" message. While the importance of the former is highlighted by our model, the latter is at the heart of secure termination. Most analyses of truncation attacks are ad-hoc, essentially cryptanalyses based on weaknesses discovered in a particular protocol. Some of these have been against the TLS protocol [27,35], leveraging and exploiting implementation faults. Other recent work on protocol termination, albeit in an unrelated aspect, highlights a growing interest in the final stages of a cryptographic protocol run [10]. Consequently, we define secure termination in the interest of providing a formal framework for modeling truncation attacks, by modeling finalization and completion guarantees on received communication flows.

Channels. To discuss secure channels and channel termination it is vital to clearly define what a channel actually is. Past work using channels has provided mixed descriptions of this concept – Hoepman [18] describes *unidirectional* and *bidirectional* channels, hence conceptually equating a channel to a transport link between entities. In this sense, a bidirectional channel for a real-world protocol such as TLS would have separate keys for each direction, but all keys would be considered to be within the same channel. Meanwhile, another line of research [25,26] defines a channel in a unidirectional sense, with messages input from a sender and output to a receiver. Ultimately, this formulation allows for a modular analysis of channel security, with channel keys being used for sending messages at one end of the channel and for receiving messages at the other end. This practice has met with wide-spread acceptance, with channels generally being modeled by three interfaces (sender, receiver, and adversary) based on various adversarial capabilities [2].

In 2001, Canetti and Krawczyk [9] defined a *secure channel* as "a link between a pair of parties" which provides message authentication and confidentiality via a key obtained via a key-exchange protocol. As in many other works on key exchange and secure channel analysis [4,20,23], the authors consider *sessions* at principals as participants in the key exchange protocol, and call the resulting key the *session key*. This session key is then used to secure the channel (e.g. encryption and authentication keys are derived from the session key).

One salient issue arises when the standard conceptualization of a session key is compared with the modeling of a channel, as discussed above. Namely, a key exchange protocol should minimally result in a set of two channel keys. This assumption follows from standard real-world protocols which maintain separate session keys for sending channels and receiving channels [11,19,31]. In consideration of this, we undertake to formalize channels in the context of sessions for bi-directional communication. With sent messages at a session being not necessarily independent from received messages (particularly, as we will see, in the context of secure termination), this new, "big picture" view of session modeling raises interesting questions for channel analysis. One recent work [24] similarly aims to address bi-directional channels, but does not consider sub-connections (parallel channels after key derivation) or channel termination.

While TLS and similar protocols have been analyzed under the assumption of discrete messages, important work has been done considering AEAD in the streaming setting [12]. We view our work as easily adaptable to the streaming security context, since the security of our channel protocol model is reliant upon underlying, "plug-in" primitives and their security games.

Cryptographic Agility. While channels generally use separate keys for sending and receiving, these keys are often generated from the same master session key. This is indeed the case in many real-world protocols such as TLS. Moreover, it is possible that the same master session key could be re-used with different concrete cryptographic algorithms, which may be controllable by the adversary. We account for this possibility by requiring *agile* [1,15] channel key derivation in our channel security analysis. Bhargavan et al. [6] analyzed cryptographic agility in TLS, focusing on the public key algorithms used in the handshake protocol. Agility definitions appear in the full version due to space restrictions. We apply agile key derivation functions in our results in order to provide strong channel security.

Paper Outline. Introducing keyed two-party controllable channel protocols, Sect. 2 defines sessions, connections, schemes, channels, and connection/channel closure, outlining the fundamental structure of the channel environment even before consideration of security. Combinations of security schemes and key derivation functions (for the channel key) comprise *suites*.

Subsequently, Sect. 3 describes security. We focus on channel stLHAE security due to it being a frequent real-world objective. Our security experiments here are broad, and encompass the situation where parallel and consecutive connections may employ various suites. We expect that this work can be extended to situations where parallel and consecutive connections may employ combinations of various authentication suites, stLHAE suites, AEAD suites, etc.

Additionally, we provide constructions of channel protocol environments where channels are constructed from various stLHAE schemes. Proving security for our constructions, we provide a reduction from the channel security to the security of the underlying schemes used in the construction.

Linking our definitions and constructions to the ACCE model, we furthermore demonstrate that channel stLHAE security can be reduced to ACCE security in the post-accept phase (channel phase of ACCE), when the session key is used directly as the channel key and only one connection for the session is initialized (Sect. 5.1). Thus our channel protocol can be used as a refined post-accept phase for the ACCE model, if such a model is necessary due to lack of key indistinguishability. Formally, the one-connection and session key restrictions on the reduction arise from the formalization of the ACCE model, as keyed two-party controllable channel protocols encompass a wider vision of protocol interaction, based on real-world protocol implementations.

In Sect. 4 secure termination and the secure termination experiment are defined. Additionally, we associate secure termination and channel protocol security by reductions between the former and the latter, under the generic case of parallel and consecutive connections constructed from various stLHAE suites. We demonstrate that TLS 1.2 achieves secure termination on receipt of Alert or `close_notify` messages by combining our work on secure channels with previous analyses of the TLS 1.2 protocol in the ACCE model.

While presented in detail in the following sections, the notation for channel protocols, schemes, and respective security games is summarized in Table 1. This provides a reference point, highlighting the differences between similar terms and notation, and is an extension of previously established notation.

Table 1. Notation reference for protocols, schemes, and experiments.

ChannelSnd	Send and receive algorithms for a keyed two-party controllable
ChannelRcv	channel protocol $\mathrm{CHNL}[\{(\Pi, \mathrm{KDF})\}]$
ChnlEnc	Security experiment oracles for a keyed two-party controllable
ChnlDec	channel protocol $\mathrm{CHNL}[\{(\Pi, \mathrm{KDF})\}]$, where $\{\Pi\}$ are stLHAE schemes.
Send$_\mathrm{T}$	Security experiment oracles for the secure termination of a channel
Receive$_\mathrm{T}$	protocol experiment.
Enc & Dec	Encrypt and decrypt algorithms for a stLHAE scheme

2   Channels

In this section we formalize the natural real-world protocol environment of sessions, connections, and channels. Figure 1 provides a depiction of this environment.

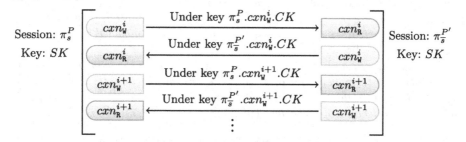

Fig. 1. Communication diagram with sessions π_s^P and $\pi_{\overline{s}}^{P'}$, write and read connections $cxn_\mathtt{W}$ and $cxn_\mathtt{R}$ for each session, and channels between connections protected by the channel keys $\pi_s^P.cxn_\mathtt{W}^i.CK$, etc. Each principal may be modeled by multiple sessions.

2.1   Definitions

Every channel protocol will be associated with one or more cryptographic *schemes*. Typical schemes include authentication schemes, under a message authentication code, and stLHAE, but many other types are possible. We define abstractly the elements of any such scheme.

Definition 1. (Scheme). *Let $\mathcal{M}$ be a message space, $\mathcal{K}$ a key space, and $\mathcal{C}$ an output space, and let the elements of $\mathcal{C}$ be called ciphertexts. A scheme Π is a tuple of algorithms:*

- $\mathrm{Kgn}() \xrightarrow{\$} k$: *A probabilistic key gen. algorithm that outputs a key $k \in \mathcal{K}$.*
- $\mathrm{Snd}(k, m, st_\mathsf{S}) \xrightarrow{\$} (c, st_\mathsf{S}')$: *A probabilistic send algorithm that takes as input a key $k \in \mathcal{K}$, a message $m \in \mathcal{M}$, and a write state st_S, and outputs an outgoing ciphertext $c \in \mathcal{C}$ or an error symbol $\perp$, and an updated state st_S'.*
- $\mathrm{Rcv}(k, c, st_\mathsf{R}) \rightarrow (m, st_\mathsf{R}')$: *A deterministic receive algorithm that takes as input a key $k \in \mathcal{K}$, a ciphertext $c \in \mathcal{C}$, and a read state st_R, and outputs either a message $m \in \mathcal{M}$ or a error symbol $\perp$, and an updated state st_R'.*

On first use, st_S and st_R are initialized to st_S^0 and st_R^0, resp. If, for $\mathrm{Snd}(k, m, st_\mathsf{S}) \xrightarrow{\$} (c, st_\mathsf{S}')$ and $\mathrm{Rcv}(k, c, st_\mathsf{R}) \rightarrow (m, \alpha, st_\mathsf{R}')$, $st_\mathsf{S}' = \perp$ and $st_\mathsf{R}' = \perp$, then Π is said to be stateless. Otherwise Π is said to be stateful.

Correctness Consider the following: $i \geq 0$, all $m_i \in \mathcal{M}$, all $k \xleftarrow{\$} \mathrm{Kgn}()$, initial states st_S^0 and st_R^0, and a sequence $(c_i, st_\mathsf{S}^{i+1}) \xleftarrow{\$} \mathrm{Snd}(k, m_i, st_\mathsf{S}^i)$, where

$c_i \neq \perp$ for all i. Then, for a matching sequence of message receipts, we have $(m_i, st_R^{i+1}) \leftarrow \text{Rcv}(k, c_i, st_R^i)$. Further correctness requirements may hold, dependent on the scheme. In Sect. 3, stLHAE schemes will be considered; however, many scheme types are possible. Other types of schemes include signatures schemes and authentication schemes.

Definition 2 (Principals and Sessions). *For a collection of principals* $\{P_1, \ldots, P_p\}$, *where* $p \in \mathbb{N}$, *each* $P_l \in \{P_1, \ldots, P_p\}$ *is (potentially) in possession of a long-term private/public key pair* (sk_P, pk_P), *and is modeled by a collection of session oracles* $\{\pi_{s_1}^{P_l}, \ldots, \pi_{s_n}^{P_l}\}$.

Correspondingly and wlog, each session π_s^P *is an oracle with access to the (potential) long-term key pair of* P *and the (potential) long-term public keys* $pk_1, \ldots, pk_p$ *of all other principals. Furthermore, a session* π_s^P *at a principal* P *maintains a collection of variables* $(\{\pi_s^P.cxn_{role}^i\}, \pi_s^P.(P', \bar{s}), \pi_s^P.\alpha, \pi_s^P.SK)$:

- $\{cxn_{role}^i\}$: *A collection of connections, where* role $\in \{W, R\}$, *representing 'write' and 'read' connections, respectively.*
  If role $= W$, *then* $\overline{role}$ *denotes* R, *and vice versa.*
- $(P', [\bar{s}])$: *An identifier for the partner and (optionally) the partner's session.*
- α: *A status variable in* $\{0, 1\}$, *where the session is active if* $\alpha = 1$ *and inactive if* $\alpha = 0$. *A session must be active to send or receive messages.*
- *SK*: *A session key shared with the partner session.*

Any P *may maintain several sessions, both in parallel and consecutively.*

The following definition uses a key derivation function (KDF). We follow standard assumptions by requiring KDF to be a PRF [8]; KDFs may also be defined more explicitly (see [22]).

Definition 3 (Connection). *A connection* cxn_{role} *with* role $\in \{W, R\}$ *is defined by a set of variables* $(cxn_{role}.CK, cxn_{role}.status, cxn_{role}.suite, cxn_{role}.substate)$. *Let the notation e.g.* $cxn_{role}.CK$ *denote variables at a specific connection:*

- *CK*: *A channel key corresponding to the connection and role.*
- *status*: *A status variable in* {active, terminated}.
- *suite*: *A variable identifying the scheme/KDF pair* (Π, KDF) *implemented on the connection. If no pair is specified for the connection, then* $cxn_{role}.suite \leftarrow \perp$.
- *substate*: *Any additional scheme-specific connection state variables.*

The connection *substate* variable models other state information, which may be defined by *suite*. For example, this variable may handle protocol state if Π is a stLHAE scheme. Exact use of this variable can be seen in the concrete constructions provided in Sect. 3. We abuse notation and use cxn_{role} as an identifier by which an entity may refer to the collection of variables, without having access to them.

Definition 4 (Keyed Two-Party Controllable Channel Protocol). *Let* $\mathcal{M} = \mathcal{AD} \times \mathcal{AED}$ *be a message space and* $\mathcal{L}$ *an optional length space. A keyed two-party controllable channel protocol* $\text{CHNL}[\{(\Pi, \text{KDF})\}]$ *over a set of scheme, key derivation function pairs* $\{(\Pi, \text{KDF})\}$ *is a tuple of algorithms:*

- $\text{SessionKeyGen}(1^{\lambda}, P, P', s, \overline{s}) \xrightarrow{\$} SK$: *A probabilistic* session key generation algorithm *that takes as input a security parameter* λ, *identities* P *and* P', *and session indices* s *and* $\overline{s}$. *It sets the respective partner identifiers and session status* $\pi_s^P.\alpha \leftarrow 1$, *and outputs a shared session key* SK.
- $\text{ConnectionInit}(SK, \pi_s^P, [\Pi], [\text{KDF}], i) \xrightarrow{\$} (\pi_s^P.cxn_W^i, \pi_s^P.cxn_R^i)$: *A probabilistic* connection initiation algorithm *that takes as input a tuple of a shared session key* SK, *a session* π_s^P, *an optional scheme* Π, *an optional key derivation function* KDF *used to derive* CK, *and connection index* i, *and outputs the* i-th *'read' and 'write' connections at the session,* $\pi_s^P.cxn_W^i$ *and* $\pi_s^P.cxn_R^i$, *or a distinguishing failure symbol* $\perp$.
- $\text{ChannelSnd}(m, [\ell], cxn_W^i) \xrightarrow{\$} (c, cxn_W^{i\,'})$: *A probabilistic* channel sending algorithm *that takes as input a message* $m \in \mathcal{M} = \mathcal{AD} \times \mathcal{AED}$, *an optional output length* $\ell \in \mathcal{L}$, *and a connection* cxn_W^i, *and outputs a ciphertext* $c \in \mathcal{C}$ *or a distinguishing failure symbol* $\perp$, *and an updated connection* $cxn_W^{i\,'}$.
- $\text{ChannelRcv}(p, cxn_R^i) \rightarrow (m, cxn_R^{i\,'})$: *A deterministic* channel receiving algorithm *that takes as input a packet* $p \in \mathcal{P} = \mathcal{AD} \times \mathcal{C}$ *and a connection* cxn_R^i, *and outputs a message* $m \in \mathcal{M} = \mathcal{AD} \times \mathcal{AED}$ *or a distinguishing failure symbol* $\perp$, *and an updated connection* $cxn_R^{i\,'}$.

The packet space $\mathcal{P}$ *is a set induced by* $\text{CHNL}[\Pi, \text{KDF}]$ *for each* $\Pi \in \{\Pi\}$, *the length space* $\mathcal{L}$, *and the message space* $\mathcal{M}$, *where* $\mathcal{M}$ *is a tuple of the data space of authenticated transmissions* $\mathcal{AD}$, *and a data space of authenticated and encrypted transmissions* $\mathcal{AED}$. *Consequently,* $\mathcal{P}$ *is a tuple of* $\mathcal{AD}$ *and a ciphertext space* $\mathcal{C}$, *where* $\mathcal{C}$ *is defined by the scheme used on* $\mathcal{M}$. *The* i-th *read-write connection pair at a session* π_s^P *is denoted* $(\pi_s^P.cxn_W^i, \pi_s^P.cxn_R^i)$.

We define correctness in the logical way where ConnectionInit outputs the failure symbol if the session is not active, and ChannelSnd and ChannelRcv, respectively, output the failure symbol if the connection status variable is not active. Due to space restrictions, details appear in the full version.

Remark 1. Note that there is no restriction on the number of calls made to $\text{ConnectionInit}(SK, \pi_s^P, \pi_{\overline{s}}^{P'}, [\Pi], [\text{KDF}], i)$, for a given session key SK and sessions π_s^P and $\pi_{\overline{s}}^{P'}$. This models real-world protocols where session resumption is possible. Particularly, connections $\pi_s^P.cxn_{role}^i$ and $\pi_s^P.cxn_{\overline{role}}^i$ may be *terminated*, resulting in the connections being destroyed completely; later resumption based on the session keying material is possible by calling ConnectionInit again.

Remark 2. We explicitly allow ConnectionInit to be used to create connections at only one session. Matching connections can be created by using the algorithm again: $\text{ConnectionInit}(SK, \pi_{\overline{s}}^{P'}, \pi_s^P, [\Pi], [\text{KDF}], i)$. This matches real-world protocols where each session derives its connection keys independently, regardless of whether or not the partner session is still active.

CHNL may take as input several schemes which may each be used to initialize different connections. If no KDF is used to derive channel keys, then either the session key is used directly in the channel, or no security scheme Π is implemented (i.e. the $([], [])$ suite). In either case $[]$ is included in the list of functions $\{\text{KDF}\}$, and represents the identity function.

Definition 5 (Channel). *If* CHNL *is a keyed two-party controllable channel protocol, and* $\pi_s^P.cxn_\mathsf{W}^i$ *and* $\pi_{\bar{s}}^{P'}.cxn_\mathsf{R}^j$

- *share a channel key* $\pi_s^P.cxn_\mathsf{W}^i.CK = \pi_{\bar{s}}^{P'}.cxn_\mathsf{R}^j.CK$ *and*
- *implement the same scheme/KDF suite such that* $\pi_s^P.cxn_\mathsf{W}^i.suite = \pi_{\bar{s}}^{P'}.cxn_\mathsf{R}^j.suite,$

then we say that $\pi_s^P.cxn_\mathsf{W}^i$ *has a channel to* $\pi_{\bar{s}}^{P'}.cxn_\mathsf{R}^j$. *Moreover, if* $\pi_s^P.cxn_\mathsf{W}^i.suite = (\Pi, \text{KDF}) = \pi_{\bar{s}}^{P'}.cxn_\mathsf{R}^j.suite$, *then we say that* $\pi_s^P.cxn_\mathsf{W}^i$ *has a* Π-*channel to* $\pi_{\bar{s}}^{P'}.cxn_\mathsf{R}^j$.

By not demanding that $i = j$ in Definition 5, we enable modeling of unknown key share. Namely, *any* two connections using the same channel key and suite share a channel, regardless if they were correctly initiated via ConnectionInit.

3   Keyed Two-Party StLHAE Channel Protocol Security

As discussed in the introduction and Sect. 2, channel protocols may take as input Π-schemes of various types as well as various KDF-functions. In this section, we introduce stateful length-hiding authenticated encryption (stLHAE) channel security and provide concrete constructions of channels where the set $\{\Pi\}$ is comprised of stLHAE schemes (see Appendix A).

While the following definition, Definition 6, is not necessary for defining the channel protocol environment, it is essential for consideration of its security. Termination messages affect connection status, and therefore the ability to send or receive messages. Consequently, an adversary could use the encryption of such messages to distinguish between ciphertexts (see Fig. 2).

Definition 6 (Terminate Message). *Let* CHNL *be a keyed two-party controllable channel protocol, and let* $\mathcal{T} \subset \mathcal{M}$, *the message space of* CHNL. *Then, for* $m \in \mathcal{T}$, *m is called a* **terminate** *message and, for all* $m \in \mathcal{T}$, *we add the following to the* correctness *requirements of* CHNL:

- *if* $(c, \pi_s^P.cxn_\mathsf{W}^{i}{}') \leftarrow \text{ChannelSnd}(m, [\ell], \pi_s^P.cxn_\mathsf{W}^i)$ *and* $\pi_s^P.cxn_\mathsf{W}^i.status = $ active, *then* $\pi_s^P.cxn_\mathsf{W}^{i}{}'.status \leftarrow$ terminated, *and*
- *if* $(m, \pi_s^P.cxn_\mathsf{R}^{i}{}') \leftarrow \text{ChannelRcv}(p, \pi_s^P.cxn_\mathsf{R}^i)$ *and* $\pi_s^P.cxn_\mathsf{R}^i.status = $ active, *then* $\pi_s^P.cxn_\mathsf{R}^{i}{}'.status \leftarrow$ terminated.

We define *secure stLHAE channels* in Definition 7. Note that we do not present a single, generic *secure channel* definition since security for channel protocols must be considered with respect to the Π-scheme goals (stLHAE, authentication, signatures, etc.). We envisage protocols possibly implementing several Π-schemes. For example, an encryption scheme Π_1 and authentication scheme Π_2. Connections would be initiated using (Π_1, KDF_1), (Π_2, KDF_2), or no security scheme $([],[])$, denoted $\textsc{Chnl}[(\Pi_1, \mathrm{KDF}_1), (\Pi_2, \mathrm{KDF}_2), ([],[])]$. In terms of real-world communication, a session could have, and close, connections running HTTPS, while maintaining other connections that send and receive information unprotected via HTTP (i.e. the $([],[])$ suite). It may then, via a TLS key-renegotiation under the existing session key, initiate new connections for channels that will be protected under an stLHAE Π-scheme. Such possibilities extend the current security considerations and are left for future work.

Definition 7 (stLHAE Channel Security). *Let* $\textsc{Chnl}[\{(\Pi, \mathrm{KDF})\}]$ *be a keyed two-party controllable channel protocol such that* $\{\Pi\}$ *are stLHAE schemes, and let* $\mathcal{A}$ *be a PPT adversarial algorithm. The stLHAE experiment for* $\textsc{Chnl}[\{(\Pi, \mathrm{KDF})\}]$ *is given by* $\mathsf{Exp}^{\text{stlhae-chnl}}_{\textsc{Chnl}[\{(\Pi, \mathrm{KDF})\}]}$ *in Fig. 2. We define*

$$\mathbf{Adv}^{\text{stlhae-chnl}}_{\textsc{Chnl}[\{(\Pi, \mathrm{KDF})\}]}(\mathcal{A}) = 2\Pr\left[\mathsf{Exp}^{\text{stlhae-chnl}}_{\textsc{Chnl}[\{(\Pi, \mathrm{KDF})\}], \mathcal{A}}(\lambda)\right] - 1 \;.$$

An channel protocol $\textsc{Chnl}[\{(\Pi, \mathrm{KDF})\}]$ *is a secure channel stLHAE protocol if* $\mathbf{Adv}^{\text{stlhae-chnl}}_{\textsc{Chnl}[\{(\Pi, \mathrm{KDF})\}]}(\mathcal{A})$ *is a negligible function in* λ *for all PPT adversaries* $\mathcal{A}$.

In the security game for $\textsc{Chnl}[\{(\Pi, \mathrm{KDF})\}]$ in Fig. 2, the adversary may select (Π, KDF) pairs used to initiate the channel connections. However, if the pair is not valid – in the set $\{(\Pi, \mathrm{KDF})\}$ – no connection will be initiated. ChnlSnd may be called on any connection as ChnlSnd adaptively uses ChannelSnd constructed from the scheme Π from the connection's internal variable $\pi_s^P.cxn_u^i.suite$ (analogously ChnlRcv). For agility between suites, every connection pair is initialized with the same session key SK.

Remark 3. Since multiple Π schemes may be implemented by $\textsc{Chnl}[\{(\Pi, \mathrm{KDF})\}]$, we envisage that it is possible to run various but simultaneous (or consecutive) experiments on the different connections – all linked to the master session key. Note the applications to real-world protocols: in 802.11 [19], TKIP uses a pairwise master key to derive 2 sets of MAC and 2 sets of encryption keys for EAPOL and application data protection. Different, simultaneous experiments can also be considered for the MAC and encryption goals. This is left for future work.

Definition 8 (Channel Construction from stLHAE). *Let* $\{\Pi\}$, *where* $\Pi = (\mathrm{Kgn}, \mathrm{Enc}, \mathrm{Dec})$, *be stLHAE scheme(s) and let* $\{\mathrm{KDF}\}$ *be key derivation function(s). A keyed two-party controllable channel protocol* $\textsc{Chnl}[\{(\Pi, \mathrm{KDF})\}]$

$\mathrm{Exp}_{\mathrm{CHNL}[\{(\Pi,\mathrm{KDF})\}],\mathcal{A}}^{\text{stlhae-chnl}}(\lambda):$

1: $\mathrm{list} \leftarrow \bot$
2: $b'_{(P^*,s^*,i^*)}$
   $\leftarrow \mathcal{A}^{\mathsf{SnPairInit}(\cdot),\mathsf{CxnInit}(\cdot),\mathsf{ChnlEnc}(\cdot),\mathsf{ChnlDec}(\cdot)}()$
3: $\mathbf{return}$ $(b'_{(P^*,s^*,i^*)} = b_{(P^*,s^*,i^*)})$

$\mathsf{CxnInit}(\pi_s^P,\Pi^*,\mathrm{KDF}^*,i):$

1: $\mathbf{if}$ $(\Pi^*,\mathrm{KDF}^*) \notin \{(\Pi,\mathrm{KDF})\}$ $\mathbf{then}$
2:    $\mathbf{return}$ $\bot$
3: $\mathbf{if}$ $(\pi_s^P.cxn_{\mathbb{W}}^i \in \mathrm{list}) \vee (\pi_s^P.cxn_{\mathbb{R}}^i \in \mathrm{list})$ $\mathbf{then}$
4:    $\mathbf{return}$ $\bot$
5: $(\pi_s^P.cxn_{\mathbb{W}}^i, \pi_s^P.cxn_{\mathbb{R}}^i) \leftarrow \mathrm{ConnectionInit}(SK, \pi_s^P, \Pi^*, \mathrm{KDF}^*, i)$
6: $\mathrm{list} \leftarrow \mathrm{list}|\pi_s^P.cxn_{\mathbb{W}}^i|\pi_s^P.cxn_{\mathbb{R}}^i$
7: $u_{(P,s,i)} \leftarrow 0$, $v_{(P,s,i)} \leftarrow 0$, $\mathbf{phase}_{(P,s,i)} \leftarrow 0$
8: $b_{(P,s,i)} \xleftarrow{\$} \{0,1\}$
9: $\mathbf{return}$ $(\pi_s^P.cxn_{\mathbb{W}}^i, \pi_s^P.cxn_{\mathbb{R}}^i)$

$\mathsf{ChnlEnc}((\mathbf{ad}, (m_0, m_1)), \ell, \pi_s^P.cxn_{\mathbb{W}}^i):$

1: $u \leftarrow u + 1$
2: $\mathbf{if}$ $((\mathbf{ad}, m_0) \in \mathcal{T}) \wedge ((\mathbf{ad}, m_1) \notin \mathcal{T})$ or
   $((\mathbf{ad}, m_1) \in \mathcal{T}) \wedge ((\mathbf{ad}, m_0) \notin \mathcal{T})$ $\mathbf{then}$
3:    $\mathbf{return}$ $(\bot, \pi_s^P.cxn_{\mathbb{W}}^i.status)$
4: $(c^{(0)}, \pi_s^P.cxn_{\mathbb{W}\cdot(0)}^i)$
   $\leftarrow \mathrm{ChannelSnd}((\mathbf{ad}, m_0), [\ell], \pi_s^P.cxn_{\mathbb{W}}^i)$
5: $(c^{(1)}, \pi_s^P.cxn_{\mathbb{W}\cdot(1)}^i)$
   $\leftarrow \mathrm{ChannelSnd}((\mathbf{ad}, m_1), [\ell], \pi_s^P.cxn_{\mathbb{W}}^i)$
6: $\mathbf{if}$ $c^{(0)} = \bot$ or $c^{(1)} = \bot$ $\mathbf{then}$
7:    $\mathbf{return}$ $(\bot, \pi_s^P.cxn_{\mathbb{W}}^i.status)$
8: $(sent.ad_u, sent.c_u) := (\mathbf{ad}, c^{(b)})$
9: $\pi_s^P.cxn_{\mathbb{W}}^i \leftarrow \pi_s^P.cxn_{\mathbb{W}\cdot(b)}^i$
10: $\mathbf{return}$ $(sent.c_u, \pi_s^P.cxn_{\mathbb{W}}^i.status)$

$\mathsf{SnPairInit}((P,s), (P',\bar{s})):$

1: $SK \leftarrow \mathrm{SessionKeyGen}(1^\lambda, P, P', s, \bar{s})$
2: $\mathbf{return}$ $\bot$

$\mathsf{ChnlDec}((\mathbf{ad}, c), \pi_s^P.cxn_{\mathbb{R}}^i):$

1: $\mathbf{if}$ $b = 0$ $\mathbf{then}$
2:    $\mathbf{return}$ $(\bot, \pi_s^P.cxn_{\mathbb{R}}^i.status)$
3: $v \leftarrow v + 1$
4: $((\mathbf{ad}, m), \pi_s^P.cxn_{\mathbb{R}}^i)$
   $\leftarrow \mathrm{ChannelRcv}((\mathbf{ad}, c), \pi_s^P.cxn_{\mathbb{R}}^i)$
5: $\mathbf{if}$ $(\exists \pi_{\bar{s}}^{P'}.cxn_{\mathbb{W}}^i: \pi_{\bar{s}}^{P'}.cxn_{\mathbb{W}}^i$ has a channel
   to $\pi_s^P.cxn_{\mathbb{R}}^i) \wedge (\nexists j, j \neq i : \pi_{\bar{s}}^{P'}.cxn_{\mathbb{W}}^j$
   has a channel to $\pi_s^P.cxn_{\mathbb{R}}^i)$ $\mathbf{then}$
6:    $u \leftarrow u_{(P',\bar{s},i)}$
7: $\mathbf{else}$
8:    $u \leftarrow 0$
9: $\mathbf{if}$ $(u < v) \vee (c \neq sent.c_v) \vee (\mathbf{ad} \neq sent.ad_v)$ $\mathbf{then}$
10:    $\mathbf{phase} \leftarrow 1$
11: $\mathbf{if}$ $\mathbf{phase} = 1$ $\mathbf{then}$
12:    $\mathbf{return}$ $((\mathbf{ad}, m), \pi_s^P.cxn_{\mathbb{R}}^i.status)$
13: $\mathbf{return}$ $(\bot, \pi_s^P.cxn_{\mathbb{R}}^i.status)$

Fig. 2. Oracles of the stLHAE $\mathrm{CHNL}[\{(\Pi, \mathrm{KDF})\}]$ security experiment, where Π is specified in $\pi_s^P.cxn_{\mathbb{W}}^i.suite$ (resp. $\pi_s^P.cxn_{\mathbb{R}}^i.suite$). For conciseness, the synchronization variable $u_{(P,s,i)}$ is referenced as u in $\mathsf{ChnlEnc}$ (resp. for $v_{(P,s,i)}$). Similarly $b_{(P,s,i)}$ is referenced as b.

is constructed to achieve a pair of linked stLHAE channels, with message space $\mathcal{M} = \mathcal{AD} \times \mathcal{AED}$ and packet space $\mathcal{P} = \mathcal{AD} \times \mathcal{C}$, as follows:

- $\mathrm{SessionKeyGen}(1^\lambda, P, P', s, \bar{s}):$
  - Selects a shared session key SK according to the distribution of key space,
  - sets $\pi_s^P.\alpha \leftarrow 1$, $\pi_{\bar{s}}^{P'}.\alpha \leftarrow 1$,
  - sets respective partner identifiers $\pi_s^P.(P', \bar{s})$ and $\pi_{\bar{s}}^{P'}.(P, s)$,
  - sets $\pi_s^P.SK \leftarrow SK$ and $\pi_{\bar{s}}^{P'}.SK \leftarrow SK$.

Return SK.

- ConnectionInit$(SK, \pi_s^P, \Pi, \text{KDF}, i)$:

  If ConnectionInit$(\cdot, \pi_s^P, \cdot, \cdot, i)$ *has previously been called, return* $\perp$.
  - *Compute* $\pi_s^P.cxn_{\mathsf{W}}^i.CK \leftarrow \text{KDF}(SK, (P, s), (P', \overline{s}), i)$ *and*
  - $\pi_s^P.cxn_{\mathsf{R}}^i.CK \leftarrow \text{KDF}(SK, (P', \overline{s}), (P, s), i)$.

  If $\pi_s^P.cxn_{\mathsf{W}}^i.CK$ *or* $\pi_s^P.cxn_{\mathsf{R}}^i.CK$ *are not in key space* $\mathcal{K}$ *of* Π, *return* $\perp$.
  - *Set status* $\pi_s^P.cxn_{\mathsf{W}}^i.status = \mathbf{active}$ *and* $\pi_s^P.cxn_{\mathsf{R}}^i.status = \mathbf{active}$,
  - *set suite* $\pi_s^P.cxn_{\mathsf{W}}^i.suite \leftarrow (\Pi, \text{KDF})$, *and* $\pi_s^P.cxn_{\mathsf{R}}^i.suite \leftarrow (\Pi, \text{KDF})$,
  - $\pi_s^P.cxn_{\mathsf{W}}^i.substate \leftarrow 0$, *and* $\pi_s^P.cxn_{\mathsf{R}}^i.substate \leftarrow 0$.

  Return $(\pi_s^P.cxn_{\mathsf{W}}^i, \pi_s^P.cxn_{\mathsf{R}}^i)$.

- ChannelSnd$((\mathsf{ad}, m), \ell, \pi_s^P.cxn_{\mathsf{W}}^i)$:

  If $\pi_s^P.cxn_{\mathsf{W}}^i.status \neq \mathbf{active}$, *return* $(\perp, \pi_s^P.cxn_{\mathsf{W}}^i)$.

  Otherwise,
  - *compute:*

    $(c, \pi_s^P.cxn_{\mathsf{W}}^i.substate') \xleftarrow{\$} \text{Enc}(\pi_s^P.cxn_{\mathsf{W}}^i.CK, \ell, \mathsf{ad}, m, \pi_s^P.cxn_{\mathsf{W}}^i.substate)$, *where* Enc *is specified by the scheme* Π *defined in* $\pi_s^P.cxn_{\mathsf{W}}^i.suite$.
  - *If* $(\mathsf{ad}, m) \in \mathcal{T}$, *set* $\pi_s^P.cxn_{\mathsf{W}}^i.status \leftarrow \mathbf{terminated}$.

  Return $(c, \pi_s^P.cxn_{\mathsf{W}}^{i}{}')$.

- ChannelRcv$((\mathsf{ad}, c), \pi_s^P.cxn_{\mathsf{R}}^i)$:

  If $\pi_s^P.cxn_{\mathsf{R}}^i.status \neq \mathbf{active}$, *return* $(\perp, \pi_s^P.cxn_{\mathsf{W}}^i)$.

  Otherwise,
  - *compute:*

    $(m, \pi_s^P.cxn_{\mathsf{R}}^i.substate') \leftarrow \text{Dec}(\pi_s^P.cxn_{\mathsf{R}}^i.CK, \mathsf{ad}, c, \pi_s^P.cxn_{\mathsf{R}}^i.substate)$, *where* Dec *is specified by the scheme* Π *in* $\pi_s^P.cxn_{\mathsf{R}}^i.suite$.

  If $m = \perp$, *return* $(\perp, \pi_s^P.cxn_{\mathsf{W}}^i)$.

  If $(\mathsf{ad}, m) \in \mathcal{T}$, *set* $\pi_s^P.cxn_{\mathsf{R}}^i.status \leftarrow \mathbf{terminated}$. *Return* $((\mathsf{ad}, m), \pi_s^P.cxn_{\mathsf{R}}^{i}{}')$.

Naturally, stLHAE security of a channel protocol construction ought to be reducible to the security of the stLHAE scheme(s) $\{\Pi\}$ underlying the construction. Yet there is an additional consideration. While each Π uses connection keys derived via the KDF, all KDFs use the same shared master session key SK. Consequently, we require *agility* for $\{\text{KDF}\}$. Agility for the entire set $\{\text{KDF}\}$ implies that the individual primitives can share SK securely [1].

Theorem 1. *Let* $\text{CHNL}[\{(\Pi_j, \text{KDF})\}]$ *be a keyed two-party controllable channel protocol constructed from stLHAE scheme(s)* $\{\Pi_j\}$ *and key derivation function(s)* $\{\text{KDF}\}$, *such that* $\{\text{KDF}\}$ *is a compatible, finite set which is agile with respect to pseudo-randomness.*

Let $\mathcal{A}$ *be an adversarial algorithm against the* $\text{Exp}_{\text{CHNL}[\{(\Pi, \text{KDF})\}], \mathcal{A}}^{\text{stlhae-chnl}}(\lambda)$ *experiment in Fig. 2. Let* p *be the number of identities and* n *be the maximum number of sessions at an identity. Then we can construct a* $\{\text{KDF}\}$-*restricted adversarial algorithm* $\mathcal{B}_0$ *against the pseudo-randomness agility of* $\{\text{KDF}\}$ *in* $\text{Exp}_{\{\text{KDF.F}\}}^{\text{agile-prf}}$, *and adversarial algorithms* $\mathcal{B}_j$ *against* $\text{Exp}_{\Pi_j}^{\text{stlhae}}$ *from Fig. 6, such that*

$$\mathbf{Adv}_{\text{CHNL}[\{(\Pi, \text{KDF})\}]}^{\text{stlhae-chnl}}(\mathcal{A}) \leq p^2 \cdot n^2 \cdot \left(\mathbf{Adv}_{\{\text{KDF.F}\}}^{\text{agile-prf}}(\mathcal{B}_0) + \max_j \{\mathbf{Adv}_{\Pi_j}^{\text{stlhae}}(\mathcal{B}_j)\}\right).$$

Due to space restrictions, the proof of Theorem 1 appears in the full version.

4   Secure Termination

Ultimately, the goal of secure termination is a guarantee to the receiver connection that no further messages are being sent. We define *closure* in the contexts of both connections and channels before presenting the secure termination adversarial advantage and experiment.

4.1   Closure Alerts and Channel Closure

Inherently, secure termination is the closure of connections, controlled by the sending and receipt of signifying messages from a subset of the message space.

Definition 9 (Connection Closure). *Let* CHNL *be a keyed two-party controllable channel protocol and π_s^P be a session of* CHNL.

- *The i-th write channel connection at π_s^P is said to be* closed *if $\pi_s^P.cxn_{\mathtt{W}}^i.status = \mathtt{terminated}$.*
- *The i-th read channel connection at π_s^P is said to be* closed *if $\pi_s^P.cxn_{\mathtt{R}}^i.status = \mathtt{terminated}$.*

If all channels at a given session are closed, the session is said to be closed.

Definition 10 (Channel Closure). *We say that a channel from $\pi_s^P.cxn_{\mathtt{W}}^i$ to $\pi_{\bar{s}}^{P'}.cxn_{\mathtt{R}}^i$ closes using a message $m^* \in \mathcal{M}$ if*

- $(c, \pi_s^P.cxn_{\mathtt{W}}^{i\,'}) \xleftarrow{\$} \mathrm{ChannelSnd}(m^*, [\ell], \pi_s^P.cxn_{\mathtt{W}}^i)$, *for some $c \in \mathcal{C}$,*
  where $\pi_s^P.cxn_{\mathtt{W}}^i.status = \mathtt{active}$, and $\pi_s^P.cxn_{\mathtt{W}}^{i\,'}.status = \mathtt{terminated}$, and
- $(m^*, \pi_{\bar{s}}^{P'}.cxn_{\mathtt{R}}^{i\,'}) \leftarrow \mathrm{ChannelRcv}(p, \pi_{\bar{s}}^{P'}.cxn_{\mathtt{R}}^i)$, *for some $p \in \mathcal{P}$,*
  where $\pi_{\bar{s}}^{P'}.cxn_{\mathtt{R}}^i.status = \mathtt{active}$ and $\pi_{\bar{s}}^{P'}.cxn_{\mathtt{R}}^{i\,'}.status = \mathtt{terminated}$.

The sending, resp. receiving, of any **terminate** *in the set of termination messages $\mathcal{T} \subset \mathcal{M}$ results in channel closure. Moreover, if the channel from π_s^P to $\pi_{\bar{s}}^{P'}$ closes using a* **terminate** *message, we say that π_s^P initiated the channel closure.*

Note that the sending, resp. receiving, of a **terminate** message $m \in \mathcal{T}$ results in *connection closure*; however, *channel closure* demands a causal relationship between both end connections based on m.

Remark 4. While a session may consist of multiple channel connections at any given time, it may also consist of no connections (this may occur when no channel parameters have been negotiated, or all channels have been *closed*). The number of channel connections may change during a session's lifespan, namely by means of session *closure* and *resumption*. Resumption is realized via ConnectionInit.

4.2   Secure Termination Experiment

Definition 11 (Secure Termination Experiment). *Let* CHNL *be a keyed two-party controllable channel protocol with message space* $\mathcal{M}$, *and let* $\mathcal{A}$ *be an adversary algorithm. Let* terminate *be an element of* $\mathcal{T} \subset \mathcal{M}$, *where* $\mathcal{T}$ *is the set of all termination messages. With the secure termination experiment for* CHNL *given by* $\mathrm{Exp}^{\mathsf{sc.t}}_{\mathrm{CHNL}}$ *in Fig. 3, define*

$$\mathbf{Adv}^{\mathsf{sc.t}}_{\mathrm{CHNL}}(\mathcal{A}) = \Pr\left[\mathrm{Exp}^{\mathsf{sc.t}}_{\mathrm{CHNL},\mathcal{A}}(\lambda) = 1\right] \ .$$

The existence of a signifying terminate message (i.e. $\mathcal{T} \neq \emptyset$) is insufficient for claiming that a protocol *always* securely terminates connections. Only connection closure with such a terminate message yields secure termination of the connection. Intrinsically, secure termination is a property of the read side of a channel, which is achieved upon receipt of terminate.

Remark 5. Secure termination is a per-connection goal, achieved on message receipt, and handles adversarial intervention in channel closure – what is commonly referred to as a *truncation attack*. Truncation, malicious or otherwise, can happen via various means; for example, closure of the underlying TCP connection as a means of closing a TLS channel. The adversary wins the secure termination security game only if it is able to make an honest party accept that the connection has been correctly terminated when it has not been. Thus malicious closure of the TCP connection is not a valid attack.

Remark 6. Some protocols have "terminate"-looking messages that may not be authenticated at all or authenticated properly, and our model aids in understanding and comparing the security of such protocols against truncation attacks. For example, the DeauthenticationRequest of 802.11 *may* meet termination message requirements, but that is dependent on statefulness and whether or not the requests are protected as Robust Management Frames (RMF). A session that does not negotiate to send such requests as RMFs is susceptible to truncation attacks. Similarly, the security implications of 802.11's DisassociationRequest should be questioned. Many protocols have specified messages which appear to indicate termination; however, exactly what cryptographic guarantees are provided on receipt has not been well understood, in the absence of a secure termination model. Hence the success of truncation attacks.

Definition 12 (Secure Termination of a Protocol). *Let* CHNL *be a two-party controllable channel protocol, let* π^P_s *and* $\pi^{P'}_{\bar{s}}$ *be any two sessions of* CHNL, *and let* π_s *have a channel to* $\pi_{\bar{s}}$ *according to Definition 5.*
We say that CHNL *achieves secure termination on the channel from* π_s *to* $\pi_{\bar{s}}$ *with* terminate *if*

- *the channel from* π^P_s *to* $\pi^{P'}_{\bar{s}}$ *closes using a termination message* terminate $\in$ $\mathcal{T}$, *according to Definition 10, and*
- $\mathbf{Adv}^{\mathsf{sc.t}}_{\mathrm{CHNL}}(\mathcal{A})$ *is a negligible function in* λ *for all PPT adversaries* $\mathcal{A}$.

$\mathsf{Exp}^{\text{sc.t}}_{\text{CHNL}[\{(\Pi,\text{KDF})\}],\mathcal{A}}(\lambda):$

1: **phase** $\leftarrow 0$, **list** $\leftarrow \perp$
2: $\mathcal{A}^{\mathsf{SnPairInit}(\cdot),\mathsf{ConnectionInit}(\cdot),\mathsf{Send}_{\mathsf{T}}(\cdot),\mathsf{Receive}_{\mathsf{T}}(\cdot)}()$
3: **return phase**

$\mathsf{SnPairInit}((P,s),(P',\bar{s})):$

1: $SK \leftarrow \text{SessionKeyGen}(1^\lambda, P, P', s, \bar{s})$
2: **return** $\perp$

$\mathsf{ConnectionInit}(\pi_s^P, \Pi^*, \text{KDF}^*, i):$

1: **if** $(\Pi^*, \text{KDF}^*) \notin \{(\Pi, \text{KDF})\}$ **then**
2:     **return** $\perp$
3: **if** $(\pi_s^P.cxn_{\mathsf{W}}^i \in \texttt{list}) \vee (\pi_s^P.cxn_{\mathsf{R}}^i \in \texttt{list})$ **then**
4:     **return** $\perp$
5: $(\pi_s^P.cxn_{\mathsf{W}}^i, \pi_s^P.cxn_{\mathsf{R}}^i) \leftarrow \text{ConnectionInit}(SK, \pi_s^P, \Pi^*, \text{KDF}^*, i)$
6: $\texttt{list} \leftarrow \texttt{list}|\pi_s^P.cxn_{\mathsf{W}}^i|\pi_s^P.cxn_{\mathsf{R}}^i$
7: **return** $(\pi_s^P.cxn_{\mathsf{W}}^i, \pi_s^P.cxn_{\mathsf{R}}^i)$

$\mathsf{Send}_{\mathsf{T}}(m, [\ell], \pi_s^P.cxn_{\mathsf{W}}^i):$

1: $(c, \pi_s^P.cxn_{\mathsf{W}}^i)$
    $\leftarrow \text{ChannelSnd}(m, [\ell], \pi_s^P.cxn_{\mathsf{W}}^i)$
2: **return** $(c, \pi_s^P.cxn_{\mathsf{W}}^i.status)$

$\mathsf{Receive}_{\mathsf{T}}(p, \pi_s^P.cxn_{\mathsf{R}}^i):$

1: $(m, \pi_s^P.cxn_{\mathsf{R}}^i)$
    $\leftarrow \text{ChannelRcv}(p, \pi_s^P.cxn_{\mathsf{R}}^i)$
2: **if** $(m \in \mathcal{T}) \wedge (\pi_s^P.cxn_{\mathsf{R}}^i.status =$
    terminated$) \wedge \big((\exists \pi_{\bar{s}}^{P'}.cxn_{\mathsf{W}}^i :$
    $\pi_{\bar{s}}^{P'}.cxn_{\mathsf{W}}^i$ has a channel to $\pi_s^P.cxn_{\mathsf{R}}^i)$
    $\implies (\pi_{\bar{s}}^{P'}.cxn_{\mathsf{W}}^i.status \neq$
    terminated$)\big)$ **then**
3:     **phase** $\leftarrow 1$
4:     **return phase** from experiment
5: **return** $\pi_s^P.cxn_{\mathsf{R}}^i.status$

Fig. 3. Secure termination experiment for a protocol $\text{CHNL}[\{(\Pi, \text{KDF})\}] =$ (SessionGen, ConnectionInit, ChannelSnd, ChannelRcv) with message space $\mathcal{M}$, $\mathcal{T} \subset \mathcal{M}$, and adversary $\mathcal{A}$, where $\mathsf{Send}_{\mathsf{T}}$ and $\mathsf{Receive}_{\mathsf{T}}$ are constructed from (Π, KDF) as defined by $\pi_s^P.cxn_{\mathsf{W}}^i.suite$ and $\pi_s^P.cxn_{\mathsf{R}}^i.suite$.

Naturally, the fact that the read connection of the closure-initiator's session may not necessarily be required to close when the write connection sends a **terminate** message gives rise to the concepts of *fatal* and *graceful secure termination*. When a session π_s^P initiates closure with **terminate** $\in \mathcal{T}$ such that only the write connection closes, graceful closure *can* be achieved by waiting for a corresponding **terminate** message to be sent to the read connection of π_s^P before the read connection closes. Thus both sessions sharing the channels *may* achieve secure termination. Comparatively, if π_s^P initiates closure with a fatal **terminate** message, it *cannot* achieve secure termination– only the receiving session may achieve it.

Definition 13 (Fatal and Graceful Secure Termination). *Let π_s^P and $\pi_{\bar{s}}^{P'}$ be sessions of a two-party controllable channel protocol CHNL such that π_s^P has an channel to $\pi_{\bar{s}}^{P'}$ according to Definition 5. Let* **terminate** $\in \mathcal{T}$.

- *If, upon running $(c, \pi_s^P.cxn_{\mathsf{W}}^i{}') \xleftarrow{\$} \text{ChannelSnd}($**terminate**$, \pi_s^P.cxn_{\mathsf{W}}^i)$, both the write and read connections at π_s^P are closed according to Definition 9, then* **terminate** *is said to be a* fatal termination message.

– *If, upon running* $(c, \pi_s^P.cxn_W^{i\,\prime}) \xleftarrow{\$} \mathsf{ChannelSnd}(\texttt{terminate}, \pi_s^P.cxn_W^i)$, *only the write connection at* π_s *is closed according to Definition 9, then* terminate *is said to be a* graceful termination message.

4.3   Reduction to StLHAE Security

Secure termination depends upon the relay of messages with unaltered content and therefore its security is reducible to that of the authentication guarantees of the channel.

Theorem 2. *Let* $\mathrm{CHNL}[\{(\Pi, \mathrm{KDF})\}]$ *be a keyed two-party controllable channel protocol constructed from authentication scheme(s)* $\{\Pi\}$, *with a message space* $\mathcal{M}$ *and* $\mathcal{T} \subset \mathcal{M}$, *and let* $\mathcal{A}$ *be an adversarial algorithm in the* $\mathsf{Exp}_{\mathrm{CHNL}[\{(\Pi, \mathrm{KDF})\}]}^{\mathrm{sc.t}}$ *experiment. Then we can construct an adversarial algorithm* $\mathcal{B}$ *against* $\mathsf{Exp}_{\mathrm{CHNL}[\{(\Pi, \mathrm{KDF})\}]}^{\mathrm{stlhae\text{-}chnl}}$ *such that*

$$\mathbf{Adv}_{\mathrm{CHNL}[\{(\Pi, \mathrm{KDF})\}]}^{\mathrm{sc.t}}(\mathcal{A}) \leq \mathbf{Adv}_{\mathrm{CHNL}[\{(\Pi, \mathrm{KDF})\}]}^{\mathrm{stlhae\text{-}chnl}}(\mathcal{B}) \ .$$

Due to space restrictions, the proof of Theorem 2 appears in the full version.

5   Secure Channels and Termination in TLS 1.2

TLS is one of the most important security protocols in the world today and serves as the backbone of internet security. Due to the lack of key indistinguishability in TLS 1.2, many works analyzing it rely on the ACCE model [20]. We show that the *post-accept* phase channel ACCE security model can be viewed as a highly restricted case of channel protocol stateful length-hiding AE (stLHAE) security, and provide positive secure termination results for TLS 1.2 under this restricted case. Note that the use of the *post-accept* ACCE model, together with the coinciding channel restrictions, is not inherent; we demonstrate the correlation to bypass a reanalysis of TLS and directly consider secure termination. Analyzing TLS in our channel protocol model would allow for consideration of parallel sessions and connections, as well as resumption, key derivation functions, etc.

5.1   Comparing Channel Protocols and ACCE

ACCE employs a *pre-accept* phase and a *post-accept* phase. While the former handles all protocol interactions before a session key has been accepted, the latter is correlated to channel security under the agreed-upon session key. Breaking ACCE security is described in terms of either getting a session oracle to accept maliciously, or correctly answering a stLHAE encryption challenge.

Since CHNL session keys need not be sampled uniformly at random, it is possible to adapt the CHNL stLHAE construction (Definition 8) and allow for SK to be derived by other means (e.g. as the output of a handshake in the ACCE *pre-accept* phase). Thus we can link the CHNL stLHAE security experiment to the ACCE *post-accept* phase experiment (see [20]). The ACCE model uses the session key directly for the stLHAE primitive, with key derivation consisting of splitting the session key into two in order to obtain write/read keys. Since only one session key exists and is used directly as the connection keys (e.g. on cxn_W, cxn_R), only one connection pair is allowed per session. Another session key would be required for further connections if key separation is to be achieved. This assumption is inherent to the ACCE model TLS analyses to date, where SK is assumed to be a concatenation of the write and read keys (e.g. [23]).

Theorem 3. *Let* $\text{CHNL}[(\Pi, [])]$ *be a keyed two-party controllable channel protocol constructed from a single stLHAE scheme* Π, *using the identity KDF* $[]$. *Let* p *be the number of principals,* n *be the maximum number of sessions at a principal, and let* $\mathcal{A}$ *be an adversarial algorithm against the* $\text{Exp}^{\text{stlhae-chnl}}_{\text{CHNL}[(\Pi,[])]}()$ *experiment in Fig. 2. Then we can construct an adversarial algorithm* $\mathcal{B}$ *against* $\text{Exp}^{ACCE}_{\Pi}()$ *such that*

$$\mathbf{Adv}^{\text{stlhae-chnl}}_{\text{CHNL}[(\Pi,[])]}(\mathcal{A}) \leq p^2 \cdot n^2 \cdot \mathbf{Adv}^{ACCE}_{\Pi}(\mathcal{B}) \ .$$

Due to space restrictions, the proof of Theorem 3 appears in the full version.

5.2   Secure Termination in TLS

According to specification, the Alert Protocol in TLS falls into three categories: fatal alerts, warning alerts, and `close_notify` alerts. Unlike fatal alerts, which upon sending/receipt close both write and read connections at a session, `close_notify` alerts do not necessarily close the initiator's receive connection immediately, but *may* wait until receipt of the reciprocal `close_notify` alert. Figures 4 and 5 illustrate fatal and `close_notify` alert behavior. According to the TLS 1.2 standard, the determination of whether or not the initiator's read connection should be closed when a `close_notify` is sent is left to the usage profile [11, p. 28]. However, upon receipt of a `close_notify` alert, the responder *must* close its read connection and *must* send a corresponding `close_notify` alert on its send connection, before closing it also. Receipt of the reciprocal alert results in the closure of the original initiator's read connection.

Ostensibly, TLS fatal alerts are *fatal termination messages* per Definition 13 and the TLS 1.2 specification [11]. Comparatively, `close_notify` alerts are either *fatal* or *graceful termination messages*, depending on the implementation. Per specification, "It is not required for the initiator of the close to wait for the responding `close_notify` alert before closing the read side of the connection."

Remark 7. It is crucial to note that Alert Protocol messages are in fact, within the message space of the TLS protocol according to Definitions 5 and 8, despite the Alert Protocol running on top of the Record Layer Protocol. This is due to the fact that TLS 1.2 encrypts and sequences these messages in the same manner as application messages [11, Sect. 7.2].

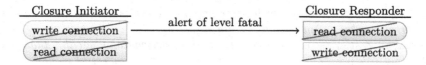

Fig. 4. TLS fatal alert behavior, where *initiator* is the session initiating a channel closure. Both the read and write *cxn* of the initiator close immediately upon sending.

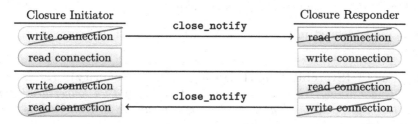

Fig. 5. TLS `close_notify` behavior. The write *cxn* of the initiator closes upon sending of `close_notify`. Upon receipt, the read *cxn* at the responder closes. Subsequently, the responder sends a corresponding `close_notify` alert and closes its write *cxn*.

We conclude with the following theorem on secure termination in TLS, under the restricted (ACCE-induced) channel environment of prior TLS analyses.

Theorem 4. *For TLS 1.2, TLS-RSA, TLS-CCA, TLS-DH, and TLS-DHE achieve secure termination under any fatal alert or* `close_notify` *alert, where each TLS session consists of a single connection pair with connection keys derived from the session key via the identity KDF.*

Theorem 4 follows by combining previous ACCE analyses of TLS 1.2 [7, 20,23,29], Theorems 3, and 2, and applying the observation above that *fatal* and `close_notify` alerts satisfy the definition of **terminate** messages within $\mathcal{T} \subset \mathcal{M}$, where $\mathcal{M}$ is the protocol message space.

From previous analyses of TLS 1.2 in the ACCE model, Theorem 4 inherits the restriction that sessions consist of a single connection pair. However this is not intrinsic to the design of TLS and it may be analyzed in the keyed two-party controllable channel model for better consideration of the full protocol.

A   stLHAE Syntax and Security

Definition 14 (Stateful Length-Hiding AEAD). *A stateful length-hiding AEAD scheme Π for a message space $\mathcal{M}$, an associated data space $\mathcal{AD}$, a key space $\mathcal{K}$, and a ciphertext space $\mathcal{C}$, is a tuple of algorithms:*

- $\mathrm{Kgn}() \xrightarrow{\$} k$: *A probabilistic key generation algorithm that outputs a key k.*
- $\mathrm{Enc}(k, \ell, \mathsf{ad}, m, st_{\mathsf{S}}) \xrightarrow{\$} (c, st'_{\mathsf{S}})$: *A probabilistic encryption algorithm that takes as input a key $k \in \mathcal{K}$, a length $\ell \in \mathbb{Z} \cup \{\bot\}$, associated data $\mathsf{ad} \in \mathcal{AD}$, a*

message $m \in \mathcal{M}$, and an write state st_S, and outputs a ciphertext $c \in \mathcal{C}$ or an error symbol $\perp$, and updated state st'_S.

- $\mathrm{Dec}(k, \mathrm{ad}, c, st_R) \to (m, st'_R)$: *A deterministic decryption algorithm that takes as input a key $k \in \mathcal{K}$, associated data $\mathrm{ad} \in \mathcal{AD}$, a ciphertext c, and a read state st_R, and outputs a message $m \in \mathcal{M}$ or an error symbol $\perp$, and an updated state st'_R.*

If $\ell \neq \perp$, then we say that Π is length-hiding.

Correctness is defined in the obvious way, based on scheme correctness from Definition 1.

Definition 15 (Stateful Length-Hiding AEAD Security). *Let Π be a stateful length-hiding AEAD scheme and let $\mathcal{A}$ be an PPT adversarial algorithm. The stateful length-hiding AEAD experiment for Π with bit b is given by* $\mathrm{Exp}_{\Pi}^{\mathsf{stlhae}}(\mathcal{A})$ *in Fig. 6. We define*

$$\mathbf{Adv}_{\Pi}^{\mathsf{stlhae}}(\mathcal{A}) = 2\Pr\left[\mathrm{Exp}_{\Pi}^{\mathsf{stlhae}}(\mathcal{A})\right] - 1 \ .$$

Note that the state variables st_S, st_R in Fig. 6 are considered substate variables in terms of the channel environment (e.g. $\pi_s^P.cxn_W^i.substate$, $\pi_s^P.cxn_R^i.substate$). This is due to the increased state considerations of the environment.

$\underline{\mathrm{Exp}_{\Pi}^{\mathsf{stlhae}}(\mathcal{A})\colon}$

1: $k \xleftarrow{\$} \mathrm{Kgn}()$
2: $b \xleftarrow{\$} \{0,1\}$
3: $st_S \leftarrow \perp, st_R \leftarrow \perp$
4: $u \leftarrow 0, v \leftarrow 0$
5: **phase** $\leftarrow 0$
6: $b' \xleftarrow{\$} \mathcal{A}^{\mathsf{Encrypt}(\cdot), \mathsf{Decrypt}(\cdot)}()$
7: **return** $(b' = b)$

$\underline{\mathrm{Enc}(\ell, \mathrm{ad}, (m_0, m_1))\colon}$

1: $u \leftarrow u + 1$
2: $(sent.c^{(0)}, st_S^{(0)}) \leftarrow \mathrm{Enc}(k, \ell, \mathrm{ad}, m_0, st_S)$
3: $(sent.c^{(1)}, st_S^{(1)}) \leftarrow \mathrm{Enc}(k, \ell, \mathrm{ad}, m_1, st_S)$
4: **if** $sent.c^{(0)} = \perp$ **or** $sent.c^{(1)} = \perp$ **then**
5:    **return** $\perp$
6: $(sent.ad_u, sent.c_u, st_S) := (\mathrm{ad}, sent.c^{(b)}, st_S^{(b)})$
7: **return** $sent.c_u$

$\underline{\mathrm{Dec}(\mathrm{ad}, c)\colon}$

1: **if** $b = 0$ **then**
2:    **return** $\perp$
3: $v \leftarrow v + 1$
4: (m, st_R)
        $\leftarrow \mathrm{Dec}(k, \mathrm{ad}, c, st_R)$
5: **if** $(u < v) \vee (c \neq sent.c_v) \vee$
        $(\mathrm{ad} \neq sent.ad_v)$ **then**
6:    **phase** $\leftarrow 1$
7: **if phase** $= 1$ **then**
8:    **return** m
9: **return** $\perp$

Fig. 6. Stateful length-hiding AEAD experiment stlhae for stateful length-hiding AEAD scheme $\Pi = (\mathrm{Kgn}, \mathrm{Enc}, \mathrm{Dec})$ and adversary $\mathcal{A}$.

References

1. Acar, T., Belenkiy, M., Bellare, M., Cash, D.: Cryptographic agility and its relation to circular encryption. In: Gilbert, H. (ed.) EUROCRYPT 2010. LNCS, vol. 6110, pp. 403–422. Springer, Heidelberg (2010). https://doi.org/10.1007/978-3-642-13190-5_21

2. Badertscher, C., Matt, C., Maurer, U., Rogaway, P., Tackmann, B.: Augmented secure channels and the goal of the TLS 1.3 record layer. In: Au, M.-H., Miyaji, A. (eds.) ProvSec 2015. LNCS, vol. 9451, pp. 85–104. Springer, Cham (2015). https://doi.org/10.1007/978-3-319-26059-4_5

3. Bellare, M., Namprempre, C.: Authenticated encryption: relations among notions and analysis of the generic composition paradigm. J. Cryptol. 21(4), 469–491 (2008)

4. Bergsma, F., Dowling, B., Kohlar, F., Schwenk, J., Stebila, D.: Multi-ciphersuite security of the secure shell (SSH) protocol. In: Proceedings of the 2014 ACM SIGSAC Conference on Computer and Communications Security, CCS 2014, pp. 369–381. ACM (2014). https://doi.org/10.1145/2660267.2660286

5. Bhargavan, K., Delignat-Lavaud, A., Fournet, C., Pironti, A., Strub, P.Y.: Triple handshakes and cookie cutters: Breaking and fixing authentication over TLS. In: 2014 IEEE Symposium on Security and Privacy, pp. 98–113. IEEE Computer Society Press, May 2014

6. Bhargavan, K., Fournet, C., Kohlweiss, M., Pironti, A., Strub, P.-Y., Zanella-Béguelin, S.: Proving the TLS handshake secure (As It Is). In: Garay, J.A., Gennaro, R. (eds.) CRYPTO 2014. LNCS, vol. 8617, pp. 235–255. Springer, Heidelberg (2014). https://doi.org/10.1007/978-3-662-44381-1_14

7. Boyd, C., Hale, B., Mjølsnes, S.F., Stebila, D.: From stateless to stateful: generic authentication and authenticated encryption constructions with application to TLS. In: Sako, K. (ed.) CT-RSA 2016. LNCS, vol. 9610, pp. 55–71. Springer, Cham (2016). https://doi.org/10.1007/978-3-319-29485-8_4

8. Brier, E., Peyrin, T.: A forward-secure symmetric-key derivation protocol. In: Abe, M. (ed.) ASIACRYPT 2010. LNCS, vol. 6477, pp. 250–267. Springer, Heidelberg (2010). https://doi.org/10.1007/978-3-642-17373-8_15

9. Canetti, R., Krawczyk, H.: Analysis of key-exchange protocols and their use for building secure channels. In: Pfitzmann, B. (ed.) EUROCRYPT 2001. LNCS, vol. 2045, pp. 453–474. Springer, Heidelberg (2001). https://doi.org/10.1007/3-540-44987-6_28

10. Cohen, R., Coretti, S., Garay, J., Zikas, V.: Probabilistic Termination and Composability of Cryptographic Protocols (2016). http://eprint.iacr.org/

11. Dierks, T., Rescorla, E.: The Transport Layer Security (TLS) Protocol Version 1.2 (2008). https://tools.ietf.org/html/rfc5426. RFC 5426

12. Fischlin, M., Günther, F., Marson, G.A., Paterson, K.G.: Data is a stream: security of stream-based channels. In: Gennaro, R., Robshaw, M. (eds.) CRYPTO 2015. LNCS, vol. 9216, pp. 545–564. Springer, Heidelberg (2015). https://doi.org/10.1007/978-3-662-48000-7_27

13. Giesen, F., Kohlar, F., Stebila, D.: On the security of TLS renegotiation. In: Sadeghi, A.R., Gligor, V.D., Yung, M. (eds.) ACM CCS 13, pp. 387–398. ACM Press, November 2013

14. Günther, F., Mazaheri, S.: A formal treatment of multi-key channels. In: Katz, J., Shacham, H. (eds.) CRYPTO 2017. LNCS, vol. 10403, pp. 587–618. Springer, Cham (2017). https://doi.org/10.1007/978-3-319-63697-9_20

15. Haber, S., Pinkas, B.: Securely combining public-key cryptosystems. In: ACM CCS 2001, pp. 215–224. ACM Press, November 2001

16. Hoang, V.T., Krovetz, T., Rogaway, P.: Robust authenticated-encryption AEZ and the problem that it solves. In: Oswald, E., Fischlin, M. (eds.) EUROCRYPT 2015. LNCS, vol. 9056, pp. 15–44. Springer, Heidelberg (2015). https://doi.org/10.1007/978-3-662-46800-5_2

17. Hoang, V.T., Reyhanitabar, R., Rogaway, P., Vizár, D.: Online authenticated-encryption and its nonce-reuse misuse-resistance. In: Gennaro, R., Robshaw, M.J.B. (eds.) CRYPTO 2015, Part I. LNCS, vol. 9215, pp. 493–517. Springer, Heidelberg (Aug (2015)

18. Hoepman, J.-H.: The ephemeral pairing problem. In: Juels, A. (ed.) FC 2004. LNCS, vol. 3110, pp. 212–226. Springer, Heidelberg (2004). https://doi.org/10.1007/978-3-540-27809-2_22

19. IEEE 802.11: Wireless LAN Medium Access Control (MAC) and Physical Layer (PHY) Specifications (2012). https://doi.org/10.1109/IEEESTD.2012.6178212

20. Jager, T., Kohlar, F., Schäge, S., Schwenk, J.: On the security of TLS-DHE in the standard model. In: Safavi-Naini, R., Canetti, R. (eds.) CRYPTO 2012. LNCS, vol. 7417, pp. 273–293. Springer, Heidelberg (2012). https://doi.org/10.1007/978-3-642-32009-5_17

21. Katz, J., Yung, M.: Unforgeable encryption and chosen ciphertext secure modes of operation. In: Goos, G., Hartmanis, J., van Leeuwen, J., Schneier, B. (eds.) FSE 2000. LNCS, vol. 1978, pp. 284–299. Springer, Heidelberg (2001). https://doi.org/10.1007/3-540-44706-7_20

22. Krawczyk, H.: Cryptographic Extraction and key derivation: the HKDF scheme. In: Rabin, T. (ed.) CRYPTO 2010. LNCS, vol. 6223, pp. 631–648. Springer, Heidelberg (2010). https://doi.org/10.1007/978-3-642-14623-7_34

23. Krawczyk, H., Paterson, K.G., Wee, H.: On the security of the TLS protocol: a systematic analysis. In: Canetti, R., Garay, J.A. (eds.) CRYPTO 2013. LNCS, vol. 8042, pp. 429–448. Springer, Heidelberg (2013). https://doi.org/10.1007/978-3-642-40041-4_24

24. Marson, G., Poettering, B.: Security Notions for Bidirectional Channels. In: IACR Transactions on Symmetric Cryptology. vol. 2017, pp. 405–426. http://ojs.ub.rub.de/index.php/ToSC/article/view/602

25. Maurer, U., Tackmann, B.: On the soundness of authenticate-then-encrypt: formalizing the malleability of symmetric encryption. In: Al-Shaer, E., Keromytis, A.D., Shmatikov, V. (eds.) ACM CCS 2010, pp. 505–515. ACM Press, October 2010

26. Maurer, U.M.: Perfect cryptographic security from partially independent channels. In: 23rd ACM STOC, pp. 561–571. ACM Press, May 1991

27. Microsoft-Inria Joint Centre: miTLS: A verified reference TLS implementation (2012). https://www.mitls.org/pages/attacks

28. Namprempre, C.: Secure channels based on authenticated encryption schemes: a simple characterization. In: Zheng, Y. (ed.) ASIACRYPT 2002. LNCS, vol. 2501, pp. 515–532. Springer, Heidelberg (2002). https://doi.org/10.1007/3-540-36178-2_32

29. Paterson, K.G., Ristenpart, T., Shrimpton, T.: Tag size *Does* matter: attacks and proofs for the TLS record protocol. In: Lee, D.H., Wang, X. (eds.) ASIACRYPT 2011. LNCS, vol. 7073, pp. 372–389. Springer, Heidelberg (2011). https://doi.org/10.1007/978-3-642-25385-0_20

30. Rescorla, E.: The Transport Layer Security (TLS) Protocol Version 1.3: draft-ietf-tls-tls13-20, April 2017. https://tools.ietf.org/pdf/draft-ietf-tls-tls13-20.pdf. Expires 30 October 2017
31. Rescorla, E., Modadugu, N.: Datagram Transport Layer Security (2006). https://tools.ietf.org/html/rfc4347. RFC 4347
32. Rogaway, P.: Authenticated-encryption with associated-data. In: Atluri, V. (ed.) ACM CCS 2002, pp. 98–107. ACM Press, November 2002
33. Rogaway, P., Shrimpton, T.: Deterministic authenticated-encryption: a provable-security treatment of the key-wrap problem. Cryptology ePrint Archive, Report 2006/221 (2006). http://eprint.iacr.org/2006/221
34. Shrimpton, T.: A characterization of authenticated-encryption as a form of chosen-ciphertext security. Cryptology ePrint Archive, Report 2004/272 (2004). http://eprint.iacr.org/2004/272
35. Smyth, B., Pironti, A.: Truncating TLS connections to violate beliefs in web applications. In: 7th USENIX Workshop on Offensive Technologies, WOOT 2013 (2013)

Improved Security Notions for Proxy Re-Encryption to Enforce Access Control

Ela Lee[(✉)]

Royal Holloway, University of London, Egham, UK
`Ela.Berners-Lee.2010@live.rhul.ac.uk`

Abstract. Proxy Re-Encryption (PRE) allows a ciphertext encrypted under Alice's public key to be transformed to an encryption under Bob's public key without revealing either the plaintext or the decryption keys. PRE schemes have clear applications to cryptographic access control by allowing outsourced data to be selectively shared to users via re-encryption to appropriate keys. One concern for this application is that the server should not be able to perform unauthorised re-encryptions. We argue that current security notions do not adequately address this concern. We revisit existing definitions for PRE, starting by challenging the concept of unidirectionality, which states that re-encryption tokens from A to B cannot be used to re-encrypt from B to A. We strengthen this definition to reflect realistic scenarios in which adversaries may try to reverse a re-encryption by retaining information about prior ciphertexts and re-encryption tokens. We then strengthen the adversarial model to consider malicious adversaries that may collude with corrupt users and attempt to perform unauthorised re-encryptions; this models a malicious cloud service provider aiming to subvert the re-encryption process to leak sensitive data. Finally we revisit the notion of authenticated encryption for PRE. This currently assumes the same party who created the message also encrypted it, which is not necessarily the case in re-encryption. We thus introduce the notion of *ciphertext origin authentication* to determine who encrypted the message (initiated a re-encryption) and show how to fulfil this requirement in practice.

Keywords: Proxy re-encryption · Applied cryptography ·
Unidirectional · Multi-hop · Malicious model · Access control

1 Introduction

There are many practical situations in which a ciphertext encrypted under one key must be re-encrypted such that it becomes an encryption of the same message under a different key. This is trivial when data is stored locally, but is less

The author was supported by the EPSRC and the UK government as part of the Centre for Doctoral Training in Cyber Security at Royal Holloway, University of London (EP/K035584/1).

© Springer Nature Switzerland AG 2019
T. Lange and O. Dunkelman (Eds.): LATINCRYPT 2017, LNCS 11368, pp. 66–85, 2019.
https://doi.org/10.1007/978-3-030-25283-0_4

straightforward when data is stored remotely by an untrusted server such as a cloud service provider. Proxy Re-Encryption (PRE) [5] enables a third party to re-encrypt a ciphertext using an *update token* generated by the client, in such a way that neither the decryption keys nor plaintext are revealed.

A common motivation cited for PRE is *email forwarding* [2,3,5,7,8,18], where Alice wants to forward her emails to Bob and have him read them on her behalf, without revealing her secret key. With PRE, she can generate an update token which the email server uses to re-encrypt ciphertexts under Alice's key to ciphertexts under Bob's key, without the server reading her emails. Another motivation, which we focus on in this paper, is enforcing cryptographic access control over remotely stored files [3,17]. If data is given a classification level, and keys are shared with users according to access control policy, then re-encryption is used to enforce changes to the policy. In particular, re-encryption can signify a change in user access rights, revocation or key expiry.

In this paper, we revisit the security notions for PRE with a particular focus on enforcing access control as an application. The main issue not addressed by existing literature is that a malicious server should not be able to perform an unauthorised re-encryption. We aim to strengthen security from previous work which mainly considers *honest-but-curious* adversaries that follow the protocol honestly but try to learn the underlying plaintexts. We break unauthorised re-encryptions down into two main security notions: the inability to create a valid update token even given having seen a number of valid tokens, and a stronger notion of unidirectionality which considers reversal attacks. Our main contributions are as follows:

Token Robustness. Existing work [11] tackles the issue of controlling which ciphertexts are re-encrypted by defining *ciphertext dependence*, where tokens are created to only be valid for specific ciphertexts. We strengthen this definition to create a security notion which states that an adversary cannot generate a valid update token which re-encrypts to a previously unused key, even having seen a number of legitimate tokens. We then give an example which shows that this notion is stronger than ciphertext dependence. We call this *token robustness*.

Unidirectionality. To tackle re-encryptions to keys which a ciphertext has previously been encrypted under, we revisit the existing notion of unidirectionality, which states that a re-encryption token can only be used to transform a ciphertext under pk_i to pk_j and not from pk_j to pk_i (otherwise the scheme is *bidirectional*). The ability to re-encrypt back to the old key can grant access back to an unauthorised user or re-encrypt to an expired key. Current notions do not consider reversal attacks where a server may retain some limited information about an old ciphertext and update token to reverse the re-encryption. This consideration is particularly important for token robust schemes where the token used to perform the update is crucial in reverting a ciphertext back to an expired key. We formally define reversal attacks with respect to the size of the state the server must retain in order to reverse a re-encryption, and use this to form an upper bound on security definitions for directionality. This is stronger than existing notions for unidirectionality as it gives the adversary more control over the information they have access to than traditional notions, which only consider tokens given to the adversary. We then use this together with token robustness define *best-achievable unidirectionality*. Overall, our security model covers a wider range of attacks than prior definitions. A simple adaptation of ElGamal-based PRE that shows these definitions can be met is given in Appendix B.

Ciphertext Origin Authentication. Finally we revisit the notion of data origin authentication for PRE. Typically, data origin authentication assumes that the same party who created the message also encrypted it, so tying the data owner's identity to the message within the ciphertext is suffient. Whilst this is a valid assumption for many encryption scenarios, for access control where more than one party shares a key, the same assumption cannot be made. We create a new notion of *ciphertext origin authentication* where the encryptor/re-encryption initiator's identity is tied to the ciphertext as opposed to the message, and re-encryption updates this accordingly. We offer an extension to our unidirectional token robust scheme, and show how to develop similar extensions for other schemes [4].

The structure of this paper is as follows: In Sects. 2 and 3 we formally discuss existing work and current notions of security for PRE. We define *token robustness* in Sect. 4 and *maximal irreversibility* in Sect. 5. We then build on these to define *best-achievable unidirectionality*. In Sect. 6 we define the requirements for a PRE scheme to be secure for a malicious server and define *token robustness*. In Sect. 5 we critique existing notions of unidirectionality, and present the first security definition for that considers reversibility. A formal security definition for unidirectionality as it is currently considered is given in the full version [4]. We then use this to create a stronger definition for *best-achievable unidirectionality*. In Sect. 7 we define ciphertext origin authentication to provide authenticated PRE and discuss how to achieve this.

2   Preliminaries

In this work we only consider an IND-CPA schemes with a randomised encryption algorithm.

Definition 1 (multi-hop PRE scheme). *A* (multi-hop) proxy re-encryption (PRE) scheme *consists of the following algorithms:*

- Setup$(1^\lambda) \to param$: *Takes the security parameter* 1^λ *and outputs the set of parameters param, including a description of the message space* $\mathcal{M}$ *and token space* $\mathcal{D}$. *We note that param is an input for all subsequent algorithms but we leave it out for compactness of notation.*
- KeyGen$(1^\lambda) \xrightarrow{\$} (\mathsf{pk}, \mathsf{sk})$: *Generates a public-private key pair.*
- Enc$(\mathsf{pk}, m) \xrightarrow{\$} C$: *Given a public key* pk *and message* $m \in \mathcal{M}$, *returning the ciphertext* C.

- $\mathsf{Dec}(\mathsf{sk}, C) \rightarrow m$ or $\perp$: *Given a secret key* sk *and a ciphertext* C, *returns either a message* m *or the error symbol* $\perp$.
- $\mathsf{ReKeyGen}(\mathsf{sk}_1, \mathsf{pk}_2) \rightarrow \Delta_{1,2}$: *For two keypairs* $(\mathsf{pk}_1, \mathsf{sk}_1), (\mathsf{pk}_2, \mathsf{sk}_2)$, *outputs an update token* $\Delta_{1,2}$.
- $\mathsf{ReEnc}(\Delta_{1,2}, C_1) \rightarrow C_2$: *Takes a ciphertext* C_1 *and a token* $\Delta_{1,2}$ *and translates the ciphertext to output a new ciphertext* C_2.

A PRE scheme is correct *if for every message* $m \in \mathcal{M}$, *any sequence of* κ *keypairs* $(\mathsf{pk}_1, \mathsf{sk}_1), \ldots, (\mathsf{pk}_\kappa, \mathsf{sk}_\kappa) \leftarrow \mathsf{KeyGen}(1^\lambda)$, *all ciphertexts* $C_1 \leftarrow \mathsf{Enc}(\mathsf{pk}_1, m)$, *and all transformed ciphertexts* $\{C_i \leftarrow \mathsf{ReEnc}(\mathsf{ReKeyGen}(\mathsf{sk}_{i-1}, \mathsf{pk}_i), C_{i-1})\}_{i=1}^\kappa$:

$$\Pr\left[\mathsf{Dec}(\mathsf{sk}_i, C_i)) \neq m\right] \leq \mathsf{negl}(\lambda),$$

for some negligible function $\mathsf{negl}(\lambda)$.

In other words, ciphertexts decrypt correctly, including ciphertexts which are re-encryptions of other correct ciphertexts. Definition 1 can be intuitively adapted to the symmetric key setting, where token generation requires knowledge of both secret keys.

2.1 Additional Properties

There are some additional properties which a PRE scheme can have. Whether or not these properties are required depends on the security model and the application. We define some of these properties below.

Directionality: A PRE scheme is *bidirectional* if a re-encryption token from pk_i to pk_j can be used to re-encrypt from pk_j to pk_i and we write $\Delta_{i\leftrightarrow j}$. Otherwise, it is *unidirectional* and we write $\Delta_{i\rightarrow j}$. We reserve the notation $\Delta_{i,j}$ for the general case where directionality is not specified.

Single/Multi-hop: Some PRE schemes are *single-hop* meaning ciphertexts can only be re-encrypted once. In contrast a *multi-hop* scheme can be re-encrypted multiple times. Single-hop schemes only have limited use and are mainly considered for unidirectionality purposes. Since we focus on the practical application of access control as a motivation, we will assume multi-hop as a necessary requirement of a PRE scheme in the remainder of this work.

Ciphertext Dependence: Informally, ReKeyGen takes some additional information as input about the ciphertext that is to be re-encrypted under a new key. The resulting token can only correctly re-encrypt the specified ciphertext. Let ReKeyGen in a PRE scheme be redefined to take additional information $\tilde{C}$ about ciphertext C as input: $\mathsf{ReKeyGen}(\mathsf{sk}_i, \mathsf{pk}_j, \tilde{C}) \rightarrow \Delta_{i,j,C}$. This PRE scheme is *ciphertext dependent* if for all $C_i^1 \overset{\$}{\leftarrow} \mathsf{Enc}(\mathsf{pk}_i, m_1)$ and $C_i^2 \overset{\$}{\leftarrow} \mathsf{Enc}(\mathsf{pk}_i, m_2)$ such that $C_i^1 \neq C_i^2$, and all re-encryption tokens $\Delta_{i,j,C_i^1} \overset{\$}{\leftarrow} \mathsf{ReKeyGen}(\mathsf{sk}_i, \mathsf{pk}_j, \tilde{C}_i^1)$, then:

$$\Pr\left[\mathsf{Dec}(\mathsf{sk}_j, \mathsf{ReEnc}(\Delta_{i,j,C_i^1}, C_i^2)) = \mathsf{Dec}(\mathsf{sk}_i, C_i^2)\right] \leq \mathsf{negl}(\lambda). \tag{1}$$

In existing work [11] and in our scheme, $\tilde{C}$ is the header of the ciphertext, and for simplicity we assume this is the case in the remainder of this paper. We note that not all applications require ciphertext dependence, such as key expiry, where all ciphertexts under the old key must be re-encrypted. In subsequent definitions we will assume ciphertext dependence, but we note that these definitions can easily be extended to ciphertext independent schemes by setting $\tilde{C} = \emptyset$.

2.2 Existing Work

PRE was first introduced in [5]. The common approach to PRE in practice is the key encapsulation approach, where the ciphertext header contains the data encryption key k_D, encrypted with a key encryption key k_K. Typically, such schemes perform re-encryption by replacing k_K—so the ciphertext header now contains the same k_D encrypted with the new key encryption key k'_K and the body of the ciphertext remains unchanged:

$$C = ([k_D]_{k_K}, [m]_{k_D}) \xrightarrow{\text{ReEnc}(\varDelta, C)} C' = ([k_D]_{k'_K}, [m]_{k_D})$$

The appeal of this approach is that it is efficient and can use hybrid encryption. It is used widely, for example in Amazon's Key Management Service [1]. Whilst these schemes are simple and easy to implement, they do not completely re-randomise a ciphertext during re-encryption. A particular concern with the key encapsulation approach is that a malicious user can simply retain k_D and be able to decrypt the message, regardless of how many times it is re-encrypted.

Other indistinguishability notions for PRE are described in [8] and [11]. A similar definition for CCA-security is used in [3,7,16]. Existing notions which imply complete re-randomisation for public-key PRE include *unlinkability* in [7], and for symmetric key PRE include *ciphertext independence*[1] in [6] and UP-REENC security in [11]. Ciphertext dependence was first introduced in [11] for symmetric PRE, but has not yet been picked up by subsequent work. However their work does not explicitly consider unauthorised re-encryptions or unidirectionality.

One attempt to formalise the definition of directionality is given in [13], but they do not view directionality as a security definition, rather a classification of PRE schemes. They therefore define unidirectional PRE schemes and bidirectional PRE schemes as opposed to defining directionality separately. As a consequence of this, the definition of unidirectionality in [13] assumes that a unidirectional scheme is single-hop, which is not necessarily the case. Other more recent work which informally describes unidirectionality say no PPTalgorithm can out output a token that can re-encrypt to the old key [11], whereas other works [17] say no PPTalgorithm can output an equivalent encryption of the old ciphertext. This inconsistency is problematic for analysing security.

For a long time it was an open problem to create a scheme which is both unidirectional and multi-hop and, as such, there exist a number of PRE schemes which are unidirectional and single-hop [8,16,18]. They achieve unidirectionality

---

[1] As in [11], we reserve this terminology for PRE schemes for which token generation is not specific to a given ciphertext as in Sect. 2.1.

by having two distinct levels of ciphertext which have different formats—level 2 for ciphertexts which can be re-encrypted, and level 1 for ciphertexts which cannot be re-encrypted. It is this format change which prevents a ciphertext from being re-encrypted more than once. This approach is undesirable, since it does not allow for multiple re-encryptions and therefore has limited practical application. Furthermore it does not convey how easy it is for a malicious server to reverse the re-encryption process. We discuss this in Sect. 5.

In many multi-hop schemes the number of re-encryptions is fixed, and the size of the ciphertext grows linearly with each re-encryption [7,14]. The related problem of multi-hop unidirectional proxy re-signatures has a solution given in [15], however the message must be provided with the signature and thus such a scheme cannot be easily adapted to re-encryption. The first PRE scheme which is both unidirectional and multi-hop was given in [17], but does not address ciphertext dependence and current methods for achieving this cannot be applied to their scheme.

To our knowledge, there is no existing work in PRE that considers a malicious server which may perform unauthorised re-encryptions.

3 Indistinguishability

The most common notion of indistinguishability for PRE is that a re-encryption of a ciphertext should *preserve* the indistinguishability given by the underlying encryption scheme, which we call pres-IND-CPA (more details are given in Appendix A). It is not usually considered a requirement that re-encryption fully re-randomises a ciphertext. However full re-randomisation is a necessary security property for applications such as access control (revocation) and key expiry. We address this in Definition 2, based on UP-REENC in [11] adapted to the public-key setting, which models a revoked user trying to distinguish a re-encrypted ciphertext from two potential original ciphertexts. In this game, challenge ciphertexts are given using a left-right-oracle, LR-ReEnc which the adversary can query adaptively. For stronger security, the adversary has access to a token generation oracle, OReKeyGen. The adversary is also given t secret keys, to model revocation scenarios where a user knows the old key and oracles have the restriction that they will not return tokens to a compromised key.

Definition 2. *A PRE scheme $\mathcal{PRE}$ is* re-encryption indistinguishable against chosen plaintext attack *(ReEnc-IND-CPA) if for all* PPT *adversaries $\mathcal{A}$ there exists a negligible function* negl(λ) *such that:*

$$\Pr\left[\mathsf{ReEnc\text{-}IND\text{-}CPA}_{\mathcal{PRE}}^{\mathcal{A}}(\lambda) = 1\right] \leq \frac{1}{2} + \mathsf{negl}(\lambda),\qquad(2)$$

where ReEnc-IND-CPA *is given in Fig. 1.*

This definition can be easily extended to symmetric PRE by providing the adversary with encryption oracles for both keys, see [11]. If ReKeyGen is deterministic, the adversary can win by calling OReKeyGen(i, j, C_0) to obtain Δ, compute

$$
\boxed{
\begin{array}{l}
\textbf{ReEnc-IND-CPA}^{\mathcal{A}}_{\mathcal{PRE}}(\lambda) \\
\hline
param \leftarrow \mathsf{Setup}(\lambda) \\
b \xleftarrow{\$} \{0,1\} \\
(\mathsf{pk}_1, \mathsf{sk}_1), \dots (\mathsf{pk}_\kappa, \mathsf{sk}_\kappa) \leftarrow \mathsf{KeyGen}(1^\lambda) \\
\text{compromised} = \{\mathsf{sk}_1, \dots, \mathsf{sk}_t\} \\
b' \leftarrow \mathcal{A}^{\mathsf{LR\text{-}ReEnc}, \mathsf{OReKeyGen}}(1^\lambda, \text{compromised}, \mathsf{pk}_1, \dots, \mathsf{pk}_\kappa) \\
\quad \textbf{return } b' = b
\end{array}
}
$$

$\mathsf{LR\text{-}ReEnc}(i,j,C_0,C_1)$	$\mathsf{OReKeyGen}(i,j,C)$
if $|C_0| \neq |C_1|$ **or** $\mathsf{sk}_j \in$ compromised	**if** $\mathsf{sk}_j \in$ compromised
$\quad$ **return** $\perp$	$\quad$ **return** $\perp$
$\Delta_{i,j,C_b} \xleftarrow{\$} \mathsf{ReKeyGen}(\mathsf{sk}_i, \mathsf{pk}_j, \tilde{C}_b)$	$\Delta_{i,j,C} \xleftarrow{\$} \mathsf{ReKeyGen}(\mathsf{sk}_i, \mathsf{pk}_j, \tilde{C})$
$C' \leftarrow \mathsf{ReEnc}(\Delta_{i,j,C}, C_b)$	**return** $\Delta_{i,j,C}$
return (C')	

Fig. 1. ReEnc-IND-CPA game. Schemes that meet this definition must fully rerandomise a ciphertext upon re-encryption.

$\mathsf{ReEnc}(\Delta, C_1)$ and compare this to $\mathsf{LR\text{-}ReEnc}(i,j,C_0,C_1)$. Since we consider re-randomisation a necessary property, from now on we will assume that $\mathsf{ReKeyGen}$ is randomised.

4 Token Robustness

This section defines *token robustness* - a stronger notion than ciphertext dependence. Informally, token robustness states that even with access to a token generation oracle, an adversary cannot create a new valid token which re-encrypts a ciphertext to a key it was never previously encrypted under. We cover re-encryption to keys a ciphertext was previously encrypted under in Sect. 5. Before we define token robustness, we need to define token validity.

Definition 3 (Token validity). *Let* $\delta \in \mathcal{D}$. *We say that* δ *is a* valid update token *if there exist keys* $(\mathsf{pk}_1, \mathsf{sk}_1), (\mathsf{pk}_1, \mathsf{sk}_2) \leftarrow \mathsf{KeyGen}(1^\lambda)$ *and a ciphertext* $C \xleftarrow{\$} \mathsf{Enc}(\mathsf{pk}_1, m)$ *for some* $m \in \mathcal{M}$ *such that:*

$$\Pr[\mathsf{Dec}(\mathsf{sk}_2, \mathsf{ReEnc}(\delta, C)) \neq m] \leq \mathsf{negl}(\lambda). \tag{3}$$

In the token robustness game Fig. 2, the adversary has access to a token generation oracle $\mathsf{OReKeyGen}$ and an encryption oracle OEnc, and attempts to output a valid token $\delta^{\mathcal{A}}$ which re-encrypts a target ciphertext $C_i^{\mathcal{A}}$ from being under pk_i to being under pk_j. The list chain records which messages have been encrypted under which keys by adding the appropriate keys to $\mathsf{chain}(m)$ whenever OEnc or $\mathsf{OReKeyGen}$ are called. This means the adversary cannot trivially

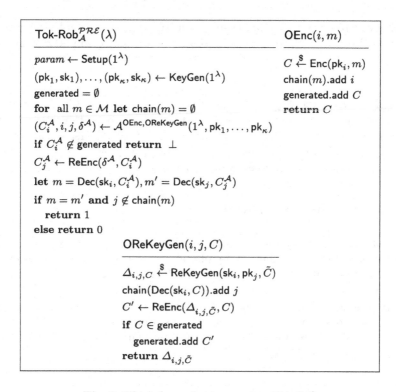

Fig. 2. The token robustness game Tok-Rob

win by submitting a token which was the output of an OReKeyGen query. Another condition is the adversarys target ciphertext $C_i^{\mathcal{A}}$ must be an output of the OEnc oracle (or a re-encryption of such a ciphertext) to ensure that the adversary has no additional advantage from storing information created when encrypting the ciphertext. For example, in our scheme in Appendix B, encryption selects a random y and sets $\tilde{C} = g^y$. If the adversary encrypts the message for themselves then they learn y, which the server would not know in the cloud storage application. The function **generated** is used to keep track of these ciphertexts.

Definition 4. *We say that a PRE scheme $\mathcal{PRE}$ has* token robustness *if for all PPT adversaries $\mathcal{A}$, there exists a negligible function $\mathsf{negl}(\lambda)$ such that*

$$\Pr\left[\mathsf{Tok\text{-}Rob}_{\mathcal{PRE}}^{\mathcal{A}}(\lambda) = 1\right] \le \mathsf{negl}(\lambda),\tag{4}$$

where Tok-Rob *is given in Fig. 2.*

Theorem 1. *No ciphertext independent PRE scheme has token robustness.*

Proof. If a PRE scheme is not ciphertext dependent, then the same update token can be used to re-encrypt more than one ciphertext. In the Tok-Rob game, let $C_1 \leftarrow \mathsf{OEnc}(i, m_1), C_2 \leftarrow \mathsf{OEnc}(i, m_2)$. Then the adversary can submit (i, j, C_1)

to OReKeyGen to obtain $\Delta_{i,j}$ and then submit $(C_2, i, j, \Delta_{i,j})$ (in other words, set $C^{\mathcal{A}} = C_2, \delta^{\mathcal{A}} = \Delta_{i,j})$. Since $j \neq \mathsf{chain}(m_2)$, the adversary wins the game with probability 1. □

Ciphertext dependence alone does not imply token robustness. For example, suppose that $\mathsf{ReKeyGen}(\mathsf{pk}_i, \mathsf{sk}_j, \tilde{C}_1)$ outputs $\Delta_{i,j,C_1} = (\Delta_0 = \tilde{C}_1, \Delta_1)$, and that $\mathsf{ReEnc}(\Delta, C)$ incorporates ciphertext dependence by verifying that $\Delta_0 = \tilde{C}$, with re-encryption only proceeding if this is true. Then an adversary can trivially craft a valid token for a different ciphertext by setting $\delta^{\mathcal{A}} = (\tilde{C}_2, \Delta_1)$. Token robustness is therefore a stronger notion than ciphertext dependence.

5   Directionality Revisited

Recall that the existing definition of unidirectionality states that an update token $\Delta_{i \to j}$ cannot be used to re-encrypt a ciphertext under pk_j to pk_i. We argue that this notion is not sufficient for access control as it is lacks the formality of a security definition and does not consider reversal attacks where the adversary may have retained information on the old ciphertext. It also does not couple well with ciphertext dependence or token robustness. In this section we will elaborate on this claim before offering a security definition which covers reversal attacks, which we call $\bar{\lambda}$-*reversibility*.

5.1   Problems with Traditional Directionality

Unidirectionality is required in a number of applications for security reasons, but is currently defined as a class of PRE schemes as opposed to a security property. In the full version [4], we give a security definition for the current understanding of unidirectionality. However, this notion does not consider reversal attacks where the server has a re-encrypted ciphertext and the information used to perform the re-encryption. However this is a possible means of a malicious server performing an unauthorised re-encryption and so warrants further consideration. Whilst this is not of any concern for email forwarding, it is an important consideration for access control as reversing a re-encryption can mean regranting access to a revoked user. Particularly for ciphertext dependent schemes where update tokens are randomised, reversal attacks become more significant as each re-encryption token should only be able to reverse one specific ciphertext. Therefore existing notions of unidirectionality do not couple well with ciphertext dependence.

There are schemes for which storage of the update token alone cannot reverse the re-encryption, but retaining components of the update token and components of the original ciphertext can reverse a re-encryption. We provide more explicit examples in Sect. 5.3. If storing some component of the original ciphertext makes a reversal attack successful, then we should assume that the adversary will do so, especially if the amount of storage needed is at most the size of the update token (which they are presumed to retain in existing notions of unidirectionality). This shows that unidirectional schemes do not prevent an adversary from reversing a re-encryption. For practical reasons, header values and update tokens are often designed to be small, and thus they can easily be retained. Given that current models of unidirectionality permit an adversary to retain the update token in order to attempt to re-encrypt, we argue that there is no reason to restrict the information an adversary may store to update tokens alone when adversarial sucess may be greater by retaining other information that was previously available, particularly in the case of a malicious server.

5.2   Directionality Reconsidered

Now that we have argued that current notions of unidirectionality are not suitable for access control, we present a security defintion for reversal attacks. Before we define this, we explain the key principles behind the motivation of the definition.

Principle 1: *Malicious storage cannot be prevented.* It is impossible for one party to prevent another from storing extra information without additional assumptions. In particular we cannot prevent the server from retaining the old ciphertext.

Principle 2: *The amount of storage needed to reverse a process has a lower bound.* Whilst we cannot prevent a malicious server from retaining an old ciphertext, we can ensure there is no 'easier' way for them to obtain the old ciphertext. By 'easier', we mean that the server needs significantly less storage than keeping the components of the original ciphertext that were updated. This is similar to the motivation behind an *economically rational server* considered in [10].

This definition is important in that if a scheme is token robust and we can prove that the only way of reversing a re-encryption is by storing a state the size of the original ciphertext then this is the best notion of unidirectionality that can be achieved without assuming that the adversary honestly deletes old ciphertext. In Sect. 6 we define this as *best-achievable unidirectionality.*

By considering unidirectionality in this way, the problem of creating a unidirectional multi-hop PRE scheme may be solved more easily using token robustness and could therefore lead to more unidirectional multi-hop schemes that are practically implementable.

We now define a reversal attack game Rev-ReEnc which takes into account the amount of information the adversarial server may have retained during the re-encryption process using a storage parameter $\bar{\lambda}$.

The following game has an adversary in three stages. All three adversaries receive the security parameter λ, storage parameter $\bar{\lambda}$, public keys and system parameters as input. The first stage adversary A_0 receives a randomly chosen message and decides which keys should be used for encryption and re-encryption. The second stage adversary A_1 receives the ciphertext and update token and determines what should be retained in the state st_A, which is bounded by a storage parameter $\bar{\lambda}$. Note this adversary never receives the message. Since this adversary knows the storage bound, it can compute many potential states before selecting which one will be passed on to A_2. The final adversary A_2 receives the re-encrypted ciphertext C' and state st_A, and uses this to try to output a ciphertext which is an encryption of the same message under the original key. This adversary never receives the message, original ciphertext or the update token—they only receive the information retained by $\mathcal{A}_1$. Note that this does not need to be the original ciphertext, it can be any encryption of the message under the original key (an equivalent ciphertext). This emulates the scenario where the server must decide how much information to retain about the old ciphertext and update token, before later attempting to reverse the re-encryption (or revert to an equivalent ciphertext).

Definition 5. *Given a PRE scheme $\mathcal{PRE}$, let s be the size of the components in ciphertexts as estabilished by the scheme and let c be the number of ciphertext components updated by* ReEnc. *Then for $\bar{\lambda} \in \{0, s, \dots, cs\}$, we define the advantage of an adversary $\mathcal{A} = (\mathcal{A}_0, \mathcal{A}_1, \mathcal{A}_2)$ in winning the* Rev-ReEnc *game given in Fig. 3 as:*

$$\mathbf{adv}_{\mathcal{A},\bar{\lambda}}^{\mathsf{Rev\text{-}ReEnc}}(\lambda) = \left| \Pr\left[\mathsf{Rev\text{-}ReEnc}_{\mathcal{A},\bar{\lambda}}^{\mathcal{PRE}}(\lambda) = 1 \right] - \frac{1}{2^{cs-\bar{\lambda}}} \right|, \qquad (5)$$

where $\frac{1}{2^{cs-\bar{\lambda}}}$ is the probability that an adversary who has retained $\bar{\lambda}$ bits of (the updatable components of) C can correctly guess the remaining bits.

We say that a proxy re-encryption scheme $\mathcal{PRE}$ is $\bar{\lambda}$-irreversible *if for all* PPT *adversaries $\mathcal{A} = (\mathcal{A}_0, \mathcal{A}_1, \mathcal{A}_2)$, the advantage of winning the game is negligible:*

$$\mathbf{adv}_{\mathcal{A},\bar{\lambda}}^{\mathsf{Rev\text{-}ReEnc}}(\lambda) \leq \mathsf{negl}(\lambda). \qquad (6)$$

$\mathsf{Rev\text{-}ReEnc}_{\mathcal{A},\bar{\lambda}}^{\mathcal{PRE}}(\lambda)$

$param \leftarrow \mathsf{Setup}(\lambda)$

$(\mathsf{pk}_1, \mathsf{sk}_1), \dots (\mathsf{pk}_\kappa, \mathsf{sk}_\kappa) \xleftarrow{\$} \mathsf{KeyGen}(1^\lambda)$

$m \xleftarrow{\$} \mathcal{M}$

$(i, j) \leftarrow \mathcal{A}_0(1^\lambda, 1^{\bar{\lambda}}, \mathsf{pk}_1, \dots \mathsf{pk}_\kappa, m)$

$C \xleftarrow{\$} \mathsf{Enc}(\mathsf{pk}_i, m)$

$\Delta_{i,j,C} \xleftarrow{\$} \mathsf{ReKeyGen}(\mathsf{sk}_i, \mathsf{pk}_j, \tilde{C})$

$st_{\mathcal{A}} \leftarrow \mathcal{A}_1(1^\lambda, 1^{\bar{\lambda}}, \mathsf{pk}_1, \dots \mathsf{pk}_\kappa, \Delta, C)$

if $|st_{\mathcal{A}}| > \bar{\lambda}$ **return** $\perp$

$C' \leftarrow \mathsf{ReEnc}(\Delta_{i,j,C}, C)$

$C_{\mathcal{A}} \leftarrow \mathcal{A}_2(1^\lambda, 1^{\bar{\lambda}}, \mathsf{pk}_1, \dots \mathsf{pk}_\kappa, st_{\mathcal{A}}, C')$

return $\mathsf{Dec}(\mathsf{sk}_i, C_{\mathcal{A}}) = \mathsf{Dec}(\mathsf{sk}_j, C')$

Fig. 3. The reversal game Rev-ReEnc.

Conversely, a PRE scheme is $\bar{\lambda}$-reversible if there exists a PPT *algorithm $\mathcal{A}$ that can win the* Rev-ReEnc$_{\mathcal{A},\bar{\lambda}}^{\mathcal{PRE}}(\lambda)$ *game with state $st_{\mathcal{A}}$ of size at most $\bar{\lambda}$ with non-negligible probability.*

We briefly note constructing this notion as an indistinguishability game is difficult as the adversary has control over what form the state has. For example, if the adversary stores a truncated hash of the original ciphertext then the game cannot compute another ciphertext that makes indistinguishability difficult. Since this definition aims to convey that an adversary should not be able to re-encrypt back to the old key, we do not consider the lack of indistinguishability to hinder this.

We now formulate a definition for *maximal irreversibility*. Informally, the amount of storage needed to reverse a re-encryption is at least the size of the updated ciphertext components

Definition 6. *A PRE scheme is* maximally irreversible *if it is cs-reversible, where c is the number of the number of ciphertext components updated by* ReEnc *and s is the component size.*

Clearly, *maximal irreversibility* is stronger than traditional notions of unidirectionality as it covers directionality attacks for ciphertext dependent schemes as well as ciphertext independent schemes. In Sect. 6 we use this notion together with token robustness (which is stronger than ciphertext dependence) to form a definition for best-achievable unidirectionality.

Observations

1. The storage bound $\bar{\lambda}$ can be considered similarly to the security parameter λ in that the larger $\bar{\lambda}$ is, the more secure the scheme is. However, even small values for $\bar{\lambda}$ are still meaningful since they convey how easy it is to reverse a re-encryption and can therefore be used to compare different schemes.
2. The most useful values which $\bar{\lambda}$ can take are $\bar{\lambda} = |\Delta|$ as this is comparable to traditional bidirectionality or $\bar{\lambda} = cs$ as this makes a scheme maximally irreversable. In general, useful values are in the range $|\Delta| \leq \bar{\lambda} \leq |C|$.
3. If a scheme is both ReEnc-IND-CPA and maximally irreversible then it is $|C|$-irreversible.
4. All traditionally bidirectional schemes can be shown to be $|\Delta|$-reversible, but there also exist $|\Delta|$-reversible schemes which are *not* traditionally bidirectional, as we shall see in Sect. 5.3. Since more attacks are covered, saying that a scheme is $|\Delta|$-reversible is stronger than saying it is bidirectional in the traditional sense.

5.3 Existing Schemes Under the New Definition

Some traditionally unidirectional schemes are $|\Delta|-reversible$. In both [11] and [6], the update token consists of the new header and another value used to change the body of the ciphertext using an arithmetic operation. We can generalise this by saying $\Delta = (\Delta_0, \Delta_1)$, where $\Delta_0 = \tilde{C}'$ and $(\Delta_1)^{-1}$ is easily computable. To reverse the re-encryption, the adversary $\mathcal{A}_1$ retains the old header $\tilde{C}$, and computes the inverse of Δ_1, and sets $st_{\mathcal{A}} = (\tilde{C}, \Delta_1^{-1})$, which is equivalent to $st_{\mathcal{A}} = \Delta^{-1}$. Then $\mathcal{A}_2$ can recover $C \leftarrow \mathsf{ReEnc}(st_{\mathcal{A}}, C')$ to win the game. Note that $\mathcal{A}$ does not need to retain Δ_0 as this is contained in the new ciphertext. The state $st_{\mathcal{A}}$ is clearly the same size as $\Delta = (\tilde{C}', \Delta_1)$, and we can therefore consider such schemes to be $|\Delta|$-reversible. Since any adversary willing to store information of size up to $|\Delta|$ will not restrict themselves to retaining Δ alone, our definition reflects stronger security than traditional bidirectionality. In particular, because [11] is ciphertext-dependent, it should be considered bidirectional under these realistic assumptions.

Some existing bidirectional schemes are maximally irreversible. In the multi-hop PRE scheme of [7], ReKeyGen takes two secret keys as input and the ciphertext includes a number of components including $B = (g^a)^r$, where $\mathsf{pk} = g^a, \mathsf{sk} = a$ and $r \xleftarrow{\$} \mathbb{Z}_q$. The re-encryption token takes as input two secret keys a, b and outputs $\Delta_{a,b} = b/a$, which is then used to update B and no other part of the ciphertext. Since both the ciphertext component B and the re-keying token $\Delta_{a,b}$ are integers modulo q, an adversary hoping to reverse the re-encryption by storing $\Delta_{a,b}$ could have simply retained B. Particularly for applications where there is one message per keypair, the server would need to store one token per re-encrypted ciphertext in which case they could have retained every original ciphertext[2]. Similarly, the original symmetric proxy re-encryption scheme [5] may also be considered maximally irreversible.

6 Proxy Re-Encryption in the Malicious Model

We now describe the requirements for a PRE scheme to be secure in the malicious model. We discuss some conditions which apply to re-encryption generally, before explaining the stronger conditions specific to our setting. Clearly, *correctness* is a necessary property of all PRE schemes. We consider ReEnc-IND-CPA as another necessary condition for revocation and key expiry, despite the fact that this is not the case in much existing work [3,5,7,8,15].

In the malicious model, we must ensure that giving the server the ability to perform some re-encryptions does not mean they can perform unauthorised re-encryptions. In particular, we want to consider revoked users who are honest-but-curious in that they may try to decrypt re-encrypted ciphertexts, but not collude with the server directly. We thus require a means of ensuring that only authorised re-encryptions are possible. The inability to perform unauthorised re-encryptions breaks down to two properties:

Maximal Irreversibility: *The token used to perform a re-encryption cannot be used to reverse that re-encryption.* If re-encryption has been performed to revoke

---

[2] As the value B is unique for each ciphertext, retaining B for one ciphertext does not allow a different ciphertext to be re-encrypted whereas the update token can re-encrypt any ciphertext in either direction. This further demonstrates why token robustness is a necessary requirement.

access, then reversing that re-encryption regrants access to the revoked user. Our definition of maximal irreversability conveys this under realistic assumptions.

Token Robustness: *No matter how many re-encryption tokens the server sees, the server cannot use these to form a token which encrypts a ciphertext to a new key.* This means the adversary is unable to share messages with users who have not had access to them before.

We combine these definitions to form the following definition which is a requirement for a PRE scheme used to enforce changes to access control policy on a malicious server.

Definition 7. *A PRE scheme is* best-achievable unidirectional *if it is both token robust and maximally irreversable.*

Token robustness implies that a token Δ_{i,j,C_1} cannot be used to re-encrypt a ciphertext $C_2 \overset{\$}{\leftarrow} \mathsf{Enc}(\mathsf{pk}_j, m)$ where $C_2 \neq C_1$ (except with negligible probability), which covers the traditional notion of unidirectionality. Coupled with maximal irreversability, this means that given a re-encrypted ciphertext C_2 under pk_j, the only way that the adversary can produce a ciphertext C_A such that $\mathsf{Dec}(\mathsf{sk}_i, C_A) = \mathsf{Dec}(\mathsf{sk}_j, C_2)$ where pk_i is the original key is by retaining a state the size of the original ciphertext during the re-encryption process.

Ciphertext dependence is reasonably trivial to achieve for ElGamal-based schemes by having the randomness used to encrypt the message input to ReKeyGen. We build on the existing technique given in [11] to create a token robust scheme in Appendix B which is a simple adaptation of ElGamal-based PRE, and outline its security proof which relies on the CDH assumption.

7 Ciphertext Origin Authentication

We now revisit the traditional notion of data origin authentication and how this needs tweaking for PRE. Traditionally, data origin authentication is intended for settings where the party who created the message also encrypts it. However, for PRE this is not always the case. Particularly in applications where more than one party shares an encryption key, proof of having used this key is not sufficient to authenticate the encryptor/re-encryption initiator.

In some scenarios, it may be beneficial to use individual signature keys to verify specific identities, in addition to the encryption keys for confidentiality. Both signatures and PRE could be combined to create an authenticated PRE scheme. This is useful in auditing changes to access control policy, or enabling users to verify which user has revoked their access.

Now that we have outlined this distinction, we formulate the notion of *Ciphertext Origin Authentication* (COA).

7.1 Authentication with Corrupted Users

Many authenticated encryption schemes including Signcryption [19] implement data origin authentication by having a check during decryption which terminates the process if the check fails. Such a check is also made in [11] which to our knowledge is the only ReEnc-IND-CPA scheme to provide authentication. However, if corrupted users are being considered then honest termination of a process is not guaranteed. Therefore compulsory COA provides stronger security against users who want to change policy without being caught, as the message can *only* be derived if identity is verified correctly. We call this *correctness upon verification* and consider it a secondary goal.

7.2   Correctness upon Verification

The most intuitive way of proving which entity encrypted a message is to show proof of knowledge of the secret information used to form the new ciphertext. In ElGamal-based schemes such as the one we give in Appendix B, this is the value y. However, the COA check must not leak y as this will enable decryption using the public key. Therefore, we need the initiator to prove that they know y without revealing it.

Recall the basic ElGamal signature scheme:

1. $\mathsf{Sign}(\mathbf{x}, m) \rightarrow \sigma = (r, s)$: $r = g^k$ for $k \xleftarrow{\$} \mathbb{Z}_p$ and $s = (h(m) - \mathbf{x}r)k^{-1}$ mod $p - 1$, for hash function $h()$.
2. $\mathsf{Verify}(\mathbf{X}, \sigma, m) \rightarrow \{0, 1\}$: if $g^{h(m)} = \mathbf{X}^r \cdot r^s$ return 1, else return 0.

We can obtain a non-optional COA check by replacing g^y in our original scheme (Fig. 5) with an ElGamal signature on y signed using the initiator's public key. We also adapt the Verify algorithm so that it derives a specific value a. We call the resulting algorithm VerRetrieve.

sigKeyGen(1^λ)	Sign($\mathbf{x}, y$)	VerRetrieve($\mathbf{X}, \sigma$)
$\mathbf{x} \xleftarrow{\$} \mathbb{Z}_p^*$	$k \xleftarrow{\$} \mathbb{Z}_p, r = g^k$	$(r, s) = \sigma$
$\mathbf{X} = g^{\mathbf{x}}$	$s = (y - \mathbf{x}r)k^{-1} \quad \mod p - 1$	$a = \mathbf{X}^r \cdot r^s$
$\mathsf{ssk} = \mathbf{x}, \mathsf{svk} = \mathbf{X}$	$\sigma = (r, s)$	**return** a
return $(\mathbf{x}, \mathbf{X})$	**return** σ	

Ciphertexts now have the form $C = (\sigma, m \cdot g^{xy})$. By the correctness of ElGamal signatures, VerRetrieve should return $a = g^y$, since $\mathbf{X}^r \cdot r^s = g^{\mathbf{x}r} \cdot g^{k(y - \mathbf{x}r)k^{-1}} = g^y$. Since obtaining g^y is necessary for decryption, and this can only be learned by successfully computing the VerRetrieve operation described above using the encryptor's public key, verification is compulsory.

However, if the scheme is only adapted with the change outlined above then there is no confirmation that the obtained g^y was correct, as the decryptor has no means verifying the message. Therefore in order to have COA, we also need a message integrity check.

We propose adapting the encryption mechanism to replace $\bar{C} = m \cdot g^{xy}$ with $\bar{C} = (g^{x\hat{y}h(m)}, m \cdot g^{xy})$ where $\hat{y} \xleftarrow{\$} \mathbb{Z}_p^*$ and adding the matching signature to the header.

7.3 COA in Other Schemes

We note that COA is not restricted to our scheme. It is sufficient to create a signature using the encryptor's signing key and the randomness used to form the ciphertext and changing re-encryption and decryption accordingly. For other ElGamal-based schemes including [5], a similar adaptation to the above can be made. Such adaptations are not restricted to ElGamal-based schemes however, as we demonstrate in the full version [4] by giving both optional and compulsory COA extensions for [11].

8 Conclusions and Open Problems

We revisited the notion of unidirectionality in PRE schemes and provided a formal security definition that covers reversal attacks. We have shown how, under this new definition, existing PRE schemes which are considered traditionally bidirectional may be considered unidirectional and vice versa. We also outlined properties a PRE scheme needs to be considered secure in the malicious model, in particular defining token robustness—the inability of the server to forge update tokens. Finally, we introduced a new notion of ciphertext origin authentication for authenticated PRE and discuss how to implement this. Schemes meeting these definitions are given in the appendices.

A useful extension of this work is to create a best-achievable unidirectional token robust scheme which can be used for longer messages. This could be achieved trivially by having the update token be as long as the ciphertext, but this is an inefficient solution, going against the motivations of outsourcing re-encryption. Developing a best-achievable unidirectional PRE scheme with small update tokens has similar challenges to white-box cryptography and obfuscation [12]. Another related challenge is to create a best-achievable unidirectional token robust symmetric PRE scheme. We leave these as open problem.

We also leave to future work creating a CCA secure PRE scheme which is best-achievable unidirectional and token robust, as well as defining what it means for a PRE scheme to be post-compromise secure [9] and creating a post-compromise secure PRE scheme.

Acknowledgements. Many thanks to my supervisor Keith Martin for guiding my ideas into a worthwhile piece of work and helping me improve my writing. Also many thanks to those who gave up their time to proofread my work and taught me how to better explain technical definitions, especially Christian Janson, Kenny Paterson, Martin Albrecht and James Alderman.

A Common Definitions for Confidentiality in PRE

Since [7], the main notion for security in PRE schemes is against chosen-ciphertext attacks (CCA) as opposed to chosen-plaintext (CPA) attacks. However since the focus of this paper is to revisit definitions with respect to unauthorised re-encryptions, for simplicity we restrict security to CPA and leave

IND-CCA to future work. We further note that since authors of recent practical unidirectional and multi-hop schemes focus on CPA security [17], this not a significant weakening of security in comparison with existing practical schemes.

The following definition is a formalism of the preservation of indistinguishability introduced in [7] adapted to CPA security. We note that this definition does not consider compromised keys.

Definition 8. *A PRE scheme* $\mathcal{PRE}$ *preserves* IND-CPA *if for all* PPT *algorithms* $\mathcal{A}$ *there exists a negligible function* $\mathsf{negl}(\lambda)$ *such that:*

$$\Pr\left[\mathsf{pres\text{-}IND\text{-}CPA}_{\mathcal{PRE}}^{\mathcal{A}}(\lambda) = 1\right] \leq \frac{1}{2} + \mathsf{negl}(\lambda)\,,$$

where pres-IND-CPA *is given in Fig. 4.*

$\mathsf{pres\text{-}IND\text{-}CPA}_{\mathcal{PRE}}^{\mathcal{A}}(\lambda)$	$\mathsf{LR}(i, m_0, m_1)$
$param \leftarrow \mathsf{Setup}(1^\lambda)$	**if** $|m_0| \neq |m_1|$
$b \xleftarrow{\$} \{0,1\}$	$\quad$ **return** $\perp$
$(\mathsf{pk}_1, \mathsf{sk}_1), \ldots (\mathsf{pk}_\kappa, \mathsf{sk}_\kappa) \leftarrow \mathsf{KeyGen}(1^\lambda)$	$C \xleftarrow{\$} \mathsf{Enc}(\mathsf{pk}_i, m_b)$
$b' \leftarrow \mathcal{A}^{\mathsf{LR}, \mathsf{OReKeyGen}, \mathsf{OReEnc}}(1^\lambda, \mathsf{pk}_1, \ldots, \mathsf{pk}_\kappa)$	**return** C
return $b' = b$	
$\mathsf{OReKeyGen}(i, j, C)$	$\mathsf{OReEnc}(i, j, C)$
$\Delta_{i,j,C} \xleftarrow{\$} \mathsf{ReKeyGen}(\mathsf{sk}_i, \mathsf{pk}_j, \tilde{C})$	$\Delta_{i,j,C} \xleftarrow{\$} \mathsf{ReKeyGen}(\mathsf{sk}_i, \mathsf{pk}_j, \tilde{C})$
return $\Delta_{i,j,C}$	$C' \leftarrow \mathsf{ReEnc}(\Delta_{i,j,C}, C)$
	return C'

Fig. 4. The pres-IND-CPA game which reflects the most common notion of indistinguishability for PRE.

Informally, the PRE scheme is still IND-CPA secure even when the adversary is given access to a re-encryption and token generation oracle. Clearly the underlying PKE scheme must be IND-CPA in order for the PRE scheme to be pres-IND-CPA.

Observe that the above definition applies whether or not the PRE scheme is ciphertext-dependent or unidirectional. It can be easily extended to symmetric PRE by providing the adversary with encryption oracles for both keys, see [11].

B   A Secure PRE Scheme in the Malicious Model

Recall that PRE suitable for access control must be multi-hop. For the malicious model we require a unidirectional and token robust scheme. A multi-hop, ciphertext dependent scheme is given in Fig. 5. We use Definitions 4 and 5 to assess the unidirectionality and token robustness.

Setup$(1^\lambda) \to param$	KeyGen$(1^\lambda) \overset{\$}{\to} (X, x)$	Enc$(X, m) \overset{\$}{\to} C$
p large prime	$x \overset{\$}{\leftarrow} \mathbb{Z}_p^*$	$y \overset{\$}{\leftarrow} \mathbb{Z}_p^*$
g a generator of $\mathbb{Z}_p$	$X = g^x$	$\tilde{C} = g^y$
$\mathcal{M} = \mathbb{Z}_p$	$\mathsf{pk} = X, \mathsf{sk} = x$	$\bar{C} = m \cdot X^y$
$\mathcal{D} = \mathcal{K} = \mathbb{Z}_p^*$	return $(\mathsf{pk}, \mathsf{sk})$	
return $param = (p, g, \mathcal{M}, \mathcal{K}, \mathcal{D})$		return $C = (\tilde{C}, \bar{C})$

Dec$(x, C) \to m$	ReKeyGen$(x_i, X_j, \tilde{C}) \overset{\$}{\to} \Delta_{i,j,C}$	ReEnc$(\Delta_{i,j,C}, C) \to C'$
$m = \bar{C}^{-x} \cdot \bar{C}$	$y' \overset{\$}{\leftarrow} \mathbb{Z}_p^*$	$C = (\tilde{C}, \bar{C})$
return m	$\Delta_{i,j,C}^0 = g^{y'}$	$\tilde{C}' = \Delta_{i,j,C}^0 = g^{y'}$
	$\Delta_{i,j,C}^1 = X_j^{y'} \cdot \tilde{C}^{-x_i} = g^{x_j y' - x_i y}$	$\bar{C}' = \bar{C} \cdot \Delta_{i,j,C}^1 = m \cdot X_j^{y'}$
	return $\Delta_{i,j,C} = (\Delta_{i,j,C}^0, \Delta_{i,j,C}^1)$	return $C' = (\tilde{C}', \bar{C}')$

Fig. 5. An ElGamal-based scheme similar to [5] which is best-achievable unidirectional and token robust.

Correctness: Let $C_i = (g^y, m \cdot g^{x_i y})$ be an encryption of m under g^{x_i}. The update token resulting from ReEnc(x_i, g^{x_j}, g^y) has the form $\Delta_{i,j,C} = (g^{y'}, X_j^{y'} \cdot (g^y)^{-x_i}) = (g^{y'}, g^{x_j y' - x_i y})$. Then re-encryption derives a ciphertext of the form $C_j = (g^{y'}, m \cdot g^{x_i y} \cdot g^{x_j y' - x_i y}) = (g^{y'}, m \cdot g^{x_j y'})$.

B.1   Security Analysis

First we show that this scheme is ReEnc-IND-CPA, then best-achievable unidirectional. Here we give proof sketches, but note that the full proofs can be found in [4].

Theorem 2. *The scheme described in Fig. 5 is ReEnc-IND-CPA under the decisional Diffie-Hellman assumption.*

Proof sketch. Re-encrypted ciphertexts under x_j are identically distributed to ciphertexts encrypted for the first time under x_j. Therefore the problem reduces to ElGamal being IND-CPA, so we can assume the scheme is ReEnc-IND-CPA. □

Theorem 3. *The scheme in Fig. 5 is best-achievable unidirectional.*

We prove this through two lemmas, first proving maximal irreversibility and then token robustness.

Lemma 1. *The scheme described in Fig. 5 is maximally irreversible under the Computational Diffie-Hellman (CDH) assumption.*

We assume $\bar{\lambda} \in \{0, s, \ldots cs\}$ where s is the size of components in the ciphertext and c is the number of components updated during re-encryption, as in Definition 5. In [4] we provide a proof showing the unidirectionality of the scheme when $\bar{\lambda} \in \{0, s, \ldots, cs\}$.

Proof sketch. The CDH assumption states that, given (g^a, g^b), it is computationally infeasible to compute g^{ab}. To prove this, show that an adversary who only retains $\Delta^1_{i,j,C} = g^{x_i y - x_j y'}$ cannot derive $\tilde{C} = g^y$ without breaking the CDH assumption. Analogously, an adversary who only retains g^y cannot calculate $g^{x_i y - x_j y'}$.   □

Lemma 2. *The scheme in Fig. 5 has token robustness under the CDH assumption.*

Proof sketch. To win the token robustness game, the adversary must output a token which re-encrypts an honestly-generated ciphertext so that it is under a key which it has been encrypted under before.

The adversary must output a token $(g^{y'}, g^{x_j y' - x_i y})$, where $j \notin \mathsf{chain}(m)$. It is trivial for the adversary to calculate $g^{x_j y'} = \mathsf{pk}_j^{y'}$ for some $y' \xleftarrow{\$} \mathbb{Z}_p^*$ from pk_j. It remains for the adversary to calculate $g^{x_i y}$, which requires either factoring or finding the most common factor modulo p, which are hard problems.   □

This shows our scheme is suitable for the malicious model according to the goals outlined in Sect. 1, namely that a malicious server is unable to perform unauthorised re-encryptions on stored files as much as can be guaranteed given realistic storage assumptions. Full details and an explicit construction for the adapted scheme with COA can be found in [4].

References

1. Amazon Web Services: Protecting data using client-side encryption (2017). http://docs.aws.amazon.com/AmazonS3/latest/dev/UsingClientSideEncryption.html
2. Ateniese, G., Benson, K., Hohenberger, S.: Key-private proxy re-encryption. In: Fischlin, M. (ed.) CT-RSA 2009. LNCS, vol. 5473, pp. 279–294. Springer, Heidelberg (2009). https://doi.org/10.1007/978-3-642-00862-7_19
3. Ateniese, G., Fu, K., Green, M., Hohenberger, S.: Improved proxy re-encryption schemes with applications to secure distributed storage. ACM Trans. Inf. Syst. Secur. 9(1), 1–30 (2006). https://doi.org/10.1145/1127345.1127346
4. Berners-Lee, E.: Improved security notions for proxy re-encryption to enforce access control. Cryptology ePrint Archive, Report 2017/824 (2017). http://eprint.iacr.org/2017/824
5. Blaze, M., Bleumer, G., Strauss, M.: Divertible protocols and atomic proxy cryptography. In: Nyberg, K. (ed.) EUROCRYPT 1998. LNCS, vol. 1403, pp. 127–144. Springer, Heidelberg (1998). https://doi.org/10.1007/BFb0054122
6. Boneh, D., Lewi, K., Montgomery, H., Raghunathan, A.: Key Homomorphic PRFs and their applications. In: Canetti, R., Garay, J.A. (eds.) CRYPTO 2013. LNCS, vol. 8042, pp. 410–428. Springer, Heidelberg (2013). https://doi.org/10.1007/978-3-642-40041-4_23

7. Canetti, R., Hohenberger, S.: Chosen-ciphertext secure proxy re-encryption. In: Ning, P., di Vimercati, S.D.C., Syverson, P.F. (eds.) Proceedings of the 2007 ACM Conference on Computer and Communications Security, CCS 2007, Alexandria, Virginia, USA, 28–31 October 2007, pp. 185–194. ACM (2007). https://doi.org/ 10.1145/1315245.1315269

8. Chow, S.S.M., Weng, J., Yang, Y., Deng, R.H.: Efficient unidirectional proxy re-encryption. In: Bernstein, D.J., Lange, T. (eds.) AFRICACRYPT 2010. LNCS, vol. 6055, pp. 316–332. Springer, Heidelberg (2010). https://doi.org/10.1007/978-3-642-12678-9_19

9. Cohn-Gordon, K., Cremers, C.J.F., Garratt, L.: On post-compromise security. In: IEEE 29th Computer Security Foundations Symposium, CSF 2016, Lisbon, Portugal, 27 June – July 1 (2016), pp. 164–178. IEEE Computer Society (2016). https:// doi.org/10.1109/CSF.2016.19

10. van Dijk, M., Juels, A., Oprea, A., Rivest, R.L., Stefanov, E., Triandopoulos, N.: Hourglass schemes: how to prove that cloud files are encrypted. In: Yu, T., Danezis, G., Gligor, V.D. (eds.) The ACM Conference on Computer and Communications Security, CCS'12, Raleigh, NC, USA, 16–18 October 2012, pp. 265–280. ACM (2012). https://doi.org/10.1145/2382196.2382227

11. Everspaugh, A., Paterson, K.G., Ristenpart, T., Scott, S.: Key rotation for authenticated encryption. IACR Cryptology ePrint Archive 2017, 527 (2017). http:// eprint.iacr.org/2017/527

12. Hohenberger, S., Rothblum, G.N., Shelat, A., Vaikuntanathan, V.: Securely obfuscating re-encryption. J. Cryptol. **24**(4), 694–719 (2011)

13. Ivan, A., Dodis, Y.: Proxy cryptography revisited. In: Proceedings of the Network and Distributed System Security Symposium, NDSS 2003, San Diego, California, USA. The Internet Society (2003). http://www.isoc.org/isoc/conferences/ ndss/03/proceedings/papers/14.pdf

14. Liang, X., Cao, Z., Lin, H., Shao, J.: Attribute based proxy re-encryption with delegating capabilities. In: Li, W., Susilo, W., Tupakula, U.K., Safavi-Naini, R., Varadharajan, V. (eds.) Proceedings of the 2009 ACM Symposium on Information, Computer and Communications Security, ASIACCS 2009, Sydney, Australia, 10–12 March 2009, pp. 276–286. ACM (2009). https://doi.org/10.1145/1533057.1533094

15. Libert, B., Vergnaud, D.: Multi-use unidirectional proxy re-signatures. In: Ning, P., Syverson, P.F., Jha, S. (eds.) Proceedings of the 2008 ACM Conference on Computer and Communications Security, CCS 2008, Alexandria, Virginia, USA, 27–31 October 2008, pp. 511–520. ACM (2008). https://doi.org/10.1145/1455770. 1455835

16. Libert, B., Vergnaud, D.: Unidirectional Chosen-ciphertext secure proxy re-encryption. In: Cramer, R. (ed.) PKC 2008. LNCS, vol. 4939, pp. 360–379. Springer, Heidelberg (2008). https://doi.org/10.1007/978-3-540-78440-1_21

17. Polyakov, Y., Rohloff, K., Sahu, G., Vaikuntanthan, V.: Fast proxy re-encryption for publish/subscribe systems. IACR Cryptology ePrint Archive 2017, 410 (2017). http://eprint.iacr.org/2017/410

18. Shao, J., Cao, Z.: CCA-secure proxy re-encryption without pairings. In: Jarecki, S., Tsudik, G. (eds.) PKC 2009. LNCS, vol. 5443, pp. 357–376. Springer, Heidelberg (2009). https://doi.org/10.1007/978-3-642-00468-1_20

19. Zheng, Y.: Digital signcryption or how to achieve cost(signature & encryption) << cost(signature) + cost(encryption). In: Kaliski, B.S. (ed.) CRYPTO 1997. LNCS, vol. 1294, pp. 165–179. Springer, Heidelberg (1997). https://doi.org/10. 1007/BFb0052234

Public-Key Implementation

Optimal 2-3 Chains for Scalar Multiplication

Cristobal Leiva and Nicolas Thériault[✉]

Departamento de Matemática y ciencia de la Computación,
Universidad de Santiago de Chile, Santiago, Chile
{cristobal.leiva,nicolas.theriault}@usach.cl

Abstract. Using double-base chains to represent integers, in particular chains with bases 2 and 3, can be beneficial to the efficiency of scalar multiplication. However, finding an optimal 2-3 chain as long been thought to be more expensive than the scalar multiplication itself, complicating the use of 2-3 chains in practical applications where the scalar is used only a few time (as in the Diffie-Hellman key exchange).

In the last few years, important progress has been made in obtaining the shortest possible double-base chain for a varying integer n. In 2008, Doche and Habsieger used a binary-tree based approach to get a (relatively close) approximation of the minimal chain. In 2015, Capuñay and Thériault presented the first deterministic polynomial-time algorithm to compute the minimal chain for a scalar, but the complexity of $O((\log n)^{3+\epsilon})$ is too high for use with a varying scalars. More recently, Bernstein, Chuengsatiansup, and Lange used a graph-based approach to obtain an algorithm with running time $O((\log n)^{2.5+\epsilon})$.

In this work, we adapt the algorithm of Capuñay and Thériault to obtain minimal chains in $O((\log n)^2 \log \log n)$ bit operations and $O((\log n)^2)$ bits of memory. This allows us to obtain minimal chains for 256-bits integers in the 0.280 ms range, making it useful to reduce scalar multiplication costs randomly-selected scalars.

We also show how to extend the result to other types of double-base and triple-base chains (although the complexity for triple-base chains is cubic instead of quadratic). In the case of environments with restricted memory, our algorithm can be adapted to compute the minimal chain in $O((\log n)^2 (\log \log n)^2)$ bit operations with only $O(\log n (\log \log n)^2)$ bits of memory.

Keywords: Integer representations · Double-base chains · Scalar multiplication

1 Introduction

Scalar multiplication is an integral part of group-based cryptosystems, and ever since the introduction of elliptic curves for cryptographic applications [11,12],

N. Thériault—This research was supported by FONDECYT grant 1151326 (Chile).

T. Lange and O. Dunkelman (Eds.): LATINCRYPT 2017, LNCS 11368, pp. 89–108, 2019.
https://doi.org/10.1007/978-3-030-25283-0_5

there has been constant efforts to improve the efficiency of scalar multiplication, mainly by improving the group operations or using a representation of the secret scalar n that reduces the number of these group operations.

In 1998, Dimitrov et al. [8] proposed the use of double-base chains to reduce the cost of scalar multiplications in certain groups. Several families of elliptic curves are known to be interesting for double-base chains in base 2-3 as they have a very favorable ratio between the costs of group doublings and triplings [2,3,6,7]. An obvious problem with the implementation of such systems is the need to find a chain with low Hamming weight, ideally one with the minimal possible Hamming weight.

An exhaustive search is clearly out of the question, so alternative approaches need to be found. Although a greedy algorithm easily produces double-base chains, they are far from optimal. The first step to obtaining optimal chains was taken by Doche and Habsieger [9], producing much better chains than the greedy approach, although the chains produced are still slightly sub-optimal in general.

In recent years, two approaches have been proposed to find optimal chains in polynomial time, first by Capuñay and Thériault, with complexity $O((\log n)^{3+\epsilon})$, and then by Bernstein, Chuengsatiansup, and Lange [4], decreasing the complexity to $O((\log n)^{2.5+\epsilon})$.

This paper aims at reducing the cost of obtaining optimal double base chains, lowering it to $O((\log n)^2 \log \log n)$ bit operations. Reducing to this complexity should be considered essential to the application of double-base chains in cases where the scalar changes at every use or after a fixed number of uses, as in the Diffie-Hellman key exchange.

The paper is organized as follows: a background on double-base chains and the algorithms to compute them is given in Sect. 2. In Sect. 3 we show how to improve the algorithm of Capuñay and Thériault to obtain quadratic complexity. We then provide generalizations to other double-base systems in Sect. 4 (and triple-base in Appendix A) and in Sect. 5 we show how to adapt the algorithm to restricted-memory environments at the cost of an extra $\log \log n$ factor in complexity. We give experimental results for the fastest form of the algorithm in Sect. 6, showing how effective it can be even at various integer sizes. We conclude in Sect. 7.

2   Background

2.1   Double-Base Chains

Definition 1. *Given p and q, two distinct prime numbers, a double-base number system (DBNS), is a representation scheme in which every positive integer n is represented as the sum or difference of numbers of the form $p^a q^b$, i.e.*

$$n = \sum_{i=1}^{m} s_i p^{a_i} q^{b_i}, \quad \text{with } s_i \in \{-1, 1\}, \text{ and } a_i, b_i \geq 0. \tag{1}$$

The Hamming weight of a DBNS representation is the number m of terms in (1).

The main interest of DBNS comes from the possibility of decreasing the Hamming weight of the representation of the scalar n. In [8], Dimitrov *et al.* showed that for any integer n, it is possible to use a greedy algorithm to obtain a DBNS expansion of n having at most $O\left(\frac{\log n}{\log \log n}\right)$ terms.

However, this representation is usually not suited for scalar multiplications as it minimizes the number of group additions but does not worry about the number of multiplications by p and q required to reach these additions. In effect, the DBNS representations of n with minimized Hamming weight will typically be more costly then the corresponding single-base representations. To avoid this problem, Dimitrov *et al.* [7] proposed the use of double-base chains.

Definition 2. *A double-base chain (DBC) for n (or simply called a p-q chain for n) is an expansion of the form*

$$n = \sum_{i=1}^{m} s_i p^{a_i} q^{b_i}, \quad \text{with } s_i \in \{-1, 1\}, \tag{2}$$

such that $a_1 \geq a_2 \geq \cdots \geq a_m \geq 0$ and $b_1 \geq b_2 \geq \cdots \geq b_m \geq 0$.

The monotone form of the sequence of exponents makes it more easily applicable to scalar multiplication by minimizing the number of multiplications by p and q while still reducing the Hamming weight.

Note that most DBNS representations cannot be written as chains since the degrees in a DBNS representation can vary independently (for example $59 = 2^5 + 3^3$), so chains are more restrictive representations.

The simplest case (in terms of group operations) comes from 2-3 chains. There are several example of algebraic groups where the ratio between the costs of doublings and tripling are close enough to the theoretical proportion of $\ln 2/\ln 3$ for an ideal interchange between the two bases. Experimental results in [5] show that the Hamming weight for 2-3-chains is lower than other integer recodings with the same digit sets, but still linear in $\log n$, coming close to $0.19 \log_2 n$.

A number of technique to obtain double-base chains of low Hamming weight have been developed in the last few years. In the following subsections, we describe the algorithm of Capuñay and Thériault (which will be the basis of our result) and give a brief overview of alternative approaches.

2.2 Algorithm of Capuñay and Thériault

We now describe the algorithm of Capuñay and Thériault, simplifying some of the notation to the minimal required to follow the current work. The proofs of the different results can be found in [5].

Definition 3. *Given a positive integer n, we denote by $n_{i,j}$ the (unique) integer in $\{0, 1, \ldots, (2^i 3^j - 1)\}$ such that $n_{i,j} \equiv n \bmod 2^i 3^j$, and by $\overline{n}_{i,j}$ the (unique) integer in $\{-1, -2, \ldots, -2^i 3^j\}$ such that $\overline{n}_{i,j} \equiv n \bmod 2^i 3^j$.*

Note that this definition differs slightly from that of [5] (where $\overline{n}_{i,j}$ is the (unique) integer in $\{0, -1, \ldots, -(2^i 3^j - 1)\}$ such that $\overline{n}_{i,j} \equiv n \bmod 2^i 3^j$). We will discuss this change in Remark 1, however, this new definition clearly implies that $\overline{n}_{i,j} = n_{i,j} - 2^i 3^j$, so the discussion can naturally be restricted to the positive values $(n_{i,j})$.

Definition 4. *We denote by* $\mathcal{C}_{i,j}$ *a minimal 2-3 chain for* $n_{i,j}$ *in which all terms are strict divisors of* $2^i 3^j$ *(that is to say, any term in the chain is of the form* $\pm 2^a 3^b$ *with at least* $a < i$ *or* $b < j$), *and by* $\overline{\mathcal{C}}_{i,j}$ *a minimal 2-3 chain for* $\overline{n}_{i,j}$ *in which all terms are strict divisors of* $2^i 3^j$. *If no such chain is possible, we write* $\mathcal{C}_{i,j} = \emptyset$, *or* $\overline{\mathcal{C}}_{i,j} = \emptyset$.

Note that there may be several choices of optimal chains for $\mathcal{C}_{i,j}$ and/or $\overline{\mathcal{C}}_{i,j}$ if more than one chain has the same (minimal) Hamming weight. However, all of them are equivalent and interchangeable in terms of the desired solution, so only one needs be taken into account. We also write $\emptyset \pm 2^i 3^j = \emptyset$ since it is not possible to extend a non-existing chain.

To ensure the first steps of recursive arguments follow the general pattern, we also write $\mathcal{C}_{-1,j} = \overline{\mathcal{C}}_{-1,j} = \mathcal{C}_{i,-1} = \overline{\mathcal{C}}_{i,-1} = \emptyset$.

The inductive process of the algorithm of Capuñay and Thériault relies on the observation that subchains of minimal chains must also be minimal (for the corresponding $n_{i,j}$ or $\overline{n}_{i,j}$. It also uses the recursive relations between the values $n_{i,j}$ and $\overline{n}_{i,j}$. By definition of $n_{i,j}$ and $\overline{n}_{i,j}$, it is clear that if $i > 0$ then

$$n_{i,j} \in \{n_{i-1,j}, n_{i-1,j} + 2^{i-1} 3^j\}, \quad \overline{n}_{i,j} \in \{\overline{n}_{i-1,j}, \overline{n}_{i-1,j} - 2^{i-1} 3^j\}$$

and if $j > 0$ then

$$n_{i,j} \in \{n_{i,j-1}, n_{i,j-1} + 2^i 3^{j-1}, n_{i,j-1} + 2 \cdot 2^i 3^{j-1}\}$$
$$\overline{n}_{i,j} \in \{\overline{n}_{i,j-1}, \overline{n}_{i,j-1} - 2^i 3^{j-1}, \overline{n}_{i,j-1} - 2 \cdot 2^i 3^{j-1}\}$$

The algorithm looks at the evolution of the values of $n_{i,j}$ and $\overline{n}_{i,j}$. However, under the definition of double-base chains used, terms of the form $\pm 2 \cdot 2^i 3^{j-1}$ are not allowed in a 2-3 chain (unless we write them as $\pm 2^{i+1} 3^{j-1}$), so they incompatible with our definition of $\mathcal{C}_{i,j}$ and $\overline{\mathcal{C}}_{i,j}$.

Given a chain for $n_{i,j}$ (where all terms are decreasing divisors $2^i 3^j$, all smaller than $2^i 3^j$ in absolute value), we can extract a chain for one of $n_{i-1,j}$, $\overline{n}_{i-1,j}$, $n_{i,j-1}$ or $\overline{n}_{i,j-1}$, and this gives us inductive relationships.

Lemma 1. *[Lemma 3 of [5]]* $\mathcal{C}_{i,j} \neq \emptyset$ *if and only if one (or more) of the following cases occurs:*

1. $\mathcal{C}_{i,j} = \mathcal{C}_{i-1,j}$ *(only if* $n_{i,j} = n_{i-1,j}$);
2. $\mathcal{C}_{i,j} = 2^{i-1} 3^j + \mathcal{C}_{i-1,j}$ *(only if* $n_{i,j} = 2^{i-1} 3^j + n_{i-1,j}$);
3. $\mathcal{C}_{i,j} = 2^{i-1} 3^j + \overline{\mathcal{C}}_{i-1,j}$ *(only if* $n_{i,j} = 2^{i-1} 3^j + \overline{n}_{i-1,j}$);
4. $\mathcal{C}_{i,j} = \mathcal{C}_{i,j-1}$ *(only if* $n_{i,j} = n_{i,j-1}$);
5. $\mathcal{C}_{i,j} = 2^i 3^{j-1} + \mathcal{C}_{i,j-1}$ *(only if* $n_{i,j} = 2^i 3^{j-1} + n_{i,j-1}$);
6. $\mathcal{C}_{i,j} = 2^i 3^{j-1} + \overline{\mathcal{C}}_{i,j-1}$ *(only if* $n_{i,j} = 2^i 3^{j-1} + \overline{n}_{i,j-1}$);

Similar cases occur for negative chains (after interchanging the signs).

Proof. See [5], Lemma 3.

Lemma 1 gives relations between the chains $C_{i,j}$ in terms of decreasing values of i or j (or both). However, to construct the chains it is more convenient to build relations on increasing values of i and j, and hence (in general) increasing values of $n_{i,j}$ (since optimal chains are more easily obtained for smaller values of n).

However, increasing the values of the pair (i, j) has a disadvantage: whereas subchains of an optimal chain are also optimal, the same does not necessarily hold when extending a subchain. As a result, the extended subchains will be candidates for the optimal chains $\mathcal{C}_{i,j}$ and $\overline{\mathcal{C}}_{i,j}$, leading to the following definition:

Definition 5. *A double-base chain C is called a* (possible) source *for $\mathcal{C}_{i,j}$ (resp. $\overline{\mathcal{C}}_{i,j}$) if C sums up to $n_{i,j}$ (resp. $\overline{n}_{i,j}$), and one of the following holds:*

- *If the largest term is of the form $\pm 2^{i-1}3^{j}$, then the subchain obtained from C by removing this term is optimal for $n_{i-1,j}$ or $\overline{n}_{i-1,j}$;*
- *If the largest term is of the form $\pm 2^{i}3^{j-1}$, then the subchain obtained from C by removing this term is optimal for $n_{i,j-1}$ or $\overline{n}_{i,j-1}$;*
- *If the largest term is neither of the form $\pm 2^{i-1}3^{j}$ or $\pm 2^{i}3^{j-1}$, then C is optimal for either $n_{i-1,j}$ or $n_{i,j-1}$ (resp. $\overline{n}_{i-1,j}$ or $\overline{n}_{i,j-1}$).*

The set of possible sources for $\mathcal{C}_{i,j}$ is denoted $\mathcal{S}_{i,j}$ (resp. $\overline{\mathcal{S}}_{i,j}$ for $\overline{\mathcal{C}}_{i,j}$).

Although not all sources are optimal chains for $n_{i,j}$ (resp. $\overline{n}_{i,j}$), as soon as there are some sources at least one of them must be optimal, since the subchains of an optimal chain are optimal and therefore can produce a source of $\mathcal{C}_{i,j}$ (resp. $\overline{\mathcal{C}}_{i,j}$).

Remark 1. Our use of Definition 3 rather than that of [5] has the following motivation. For $n_{i,j} \neq 0$, both definitions coincide, so the only difference comes for $n_{i,j} = 0$.

- From both definitions, $\mathcal{C}_{i,j} = 0$ if and only if $n_{i,j} = 0$.
- From the definition of $\overline{n}_{i,j}$ in [5], $\overline{\mathcal{C}}_{i,j} = 0$ if and only if $\overline{n}_{i,j} = 0 = n_{i,j}$.
- $\mathcal{C}_{i,j} = 0$ and $\overline{\mathcal{C}}_{i,j} = 0$ are completely interchangeable in the construction of larger chains, and we can safely assume that priority is given to the positive chain.
- From Definition 3, if $n_{i,j} = 0$, then $\overline{n}_{i,j} = -2^{i}3^{j}$ so $\overline{\mathcal{C}}_{i,j} = \emptyset$: consecutive terms in a chain grow (in absolute value) by a factor of at least 2 and the largest one is $\leq 2^{i-1}3^{j}$ (in absolute value), so the sum of the chain cannot sum up to $-2^{i}3^{j}$.

The change in definition will therefore have no impact on the terms of the chain produced by the algorithm.

With our definition of $n_{i,j}$ and $\overline{n}_{i,j}$, the corollary that allows the construction of optimal chains from [5] becomes:

Table 1. Possible sources of $\mathcal{C}_{i,j}$ and $\overline{\mathcal{C}}_{i,j}$ when multiplying by 2.

$n_{i,j}$	Possible $\mathcal{C}_{i,j}$		Possible $\overline{\mathcal{C}}_{i,j}$
$n_{i-1,j}$	$\mathcal{C}_{i-1,j},$	$2^{i-1}3^j + \overline{\mathcal{C}}_{i-1,j}$	$-2^{i-1}3^j + \overline{\mathcal{C}}_{i-1,j}$
$n_{i-1,j} + 2^{i-1}3^j$	$2^{i-1}3^j + \mathcal{C}_{i-1,j}$		$\overline{\mathcal{C}}_{i-1,j},$ $\quad -2^{i-1}3^j + \mathcal{C}_{i-1,j}$

Table 2. Possible sources of $\mathcal{C}_{i,j}$ and $\overline{\mathcal{C}}_{i,j}$ when multiplying by 3.

$n_{i,j}$	Possible $\mathcal{C}_{i,j}$		Possible $\overline{\mathcal{C}}_{i,j}$
$n_{i,j-1}$	$\mathcal{C}_{i,j-1},$	$2^i3^{j-1} + \overline{\mathcal{C}}_{i,j-1}$	$\emptyset$
$n_{i,j-1} + 2^i3^{j-1}$	$2^i3^{j-1} + \mathcal{C}_{i,j-1}$		$-2^i3^{j-1} + \overline{\mathcal{C}}_{i,j-1}$
$n_{i,j-1} + 2 \cdot 2^i3^{j-1}$	$\emptyset$		$\overline{\mathcal{C}}_{i,j-1},$ $\quad -2^i3^{j-1} + \mathcal{C}_{i,j-1}$

Corollary 1. *[Corollary 1 of [5]] Given chains $\mathcal{C}_{i-1,j}$, $\overline{\mathcal{C}}_{i-1,j}$, $\mathcal{C}_{i,j-1}$ and $\overline{\mathcal{C}}_{i,j-1}$, then the possible sources for $\mathcal{C}_{i,j}$ and $\overline{\mathcal{C}}_{i,j}$ can be found in Tables 1 and 2.*

Proof. See [5], Corollary 1, adjusting to Definition 3.

In order to simplify the final step of our algorithm, we introduce one more notation:

Definition 6. *For every integer $0 \leq j \leq \lceil \log_3 n \rceil$, we set the (optimal) chains C_j and $\overline{C}_j$ as $C_j = \mathcal{C}_{i,j}$ and $\overline{C}_j = 2^i3^j + \overline{\mathcal{C}}_{i,j}$, where i is the smallest non-negative integer such that $2^i3^j > n$.*

Algorithm 1 compute optimal subchains $\mathcal{C}_{i,j}$ (for $n_{i,j}$) and $\overline{\mathcal{C}}_{i,j}$ (for $\overline{n}_{i,j}$) for increasing values of i until $n \leq 2^i3^j < 2n$ (after which $\mathcal{C}_{i,j}$ remains fixed) and $\overline{C}_j$ is replaced by $2^i3^j + \overline{\mathcal{C}}_{i,j}$.

Theorem 1. *[Therorem 1 of [5]] The set S defined as*

$$S = \{C_j \mid 0 \leq j \leq \lceil \log_3(n+1) \rceil \} \cup \{\overline{C}_j \mid 0 \leq j \leq \lceil \log_3(n+1) \rceil \}$$

obtained from Algorithm 1 contains a minimal 2-3 chain for n.

Proof. See [5], Theorem 1.

Theorem 2. *[Theorem 2 of [5]] Let n be a positive integer, then Algorithm 1 returns a minimal 2-3 chain in $O((\log n)^4)$ bit operations ($O((\log n)^{3+\epsilon})$ if fast arithmetic is used), and requires $O((\log n)^3)$ bits of memory.*

Proof. See [5], Theorem 2.

Algorithm 1. Algorithm to compute a minimal 2-3 chain.

Input: Integer $n > 0$.
Output: Minimal 2-3 chain $\mathcal{C}$ for n.

1   $C_j \leftarrow \emptyset, \overline{C}_j \leftarrow \emptyset$ for every j

2   **for** $i \leftarrow 0$ **to** $\lceil \log_2(n+1) \rceil$ **do**

3     $m \leftarrow \lceil \log_3((n+1)/2^i) \rceil, \ i_m \leftarrow \lceil \log_2((n+1)/3^m) \rceil$

4   **if** $i_m < i$ **then**

5       $m \leftarrow m - 1$

6   **for** $j \leftarrow 0$ **to** m **do**

7       $n_{i,j} \leftarrow n \bmod 2^i 3^j$

8       $\mathcal{P}_{i,j} \leftarrow \emptyset, \overline{\mathcal{P}}_{i,j} \leftarrow \emptyset$

9   **if** $i > 0$ **then**

10         $n_{i-1,j} \leftarrow n \bmod 2^{i-1} 3^j$

11   **if** $n_{i,j} = n_{i-1,j}$ **then**

12   Include C_j and $2^{i-1} 3^j + \overline{C}_j$ in $\mathcal{P}_{i,j}$

13   Include $-2^{i-1} 3^j + \overline{C}_j$ in $\overline{\mathcal{P}}_{i,j}$

14   **else**

15   Include $2^{i-1} 3^j + C_j$ in $\mathcal{P}_{i,j}$

16   Include $\overline{C}_j$ and $-2^{i-1} 3^j + C_j$ in $\overline{\mathcal{P}}_{i,j}$

17   **if** $j > 0$ **then**

18         $n_{i,j-1} \leftarrow n \bmod 2^i 3^{j-1}$

19   **if** $n_{i,j} = n_{i,j-1}$ **then**

20   Include C_{j-1} and $2^i 3^{j-1} + \overline{C}_{j-1}$ in $\mathcal{P}_{i,j}$

21   No change to $\overline{\mathcal{P}}_{i,j}$

22   **else if** $n_{i,j} = n_{i,j-1} + 2^i 3^{j-1}$ **then**

23   Include $2^i 3^{j-1} + C_{j-1}$ in $\mathcal{P}_{i,j}$

24   Include $-2^i 3^{j-1} + \overline{C}_{j-1}$ in $\overline{\mathcal{P}}_{i,j}$

25   **else**

26   No change to $\mathcal{P}_{i,j}$

27   Include $\overline{C}_{j-1}$ and $-2^i 3^{j-1} + C_{j-1}$ in $\overline{\mathcal{P}}_{i,j}$

28       $C_j \leftarrow$ shortest chain in $\mathcal{P}_{i,j}$ and update its length

29   **if** $i = j = 0$ **then**

30         $C_0 \leftarrow 0$ of length 0

31       $\overline{C}_j \leftarrow$ shortest chain in $\overline{\mathcal{P}}_{i,j}$ and update its length

32   **if** $i = i_m$ **then**

33       $\overline{C}_m \leftarrow 2^i 3^m + \overline{C}_m.$

34 $\mathcal{C} \leftarrow$ shortest chain among the C_j and $\overline{C}_j$

35 **return** $\mathcal{C}$

2.3 Other Approaches

Over the years, two other approaches have been proposed to compute double-base chains. The first one, by Doche and Habsieger [9], uses a binary tree to

compute the shortest double-base chain it can find (under the restriction doublings and/or triplings are given priority over group additions, producing slightly
sub-optimal chains). As pointed out in [4], this algorithm can be made polynomial time if it is taken into account that the values of the nodes correspond to
the $n_{i,j}$ and $\overline{n}_{i,j}$ in Algorithm 1, and hence there are polynomialy many of them.
The tree should therefore keep track of all the values encountered at previous
level (discarding repeated ones) to limit its growth. Although the complexity of
this approach can be controlled, the sub-optimality of the result does not appear
to be avoidable with a binary tree-based approach.

A more recent algorithm by Bernstein, Chuengsatiansup, and Lange [4] uses
a graph-based approach to search for the optimal chain. This algorithm produces
optimal chains just as Algorithm 1, but its complexity is $O((\log n)^{2.5+\epsilon})$, making
it more efficient. Nonetheless, it will still grow asymptotically faster than scalar
multiplication with fast arithmetic techniques ($O((\log n)^{2+\epsilon})$).

3 Reducing the Complexity

In this section, we describe our improvements to the algorithm of Capuñay and
Thériault to obtain quadratic complexity. For the description and analysis, we
consider the whole set of steps (optimal subchains $\mathcal{C}_{i,j}$ and $\overline{\mathcal{C}}_{i,j}$ for all valid pairs
(i,j)), referring to *horizontal* steps those corresponding to doublings (increase in
the index i) and *vertical* steps those corresponding to triplings (increase in the
index j). This horizontal-vertical look will simplify the generalization to other
basis in the next section.

Even if the algorithm of Capuñay and Thériault does not keep information about previous subchains (in fact, it overwrites these subchains), we will
sometime consider that they are all available for the sake of discussion while
developing the new algorithm, and then clarify what minimal information needs
to be kept.

3.1 Reduced Memory by Retracing the Steps

Since our goal is to obtain an algorithm with at most quadratic complexity, a
first problem encountered with Algorithm 1 comes from obtaining $O(\log n)$ final
chains, each of $O(\log n)$ terms (from the growth of the Hamming weight) of size
$O(\log n)$, for a total memory cost of $O((\log n)^3)$.

Obviously this must be reduced before we can hope to come close to quadratic
time complexity. Keeping the terms of the chains solely in terms of their exponents reduces the memory to $O((\log n)^2 \log n)$, but we can do better.

Rather than keep complete minimal chains at every step (removing or overwriting the previous incomplete chain), we can keep track of all the movements
in the two-dimensional array corresponding to the algorithm steps. The information required at each step is:

– Whether the chain comes from a horizontal or vertical step (1 bit);

- Whether the previous chain was a positive or negative chain (1 bit);
- Whether the current chain has the same terms or one more term than the previous chain (1 bit);
- (If the number of terms increased), the sign of the latest term (1 bit).

Note that if the current chain has one more term than the previous chain, then the sign of the term is clear from the current and previous positions (knowing whether they are positive or negative chains). We could therefore record all the information for each step with 3 bits instead of 4.

The information is allocated as a block for each case of the step (for example, "15" for a chain due to a vertical move from a negative chain, adding a negative term), so the cost (in time) is the same for 3 or 4 bits of information. We preferred to use 4 bits to simplify the backtracking process and because of a more natural fit into the architecture.

This new *movements array* takes $\approx 4 \log_2 n \log_3 n$ bits (in a rectangular array, $\approx 2 \log_2 n \log_3 n$ if it can be stored in a triangular array corresponding to the maximal exponents). The associated Hamming weight array would be of size $O((\log n)^2 \log \log n)$ due to the bound on the exponents, however the algorithm only needs to keep track of the Hamming weights for two of the inner loops at a time since the optimal chains for a pair (i,j) only depend on the chains for $(i-1,j)$ and $(i,j-1)$, giving us size $O((\log n) \log \log n)$ for the Hamming weights.

Once we know which chain has the lowest Hamming weight, it can be written by retracing our steps (backtracking through the new *movements array*), which takes time $O(\log n \log \log n)$. That is to say: Step 34 compares $O(\log n)$ values of size $\leq \log_2 n$, and then Step 35 retraces the selected chain to write it out.

As an added bonus, the computational complexity, over the whole algorithm, spent on keeping track of the shortest chains (Steps 28, 31, and 33 of Algorithm 1) also decrease to $O((\log n)^2 \log \log n)$.

3.2   Order of the Steps

In [5], the double "for" loop (Steps 2 and 6) is done such that all the subchains for a given i (power of 2) are computed before increasing the value of i. For all intents and purposes, this ordering has little effect on the algorithm, except on the number of subchains for a given index. By setting the first loop in i rather than j, then the number of (positive and negative) subchains to store is $\approx 2 \log_3 n$ instead of $\approx 2 \log_2 n$, which gives a small reducing in memory.

For our improvements to work efficiently, we first invert this order, computing all the subchains for a given j (power of 3) before increasing the value of j. The reason for this choice will become clear in the next subsections.

In term of notation, the algorithm will then be written in terms of C_i and $\overline{C}_i$ instead C_j and $\overline{C}_j$, with the equivalent definition:

Definition 7. *For every integer $j \geq 0$ such that $2^i 3^j < 4n$, we denote by C_i and $\overline{C}_i$ the minimal positive and negative subchains for the current $n_{i,j}$ and $\overline{n}_{i,j}$. If $2^i 3^j \geq 4n$, then C_i remains unchanged from previous values of j.*

We could bound j such that $2^i 3^j \leq 2n$ as a parallel to Definition 6, however the bound $2^i 3^j < 4n$ (which leads to the final j satisfying $2n \leq 2^i 3^j < 4n$) has the advantage that the negative chain $\overline{\mathcal{C}}_{i-1,j}$ for $n_{i-1,j} = n$ produces a chain $2^{i-1} 3^j + \overline{\mathcal{C}}_{i-1,j}$ for n. As a result, the negative subchains $\overline{C}_i$ need not be considered in the final step of the algorithm.

3.3 Efficient Computation of the Possible Sources

To reduce the computational complexity, we first look at how the different cases for the doubling steps (going from $(i-1,j)$ to (i,j), Steps 10 to 16 of Algorithm 1) can be distinguished more efficiently.

Identifying the case of horizontal steps (increasing the index i) consists in determining if $n_{i,j} = n_{i-1,j}$ or $n_{i-1,j} + 2^{i-1} 3^j$. If all the values of $n_{i,j}$ or computed separately, each cost $O((\log n)^{1+\epsilon})$ for a total cost of $O((\log n)^{3+\epsilon})$ over the whole algorithm.

Since $n_{i-1,j} \equiv n \bmod 2^{i-1} 3^j$ and $n_{i,j} \equiv n \bmod 2^i 3^j$, then

$$\frac{n_{i,j} - n_{i-1,j}}{2^{i-1} 3^j} = \frac{(n - (n \bmod 2^{i-1} 3^j)) \bmod 2^i 3^j}{2^{i-1} 3^j}$$
$$= (n \operatorname{div} 2^{i-1} 3^j) \bmod 2$$
$$= (i-1)\text{-th bit of } (n \operatorname{div} 3^j). \tag{3}$$

For a given j, we can then extract all the horizontal steps (sources of minimal chains coming from doublings) from the binary representation of $n \operatorname{div} 3^j$. Since the algorithm already does a recursion in j (from 0 to m), we compute the binary expansions of $n \operatorname{div} 3^j$ as

$$n \operatorname{div} 3^j = (n \operatorname{div} 3^{j-1}) \operatorname{div} 3,$$

which requires a total of m divisions by 3. Furthermore, division by 3 can be implemented in linear time since we are dealing with a small, fixed denominator. We can therefore compute all the binary expansions of the form $n \operatorname{div} 3^j$ in time $O((\log n)^2)$ bit operations (without requiring fast arithmetic techniques).

Also note that the largest value of i to consider for the current j is obtained directly from the binary representation of $n \operatorname{div} 3^j$: it is simply the number of bits in this binary representation.

Steps 10 to 16, identifying the possible horizontal sources for $\mathcal{C}_{i,j}$ and $\overline{\mathcal{C}}_{i,j}$, can then be completed in $O(\log \log n)$ time ($O(1)$ time except for the Hamming weight counter which is $\leq \log_2 n$). Over the whole algorithm, the cost associated to Steps 10 to 16 then decreases to $O((\log n)^2 \log \log n)$.

3.4 Using Only the Binary Representations

To identify the cases associated to tripling steps (changes in j, Steps 18 to 27 of Algorithm 1), we could apply the same approach as in the previous subsection, working in base 3 instead of base 2, again obtaining quadratic time. However, the following lemma shows how to obtain the same result directly from the binary expansions of $n \operatorname{div} 3^j$.

Lemma 2. *Let a_i and b_i be the i-th bits of $(n \text{ div } 3^{j-1})$ and $(n \text{ div } 3^j)$ respectively:*

- *If $a_i + b_i \equiv 1 \bmod 2$, then $n_{i,j} = n_{i,j-1} + 2^i 3^{j-1}$;*
- *If $a_i + b_i \equiv 0 \bmod 2$, then $n_{i,j} = n_{i,j-1}$ or $n_{i,j-1} + 2 \cdot 2^i 3^{j-1}$:*
  - *If $a_i + a_{i+1} + b_{i+1} \equiv 0 \bmod 2$, then $n_{i,j} = n_{i,j-1}$;*
  - *If $a_i + a_{i+1} + b_{i+1} \equiv 1 \bmod 2$, then $n_{i,j} = n_{i,j-1} + 2 \cdot 2^i 3^{j-1}$.*

Proof. Let $m = n \text{ div } (2^i 3^{j-1})$. By a similar argument as in the previous section, $(n_{i,j} - n_{i,j-1})/2^i 3^{j-1}$ is equal to $m \bmod 3$, so the binary expansion of $a = n \text{ div } 3^{j-1}$ contains the essential information about the tripling case. Since $n \text{ div } (2^i 3^j) = m \text{ div } 3$, we can also use the binary expansion of $b = n \text{ div } 3^j$ to help identify the current tripling case without doing divisions by 3 for position i. Then $a_i \equiv m \bmod 2$, $b_i \equiv (m \text{ div } 3) \bmod 2$, $a_{i+1} \equiv (m \text{ div } 2) \bmod 2$, and $b_{i+1} \equiv (m \text{ div } 6) \bmod 2$, which naturally leads us to consider $m \bmod 12$.

$m \bmod 12$	0	1	2	3	4	5	6	7	8	9	10	11
$m \bmod 3$	0	1	2	0	1	2	0	1	2	0	1	2
a_i	0	1	0	1	0	1	0	1	0	1	0	1
b_i	0	0	0	1	1	1	0	0	0	1	1	1
a_{i+1}	0	0	1	1	0	0	1	1	0	0	1	1
b_{i+1}	0	0	0	0	0	0	1	1	1	1	1	1

We observe that $a_i \neq b_i$ if and only if $m \equiv 1 \bmod 3$, which allows us to identify the first case. To distinguish the other two cases (where $a_i = b_i$), we note that $a_{i+1} = b_{i+1}$ if $a_i = 0$ and $m \equiv 0 \bmod 3$ or $a_i = 1$ and $m \equiv 1 \bmod 3$. Similarly, $a_{i+1} \neq b_{i+1}$ if $a_i = 1$ and $m \equiv 0 \bmod 3$ or $a_i = 0$ and $m \equiv 1 \bmod 3$. The statement of the lemma then follows directly. □

An important effect of this lemma is that we can determine all the cases for doubling (horizontal) steps and tripling (vertical) steps for a given value of j knowing only the states (Hamming weight of the subchains) of the previous value of j and the binary expansions of $n \text{ div } 3^{j-1}$ and $n \text{ div } 3^j$. As a result, the memory that would be required to run the algorithm without retracing the chains (i.e. finding only the Hamming weight of the chain) is $O(\log n \log \log n)$ bits (since the Hamming weight are all bounded by $\log_2 n$).

3.5 Algorithm

Combining the improvements in the previous subsections, we obtain Algorithm 2. To simplify the pseudocode (so all values of i and j are treated uniformly), we write a_{-1} for the -1-th bit (NULL), and bits of the NULL value (also NULL), under the assumption that NULL bits in a conditional statement implies the algorithm skips the whole statement. The discussion leading to Algorithm 2 leads directly to its complexity:

Theorem 3. *Let n be a positive integer, then Algorithm 2 returns a minimal 2-3 chain in $O((\log n)^2 \log \log n)$ bit operations, and requires $O((\log n)^2)$ bits of memory.*

Proof. The complexity is straightforward: the double loop in i and j runs through $O((\log n)^2)$ steps. As explained, each step requires $O(\log \log n)$ bit operations for Hamming weight updates – all other operations (bit extraction and comparisons for case selections and updates of the *movements array*) being $O(1)$.

The correctness of the algorithm is a direct consequence of Theorem 1, the changes having to do with the order in which the loops are performed (which does not affect the operations at each step), how the different cases are distinguished (given by Eq. 3 and Lemma 2), and representation of the chains (through the *movements array*). □

Note that the actual implementation benefits from the following ideas (although these do not change the asymptotic complexity):

- Instead of building the sets $\mathcal{P}_{i,j}$ and $\overline{\mathcal{P}}_{i,j}$, each new source is compared the previous best (initially to $\emptyset$) and replaces it if it is shorter.
- Rather than looking at chains going to the position (i,j), we look at chains produced by that position (sources coming from $\mathcal{C}_{i,j}$ and $\overline{\mathcal{C}}_{i,j}$):
  - This allows us to avoid dealing with special cases when positions with $i = -1$ and $j = -1$ would be required.
  - Doubling steps from (i,j) to $(i+1,j)$ are performed first (thus finalizing the work for position $(i+1,j)$), after which tripling steps from (i,j) to $(i,j+1)$ (giving the initial sources for position $(i,j+1)$).
  - Only the bits a_i, b_i, a_{i+1} and b_{i+1} are used at position (i,j), reducing the number of bit extractions.
- Step 28 is in fact performed on-the-go at the end of Step 4, once the last C_i for the current j has been obtained. This also simplifies determining the starting position in the *movements array* at Step 29, by recording the pair (i,j) for this minimal Hamming weight.
- While performing Step 4, we check if all the current Hamming weights for the C_i and $\overline{C}_i$ associated to j are bigger then the current candidate for the optimal chain. If this occurs, then the loop in j is terminated as none of the remaining chains can have lower Hamming weight.

The final change has little impact on the asymptotic cost of the algorithm, but in practice it usually reduces the running time by 3 to 9% (the savings are more important for smaller values of n).

Our C++ implementation of Algorithm 2 can be found at the following site: https://github.com/leivaburto/23chains/blob/master/23.cpp

---

Algorithm 2. Algorithm to compute a minimal 2-3 chain.

Input: Integer $n > 0$.
Output: Minimal 2-3 chain $\mathcal{C}$ for n.

1   $C_i \leftarrow \emptyset$, $\overline{C}_i \leftarrow \emptyset$ for every i, all with length NULL
2   $C_0 \leftarrow 0$ with length 0, $a \leftarrow n$, $b \leftarrow NULL$ $[j = 0]$
3   **while** $a > 0$ **do**
4   **for** $i \leftarrow 0$ *to* size(a) **do**
5        $a_{i-1} \leftarrow (i-1)$-th bit of a, $a_i \leftarrow i$-th bit of a, $a_{i+1} \leftarrow (i+1)$-th bit of a
6        $b_i \leftarrow i$-th bit of b, $b_{i+1} \leftarrow (i+1)$-th bit of b
7        $\mathcal{P}_i \leftarrow \emptyset$, $\overline{\mathcal{P}}_i \leftarrow \emptyset$ $[\mathcal{P}_i = \mathcal{P}_{i,j}, \overline{\mathcal{P}}_i = \overline{\mathcal{P}}_{i,j}]$
8   **if** $a_{i-1} = 1$ **then**
9   Include C_{i-1} and $2^{i-1}3^j + \overline{C}_{i-1}$ in $\mathcal{P}_i$ $[n_{i,j} = n_{i-1,j}]$
10   Include $-2^{i-1}3^j + \overline{C}_{i-1}$ in $\overline{\mathcal{P}}_i$
11   **else**
12   Include $2^{i-1}3^j + C_{i-1}$ in $\mathcal{P}_i$ $[n_{i,j} = n_{i-1,j} + 2^{i-1}3^j]$
13   Include $\overline{C}_{i-1}$ and $-2^{i-1}3^j + C_{i-1}$ in $\overline{\mathcal{P}}_i$
14   **if** $a_i + b_i \equiv 1 \bmod 2$ **then**
15   Include $2^i3^{j-1} + C_i$ in $\mathcal{P}_i$ $[n_{i,j} = n_{i,j-1} + 2^i3^{j-1}]$
16   Include $-2^i3^{j-1} + \overline{C}_i$ in $\overline{\mathcal{P}}_i$
17   **else**
18   **if** $a_i + a_{i+1} + b_{i+1} \equiv 0 \bmod 2$ **then**
19   Include C_i and $2^i3^{j-1} + \overline{C}_i$ in $\mathcal{P}_i$ $[n_{i,j} = n_{i,j-1}]$
20   No change to $\overline{\mathcal{P}}_i$
21   **else**
22   No change to $\mathcal{P}_i$ $[n_{i,j} = n_{i,j-1} + 2 \cdot 2^i3^{j-1}]$
23   Include $\overline{C}_i$ and $-2^i3^{j-1} + C_i$ in $\overline{\mathcal{P}}_i$
24        $C_i \leftarrow$ shortest chain in $\mathcal{P}_i$ and update its length
25        $\overline{C}_i \leftarrow$ shortest chain in $\overline{\mathcal{P}}_i$ and update its length
26   Update the *movements array* as in Section 3.1
27     $b \leftarrow a$ $[j = j + 1]$
28     $a \leftarrow a$ div 3
29   $C \leftarrow$ shortest chain in $\{C_i\}$
30   $\mathcal{C} \leftarrow$ retrace the steps for chain C using the *movements array*
31   **return** $\mathcal{C}$

---

4   Other Double-Base and Triple-Base Systems

It is relatively easy to adapt Algorithm 2 to other double bases. To do so, we first observe that Table 1 can be used for the steps in the construction of a $2-q$ chain (with $q > 3$) simply by replacing powers of 3 by powers of q. Similarly, Table 2 can be used for the steps in the construction of a $3-q$ chain (with $q > 3$) simply by replacing powers of 2 by powers of q (and changing the order of indices).

The equivalent to Corollary 1 for base q is the following lemma. Note that Tables 1 and 2 can be seen as collapsed cases of Table 3 (where some of the cases overlap if $q \leq 3$).

Lemma 3. *Given double-base chains* $\mathcal{C}_{i-1,j}$, $\overline{\mathcal{C}}_{i-1,j}$, $\mathcal{C}_{i,j-1}$ *and* $\overline{\mathcal{C}}_{i,j-1}$ *in bases* p *and* q *where the index* j *correspond to base* q, *then the possible sources for* $\mathcal{C}_{i,j}$ *and* $\overline{\mathcal{C}}_{i,j}$ *can be found in Table 3.*

Table 3. Possible sources of $\mathcal{C}_{i,j}$ and $\overline{\mathcal{C}}_{i,j}$ when multiplying by $q > 3$.

$n_{i,j}$	Possible $\mathcal{C}_{i,j}$	Possible $\overline{\mathcal{C}}_{i,j}$
$n_{i,j-1}$	$\mathcal{C}_{i,j-1}, \quad p^i q^{j-1} + \overline{\mathcal{C}}_{i,j-1}$	$\emptyset$
$n_{i,j-1} + p^i q^{j-1}$	$p^i q^{j-1} + \mathcal{C}_{i,j-1}$	$\emptyset$
$n_{i,j-1} + (q-1) \cdot p^i q^{j-1}$	$\emptyset$	$\overline{\mathcal{C}}_{i,j-1}, \quad -p^i q^{j-1} + \mathcal{C}_{i,j-1}$
$n_{i,j-1} + (q-2) \cdot p^i q^{j-1}$	$\emptyset$	$-p^i q^{j-1} + \overline{\mathcal{C}}_{i,j-1}$
Other cases	$\emptyset$	$\emptyset$

Proof. Similar to the arguments for Corollary 1.   □

We also observe that our these techniques can be applied to double-base chains that consider coefficient sets other than ± 1 for example $\{\pm 1, \pm 2, \ldots, \pm k\}$ (these chains have been studied in [10] and [4]). To do so, it would be sufficient to adjust Tables 1, 2, and 3 to include the new possible sources, and increase the number of layers for each coordinates (i, j) (each layer corresponding to a distinct nonzero coefficient) to consider chains for $n_{i,j}^{(\ell)} \equiv n \bmod p^i q^j$ in the interval $[(\ell-1)p^i q^j, \ell p^i q^j[$ (with $n_{i,j}^{(1)} = n_{i,j}$) and $\overline{n}_{i,j}^{(\ell)} \equiv n \bmod p^i q^j$ in the interval] $- \ell p^i q^j, -(\ell-1)p^i q^j]$ (with $\overline{n}_{i,j}^{(1)} = \overline{n}_{i,j}$). The increased number of layers is required to account for the increased number of final corrections to n, i.e. $n = n_{i,j}^{(\ell)} - (\ell-1)p^i q^j$ or $n = \overline{n}_{i,j}^{(\ell)} + \ell p^i q^j$.

In the following discussion, we only consider the detailed adaptation for the case $q = 5$ with the coefficient set ± 1.

4.1   2-5 Chains

When working in base 2-5, Algorithm 2 can be used almost as-is, replacing base 3 by base 5 and the application of Table 2 in Steps 14 to 23 by an application of Table 3 with $q = 5$. This means divisions by 3 in Step 28 are replaced with divisions by 5 (which still have cost linear in the size of a).

However, using the bits of a and b to extract the vertical cases in Steps 14 to 23 requires a complete re-write of Lemma 2:

Lemma 4. *Let a_i and b_i be the i-th bits of $(n \text{ div } 5^{j-1})$ and $(n \text{ div } 5^j)$ respectively:*

- *If $a_i + b_i \equiv 0 \bmod 2$, then $n_{i,j} = n_{i,j-1}k \cdot 2^i 5^{j-1}$ with $k \in \{0, 2, 4\}$:*
  - *If $a_{i+1} + b_{i+1} \equiv 1 \bmod 2$, then $n_{i,j} = n_{i,j-1} + 2 \cdot 2^i 5^{j-1}$;*
  - *If $a_{i+1} + b_{i+1} \equiv 0 \bmod 2$, then $n_{i,j} = n_{i,j-1}$ or $n_{i,j-1} + 4 \cdot 2^i 5^{j-1}$:*
    * *If $a_i + a_{i+2} + b_{i+2} \equiv 1 \bmod 2$, then $n_{i,j} = n_{i,j-1}$;*
    * *If $a_i + a_{i+2} + b_{i+2} \equiv 0 \bmod 2$, then $n_{i,j} = n_{i,j-1} + 4 \cdot 2^i 5^{j-1}$;*
- *If $a_i + b_i \equiv 1 \bmod 2$, then $n_{i,j} = n_{i,j-1} + 2^i 5^{j-1}$ or $n_{i,j-1} + 3 \cdot 2^i 5^{j-1}$:*
  - *If $a_i + a_{i+1} + b_{i+1} \equiv 1 \bmod 2$, then $n_{i,j} = n_{i,j-1} + 2^i 5^{j-1}$;*
  - *If $a_i + a_{i+1} + b_{i+1} \equiv 0 \bmod 2$, then $n_{i,j-1} = n_{i,j-1} + 3 \cdot 2^i 5^{j-1}$.*

Proof. Similar to the proof of Lemma 2, working modulo 40. □

Since all changes are $O(1)$ proportional to the work done in Algorithm 2, the cost of the resulting algorithm will still be quadratic in $\log n$ (with the same $\log \log n$ term due to keeping track of the Hamming weights).

4.2   3-5 Chains

To work in base 3-5, we use base-3 representations for n and $n \text{ div } 5^j$, whose trits (trinary digits) give the cases for the horizontal (tripling) steps in Table 2. To determine the cases in Table 3 with $q = 5$ (for the vertical/quintupling steps), we again re-work Lemma 2:

Lemma 5. *Let a_i and b_i be the i-th trits of $(n \text{ div } 5^{j-1})$ and $(n \text{ div } 5^j)$ respectively:*

- *If $a_i + b_i \equiv 2 \bmod 3$, then $n_{i,j} = n_{i,j-1} + 2 \cdot 3^i 5^{j-1}$;*
- *If $a_i + b_i \equiv 0 \bmod 3$, then $n_{i,j} = n_{i,j-1}$ or $n_{i,j-1} + 4 \cdot 3^i 5^{j-1}$:*
  - *If $(a_i + 1)^2 + a_{i+1} + b_{i+1} \equiv 1 \bmod 3$, then $n_{i,j} = n_{i,j-1}$;*
  - *If $(a_i + 1)^2 + a_{i+1} + b_{i+1} \equiv 2 \bmod 3$, then $n_{i,j} = n_{i,j-1} + 4 \cdot 3^i 5^{j-1}$;*
- *If $a_i + b_i \equiv 1 \bmod 3$, then $n_{i,j} = n_{i,j-1} + 3^i 5^{j-1}$ or $n_{i,j-1} + 3 \cdot 3^i 5^{j-1}$:*
  - *If $a_i^2 + a_{i+1} + b_{i+1} \equiv 1 \bmod 3$, then $n_{i,j} = n_{i,j-1} + 3^i 5^{j-1}$;*
  - *If $a_i^2 + a_{i+1} + b_{i+1} \equiv 0 \bmod 3$, then $n_{i,j} = n_{i,j-1} + 3 \cdot 3^i 5^{j-1}$;*

Proof. Similar to the proof of Lemma 2, working modulo 45. □

Once again, we obtain an algorithm of $O((\log n)^2 \log \log n)$ bit operations and $O((\log n)^3)$ bits of memory.

5   Implementation with Limited Memory

The memory requirements of Algorithm 2 may still be too high for practical application in certain cases: For n of common cryptographic sizes in embedded devices, the $O((\log n)^2)$ bits of memory may already impractical; and even for high-end computers, pushing beyond the 2^{16} bits range becomes highly problematic. Considering that almost all of the operations performed in the algorithm are at the bit-level (with the exception of keeping track of the Hamming weights), it would be reasonable to expect hardware implementations to perform even better than in software, but only once the memory has been reduced further.

In fact, this problem can be resolved rather easily, at the cost of a slight increase in complexity. As we stated in Sect. 3.4, the memory required for the algorithm to compute the minimal Hamming weight without retracing the actual chain is $O(\log n \log \log n)$, which is the amount of memory required to run Steps 4 to 28 for one value of j. Also, given the complete information for a given j, it would be possible to restart the algorithm at that point in order to finish the search. Furthermore, to retrace one step of a subchain from a given position (i, j) it is sufficient to have the running information for the current and previous value of j (in fact, that information would be enough to retrace all steps which go back at most one value of j).

These observation lead to a straightforward divide-and-conquer approach in which the length of the loop in j is divided in 2, and the information for the middle step is stored in memory. Repeating this inductively (on the second half of the interval when going forward, on the first half when backtracking), we are able to retrace the whole chain using the information for $O(\log \log n)$ values of j at any time, for a total of $O(\log n (\log \log n)^2)$ bits of memory. For a given j, this process performs the computations at most $O(\log \log n)$ times, so the complexity increases by a factor of $O(\log \log n)$ (to a total of $O((\log n)^2 (\log \log n)^2)$).

Note that in some cases where the memory requirements are less limited, we could perform a one-off division of the interval into $O(\sqrt{\log n})$ sub-intervals and retrace the chain in at most twice the time of Algorithm 2, but with $O((\log n)^{1.5} \log \log n)$ memory.

6   Experimental Results

The $O((\log n)^2 \log \log n)$ complexity of the double-base chain search is certainly comparable to the best possible complexity for scalar multiplication, which is asymptotically at least $O((\log n)^2 \log \log n)$ assuming FFT multiplication is applicable on the underlying ring structures. Taking into account that for practical cryptographic sizes the asymptotic results for fast arithmetic for scalar multiplication are overly optimistic, whereas our complexity does not depend on fast arithmetic, one can reasonably expect the search algorithm to perform very well. It should also perform much better than alternative approach since its complexity grows much more slowly.

To determine the actual efficiency of the algorithm, we experimented it for different scalars of varying sizes. Table 4 gives the running time for integers of sizes going up to 512 bits (with 1000 samples at each size). We recall that for double-base chains to be competitive, the combined cost of obtaining the optimal chain and the scalar multiplication using that chain should be lower than the cost of a scalar multiplication using a single base representation (typically a NAF, taking into account the coefficient sets considered). The experiments were done on a 3.7 GHz Intel Xeon E5.

Since 2-3-chains appear to have Hamming density close to 0.19 instead of the 0.333 density of the NAF representation (see [5] for experimental results), using optimal double-base chains reduces the number of group additions by roughly 43%. For the use of double-base chains to be successful, the search for the optimal chain should take less than $0.143 \log_2 n$ group doublings. A complete cost comparison would depend on the specific group implementation, and is therefore beyond the scope of this paper. Instead, we report on direct computational costs.

The timings obtained in our experiments indicate that using double-base chains could indeed reduce costs for all but the fastest scalar multiplication implementations, and certainly for groups where 2-3 chains would be of interest (the fastest scalar multiplication implementations being in groups where doublings are particularly cheap).

Table 4. Average time (microseconds) to compute optimal 2-3-chains for n of k bits.

k	64	128	192	256	320	384	448	512
μsec	24.813	82.827	167.69	279.96	421.08	575.04	784.72	1023.8

To better illustrate the quadratic growth of the complexity, we performed similar experiments for integers of 2^ℓ bits, with ℓ going up to 15. The results can be seen in Table 5.

Table 5. Average time (milliseconds) to compute optimal 2-3-chains for n of k bits.

k	2^8	2^9	2^{10}	2^{11}	2^{12}	2^{13}	2^{14}	2^{15}
msec	0.27996	1.0238	3.9304	15.580	63.911	255.56	1021.1	4149.9

7   Conclusion

We presented a $O((\log n)^2 \log \log n)$ algorithm to compute optimal 2-3 chains that is significantly faster than scalar multiplication, so it can be used for on-the-go computation of the optimal chain as part as the overall scalar multiplication. This algorithm requires $O((\log n)^2)$ bits of memory, but the algorithm can be adapted to compute the optimal chain in time $O((\log n)^2 (\log \log n)^2)$ with $O(\log n (\log \log n)^2)$ bits of memory.

We also extended the result to other double-base systems, especially bases 2-5 and 3-5, both with the same $O((\log n)^2 \log \log n)$ complexity. These results also extend to the search of optimal triple base chains for base 2-3-5 in time $O((\log n)^3 \log \log n)$ and memory $O((\log n)^3)$.

Side-channel security (especially against SPA attacks) can a concern for the security of scalar multiplication when using double-base chains. In some groups, uniform operations (using atomic blocks) without dummy operations have been constructed (see for example [1]). The design of such group operations is beyond the scope of this paper, and in a sense this paper could be seen as a pre-requisite do such work: in the past, improving the efficiency of obtaining optimal double-base chains has been a bottleneck to increase the interest in developing better (SPA-secure) triplings. Nevertheless, the algorithm presented here can easily be adapted to be SPA-secure at a relatively low cost (25–30% increase in running time)[1].

Acknowledgements. The authors would like to thanks the anonymous referees for their useful comments and suggestions.

A   Triple-base chains

The algorithms to obtain optimal 2-3-chains and 2-5-chains in Sects. 3 and 4 can be combined to obtain a polynomial time algorithm to compute optimal tripple-base (2-3-5) chains for n, which is described in Algorithm 3.

Since we are now working in three dimension, each plane corresponding a coordinate k (the power of 5 in $2^i 3^j 5^k$) must have access to the subchains for $k-1$, so the array C_i is replaced by a double array $C_{i,j}$.

Theorem 4. *Let n be a positive integer, then Algorithm 3 returns a minimal 2-3-5 chain in $O((\log n)^3 \log \log n)$ bit operations, and requires $O((\log n)^3)$ bits of memory.*

Proof. Similar to the proof of Theorem 3.

The ideas of Sect. 5 can also be applied to Algorithm 3, reducing its memory requirements to $O((\log n)^2 (\log \log n)^2)$ bits, at the expense of increasing its complexity to $O((\log n)^3 (\log \log n)^2)$.

---

[1] A C++ implementation for the SPA-secure algorithm can be found at: https://github.com/leivaburto/23chains/blob/master/23_spa.cpp.

Algorithm 3. Algorithm to compute a minimal 2-3-5 chain.

Input: Integer $n > 0$.
Output: Minimal 2-3-5 chain $\mathcal{C}$ for n.

1   $C_{i,j} \leftarrow \emptyset$, $\overline{C}_{i,j} \leftarrow \emptyset$ for every i, j, all with length NULL
2   $C_{0,0} \leftarrow 0$, $a_5 \leftarrow n$, $c_5 \leftarrow NULL$ $[k = 0]$
3   **while** $a_5 > 0$ **do**
4     $a \leftarrow a_5$, $c \leftarrow c_5$, $j \leftarrow 0$, $b \leftarrow NULL$
5   **while** $a > 0$ **do**
6   **for** $i \leftarrow 0$ *to* size(a) **do**
7         $a_{i-1} \leftarrow (i-1)$-th bit of a, $a_i \leftarrow i$-th bit of a
8         $a_{i+1} \leftarrow (i+1)$-th bit of a, $a_{i+2} \leftarrow (i+2)$-th bit of a
9         $b_i \leftarrow i$-th bit of b, $b_{i+1} \leftarrow (i+1)$-th bit of b
10        $c_i \leftarrow i$-th bit of c, $c_{i+1} \leftarrow (i+1)$-th bit of c, $c_{i+2} \leftarrow (i+2)$-th bit of c
11        $\mathcal{P}_{i,j} \leftarrow \emptyset$, $\overline{\mathcal{P}}_{i,j} \leftarrow \emptyset$ $[\mathcal{P}_{i,j} = \mathcal{P}_{i,j,k}, \overline{\mathcal{P}}_{i,j} = \overline{\mathcal{P}}_{i,j,k}]$
12   Use Steps 8 to 13 of Algorithm 2 for moves $(i-1, j, k) \rightarrow (i, j, k)$
13   Use Steps 14 to 23 of Algorithm 2 for moves $(i, j-1, k) \rightarrow (i, j, k)$
14   **if** $a_i + c_i \equiv 0 \bmod 2$ **then**
15   **if** $a_{i+1} + c_{i+1} \equiv 0 \bmod 2$ **then**
16   **if** $c_i + a_{i+2} + c_{i+2} \equiv 0 \bmod 2$ **then**
17   Include $\overline{C}_{i,j}$ and $-2^i 3^j 5^{k-1} + C_{i,j}$ in $\overline{\mathcal{P}}_{i,j}$
18   **else**
19   Include $C_{i,j}$ and $2^i 3^j 5^{k-1} + \overline{C}_{i,j}$ in $\mathcal{P}_{i,j,k}$
20   **else**
21   **if** $c_i + a_{i+1} + c_{i+1} \equiv 0 \bmod 2$ **then**
22   Include $-2^i 3^j 5^{k-1} + \overline{C}_{i,j}$ in $\overline{\mathcal{P}}_{i,j}$
23   **else**
24   Include $2^i 3^j 5^{k-1} + C_{i,j}$ in $\mathcal{P}_{i,j}$
25        $C_{i,j} \leftarrow$ shortest chain in $\mathcal{P}_{i,j}$ and update its length
26        $\overline{C}_{i,j} \leftarrow$ shortest chain in $\overline{\mathcal{P}}_{i,j}$ and update its length
27   Update the *movements array* (3-dimensional version of Section 3.1)
28       $b \leftarrow a$, $j \leftarrow j+1$
29       $a \leftarrow a$ div 3, $c \leftarrow c$ div 3
30     $c \leftarrow a_5$ $[k = k+1]$
31     $a_5 \leftarrow a$ div 5
32 $C \leftarrow$ shortest chain in $\{C_{i,j}\}$
33 $\mathcal{C} \leftarrow$ retrace the steps for chain C using the *movements array*
34 **return** $\mathcal{C}$

References

1. Abarzúa, R., Thériault, N.: Complete atomic blocks for elliptic curves in jacobian coordinates over prime fields. In: Hevia, A., Neven, G. (eds.) LATINCRYPT 2012. LNCS, vol. 7533, pp. 37–55. Springer, Heidelberg (2012). https://doi.org/10.1007/978-3-642-33481-8_3

2. Bernstein, D.J., Birkner, P., Lange, T., Peters, C.: Optimizing double-base elliptic-curve single-scalar multiplication. In: Srinathan, K., Rangan, C.P., Yung, M. (eds.) INDOCRYPT 2007. LNCS, vol. 4859, pp. 167–182. Springer, Heidelberg (2007). https://doi.org/10.1007/978-3-540-77026-8_13

3. Bernstein, D.J., Chuengsatiansup, C., Kohel, D., Lange, T.: Twisted hessian curves. In: Lauter, K., Rodríguez-Henríquez, F. (eds.) LATINCRYPT 2015. LNCS, vol. 9230, pp. 269–294. Springer, Cham (2015). https://doi.org/10.1007/978-3-319-22174-8_15

4. Bernstein, D.J., Chuengsatiansup, C., Lange, T.: Double-base scalar multiplication revisited. IACR eprint archive 2017/037 (2017)

5. Capuñay, A., Thériault, N.: Computing optimal 2-3 chains for pairings. In: Lauter, K., Rodríguez-Henríquez, F. (eds.) LATINCRYPT 2015. LNCS, vol. 9230, pp. 225–244. Springer, Cham (2015). https://doi.org/10.1007/978-3-319-22174-8_13

6. Ciet, M., Joye, M., Lauter, K., Montgomery, P.L.: Trading inversions for multiplications in elliptic curve cryptography. Des. Codes Crypt. **39**(2), 189–206 (2006). https://doi.org/10.1007/s10623-005-3299-y

7. Dimitrov, V., Imbert, L., Mishra, P.K.: Efficient and secure elliptic curve point multiplication using double-base chains. In: Roy, B. (ed.) ASIACRYPT 2005. LNCS, vol. 3788, pp. 59–78. Springer, Heidelberg (2005). https://doi.org/10.1007/11593447_4

8. Dimitrov, V.S., Jullien, G.A., Miller, W.C.: An algorithm for modular exponentiation. Inform. Process. Lett. **66**(3), 155–159 (1998). https://doi.org/10.1016/S0020-0190(98)00044-1

9. Doche, C., Habsieger, L.: A tree-based approach for computing double-base chains. In: Mu, Y., Susilo, W., Seberry, J. (eds.) ACISP 2008. LNCS, vol. 5107, pp. 433–446. Springer, Heidelberg (2008). https://doi.org/10.1007/978-3-540-70500-0_32

10. Doche, C., Imbert, L.: Extended double-base number system with applications to elliptic curve cryptography. In: Barua, R., Lange, T. (eds.) INDOCRYPT 2006. LNCS, vol. 4329, pp. 335–348. Springer, Heidelberg (2006). https://doi.org/10.1007/11941378_24

11. Koblitz, N.: Elliptic curve cryptosystems. Math. Comput. **48**, 203–209 (1987). https://doi.org/10.1090/S0025-5718-1987-0866109-5

12. Miller, V.S.: Use of elliptic curves in cryptography. In: Williams, H.C. (ed.) CRYPTO 1985. LNCS, vol. 218, pp. 417–426. Springer, Heidelberg (1986). https://doi.org/10.1007/3-540-39799-X_31

Curve25519 for the Cortex-M4
and Beyond

Hayato Fujii[✉] and Diego F. Aranha

Institute of Computing, University of Campinas, Campinas, Brazil
hayato@lasca.ic.unicamp.br, dfaranha@ic.unicamp.br

Abstract. We present techniques for the implementation of a key
exchange protocol and digital signature scheme based on the Curve25519
elliptic curve and its Edwards form, respectively, in resource-constrained
ARM devices. A possible application of this work consists of TLS deployments in the ARM Cortex-M family of processors and beyond. These
devices are located towards the lower to mid-end spectrum of ARM
cores, and are typically used on embedded devices. Our implementations improve the state-of-the-art substantially by making use of novel
implementation techniques and features specific to the target platforms.

Keywords: ECC · Curve25519 · X25519 · Ed25519 · ARM Cortex-M

1 Introduction

The growing number of devices connected to the Internet collecting and storing
sensitive information raises concerns about the security of their communications
and of the devices themselves. Many of them are equipped with microcontrollers
constrained in terms of computing or storage capabilities, and lack tamper resistance mechanisms or any form of physical protection. Their attack surface is
widely open, ranging from physical exposure to attackers and ease of access
through remote availability. While designing and developing efficient and secure
implementations of cryptography is not a new problem and has been an active
area of research since at least the birth of public-key cryptography, the application scenarios for these new devices imposes new challenges to cryptographic
engineering.

A possible way to deploy security in new devices is to reuse well-known and
well-analyzed building blocks, such as the Transport Layer Security (TLS) protocol. In comparison with reinventing the wheel using a new and possibly pro-
prietary solution, this has a major advantage of avoiding risky security decisions
that may repeat issues already solved in TLS. In RFC 7748 and RFC 8032,
published by the Internet Engineering Task Force (IETF), two cryptographic
protocols based on the Curve25519 elliptic curve and its Edwards form are rec-
ommended and slated for future use in the TLS suite: the Diffie-Hellman key
exchange using Curve25519 [2] called X25519 [3] and the Ed25519 digital signature scheme [5]. These schemes rely on a careful choice of parameters, favoring

© The Authors 2019
T. Lange and O. Dunkelman (Eds.): LATINCRYPT 2017, LNCS 11368, pp. 109–127, 2019.
https://doi.org/10.1007/978-3-030-25283-0_6

secure and efficient implementations of finite field and elliptic curve arithmetic with smaller room for mistakes due to their overall implementation simplicity.

Special attention must be given to side-channel attacks, in which operational aspects of the implementation of a cryptographic algorithm may leak internal state information that allows an attacker to retrieve secret information. Secrets may leak through the communication channel itself, power consumption, execution time or radiation measurements. Information leaked through cache latency or execution time already allows powerful timing attacks against naive implementations of symmetric and public-key cryptography [20]. More intrusive attacks also attempt to inject faults at precise execution times, in hope of corrupting execution state to reveal secret information [8]. Optimizing such implementations to achieve an ideal balance between resource efficiency and side-channel resistance further complicates matters, beckoning algorithmic advances and novel implementation strategies.

This work presents techniques for efficient, compact and secure implementation against timing and caching attacks of both X25519 and Ed25519 algorithms, with an eye towards possible application for TLS deployments on constrained ARM processors[1]. Our main target platform is the Cortex-M family of microcontrollers starting from the Cortex-M4, but the same techniques can be used in higher-end CPUs such as the ARM Cortex-A series.

Contributions. We first present an ARM-optimized implementation of the finite field arithmetic modulo the prime $p = 2^{255} - 19$. The main contribution in terms of novelty is an efficient multiplier largely employing the powerful multiply-and-accumulate DSP instructions in the target platform. The multiplier uses the full 32-bit width and allows to remove any explicit addition instructions to accumulate results or propagate carries, as all of these operations are combined with the DSP instructions. These instructions are not present in the Cortex-M0 microcontrollers, and present a variable-time execution in the Cortex-M3 [13], hence the choice of focusing out efforts on the Cortex-M4 and beyond. The same strategy used for multiplication is adapted to squarings, with similar success in performance. Following related work [11], intermediate results are reduced modulo $2p$ and ultimately reduced modulo p at the end of computation.

Finite field arithmetic is then used to implement the higher levels, including group arithmetic and cryptographic protocols. The key agreement implementation uses homogeneous projective coordinates in the Montgomery curve in order to take advantage of the constant-time Montgomery ladder as the scalar multiplication algorithm, protecting against timing attacks. The digital signature scheme implementation represents points on a Twisted Edwards curve using projective extended coordinates, benefiting of efficient and unified point addition and doubling. The most time-consuming operation in the scheme is the fixed-point scalar multiplication, which uses the signed comb method as introduced by Hamburg [15], using approximately 7.5 KiB of precomputed data and running approximately two times faster in comparison to the Montgomery ladder. Side-channel security is achieved using isochronous (constant time) code

---

[1] https://www.keil.com/pack/doc/mw/Network/html/use_mbed_tls.html.

execution and linear table scan countermeasures. We also evaluate a different way to implement the conditional selection operation in terms of their potential resistance against profiled power attacks [25]. Experiments conducted on a Cortex-M4 development board indicate that our work provides the fastest implementations of these specific algorithms for our main target architecture.

Organization. Section 2 briefly describes features of our target platform. Section 3 documents related works in this area, by summarizing previous implementations of elliptic curve algorithms in ARM microcontrollers. In Sect. 4 discusses our techniques for finite field arithmetic in detail, focusing in the squaring and multiplication operations. Section 5 describes the algorithms using elliptic curve arithmetic in the key exchange and digital signatures scenarios. Finally, Sect. 6 presents experimental results and implementation details.

Code Avaliability. For reproducibility, the prime field multiplication code is publicly available at https://github.com/hayatofujii/curve25519-cortex-m4.

2 ARMv7 Architecture

The ARMv7 architecture is a reduced instruction set computer (RISC) using a load-store architecture. Processors with this technology are equipped with 16 registers: 13 general purpose, one as the program counter (pc), one as the stack pointer (sp), and the last one as the link register (lr). The latter can be freed up by saving it in slower memory and retrieving it after the register has been used.

The processor core has a three-stage pipeline which can be used to optimize batch memory operations. Memory access involving n registers in these processors takes $n + 1$ cycles if there are no dependencies (for example, when a loaded register is the address for a consecutive store). This can happen either in a sequence of loads and stores or during the execution of instructions involving multiple registers simultaneously.

The ARMv7E-M instruction set is also comprised of standard instructions for basic arithmetic (such as addition and addition with carry) and logic operations, but differently from other lower processors classes, the Cortex-M4 has support for the so-called DSP instructions, which include *multiply-and-accumulate* (MAC) instructions:

- *Unsigned MULtiply Long:* UMULL rLO, rHI, a, b takes two unsigned integer words a and b and multiplies them; the upper half result is written back to rHI and the lower half is written into rLO.
- *Unsigned MULtiply Accumulate Long:* UMLAL rLO, rHI, a, b takes unsigned integer words a and b and multiplies them; the product is added and written back to the double word integer stored as (rHI, rLO).
- *Unsigned Multiply Accumulate Long:* UMAAL rLO, rHI, a, b takes unsigned integer words a and b and multiplies them; the product is added with the word-sized integer stored in rLO then added again with the word-sized integer rHI. This double-word integer is then written back into rLO and rHI, respectively the lower half and the upper half of the result.

ARM's Technical Reference Manual of the Cortex-M4 core [1] states that all the mentioned MAC instructions take one CPU cycle for execution in the Cortex-M4 and above. However, those instructions deterministically take an extra three cycles to write the lower half of the double-word result, and a final extra cycle to write the upper half. Therefore, proper instruction scheduling is necessary in order to avoid pipeline stalls and to make best use of the delay slots.

The ARM Cortex-A cores are computationally more powerful than their Cortex-M counterparts. Cortex-A based processors can run robust operating systems due to extra auxiliary hardware; additionally, they may have a NEON engine, which is a Single Instruction-Multiple Data (SIMD) unit. Aside from that, those processors may have sophisticated out-of-order execution and extra pipeline stages.

3   Related Work

Research in curve-based cryptography proceeds in several directions: looking for efficient elliptic curve parameters, instantiating and implementing the respective cryptographic protocols, and finding new applications. More recently, isogeny-based cryptography [18], which uses elliptic curves, was proposed as candidates for post-quantum cryptography.

3.1   Scalar Multiplication

Düll *et al.* [11] implemented X25519 and its underlying field arithmetic on a Cortex-M0 processor, equipped with a $32 \times 32 \rightarrow 32$-bit multiplier. Since this instruction only returns the lower part of the product, this multiplier is abstracted as a smaller one ($16 \times 16 \rightarrow 32$) to facilitate a 3-level Refined Karatsuba implementation, taking 1294 cycles to complete on the same processor. Their 256-bit squaring uses the same multiplier strategy with standard tricks to save up repeated operations, taking 857 cycles. Putting all together, an entire X25519 operation takes about 3.6 M cycles with approximately 8 KiB of code size.

On the Cortex-A family of processor cores, implementers may use NEON, a SIMD instruction set executed in its own unit inside the processor. Bernstein and Schwabe [7] reported 527,102 Cortex-A8 cycles for the X25519 function. In the elliptic curves formulae used in their work, most of the multiplications can be handled in a parallel way, taking advantage of NEON's vector instructions and Curve25519's parallelization opportunities.

The authors are not aware of an Ed25519 implementation specifically targeting the Cortex-M4 core. However, Bernstein's work using Cortex-A8's NEON unit reports 368,212 cycles to sign a short message and 650,102 cycles to verify its validity. The authors point out that 50 and 25 thousand cycles of signing and verification are spent by SUPERCOP-choosen SHA-512 implementation, with room for further improvements.

FourQ is an elliptic curve providing about 128 bits of security equipped with the endomorphisms ψ and ϕ, providing efficient scalar multiplication [9]. Implementations of key exchange over this elliptic curve in different software and hardware platforms show a factor-2 speedup in comparison to Curve25519 and factor-5 speedup in comparison to NIST's P-256 curve [22]. Liu et al. reported [22] a 559,200 cycle count on an ARM Cortex-M4 based processor of their 32-bit implementation of the Diffie-Hellman Key Exchange in this curve.

Generating keys and Schnorr-like signatures over FourQ takes about 796,000 cycles on a Cortex-M4 based processor, while verification takes about 733,000 cycles on the same CPU [22]. Key generation and signing are aided by a 80-point table taking 7.5KiB of ROM, and verification is assisted by a 256-point table, using 24 KiB of memory. Quotient DSA (qDSA) [27] is a novel signature scheme relying on Kummer arithmetic in order use the same key for DH and digital signature schemes. It relies only on the x-coordinate with the goal of reducing stack usage and the use of optimized formulae for group operations. When instantiated with Curve25519, it takes about 3 million cycles to sign a message and 5.7 million cycles to verify it in a Cortex-M0. This scheme does not rely on an additional table for speedups since low code size is an objective given the target architecture, although this can be done using the ideas from [26] with increased ROM usage.

3.2   Modular Multiplication

Field multiplication is usually the most performance-critical operation, because other non-trivial field operations, such as inversion, are avoided by algorithmic techniques. Multiprecision multiplication algorithms can be ranked on how many single word multiplications are performed. For example, operand scanning takes $O(n^2)$ multiplications, where n is the number of words. Product scanning takes the same number of word multiplications, but reduces the number of memory access by accumulating intermediate results in registers. One of the most popular algorithms that asymptotically reduces such complexity is the Karatsuba multiplication, which takes the computational cost down to $O(n^{\log_2 3})$. This algorithm performs three multiplications of, usually, half-sized operands, thus giving it a divide-and-conquer structure and lowering its asymptotic complexity. As an example of such an application, De Santis and Sigl [28] X25519 implementation on the Cortex-M4 features a two-level Karatsuba multiplier implementation, splitting a 256-bit multiplier down to 64-bit multiplications, each one taking four hardware-supported $32 \times 32 \rightarrow 64$ multiplication instructions.

Memory accesses can be accounted for part of the time consumed by the multiplication routine. Thus, algorithms and instruction scheduling methods which minimize those memory operations are highly desirable, specially on not-so-powerful processors with slow memory access. This problem can be addressed by scheduling the basic multiplications following the product scanning strategy, which can be seen as a rhombus-like structure. However, following this scheme in its traditional way requires multiple stores and loads from memory, since the number of registers available may be not sufficient to hold the full operands. Improvements to reduce the amount of memory operations are present in the literature: namely, Operand Caching due to Hutter and Wegner [17], further improved by the Consecutive Operand Caching [30] and the Full Operand Caching, both due to Seo *et al.* [29].

The Operand Caching technique reduces the number of memory accesses in comparison to the standard product-scanning by caching data in registers and storing part of the operands in memory. This method resembles the product scanning approach, but instead of calculating a word in its entirety, rows are introduced to compute partial sub-products from each column. This method is illustrated in Fig. 1.

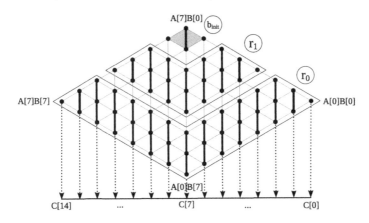

Fig. 1. Operand Caching. Each dot in the rhombus represents one-word multiplication; each column, at the end of its evaluation, is a (partial) word of the product. Vertical lines represents additions.

This method divides product scanning in two steps:

- **Initial Block.** The first step loads part of the operands, and proceeds to calculate the upper part of the rhombus using classical product-scanning.
- **Rows.** In the rightmost part, most of the necessary operands are already loaded from previous calculations, requiring only some extra, low-count operand loads, depending on row width. Product scanning is done until the row ends. Note that, at the end of each column, parts of the operands are previously loaded, hence a small quantity of loads is necessary to evaluate the next column.

At every row change, new operands needs to be reloaded, since the current operands in the registers are not useful at the start of the new row. Consecutive Operand Caching avoids those memory access by rearranging the rows and further improving the quantity of operands already in registers. This algorithm is depicted in Fig. 2.

Note that during the transition between the bottommost row and the one above, part of the operands are already available in registers, solving the reload

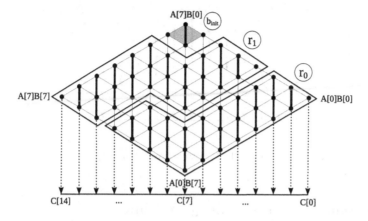

Fig. 2. Consecutive Operand Caching

problem between row changes. Let n be the number of "limbs", r the number of available working registers and number of rows e. Full Operand Caching further improves the quantity of memory access in two cases: if $n - re < e$, the Full Operand Caching structure looks like the original Operand Caching, but with a different multiplication order. Otherwise, Consecutive Operand Caching bottom row's length is adjusted in order to make full use of all available registers at the next row's processing.

3.3   Modular Squaring

The squaring routine can be built by repeating the operands and using the multiplication procedure, saving ROM space. Alternatively, writing a specialized procedure can save cycles by duplicating partial products [23]. The squaring implementation in [28] follows this strategy, specializing the 64-bit multiplication routine to 8 cycles, down from 10. Partial products are calculated then added twice to the accumulator and the resulting carry is rippled away.

Following the product scanning method, Seo's Sliding Block Doubling [30] halves the rhombus structure, allowing to use more registers to store part of the operands and doubling partial products. The algorithm is illustrated in Fig. 3 and can be divided in three parts:

- **Partial Products of the Upper Part Triangle**: an adaption of product scanning calculates partial products (represented by the black dots at the superior part of the rhombus in Fig. 3) and saves them to memory.
- **Sliding Block Doubling of Partial Products**: Each result of the column is doubled by left shifting each result by one, effectively duplicating the partial products. This process must be done in parts because the number of available registers is limited, since they hold parts of the operand.
- **Remaining Partial Products of the Bottom Line**: The bottom line multiplications are squares of part of the operand. These products must be added to their respective partial result of its above column.

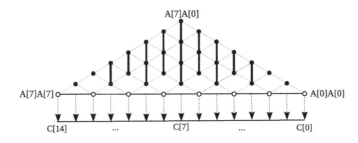

Fig. 3. Sliding Block Doubling. Black dots represent multiplications and white dots represent squarings.

4   Implementation of $\mathbb{F}_{2^{255}-19}$ Arithmetic

Our implementation aims for efficiency, so specific ARM Assembly is thoroughly used and code size is moderately sacrificed for speed. Code portability is a non-goal, so each 255-bit integer field element is densely represented, using 2^{32}-radix, implying in eight "limbs" of 32 bits, each one are in a little-endian format. This contrasts with the reference implementation [2], which use 25 or 26 bits in 32-bits words, allowing carry values requiring proper handling at the expense of more cycles.

Modular Reduction. We call as "weak" reduction a reduction modulo $2^{256} - 38$, performed at the end of every field operation in order to avoid extra carry computations between operations, as in [11]; this reduction finds a integer lesser then 2^{256} that is congruent modulo $2^{255} - 19$. When necessary, a "strong" reduction modulo $2^{255} - 19$ is performed, much like when data must be sent over the wire. This strategy is justified over the extra 10% difference between the "strong" and the "weak" reduction.

Addition and Subtraction. 256-bit addition is implemented by respectively adding each limb in a lower to higher element fashion. The carry flag, present in the ARM status registers, is used to ripple the carry across the limbs. In order to avoid extra bits generated by the final sum, the result is weakly reduced. Subtraction follows a similar strategy.

Multiplication by a 32-bit Word. Multiplication by a single word follows the algorithm described in [28], used to multiply a long integer by 121666, operation required to double a point on Curve25519.

Inversion. This operation follows the standard Itoh-Tsujii addition-chain approach to compute $a^{p-2} \equiv a^{-1} \pmod{p}$, using 11 multiplications and 254 field squarings as proposed in [2]. Adding up the costs, inversion turns to be the most expensive field operation in our implementation.

4.1   Multiplication

The $256 \times 256 \rightarrow 512$-bit multiplication follows a product-scanning like approach; more specifically, Full Operand-Caching. As mentioned in Sect. 3, parameters for this implementation are $n = 8$, $e = 3$, $r = \lfloor n/e \rfloor = 2$; since $\lfloor 3/2 \rfloor < 8 - 2 \cdot 3 \leq 3$, so Full Operand Caching with a Consecutive-like structure yields the best option.

Catching the Carry Bit. Using product scanning to calculate partial products with a double-word multiplier implies adding partial products of the next column, which in turn might generate carries. A partial column, divided in rows in a manner as described in Operand Caching, can be calculated using Algorithm 1; an example of implementation in ARM Assembly is shown in Listing 1.1. Notation follows as $(\varepsilon, z) \leftarrow w$ meaning $z \leftarrow w \bmod 2^W$ and $\varepsilon \leftarrow 0$ if $w \in [0, 2^W]$, otherwise $\varepsilon \leftarrow 1$, where W is the bit-size of a word; (AB) denotes a $2W$-bit word obtained by concatenating the W-bit words A and B.

Algorithm 1. Column computation in product scanning.

Input: Operands A, B; column index k; partial product R_k (calculated during column $k - 1$); accumulated carry R_{k+1} (generated from sum of partial products).

Output: (Partial) product $AB[k]$; sum R_{k+1} (higher half part of the partial product for column $k+1$); accumulated carry R_{k+2} (generated from sum of partial products).

$R_{k+2} \leftarrow 0$
for all $(i,j) \mid i + j = k, 0 \leq i < j \leq n - 1$ **do**
   $T \leftarrow 0$
   $(TR_k) \leftarrow A[i] \times B[j] + (T, R_k)$
   $(\varepsilon, R_{k+1}) \leftarrow T + R_{k+1}$
   $R_{k+2} \leftarrow R_{k+2} + \varepsilon$
end for
$AB[k] \leftarrow R_k$
return $AB[k]$, R_{k+1}, R_{k+2}

Listing 1.1. ARM code for calculating a column in product scanning.

```
@ k = 6
@ r5 and r4 hold R_6, R_7 respectively
@ r6, r7, r8 hold A[3], A[4] and A[5] respectively
@ r9, r10, r11 hold B[3], B[1], B[2] respectively
MOV   r12, #0
MOV   r3,  #0
UMLAL r5,  r12, r8, r10 @ A5 B1
ADDS  r4,  r4,  r12
ADC   r3,  r3,  #0
MOV   r14, #0
UMLAL r5,  r14, r7, r11 @ A4 B2
ADDS  r4,  r4,  r14
ADC   r3,  r3,  #0
MOV   r12, #0
UMLAL r5,  r12, r6, r9 @ A3 B3
ADDS  r4,  r4,  r12
ADC   r3,  r3,  #0
@ r5 holds AB[6], r4 holds R_7, @ r3 holds R_8
```

One possible optimization is **delaying the carry bit**: eliminating the last addition of Algorithm 1, this addition can be deferred to the next column with the use of a single instruction to add the partial products and the carry bit. This is easier on ARM processors, where there is fine-grained control of whether or not instructions may update the processor flags. Other optimizations involve proper register allocation in order to avoid reloads, saving up a few cycles.

Carry Elimination. Storing partial products in extra registers without adding them avoids potential carry values. In a trivial implementation, a register accumulator may be used to add the partial values, potentially generating carries. The UMAAL instruction can be employed to perform such addition, while also taking advantage of the multiplication part to further calculate more partial products. This instruction never generates a carry bit, since $(2^n-1)^2+2(2^n-1) = (2^{2n}-1)$, eliminating the need for carry handling. Partial products generated by this instruction can be forwarded to the next multiply-accumulate(-accumulate) operation; this goes on until all rows are processed. Algorithm 2 and Listing 1.2 illustrate how a column from product-scanning can be evaluated following this strategy.

Algorithm 2. Column computation in product scanning, eliminating carries.

Input: Operands A, B; column index k; m partial products $R_k[0, \ldots, m-1]$ (calculated during column $k-1$ and stored in registers).

Output: Partial product $AB[k]$; m partial products $R_{k+1}[0, \ldots, m-1]$ (higher half part of the calculated partial product for column $k+1$ stored in registers).

$t \leftarrow 1$
for all $(i, j) \mid i+j = k, 0 \leq i < j \leq n-1$ **do**
$\quad (R_k[t] R_k[0]) \leftarrow A[i] \times B[j] + R_k[0] + R_k[t]$
$\quad R_{k+1}[t-1] \leftarrow R_k[t]$
$\quad t \leftarrow t+1$
end for
$AB[k] \leftarrow R_k[0]$
return $AB[k], R_{k+1}[0, \ldots, m-1]$

Listing 1.2. ARM code for calculating a column in product scanning without carries.

```
@ k = 6
@ r3, r4, r12 and r5 hold R_6[0,1,2,3]
@ r6, r7, r8 hold A[3], A[4] and A[5] respectively
@ r9, r10, r11 hold B[3], B[1], B[2] respectively
UMAAL r3, r4,  r8, r10 @ A5 B1
UMAAL r3, r12, r7, r11 @ A4 B2
UMAAL r3, r5,  r6, r9  @ A3 B3
@ r3 holds (partially) AB[6]
@ r4, r5 and r12 hold partial products for k = 7
```

Note that this strategy is limited by the number of working registers available. These registers hold partial products without adding them up, avoiding the need of carry handling, so strategies diving columns into rows like in Operand Caching are desirable.

4.2 Squaring

The literature suggests the use of a multiplication algorithm similar to Schoolbook [30], but saving up registers and repeated multiplications. Due to its similarity with product scanning (and the possibility to apply the above optimization techniques), we choose the Sliding Block Doubling algorithm as squaring routine.

Note that, with the usage of carry flag present in some machine architectures, both *Sliding Block Doubling* and the *Bottom Line* steps (as described in Sect. 3) can be efficiently computed. In order to avoid extra memory access, one can implement those two routines without reloading operands; because of the need of the carry bit in both those operations, high register pressure may arise in order to save them into registers. We propose a technique to alleviate the register pressure: calculating a few multiplications akin to the Initial Block step as presented in the Operand Caching reduces register usage, allowing proper carry catching and handling in exchange for a few memory accesses (Fig. 4).

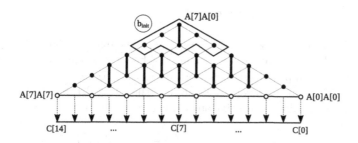

Fig. 4. Sliding Block Doubling with Initial Block

In this example, each product-scanning column is limited to height 2, meaning that only two consecutive multiplications can be handled without losing partial products. Incrementing the size of the "initial block" (or, more accurately, the initial triangle) frees up registers during the bottom row evaluation.

5 Elliptic Curves

An elliptic curve E over a field $\mathbb{F}_q$ is the set of solutions $(x, y) \in \mathbb{F}_q \times \mathbb{F}_q$ which satisfy the Weierstrass equation

$$E/\mathbb{F}_q : y^2 + a_1 xy + a_3 y = x^3 + a_2 x^2 + a_4 x + a_6, \tag{1}$$

where $a_1, a_2, a_3, a_4, a_6 \in \mathbb{F}_q$ and the curve discriminant is $\Delta \neq 0$. We restrict our attention to curves defined over prime fields which can be represented in the Montgomery [24] (or Twisted Edwards [4]) model, allowing faster formulas and unified arithmetic [6].

The set of points $E(\mathbb{F}_q) = \{(x, y) \in E(\mathbb{F}_q)\} \cup \{\mathcal{O}\} = \{P \in E(\mathbb{F}_q)\} \cup \{\mathcal{O}\}$ under the addition operation $+$ (chord and tangent) forms an additive group, with $\mathcal{O}$ as the identity element. Given an elliptic curve point $P \in E(\mathbb{F}_q)$ and an integer k, the operation kP, called scalar point multiplication, is defined by the addition of the point P to itself $k - 1$ times. This operation encodes the security assumption for Elliptic Curve Cryptography (ECC) protocols, basing their security on the hardness of solving the elliptic curve analogue of the discrete logarithm problem (ECDLP). Given a public key represented as a point Q in the curve, the problem amounts to finding the secret $k \in \mathbb{Z}$ such that $Q = kP$ for some given point P in the curve.

ECC is an efficient yet conservative option for deploying public-key cryptography in embedded systems, since the ECDLP still enjoys conjectured full-exponential security against classical computers and, consequently, reduced key sizes and storage requirements. In practice, a conservative instance of this problem can be obtained by selecting prime curves of near-prime order without supporting any non-trivial endomorphisms. Curve25519 is a popular curve at the 128-bit security level represented through the Montgomery model

$$\text{Curve25519:} \quad y^2 = x^3 + Ax^2 + x, \tag{2}$$

compactly described by the small value of the coefficient $A = 486662$. This curve model is ideal for curve-based key exchanges, because it allows the scalar multiplication to be computed using x-coordinates only. Using a birational equivalence, Curve25519 can be also represented in the twisted Edwards model using full coordinates to allow instantiations of secure signature schemes:

$$\text{edwards25519:} \quad -x^2 + y^2 = 1 - \frac{121655}{121666}x^2 y^2. \tag{3}$$

Key exchange protocols and digital signature schemes are building blocks for applications like key distribution schemes and secure software updates based on code signing. These protocols are fundamental for preserving the integrity of software running in embedded devices and establishing symmetric cryptographic keys for data encryption and secure communication.

5.1 Elliptic Curve Diffie Hellman

The Elliptic Curve Diffie Hellman protocol is an instantiation of the Diffie-Hellman key agreement protocol over elliptic curves. Modern implementations of this protocol employ x-coordinate-only formulas over a Montgomery model of the curve, for both computational savings, side-channel security and ease of implementation. Following this idea, the protocol may be implemented using the X25519 function, which is in essence a scalar multiplication of a point on the

Curve25519 [2]. In this scheme, a pair of entities generate their respective private keys, each of them 32-byte long. A public, generator point P is multiplied by the private key, generating a public key. Then, those entities exchange their public keys over an insecure channel; computing the X25519 function with their private keys and the received point generates a shared secret which may be used to generate a symmetric session key for both parties.

Since the ECDH protocol does not authenticate keys, public key authentication must be performed off-band, or an authenticated key agreement scheme such as the Elliptic Curve Menezes-Qu-Vanstone (ECMQV) [21] must be adopted.

For data confidentiality, authenticated encryption can be constructed by combining X25519 as an interactive key exchange mechanism, together with a block or stream cipher and a proper mode of operation, as proposed in the future Transport Layer Security protocol versions. Alternatively, authenticated encryption with additional data (AEAD) schemes may be combined with X25519, replacing block ciphers and a mode of operation.

5.2 Ed25519 Digital Signatures

The Edwards-curve Digital Signature Algorithm [5] (EdDSA) is a signature scheme variant of Schnorr signatures based on elliptic curves represented in the Edwards model. Like other discrete-log based signature schemes, EdDSA requires a secret value, or nonce, unique to each signature. For reducing the risk of a random number generator failure, EdDSA calculates this nonce deterministically, as the hash of the message and the private key. Thus, the nonce is very unlikely to be repeated for different signed messages. While this reduces the attack surface in terms of random number generation and improves nonce misuse resistance during the signing process, high quality random numbers are still needed for key generation. When instantiated using edwards25519 (Eq. 3), the EdDSA scheme is called Ed25519. Concretely, let H be the SHA512 hash function mapping arbitrary-length strings to 512-bit hash values. The signature of a message M under this scheme and private key k is the 512-bit string (R, S), where $R = rB$, for B a generator of the subgroup of points or order ℓ and r computed as $H(H(k), M)$; $S = r + H(R, A = aB, M) \bmod \ell$, for an integer a derived from $H(k)$. Verification works by parsing the signature components and checking if the equation $SB = R + H(R, A, M)A$ holds [5].

6 Implementation Details and Results

The focus given in this work is microcontrollers suitable for integration within embedded projects. Therefore, we choose some representative ARM architecture processors. Specifically, the implementations were benchmarked on the following platforms:

- **Teensy**: Teensy 3.2 board equipped with a MK20DX256VLH7 Cortex-M4-based microcontroller, clocked at 48 and 72 MHz.

- **STM32F401C**: STM32F401 Discovery board powered by a STM32F401C microcontroller, also based on the Cortex-M4 design, clocked at 84 MHz.
- **Cortex-A7/A15**: ODROID-XU4 board with a Samsung Exynos5422 CPU clocked at 2 GHz, containing four Cortex-A7 and four Cortex-A15 cores in a heterogeneous configuration.

Code for the Teensy board was generated using GCC version 5.4.1 compiled with the -O3 -mthumb flags; same settings apply for code compiled to the STM32F401C board, but using an updated compiler version (7.2.0). For the Cortex-A family, code was generated with GCC version 6.3.1 using the -O3 optimization flag. Cycle counts were obtained using the corresponding cycle counter in each architecture. Randomness, where required, was sampled through /dev/urandom on the Cortex-A7/A15 device. In the Cortex-M4 boards, NIST's Hash_DRBG was implemented with SHA256 and the generator is seeded by analogically sampling disconnected pins on the board.

Albeit not the most efficient for every possible target, the codebase is the same for every ARMv7 processor equipped with DSP instructions, being ideal to large heterogeneous deployments, such as a network of smaller sensors connected to a larger central server with a more powerful processor than its smaller counterparts. This helps code maintenance, avoiding possible security problems.

6.1 Field Arithmetic

Table 1 presents timings and Table 3 presents code size for field operations with implementation described in Sect. 4. In comparison to the current state-of-art [28], our addition/subtraction take 18% less cycles; the 256-bit multiplier with a weak reduction is almost 50% faster and the squaring operation takes 30% less cycles. The multiplication routine may be used in replacement of the squaring if code size is a restriction, since 1 **S** is approximately 0.9 **M**. Implementation of all arithmetic operations take less code space in comparison to [28], ranging from 20% savings in the addition to 50% from the multiplier.

As noted by Hasse [14], cycle counts on the same Cortex-M4-based controller can be different depending on the clock frequency set on the chip. Different clock frequencies set for the controller and the memory may cause stalls on the former if the latter is slower. For example, the multiplication and the squaring implementations, which rely on memory operations, use 10% more cycles when the controller is set to a 33% higher frequency. This behavior is also present on cryptographic schemes, as shown in Table 2.

6.2 X25519 Implementation

X25519 was implemented using the standard Montgomery ladder over the x-coordinate. Standard tricks like randomized projective coordinates (amounting to a 1% performance penalty) and constant-time conditional swaps were implemented for side-channel protection. Cycle counts of the X25519 function executed on the evaluated processors are shown in Table 2 and code size in Table 3.

Table 1. Timings in cycles for arithmetic in $\mathbb{F}_{2^{255}-19}$ on multiple ARM processors. Numbers for this work were taken as the average of 256 executions.

	Cortex	Add/Sub	Mult	Mult by word	Square	Inversion
De Groot [12]	M4	73/77	631	129	563	151997
De Santis [28]	M4	106	546	**72**	362	96337
This work	M4 @ 48 MHz (Teensy)	**86**	**276**	76	**252**	**66634**
	M4 @ 72 MHz (Teensy)	**86**	310	76	**280**	**75099**
	M4 @ 84 MHz (STM32F401C)	**86**	273	76	**243**	**64425**
	A7	52	290	61	233	62648
	A15	36	225	37	139	41978
	Cortex	$\mathbb{F}_{p^2}$ **Add/Sub**	$\mathbb{F}_{p^2}$ **Mult**	**Mult by word**	$\mathbb{F}_{p^2}$ **Square**	$\mathbb{F}_{p^2}$ **Inversion**
FourQ [22]	M4 (STM32F407)	84/86	358	-	215	21056

Table 2. Timings in cycles for computing the Montgomery ladder in the X25519 key exchange; and key generation, signature and verification of a 5-byte message in the Ed25519 scheme. Key generation encompasses taking a secret key and computing its public key; signature takes both keys and a message to generate its respective signature. Numbers were taken as the average of 256 executions in multiple ARM processors. Protocols are inherently protected against timing attacks (constant-time – CT) on the Cortex-M4 due to the lack of cache memory, while side-channel protection is explicitly needed in the Cortex-A. Performance penalties for side-channel protection can be obtained by comparing the implementations with CT = Y over N in the same platform.

	CT	Cortex	X25519	Ed25519 Key Gen.	Ed25519 Sign	Ed25519 Verify
De Groot [12]	Y	M4	1816351	-	-	-
De Santis [28]	Y	M4	1563852	-	-	-
This work	Y	M4 @ 48 MHz (Teensy)	**907240**	**347225**	**496039**	**1265078**
	Y	M4 @ 72 MHz (Teensy)	1003707	379734	531471	1427923
	Y	M4 @ 84 MHz (STM32F401)	894391	389480	543724	1331449
Schwabe, Bernstein [7]	Y	A8	527102	-	368212	650102
This work	N	A7	-	-	423058	1118806
	Y	A7	825914	397261	524804	-
	N	A15	-	-	264252	776806
	Y	A15	572910	245377	305797	-
eBACS ref. code [10]	Y	A15	**342477**	**241641**	**245712**	**730047**
	CT	**Cortex**	**DH**	**SchnoorQ Key Gen.**	**SchnoorQ Sign**	**SchnoorQ Verify**
FourQ [22]	Y	M4 (STM32F407)	542900	265100	345400	648600

Table 3. Code size in bytes for implementing arithmetic in $\mathbb{F}_{2^{255}-19}$, X25519 and Ed25519 protocols on the Cortex-M4. Code size for protocols considers the entire software stack needed to perform the specific action, including but not limited to field operations, hashing, tables for scalar multiplication and other algorithms.

	Add	Sub	Mult	Mult by word	Square
De Groot [12]	44	64	1284	300	1168
De Santis [28]	138	148	1264	116	882
This work	110	108	**622**	**92**	**562**
	Inversion	X25519	Ed25519 Key Gen.	Ed25519 Sign	Ed25519 Verify
De Groot [12]	388	4140	-	-	-
De Santis [28]	484	**3786**	-	-	-
This work	**328**	4152	**21265**	**22162**	**28240**

Our implementation is 42% faster than De Santis and Sigl [28] while staying competitive in terms of code size.

Note on Conditional Swaps. The classical conditional swap using logic instructions is used by default as the compiler optimizes it using function inlining, saving about 30 cycles. However, this approach opens a breach for a power analysis attack, as shown in [25], since all bits from a 32-bit long register (in ARM architectures) must be set or not depending on a secret bit.

Alternatively, the conditional swap operation can be implemented by setting the 4-bit ge-flag in the Application Program Status Register (ASPR) and then issuing the SEL instruction, which pick parts from the operand registers in byte-sized blocks and writes them to the destination [1]. Note that setting 0x0 to the ASPR.ge flag and issuing SEL copies one of the operands; setting 0xF and using SEL copies the other one. The ASPR cannot be set directly through a MOV with an immediate operand, so a Move to Special Register (MSR) instruction must be issued. Only registers may be used as arguments of this operation, so another one must be used to set the ASPR.ge flag. Therefore, at least 8 bits must be used to implement the conditional move. This theoretically reduces the attack surface of a potential side-channel analysis, down from 32 bits.

6.3   Ed25519 Implementation

Key generation and message signing requires a fixed-point scalar multiplication, here implemented through a comb-like algorithm proposed by Hamburg in [15]. The signed-comb approach recodes the scalar into its signed binary form using a single addition and a right-shift. This representation is divided in blocks and each one of those are divided in combs, much like in the multi-comb approach described in [16]. Like in the original work, we use five teeth for each of the five blocks and 10 combs for each block (11 for the last one) due to the performance balance between the direct and the linear table scan to access precomputed data if protection against cache attacks is required. To effectively calculate the scalar multiplication, our implementation requires 50 point additions and 254 point doublings. Five lookup tables of 16 points in Extended Projective coordinate format with $z = 1$ are used, adding up to approximately 7.5 KiB of data.

Verification requires a double-point multiplication involving the generator B and point A using a w-NAF interleaving technique [16], with a window of width 5 for the A point, generated on-the-fly, taking approximately 3 KiB of volatile memory. The group generator B is interleaved using a window of width 7, implying in a lookup table of 32 points stored in Extended Projective coordinate format with $z = 1$ taking 3 KiB of ROM. Note that verification has no need to be executed in constant time, since all input data is (expected to be) public. Decoding uses a standard field exponentiation for both inversion and square root to calculate the y-coordinate as suggested by [19] and [5]; this exponentiation is carried out by the Itoh-Tsujii algorithm, providing an efficient way to calculate the missing coordinate. Timings for computing a signature (both protected and unprotected against cache attacks) and verification functionality in the evaluated processors can be found in Table 2. Arithmetic modulo the group order in Ed25519-related operations relates closely to the previously shown arithmetic modulo $2^{255} - 19$, but Barrett reduction is used instead.

Final Remarks. We consider that our implementation is competitive in comparison to the mentioned works in Sect. 3, given the performance numbers shown in Tables 2 and 3. Using Curve25519 and its corresponding Twisted Edwards form in well-known protocols is beneficial in terms of security, mostly due to its maturity and its widespread usage to the point of becoming a *de facto* standard.

Acknowledgments. The authors gratefully acknowledge financial support from LG Electronics Inc. during the development of this work, under project *"Efficient and Secure Cryptography for IoT"*, and Armando Faz-Hernández for his helpful contributions and discussions during its development. We also thank the anonymous reviewers for their helpful comments.

References

1. ARM: Cortex-M4 Devices Generic User Guide (2010). http://infocenter.arm.com/help/index.jsp?topic=%2Fcom.arm.doc.dui0553a%2FCHDBFFDB.html
2. Bernstein, D.J.: Curve25519: new diffie-hellman speed records. In: Yung, M., Dodis, Y., Kiayias, A., Malkin, T. (eds.) PKC 2006. LNCS, vol. 3958, pp. 207–228. Springer, Heidelberg (2006). https://doi.org/10.1007/11745853_14
3. Bernstein, D.J.: 25519 naming, August 2014. https://www.ietf.org/mail-archive/web/cfrg/current/msg04996.html
4. Bernstein, D.J., Birkner, P., Joye, M., Lange, T., Peters, C.: Twisted edwards curves. In: Vaudenay, S. (ed.) AFRICACRYPT 2008. LNCS, vol. 5023, pp. 389–405. Springer, Heidelberg (2008). https://doi.org/10.1007/978-3-540-68164-9_26
5. Bernstein, D.J., Duif, N., Lange, T., Schwabe, P., Yang, B.: High-speed high-security signatures. J. Crypt. Eng. **2**(2), 77–89 (2012)

6. Bernstein, D.J., Lange, T.: Analysis and optimization of elliptic-curve single-scalar multiplication. Contemp. Math. Finite Fields Appl. **461**, 1–20 (2008)
7. Bernstein, D.J., Schwabe, P.: NEON crypto. In: Prouff, E., Schaumont, P. (eds.) CHES 2012. LNCS, vol. 7428, pp. 320–339. Springer, Heidelberg (2012). https://doi.org/10.1007/978-3-642-33027-8_19
8. Boneh, D., DeMillo, R.A., Lipton, R.J.: On the importance of checking cryptographic protocols for faults. In: Fumy, W. (ed.) EUROCRYPT 1997. LNCS, vol. 1233, pp. 37–51. Springer, Heidelberg (1997). https://doi.org/10.1007/3-540-69053-0_4
9. Costello, C., Longa, P.: FourQ: four-dimensional decompositions on a Q-curve over the mersenne prime. In: Iwata, T., Cheon, J.H. (eds.) ASIACRYPT 2015. LNCS, vol. 9452, pp. 214–235. Springer, Heidelberg (2015). https://doi.org/10.1007/978-3-662-48797-6_10
10. Bernstein, D.J., Lange, T. (eds.) eBACS: ECRYPT Benchmarking of Cryptographic Systems. https://bench.cr.yp.to
11. Düll, M., et al.: High-speed Curve25519 on 8-bit, 16-bit, and 32-bit microcontrollers. Des. Codes Crypt. **77**(2–3), 493–514 (2015)
12. de Groot, W.: A Performance Study of X25519 on Cortex-M3 and M4. Ph.D. thesis, Eindhoven University of Technology, September 2015
13. Großschädl, J., Oswald, E., Page, D., Tunstall, M.: Side-channel analysis of cryptographic software via early-terminating multiplications. In: Lee, D., Hong, S. (eds.) ICISC 2009. LNCS, vol. 5984, pp. 176–192. Springer, Heidelberg (2010). https://doi.org/10.1007/978-3-642-14423-3_13
14. Haase, B.: Memory bandwidth influence makes cortex m4 benchmarking difficult, September 2017. https://ches.2017.rump.cr.yp.to/fe534b32e52fcacee-026786ff44235f0.pdf
15. Hamburg, M.: Fast and compact elliptic-curve cryptography. IACR Crypt. ePrint Arch. **2012**, 309 (2012)
16. Hankerson, D., Menezes, A.J., Vanstone, S.: Guide to Elliptic Curve Cryptography. Springer-Verlag New York Inc., Secaucus (2003). https://doi.org/10.1007/b97644
17. Hutter, M., Wenger, E.: Fast multi-precision multiplication for public-key cryptography on embedded microprocessors. In: Preneel, B., Takagi, T. (eds.) CHES 2011. LNCS, vol. 6917, pp. 459–474. Springer, Heidelberg (2011). https://doi.org/10.1007/978-3-642-23951-9_30
18. Jao, D., De Feo, L.: Towards quantum-resistant cryptosystems from supersingular elliptic curve isogenies. In: Yang, B.-Y. (ed.) PQCrypto 2011. LNCS, vol. 7071, pp. 19–34. Springer, Heidelberg (2011). https://doi.org/10.1007/978-3-642-25405-5_2
19. Josefsson, S., Liusvaara, I.: Edwards-Curve Digital Signature Algorithm (EdDSA). RFC 8032, January 2017. https://rfc-editor.org/rfc/rfc8032.txt
20. Kocher, P.C.: Timing attacks on implementations of diffie-hellman, RSA, DSS, and other systems. In: Koblitz, N. (ed.) CRYPTO 1996. LNCS, vol. 1109, pp. 104–113. Springer, Heidelberg (1996). https://doi.org/10.1007/3-540-68697-5_9
21. Law, L., Menezes, A., Qu, M., Solinas, J.A., Vanstone, S.A.: An efficient protocol for authenticated key agreement. Des. Codes Crypt. **28**(2), 119–134 (2003)
22. Liu, Z., Longa, P., Pereira, G.C.C.F., Reparaz, O., Seo, H.: FourQ on embedded devices with strong countermeasures against side-channel attacks. In: Fischer, W., Homma, N. (eds.) CHES 2017. LNCS, vol. 10529, pp. 665–686. Springer, Cham (2017). https://doi.org/10.1007/978-3-319-66787-4_32
23. Liu, Z., Seo, H., Kim, H.: A synthesis of multi-precision multiplication and squaring techniques for 8-bit sensor nodes: state-of-the-art research and future challenges. J. Comput. Sci. Technol. **31**(2), 284–299 (2016)

24. Montgomery, P.L.: Speeding the pollard and elliptic curve methods of factorization. Math. Comput. **48**(177), 243–264 (1987). https://doi.org/10.2307/2007888

25. Nascimento, E., Chmielewski, L., Oswald, D., Schwabe, P.: Attacking embedded ECC implementations through cmov side channels. IACR Crypt. ePrint Arch. **2016**, 923 (2016)

26. Oliveira, T., López, J., Hışıl, H., Faz-Hernández, A., Rodríguez-Henríquez, F.: How to (Pre-)compute a ladder. In: Adams, C., Camenisch, J. (eds.) SAC 2017. LNCS, vol. 10719, pp. 172–191. Springer, Cham (2018). https://doi.org/10.1007/978-3-319-72565-9_9

27. Renes, J., Smith, B.: qDSA: small and secure digital signatures with curve-based diffie-hellman key pairs. IACR Crypt. ePrint Arch. **2017**, 518 (2017)

28. Santis, F.D., Sigl, G.: Towards side-channel protected X25519 on ARM cortex-M4 processors. In: SPEED-B. Utrecht, The Netherlands, October 2016. http://ccccspeed.win.tue.nl/

29. Seo, H., Kim, H.: Consecutive operand-caching method for multiprecision multiplication, revisited. J. Inform. Commun. Convergence Eng. **13**(1), 27–35 (2015)

30. Seo, H., Liu, Z., Choi, J., Kim, H.: Multi-precision squaring for public-key cryptography on embedded microprocessors. In: Paul, G., Vaudenay, S. (eds.) INDOCRYPT 2013. LNCS, vol. 8250, pp. 227–243. Springer, Cham (2013). https://doi.org/10.1007/978-3-319-03515-4_15

Implementing the NewHope-Simple Key Exchange on Low-Cost FPGAs

Tobias Oder[1]([✉]) and Tim Güneysu[1,2]

[1] Horst Görtz Institute for IT-Security, Ruhr-University Bochum, Bochum, Germany
{tobias.oder,tim.gueneysu}@rub.de
[2] DFKI, Bremen, Germany

Abstract. Lattice-based cryptography is one of the most promising candidates being considered to replace current public-key systems in the era of quantum computing. In 2016 Alkim, Ducas, Pöppelmann, and Schwabe proposed the lattice-based key exchange scheme NewHope. The scheme has gained some popularity in the research community as it is believed to withstand attacks by quantum computers with a comfortable security margin and provides decent efficiency and low communication cost. In this work, we evaluate the efficiency of NewHope on reconfigurable hardware. We provide the up to our knowledge first field-programmable gate array (FPGA) implementation of NewHope-Simple that is a slight modification of NewHope proposed by the authors themselves in 2016. NewHope-Simple is basically NewHope with different error correction mechanism. Our implementation of the client-side scheme requires 1,483 slices, 4,498 look-up tables (LUTs), and 4,635 flip-flops (FFs) on low-cost Xilinx Artix-7 FPGAs. The implementation of the server-side scheme takes 1,708 slices, 5,142 LUTs, and 4,452 FFs. Both cores use only two digital signal processors (DSPs) and four 18 Kb block memories (BRAMs). The implementation has a constant execution time to prevent timing attacks. The server-side operations take 1.4 ms and the client-side operations take 1.5 ms.

Keywords: Ideal lattices · NewHope · FPGA

1 Introduction

Public-key cryptography provides important security services to protect information sent over untrusted channels. Unfortunately, most well-established public-key cryptographic primitives rely either on the factorization or the discrete logarithm problem. As both problems are closely connected, a mathematical breakthrough in one of the problems would render primitives based on either of the problems insecure. In this context, the possible advent of the quantum computer is another crucial threat. A significant number of experts believe that quantum

This work was partially funded by the European Union H2020 SAFEcrypto project (grant no. 644729), European Union H2020 PQCRYPTO project (grant no. 645622).

T. Lange and O. Dunkelman (Eds.): LATINCRYPT 2017, LNCS 11368, pp. 128–142, 2019.
https://doi.org/10.1007/978-3-030-25283-0_7

computers that are large enough to pose a threat to cryptographic schemes are built within the next decade [6,23]. The National Institute of Standards and Technology (NIST) recently published a call for proposals [16] that asks to submit public-key encryption, key exchange, or digital signature schemes for standardization.

Lattice-based cryptography is a family of primitives that is believed to be secure against attacks by quantum computers. It has efficient instantiations for all three types of most relevant security services and provides reasonable parameter sizes for a decent level of security. Especially the NewHope key exchange by Alkim et al. [2] has gained significant attention from the research community and the industry. Google even tested the scheme in its Chrome browser [9]. While the original NewHope proposal contains a tricky error reconciliation, Alkim et al. proposed an improved version called NewHope-Simple [1] that avoids this error reconciliation at the price of increasing the size of the message that is sent from the client to the server from 2048 bytes to 2176 bytes.

In this work we present an implementation of NewHope-Simple for Field-Programmable Gate Arrays (FPGAs). FPGAs are widely used as platform for cryptographic hardware (e.g., also in the Internet of Things) and thus a highly interesting platform for the evaluation of NewHope-Simple. Our target platform is a low-cost Xilinx Artix-7 FPGA, but we expect similar implementation results on other reprogrammable hardware devices.

1.1   Related Work

Alkim et al. evaluated the performance of NewHope on Intel CPUs. They utilize the SIMD instructions of the AVX2 instructions set to achieve a high performance. Another implementation of NewHope targets ARM Cortex-M processors [4]. In both works [2,4] the authors implemented the original NewHope scheme and not NewHope-Simple. We are not aware of any hardware implementations of NewHope-Simple.

Besides NewHope, there is also a lattice-based key exchange called Frodo [7]. In contrast to NewHope, Frodo is based on standard lattices instead of ideal lattices. The difference between both types of lattices is that ideal lattices include a fundamental structure and thus allow a more efficient instantiation. It is, however, unclear whether this additional structure can be exploited by an attacker. So far no attacks that exploit the structure of ideal lattices and have a better runtime than the best known lattice attacks are known. Due to the higher memory consumption, Frodo is less suited for implementation on low-cost hardware. Another lattice-based key exchange has been developed by Del Pino et al. [10]. They present a generic approach and their scheme can be instantiated with any suitable signature scheme and public-key encryption scheme. Note that the scheme of [10] is an authenticated key exchange while NewHope and Frodo are unauthenticated and thus require an additional signature scheme for the authentication part.

While we are not aware of any hardware implementations of NewHope, the ring-learning with errors encryption scheme (ring-LWE) has been implemented in works like [20,21,24]. Furthermore, there is an implementation of a lattice-based identity-based encryption scheme (IBE) for Xilinx FPGAs [14]. IBE, ring-LWE, and NewHope-Simple share most operations like the number theoretic transform and the Gaussian sampling. Additionally to the operations required by ring-LWE and IBE, NewHope-Simple also requires the on-the-fly generation of the polynomial a (usually precomputed in the implementations of ring-LWE), SHAKE-128, SHA3-256, and a compression function.

1.2   Contribution

NewHope has been first proposed in late 2015 [3]. But there are still no hardware implementations of the scheme published. In this work we aim to close this gap. We present the up to our knowledge first implementation of NewHope-Simple for reconfigurable hardware devices. We optimized our implementation for area while taking care to still achieving a decent performance. Our work shows that NewHope-Simple is practical on constrained reconfigurable hardware. Our implementations takes 1,483 slices, 4,498 LUTs, and 4,635 FFs for the client and 1,708 slices, 5,142 LUTs, and 4,452 FFs for the server. Both cores use only 2 DSPs and four 18 Kb block memories. It has a constant execution time to prevent timing attacks and hamper simple power analysis. We achieved a performance of 350,416 cycles at a frequency of 117 MHz for the entire protocol run. We will also provide the source code with the publication of our work[1].

2   Preliminaries

In this chapter, we discuss the mathematical background that is crucial for the understanding of this paper.

2.1   Notation

Let $\mathbb{Z}$ be the ring of rational integers. We denote by $\mathcal{R}$ the polynomial ring $\mathbb{Z}[x]_q/\langle x^n + 1\rangle$ where n is a power of two and $x^n + 1$ is the modulus. The coefficients of the polynomials have the modulus q. In case χ is a probability distribution over $\mathcal{R}$, then $x \xleftarrow{\$} \chi$ means the sampling of x according to χ. The point-wise multiplication of two polynomials is denoted by the operator $\circ$. Polynomials in the time domain are denoted by bold lower case letters (e.g. **a**) and polynomials in the frequency domain are described by an additional hat-symbol (e.g. **â**). Polynomials that have been compressed by the NHSCompress function are marked by a bar (e.g. **ā**).

---

[1] http://www.seceng.rub.de/research/projects/pqc/.

2.2   The NewHope Scheme

In this paper we implemented the Simple version [1] of the NewHope protocol [2] that improves previous approaches to lattice-based key exchange [8,11,18]. NewHope is a server-client key exchange protocol as described in Protocol 1. Its security is based on the ring learning with errors problem. Note that NewHope is unauthenticated. Thus, an additional signature scheme is required. The scheme is parametrized by a lattice dimension n, a modulus q, and a standard deviation $\sigma = \sqrt{k/2}$ where k is used as a parameter for the binomial sampler. In this work, we implemented the scheme with the parameters $n = 1024$, $q = 12289$, and $k = 16$. As stated in [1], the security of NewHope-Simple is the same as the security of NewHope and therefore the chosen parameters yield at least a post-quantum security level of 128 bits with a comfortable margin [2], or more specifically 255 bits of security against known quantum attackers and 199 bits of security against the best plausible attackers.

Parameters: $q = 12289 < 2^{14}$, $n = 1024$
Error distribution: ψ_{16}^n

Alice (server)		Bob (client)
$seed \xleftarrow{\$} \{0,\dots,255\}^{32}$		
$\hat{a} \leftarrow$ Parse(SHAKE-128($seed$))		
$\mathbf{s},\mathbf{e} \xleftarrow{\$} \psi_{16}^n$		$\mathbf{s}',\mathbf{e}',\mathbf{e}'' \xleftarrow{\$} \psi_{16}^n$
$\hat{\mathbf{s}} \leftarrow$ NTT($\mathbf{s}$)		
$\hat{\mathbf{b}} \leftarrow \hat{\mathbf{a}} \circ \hat{\mathbf{s}} + $ NTT($\mathbf{e}$)	$\xrightarrow[\text{1824 Bytes}]{m_a = \text{encodeA}(seed,\hat{\mathbf{b}})}$	$(\hat{\mathbf{b}}, seed) \leftarrow$ decodeA(m_a)
		$\hat{\mathbf{a}} \leftarrow$ Parse(SHAKE-128($seed$))
		$\hat{\mathbf{t}} \leftarrow$ NTT($\mathbf{s}'$)
		$\hat{\mathbf{u}} \leftarrow \hat{\mathbf{a}} \circ \hat{\mathbf{t}} + $ NTT($\mathbf{e}'$)
		$\nu \xleftarrow{\$} \{0,\dots,255\}^{32}$
		$\nu' \leftarrow$ SHA3-256(ν)
		$\mathbf{k} \leftarrow$ NHSEncode(ν')
		$\mathbf{c} \leftarrow$ NTT$^{-1}(\hat{\mathbf{b}} \circ \hat{\mathbf{t}}) + \mathbf{e}'' + \mathbf{k}$
$(\hat{\mathbf{u}}, \bar{\mathbf{c}}) \leftarrow$ decodeB(m_b)	$\xleftarrow[\text{2048 Bytes}]{m_b = \text{encodeB}(\hat{\mathbf{u}},\bar{\mathbf{c}})}$	$\bar{\mathbf{c}} \leftarrow$ NHSCompress($\mathbf{c}$)
$\mathbf{c}' \leftarrow$ NHSDecompress($\bar{\mathbf{c}}$)		$\mu \leftarrow$ SHA3-256(ν')
$\mathbf{k}' \leftarrow \mathbf{c}' - $ NTT$^{-1}(\hat{\mathbf{u}} \circ \hat{\mathbf{s}})$		
$\nu' \leftarrow$ NHSDecode($\mathbf{k}'$)		
$\mu \leftarrow$ SHA3-256(ν')		

Protocol 1: A full description of the NewHope-Simple key exchange. The functions NHSEncode, NHSDecode, NHSCompress, and NHSDecompress are defined in [1]. The functions encodeA, encodeB, decodeA, and decodeB describe a simple transformation into a representation that dependents on the channel over which the information will be sent (e.g. bit-wise or byte-wise format).

The most notable difference between NewHope and NewHope-Simple is that NewHope avoids the error-reconciliation mechanism originally proposed by Ding [11]. As a consequence, NewHope-Simple is less complex but also 6.25% bigger in terms of the size of the transmitted messages. The polynomial **a** could be fixed to a constant. The authors of NewHope decided to generate a fresh **a** for every run to prevent backdoors and all-for-the-price-of-one attacks.

The idea behind the key exchange is that the server generates an ephemeral key pair and transmits the public key to the client. The client uses the public key to encrypt a secret symmetric key and transmits the ciphertext to the server. The server decrypts the ciphertext to retrieve the same symmetric key that can be used for further communication. As the scheme is based on the ring learning with errors problem, error polynomials are used to hide the symmetric key in the ciphertext. Therefore an error correction mechanism is required to recover the symmetric key. NewHope-Simple itself has no built-in authentication, it relies on external authentication, for instance with a signature scheme. The major components of the scheme are a Parse function that is used to generate **a**, a binomial sampler to generate error polynomials, the number-theoretic transform (NTT) to speed up polynomial multiplication, and the Keccak function that is used to compute SHA3-256 hashes and for the SHAKE-128 extendable output function.

2.3 Binomial Sampling

In [2] a binomial sampler is used as substitution for the Gaussian sampler that is required in many lattice-based schemes. The discrete, centered Gaussian distribution is defined by assigning a weight proportional to $\exp(\frac{-x^2}{2\sigma^2})$ where σ is the standard deviation of the Gaussian distribution. According to [2] the binomial distribution that is parametrized by $k = 2\sigma^2$ is sufficiently close to a discrete Gaussian distribution with standard deviation σ and does not significantly decrease the security level. A binomial sampler is basically realized by uniformly sampling two k-bit vectors and computing their respective Hamming weights. The binomial distributed result is obtained by subtracting the Hamming weights of both bit vectors. Binomial sampling does not require any look-up tables and has a constant runtime. But as k scales quadratically with σ the binomial approach is only suited for small σ as used in lattice-based encryption or key exchange schemes. Signature schemes usually require larger standard deviations.

2.4 Number-Theoretic Transform (NTT)

The number-theoretic transform (NTT) is a discrete Fourier transform over a finite field. An interesting property of the discrete Fourier transform, which is also highly interesting for lattice-based cryptography, is the ability to reduce the overall complexity of (polynomial) multiplication to $\mathcal{O}(n \cdot \log n)$. To allow efficient computation of the NTT the coefficient ring has to contain primitive roots of unity.

Definition 1 (Primitive root of unity [12]**).** *Let $\mathcal{R}$ be a ring, $n \in \mathbb{N}_{\geq 1}$, and $\omega \in \mathcal{R}$. The value ω is an n-th root of unity if $\omega^n = 1$. The value ω is a primitive n-th root of unity (or root of unity of order n) if it is an n-th root of unity, $n \in \mathcal{R}$ is a unit in $\mathcal{R}$, and $\omega^{n/t} - 1$ is not a zero divisor for any prime divisor t of n.*

For a given primitive n-th root of unity ω in Z_q, the NTT of a vector $a = (a_{n-1}, \ldots, a_0)$ is the vector $A = (A_{n-1}, \ldots, A_0)$ and computed as

$$A_i = \sum_{0 \leq j < n} a_j \omega^{ij} \bmod q, \, i = 0, 1, \ldots, n - 1.$$

The idea is to transform two polynomials $a = a_{n-1} \cdot x^{n-1} + \ldots + a_0$ and $b = b_{n-1} \cdot x^{n-1} + \ldots + b_0$ into their NTT representations $A = A_{n-1} \cdot x^{n-1} + \ldots + A_0$ and $B = B_{n-1} \cdot x^{n-1} + \ldots + B_0$ and computing the coefficient-wise multiplication as $C = \sum_{0 \leq i < n} A_i \cdot B_i \cdot x^i$. The result $c = a \cdot b$ is obtained after applying the inverse transform to C. For $q = 1 \bmod 2n$ the way the result has to be interpreted depends on the input.

- Assuming one expanded a and b to vectors of length $2n$ by padding n zeros, the result c equals the schoolbook multiplication of a and b without reduction.
- Without padding, the result c is already reduced modulo $f = x^n - 1$. This is called the *positive* wrapped convolution. In contrast to the first case, the resulting polynomial is only of degree n.

This reduction for free is beneficial concerning the computation time, but for `NewHope` one performs arithmetic in $\mathbb{Z}[x]/\langle x^n+1 \rangle$. Thus, the input and output have to be modified so that the *negative* wrapped convolution gets computed to exploit the reduction property. Let ψ be the square root of ω. Now one computes $a' = \sum_{0 \leq i < n} a_i \cdot \psi^i \cdot x^i$ and $b' = \sum_{0 \leq i < n} b_i \cdot \psi^i \cdot x^i$ before the polynomials are transformed into their NTT representation. To obtain $a \cdot b \bmod x^n + 1$, one also has to multiply c', the output of the inverse transform of C, by powers of the *inverse* of ψ.

There are many ways to compute the number-theoretic transform. In this work, we follow the optimized approach from [22]. For a complete description of the algorithms we refer to [22].

3   FPGA Implementation

In this chapter, we present the details of our implementation and explain our design decisions.

3.1   Overview

Our target device is a Xilinx Artix-7 FPGA. It features DSPs blocks that can multiply, add, and subtract and have a configurable number of pipeline stages. It furthermore has several 18 Kb block memories that can be used in dual-port mode. The LUTs of the Artix-7 can either be used as 6-input LUTs or

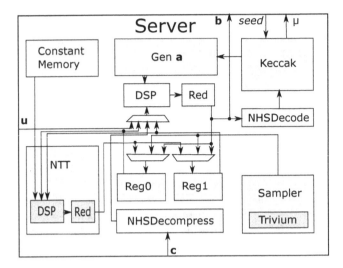

Fig. 1. Our server architecture

5-input LUTs with two outputs. Figures 1 and 2 provide an overview of our server architecture and the client architecture. We incorporated two read/write-BRAM blocks with a width of 14 bits and a depth of $n = 1024$ in dual-port mode to store polynomials ($Reg0$ and $Reg1$). Two read-only memories are used to store the twiddle factors used in the NTT. One DSP block with subsequent modular reduction serves as general-purpose DSP that is used in most sub-modules, like the NTT or the point-wise multiplication.

The client and the server side of the scheme contain almost the same set of operations. However there are slight differences, for instance the decoding operation is replaced by an encoding and the decompression is replaced by a compression module. We decided to develop two separate modules for the server and the client side as we expect an embedded device to usually be either server or client but not both. Applications that require both sides can share many of the components, like the NTT or the sampler. A neat solution for such an applications could be to replace the components that are required by only one side through dynamic partial reconfiguration. In Algorithm 1 we present the temporal structure of our implementation in pseudocode. Each line of Algorithm 1 lists operations that are executed simultaneously. All operations are constant-time, i.e. the execution time is independent from data that is processed and thus the implementation is invulnerable to timing attacks. We employed the modular reduction from [19] for the prime $q = 12289$.

3.2 Efficient Implementation of NTT

The optimized NTT approach from [22] uses a Cooley-Tukey butterfly for the forward transformation and a Gentleman-Sande butterfly for the backwards transformation. A butterfly takes two coefficients as input and combines them

Algorithm 1. Pseudocode for our implementation. Operations in the same line are executed simultaneously.

```
procedure NewHope(Registers R0, R1)
    Server-side computations:
    R0←Sample()
    R0←NTT(R0); R1←Sample()
    R1←NTT(R1)
    R1←Parse(SHAKE-128(seed)) ∘ R0 + R1
    Transmit seed and b̂ = R1
    Client-side computations:
    R0←Sample()
    R0←NTT(R0); R1←Sample()
    R1←NTT(R1)
    R1←Parse(SHAKE-128(seed)) ∘ R0 + R1
    Transmit û = R1
    R0←R0 ∘ b̂
    R0←NTT^-1(R0); R1←Sample()
    R0←NHSCompress(R0 + R1 + NHSEncode(ν')); ν'←SHA3-256(random)
    μ←SHA3-256(ν')
    Transmit c̄ = R0
    Server-side computations:
    R0←û ∘ R0
    R0←NHSDecompress(c̄) − NTT^-1(R0)
    μ←SHA3-256(NHSDecode(R0))
end procedure
```

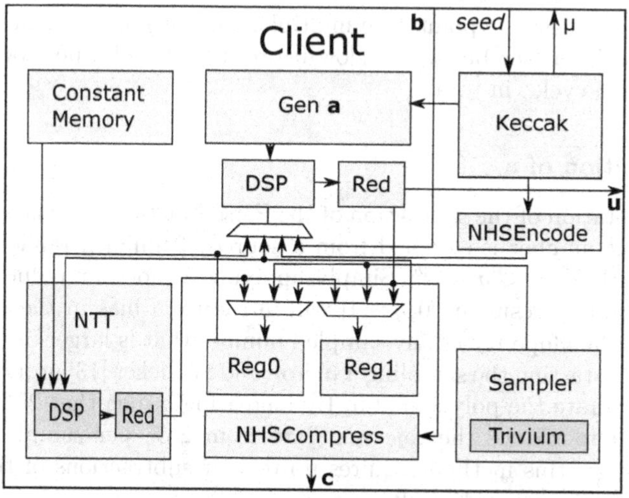

Fig. 2. Our client architecture

according to the butterfly instructions. As the transformation operates in-place, it outputs two coefficients that replace the input coefficients. Both butterfly constructions can be computed with a regular Artix-7 DSP block. To accelerate the butterfly computation, we use two DSP blocks and compute both output coefficients in parallel. We use the multi-purpose DSP of our NewHope-Simple core and add another DSP to the NTT core. As the lattice dimension in NewHope-Simple is $n = 1024$, the computation of the NTT could be further parallelized, i.e. up to 512 butterflies could be computed in parallel. However, this would require more DSPs and a complicated memory scheduling as we can only access two coefficients at the same time with a dual-port memory block. Therefore we decided to compute the butterflies serially to keep the area consumption of the implementation low. The only other difference between the forward and the backward transformation is the address generation for the memory blocks storing the input coefficients. Hence minimal changes to the state machine allow our NTT core to be able to perform both operations, the forward and the backward transformation. The computation of a butterfly takes 7 clock cycles that consist of 2 cycles for the memory access, 1 cycle for the DSP calculation and 4 cycles for the modular reduction. In total, $\frac{n}{2} \log(n)$ butterfly computation per transformation are necessary, therefore $512 \cdot 10 \cdot 7 = 35,840$ cycles.

3.3 Point-Wise Multiplication

Our implementation of the point-wise multiplication is straight-forward. We use the multi-purpose DSP of our NewHope-Simple core with subsequent modular reduction to serially compute the product of two coefficients. Therefore the point-wise multiplication is a simple counter to access the coefficients of the polynomials to be multiplied iteratively. A point-wise multiplication of two coefficients takes 9 cycles. It could be sped up to take only 7 cycles like a butterfly operation but to keep the point-wise multiplication in sync with the generation of the polynomial **a** (see below) we slow it down to 9 cycles per coefficient, i.e. $1024 \cdot 9 = 9,216$ cycles in total.

3.4 Generation of a

The implementation of the generation of the Parse function is a challenging task. Usually a b-bit number is sampled from a source of uniform randomness for a modulus q with $2^{b-1} < q < 2^b$. Simply applying a modular reduction to this number to obtain a result in $[0, q-1]$ will introduce a bias in the result. Thus the authors of NewHope reject any sampled number that is larger or equal to the modulus and restarting the sampling. Gueron and Schlieker [13] proposed a faster method to generate the polynomial **a**. By increasing b such that $2^{b-1} < 5q < 2^b$ they managed to reduce the rejection rate from 25% per sample to 6% per sample. However, this method requires up to four subtractions of the modulus q to get a properly reduced result.

We avoided these subtractions and sampled $\lceil \log_2 12289 \rceil = 14$ bits for our implementation. But we still want to achieve a lower rejection rate.

Thus we perform one execution of SHAKE-128 that gives us 1344 bits of pseudo-randomness. Three processes analyze this randomness buffer word-by-word in parallel and store 14-bit words that are smaller than the modulus in a buffer. As 96 14-bit words fit into the 1344-bit output of SHAKE-128, the probability that less than three words are found that are smaller than the modulus is $0.25^{96} + 96 \cdot 0.75 \cdot 0.25^{95} + \frac{96 \cdot 95}{2} \cdot 0.75^2 \cdot 0.25^{94} \approx 2^{-178}$ and can therefore be neglected.

To generate the 1344-bit output of SHAKE-128 we need 27 cycles. As the point-wise multiplication takes 9 cycles, we can run it three times during the execution of SHAKE-128. Therefore, the runtime of the generation of a is equal to the runtime of the point-wise multiplication, i.e. $9,216$ cycles.

3.5   Binomial Sampling

We implemented a binomial sampler that counts the Hamming weight of two k-bit vectors and subtracts theses Hamming weights. The required randomness is generated by a Trivium PRNG [19] that outputs one bit per clock cycle. This implementation of Trivium uses a fixed seed that in practice would have to be generated from a secure random number generator. However, true random number generators in FPGAs is a research field on its own and out of scope for this work. As $k = 16$ the generation of a binomial distributed sample takes 33 cycles and thus $33,792$ cycles for an entire polynomial. More instances of the Trivium PRNG would accelerate the generation of the samples. However, we refrained from applying this optimization to keep the implementation small. Only the generation of the first error polynomial of each party has an influence on the performance as the remaining error polynomials can be generated during other computations (like the NTT). One possible optimization would be to perform the generation of the first error polynomial in an offline computation so that every time a key exchange is triggered, an error polynomial is already available.

3.6   Hash Function

NewHope-Simple requires the instantiation of a hash function and an extendable output function. Thus our design contains a Keccak core that is able to compute both, SHA3-256 and SHAKE-128. Our implementation of Keccak executes one round per clock cycle. To synchronize it with the generation of a, we slow it down to take 27 cycles for the entire 24 rounds of Keccak.

3.7   Compression

The compression function as described in [1] requires a division by q. However, as the modulus q is fixed and the result is limited to [0,8], we precompute the thresholds at which the result of the division changes and use a simple multiplexer cascade to implement the division. By doing so we obtain the compressed result in two clock cycles. Similarly, the decompression requires a multiplication by q. Again, we use multiplexers as the input is limited to [0,7].

4   Results and Comparison

In this chapter, we discuss the results of our implementation and compare it with others.

4.1   Evaluation Methodology

We implemented `NewHope-Simple` for a Xilinx Artix-7 FPGA with the part number XC7A35TCPG236. Our development environment was Xilinx Vivado v2015.3. If not stated otherwise all results were obtained after post-place and route (Post-PAR).

4.2   Results

We optimized our implementation for area-efficiency. Our implementation takes 1,483 slices, 4,498 LUTs, and 4,635 FFs for the client and 1,708 slices, 5,142 LUTs, and 4,452 FFs for the server. We restricted our design to two DSPs to address a use-case for moderate throughput. Note that the use of additional DSPs will lead to a considerable speed-up. Our implementation uses four 18 Kb block memories, two for the NTT twiddle factors and two as temporary storage for intermediate polynomials. The overall runtime of 350,416 cycles is divided into 115,784 cycles for the first set of server-side operations, 179,292 cycles for the client-side operations, and 55,340 cycles for the second set of server-side operations. The client-side design was successfully placed and routed with a maximum frequency of 117 MHz. The maximum path delay is 8.037 ns and is

Table 1. This table presents the exact cycle counts for our implementation. The line numbers given in the table refer to the line numbers of Algorithm 1 and are followed by a short summary of the respective step.

Operations (server)	Cycles	Operations (client)	Cycles
Line 3: Sampling	33,794	Line 10: Sampling	33,794
Line 4: Sampling + NTT	35,843	Line 11: NTT + Sampling	35,843
Line 5: NTT	35,845	Line 12: NTT	35,845
Line 6: Parse+Multiplication	9,277	Line 13: Parse + Multiplication	9,277
Line 7: Output $\hat{b}$	1,025	Line 14: Output $\hat{u}$	1,025
Total	**115,784**	Line 15: Multiplication	9,220
		Line 16: Inverse NTT+Sampling	35,845
Line 22: Multiplication	9,219	Line 16: Multiplication with n^{-1}	9,221
Line 23: Inverse NTT	35,845	Line 17-19: Encode + Output $\bar{c}$	9,219
Line 23: Multiplication with n^{-1}	9,219	**Total**	**179,292**
Line 24: Decode	1,028		
Line 25: Hashing	29		
Total	**55,340**		

located between the DSP output and the modular reduction. The server-side design achieved a slightly better performance and was successfully placed and routed with a frequency of 125 MHz. In this case the maximum path delay is 7.179 ns and located between the output of the modular reduction and the input of the BRAM. The actual cycle counts for our implementation are listed in Table 1.

4.3   Comparison

To the best of our knowledge, this is the first hardware implementation of NewHope or NewHope-Simple. Hence, a comparison with previous work is somewhat difficult. We therefore add references to works that implement basic encryption schemes, such as ring-LWE or lattice-based IBE. Table 2 summarizes our results and previous related work. However, please note again that a straight comparison of the presented schemes is neither fair nor possible, for the following reasons:

- **Parameter sizes.** When comparing the implementations we have to consider that in our implementation the lattice dimension is $n = 1024$ while most other implementations use $n = 512$ or even $n = 256$. The lattice dimension n determines how much memory is needed to store polynomials. It furthermore has a linear influence on the run time of every module beside the Keccak core. The NTT is even slowed down by a factor of 2.22. when increasing n from 512 to 1024.
- **Additional components.** The implementation of NewHope-Simple requires a number of components that are not present in ring-LWE, standard-LWE, and IBE. Especially NHSCompress, NHSDecompress, SHA3-256, and SHAKE-128 are required by NewHope-Simple only and thus lead to a higher resource consumption.
- **Key generation.** The NewHope-Simple protocol basically performs all three ring-LWE operations: key generation, encryption, decryption. The works of [14,15,24] only present implementations of the encryption and the decryption. Thus, the cost of the key generation would have to be added first for a fair comparison.
- **Precomputation.** NewHope-Simple requires the on-the-fly generation of the public polynomial a, while previous work usually assumes that a is a global constant and is thus treated as precomputed value. In contrast to that, NewHope-Simple requires the implementation of a Parse function. Furthermore, to minimize the communication cost, both parties have to generate a while in lattice-based encryption schemes, a is usually generated only once during the key generation if not assumed to be a global constant anyway. Thus, we have to spend additional cycles and FPGA resources to meet the requirement of generating a on-the-fly.
- **Security level.** The authors of NewHope-Simple claim a security level of 255 bits against known quantum attackers [2] while the works on ring-LWE have a much lower security level of 131 bits against known quantum attackers [17].

The work of Roy et al. [24] further reduces the security as they limit the secret key to have binary coefficients instead of Gaussian distributed coefficients without discussing the implications on the security level. Such a limitation has a huge impact on the performance as a polynomial multiplication can be replaced by simple additions. We decided to stick to the recommendations of [2] as we do not want to lower the security level significantly. The parameters for lattice-based IBE are chosen to have a 80-bit resp. 192-bit security level against *classical* attackers.

Considering the aforementioned factors, our implementation compares well to other lattice-based schemes. Further optimization might even lead to a smaller implementation or better performance.

Table 2. Our implementation results in comparison with implementations of similar schemes. The first row denotes the server-side operations for key exchange and encryption for encryption schemes. The second row denotes the client-side operation for key exchange and decryption for encryption schemes. If only one of the two rows contains numbers for the resource consumption, the authors of the respective work present a combined implementation for both operations. The clock frequency is given in MHz.

Implementation	Clock	(LUT-FF-BRAM-DSP)	Cycles
NewHope-Simple (XC7A35T, **this work**)	125	(5,142 - 4,452 - 4 - 2)	171,124
(1024/12289)	117	(4,498 - 4,635 - 4 - 2)	179,292
IBE (S6LX25, [14])	174	(7,023 - 6,067 - 16 - 4)	13,958
(512/16813057)			9,530
IBE (S6LX25, [14])	174	(8,882 - 8,686 - 27 - 4)	28,586
(1024/134348801)			19,535
ring-LWE (V6LX75T, [20])	251	(5,595 - 4,760 - 14 - 1)	13,769
(512/12289)			8,883
ring-LWE (V6LX75T, [24])	278	(1,536 - 953 - 3 - 1)	13,300
(512/12289)			5,800
standard-LWE (S6LX45, [15])	125	(6,078 - 4,676 - 73 - 1)	98,304
(256/4096)	144	(63 - 58 - 13 - 1)	32,768

5   Conclusion

In this work, we presented the first implementation of the NewHope-Simple key exchange. The scheme is arguably one of the most promising candidates for quantum-secure key exchange. Hence, we expect a high interest in an instantiation of NewHope-Simple in hardware. We demonstrate that NewHope-Simple is well suited for implementations on constrained hardware devices and still maintains a decent performance on available platforms.

For future work, we plan to further improve the performance of the implementation. Especially the NTT could benefit from some ideas that Roy et al. incorporated in their implementation of ring-LWE [24]. Furthermore an in-depth analysis of side-channel vulnerabilities of the scheme is required before NewHope hardware accelerators could be deployed in the field. Due to the ephemeral nature of the scheme, an attacker is limited to a single execution to gain side-channel information. Nevertheless, simple power analysis or template attacks should be considered.

References

1. Alkim, E., Ducas, L., Pöppelmann, T., Schwabe, P.: NewHope without reconciliation (2016). http://cryptojedi.org/papers/#newhopesimple
2. Alkim, E., Ducas, L., Pöppelmann, T., Schwabe, P.: Post-quantum key exchange - a new hope. In: Proceedings of the 25th USENIX Security Symposium. USENIX Association (2016), document ID: 0462d84a3d34b12b75e8f5e4ca032869. http://cryptojedi.org/papers/#newhope
3. Alkim, E., Ducas, L., Pppelmann, T., Schwabe, P.: Post-quantum key exchange - a new hope. Cryptology ePrint Archive, Report 2015/1092 (2015). http://eprint.iacr.org/2015/1092
4. Alkim, E., Jakubeit, P., Schwabe, P.: A new hope on ARM cortex-m. IACR Cryptology ePrint Archive 2016, 758 (2016). http://eprint.iacr.org/2016/758
5. Batina, L., Robshaw, M. (eds.): Cryptographic Hardware and Embedded Systems - CHES 2014–16th International Workshop, Busan, South Korea, 23–26 September 2014. Proceedings, LNCS, vol. 8731. Springer (2014)
6. Bauer, B., Wecker, D., Millis, A.J., Hastings, M.B., Troyer, M.: Hybrid quantum-classical approach to correlated materials. Phys. Rev. X **6**(3), 031045 (2016)
7. Bos, J., et al.: Frodo: take off the ring! practical, quantum-secure key exchange from LWE. In: Proceedings of the 2016 ACM SIGSAC Conference on Computer and Communications Security. pp. 1006–1018. ACM (2016)
8. Bos, J.W., Costello, C., Naehrig, M., Stebila, D.: Post-quantum key exchange for the TLS protocol from the ring learning with errors problem. In: 2015 IEEE Symposium on Security and Privacy, SP 2015, San Jose, CA, USA, 17–21 May 2015. pp. 553–570. IEEE Computer Society (2015). https://doi.org/10.1109/SP.2015.40
9. Braithwaite, M.: Experimenting with post-quantum cryptography. Google Security Blog 7 (2016)
10. del Pino, R., Lyubashevsky, V., Pointcheval, D.: The whole is less than the sum of its parts: constructing more efficient lattice-based AKEs. In: Zikas, V., De Prisco, R. (eds.) SCN 2016. LNCS, vol. 9841, pp. 273–291. Springer, Cham (2016). https://doi.org/10.1007/978-3-319-44618-9_15
11. Ding, J.: A simple provably secure key exchange scheme based on the learning with errors problem. IACR Cryptology ePrint Archive 2012, 688 (2012). http://eprint.iacr.org/2012/688
12. Gathen, J.V.Z., Gerhard, J.: Modern Computer Algebra, 2nd edn. Cambridge University Press, New York (2003)
13. Gueron, S., Schlieker, F.: Speeding up R-LWE post-quantum key exchange. IACR Cryptology ePrint Archive 2016, 467 (2016). http://eprint.iacr.org/2016/467

14. Güneysu, T., Oder, T.: Towards lightweight identity-based encryption for the post-quantum-secure internet of things. In: 18th International Symposium on Quality Electronic Design, ISQED 2017, Santa Clara, CA, USA, 14–15 March 2017. pp. 319–324. IEEE (2017). https://doi.org/10.1109/ISQED.2017.7918335

15. Howe, J., Moore, C., O'Neill, M., Regazzoni, F., Güneysu, T., Beeden, K.: Standard lattices in hardware. In: Proceedings of the 53rd Annual Design Automation Conference, DAC 2016, Austin, TX, USA, 5–9 June 2016. pp. 162:1–162:6. ACM (2016). https://doi.org/10.1145/2897937.2898037

16. National Institute of Standards and Technology: Submission requirements and evaluation criteria for the post-quantum cryptography standardization process (2016). http://csrc.nist.gov/groups/ST/post-quantum-crypto/documents/call-for-proposals-final-dec-2016.pdf

17. Oder, T., Schneider, T., Pppelmann, T., Gneysu, T.: Practical CCA2-secure and masked ring-LWE implementation. Cryptology ePrint Archive, Report 2016/1109 (2016). http://eprint.iacr.org/2016/1109

18. Peikert, C.: Lattice cryptography for the internet. In: Mosca, M. (ed.) PQCrypto 2014. LNCS, vol. 8772, pp. 197–219. Springer, Cham (2014). https://doi.org/10.1007/978-3-319-11659-4_12

19. Pöppelmann, T., Ducas, L., Güneysu, T.: Enhanced lattice-based signatures on reconfigurable hardware. In: Batina and Robshaw [5], pp. 353–370

20. Pöppelmann, T., Güneysu, T.: Towards practical lattice-based public-key encryption on reconfigurable hardware. In: Lange, T., Lauter, K., Lisoněk, P. (eds.) SAC 2013. LNCS, vol. 8282, pp. 68–85. Springer, Heidelberg (2014). https://doi.org/10.1007/978-3-662-43414-7_4

21. Pöppelmann, T., Güneysu, T.: Area optimization of lightweight lattice-based encryption on reconfigurable hardware. In: IEEE International Symposium on Circuits and Systems, ISCAS 2014, Melbourne, Victoria, Australia, 1–5 June 2014. pp. 2796–2799. IEEE (2014). https://doi.org/10.1109/ISCAS.2014.6865754

22. Pöppelmann, T., Oder, T., Güneysu, T.: High-performance ideal lattice-based cryptography on 8-Bit ATxmega microcontrollers. In: Lauter, K., Rodríguez-Henríquez, F. (eds.) LATINCRYPT 2015. LNCS, vol. 9230, pp. 346–365. Springer, Cham (2015). https://doi.org/10.1007/978-3-319-22174-8_19

23. PQCRYPTO-EU-project: TU Eindhoven leads multi-million euro project to protect data against quantum computers (2016). https://pqcrypto.eu.org/press/press-release-post-quantum-cryptography-ENGLISH.docx

24. Roy, S.S., Vercauteren, F., Mentens, N., Chen, D.D., Verbauwhede, I.: Compact Ring-LWE cryptoprocessor. In: Batina and Robshaw 5, pp. 371–391

Cryptanalysis

Theoretical Security Evaluation Against Side-Channel Cube Attack with Key Enumeration

Haruhisa Kosuge[(✉)] and Hidema Tanaka

National Defence Academy of Japan, Yokosuka, Japan
{ed16005,hidema}@nda.ac.jp

Abstract. Side-channel cube attack (SCCA) is executed in a situation where an adversary can access some information about the internal states of the cipher. The adversary can obtain a system of linear equations by a set of chosen plaintexts called cube and recover the secret key using the system. Error tolerance is a challenging problem in SCCA. To recover the secret key based on likelihoods under an error-prone environment, we propose SCCA with key enumeration (SCCA-KE). Precise likelihoods are computed to obtain lists for sub-key candidates and an optimal list for the complete key candidate is generated by key enumeration. Then, we propose an evaluation method for SCCA-KE which includes information-theoretic evaluation and experimental evaluation by rank estimation. We apply the proposed evaluation method to PRESENT and show some conditions required to thwart SCCA-KE in realistic assumptions. Using the evaluation method, we can consider countermeasures with a sufficient security margin.

Keywords: Block cipher · Side-channel attack ·
Side-channel cube attack · Key enumeration · Rank estimation ·
Guessing entropy · PRESENT

1 Introduction

1.1 Background

Conventionally, security of block ciphers is analyzed under an assumption that an adversary is given a black-box access to cryptosystems. However, security of cryptographic devices against side-channel attacks can not be assured by the analysis. In contrast to side-channel attacks to recover the secret key directly from leaked values (internal states of the cipher) [12], some attacks which exploit an algebraic structure of block cipher (algebraic attacks) are proposed [21,26]. Side-channel cube attack (SCCA) is also an algebraic attack proposed by Dinur and Shamir [8]. SCCA can overcome protections on the first round function such as random delay [27], since the attack exploits internal states passing through multiple round functions. Also, SCCA can recover the secret key under an assumption

© Springer Nature Switzerland AG 2019
T. Lange and O. Dunkelman (Eds.): LATINCRYPT 2017, LNCS 11368, pp. 145–165, 2019.
https://doi.org/10.1007/978-3-030-25283-0_8

that the adversary can access small information of bits of internal states. In this paper, we study SCCA as a theoretical evaluation. In the evaluation, it is assumed that the adversary can access only 1-bit information of internal states. Even in such condition, the adversary can recover the secret key using a set of chosen plaintexts called *cube*. Obviously there are more advantageous bits (containing many information on the secret key) than other ones. As an *evaluator* (of which the goal is to analyze security of his cryptographic device), it is important to locate such advantageous bits, since he can take countermeasures efficiently.

In SCCA, a measured value is represented by a multivariate polynomial with variables of secret-key and plaintext bits. From the polynomial, the adversary attempts to obtain a linear equation by a cube. Using multiple cubes, he can obtain a system of linear equations. Cubes can be searched by computer experiments (*cube search*). In an error-free environment, he can recover the secret key if the number of independent equations is more than or equal to the one of the variables (secret-key bits).

If the measurements are prone to error, the analysis becomes complicated. There are two error models which suppose binary erasure channel (BEC model) [8] and binary symmetric channel (BSC model) [14]. In this paper, we investigate SCCA under BSC model. BSC model assumes that a measured value is different from the correct value with a crossover probability ρ. In CHES2013, Li et al. proposed an attack using maximum likelihood decoding (ML decoding) [14]. We call the attack *previous method*.

1.2   Contribution

First, we propose a new algorithm, SCCA with *key enumeration* [24] (SCCA-KE), which takes divide-and-conquer strategy (DC strategy) in a similar way to the previous method. In the previous method, lists for sub-key candidates (*sub lists*) are sorted by hamming distance from measured values; however, such sub lists are not enumerated based on precise likelihoods (the method is not based on ML decoding). In SCCA-KE, precise likelihoods are computed to construct optimal sub lists. Then, an optimal list for the secret-key (complete key) candidates is generated from the sub lists by key enumeration [24]. Using the optimal list, the number of times to test candidates is minimized.

Next, we propose an evaluation method for SCCA-KE. In the beginning, brute-force search for cubes of relatively small sizes is executed. Based on the searched cubes, two evaluations are executed, information-theoretic evaluation and experimental evaluation by *rank estimation* [25]. The former evaluation is to obtain a lower bound of *guessing entropy* which is equal to an expected time complexity. The latter evaluation is to obtain a success rate of SCCA-KE. Rank estimation is an evaluation method to estimate a time complexity of key enumeration. Note that we use a rank estimation algorithm proposed by Glowacz et al. [10] for its efficiency and preciseness. We set t_{adv} as the number of secret-key candidates which the adversary can test (it indicates his computing power). If a lower bound of guessing entropy is sufficiently larger than t_{adv}, the evaluator can assure security. Also, t_{adv} is a threshold in the experimental evaluation.

If a rank is lower than t_{adv}, the attack is regarded as successful. We execute the experiment a sufficient number of times to obtain a reliable success rate.

We apply the proposed evaluation method to PRESENT [4]. In the evaluations, we set $t_{adv} = 2^{60}$ and the number of leaked values is $q_{adv} = 2^{15}$ at most. We consider three *leakage models*, single bit [28], least significant bit (LSB) of hamming weight (HW) of 8-bit internal state [14] and LSB of HW of 4-bit internal state. Note that HW is in binary representation and 4 or 8-bit internal state corresponds to a register size. We obtain lower bounds of guessing entropy and success rates by changing crossover probability ρ.

As a result of the evaluation in PRESENT, we conclude that intensive protections for the second and third round are required to thwart SCCA-KE under $t_{adv} = 2^{60}$ and $q_{adv} = 2^{15}$. If it is difficult, noise insertion to achieve $\rho \geq 0.4$ is required. In this way, the evaluation method contributes to an efficient evaluation for SCCA in various settings, and the evaluator can consider a countermeasure with a sufficient security margin.

Notations. We use bold fonts for vectors, sans serif ones for functions and calligraphic ones for sets or lists (list is a set of elements with order).

2   Side-Channel Cube Attack

2.1   Outline of Side-Channel Cube Attack [7]

A side-channel leakage is represented by a nonlinear multivariate polynomial whose variables are plaintext and secret-key bits (we call *plaintext* and *secret-key variables*). The adversary can obtain a linear equation by a set of chosen plaintexts called *cube*. If he has a sufficient number of linear equations whose terms include secret-key variables, he can recover their values with trivial complexity in an error-free environment. Note that it is not trivial if measurements are prone to error (see Sect. 2.2).

Let $f : \mathbb{F}_2^M \times \mathbb{F}_2^N \to \mathbb{F}_2$ be a multivariate polynomial of plaintext variables $\mathbf{v} = (v_1, v_2, ..., v_M) \in \mathbb{F}_2^M$ and secret-key variables $\mathbf{k} = (k_1, k_2, ..., k_N) \in \mathbb{F}_2^N$. We define a cube by an index set of plaintext variables $\mathcal{I} \subset \{1, 2, ..., M\}$. Using a term $\prod_{i \in \mathcal{I}} v_i$ called *maxterm*, f is divided into two polynomials:

$$f(\mathbf{v}, \mathbf{k}) = \left(\prod_{i \in \mathcal{I}} v_i\right) \cdot q_{\mathcal{I}}(\mathbf{v}, \mathbf{k}) + r(\mathbf{v}, \mathbf{k}), \tag{1}$$

where $q_{\mathcal{I}}$ is called *superpoly* of $\mathcal{I}$, and r is a polynomial in which there is no term divisible by $\prod_{i \in \mathcal{I}} v_i$.

We denote a cube by $\mathcal{C}_{\mathcal{I}}$ such that plaintext variables indexed by $\mathcal{I}$ take all possible combinations and the other plaintext variables are 0 (constant), e.g., $\mathcal{C}_{\{0,1\}} = \{(0, 0, ..., 0), (1, 0, ..., 0), (0, 1, ..., 0), (1, 1, ..., 0)\}$. Note that we call $|\mathcal{I}|$ as *cube size*. Then, we have:

$$q_{\mathcal{I}}'(\mathbf{k}) = \bigoplus_{\mathbf{v} \in \mathcal{C}_{\mathcal{I}}} f(\mathbf{v}, \mathbf{k}), \tag{2}$$

where $q'_\mathcal{I}(\mathbf{k}) = q_\mathcal{I}(\mathbf{v}, \mathbf{k})$ such that any plaintext variable included in $q'_\mathcal{I}(\mathbf{v}, \mathbf{k})$ is 0, e.g., if $q_\mathcal{I}(\mathbf{v}, \mathbf{k}) = k_1 k_2 \oplus v_1 k_3$ and $1 \notin \mathcal{I}$ then $q'_\mathcal{I}(\mathbf{k}) = k_1 k_2$. In this way, a value of right-hand side (RHS) of a superpoly $q'_\mathcal{I}$ is obtained by the summation of $f(\mathbf{v}, \mathbf{k})$. If the following two conditions hold, the adversary can recover the key efficiently.

1. $q'_\mathcal{I}$ is not a constant polynomial: If $q'_\mathcal{I}(\mathbf{k})$ is constant for a sufficient large number of randomly chosen $\mathbf{k}$, $q'_\mathcal{I}$ is regarded as a constant polynomial and rejected.
2. $q'_\mathcal{I}$ is a linear polynomial: Linearity test known as BLR test [3] is used. When the following equation holds for a sufficient large number of randomly chosen $\mathbf{k}^o$ and $\mathbf{k}^{o'}$, $q'_\mathcal{I}$ is regarded as a linear function and accepted.

$$q'_\mathcal{I}(\mathbf{k}^o) \oplus q'_\mathcal{I}(\mathbf{k}^{o'}) \oplus q'_\mathcal{I}(\mathbf{0}) = q'_\mathcal{I}(\mathbf{k}^o \oplus \mathbf{k}^{o'}), \tag{3}$$

where $\mathbf{0}$ denotes a secret-key whose values are all 0.

We call the tests to check the above conditions as *cube test* and $q'_\mathcal{I}(\mathbf{k})$ is generally computed for 100 times to obtain reliable cubes [8].

Let $x_\mathbf{v} = f(\mathbf{v}, \mathbf{k})$ be a leaked value. Suppose that the adversary obtains a system of L linear equations by using L cubes as follows.

$$a_{1,1} \cdot k_1 \oplus a_{1,2} \cdot k_2 \oplus ... \oplus a_{1,n} \cdot k_n = x_1$$
$$a_{2,1} \cdot k_1 \oplus a_{2,2} \cdot k_2 \oplus ... \oplus a_{1,n} \cdot k_n = x_2$$
$$\vdots$$
$$a_{L,1} \cdot k_1 \oplus a_{L,2} \cdot k_2 \oplus ... \oplus a_{L,n} \cdot k_n = x_L \tag{4}$$

Note that $a_{i,j} \in \mathbb{F}_2$ ($i \in \{1, 2, ..., L\}$, $j \in \{1, 2, ..., n\}$) is a coefficient of i-th linear equation. A RHS value x_i is obtained by $x_i = \bigoplus_{\mathbf{v} \in \mathcal{C}_{\mathcal{I}_i}} x_\mathbf{v} \oplus q'_{\mathcal{I}_i}(\mathbf{0})$ $(= q'_{\mathcal{I}_i}(\mathbf{k}) \oplus q'_{\mathcal{I}_i}(\mathbf{0}))$, where $q'_{\mathcal{I}_i}(\mathbf{0})$ is a constant. If the number of independent equations is more than or equal to the one of secret-key variables n, $\mathbf{k}$ is uniquely recovered.

Generally, not all secret-key variables are obtained from a system of linear equations, since there are remaining variables for which the adversary has no information. Let $\mathbf{sk}$ ($= \mathbf{k} || \mathbf{rk}$) and $\mathbf{rk}$ be the complete N-bit variables and n'-bit remaining variables, respectively ($N = n + n'$ is the secret-key length).

2.2   Error-Tolerant Side-Channel Cube Attack

In SCCA, there are many works which assume that measurements are error-free [1,9,11,28,29]; therefore, error tolerance is not well studied. This is the drawback of the entire study for SCCA. We adopt BSC model [14] to study error-tolerance of SCCA. In BSC model, each measured value $y_\mathbf{v}$ follows crossover probability $\rho = Pr[x_\mathbf{v} \oplus y_\mathbf{v} = 1] = 1/2 - \mu$ ($x_\mathbf{v}$ is a correct value). Using piling-up lemma [19], crossover probability for $x_i = \bigoplus_{\mathbf{v} \in \mathcal{C}_{\mathcal{I}_i}} x_\mathbf{v} \oplus q'_{\mathcal{I}_i}(\mathbf{0})$ is obtained as [14]:

$$p_i = Pr[x_i \oplus y_i = 1] = \frac{1}{2} - 2^{|\mathcal{C}_{\mathcal{I}_i}|-1} \mu^{|\mathcal{C}_{\mathcal{I}_i}|}, \tag{5}$$

where $y_i = \bigoplus_{\mathbf{v} \in \mathcal{C}_{\mathcal{I}_i}} y_{\mathbf{v}} \oplus q'_{\mathcal{I}_i}(0)$ is obtained by summation of measured values of $y_{\mathbf{v}}$. Note that we call $\mathbf{x}$ (resp. $\mathbf{y}$) a vector of correct (resp. measured) RHS values.

2.3   Previous Method for BSC Model [14]

In order to recover n-bit secret-key variables from a system of linear equations of Eq. (4) under BSC model with crossover probability p_i ($i \in \{1, 2, ..., L\}$), the authors of [14] proposed a method based on ML decoding (previous method). The key-recovery problem can be reduced to a decoding problem of $[L,n]$ linear block code following the idea of Siegenthaler's cryptanalysis of stream ciphers [22].

Let $A = (a_{i,j})$ ($i \in \{1, 2, ..., L\}$, $j \in \{1, 2, ..., n\}$) be $L \times n$ matrix (a generator matrix of $[L,n]$ linear block code), and $\mathbf{a}_i$ be i-th column vector of A. A correct RHS value is obtained by $x_i = \mathbf{k} \cdot \mathbf{a}_i$, and the adversary is given y_i. We denote a system of linear equations by $(A, \mathbf{k}, \mathbf{x})$ or $(A, \mathbf{k}, \mathbf{y})$. In the previous method, the adversary selects a key candidate $\mathbf{k}^o$ based on the hamming distance $\mathsf{HD}(\mathbf{k}^o)$ as:

$$\arg \min_{\mathbf{k}^o} \mathsf{HD}(\mathbf{k}^o), \quad \mathsf{HD}(\mathbf{k}^o) = \sum_{i=1}^{L} (x_i^o \oplus y_i), \tag{6}$$

where $x_i^o = \mathbf{k}^o \cdot \mathbf{a}_i$. If a crossover probability p_i is constant for any $i \in \{1, 2, ..., L\}$, this decoding algorithm is ML decoding. This algorithm is not ML decoding if p_i is different for $|\mathcal{C}_{\mathcal{I}_i}|$ (see detail in Sect. 3.1).

Since a general decoding problem is NP-complete, time complexity increases exponentially on n. If n is large, it is intractable for the adversary to execute ML decoding. In order to reduce time complexity, the previous method takes DC strategy to divide $\mathbf{k}$ into η sub keys $\{\mathbf{k}_1, \mathbf{k}_2, ..., \mathbf{k}_\eta\}$. Gathering row vectors of A whose variables include at least a variable of $\mathbf{k}_j$, a matrix A_j is defined and a vector of correct (resp. measured) RHS is $\mathbf{x}_j$ (resp. $\mathbf{y}_j$). Hereinafter, $(A_j, \mathbf{k}_j, \mathbf{x}_j)$ or $(A_j, \mathbf{k}_j, \mathbf{y}_j)$ is referred to as *sub system*. The adversary computes hamming distances in each matrix A_j and secret-key variables of sub key $\mathbf{k}_j$.

In order to keep multiple candidates without narrowing down to a single candidate, the method chooses τ_{const} candidates in ascending order by $\mathsf{HD}(\mathbf{k}_j)$ in each sub system of linear equations. Let $\mathcal{T}_{\mathbf{k}_j}$ be a sub list of τ_{const} candidates for $\mathbf{k}_j$. Since $\mathbf{k}$ is reconstructed from η sub keys, the adversary has $(\tau_{const})^\eta$ candidates after the procedures, and we denote a set of the candidates by $\mathcal{T}_{\mathbf{k}}(= \mathcal{T}_{\mathbf{k}_1} \times \mathcal{T}_{\mathbf{k}_2} \times ... \times \mathcal{T}_{\mathbf{k}_\eta})$. Also, there are $2^{n'}$ candidates for the remaining variables $\mathbf{rk}$. We denote a list for $\mathbf{rk}$ as $\mathcal{T}_{\mathbf{rk}}$. The correct key is searched from the candidates of $\mathcal{T}_{\mathbf{k}} \times \mathcal{T}_{\mathbf{rk}}$ ($|\mathcal{T}_{\mathbf{k}} \times \mathcal{T}_{\mathbf{rk}}| = (\tau_{const})^\eta \cdot 2^{n'}$), by using some actual plaintext-ciphertext pairs. Hence, it requires a time complexity $(\tau_{const})^\eta \cdot 2^{n'}$.

The authors recommend to use overlapping sub keys where each vector shares several variables with neighboring vectors. We call the strategy *overlapping* DC strategy. The authors claim that it is possible to reduce time complexity since only candidates that agree in the overlapping secret-key variables are tested in overlapping DC strategy.

3   Side-Channel Cube Attack with Key Enumeration

We consider SCCA-KE under BSC model. SCCA-KE is applicable if a conditional probability distribution of leaked values given a key candidate, i.e., $Pr[\mathbf{y}|\mathbf{k}]$, is approximated. Note that asymmetric crossover probability ($Pr[y_i = 0|x_i = 1] \neq Pr[y_i = 1|x_i = 0]$) can be handled by SCCA-KE.

3.1   Divide-and-Conquer Strategy and Key Enumeration

Let $\mathcal{T}_{\mathbf{sk}} = \{\mathbf{sk}^1, \mathbf{sk}^2, ..., \mathbf{sk}^\tau\}$ be a list of secret-key candidates which can be obtained by measurements. The adversary tests secret-key candidates from $\mathbf{sk}^1$ to $\mathbf{sk}^\tau$ and disregard other candidates not in $\mathcal{T}_{\mathbf{sk}}$, where τ is determined by his computing power. Likelihood or posterior probability is used to make the list $\mathcal{T}_{\mathbf{sk}}$. We get the same list if a uniform prior distribution can be assumed [15]. In this paper, we use log likelihood for the convenience of implementation.

Taking DC strategy, we use key enumeration to obtain $\mathcal{T}_{\mathbf{sk}}$ from η sub lists $\{\mathcal{T}_{\mathbf{k}_1}, \mathcal{T}_{\mathbf{k}_2}, ..., \mathcal{T}_{\mathbf{k}_\eta}\}$ and a sub list for the remaining variables $\mathcal{T}_{\mathbf{rk}}$. Since there is no information on $\mathbf{rk}$, candidates of $\mathcal{T}_{\mathbf{rk}}$ are randomly sorted (all candidates have the same log likelihood). SCCA-KE uses the following *optimal list* for $\mathbf{k}$.

Definition 1 (optimal list). *Let $\mathbf{y}$ be a vector of RHS values of a system of linear equations obtained by independent measurements. In the list of candidates $\mathcal{T}_{\mathbf{k}} = \{\mathbf{k}_1, \mathbf{k}_2, ..., \mathbf{k}_\tau\}$, the list $\mathcal{T}_{\mathbf{k}}$ is an optimal list of key candidates if the following conditions hold.*
For any (o, o') such that $\mathbf{k}^o, \mathbf{k}^{o'} \in \mathcal{T}_{\mathbf{k}}$ and $o < o'$,

$$\sum_{i=1}^{L} \log_2(Pr[y_i|\mathbf{k}^o]) \geq \sum_{i=1}^{L} \log_2(Pr[y_i|\mathbf{k}^{o'}]), \tag{7}$$

and for any (o, o'') such that $\mathbf{k}^o \in \mathcal{T}_{\mathbf{k}}$, $\mathbf{k}^{o''} \notin \mathcal{T}_{\mathbf{k}}$,

$$\sum_{i=1}^{L} \log_2(Pr[y_i|\mathbf{k}^o]) \geq \sum_{i=1}^{L} \log_2(Pr[y_i|\mathbf{k}^{o''}]). \tag{8}$$

Note that $Pr[y_i|\mathbf{k}^o] = Pr[x_i^o \oplus y_i]$, where $\mathbf{x}^o = (x_1^o, x_2^o, ..., x_L^o) = \mathbf{k}^o \cdot A$. The optimal list is in descending order by log likelihood and all candidates has higher log likelihoods than any candidates not in the optimal list. Obviously, the optimal list can function as ML decoding.

We construct η optimal sub lists $\{\mathcal{T}_{\mathbf{k}_1}, \mathcal{T}_{\mathbf{k}_2}, ..., \mathcal{T}_{\mathbf{k}_\eta}\}$. Note that there is no overlapping variables among sub keys (overlapping DC strategy is not taken). Then, a log likelihood of $\mathbf{k}^o = \mathbf{k}_1^o||\mathbf{k}_2^o||...||\mathbf{k}_\eta^o$ is obtained by:

$$\sum_{j=1}^{\eta} \sum_{i=1}^{L_j} \log_2(Pr[y_{j,i}|\mathbf{k}_j^o]), \tag{9}$$

where L_j is the number of linear equations of j-th sub system. Note that $\mathcal{T}_{\mathbf{rk}}$ is always optimal, since there is no information on $\mathbf{rk}$. Therefore, $\mathcal{T}_{\mathbf{sk}} = \mathcal{T}_{\mathbf{k}} \times \mathcal{T}_{\mathbf{rk}}$ is an optimal list if $\mathcal{T}_{\mathbf{k}}$ is optimal.

In the previous method [14], $\mathcal{T}_{\mathbf{k}}$ is not optimal as follows.

1. If a crossover probability p_i is different for $|\mathcal{C}_{\mathcal{I}_i}|$, a list sorted by hamming distance (see Eq. (5)) is not optimal. In other word, this method is not based on ML decoding. In general, the adversary exploits cubes of various sizes.
2. Since log likelihoods for η sub systems are not independent in the overlapping DC strategy, a total log likelihood is not calculated by simple summation such as Eq. (9). To calculate it, log likelihoods for overlapping sub-key candidates should be subtracted after the summation. No existing key-enumeration algorithm support the calculation.

3.2   Proposed Algorithm

We show a proposed algorithm for SCCA-KE in Algorithm 1. Note that we use a notation $(\mathbf{k}^o, \lambda_{\mathbf{k}^o}) \in \mathcal{U}_{\mathbf{k}}$ instead of $\mathbf{k}^o \in \mathcal{T}_{\mathbf{k}}$, since log likelihoods are used in key enumeration (see Eq. (9)). Algorithm 1 has three steps as follows.

Step-1. A system of linear equations $(A, \mathbf{k}, \mathbf{y})$ is divided into η sub systems. We show a toy example as follows.

$$\left(\begin{pmatrix} 1\,0\,0\,0\,0\,0\,1 \\ 0\,1\,1\,0\,0\,0\,0 \\ 0\,0\,0\,1\,0\,0\,0 \\ 0\,0\,0\,0\,0\,0\,1 \\ 0\,0\,1\,0\,1\,0\,0 \\ 0\,0\,0\,1\,0\,1\,0 \end{pmatrix}, (k_1, k_2, k_3, k_4, k_5, k_6), (y_1, y_2, y_3, y_4, y_5, y_6, y_7, y_8) \right)$$

$$\Rightarrow \left(\begin{pmatrix} 1\,1 \\ 0\,1 \end{pmatrix}, (k_1, k_4), (y_1, y_7) \right), \left(\begin{pmatrix} 1\,1\,0 \\ 0\,1\,1 \end{pmatrix}, (k_2, k_5), (y_2, y_3, y_5) \right), \left(\begin{pmatrix} 1\,0 \\ 1\,1 \end{pmatrix}, (k_3, k_6), (y_4, y_6) \right)$$

Step-2. In each sub system, log likelihoods $\lambda_{\mathbf{k}^o_j}$ of all sub-key candidates are computed. Sub-key candidates and their log likelihoods $(\mathbf{k}^o_j, \lambda_{\mathbf{k}^o_j})$ are stored in $\mathcal{U}_{\mathbf{k}_j}$ in descending order by $\lambda_{\mathbf{k}^o_j}$. As mentioned in Sect. 2.1, there are n' remaining secret-key variables $\mathbf{rk}$; therefore, $\mathcal{U}_{\mathbf{rk}}$ for $\mathbf{rk}$ is prepared. Since there is no information on $\mathbf{rk}$, all sub-key candidates have the same log likelihood $\log_2(2^{-n'}) = -n'$.

Step-3. Using key enumeration, the correct key $\mathbf{sk}^{\psi}$ is searched. Note that the adversary determines τ as the number of candidates to enumerate and test. If the correct key can not be found in τ enumerated candidates, Algorithm 1 fails. Note that the optimal algorithm of [24] is used for KE. If another algorithm is used, $\mathcal{U}_{\mathbf{sk}}$ and $\mathcal{U}_{\mathbf{k}}$ are not optimal (they become sub optimal).

Contrary to the previous method shown in Sect. 3.1, optimal lists are generated in SCCA-KE for the following reasons.

Algorithm 1. Side-channel cube attack with key enumeration (SCCA-KE).

---

input A system of linear equations $(A, \mathbf{k}, \mathbf{y})$.
Divide $(A, \mathbf{k}, \mathbf{y})$ into η sub-systems $(A_j, \mathbf{k}_j, \mathbf{y}_j)$ $(j \in \{1, 2, ..., \eta\})$.
for $j = 1 \rightarrow \eta$ **do**
    for $o = 1 \rightarrow 2^{n_j}$ **do**
        $\mathbf{x}_j^o \leftarrow \mathbf{k}_j^o \cdot A_j$
        $\lambda_{\mathbf{k}_j^o} \leftarrow \sum_{i=1}^{L_j} \log_2(Pr[x_{j,i}^o \oplus y_{j,i}])$ $\triangleright$ $Pr[x_{j,i}^o \oplus y_{j,i}]$ is obtained by Eq.(5).
    end for
    Store all $(\mathbf{k}_j^o, \lambda_{\mathbf{k}_j^o})$ in $\mathcal{U}_{\mathbf{k}_j}$ in descending order by $\lambda_{\mathbf{k}_j^o}$.
end for
Store all $(\mathbf{rk}^o, -n')$ in $\mathcal{U}_{\mathbf{rk}}$ $(o \in \{1, 2, ..., 2^{n'}\})$.
$\mathbf{sk}^\psi \leftarrow \mathsf{KE}(\mathcal{U}_{\mathbf{k}_1}, \mathcal{U}_{\mathbf{k}_2}, ..., \mathcal{U}_{\mathbf{k}_\eta}, \mathcal{U}_{\mathbf{rk}}, \tau)$ $\triangleright$ KE is a key enumeration algorithm of [24].
return $\mathbf{sk}^\psi$ or *"failure"* $\triangleright$ *"failure"* indicates $\mathbf{sk}^\psi$ is not found in τ candidates.

---

1. Log likelihoods of candidates are obtained by considering cube sizes. If a conditional probability distribution for leaked values given a key candidate is well approximated, a list $\mathcal{U}_{\mathbf{k}}$ sorted by log likelihoods is optimal and the secret key can be recovered based on ML-decoding.
2. SCCA-KE does not take the overlapping DC strategy. Therefore, the key enumeration algorithm [24] can be executed to obtain $\mathcal{U}_{\mathbf{k}}$.

3.3 Complexity Estimation

The total complexity for SCCA-KE is estimated as:

$$t = t_{prep} + t_{ke} + \tau,$$
$$m = m_{prep} + m_{ke}, \tag{10}$$

where t_{prep} and t_{ke} (resp. m_{prep} and m_{ke}) are time (resp. memory) complexity for constructing the optimal sub lists (preparation for key enumeration) and execution of key enumeration.

Taking DC strategy, complexity for constructing the sub lists become:

$$t_{prep} = \sum_{j=1}^{\eta} L_j \cdot 2^{n_j},$$
$$m_{prep} = \sum_{j=1}^{\eta} 2^{n_j}, \tag{11}$$

where n_j is the number of variables in a sub system. Note that this computation is required for the evaluation method shown in Sect. 4.3; therefore, it should be tractable in practice. If there is a sub system with large n_j, it is still hard to obtain a sub list. On this point, we have an observation as follows (see Appendix A for its intuitive explanation).

Observation. Suppose that a system of linear equations is divided into η sub systems which do not contain any overlapping variables. The number of secret-key variables n_j is generally small ($j \in \{1, 2, ..., \eta\}$).

This is the observation obtained by experiments on PRESENT (see in Sect. 5.1) and other works [1,11].

Using the optimal algorithm [24], t_{ke} and m_{ke} increase in the number of key candidates to enumerate and test τ. Especially, high memory complexity for key enumeration becomes a practical limitation [5]. In order to reduce complexity for key enumeration, efficient algorithms [5,6,16,17,20] can be used even if they are sub-optimal algorithms.

Since our goal is to propose an evaluation method for SCCA-KE, we only consider time complexity to test key candidates τ. Any key-enumeration algorithm can not achieve a time complexity less than τ; therefore, τ is the lower bound of time complexity. Also, we do not consider memory complexity, since there are sub-optimal algorithms with constant memory complexity. By considering security against SCCA-KE with all key-enumeration algorithms, we only consider the time complexity τ in the security evaluation against SCCA-KE.

4   Evaluation Method for Side-Channel Cube Attack with Key Enumeration

In this section, we propose an evaluation method for SCCA-KE. The evaluator considers the most effective attack to take countermeasures with a sufficient security margin. For any given leaked values which are measured using cubes, SCCA-KE is the most effective (error tolerant) key-recovery method, since it is based on the optimal list of Definition 1. Note that the above statement is true if an approximation of conditional probability distribution $Pr[\mathbf{y}|\mathbf{k}]$ is accurate. We evaluate a security against SCCA-KE under an assumption that the approximation is accurate. The proposed evaluation method has three steps.

Step-1. (Sect. 4.1) Cubes are searched by a computer experiment. The evaluator should simulate any leakage which possibly occurs in his device.

Step-2. (Sect. 4.2) The expected time complexity is information-theoretically estimated. We consider *guessing entropy* which is equal to an expected time complexity. Since guessing entropy is computationally hard to obtain, we compute the lower bound [18], alternatively.

Step-3. (Sect. 4.3) Success rates of attacks are experimentally estimated by rank estimation. The evaluator uses rank estimation instead of key enumeration, since it can efficiently estimate time complexity of the attack. As an efficient and precise algorithm, we use a rank estimation algorithm proposed by Glowacz et al. [10] (see Appendix B).

As mentioned in Sect. 3.3, we assume that the time complexity of SCCA-KE is $t = \tau$ (the number of key candidates to test) and ignore the memory complexity. The evaluator sets a threshold of time complexity t_{adv} which is the number of candidates that the adversary can enumerate and test. The threshold is used in

Step-2 and 3, and it should be determined in light of situations such as future computer technology and usages of the cryptographic device.

4.1 Cube Search

A cube search algorithm has not been established. There are two existing strategies, random-walk search [8,14] and brute-force search [11]. We recommend the evaluator to execute brute-force search, since a sufficient number of trials to find all cubes has not been proven in the current random-walk search.

The brute-force search of cubes executes cube tests $\binom{N}{|\mathcal{I}|}$ times (see Sect. 2.1). A cube test executes a reduced-round cipher function $100 \times 2^{|\mathcal{I}|}$ times to obtain reliable results. We summarize the numbers of trials in Table 1 when $N = 64$.

We claim that it is not necessary to search cubes of large sizes if measurements are error-prone such as $\rho \geq 0.1$. Figure 1 shows relations between crossover probability for RHS p_i and cube size $|\mathcal{I}|$ for $\rho \in (0:0.5]$ (see Eq. (5)). When the crossover probability is $\rho \geq 0.1$, the one for RHS becomes $p_i \approx 0.5$ if a cube of $|\mathcal{I}| > 6$ is used. In the evaluation of PRESENT shown in Sect. 5, we obtain a sufficient condition of ρ (closer to 0.5 than 0.1) to thwart SCCA-KE. Hence, we set a restriction, i.e., $|\mathcal{I}| \leq 6$, in the computer experiment of Sect. 5.1.

4.2 Information-Theoretic Evaluation

As a security metric, guessing entropy [18] was introduced to side-channel attack [13]. We define guessing entropy as follows.

Definition 2 (guessing entropy [18,23]). *Suppose that the adversary obtains a list of candidates* $\mathcal{T}_{\mathbf{sk}} = \{\mathbf{sk}^1, \mathbf{sk}^2, ..., \mathbf{sk}^{2^N}\}$ *given a vector of leaked values* $\mathbf{y}$. *Guessing entropy for the adversary is:*

$$G = \underset{\mathbf{y}}{\mathbb{E}} \underset{\mathbf{sk}^\psi}{\mathbb{E}} [\mathsf{I}(\mathcal{T}_{\mathbf{sk}})], \tag{12}$$

where $\mathsf{I}(\mathcal{T}_{\mathbf{sk}})$ *is an index o such that* $\mathbf{sk}^o \in \mathcal{T}_{\mathbf{sk}}$ *is the correct key* $\mathbf{sk}^\psi$.

Guessing entropy is equal to an expected time complexity for key enumeration (t_{ke} is ignored), since $\mathsf{I}(\mathcal{T}_{\mathbf{sk}})$ indicates the number of times to test candidates until the correct key is found. From the assumption mentioned in Sect. 3.3, an expected time complexity of SCCA-KE is $\mathbb{E}[t] = G$.

In SCCA-KE, guessing entropy G is obtained as [13]:

$$G = \sum_{\mathbf{y}} Pr[\mathbf{y}] \sum_{o=1}^{2^N} o \cdot Pr[\mathbf{sk}^o|\mathbf{y}]$$

$$= 2^{n'} \sum_{\mathbf{y}} Pr[\mathbf{y}] \sum_{o'=1}^{2^n - 1} o' \cdot Pr[\mathbf{k}^{o'}|\mathbf{y}] + \frac{2^{n'} + 1}{2}. \tag{13}$$

It is computationally hard if n is large, since we should compute posterior probabilities of 2^n candidates. We use a lower bound of guessing entropy LG [2] ($G \geq LG$). In SCCA-KE, we can reduce time complexity for LG as follows.

Table 1. The number of trials for the brute-force cube search.

Cube size $|\mathcal{I}|$	#trials
3	$2^{24.99}$
4	$2^{29.92}$
5	$2^{34.51}$
6	$2^{38.80}$
7	$2^{42.85}$
8	$2^{46.69}$

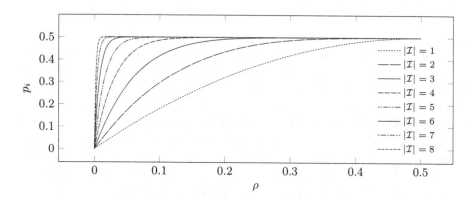

Fig. 1. Cross over probabilities for different cube sizes.

Proposition 1. *In SCCA-KE, we can compute a lower bound of guessing entropy LG as follows.*

$$LG = \frac{1}{1+N} \sum_{\mathbf{y}} \left(\sum_{\mathbf{sk}^\psi} Pr[\mathbf{sk}^\psi, \mathbf{y}]^{\frac{1}{2}} \right)^2$$

$$= \frac{2^{n'}}{1+N} \prod_{j=1}^{\eta} \left(2^{-n_j} \sum_{o=1}^{2^{n_j}} \sum_{\substack{o'=1 \\ o'\neq o}}^{2^{n_j}} \left(\prod_{\substack{i=1 \\ x_{j,i}^o \neq x_{j,i}^{o'}}}^{L_j} 2 \cdot p_{j,i}^{\frac{1}{2}} \cdot (1 - p_{j,i})^{\frac{1}{2}} \right) + 1 \right), \quad (14)$$

where $\mathbf{x}_j^o = \mathbf{k}_j^o \cdot A_j = (x_{j,1}^o, x_{j,2}^o, ..., x_{j,L_j}^o)$ *be a vector of correct RHS values for a sub-key candidate* $\mathbf{k}_j^o$ *and* $p_{j,i} = Pr[x_{j,i}^o \oplus y_{j,i} = 1]$.

See Appendix C for the proof. If sub systems of linear equations $(A_j, \mathbf{k}_j, \mathbf{x}_j)$ are given, Eq. (14) is computed by $\sum_{j=1}^{\eta} L_j \cdot 2^{n_j} \cdot (2^{n_j} - 1)$ times of multiplications. If the observation shown in Sect. 3.3 is correct, the computation is tractable.

The evaluator obtains a lower bound of expected time complexity of SCCA-KE from Eq. (14). If this is sufficiently larger than t_{adv}, he can assure security of his device. Therefore, he should consider countermeasures which can increase

LG. Note that guessing entropy can not prove that the success rate is negligible. Hence, it is important to execute an experimental evaluation shown in Sect. 4.3.

4.3 Experimental Evaluation by Rank Estimation

Rank estimation is an evaluation tool for side-channel attacks enhanced by key enumeration [25]. The algorithm is to evaluate the rank of a correct key when the evaluator knows the correct key. We show the algorithm for the experimental evaluation in Algorithm 2. The algorithm outputs a success rate SR for randomly chosen correct keys and leakages (these two values are not independent). Algorithm 2 has three steps as follows.

Step-1. In the same manner as Algorithm 1, a system of linear equations is divided. Also, a vector of crossover probabilities $\mathbf{p}$ is divided into η vectors $\mathbf{p}_j = (p_{j,1}, p_{j,2}, ..., p_{j,L_j})$. The evaluator repeats **Step-2** and **3** for s_{all} times by changing a value of the correct key $\mathbf{sk}^\psi = \mathbf{k}^\psi || \mathbf{rk}^\psi$.

Step-2. The following procedures are repeated for all $j \in \{1, 2, ..., \eta\}$. A correct sub key $\mathbf{k}_j^\psi$ is chosen at random, and a vector of correct RHS values $\mathbf{x}_j^\psi$ is obtained by $\mathbf{k}_j^\psi \cdot A_j$. A vector of measured RHS values $\mathbf{y}$ are chosen at random according to $\mathbf{p}_j$. A log likelihood of the correct sub key $\lambda_{\mathbf{k}_j^\psi}$ is derived. For all candidates of $\mathbf{k}_j$, log likelihoods are computed. All results are stored in a list $\mathcal{U}_{\mathbf{k}_j}$ and $(\mathbf{k}_j^o, \lambda_{\mathbf{k}_j^o})$ is sorted in descending order by $\lambda_{\mathbf{k}_j^o}$.

Step-3. From $\mathcal{U}_{\mathbf{k}_j}$ and $\lambda_{\mathbf{k}_j^\psi}$ ($j \in \{1, 2, ..., \eta\}$), a rank τ of the correct key is estimated by a rank-estimation algorithm RE. We use a rank estimation algorithm proposed by Glowacz et al. [10] (see Appendix B). If a total complexity τ is less than t_{adv}, the attack is regarded as successful and s increases by 1. Return to **Step-1**.

Step-4. After s_{all} times of trials, a success rate $SR = s/s_{all}$ is outputted.

The time complexity of Algorithm 2 is estimated as $s_{all} \cdot (t_{prep} + t_{re})$, where t_{prep} is obtained by Eq. (11) and t_{re} is a time complexity for rank estimation (see Eq. (15) of Appendix B).

5   Application to PRESENT

We apply the evaluation method shown in Sect. 4 to PRESENT [4]. We suppose that PRESENT is implemented on a device encrypting a small amount of data (e.g., smart card). As a realistic assumption for the device, we set the adversary's condition as $t_{adv} = 2^{60}$ and $q_{adv} = 2^{15}$ (the number of leaked values at most). Note that $q = 2^{15}$ requires 256 KB of data to be encrypted and measured . Using the assumption, we can assure sufficient security of the device. In Sect. 5.1, we show the results of cube search. In Sect. 5.2, we evaluate the security of PRESENT against SCCA-KE.

Algorithm 2. Experimental evaluation for SCCA-KE by rank estimation.

---

input Threshold t_{adv}, a matrix A with variables $\mathbf{k}$ and probabilities $\mathbf{p}$.
Divide $(A, \mathbf{k}, \mathbf{y})$ into η sub-systems $(A_j, \mathbf{k}_j, \mathbf{y}_j)$ $(j \in \{1, 2, ..., \eta\})$.
Divide $\mathbf{p}$ into η vectors $\mathbf{p}_j$ corresponding to $(A_j, \mathbf{k}_j, \mathbf{y}_j)$ $(j \in \{1, 2, ..., \eta\})$.
$s \leftarrow 0$ $\triangleright$ s: counter variable for *success*.
for $trial = 1 \rightarrow s_{all}$ **do**
    for $j = 1 \rightarrow \eta$ **do**
        Choose a value of the correct sub key $\mathbf{k}_j^\psi$ at random.
        $\mathbf{x}_j^\psi \leftarrow \mathbf{k}_j^\psi \cdot A_j$
        Obtain $\mathbf{y}_j$ from $\mathbf{x}_j^\psi$ at random according to $\mathbf{p}_j$.
        $\lambda_{\mathbf{k}_j^\psi} \leftarrow \sum_{i=1}^{L_j} \log_2(Pr[x_{j,i}^\psi \oplus y_{j,i}])$ $\triangleright$ $\lambda_{\mathbf{k}_j^\psi}$: log likelihood of the correct sub key.
        for $o = 1 \rightarrow 2^{|n_j|}$ **do** $\triangleright$ $Pr[x_{j,i}^o \oplus y_{j,i} = 1] = p_{j,i}$.
            $\mathbf{x}_j^o \leftarrow \mathbf{k}_j^o \cdot A_j$ and $\lambda_{\mathbf{k}_j^o} \leftarrow \sum_{i=1}^{L_j} \log_2(Pr[x_{j,i}^o \oplus y_{j,i}])$
        end for
        Store all $(\mathbf{k}_j^o, \lambda_{\mathbf{k}_j^o})$ in $\mathcal{U}_{\mathbf{k}_j}$ in descending order by $\lambda_{\mathbf{k}_j^o}$.
    end for $\triangleright$ RE: rank estimation algorithm of [10].
    $\tau \leftarrow \mathsf{RE}(\mathcal{U}_{\mathbf{k}_1}, \mathcal{U}_{\mathbf{k}_2}, ..., \mathcal{U}_{\mathbf{k}_\eta}, \lambda_{\mathbf{k}_1^\psi}, \lambda_{\mathbf{k}_2^\psi}, ..., \lambda_{\mathbf{k}_\eta^\psi}, n')$
    if $t_{adv} \geq \tau$ **then** $s \leftarrow s + 1$
    end if
end for
return $SR = s/s_{all}$

5.1 Cubes of PRESENT

As mentioned in Sect. 4.1, we execute brute-force cube search by restricting the cube size, i.e., $|\mathcal{I}| \leq 6$. We experiment under the following *leakage models*, where w_i $(i \in \{1, 2, ..., 64\})$ denotes an output bit of internal rounds of PRESENT.

1. Single-bit leakage [28]: An output bit of an internal round is leaked as w_i $(i \in \{1, 2, ..., 64\})$.
2. LSB leakage of HW (binary representation) of 8-bit state [14]: A LSB of HW of 8-bit internal states (output of two S-boxes) of PRESENT is leaked as $\bigoplus_{j=1}^{8} w_{8 \cdot (i-1)+j}$ $(i \in \{1, 2, ..., 8\})$. PRESENT is assumed to be implemented on an 8-bit processor.
3. LSB leakage of HW of 4-bit state: A LSB of HW of 4-bit internal states (output of one S-box) of PRESENT is leaked as $\bigoplus_{j=1}^{4} w_{4 \cdot (i-1)+j}$ $(i \in \{1, 2, ..., 16\})$. PRESENT is assumed to be implemented on a 4-bit processor.

Since LSB can be represented by the lowest-degree polynomial among all HW bits, this leakage model is the most advantageous for the adversary. For all (r, i) (i-th bit/LSB of r-th round), we execute brute-force search.

As a result, we have results shown in Tables 2, 3 and 4. We show cubes with $n \geq 20$, since this is the necessary condition for the successful attack ($t_{adv} = 2^{60}$ and secret-key length is 80). Even if the adversary can recover n ($n < 20$) secret-key variables with negligible complexity, he should recover $80 - n$ secret-key

Table 2. The results of cube search for single bit leakage.

r	i	#cubes of each cube size						n	L	$\max n_j$	$\max L_j$
		1	2	3	4	5	6				
3	1	8	48	120	160	0	48	32	384	1	30
3	5	0	0	144	144	0	3456	32	3744	1	288
3	26	0	0	0	2880	0	0	32	2880	1	144
3	33	0	0	0	1920	0	0	32	1920	1	96
3	49	0	0	0	2880	0	0	32	2880	1	144
4	17	0	0	0	231	731	4813	51	5775	16	2209
4	49	0	0	0	240	731	4815	51	5786	16	2220

Table 3. The results of cube search for LSB leakage of 8-bit state.

r	i	#cubes of each cube size						n	L	$\max n_j$	$\max L_j$
		1	2	3	4	5	6				
2	1	0	48	0	0	144	0	64	192	3	9
2	2	8	24	0	48	96	0	56	176	8	36
3	1	0	0	0	0	0	108	24	108	3	18
3	2	0	0	0	68	80	36	30	184	3	26

Table 4. The results of cube search for LSB leakage of 4-bit state.

r	i	#cubes of each cube size						n	L	$\max n_j$	$\max L_j$
		1	2	3	4	5	6				
2	1	16	32	16	0	0	0	32	64	1	3
2	2	0	48	0	0	144	0	64	192	3	9
2	3	0	40	0	0	80	0	64	120	2	4
2	4	0	48	0	0	144	0	64	192	3	9
2	5	0	0	288	288	72	0	32	648	1	27
3	1	0	20	0	102	120	72	60	314	4	52
3	2	0	0	0	0	0	108	24	108	3	18
3	3	0	0	0	0	0	72	24	72	3	12
3	4	0	0	0	0	0	108	24	108	3	18
3	5	0	0	0	0	0	432	24	432	3	72
3	9	0	0	0	0	0	288	24	288	3	48
3	13	0	0	0	0	0	432	24	432	3	72

variables without any advantage. Note that "$\max n_j$" and "$\max L_j$" denotes the maximum values of n_j and L_j among all sub systems ($j \in \{1, 2, ..., \eta\}$). Both values determine whether execution of information-theoretic and experimental evaluations are tractable. Since $\max n_j = 16$ and $\max L_j = 2220$ at most in the tables, the above execution time is relatively small and this fact supports our observation shown in Sect. 3.3.

5.2   Security Evaluation of PRESENT

We use six conditions which are advantageous for the adversary, and Table 5 shows them. In order to satisfy $q \leq q_{adv}$ ($q_{adv} = 2^{15}$), some cubes should be reduced (see underlined number of Table 5). Also, some cubes are used multiple times if the number of leaked values are smaller than q_{adv}. For simplicity, we use all cubes for the same number of times, and d denotes the number.

Choosing two conditions from each leakage model, we show the results for information-theoretic and experimental evaluations in Figs. 2 and 3, respectively. In the latter, we execute the experiment for 1,000 times ($s_{all} = 1,000$ in Algorithm 2) changing the correct key $\mathbf{sk}^\psi$ and RHS values $\mathbf{y}$.

Table 5. Cubes used in the evaluation.

Leakage model	r	i	#cubes of each cube size						n	L	$\max n_j$	$\max L_j$	q	d
			1	2	3	4	5	6						
Single bit	3	1	8	48	120	160	720	48	32	384	1	30	$2^{14.86}$	1
	4	49	0	0	0	240	731	<u>0</u>	32	971	16	780	$2^{14.73}$	1
LSB of HW of 8-bit state	2	2	64	192	0	384	768	0	56	1408	8	288	$2^{14.94}$	8
	3	2	0	0	0	340	400	180	30	920	3	130	$2^{14.86}$	5
LSB of HW of 4-bit state	2	1	1808	3616	1808	0	0	0	32	7232	1	339	$2^{14.81}$	113
	3	1	0	60	0	306	360	216	60	942	4	156	$2^{14.89}$	3

From the results of evaluation, we have the following observations.

1. In PRESENT, SCCA is error tolerant when leakages are from early rounds such as the second and third rounds. This is a general statement for block cipher. Since an algebraic degree increases round by round, linear superpolies can not be obtained by cubes of small sizes.
2. The second and third rounds give an advantage to the adversary. Therefore, SCCA can be thwarted by sufficient protections for the above rounds. Also, $\rho \geq 0.4$ is sufficient to prevent SCCA-KE from Figs. 2 and 3.

5.3 Comparison with the Previous Method

In Fig. 4, we show a comparison to the previous method by using a leakage model used in [14] (LSB leakage of HW of 8-bit state and $(r, i) = (2, 1)$, see Table 3). The experiment is executed under the same condition as Sect. 5.2 ($t_{adv} = 2^{60}$ and $q_{adv} = 2^{15}$), and all cubes are used $d = 6$ times. Obviously, we can conclude that SCCA-KE is more error tolerant than the previous method. Since guessing

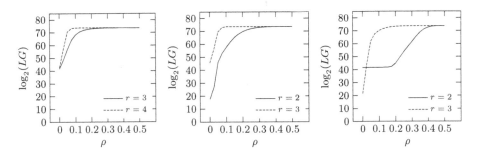

Fig. 2. Lower bounds of guessing entropy of single-bit leakage (left), LSB leakage of 8-bit state (middle) and LSB leakage of 4-bit state (right).

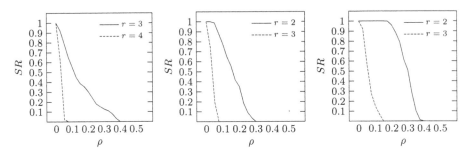

Fig. 3. Success rates of single-bit leakage (left), LSB leakage of 8-bit state (middle) and LSB leakage of 4-bit state (right).

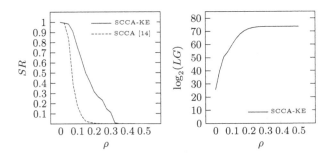

Fig. 4. Success rates of SCCA-KE and the previous method [14] under LSB leakage of HW of 8-bit state and $(r, i) = (2, 1)$ (left), and lower bounds of guessing entropy of SCCA-KE in the same condition (right).

entropy can not be defined in the previous method, we only show LG for SCCA-KE as a reference.

We execute experiments for the previous method by computing hamming distances of the correct key and the last candidate of the list of secret-key candidates $\mathcal{T}_{\mathbf{sk}}$ ($|\mathcal{T}_{\mathbf{sk}}| = t_{adv} = 2^{60}$). If the former value is less than the latter one, we regard the attack as success. A system of linear equations for 64 secret-key variables is divided into four sub systems in the same manner as [14].

6   Conclusions and Open Problems

We propose SCCA-KE which improves error tolerance of the previous method [14]. Then, we propose an evaluation method with information-theoretic and experimental evaluations. Using the evaluation method, the evaluator can consider a countermeasure with a sufficient security margin. In this paper, we evaluate PRESENT in various situations under BSC model fixing the adversary's condition. It is also possible to evaluate the security for various adversary.

For further study, we list open problems.

1. Cube search strategy has not been established. Since it is computationally hard to execute brute-force cube search in larger cube sizes, more efficient algorithms should be designed.
2. After the cube search, we should select cubes in order to maximize the success rate considering the restriction of the number of leaked values and computing power. In other word, selection of cubes should be optimized.

Acknowledgment. This work was supported by JSPS KAKENHI Grant Number 17K0645.

A   Intuitive Explanation for the Observation

If the number of variables in a linear equation is large, it shares variables with other equations and n^j becomes large. In early rounds, the number of secret-key variables are small in all superpolies since diffusion of key variables is not enough. In other rounds, the number of secret-key variables in each superpoly increases. However, superpolies with many secret-key variables tend to be non-linear in these rounds. Therefore, the number of secret-key variables in each linear equation is small in any round and n^j tends to be small.

B   Rank Estimation Algorithm of [10]

Algorithm 3 shows the rank estimation algorithm. The rank-estimation algorithm outputs an estimated rank. The algorithm executes t_{re} times additions in the convolution:

$$t_{re} = \sum_{j=2}^{m} \sum_{b=j-1}^{j \cdot n_{bin} - (j-1)} n_{bin}. \tag{15}$$

Algorithm 3. Rank estimation algorithm of [10].

---

input Sub-key lists $\mathcal{U}_{\mathbf{k}_1}, \mathcal{U}_{\mathbf{k}_2}, ..., \mathcal{U}_{\mathbf{k}_\eta}$, log likelihoods of the correct sub keys $\lambda_{\mathbf{k}_1^\psi}, \lambda_{\mathbf{k}_2^\psi}, ..., \lambda_{\mathbf{k}_\eta^\psi}$ and the number of remaing variables n'.

for $j = 1 \rightarrow \eta$ **do**   ▷ b^ψ: index of bin which the correct key belongs to.
  $b^\psi \leftarrow b^\psi + \lfloor \lambda_{\mathbf{k}_j^\psi} / l_{bin} \rfloor$
  for $o = 1 \rightarrow 2^{n_j}$ **do**
    $b \leftarrow \lfloor \lambda_{\mathbf{k}_j^o} / l_{bin} \rfloor$ and $\mathsf{H}_j(b) \leftarrow \mathsf{H}_j(b) + 1$ ▷ l_{bin}: width of a bin.
  end for
end for
$\mathsf{H}_{1:1} \leftarrow \mathsf{H}_1$.
for $j = 2 \rightarrow \eta$ **do**
  for $b = (j-1) \rightarrow j \cdot n_{bin} - (j-1)$ **do**   ▷ n_{bin}: size of a bin.
    for $b' = 1 \rightarrow n_{bin}$ **do**
      $\mathsf{H}_{1:j}(b+b') \leftarrow \mathsf{H}_{1:j}(b+b') + \mathsf{H}_{1:j-1}(b) \cdot \mathsf{H}_j(b')$
    end for
  end for
end for
return $\tau \leftarrow \sum_{b=b^\psi}^{\eta \cdot n_{bin} - (\eta - 1)} \mathsf{H}_{1:\eta}(b) + n'$

There is an estimation error caused by the convolution of histograms; however, the rank can be lower bounded by $\sum_{b=b^\psi + \lceil \eta/2 \rceil}^{\eta \times n_{bin} - (\eta - 1)} \mathsf{H}_{1:\eta}(b)$ and upper bounded by $\sum_{b=b^\psi - \lceil \eta/2 \rceil}^{\eta \times n_{bin} - (\eta - 1)} \mathsf{H}_{1:\eta}(b)$.

C   Proof for Proposition 1

A lower bound of guessing entropy can be computed in each sub system.

$$
\begin{aligned}
LG &= \frac{1}{1+N} \sum_{\mathbf{y}} \left(\sum_{\mathbf{sk}^\psi} Pr[\mathbf{sk}^\psi, \mathbf{y}]^{\frac{1}{2}} \right)^2 \\
&= \frac{1}{1+N} \sum_{\mathbf{y}} \left(\sum_{\mathbf{k}^\psi} \prod_{j=1}^{\eta} Pr[\mathbf{y}_j | \mathbf{k}_j^\psi]^{\frac{1}{2}} \cdot Pr[\mathbf{k}_j^\psi]^{\frac{1}{2}} \right)^2 \cdot \left(\sum_{\mathbf{rk}^\psi} Pr[\mathbf{rk}^\psi]^{\frac{1}{2}} \right)^2 \\
&= \frac{2^{n'}}{1+N} \sum_{\mathbf{y}} \left(\prod_{j=1}^{\eta} 2^{-\frac{n_j}{2}} \sum_{\mathbf{k}_j^\psi} Pr[\mathbf{y}_j | \mathbf{k}_j^\psi]^{\frac{1}{2}} \right)^2 \\
&= \frac{2^{n'}}{1+N} \prod_{j=1}^{\eta} 2^{-n_j} \sum_{\mathbf{y}_j} \left(\sum_{\mathbf{k}_j^\psi} Pr[\mathbf{y}_j | \mathbf{k}_j^\psi]^{\frac{1}{2}} \right)^2 \\
&= \frac{2^{n'}}{1+N} \prod_{j=1}^{\eta} LG_j
\end{aligned}
$$

Note that we assume that uniform prior distribution holds ($Pr[\mathbf{k}_j] = 2^{-n_j}$, $Pr[\mathbf{rk}] = 2^{-n'}$). Then, we can simplify LG_j by expanding the square part as follows.

$$LG_j = 2^{-n_j} \sum_{\mathbf{y}_j} \sum_{o=1}^{2^{n_j}} \sum_{o'=1}^{2^{n_j}} Pr[\mathbf{y}_j | \mathbf{k}_j^o]^{\frac{1}{2}} \cdot Pr[\mathbf{y}_j | \mathbf{k}_j^{o'}]^{\frac{1}{2}}$$

$$= 2^{-n_j} \sum_{o=1}^{2^{n_j}} \sum_{o'=1}^{2^{n_j}} \prod_{i=1}^{L_j} \sum_{y_{j,i}} Pr[y_{j,i} \oplus x_{j,i}^o]^{\frac{1}{2}} \cdot Pr[y_{j,i} \oplus x_{j,i}^{o'}]^{\frac{1}{2}}$$

$$= 2^{-n_j} \sum_{o=1}^{2^{n_j}} \sum_{o'=1}^{2^{n_j}} \prod_{i=1}^{L_j} \left(Pr[0 \oplus x_{j,i}^o]^{\frac{1}{2}} \cdot Pr[0 \oplus x_{j,i}^{o'}]^{\frac{1}{2}} + Pr[1 \oplus x_{j,i}^o]^{\frac{1}{2}} \cdot Pr[1 \oplus x_{j,i}^{o'}]^{\frac{1}{2}} \right)$$

$$= 2^{-n_j} \sum_{\substack{o=1 \\ o' \neq o}}^{2^{n_j}} \sum_{o'=1}^{2^{n_j}} \left(\prod_{\substack{i=1 \\ x_{j,i}^o \neq x_{j,i}^{o'}}}^{L_j} 2 \cdot p_{j,i}^{\frac{1}{2}} \cdot (1 - p_{j,i})^{\frac{1}{2}} \right) + 1 \qquad (16)$$

In the last rearrangement, we only consider products of probabilities such that $x_{j,i}^o \neq x_{j,i}^{o'}$, since a product of probabilities is always 1 if $x_{j,i}^o = x_{j,i}^{o'}$. If $o = o'$, the above product is always 1 and there are 2^{n_j} pairs of the same candidate; therefore, $2^{n_j} \cdot 2^{-n_j} = 1$ is added in the last. $\qquad \square$

References

1. Abdul-Latip, S.F., Reyhanitabar, M.R., Susilo, W., Seberry, J.: On the security of NOEKEON against side channel cube attacks. In: Kwak, J., Deng, R.H., Won, Y., Wang, G. (eds.) ISPEC 2010. LNCS, vol. 6047, pp. 45–55. Springer, Heidelberg (2010). https://doi.org/10.1007/978-3-642-12827-1_4
2. Arikan, E.: An inequality on guessing and its application to sequential decoding. IEEE Trans. Inf. Theor. **42**(1), 99–105 (1996)
3. Bellare, M., Coppersmith, D., Hastad, J., Kiwi, M., Sudan, M.: Linearity testing in characteristic two. IEEE Trans. Inf. Theor. **42**(6), 1781–1795 (1996)
4. Bogdanov, A., et al.: PRESENT: an ultra-lightweight block cipher. In: Paillier, P., Verbauwhede, I. (eds.) CHES 2007. LNCS, vol. 4727, pp. 450–466. Springer, Heidelberg (2007). https://doi.org/10.1007/978-3-540-74735-2_31
5. Bogdanov, A., Kizhvatov, I., Manzoor, K., Tischhauser, E., Witteman, M.: Fast and memory-efficient key recovery in side-channel attacks. In: Dunkelman, O., Keliher, L. (eds.) SAC 2015. LNCS, vol. 9566, pp. 310–327. Springer, Cham (2016). https://doi.org/10.1007/978-3-319-31301-6_19
6. David, L., Wool, A.: A bounded-space near-optimal key enumeration algorithm for multi-dimensional side-channel attacks. IACR Cryptology ePrint Archive 2015, 1236 (2015)
7. Dinur, I., Shamir, A.: Cube attacks on tweakable black box polynomials. In: Joux, A. (ed.) EUROCRYPT 2009. LNCS, vol. 5479, pp. 278–299. Springer, Heidelberg (2009). https://doi.org/10.1007/978-3-642-01001-9_16

8. Dinur, I., Shamir, A.: Side channel cube attacks on block ciphers. IACR Cryptology ePrint Archive 2009, 127 (2009)

9. Faisal, S., Reza, M., Susilo, W., Seberry, J.: Extended cubes: enhancing the cube attack by extracting low-degree non-linear equations (2011)

10. Glowacz, C., Grosso, V., Poussier, R., Schüth, J., Standaert, F.-X.: Simpler and more efficient rank estimation for side-channel security assessment. In: Leander, G. (ed.) FSE 2015. LNCS, vol. 9054, pp. 117–129. Springer, Heidelberg (2015). https://doi.org/10.1007/978-3-662-48116-5_6

11. Islam, S., Afzal, M., Rashdi, A.: On the security of lblock against the cube attack and side channel cube attack. In: Cuzzocrea, A., Kittl, C., Simos, D.E., Weippl, E., Xu, L. (eds.) CD-ARES 2013. LNCS, vol. 8128, pp. 105–121. Springer, Heidelberg (2013). https://doi.org/10.1007/978-3-642-40588-4_8

12. Kocher, P., Jaffe, J., Jun, B.: Differential power analysis. In: Wiener, M. (ed.) CRYPTO 1999. LNCS, vol. 1666, pp. 388–397. Springer, Heidelberg (1999). https://doi.org/10.1007/3-540-48405-1_25

13. Köpf, B., Basin, D.: An information-theoretic model for adaptive side-channel attacks. In: Proceedings of the 14th ACM Conference on Computer and Communications Security, pp. 286–296. ACM (2007)

14. Li, Z., Zhang, B., Fan, J., Verbauwhede, I.: A new model for error-tolerant side-channel cube attacks. In: Bertoni, G., Coron, J.-S. (eds.) CHES 2013. LNCS, vol. 8086, pp. 453–470. Springer, Heidelberg (2013). https://doi.org/10.1007/978-3-642-40349-1_26

15. MacKay, D.J.: Information Theory, Inference and Learning Algorithms. Cambridge University Press, Cambridge (2003)

16. Manzoor, K., et al.: Efficient practical key recovery for side-channel attacks. Master's thesis, Aalto University, June 2014. http://cse. aalto. fi/en/personnel/antti-yla-jaaski/msc-thesis/2014-msc-kamran-manzoor. pdf (2014)

17. Martin, D.P., O'Connell, J.F., Oswald, E., Stam, M.: Counting keys in parallel after a side channel attack. In: Iwata, T., Cheon, J.H. (eds.) ASIACRYPT 2015. LNCS, vol. 9453, pp. 313–337. Springer, Heidelberg (2015). https://doi.org/10. 1007/978-3-662-48800-3_13

18. Massey, J.L.: Guessing and entropy. In: 1994 IEEE International Symposium on Information Theory, 1994. Proceedings., p. 204. IEEE (1994)

19. Matsui, M.: Linear cryptanalysis method for DES cipher. In: Helleseth, T. (ed.) EUROCRYPT 1993. LNCS, vol. 765, pp. 386–397. Springer, Heidelberg (1994). https://doi.org/10.1007/3-540-48285-7_33

20. Poussier, R., Standaert, F.-X., Grosso, V.: Simple key enumeration (and Rank Estimation) using histograms: an integrated approach. In: Gierlichs, B., Poschmann, A.Y. (eds.) CHES 2016. LNCS, vol. 9813, pp. 61–81. Springer, Heidelberg (2016). https://doi.org/10.1007/978-3-662-53140-2_4

21. Renauld, M., Standaert, F.-X.: Algebraic side-channel attacks. In: Bao, F., Yung, M., Lin, D., Jing, J. (eds.) Inscrypt 2009. LNCS, vol. 6151, pp. 393–410. Springer, Heidelberg (2010). https://doi.org/10.1007/978-3-642-16342-5_29

22. Siegenthaler, T.: Decrypting a class of stream ciphers using ciphertext only. IEEE Trans. Comput. **34**(1), 81–85 (1985)

23. Standaert, F.-X., Malkin, T.G., Yung, M.: A unified framework for the analysis of side-channel key recovery attacks. In: Joux, A. (ed.) EUROCRYPT 2009. LNCS, vol. 5479, pp. 443–461. Springer, Heidelberg (2009). https://doi.org/10.1007/978-3-642-01001-9_26

24. Veyrat-Charvillon, N., Gérard, B., Renauld, M., Standaert, F.-X.: An optimal key enumeration algorithm and its application to side-channel attacks. In: Knudsen, L.R., Wu, H. (eds.) SAC 2012. LNCS, vol. 7707, pp. 390–406. Springer, Heidelberg (2013). https://doi.org/10.1007/978-3-642-35999-6_25

25. Veyrat-Charvillon, N., Gérard, B., Standaert, F.-X.: Security evaluations beyond computing power. In: Johansson, T., Nguyen, P.Q. (eds.) EUROCRYPT 2013. LNCS, vol. 7881, pp. 126–141. Springer, Heidelberg (2013). https://doi.org/10.1007/978-3-642-38348-9_8

26. Veyrat-Charvillon, N., Gérard, B., Standaert, F.-X.: Soft analytical side-channel attacks. In: Sarkar, P., Iwata, T. (eds.) ASIACRYPT 2014. LNCS, vol. 8873, pp. 282–296. Springer, Heidelberg (2014). https://doi.org/10.1007/978-3-662-45611-8_15

27. Xinjie, Z., Shize, G., Zhang, F., Tao, W., Zhijie, S., Hao, L.: Enhanced side-channel cube attacks on PRESENT. IEICE Trans. Fundam. Electron., Commun. Comput. Sci. **96**(1), 332–339 (2013)

28. Yang, L., Wang, M., Qiao, S.: Side channel cube attack on PRESENT. In: Garay, J.A., Miyaji, A., Otsuka, A. (eds.) CANS 2009. LNCS, vol. 5888, pp. 379–391. Springer, Heidelberg (2009). https://doi.org/10.1007/978-3-642-10433-6_25

29. Zhao, X.j., Wang, T., Guo, S.: Improved side channel cube attacks on PRESENT. IACR Cryptology ePrint Archive 2011, 165 (2011)

On the Hardness of the Mersenne Low Hamming Ratio Assumption

Marc Beunardeau, Aisling Connolly$^{(\boxtimes)}$, Rémi Géraud, and David Naccache

Département d'informatique de l'ENS, École normale supérieure,
PSL Research University, Paris, France
{marc.beunardeau,aisling.connolly,remi.geraud,david.naccache}@ens.fr

Abstract. In a recent paper [1], Aggarwal, Joux, Prakash, and Santha (AJPS) describe an ingenious public-key cryptosystem mimicking NTRU over the integers. This algorithm relies on the properties of Mersenne primes rather than polynomial rings. The security of the AJPS cryptosystem relies on the conjectured hardness of the Mersenne Low Hamming Ratio Assumption, defined in [1].

This work shows that AJPS' security estimates are too optimistic and describes an algorithm allowing to recover the secret key from the public key much faster than foreseen in [1].

In particular, our algorithm is *experimentally practical* (within the reach of the computational capabilities of a large organization), at least for the parameter choice $\{n = 1279, h = 17\}$ conjectured in [1] as corresponding to a 2^{120} security level. The algorithm is fully parallelizable.

1 Introduction

A Mersenne prime is a prime of the form $2^n - 1$, where n itself is prime.

In a recent paper [1], Aggarwal, Joux, Prakash, and Santha (AJPS) describe a public-key cryptosystem mimicking NTRU over the integers. This algorithm relies on the properties of Mersenne numbers instead of polynomial rings. Their scheme is defined by the following algorithms:

- Setup(1^λ) → pp, which chooses the public parameters pp $= (n, h)$ such that $p = 2^n - 1$ is prime and so as to achieve a λ-bit security level. In [1] the following lower bound is derived

$$\binom{n-1}{h-1} > 2^\lambda$$

which, for instance, is satisfied by $\lambda = 120$, pp $= (n = 1279, h = 17)$.

- KeyGen(pp) → (sk, pk), which picks F, G two n-bit strings chosen independently and uniformly at random from all n-bit strings of Hamming weight h, and returns sk ← G and pk ← $H = F/G \bmod (2^n - 1)$.

T. Lange and O. Dunkelman (Eds.): LATINCRYPT 2017, LNCS 11368, pp. 166–174, 2019.
https://doi.org/10.1007/978-3-030-25283-0_9

- Encrypt(pp, pk, $b \in \{0, 1\}$) $\rightarrow c$, which picks A, B two n-bit strings chosen independently and uniformly at random from all n-bit strings of Hamming weight h, then computes

$$c \leftarrow (-1)^b (AH + B) \bmod (2^n - 1).$$

- Decrypt(pp, sk, c) $\rightarrow \{\perp, 0, 1\}$, which computes $D = \|Gc \bmod (2^n - 1)\|$ and returns

$$\begin{cases} 0 & \text{if } D \leq 2h^2, \\ 1 & \text{if } D \geq n - 2h^2, \\ \perp & \text{otherwise} \end{cases}$$

We refer the reader to [1] for more details on this cryptosystem which does not require further overview as we directly attack the public key to infer the secret key.

In particular, security rests upon the conjectured intractability of the following problem:

Definition 1. *The* Mersenne Low Hamming Ratio Assumption *states that given an n-bit Mersenne prime $p = 2^n - 1$ and an integer h, the advantage of any probabilistic polynomial time adversary attempting to distinguish between F/G mod p and R is at most $\frac{\mathrm{poly}(n)}{2^\lambda}$, where R is a uniformly random n-bit string, and (F, G) are independently chosen n-bit strings each having Hamming weight h.*

We argue that (F, G) can be *experimentally* computed from H, at least for the parameter choice $\{n = 1279, h = 17\}$ conjectured in [1] as corresponding to a 2^{120} security level.

The full code (Python for partition sampling and Mathematica for lattice reduction) is available from the authors upon request.

2 Outline of the Analysis

The analysis uses the Lenstra–Lenstra–Lovász lattice basis reduction algorithm (LLL, [3]). We do not recall here any internal details of LLL but just the way in which it can be used to solve a linear equation with k unknowns when the total size of the unknowns is properly bounded.

2.1 Using LLL to Spread Information

Let $x_1, \ldots, x_k \in \mathbb{N}^*$ be k unknowns. Let $p \in \mathbb{N}$ be a modulus and $a_0, \ldots, a_k \in \mathbb{N}$. Consider the equation:

$$a_0 = \sum_{i=1}^{k} a_i x_i \bmod p.$$

All the reader needs to know is that the LLL algorithm will find $x_1, \ldots, x_k$ if $\prod_{i=1}^{k} x_i < p$.

In particular, LLL can be adapted to provide any uneven split of sizes between the x_i as long as the sum of those sizes does not exceed the size of p. More details on the theoretical analysis of LLL in that setting and variants are given in [4, Sect. 3.2] and [2, Chap. 13], in the context of generalised knapsack problems.

2.2   Partition and Try

The first observation that attracted our attention is that the size[1] of F (and G) has an unusually small expectation $\sigma(n, h)$:

$$\sigma(n, h) = n \left(1 + \frac{(1 - \frac{h}{n})^{n+1} - 1}{\frac{h}{n}(n + 1)} \right)$$

The difference in size between $n = 1279$ and $\sigma(1279, 17)$ is not huge[2] and cannot be immediately exploited. However, the same phenomenon also occurs at the least significant bits and further shortens the expected nonzero parts of F and G by 70 bits.

Similarly, assume that in the key generation procedure, both F and G happen to have bits set to 1 only in their lower halves. When this (rare event) happens, we can directly apply LLL to H to recover F and G. We call this event T.

Is that event rare? Since F and G are chosen at random, T happens with probability at least 2^{-2h}. While T's probability is not cryptographically negligible, this pre-attack only allows to target one key out of 2^{2h}. For the first suggested parameter set ($\lambda = 120$), one public key out of 67 million can be attacked in this fashion and its F and G recovered, i.e., a total break. The question is hence, can this phenomenon be extended to any key? and if so, at what cost? In particular, can we sacrifice work to increase the size of the vulnerable key space? The answers to these questions turn out to be positive, as we will explain hereafter.

Random Partitions. Instead of a fixed partition of $\{0, \ldots, n-1\}$, we can sample random partitions, for instance by sampling (without replacement) m positions, which are interpreted as boundaries between regions of zeros and regions that possibly contain a 1. The total number of regions, $m + 1$, determines the dimension of the lattice being reduced.

For the sake of simplicity we consider *balanced* partitions:

Definition 2. *A partition P of $\{0, \ldots, n-1\}$ into type 0 blocks and type 1 blocks is* balanced *if the total length of the type 0 blocks and the total length of the type 1 blocks differ by at most one.*[3]

---

[1] That is, the length of a number, once its leading zeros are discarded.
[2] $1279 - \sigma(1279, 17) \approx 75$ bits.
[3] Since n is odd, we must accept a ± 1 excess.

A randomly sampled partition is not necessarily a balanced partition: we use rejection sampling to ensure the balancing property.[4] The sought-after property of these partitions is the following:

Definition 3. *Let X be a binary string of length n. A partition P of X into type 0 blocks and type 1 blocks is correct for X if the type 0 blocks contain only zeros.*

Figure 1 illustrates the partitions that we are interested in on a simple example. Also note that the definition above does not put any constraint on type 1 blocks, which may contain zeros or not; since they are not guaranteed to be zero we refer to them as "non-zero" blocks. Accordingly, blocks of type 0 in a correct partition are referred to as "zero" blocks.

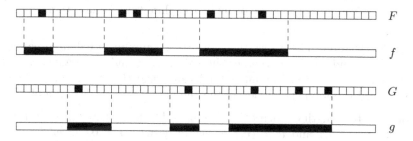

Fig. 1. An illustration of the partitions that we are interested in: in these diagrams, a black square in F or G represents a **1**, while white squares represent 0s. The partitions f and g are balanced and correct for F and G respectively, with "zero" blocks coloured white, and "non-zero" blocks coloured black. The vertical dashed lines show how F and G align with their respective partitions.

The observation at the beginning of this section is that using partitions that are both balanced and correct for F and G, we can recover F and G from H.

Since F and G are unknown, we cannot construct a correct partition from them directly; but the probability that a random balanced partition is correct for F (resp. G) is lower bounded[5] by 2^{-h}. Assuming that F and G are independent, which they should be according to the key generation procedure, we found a correct partition for *both* F and G with a probability of 2^{-2h}.

Remark 1. We may also consider imbalanced partitions which allow an extra speed-up for a subtle reason: Given that the unknowns found by LLL have a low

---

[4] There is room for improvement here as well, since rejection sampling is a very inefficient approach. Nevertheless it will be sufficient for our discussion, and any approach to generating such partitions would work without impacting the analysis.

[5] We ignore the fact that we sample without replacement here, as $h \ll n$. Under this conservative approximation, all the bits are sampled uniformly and independently, and may fall with probably 1/2 either in a type 0 or a type 1 block.

Hamming density, the odds that these numbers naturally begin by a sequence of zeros (and are hence shorter than expected) is high. The interesting point is that the total length of such natural gains sum up and allow to unbalance the partition in favor of type 1 blocks. Consider the analogy of a fishing boat that can carry up to 1000 kg of fish. The fisherman fishes with 3 nets having maximal capacities of 200, 300 and 500 kg each. Because waters are sparse in fish, the nets are expected to catch only 70% of their maximal capacity. Hence, we see that larger nets (285, 428, 714) can be used to optimize the boat's fishing capacity. However, unlike the boat, with LLL fish cannot be thrown back to the water and... excess weight sinks the boat (the attack fails). Hence if this speed-up strategy is used, we need to catch more than normal but not be too greedy. Note as well that if all variables end by at least ℓ trailing (LSB) zeros then these $m\ell$ zeros add-up to the gain as well (because there is no constant term in the equation, a division of all variables by 2 has no effect on the solution's correctness). We did not analyse or further explore this optimisation.

Trying Partitions. The attack then consists in sampling a balanced partition, running LLL, and checking whether the values of F and G obtained from the reduction have the correct Hamming weight and yield H by division. The matrix to be reduced is obtained as follows from the partitions f of F and g of G:

1. Compute the length of each of the non-zero blocks in f and g, we call these lengths $\boldsymbol{u} = \{u_i\}$ and $\boldsymbol{v} = \{v_i\}$ respectively, with $i = 0, \ldots, m/2 - 1$. Let $w = \max_i \{u_i, v_i\}$.
2. Construct the vector $\boldsymbol{s} = s_i$ as follows:

$$s_i = \begin{cases} 2^{w-v_i} & \text{if } i < m/2 \\ 2^{w-u_i} & \text{if } m/2 \le i < m \end{cases}$$

3. Construct the vector $\boldsymbol{a} = \{a_j\}$ as follows: let f_i (resp. g_i) denote the starting position of the non-zero blocks in F (resp. G), and set

$$a_j = \begin{cases} H \times 2^{g_i} \bmod p & \text{if } j < m/2 \\ p - 2^{f_i} & \text{if } m/2 \le j < m \end{cases}$$

4. Choose an integer K, and assemble the matrix $\boldsymbol{M}$ as follows:

$$\boldsymbol{M} = \begin{pmatrix} \mathrm{diag}(\boldsymbol{s}) & K\boldsymbol{a} \\ 0 & Kp \end{pmatrix}$$

where $\mathrm{diag}(\boldsymbol{s})$ is the diagonal matrix whose diagonal entries are given by $\boldsymbol{s}$. The coefficient K is a tuning parameter, which we set to 2^{1200}.

5. Finally, we use LLL on $\boldsymbol{M}$ (using the Mathematica command `LatticeReduce`) and recover the row of the reduced matrix that complies with the Hamming density of F and G. This row is expected to give the values of the non-zero blocks of F and G, and we can check its correctness by computing its Hamming weight, and checking that the ratio of the candidate values modulo p result in H.

By the above analysis, a given partition is correct with probability 2^{-2h}, which for $\lambda = 120$ is only 2^{-34}; if we can run LLL reasonably fast, which is the case for $m = 16$, an efficient attack happens to be within the reach of a well-equipped organization. Experimental evidence indeed suggests the feasibility of the attack, see Sect. 3.

Remark 2. For larger security parameters λ, the ratio h/n deduced from the analysis in [1] asymptotically vanishes. It should be checked if this influences imbalanced partition finding to the attacker's relative advantage for larger values of λ. We did not explore this avenue left to the reader as a potential research question.

3   Experiment

To illustrate the attack's feasibility, we fix a random tape in a deterministically verifiable way and implement our algorithm (see Fig. 2).

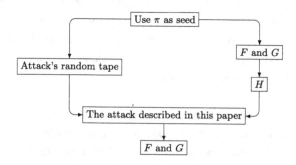

Fig. 2. The feasibility demonstration consists in deriving the attack's random tape from a verifiable source in a deterministic way, as well as the keys.

We generated a nothing-up-our-sleeves key with the procedure of Fig. 3.

1. $n, h \leftarrow \mathsf{pp}$
2. $I_1 = \{i_1, \ldots, i_h\} \leftarrow \mathsf{sample}(\{0, \ldots, n-1\}, h)$
3. $I_2 = \{i_1, \ldots, i_h\} \leftarrow \mathsf{sample}(\{0, \ldots, n-1\}, h)$
4. $F \leftarrow \sum_{i \in I_1}^{h} 2^i$
5. $G \leftarrow \sum_{i \in I_2}^{h} 2^i$
6. return $(\mathsf{sk} = G, \mathsf{pk} = F \cdot G^{-1} \bmod p)$

Fig. 3. The KeyGen(pp) procedure.

The sample(S, h) procedure selects h indices without replacement in the range S. It is implemented[6] by returning the h first entries of a deterministic Fisher–Yates shuffle of S. The randomness in sample(S, h) is simulated by iterating the SHA256 function, starting with the seed given by the ASCII representation of the 100 first decimals of π:

$$3141592653589793238462643383279502884197169399375$$
$$0582097494459230781640628620899862803482534211706$$

In a real attack we would simply use a fast non-cryptographic random number generator, but the above choice serves the purpose of reproducibility.

This gives the following (in hexadecimal notation with the zero MSBs excluded):

$I_1 = \{33, 47, 8e, 95, a1, 134, 19f, 1ab, 1ac, 1ce, 25d, 301, 30a, 3ee, 444, 46b, 471\}$

$I_2 = \{89, b5, de, 116, 141, 1dd, 1de, 2ae, 322, 37a, 388, 38a, 3f9, 48c, 48d, 4e9, 4f2\}$

$F = 2080000000001000000000000000000000004000000000000000000000000000000$
$0000000000000000000000000004020000000000000000000000000000000000000$
$0000020000000000000000000000000000000000000000400000001800800000000000$
$0000000000000001000000000000000000000000000000000000000200204000000$
$00000000000080000800000000000000$

$G = 40200000000000000000000000030000000000000000000000000000000000000020$
$0000000000000000000000000050004000000000000000000000000400000000000$
$0000000000000000040000000000000000000000000000000000000000000000000$
$000006000000000000000000000000000000000000000000002000000000040000000$
$00000400000000020000000000200000000000000000000000000000000000$

$H = 1610fecf11dbd70f5d09da1244a85c3aa7aed7de75a6d1fe4e988b5f66d66e1b$
$c27d46afd96800ff8b2b67316dff1046b88d205e620ba78a813c15f47ab8a7d2$
$a8f7eb12fe0fcff882307d92d4c0f9296a7cf4390ce3140e11e4b7c802fa67d3$
$a8517d30b00980380bdf8992ed6a2d3f74e25f14bae21786672bddae4f2bf897$
$f38741cdc10b319f8272d42f738cd296d4907331518c3439621aefad5c3d1a7c$

3.1 Recovering F and G from H

Finding a Winning Partition. At this step, we generate random balanced partitions and try LLL on the resulting decomposition. Doing so we quickly find the following partitions

---

[6] Other implementations are of course possible and do not affect the analysis. For other classical sampling without replacement algorithms, the reader may consult [5].

$f = \{2a, bf, 134, 1ec, 233, 253, 25a, 270, 2ee, 32d, 3e4, 41e, 42b, 4a7, 4f6, 4fd\}$
$g = \{7c, 142, 1d0, 22a, 289, 2c8, 2de, 2e7, 2eb, 33c, 372, 3a0, 3da, 3ff, 48a, 4fd\}$

respectively for F and G, which upon lattice reduction yield candidates of the correct Hamming weight. Their ratio indeed gives H; however one may debate our claim that this partition was found at random and argue that we constructed it from our prior knowledge of F and G.

To counter this argument and insist that finding partitions is reasonably easy, we derived them *deterministically from the same seed as the key*. To achieve this, we proceed as follows: we draw two independent sets of $m/2 - 1$ indices in the range $[0, n/2]$, which gives the lengths of the zero blocks and the non-zero blocks. This guarantees that the partitions are balanced. The randomness used for this sampling is obtained by iterating SHA256 as for key generation.

As in the example above, we construct partitions for $m = 16$ — this choice is not dictated by probability (as the likelihood to find a correct partition is, in theory, independent of m), but rather by a trade-off between the cost of LLL and the number of partitions explored. It is possible for instance to start with $m = 2$ partitions, then $m = 3$, and so forth, but we settled for a random search which is easier to implement.

We found the following partition for F at run #1,152,006 (in 116 s):

$f = \{27, b2, 10e, 13c, 198, 1cf, 24b, 27b, 2ac, 30f, 3e1, 456, 45a, 4ba, 4d6, 4fd\}$

Recovering F alone took about two minutes.[7] Given that we have a totally deterministic random tape, we regard our experiment as legitimately reflecting reality. Because F and G are independent, this brings the total effort to about the square of this number, i.e. about 2^{34} attempts to get both partitions with certainty. Each of these attempts must also involve one LLL, which is the main cost factor.

Using the same sequence, #64,249 gave a partition for G too (in 7.6 s):

$g = \{7b, 11c, 13b, 181, 1cc, 1e1, 284, 2e6, 318, 329, 36f, 3e5, 3f1, 404, 476, 4fd\}$

Finally, note that the task is fully parallelizable and would benefit from running on several independent computers, a remark that we will later use in our final workfactor estimates.

Computing the Secret Key. Running our program as explained in Sect. 2, we recover F, G, and confirm that $H = F/G \bmod p$.

---

[7] Experiments with random partitions show that this number is quite variable and follows a Poisson distribution, with a correct partition being typically found earlier, with an average of 2^{17} tries.

4 Predicting the Total Execution Time

4.1 Naive Attack

Putting all of the above together, the total expected effort is:

$$\frac{(\text{LLL\_Time} + 2 \times \text{Partition\_Time}) \times \text{Average\_Partition\_Tries}^2}{\text{Number\_of\_Processors}}$$

Where, in our basic scenario $\text{Average\_Partition\_Tries} = 2^h$.

We performed LLL on Mathematica using the `LatticeReduce` function, which took less than a second in the worst case on a simple laptop. We safely assume that this figure can be divided by 10 using a dedicated and optimized code. We also assume that a credible attacker can, for example, very easily afford to buy or rent 150 TILE-Gx72 multicore processors.

$$\frac{\frac{1}{10} \times 1{,}152{,}006 \times 64{,}249}{150 \times 72} \times \frac{1}{60 \times 60 \times 24} \approx 7 \,\text{days } 22 \,\text{hours}$$

Hence, according to the evidence exhibited in this paper, breaking a 1279 bit key takes a week using 150 currently available multicore processors (e.g., TILE-Gx72).

5 Conclusion

While we did not formally evaluate efficiency nor asymptotic complexities, our quick and dirty experiments clearly suffice to show that key recovery is fast and within reach. An obvious countermeasure consists in increasing parameter sizes. Hence a precise re-evaluation of parameter sizes and safety margins of the Mersenne Low Hamming Ratio Assumption seems in order. More systemic protections may consist in modifying the definition of H (and possibly the underlying cryptosystem) which is clearly a very interesting open problem.

Nonetheless, the AJPS idea of exploiting the fact that arithmetics modulo Mersenne numbers is (somewhat) Hamming-weight preserving, is very elegant and seems very rich in possibilities and potential cryptographic applications.

References

1. Aggarwal, D., Joux, A., Prakash, A., Santha, M.: A new public-key cryptosystem via Mersenne numbers. Cryptology ePrint Archive, Report 2017/481 (2017). http://eprint.iacr.org/2017/481
2. Joux, A.: Algorithmic Cryptanalysis. CRC Press, Boca Raton (2009)
3. Lenstra, A.K., Lenstra, H.W., Lovász, L.: Factoring polynomials with rational coefficients. Math. Ann. 261(4), 515–534 (1982)
4. Nguyen, P.Q., Stern, J.: The two faces of lattices in cryptology. In: Silverman, J.H. (ed.) CaLC 2001. LNCS, vol. 2146, pp. 146–180. Springer, Heidelberg (2001). https://doi.org/10.1007/3-540-44670-2_12
5. Stanton, D., White, D.: Constructive Combinatorics. Springer Science & Business Media, Berlin (2012)

Energy-Efficient ARM64 Cluster
with Cryptanalytic Applications
80 Cores That Do Not Cost You an ARM and a Leg

Thom Wiggers[✉]

Institute of Computing and Information Science,
Radboud University, Nijmegen, The Netherlands
thom@thomwiggers.nl

Abstract. Getting a lot of CPU power used to be an expensive undertaking. Servers with many cores cost a lot of money and consume large amounts of energy. The developments in hardware for mobile devices has resulted in a surge in relatively cheap, powerful, and low-energy CPUs. In this paper we show how to build a low-energy, eighty-core cluster built around twenty ODROID-C2 development boards for under 1500 USD. The ODROID-C2 is a 46 USD microcomputer that provides a 1.536 GHz quad-core Cortex-A53-based CPU and 2 GB of RAM. We investigate the cluster's application to cryptanalysis by implementing Pollard's Rho method to tackle the Certicom ECC2K-130 elliptic curve challenge. We optimise software from the *Breaking ECC2K-130* technical report for the Cortex-A53. To do so, we show how to use microbenchmarking to derive the needed instruction characteristics which ARM neglected to document for the public. The implementation of the ECC2K-130 attack finally allows us to compare the proposed platform to various other platforms, including "classical" desktop CPUs, GPUs and FPGAs. Although it may still be slower than for example FPGAs, our cluster still provides a lot of value for money.

Keywords: ARM · Compute cluster · Cryptanalysis ·
Elliptic curve cryptography · ECC2K-130

1   Introduction

Bigger is not always better. Traditionally large computational tasks have been deployed on huge, expensive clusters. These are often comprised of a collection of energy-hungry CPUs. In recent years, GPUs, FPGAs and other accelerators have complemented these. While they provide a decent speed boost, they do not bring down the price of acquiring the hardware. It is also more difficult to write software for GPUs and FPGAs.

The rise of portable computing in smartphones, tablets and the "Internet of Things" has coincided with a surge in relatively low-cost, powerful and low-energy CPUs. We investigate a cluster built from ARM Cortex-A53 based

© Springer Nature Switzerland AG 2019
T. Lange and O. Dunkelman (Eds.): LATINCRYPT 2017, LNCS 11368, pp. 175–188, 2019.
https://doi.org/10.1007/978-3-030-25283-0_10

Table 1. Shopping list for the complete cluster. Cost of the Lego is not included.

Item	Cost per unit (USD)	Number	Total cost
ODROID-C2	$ 46	20	$ 920
5 V Power Supply	$ 5	20	$ 100
Micro-SD cards	$ 17	20	$ 340
LAN cables	$ 1	21	$ 21
24-port switch (TL-SG1024D)	$ 85	1	$ 85
Total			$ 1466

development boards. The Cortex-A53 has been employed in many smartphones,[1] and is also the CPU powering the popular Raspberry Pi 3 [3] development board and Nintendo Switch game console [20]. We used the ODROID-C2 by Hardkernel [4]. The ODROID-C2 provides a quad-core, 1.536 GHz CPU and 2 GB of RAM for 46 US Dollars.

In this paper, we will start out by showing how to build a cheap cluster from 20 ODROID-C2 boards. This includes a "shopping list" with all of the required components. We will then discuss the characteristics of the Cortex-A53. Microbenchmarking is used to determine instruction characteristics that ARM have neglected to publish.

Next, we adapted software from the international effort to break the ECC2K-130 challenge elliptic curve [5] to run on our platform. Using Karatsuba multiplication and bitslicing techniques, we are able to run 79 million Pollard Rho iterations per second on our full cluster.

Finally, the results with our ECC2K-130 software allow us to compare the cluster to several other platforms. We will compare our efforts with the implementations of ECC2K-130 on Desktop CPUs, GPUs and FPGAs. While it may still be slower than FPGAs, our cluster still provides a lot of performance on a modest budget.

2 Building a Cheap Cluster

In this section we will explain how we built the cluster. We hope this inspires people who consider building a similar setup.

We ordered hardware as per the shopping list in Table 1. The listed prices are indicative of what we paid for the components. We did however pay a bit more for the ODROID-C2s due to European availability, shipping times and taxes. The listed price is from the manufacturer at Hardkernel.com.

We formatted the SD cards and prepared them with Arch Linux ARM. Ansible [1] was used to provision them with the appropriate settings and to

---

[1] Including the Motorola Moto G5 Plus, Moto X Play, Samsung Galaxy A3 and A5, and HTC Desire 826: https://goo.gl/aZMky5.

deploy software. The provisioning scripts and Ansible playbooks are available at thomwiggers.nl/research/armcluster/.

Inspired by Cox et al.'s Raspberry Pi cluster [13], we built a Lego enclosure for the ODROID-C2 boards as seen in Fig. 1. It allows us to mount the boards in such a way that we get a reasonably compact setup. It also prevents any unwanted contact between exposed metal parts of the boards (notably I/O pins). Finally, Legos allow to preserve some airflow as they are rigid enough to leave gaps between columns of the structure.

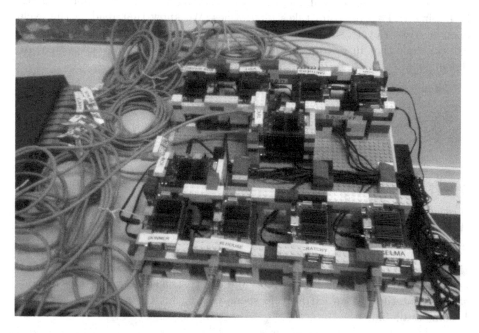

Fig. 1. The assembled Lego "rack". Cable management remains a subject for further investigation.

3   The ARM Cortex-A53

The ARM Cortex-A53 is a 64-bit CPU that implements the ARMv8-A architecture. As such it provides 32 registers, twice the number of registers in the previous ARMv7 architecture. Of special interest for high-performance applications are the 128-bit NEON registers, as we will explain in Sect. 4.3. ARMv8 provides 32 of these SIMD registers, again doubling the number available compared to ARMv7 [2].

3.1   Determining Hardware Characteristics

To be able to understand the real potential performance of a certain CPU, we need to look at how CPU instructions behave. We need to understand not only the number of cycles a certain instruction spends, but also the instruction latency, the delay before its result becomes available. This allows us to write software that uses the available circuits as efficiently as possible. Unfortunately, while ARM published very detailed information for previous generations of Cortex CPUs, we found information on the Cortex-A53 severely lacking. This meant we had to try and figure out cycle timings and instruction characteristics ourselves.

Fortunately, the Cortex-A53 does provide a cycle counter. It is precise enough to do benchmarking of small snippets of code. An example benchmark is given in Listing 1. This program takes nine cycles. We know that reading the cycle counter costs a cycle, so these four instructions cost eight cycles. From this we can conclude that in a sequence of loads, each load costs two cycles if they are independent.

```
fourloads: mrs x17, PMCCNTR_EL0    ; store cycle counter at x17
           ldr q0, [x0]            ; load q0 from address x0
           ldr q1, [x0]            ; load q1
           ldr q2, [x0]            ; load q2
           ldr q3, [x0]            ; load q3
           mrs x18, PMCCNTR_EL0    ; store cycle counter at x18
           sub x0, x18, x17        ; cycles spent = x18 - x19
           ret
```

Listing 1: Example microbenchmark subroutine that measures four independent 128-bit vector loads.

Listing 2 demonstrates a sequence of instructions where the second instruction uses the result of the first one. These two lines are measured to cost four cycles. We know that ldr is two cycles and eor costs a single cycle. This demonstrates that there is an extra cycle spent waiting for the result of the ldr to become available.

```
ldr q0, [x0]
eor v0.16b, v0.16b, v0.16b
```

Listing 2: Example microbenchmark to investigate vector load latencies. Note that q0 and v0 are the same register.

The two instructions shown in Listing 3 take only two cycles to execute. This is a cycle less than the simple addition of the two cycles of ldr and single cycle of eor. This shows that some instructions may execute simultaneously.

```
ldr q0, [x0]
eor v1.16b, v1.16b, v1.16b
```

Listing 3: Example microbenchmark to investigate the NEON execution pipelines.

We can use these details to avoid bad schedules that cost more cycles than necessary, like that in Listing 2, and try to use those that do more in fewer cycles as in Listing 3 instead. A summary our hypotheses for 128-bit vector operations can be found in Table 2. These operations are of interest to our application, which will become clear in Sect. 4. In Appendix A we will discuss some more findings for other operations and input sizes.

Detailed information on instruction characteristics is clearly of vital importance for the optimisations performed by compilers. Without it, they can hardly be expected to generate efficient instruction schedules. Unfortunately, it appears both Clang and GCC suffer from the lack of documentation. They generate arguably inefficient code in our tests with NEON programs. Consequently, to get decent performance out of the Cortex-A53 we need to hand-optimise code. We would still like to urge ARM to release better documentation for this CPU.

Table 2. Hypothesised 128-bit vector instruction characteristics on the Cortex-A53. Latencies are including the issue cycles. Vector `ldr` and `ldp` can be paired with a single arithmetic instruction for free.See Appendix A for more details.

Instruction	Issue cycles	Latency (cycles)
Binary arithmetic (`eor, and`)	1	1
Addition (`add`)	1	2
Load (`ldr`)	2	3
Store (`str`)	1	—
Load pair (`ldp`)	4	3, 4
Store pair (`stp`)	2	—

Of special interest are the instructions that load or store two registers at the same time. When using these for vector registers, they appear to be at best as fast as the two individual instructions they would replace. "Load pair" `ldp` in particular does not appear to pair up with arithmetic instructions as well as `ldr` does, making it almost always a poor choice. Unfortunately, code generated by Clang 4.9 makes heavy use of it.

Our benchmarking software is available through our website at thomwiggers.nl/research/armcluster/. We hope that it allows others to learn more about this platform, and welcome contributions.

4 Breaking ECC on the Cortex-A53

To better understand the complexity of the elliptic-curve-discrete-logarithm problem (ECDLP) underlying elliptic curve cryptography, Certicom has published several challenges [11]. Several smaller instances have been broken already, but the 131-bit challenges, the last level-I challenges, remain open. There are two challenges over $\mathbb{F}_{2^{131}}$ and one over $\mathbb{F}_p$, where p is a 131-bit prime number.

The 2009 report "Breaking ECC2K-130" [5] describes a viable attack on the Koblitz curve challenge in $\mathbb{F}_{2^{131}}$ using Pollard's Rho method [19]. They implement their approach on various hardware platforms and give estimates how many instances of those platforms would be needed to carry out the full attack. We can build on this work by adapting the attack to our platform and providing similar estimates.

We will first explain how the attack works and analyse the expected complexity. Then we will go into adapting the attack to our target platform, the Cortex-A53. Finally, we will discuss performance estimates based on real-world benchmarks of this work.

4.1 Distributed Pollard Rho

The ECDLP problem is defined as follows: given an elliptic curve E and two points P, Q on curve E such that $Q = [k]P$, find the integer k. In other words, try to find the discrete logarithm of Q with respect to the base point P on an elliptic curve E. This problem, the basis of elliptic curve cryptography, is assumed to be hard.

Pollard's Rho algorithm for logarithms [19] is a well-known and powerful method to try to find such a k in an expected $\sqrt{\pi l/2}$ steps, where l is the order of P. By performing pseudo-random walks over the curve it tries to find integers a, b, a', b' such that $R = aP + bQ = a'P + b'Q$ with $b \neq b'$. When it finds such a solution, k can be obtained as $k = \frac{a'-a}{b'-b}$.

Van Oorschot and Wiener [21] described how to distribute this algorithm over K machines to gain a $\Theta(K)$ speedup. It works by having a server collect a subset of the points (R, a, b) computed by clients performing walks over the curve. These points are known as distinguished points. The clients submit the points with a Hamming weight of the x coordinate of R that is less than or equals 34 in a normal-basis representation. The server checks for each (R, a, b) it receives if it has already received a triple (R, a', b') where $b \neq b'$. If it has, it computes the solution k as above.

We should note that the authors of *Breaking ECC2K-130* [5] expect to break ECC2K-130 in an expected number of $2^{60.9} \in \mathcal{O}\left(\sqrt{\pi l/(2 \cdot 2 \cdot 131)}\right)$ iterations. They achieve this speedup over the general case of $\sqrt{\pi l/2}$ by applying various methods that exploit the special structure of Koblitz curves.

4.2 Iteration Function

We adopted the software from [5], which we obtained from the authors. In this section we will describe the iteration function it uses to walk over the curve.

The iteration function is defined as

$$R_{i+1} = \sigma^j (R_i) + R_i$$

where $j = \mathrm{HW}((x_{R_i})/2 \mod 8) + 3$. HW is the Hamming Weight function and σ is the Frobenius endomorphism, so $\sigma^j((x,y)) = (x^{2^j}, y^{2^j})$. This group automorphism can be used because ECC2K-130 is a Koblitz curve.

As $3 \leq j \leq 10$, putting all this together means that each iteration consists of at most twenty squarings and a single elliptic curve addition. In affine coordinates this means doing this for a single point would take one inversion, two multiplications, 21 squarings and seven additions over the underlying field. "Montgomery's trick" [17] can be used to batch up N inversions, which allows us to trade the N inversions for a single inversion and $3N - 3$ multiplications. The number of multiplications per iteration thus quickly converges to five, while the number of inversions becomes negligible for large enough N.

For the full details of the attack on ECC2K-130 we will defer to [5]. This concerns more details of the iteration function, parameters and their motivation.

4.3   Bitslicing

Bitslicing is a powerful technique used by the software from [5] that allows us to perform many operations in parallel. First we unpack the 131 bits of a $\mathbb{F}_{2^{131}}$ field element into 131 separate vectors. If we do this for many of these elements, we then can take the jth bit of all these field elements and put them all in a single vector. We do this such that in the ith vector, the jth bit represents the ith bit of the jth element. As we have 128-bit NEON vector registers on ARMv8, we store 128 bits of 128 field elements in each vector. We then use the binary logic operations on these NEON registers as if they are 128-way SIMD instructions operating on each bit simultaneously.

This technique increases the latency for a single iteration as each operation needs to be decomposed into bit-wise programs. However, because of the massive increase in parallelism we achieve a much higher throughput. Effectively, we can divide our operation counts by 128, as each bit operation manipulates 128 field elements at the same time.

4.4   Optimising Multiplications

Multiplications are the most expensive operation in terms of bit operations. Naively, they scale quadratically in the size of the input. Experimental results also show that multiplications accounted for most of the runtime of our software.

Doing schoolbook multiplication of two 131-bit polynomials would take 131^2 ANDs and 130^2 XORs, adding up to 34061 bit operations in total. Karatsuba's method [16] is a well known improvement over the classic method. We followed Hutter and Schwabe's approach [15] to efficiently schedule Karatsuba with techniques from [7,10] to write 33- and 32-bit multipliers in assembly. We then compose these to form the full 131-bit multiplier.

Karatsuba's method computes the multiplication of two binary, n-bit polynomials by first splitting these polynomials in upper and lower parts. It then computes the product of the two upper parts, the two lower parts and the product of the addition of the upper and the lower part of the two inputs. These products are again computed using Karatsuba. Like [15] we use the refined Karatsuba approach from [7] to further reduce the number of operations needed. This comes together in Algorithm 1. Unlike the algorithms in Hutter and Schwabe's work, as we are working on binary polynomials, we do not need to worry about carrying bits.

Algorithm 1. Refined Karatsuba, $R = A \cdot B$

Write $A \triangleq (a_0, \ldots, a_{n-1})$, $B \triangleq (b_0, \ldots, b_{n-1})$. Let $k = \frac{n}{2}$. We distinguish the upper and lower parts as $A_l \triangleq (a_0, \ldots, a_{k-1})$, $A_h \triangleq (a_k, \ldots, a_{n-1})$, $B_l \triangleq (b_0, \ldots, b_{k-1})$, $B_h \triangleq (b_k, \ldots, b_{n-1})$. The result will be given as $R \triangleq (r_0, \ldots, r_{2n-2})$.

1. Compute $A_l \cdot B_l$. Let the result be $L = (l_0, \ldots, l_{n-2})$.
2. The lower k bits of the result R are now known: $(r_0, \ldots, r_{k-1}) = (l_0, \ldots, l_{k-1})$.
3. We now compute $(A_l + A_h)$ and $(B_l + B_h)$ so we can drop the registers holding the lower parts.
4. Compute $\bar{H} = A_h \cdot B_h + (l_k, \ldots, l_{n-2}) = (\bar{h}_0, \ldots, \bar{h}_{n-2})$. It is important to do this addition during the multiplication, to minimise the number of values kept in registers.
5. Set the upper result bits: $(r_{n+k-1}, \ldots, r_{2n-2})$.
6. Compute $M = (A_l + A_h) \cdot (B_l + B_h)$.
7. Let $U = (l_0, \ldots, l_{k-1}, \bar{h}_0, \ldots, \bar{h}_{k-1})$.
8. Compute $U = U + M + \bar{H}$.
9. Set the remaining result bits $(r_k, \ldots, r_{n+k-2}) = U$.

This approach is not the cheapest in number of operations. Bernstein [6,7] presents upper bounds for multiplication which have fewer operations. We will present a comparison in Sect. 5.1. However, the Bernstein multipliers are much harder to manually schedule, as they are presented as straight-line code with many intermediate values. The compilers we tried also struggled with it, and our assembly multipliers easily outperform the code generated for Bernstein's straight-line programs. These multipliers are available through our website at thomwiggers.nl/research/armcluster/.

4.5 Pollard Rho Iterations Per Second

With our high-speed multipliers, batching 32 inversions, and using bitslicing to perform 128 iterations in parallel, we achieve a speed of 1560 cycles per iteration. As the ODROID-C2 has four cores running at 1536 MHz, this means that a single board performs 3.94 million iterations per second. As we expect to need $2^{60.9}$ Pollard Rho iterations, we would need to have 17310 boards or 866 clusters running continuously to break the ECC2K-130 challenge curve in one year.

5   Results and Comparison

5.1 Benchmarking Multiplications

By using the cycle counters made available by the architecture we can obtain accurate cycle counts. We will compare our optimised assembly code with the number of bit operations and with the code given by Bernstein [6]. We compiled the code by Bernstein using Clang 4.9 with the settings `-Ofast -mtune=cortex-a53 -fomit-frame-pointer`. We will also give the number of bit operations needed by our Karatsuba approach. The published software includes our benchmarking program.

Table 3. Multiplication benchmarks. Cycle counts reported are the median of 200 000 measurements.

	4×4	8×8	16×16	32×32
Bit operations [6]	25	100	350	1158
Refined Karatsuba bit operations (Algorithm 1)	—	100	353	1168
Straight-line code [6] in C (cycles)	59	173	909	3698
This work (cycles)	42	137	416	2173

The results are shown in Table 3. The difference between the number of bit operations and the number of cycles needed can largely be found in the number of loads and stores that are needed. Some of these are required, such as the loads that are needed for the inputs ($2n$ for an $n \times n$ multiplier) and the store operations needed to write the result ($2n - 2$). Based on what we learnt from the microbenchmarks in Sect. 3.1 we should thus expect an additional $4n - 2$ cycles. Any further overhead results from extra spills that need to be done because not all intermediates fit into the available registers and from bad scheduling. It is not always possible to schedule the instructions in such a way that all pipeline stalls can be avoided.

The massive difference between the number of bit operations and the needed CPU cycles for the straight-line C code clearly demonstrates the poor performance of the code generated by C-compilers on the Cortex-A53. ARM would make this platform a lot more attractive if they provided the compilers with the information they need to improve instruction scheduling.

5.2 Energy Usage

We performed measurements of the energy usage of our cluster. For the measurements we used a Globaltronics GT-PM-07 Energy Meter. We measured the consumption at the wall socket, where the device or devices we were measuring were plugged in. This means that consumption includes peripheral devices like adaptors. For the measurements of multiple devices, we measured the power strip into which everything was plugged in.

Measurements were obtained for both heavy CPU load and while the cluster was idle.[2] To generate CPU load we ran our ECC2K-130 software. Results can be found in Table 4. All results have been rounded up.

---

[2] We should note that is important to remove the J2 jumper from the ODROID-C2 board when not powering it through USB: this saves a significant amount of energy.

Table 4. Energy Usage

Item		Watts
ODROID-C2	Idle	2.3 W
	CPU load	5.3 W
Switch		13 W
20 ODROID-C2s	Idle	47 W
	CPU load	108 W
Complete System	Idle	59 W
	CPU load	122 W

5.3 Comparison with Other Hardware

Because the ECC2K-130 software has been optimised for many platforms, we can use it to make a comparison. The 2009 technical report [5] and the papers discussing further improvements of implementations on various platforms [8,10,14] provide iteration counts for various systems. While these platforms are no longer state-of-the-art, we think it still provides some insight into how our cluster compares. However, we will not compare prices of the different platforms, as some are no longer available and their retail prices are not representative anymore.

To get some more modern numbers, we adapted our software to run on AVX2 as well. In the table we list the performance of the 10-core Intel

Table 5. ECC2K-130 on various platforms [5,8,10,14]

Type	Instance	Iters/s ($\times 10^6$)	Watts	Watts (10^6 iters/s)	Notes
CPU	Core 2 QX6850	22.45	130 W	5.8	CPU TDP only
CPU	E5–2630L v4	61	55 W	0.9	CPU TDP only
GPU	NVIDIA GTX 295	63	289 W	4.6	GPU only
PS3	PlayStation 3 Cell CPU	25.57	200 W	7.8	Energy use while in "normal use" [18], 380 W PSU
FPGA	Xilinx XC3S5000	111	5 W	0.045	
ARM	ODROID-C2	3.94	5 W	1.3	
	ODROID-C2 Cluster	79	122 W	1.5	

E5–2630L v4. This is a 10-core, 1.8 GHz CPU. Our implementation needs 294 cycles per iteration on this machine, for a total of 61 million iterations per second. While very fast, this CPU does come with a hefty price tag. It does illustrate that Intel CPUs also have gotten quite a bit faster.

Table 5 compares a desktop CPU, a GPU, the PlayStation 3 and a Spartan 3 FPGA with the ODROID-C2. We can see that at least per watt, the ODROID-C2 performs admirably. This conclusion is strengthened if one considers that the other platforms need more hardware. For instance, CPUs and GPUs need to be mounted on Motherboards and require additional hardware such as hard drives. These consume additional energy.

We see that FPGAs clearly outperform all competitors, including our proposal. They provide an impressive amount of iterations for very low energy. On a different curve and using a more recent FPGA, Bernstein, Engels, Lange, Niederhagen, Paar, Schwabe and Zimmermann achieve 300 million iterations per second, although we should note that their curve is only 113 bits [9]. For purely cryptanalytic purposes FPGAs thus remain the most potent candidate.

However, our cluster is composed of more general-purpose hardware and can be used using more common programming languages. This makes it much more accessible and more generally applicable. We also see applications in education, in for example teaching distributed algorithms.

A   Cortex-A53 Benchmarking Results

In this section we will provide an overview of our results with microbenchmarking. As described in Sect. 3.1 we measured the execution times of various instructions. We also looked at various combinations of instructions to learn about pipelining behaviour and execution units.

A.1   Operations On "Normal" Registers

Our findings for AArch64 instructions are shown in Table 6. When measuring two arithmetic instructions we noticed that they take the time as a single instruction. This suggests that the Cortex-A53 has two ALUs and thus can compute two arithmetic instructions at the same time. This does not hold for multiplication or the memory operations and we suspect that the architecture only has one multiplier and a single processing unit for memory access.

A.2   Operations On NEON Vector Registers

The NEON vector registers are available in different sizes. It is possible to access them as 64-bit vectors or as 128-bit vectors. Tables 7 and 8 give an overview of our results. For the 64-bit vectors we again notice that two arithmetic instructions run in the same time as a single instruction. This however is not the case with the 128-bit vectors. This suggests that there are two 64-bit execution units that are combined for the 128-bit values.

Table 6. Hypothesised instruction characteristics for instructions operating on registers. Latencies are including the issue cycles. Many instructions can be dual-issued.

Instruction	Mnemonic	Issue cycles	Latency (cycles)
Exclusive Or	eor	1	1
And	and	1	1
Or	orr	1	1
Or Not	orn	1	1
Addition	add	1	1
Subtraction	sub	1	1
Multiplication	mul	2	4
Load	ldr	1	1
Load Pair	ldp	2	first: 2, second: 3
Store	str	1	—
Store Pair	stp	2	—

Load and store operations again do not execute in parallel and we suspect there is only one load-store-unit. It is possible to pair up an arithmetic operation with a load or store.

B The ECC2K-130 Challenge Parameters

The Certicom ECC2K-130 challenge is defined in [11,12]. The challenge is to find integer k such that $Q = [k]P$ on the Koblitz curve $y^2 + xy = x^3 + 1$ defined over $\mathbb{F}_{2^{131}}$. The group order $|E(\mathbb{F}_{2^{131}})| = 4l$, where l is the 129-bit prime number

$$l = 680564733841876926932320129493409985129.$$

The coordinates of P and Q are given in a polynomial-basis representation of $F_2[z]/(F)$ where $F(z) = z^{131} + z^{13} + z^2 + z + 1$. They are represented below as hexadecimal bit strings with respect to this basis.

$$P_x = \texttt{051C99BFA6F18DE467C80C23B98C7994AA}$$
$$P_y = \texttt{042EA2D112ECEC71FCF7E000D7EFC978BD}$$
$$Q_x = \texttt{06C997F3E7F2C66A4A5D2FDA13756A37B1}$$
$$Q_y = \texttt{04A38D11829D32D347BD0C0F584D546E9A}$$

Table 7. Hypothesised instruction characteristics for instructions operating on 64-bit vectors. Latencies are including the issue cycles. Arithmetic operations can be issued together with other arithmetic instructions or with a load or store operation.

Instruction	Mnemonic	Issue cycles	Latency (cycles)
Exclusive Or	eor	1	1
And	and	1	1
Or	orr	1	1
Or Not	orn	1	1
Addition	add	1	2
Subtraction	sub	1	2
Multiplication	mul	1	4
Load	ldr	2	2
Load Pair	ldp	4	first: 3, second: 4
Store	str	2	—
Store Pair	stp	4	—

Table 8. Hypothesised instruction characteristics for instructions operating on 128-bit vectors. Latencies are including the issue cycles.

Instruction	Mnemonic	Issue cycles	Latency (cycles)
Exclusive Or	eor	1	1
And	and	1	1
Or	orr	1	1
Or Not	orn	1	1
Addition	add	1	2
Subtraction	sub	1	2
Multiplication	mul	1	4
Load	ldr	2	3
Load Pair	ldp	4	first: 4, second: 5
Store	str	2	—
Store Pair	stp	4	—

References

1. Ansible. https://docs.ansible.com/ansible/. Accessed 22 June 2017
2. ARM Cortex-A Series Programmer's Guide for ARMv8-A. Version 1.0. https://developer.arm.com/products/processors/cortex-a/cortex-a53/docs/den0024/latest/1-introduction. Accessed 22 June 2017
3. BCM2837 - Raspberry Pi documentation. https://www.raspberrypi.org/documentation/hardware/raspberrypi/bcm2837/README.md. Accessed 08 May 2017

4. ODROID-C2. http://www.hardkernel.com/main/products/prdt_info.php?g_code=G145457216438. Accessed 03 Apr 2017
5. Bailey, D.V., Batina, L., Bernstein, D.J., Birkner, P., Bos, J.W., Chen, H.-C., Cheng, C.-M., Damme, G.V., de Meulenaer, G., Perez, L.J.D., Fan, J., Güneysu, T., Gürkaynak, F., Kleinjung, T., Lange, T., Mentens, N., Niederhagen, R., Paar, C., Regazzoni, F., Schwabe, P., Uhsadel, L., Herrewege, A.V., Yang, B.-Y.: Breaking ECC2K-130. Cryptology ePrint Archive, Report 2009/514 (2009). https://eprint.iacr.org/2009/541/
6. Bernstein, D.J.: Minimum number of bit operations for multiplication. https://binary.cr.yp.to/m.html. Accessed 05 Apr 2017
7. Bernstein, D.J.: Batch binary Edwards. In: Halevi, S. (ed.) CRYPTO 2009. LNCS, vol. 5677, pp. 317–336. Springer, Heidelberg (2009). https://doi.org/10.1007/978-3-642-03356-8_19
8. Bernstein, D.J., Chen, H.-C., Cheng, C.-M., Lange, T., Niederhagen, R., Schwabe, P., Yang, B.-Y.: ECC2K-130 on NVIDIA GPUs. In: Gong, G., Gupta, K.C. (eds.) INDOCRYPT 2010. LNCS, vol. 6498, pp. 328–346. Springer, Heidelberg (2010). https://doi.org/10.1007/978-3-642-17401-8_23
9. Bernstein, J.D., Engels, S., Lange, T., Niederhagen, R., Paar, C., Schwabe, P., Zimmermann, R.: Faster discrete logarithms on fpgas (2016). http://cryptojedi.org/papers/#sect113r2
10. Bos, J.W., Kleinjung, T., Niederhagen, R., Schwabe, P.: ECC2K-130 on cell CPUs. In: Bernstein, D.J., Lange, T. (eds.) AFRICACRYPT 2010. LNCS, vol. 6055, pp. 225–242. Springer, Heidelberg (2010). https://doi.org/10.1007/978-3-642-12678-9_14
11. Certicom Corp: The Certicom ECC Challenge. https://www.certicom.com/content/certicom/en/the-certicom-ecc-challenge.html. Accessed 03 Apr 2017
12. Certicom Research. Certicom ECC Challenge. https://www.certicom.com/content/dam/certicom/images/pdfs/challenge-2009.pdf. Accessed 10 Nov 2009
13. Cox, S.J., Cox, J.T., Boardman, R.P., Johnston, S.J., Scott, M., O'Brien, N.S.: Iridis-pi: a low-cost, compact demonstration cluster. Cluster Comput. **17**(2), 349–358 (2014). https://doi.org/10.1007/s10586-013-0282-7
14. Fan, J., Bailey, D.V., Batina, L., Guneysu, T., Paar, C., Verbauwhede, I.: Breaking elliptic curve cryptosystems using reconfigurable hardware. In: 2010 International Conference on Field Programmable Logic and Applications, pp. 133–138, 8 2010. https://doi.org/10.1109/FPL.2010.34
15. Hutter, M., Schwabe, P.: Multiprecision multiplication on AVR revisited. J. Cryptogr. Eng. **5**(3), 201–214 (2015). http://cryptojedi.org/papers/#avrmul
16. Karatsuba, A., Ofman, Y.: Multiplication of multidigit numbers on automata. In: Soviet Physics Doklady, vol. 7, p. 595 (1963)
17. Montgomery, P.L.: Speeding the Pollard and elliptic curve methods of factorization. Math. Comput. **48**(177), 243–264 (1987)
18. Patel, N.: Sony says the 40GB PS3 is still using 90nm chips. https://www.engadget.com/2007/11/03/sony-says-the-40gb-ps3-is-still-using-90nm-chips/. Accessed 24 Aug 2017
19. Pollard, J.M.: Monte Carlo methods for index computation (mod p). Math. Comput. **32**(143), 918–924 (1978)
20. TechInsights. Nintendo Switch teardown. http://techinsights.com/about-techinsights/overview/blog/nintendo-switch-teardown/. Accessed 08 May 2017
21. van Oorschot, P.C., Wiener, M.J.: Parallel collision search with cryptanalytic applications. J. Cryptol. **12**(1), 1–28 (1999). https://doi.org/10.1007/PL00003816

Theory of Symmetric-Key Cryptography

Generation of 8-Bit S-Boxes Having Almost Optimal Cryptographic Properties Using Smaller 4-Bit S-Boxes and Finite Field Multiplication

Reynier Antonio de la Cruz Jiménez[(⊠)]

Institute of Cryptography, Havana University, Havana, Cuba
djr.antonio537@gmail.com

Abstract. Substitution Boxes (S-Boxes) as the only component of non-linearity in modern ciphers, play a crucial role in the protection against differential, linear and algebraic attacks. The construction of S-Boxes with cryptographic properties close to optimal is an open problem. In this article we propose a new construction for generating such 8-bit permutations with nonlinearity up to a value of 108.

Keywords: S-Box · Permutations · Vectorial Boolean functions · Finite field multiplication

1 Introduction and Motivation

Modern symmetric ciphers contain one or more cores of nonlinear operations. Often these cores are n to m Boolean mappings, called S-Boxes. Among the whole set of S-Boxes the bijective ones (also-called permutations) are particularly interesting. In the design of many block ciphers, S-Boxes are often chosen to bring confusion into ciphers. The security of these ciphers is then strongly dependent on the cryptographic properties of the S-Boxes, for this reason S-Boxes are carefully chosen and the criteria or algorithm used to build them are usually explained and justified by the designers of prospective algorithms.

The known methods for constructing S-Boxes can be divided into three main classes: algebraic constructions, pseudo-random generation and heuristic techniques. Each approach has its advantages and disadvantages respectively (see, e.g. [25]). The inversion in the finite field with 2^n elements is a good method for generating robust S-Boxes. With respect to cryptographic strength against differential and linear attacks, the inversion in the finite field, used in block ciphers like AES/Rijndael [35], Camellia [2], ARIA [30], HyRAL [23], Hierocrypt [37] has the best known values. Nevertheless, further analysis has shown that this approach leads to existence of a system of polynomial equations with low degree and "potential vulnerability" of the cipher to algebraic attacks [13]. It should be noted that the problem of solving generic systems of polynomials equations

© Springer Nature Switzerland AG 2019
T. Lange and O. Dunkelman (Eds.): LATINCRYPT 2017, LNCS 11368, pp. 191–206, 2019.
https://doi.org/10.1007/978-3-030-25283-0_11

over finite fields is NP-hard [15] already for quadratic ones, but there are obviously instances where it is not the case. This discrepancy combined with the fundamental complexity of rigorous analysis sometimes leads to certain controversy regarding the validity of the so-called algebraic attacks. However, from a designer's perspective, it is better to choose an S-Box (or several S-Boxes) that meets specific (see, Sect. 4) algebraic, linear and differential requirements. This kind of permutations has been used in the design of cryptographic algorithms like BelT [48], Kuznyechik [20] and Kalyna [38] and compared with the inversion function, which can be described by polynomial equations of degree 2, their main advantage (in terms of its cryptographic properties) is a description by a system of 441 polynomials equations of degree 3.

Motivated by specialist's work [8] of Luxembourg's university Alex Biryukov, Léo Perrin and Aleksei Udovenko on decomposition of the S-Box used in the block cipher Kuznyechik, hash function Streebog [21] and CAESAR first round candidate stribobr1 [45] we propose a new construction for generating cryptographically strong 8-bit S-Boxes using smaller ones and finite field multiplication.

In cryptography, it is not uncommon to build an S-Box from smaller ones, usually an 8-bit S-Box from several 4-bit S-Boxes. For example, S-Boxes used in CLEFIA [49], Iceberg [47], Khazad [4], Whirlpool [5] and Zorro [18] are permutations of 8 bits based on smaller S-Boxes. In many cases, such a structure is used not only to allow an efficient implementation of the S-Box in hardware or using a bit-sliced approach, but also to protect S-Boxes implemented in this way against side-channel attacks. In this work we do not investigate the implementation cost of our S-Boxes in hardware. We focus on some cryptographic properties of those S-Boxes obtained by our method.

This article is structured as follows: In Sect. 2 we give the basic definitions. In Sect. 3 we present a new method for constructing S-Boxes having almost optimal cryptographic properties. In Sect. 4 we present an algorithm for finding cryptographically strong 8-bit permutations. A summary of some available recent methods for the generation of permutations with strong cryptographic properties and some related problem with these methods are discussed in Sect. 5. New S-boxes with stronger properties, generated by our construction are given in Sect. 6. Our work is concluded in Sect. 7.

2   Definitions and Notations

Let V_n be the n-dimensional vector space over the field GF(2), by $S(V_n)$ we denote the symmetric group on set of 2^n elements. The finite field of size 2^n is denoted by GF(2^n), where GF(2^n) = GF(2)$[\xi]/g(\xi)$, for some irreducible polynomial $g(\xi)$ of degree n. We use the notation $\mathbb{Z}/2^n$ for the ring of the integers modulo 2^n. There are bijective mappings between $\mathbb{Z}/2^n, V_n$ and GF(2^n) defined by the correspondences:

$$[a_{n-1} \cdot 2^{n-1} + \ldots + a_0] \leftrightarrow (a_{n-1}, \ldots, a_0) \leftrightarrow [a_{n-1} \cdot \xi^{n-1} + \ldots + a_0].$$

Using these mapping in what follows we make no difference between vectors of V_n and the corresponding elements in $\mathbb{Z}/2^n$ and GF(2^n).

Also in the rest of this article, we shall use the following operations and notations:

$a\|b$ — concatenation of the vectors a, b of V_l, i.e. a vector from V_{2l};

0 — the null vector of V_l ;

$\oplus$ — bitwise eXclusive-OR. Addition in $\mathrm{GF}(2^l)$;

$<a, b>$ — the scalar product of vectors $a = (a_{l-1}, \ldots, a_0), b = (b_{l-1}, \ldots, b_0)$ of V_l and is equal to $<a, b> = a_{l-1}b_{l-1} \oplus \ldots \oplus a_0 b_0$;

$w_H(a)$ — the Hamming weight of a binary vector $a \in V_l$, i.e. the number of its nonzero coordinates;

$\otimes$ — finite field multiplication;

$F \circ G$ — a composition of mappings, where G is the first to operate;

F^{-1} — the inverse transformation to some bijective mapping F.

Now, we give some basic definitions, which usually are used as cryptographic tools for evaluating the strength of S-Boxes with respect to linear, differential and algebraic attack. For this purpose, we consider an n-bit S-Box Φ as a vector of Boolean functions:

$$\Phi = (f_0, \ldots, f_{n-1}), f_i : V_n \to V_1, i = 0, 1, \ldots n - 1. \tag{1}$$

For some fixed $i = 0, 1, \ldots, n - 1$, every Boolean function f_i can be written as a sum over V_1 of distinct t-order products of its arguments, $0 \leq t \leq n - 1$; this is called the algebraic normal form of f_i. Functions f_i are called coordinate Boolean functions of the S-Box Φ and it is well known that most of the desirable cryptographic properties of Φ can be defined in terms of their linear combinations. S-Box coordinate Boolean functions of Φ and all their linear combinations are referred to as the S-Box component Boolean functions.

Definition 1. For each vector $a \in V_n$ the The Walsh-Hadamard transform $W_f(a)$ of the n-variable Boolean function f is defined as

$$W_f(a) = \sum_{x \in V_n} (-1)^{f(x) \oplus <a, x>}. \tag{2}$$

Definition 2. The nonlinearity N_f of the n-variable Boolean function f is defined as

$$N_f = \min_{g \in \mathcal{A}_n} w_H(f \oplus g), \tag{3}$$

where $\mathcal{A}_n$ is the set of all n-variable affine Boolean functions and $w_H(f \oplus g)$ is the Hamming weight of the n-variable Boolean function $f \oplus g$. The nonlinearity N_f can be expressed as follows:

$$N_f = 2^{n-1} - \frac{1}{2} \max_{a \in V_n \setminus \{0\}} |W_f(a)| \tag{4}$$

Definition 3. The autocorrelation transform, taken with respect to $a \in V_n$, of an n-variable Boolean function f is denoted by $\hat{r}_f(a)$ and defined as:

$$\hat{r}_f(a) = \sum_{x \in V_n} (-1)^{f(x) \oplus f(x \oplus a)}. \tag{5}$$

Definition 4. The absolute indicator of the n-variable Boolean function f, denoted by $AC(f)_{max}$ is defined as

$$AC(f)_{max} = \max_{a \in V_n \setminus \{0\}} |\hat{r}_f(a)|. \tag{6}$$

Definition 5. For $a, b \in V_n$ the Walsh transform $W_\Phi(a, b)$ of an n-bit S-Box Φ is defined as

$$W_\Phi(a, b) = \sum_{x \in V_n} (-1)^{<b,\Phi(x)> \oplus <a,x>}. \tag{7}$$

Definition 6. The nonlinearity of an n-bit S-Box Φ, denoted by N_Φ, is defined as

$$N_\Phi = \min_{a \in V_n \setminus \{0\}} \{N_{a_0 f_0 \oplus \ldots \oplus a_{n-1} f_{n-1}}\}, \tag{8}$$

where $N_{a_0 f_0 \oplus \ldots \oplus a_{n-1} f_{n-1}}$ is the nonlinearity of each of the component Boolean functions excluding the zero one.
The nonlinearity N_Φ of an arbitrary n-bit S-Box Φ can be calculated as follows

$$N_\Phi = 2^{n-1} - \frac{1}{2} \cdot \max_{a \neq 0, b \in V_n} |W_\Phi(a, b)|. \tag{9}$$

From a cryptographic point of view S-Boxes with small values of Walsh coefficients offer better resistance against linear attacks.

Definition 7. The differential uniformity of an n-bit S-Box Φ, denoted by δ_Φ, is defined as

$$\delta_\Phi = \max_{a \neq 0, b \in V_n} \delta(a, b), \tag{10}$$

where $\delta(a, b) = |\{x \in V_n | \Phi(x \oplus a) \oplus \Phi(x) = b\}|$.
The resistance offered by an S-Box against differential attacks is related by the highest value of δ, for this reason S-Boxes must have a small value of δ-uniformity for a sufficient level of protection against this type of attacks.

Definition 8. The maximal absolute indicator and the sum-of-squares indicator of an n-bit S-Box Φ, denoted by $AC(\Phi)_{max}$ and $\sigma(\Phi)$, respectively, are defined as

$$AC(\Phi)_{max} = \max_{a \in V_n \setminus \{0\}} |\hat{r}_f(a_0 f_0 \oplus \ldots \oplus a_{n-1} f_{n-1})|, \tag{11}$$

$$\sigma(\Phi) = \sum_{a \in V_n} \hat{r}_f^2(a). \tag{12}$$

Any n-bit S-box Φ should have low autocorrelation in order to improve the avalanche effect of the cipher [16], for this reason, the absolute indicators of the component Boolean functions of the S-box should be as small as possible. In other words, the parameter $AC(\Phi)_{max}$, should be as small as possible.

The algebraic degree of the Boolean functions $f : V_n \to V_1$, denoted by $\deg f$, is the maximum order of the terms appearing in its algebraic normal form.

Definition 9. The minimum degree of an S-Box Φ, denoted by $\deg(\Phi)$, is defined as

$$\deg(\Phi) = \min_{a \in V_n \backslash \{0\}} \{\deg(a_0 f_0 \oplus \ldots \oplus a_{n-1} f_{n-1})\}. \tag{13}$$

In order to resist low order approximation [19,34] and higher order differential attacks [29] any n-bit S-Box Φ should have a minimum degree as high as possible.

Proposition 1. *For any 8-bit S-Box Φ we have,* $1 \le \deg(\Phi) \le 7$.

The annihilator of a Boolean function f with n variables is another Boolean function g with n variables such that $f \cdot g = 0$. For a given Boolean function f, the algebraic immunity $AI(f)$ is the minimum value d such that f or $f \oplus 1$ has a nonzero annihilator of degree d.

It is well known [10] that there are three kinds of definitions of the algebraic immunity for S-Boxes. At first, we present a concept of annihilating set [3]:

Definition 10. Let U be a subset of V_{2n}, then

$$\{p \in GF(2)[z_1, \ldots, z_{2n}] \big| p(U) = 0\}$$

is the annihilating set of U.

Definition 11. The algebraic immunity of U is defined as

$$AI(U) = \min \Big\{ \deg p \,\Big|\, 0 \neq p \in GF(2)[z_1, \ldots, z_{2n}], p(U) = 0 \Big\}.$$

Definition 12. Let Φ be any n-bit S-Box, and define

$$AI(\Phi) = \min \Big\{ AI(\Phi^{-1}(a)) \,\Big|\, a \in V_n \Big\} \tag{14}$$

as the basic algebraic immunity of Φ,

$$AI_{gr}(\Phi) = \min \Big\{ \deg p \,\Big|\, 0 \neq p \in GF(2)[z_1, \ldots, z_{2n}], p(gr(\Phi)) = 0 \Big\} \tag{15}$$

as the graph algebraic immunity of Φ, where $gr(\Phi) = \{(x, \Phi(x)) | x \in V_n\} \subseteq V_{2n}$,

$$AI_{comp}(\Phi) = \min_{a \in V_n \backslash \{0\}} \Big\{ AI(a_{n-1} f_{n-1} \oplus \ldots \oplus a_0 f_0) \Big\} \tag{16}$$

as the component algebraic immunity of Φ.

For any n-bit permutation Φ the bounds of these three algebraic immunity definitions (explained in [3]) are the following, $AI(\Phi) \leq 1$ (so there is no significance in analyzing the basic algebraic immunity of an S-Box), $AI_{gr}(\Phi) \leq d_{gr}$, where d_{gr} is the minimum positive integer which satisfies $\sum_{i=0}^{d_{gr}} \binom{2n}{i} > 2^n$ and $AI_{comp}(\Phi) \leq \lceil \frac{n}{2} \rceil$.

To the best of our knowledge, there is no literature that proposes any attack given the basic and component algebraic immunity rather than the graph algebraic immunity [7,13]. Thus we focus on the graph algebraic immunity of S-Box $\Phi - AI_{gr}(\Phi)$ and also on the parameter $t_{\Phi}^{(AI_{gr}(\Phi))}$ referred to as the number of all the independent equations in input and output values of the S-Box Φ, i.e., equations of the form $p(x, \Phi(x)) = 0 \ \forall x \in V_n$.

The level of protection provided by an S-Box Φ against algebraic attacks is measured by the parameters $AI_{gr}(\Phi)$ and $t_{\Phi}^{(AI_{gr}(\Phi))}$, respectively.

Proposition 2 ([11]). *For any 8-bit S-Box Φ we have $AI_{gr}(\Phi)) \leq 3$.*

Definition 13. An element $a \in V_n$ is called a fixed point of an n-bit S-Box Φ if $\Phi(a) = a$.

An n-bit substitution Φ must have no fixed point, i.e., $\Phi(a) \neq a, \forall a \in V_n$. Many ciphers have used the above mentioned notion for increasing resistance against statistical attacks.

Definition 14. Two n-bit S-Boxes Φ_1 and Φ_2 are affine/linear equivalent if there exist a pair of invertible affine/linear permutation $A_1(x)$ and $A_2(x)$, such that $\Phi_1(x) = A_2 \circ \Phi_2 \circ A_1(x)$.

The affine/linear equivalence can be used to prevent the appearance of fixed points during generation of some n-bit S-Box.

3   New Construction

Let $n = 2k$, where $k \geq 2$. Choosing the permutation polynomial (PP) $\tau_{2^k - 2}(x) = x^{2^k - 2}$ over GF(2^k) and arbitrary permutations $h_i \in S(V_k)$, $i = 1, 2$, we construct the following n-bit vectorial Boolean function $\pi : V_{2k} \to V_{2k}$ as follows

Construction of π
For the input value $(l\|r) \in V_{2k}$ we define the corresponding output value $\pi(l\|r) = (l_1\|r_1)$ where, $$l_1 = \begin{cases} h_1(l), & \text{if } r = 0; \\ \tau_{2^k-2}(l \otimes r), & \text{if } r \neq 0; \end{cases}$$ $$r_1 = \begin{cases} h_2(r), & \text{if } l_1 = 0; \\ l_1 \otimes \tau_{2^k-2}(r), & \text{if } l_1 \neq 0. \end{cases}$$

Taking into account that block ciphers based on Substitution-Permutation Networks need the inverse substitution to π for the decryption process we also give the construction of π^{-1}.

Construction of π^{-1}

For the input value $(l_1\|r_1) \in V_{2k}$ we define
the corresponding output value
$\pi^{-1}(l_1\|r_1) = (l\|r)$ where,

$$r = \begin{cases} h_2^{-1}(r_1), & \text{if } l_1 = 0; \\ l_1 \otimes \tau_{2^k-2}(r_1), & \text{if } l_1 \neq 0. \end{cases}$$

$$l = \begin{cases} h_1^{-1}(l_1), & \text{if } r = 0; \\ \tau_{2^k-2}(l_1 \otimes r), & \text{if } r \neq 0. \end{cases}$$

It should be noted, that the proposed construction is different from decomposition obtained in [8] and S-Boxes generated by our construction can achieve better properties (see, Sect. 6).

4 Generating 8-Bit Permutations from Smaller Ones and Finite Field Multiplication

In this work the substitution having almost optimal cryptographic properties refers to a permutation with

1. Absence of fixed points;
2. Maximum value of minimum degree;
3. Maximum graph algebraic immunity with the minimum number of equations;
4. Minimum value of δ-uniformity limited by parameter listed above;
5. Maximum value of nonlinearity limited by parameter listed above.

For example, for $n = 8$ an almost optimal permutation π without fixed points has:

- $\deg(\pi) = 7$;
- $AI_{gr}(\pi) = 3$ with $t_\pi^{(3)} = 441$;
- $\delta_\pi \leq 8$;
- $N_\pi \geq 100$.

For $n = 8$ in correspondence with the suggested construction of π we need to construct; the finite field $\mathrm{GF}(2^4)$, two 4-bit permutations $h_1, h_2 \in S(V_4)$ and the PP $\tau_{14}(x) = x^{14}$ over $\mathrm{GF}(2^4)$. It is well known [43] that there are only three irreducible polynomials of degree 4 over $\mathrm{GF}(2)$, $g_1(\xi) = \xi^4 + \xi + 1$, $g_2(\xi) = \xi^4 + \xi^3 + 1$ and $g_3(\xi) = \xi^4 + \xi^3 + \xi^2 + \xi + 1$. In what follows, for the sake of simplicity, we shall work in $\mathrm{GF}(2^4) = \mathrm{GF}(2)[\xi]/g_1(\xi)$. Thus, π can be written as follows

$$\pi(l\|r) = (l_1\|r_1), \tag{17}$$

where,

$$l_1 = \begin{cases} h_1(l), & \text{if } r = 0; \\ (l \otimes r)^{14}, & \text{if } r \neq 0; \end{cases}$$

$$r_1 = \begin{cases} h_2(r), & \text{if } l_1 = 0; \\ l_1 \otimes r^{14}, & \text{if } l_1 \neq 0. \end{cases}$$

Based on an exhaustive search over all affine equivalence classes for 4-bit S-Boxes [6,14,42] was checked that for 8-bit permutations constructed according to (17) the following properties holds:

$$98 \leq N_\pi \leq 108, 6 \leq \delta_\pi \leq 18.$$

The main advantage of our construction is that it allows to perform a search based on random generation of 4-bit permutations for finding 8-bit S-Boxes having almost optimal cryptographic parameters. For this purpose we propose the following generic algorithm. The basic steps of the algorithm for generating such permutations are described as follows:

Step 1. Generate randomly two 4-bit permutations $h_1, h_2 \in S(V_4)$;

Step 2. For already generated 4-bit permutations $h_1, h_2 \in S(V_4)$ construct the 8-bit permutation π according to (17);

Step 3. Test the permutation π for all criteria 1-5. If π satisfies all of them except criterion 1 then go to **Step 4**. Otherwise repeat **Step 1**;

Step 4. Apply affine/linear equivalence to π in order to achieve the required property 1;

Step 5. Output. A permutation π with the desired properties.

5   A Discussion with Respect to Some Recent Methods

In [28] Kazymyrov *et al.* presented a method for generating cryptographically strong S-Boxes called Gradient descent method. The proposed method is based on the already known [27] method of gradient descent, but was adopted for the vectorial case. It allows to generate permutations for symmetric cryptography primitives providing a high level of resistance to differential, linear and algebraic attacks. The best result obtained in this work (in terms of its cryptographic properties) was a permutation without fixed points with the following properties

- minimum degree—7;
- graph algebraic immunity—3 (with 441 equations);
- 8—uniform;
- nonlinearity—104.

Moreover, in the same work was raised the following open question: *Does there exist an 8-bit permutation with algebraic immunity (i.e., the graph algebraic immunity) 3 and nonlinearity more than 104?*

In [25] Ivanov *et al.* presented a method for generating S-Boxes with strong cryptographic properties based on Modified Immune Algorithm referred as the "*SpImmAlg*". The authors propose an S-Box generation technique using a special kind of artificial immune algorithm, namely the clonal selection algorithm, combined with a slightly modified hill climbing method for S-Boxes. The best result obtained in this work (in terms of its cryptographic properties) was a large set of permutations without fixed points with the following properties

- minimum degree—7;
- graph algebraic immunity—3 (with 441 equations);
- 6—uniform;
- nonlinearity—104.

In [31] Menyachikhin presented new methods for generating S-Boxes having almost optimal cryptographic properties called the Spectral-linear and spectral-difference methods [31]. The proposed methods are based on using linear and differential spectrum for iteratively improving a given S-Box with respect to certain cryptographic properties. These methods multiply the given S-Box with some special permutations and the resulting S-Box is then stronger. The above mentioned methods can also be applied for generating involutive S-Boxes and orthomorphisms with strong cryptographic properties. The best results obtained by A. Menyachikhin using both methods (in terms of its cryptographic properties) were S-Boxes without fixed points with the following properties

- minimum degree—7;
- graph algebraic immunity—3 (with 441 equations);
- 6—uniform;
- nonlinearity—104.

All these results show us that finding cryptographically strong 8-bit S-Boxes with graph algebraic immunity 3 and nonlinearity more than 104 is a difficult task, moreover at the time of writing no counterexample was found in the public literature. In the next section we show that our construction produce 8-bit permutations with the best cryptographic properties reported for nonlinearity and graph algebraic immunity respectively.

6   Practical Results

The algorithm described in the previous section was implemented in SAGE [44] but with the following slight modification, $h_1 = h_2 = h$. Furthermore, for the sake of simplicity 500 random generated 4-bit S-Boxes h were stored in a list. Then for each 4-bit substitution of this list we applied the rest of the steps specified in our algorithm. After several minutes 417 permutations having almost optimal cryptographic parameters were generated. A total of 56 generated permutations have graph algebraic immunity—2. The remaining 27 have differential uniformity strictly greater than 8. In this search we did not find a 4-bit substitution h for which the resulting π has $N_\pi = 108$. Then, we decide generate 2^{20} random 4-bit substitution h and abort the algorithm as soon as a permutation π with almost optimal cryptographic properties reaching a nonlinearity of 108 has been found. After 7 h 17 min on 2.3 GHz Intel Core i3-6100U processor with 4 GB RAM, we found the next 4-bit S-Box $h = (0, 1, e, 9, f, 5, c, 2, b, a, 4, 8, d, 6, 3, 7)$ for which π has almost optimal cryptographic properties with $N_\pi = 108$. So instead of trying to find a random 4-bit substitution h for which the almost optimal permutation π generated by our algorithm has the maximal possible nonlinearity it was decided to solve the problem from the other side. We started to pick in our construction some 4-bit S-Boxes $h_i, i = 1, 2$ from the well-known class

$$\left\{ x^s \middle| \gcd(s, 15) = 1, s \in \mathbb{N} \right\}$$

of Permutations Polynomials (also-called Power Functions) [43] over GF(2^4) until the expected result was achieved for $h_1 = x^{13}$ and $h_2 = x^{11}$.

Our experiments show that not any pair of 4-bit S-Boxes can generate 8-bit permutations having almost optimal cryptographic parameters. Moreover, the cryptographic quality of those 8-bit permutations not always depended on the cryptographic properties of smaller 4-bit S-Boxes, for example, if we choose $h_1 = h_2 = \tau_{14}(x) = x^{14} \in S(V_4)$ in our construction then the resulting 8-bit permutation do not possess a high value of graph algebraic immunity, even when x^{14} has optimal properties in $S(V_4)$, i.e., $N_{x^{14}} = 4, \delta_{x^{14}} = 4, \deg(x^{14}) = 3, AI_{gr}(x^{14}) = 2, r^{(2)}_{x^{14}} = 21$. But if now, $h_1 = h_2 =$(b, c, 2, 3, d, a, 7, 1, 4, 0, f, e, 5, 6, 9, 8) $\in S(V_4)$ which has $N_h = 0, \delta_h = 10, \deg(h) = 1, AI_{gr}(h) = 1, r^{(1)}_h = 1$, then, the substitution π generated by our construction is almost optimal. We can thus discard the idea that the strength of π against differential, linear and algebraic attacks relies only on the quality of each of its 4-bit S-Boxes. How to select the 4-bit components h_1, h_2 in such a way that the obtained 8-bit substitution π will be almost optimal (with respect to the chosen criteria) is an open question.

However, our method has been applied to a large number of random 4-bit permutations. As a result we have obtained a lot of new affine nonequivalent 8-bit permutations without fixed points with the following cryptographic parameters

- minimum degree—7;
- graph algebraic immunity—3 (with 441 equations);
- 6 and 8—uniform;
- nonlinearity in range of 100 up to a value of 108.

In Table 1 we show four 8-bit S-Boxes π_1, π_2, π_3 and π_4. As it can be seen, our S-Boxes provide high level of protection against differential, linear and algebraic attacks.

In Table 2 two other S-Boxes π_5 and π_6 having almost optimal cryptographic parameters are showed. As it can be seen from the table our permutations compared with π_1, π_2, π_3 and π_4 demonstrate better properties. The S-Box π_5 was produced by our algorithm and permutation π_6 was obtained choosing in construction (17) the next PPs $h_1 = x^{13}, h_2 = x^{11} \in S(V_4)$ followed by application of an affine transformation to avoid fixed points.

Finally, in Table 3 we compare our results with the state-of-the-art in design of cryptographically strong S-Boxes obtained by different available methods. In this table we have added three parameters. The first two are transparency order [39] denoted by τ_π and defined as:

$$\tau_\pi = \max_{b \in V_n} \left(|n - 2w_H(b)| - \frac{1}{2^{2n} - 2^n} \sum_{a \in V_n \setminus \{0\}} \left| \sum_{c \in V_n, w_H(c)=1} (-1)^{<c,b>} W_{\pi(x) \oplus \pi(x \oplus a)}(0, c) \right| \right),$$

and the Signal-to-Noise Ratio $SNR(DPA)(\pi)$ [22], defined as follows

$$SNR(\pi) = n2^{2n}\left(\sum_{a\in V_n}\left(\sum_{i=0}^{n-1}W_{f_i}(a)\right)^4\right)^{-\frac{1}{2}},$$

where $f_i, i = 0,\dots,7$ are the coordinate Boolean functions of the S-Box π. These parameters quantify the resistance of an n-bit S-Box π to Differential

Table 1. Some 8-bit S-Boxes generated by our construction

S-Box π_1

$N_{\pi_1} = 100, \delta_{\pi_1} = 8, \deg(\pi_1) = 7, AI_{gr}(\pi_1) = 3, t^{(3)}_{\pi_1} = 441$

1b	d4	6b	c6	a6	e4	96	59	29	94	69	19	2b	d6	5b	a4
47	88	d7	57	62	06	f6	f7	ff	31	c0	1e	c1	6f	54	ae
d0	0f	db	7a	75	b9	12	18	83	5f	d1	39	ce	51	cf	aa
af	58	23	cc	f2	a8	93	1d	45	3c	9b	0b	42	bb	ef	08
ea	d5	6d	14	60	41	53	f8	2c	36	80	79	f5	27	b1	cd
c9	d2	35	a5	f1	bf	4b	3d	ec	9d	01	cb	16	1c	4a	d8
64	32	04	33	e0	97	05	26	63	c2	55	81	48	20	d3	49
38	e9	07	7f	34	c4	b5	df	e3	e8	8e	30	1f	7e	de	e5
f3	9a	eb	fd	73	fb	e1	dd	5a	3f	90	9e	b7	b4	c8	4c
02	6e	72	ac	24	87	e2	a7	7c	8a	0d	17	76	43	c6	ad
b6	2f	9f	0a	bd	dc	6a	a1	f0	da	8b	37	86	d9	4e	fe
7d	0e	b8	03	40	82	66	6e	15	78	13	ed	44	2d	2a	f4
95	09	67	a2	70	b3	91	71	61	ca	e7	4d	50	89	3a	a9
21	8d	c5	25	9c	5d	bc	28	10	2e	7b	b0	ba	0c	99	74
5e	92	84	a3	fc	11	65	00	f9	68	ab	c7	fa	c3	b2	52
8c	85	ee	3e	3b	1a	a0	46	be	98	77	8f	5c	4f	56	22

S-Box π_2

$N_{\pi_2} = 102, \delta_{\pi_2} = 8, \deg(\pi_2) = 7, AI_{gr}(\pi_2) = 3, t^{(3)}_{\pi_2} = 441$

a7	40	bd	2c	25	fd	09	6c	d8	91	f4	98	d1	b4	49	65
a2	5d	f1	b7	84	9f	46	1b	ea	6e	d9	28	c2	75	33	ac
92	69	8d	6a	1e	90	e7	8e	03	1d	77	fa	f9	93	74	e4
54	26	bb	96	82	89	2d	0b	b0	32	a4	1f	af	39	14	9d
f6	c4	72	76	be	7e	04	c0	b2	0c	7a	08	ba	cc	c8	b6
f3	d6	b5	3d	a6	f8	88	5e	eb	4d	70	c5	2e	13	9b	63
c6	4f	36	fc	9e	19	ca	85	b3	2f	d3	e5	56	aa	60	79
61	12	c7	4b	18	86	8c	9e	59	41	0a	cd	94	df	53	d5
35	7b	4a	21	06	16	6b	10	5a	5c	7d	37	6d	4c	27	31
00	bf	38	57	b8	68	6f	d0	e8	50	07	3f	d7	80	ef	87
64	99	83	c1	3a	e1	42	db	58	62	a3	20	78	b9	fb	1a
51	f0	0e	ab	24	71	a5	55	5b	7f	d4	da	81	2a	8f	fe
97	8b	44	8a	22	67	ce	45	01	23	a9	ed	ec	66	a8	cf
30	ad	ff	1c	a0	ee	e3	4e	b1	11	0d	f2	43	5f	bc	52
05	e2	c9	e0	3c	f7	29	cb	02	3e	de	17	15	f5	dc	2b
c3	34	7c	dd	9a	0f	a1	95	e9	73	ae	d2	3b	e6	47	48

S-Box π_3

$N_{\pi_3} = 104, \delta_{\pi_3} = 8, \deg(\pi_3) = 7, AI_{gr}(\pi_3) = 3, t^{(3)}_{\pi_3} = 441$

38	90	19	14	3d	9d	30	ad	b9	29	b4	84	0d	a0	24	00
c0	2d	26	b3	63	db	95	b8	9e	fd	4e	68	f6	45	d0	0b
f8	1b	47	98	1a	de	df	c4	83	99	01	46	c5	5d	82	5c
93	aa	35	ff	42	22	ca	60	55	17	c8	dd	88	77	bd	9f
f1	d7	a3	c6	97	25	65	b2	11	86	40	e3	f2	34	51	74
ab	4b	f7	12	ac	02	e5	ae	59	f5	e7	10	49	5b	be	bc
9a	b1	72	67	58	fc	15	a4	d6	8e	e9	4d	2a	3f	c3	
31	9e	54	d4	3b	27	80	1c	48	73	a7	f3	bb	6f	ef	c8
a2	87	13	4c	21	f9	5f	d8	cb	ea	a6	b5	7e	32	6d	94
62	50	b0	8a	b6	dc	3a	6a	da	6c	e6	56	8e	06	3c	e0
c9	fa	85	75	f4	fe	f0	0a	8f	7b	0e	8b	04	71	81	7f
53	e1	c2	ee	ce	0c	2f	ce	0c	e2	0f	cd	c1	2c	03	23
6b	66	d1	a1	cf	d9	70	16	c7	08	a9	78	bf	1e	6e	b7
5a	cc	e4	5e	8d	fb	ba	76	92	1f	41	a5	37	d3	28	
09	7d	96	39	d5	07	af	d2	44	91	a8	3e	7a	43	cc	eb
89	36	61	2b	79	05	4a	7c	1d	64	4f	2e	33	18	52	57

S-Box π_4

$N_{\pi_4} = 104, \delta_{\pi_4} = 6, \deg(\pi_4) = 7, AI_{gr}(\pi_4) = 3, t^{(3)}_{\pi_4} = 441$

c9	9b	0f	2e	01	b4	0e	94	20	9a	bb	00	95	21	b5	2f
99	79	32	9f	0d	d9	ad	d4	e6	eb	74	46	a0	3f	92	4b
78	89	0c	82	c9	ce	8e	07	0b	c2	60	6c	67	c5	6b	85
dc	25	a3	d8	3b	65	7b	5e	fd	c6	1e	bd	40	98	e3	86
50	96	5d	34	9e	61	69	ff	a2	3e	08	55	f7	c3	aa	cb
6d	43	c0	f1	41	33	31	72	b2	f3	02	c2	70	81	b0	83
f4	ac	af	5a	d2	8b	09	7a	b6	24	7e	d1	27	7d	88	03
8c	d5	9d	c5	df	52	58	8d	10	cf	0a	97	87	42	1a	48
b1	5c	91	47	36	bc	d6	8a	1b	2d	6a	fb	e0	a7	71	cd
3d	ca	cc	73	a8	dd	bf	75	b9	11	62	ae	17	64	db	06
45	ef	6f	ab	93	b8	c4	2b	44	d7	7c	13	57	fc	38	80
ba	66	63	29	7a	56	84	2e	4f	35	1c	7f	30	19	53	05
e1	3a	f2	6e	4c	ea	9c	a6	54	18	76	84	d0	be	22	c8
28	1f	51	b6	77	8f	e7	f8	a9	de	68	39	90	26	c1	4e
a4	b3	fe	ce	a5	04	12	a1	5f	fa	16	e8	b7	5b	49	4d
15	f0	3e	1d	e4	37	23	d3	cd	09	14	2a	c7	da	f9	ce

Table 2. The best S-Boxes produced by our construction

S-Box π_5

$N_{\pi_5} = 106, \delta_{\pi_5} = 6, \deg(\pi_5) = 7, AI_{gr}(\pi_5) = 3, t^{(3)}_{\pi_5} = 441$

96	24	63	c0	ab	1f	a3	6b	2c	47	ec	c8	08	e4	8f	87
25	bc	20	d4	82	ca	f4	48	68	ea	3e	1e	76	a2	56	9c
12	c4	a6	c7	9d	be	7a	dc	3b	23	85	59	41	ff	62	
98	14	5f	ce	f1	54	b1	a5	fa	0b	c5	ba	40	ae	1f	4b
2b	05	8e	7e	f0	07	f2	f7	7b	8b	f5	79	02	7c	8e	89
bd	69	55	5c	64	04	09	60	35	51	6d	58	6d	31	38	3c
1c	d0	f9	f6	16	c9	0f	df	26	30	c6	3f	19	ef	e0	29
0e	6c	d9	22	94	03	fb	97	4e	da	f8	21	6f	4d	b6	b5
8a	a8	7f	3a	73	9e	45	ef	92	e1	db	a4	36	0c	49	d7
af	ad	f3	a4	83	99	b7	1a	e9	6a	3e	44	70	c7	5e	
b3	b9	ac	aa	72	cd	06	bf	13	61	cb	67	74	de	d8	15
a1	7d	0a	b2	95	50	b8	c5	cf	5a	e8	e2	2d	9f	27	77
37	d5	75	88	e0	ce	fd	28	5d	bb	33	46	1b	93	6e	4d
39	c1	2a	66	17	9a	4c	8d	a7	b0	d6	fc	5b	3d	71	eb
84	11	d3	90	01	53	43	52	81	80	10	c3	42	d2	91	c2
00	78	86	ee	65	57	4a	32	b4	d1	1d	9b	2f	e3	a9	fe

S-Box π_6

$N_{\pi_6} = 108, \delta_{\pi_6} = 6, \deg(\pi_6) = 7, AI_{gr}(\pi_6) = 3, t^{(3)}_{\pi_6} = 441$

1b	58	81	db	94	8d	41	02	98	17	d7	4d	ce	0e	54	c2
9e	dd	ad	c3	7b	d3	75	b3	05	65	bd	0b	15	cd	a3	6b
e1	fb	38	b9	93	f2	9a	7a	59	d1	73	50	12	b0	31	d8
13	d6	a0	90	19	e4	2b	e6	5d	5f	d4	6f	29	a2	92	6d
4c	77	53	8f	80	30	c7	ab	e3	78	ee	a4	5c	c8	14	3f
3b	9c	7d	7e	6a	ee	18	9f	f9	88	cd	8b	69	0c	0f	fa
e9	36	83	32	91	0d	aa	87	1f	95	bc	24	20	09	b8	ae
6c	f0	35	ea	f1	c5	c4	db	5c	c4	db	03	fd	06	ae	17
96	10	16	48	79	2e	45	4e	43	21	72	7f	27	74	2a	1d
c1	7e	5e	dc	c2	07	99	fe	bb	42	85	c0	60	a7	25	39
c9	b1	e5	57	e0	43	56	a4	03	fd	06	a4	b4	52	1e	ac	4f
33	51	e6	f5	68	11	28	62	bf	cc	22	ff	5b	b5	86	8c
be	5a	e6	a6	0a	26	76	37	e7	f6	4b	9b	67	da	b7	8a
b6	97	70	2d	08	d9	46	ca	a1	b2	84	ef	55	63	3e	fc
44	ba	c8	04	82	cf	f7	56	a5	3e	23	d0	6e	71	9d	49
64	3d	8e	61	f3	3a	f4	d2	47	af	d5	40	1c	66	89	a8

Power Analysis (DPA). The last one is the well-known robustness *to differential cryptanalysis* (see, e.g. [46]).

Table 3. A comparison between the cryptographic properties of 8-bit S-Boxes produced by different modern generation methods (NR means "not reported")

Methods/Cryptographic properties	N_π	δ_π	$deg(\pi)$	$AI_{gr}(\pi)\left(t^{(AI_{gr}(\pi))}\right)$	$AC(\pi)_{max}\left(\sigma(\pi)\right)$	τ_π	$SNR(\pi)$	rdc
Finite Field Inversion [36] (AES S-Box)	112	4	7	2(39)	32(133120)	7,860	9,600	0,984
Exponential method [1] (BelT S-Box)	102	8	6	3(441)	88(232960)	7,833	8,318	0,969
4-uniform permutations method [40,41]	98	4	NR	NR	NR	NR	NR	NR
Gradient descent method [28]	104	8	7	3(441)	72(206464)	7,823	9,208	0,969
GA/HC [33]	100	NR	NR	NR	NR	NR	NR	NR
GaT [50]	104	NR	NR	NR	NR	NR	NR	NR
GA1 [26]	106	6	6	2(32)	56(151936)	7,850	9,458	0,977
	108	6	6	2(34)	48(148864)	7,849	9,768	0,977
	110	6	7	2(36)	40(145024)	7,855	9,850	0,977
GA2 [26]	112	6	7	2(38)	32(138112)	7,858	9,866	0,977
Hill Climbing [32]	100	NR	NR	NR	NR	NR	NR	NR
Hybrid Heuristic	102	6	4	3(441)	96(255872)	7,833	8,650	0,977
Methods [24]	104	6	4	3(441)	96(242176)	7,824	8,467	0,977
Simulated Annealing [12]	102	NR	NR	NR	80(NR)	NR	NR	NR
SpImmAlg [25]	104	6	7	3(441)	88(216448)	7,822	9,038	0,977
Spectral-linear and Spectral-difference methods [31]	104	6	7	3(441)	NR	NR	NR	NR
Tweaking [17]	106	6	7	2(27)	56(171520)	7,854	9,481	0,977
New[S-Box π_1]	100	8	7	3(441)	72(186112)	7,770	8,220	0,969
New[S-Box π_2]	102	8	7	3(441)	80(227584)	7,783	8,751	0,969
New[S-Box π_3]	104	8	7	3(441)	72(193024)	7,806	8,169	0,969
New[S-Box π_4]	104	6	7	3(441)	80(192256)	7,818	8,745	0,977
New[S-Box π_5]	106	6	7	3(441)	72(191104)	7,816	9,013	0,977
New[S-Box π_6]	108	6	7	3(441)	64(185344)	7,838	9,335	0,977

This comparison shows that:

1. Our construction produces 8-bit permutations with the same properties reported in [1,12,17,24,25,28,31–33,50];
2. The GA1 and GA2 methods (with the exception of the AES' S-Box) have the best values reported for nonlinearity, maximal absolute indicator and sum-of-squares indicators. But these S-Boxes do not possess a high value of graph algebraic immunity;
3. The transparency order and SNR(DPA) for the proposed S-Boxes in this work $\pi_i, i = 1, \ldots, 6$ are lesser than that of AES S-Box and GA1,GA2 methods;
4. Finite Field Inversion (AES S-Box) and 4-uniform permutations methods have the smallest known values of differential uniformity but the other methods present good values for this parameter;

5. Finite Field Inversion method (AES S-Box) has the best value for robustness *to differential cryptanalysis* but the other methods exhibits acceptable values for this parameter;
6. With respect to cryptographic strength against differential, linear and algebraic attacks S-Boxes π_5 and π_6 establish up to date a new record in the public available literature on generation of S-boxes with strong cryptographic properties.

The S-Boxes $\pi_i, i = 1, \ldots, 6$ generated by our method were selected in order to have good resistive properties both towards classical cryptanalysis as well as DPA attacks.

7   Conclusion and Future Work

In this article was presented a new method for constructing S-Boxes of dimension $n = 2k, k \geq 2$. In particular, we proposed a special algorithmic-algebraic scheme which utilizes inversion in $GF(2^4)$ and two arbitrary permutations from $S(V_4)$ for generating 8-bit S-boxes having almost optimal cryptographic properties. Our work solves the question raised in [28] about existence of permutations with graph algebraic immunity 3 and nonlinearity more than 104, providing new 8-bit S-Boxes which have better resistance to algebraic and DPA attacks in terms of algebraic immunity, transparency order and SNR(DPA) than AES S-box while having comparable classical cryptographic properties. These substitutions can be appropriate in the design of stream cipher, block cipher and hash functions. It will be interesting to obtain theoretical results on cryptographic properties of the proposed construction for $n = 2k, k \geq 2$. Our work raised the following

Open Question: *Does there exist an 8-bit permutation with graph algebraic immunity 3 and nonlinearity more than 108?*

Acknowledgements. The author is very grateful to the anonymous reviewers for their useful comments and valuable observations, which helped to improve the final version of this article.

References

1. Agievich S., Afonenko A.: Exponential s-boxes. Cryptology ePrint Archive, Report 2004/024 (2004). http://eprint.iacr.org/2004/024
2. Aoki, K., et al.: *Camellia*: a 128-bit block cipher suitable for multiple platforms — design and analysis. In: Stinson, D.R., Tavares, S. (eds.) SAC 2000. LNCS, vol. 2012, pp. 39–56. Springer, Heidelberg (2001). https://doi.org/10.1007/3-540-44983-3_4
3. Armknecht, F., Krause, M.: Constructing single and multioutput Boolean functions with maximal algebraic immunity. In: Bugliesi, M., Preneel, B., Sassone, V., Wegener, I. (eds.) ICALP 2006, Part II. LNCS, vol. 4052, pp. 180–191. Springer, Heidelberg (2006). https://doi.org/10.1007/11787006_16
4. Barreto, P., Rijmen, V.: The Khazad legacy-level block cipher. Primitive submitted to NESSIE (2000)

5. Barreto, P., Rijmen, V.: The Whirlpool hashing function. In: First open NESSIE Workshop, Leuven, Belgium, vol. 13 (2000)

6. Bilgin, B., Nikova, S., Nikov, V., Rijmen, V., Stutz, G.: Threshold Implementations of all 3×3 and 4×4 S-Boxes, http://eprint.iacr.org/2012/300/ (2012)

7. Biryukov, A., De Cannière, C.: Block ciphers and systems of quadratic equations. In: Johansson, T. (ed.) FSE 2003. LNCS, vol. 2887, pp. 274–289. Springer, Heidelberg (2003). https://doi.org/10.1007/978-3-540-39887-5_21

8. Biryukov, A., Perrin, L., Udovenko, A.: Reverse-engineering the S-box of Streebog, Kuznyechik and STRIBOBr1. In: Fischlin, M., Coron, J.-S. (eds.) EUROCRYPT 2016, Part I. LNCS, vol. 9665, pp. 372–402. Springer, Heidelberg (2016). https://doi.org/10.1007/978-3-662-49890-3_15

9. Canteaut, A., Duval, S., Leurent, G.: Construction of lightweight S-boxes using Feistel and MISTY structures. In: Dunkelman, O., Keliher, L. (eds.) SAC 2015. LNCS, vol. 9566, pp. 373–393. Springer, Cham (2016). https://doi.org/10.1007/978-3-319-31301-6_22

10. Carlet, C.: Vectorial Boolean functions for cryptography. Boolean Models and Methods in Mathematics, Computer Science, and Engineering. Cambridge University Press, New York (2010)

11. Carlet, C.: On the Algebraic Immunities and Higher Order Nonlinearities of Vectorial Boolean Functions. Enhancing Cryptographic Primitives with Techniques from Error Correcting Codes, pp. 104–116. IOS Press, Amsterdam (2009)

12. Clark, J.A., Jacob, J.L., Stepney, S.: The design of s-boxes by simulated annealing. New Gener. Comput. Arch. **23**(3), 219–231 (2005)

13. Courtois, N.T., Pieprzyk, J.: Cryptanalysis of Block Ciphers with Over defined Systems of Equations. http://eprint.iacr.org/2002/044/ (2002)

14. De Cannière, C.: Analysis and design of symmetric encryption algorithms, Ph.D. thesis (2007)

15. Garey, M.R., Johnson, D.S.: Computers and Intractability - A Guide to the Theory of NP-Completeness. W.H Freeman and Company, San Francisco (1979)

16. Feistel, H.: Cryptography and computer privacy. Sci. Am. **228**(5), 15–23 (1973)

17. Fuller, J., Millan, W.: Linear redundancy in S-boxes. In: Johansson, T. (ed.) FSE 2003. LNCS, vol. 2887, pp. 74–86. Springer, Heidelberg (2003). https://doi.org/10.1007/978-3-540-39887-5_7

18. Gérard, B., Grosso, V., Naya-Plasencia, M., Standaert, F.-X.: Block ciphers that are easier to mask: how far can we go? In: Bertoni, G., Coron, J.-S. (eds.) CHES 2013. LNCS, vol. 8086, pp. 383–399. Springer, Heidelberg (2013). https://doi.org/10.1007/978-3-642-40349-1_22

19. Golić, J.D.: Fast low order approximation of cryptographic functions. In: Maurer, U. (ed.) EUROCRYPT 1996. LNCS, vol. 1070, pp. 268–282. Springer, Heidelberg (1996). https://doi.org/10.1007/3-540-68339-9_24

20. GOST R 34.12-2015 Information technology. Cryptographic protection of information. Block ciphers. Moscow, Standartinform (2015)

21. GOST R 34.11-2012 Information technology. Cryptographic protection of information. Hash function. Moscow, Standartinform (2012)

22. Guilley, S., Hoogvorst, P., Pacalet, R.: Differential power analysis model and some results. In: CARDIS, pp. 127–142 (2004)

23. Hirata, K.: The 128-bit block cipher HyRAL (hybrid randomization algorithm): common keyblock cipher. In: International Symposium on Intelligence Information Processing and Trusted Computing, pp. 9–14, October 2010

24. Isa, H., Jamil, N., Z'aba, M.: Hybrid heuristic methods in constructing cryptographically strong S-boxes. Int. J. Cryptol. Res. **6**(1), 1–15 (2016)

25. Ivanov, G., Nikolov, N., Nikova, S.: Cryptographically strong S-boxes generated by modified immune algorithm. In: Pasalic, E., Knudsen, L.R. (eds.) BalkanCryptSec 2015. LNCS, vol. 9540, pp. 31–42. Springer, Cham (2016). https://doi.org/10.1007/978-3-319-29172-7_3

26. Ivanov, G., Nikolov, N., Nikova, S.: Reversed genetic algorithms for generation of bijective S-Boxes with good cryptographic properties. IACR Cryptology ePrint Archive (2014), Report 2014/801, http://eprint.iacr.org/2014/801.pdf

27. Izbenko, Y., Kovtun, V., Kuznetsov, A.: The Design of Boolean Functions by Modified Hill Climbing Method. http://eprint.iacr.org/2008/111.pdf

28. Kazymyrov, O.V., Kazymyrova, V.N., Oliynykov, R.V.: A method for generation of high-nonlinear S-Boxes based on gradient descent. Mat. Vopr. Kriptogr. **5**(2), 71–78 (2014)

29. Knudsen, L.R.: Truncated and higher order differentials. In: Preneel, B. (ed.) FSE 1994. LNCS, vol. 1008, pp. 196–211. Springer, Heidelberg (1995). https://doi.org/10.1007/3-540-60590-8_16

30. Kwon, D., et al.: New block cipher: ARIA. In: Lim, J.-I., Lee, D.-H. (eds.) ICISC 2003. LNCS, vol. 2971, pp. 432–445. Springer, Heidelberg (2004). https://doi.org/10.1007/978-3-540-24691-6_32

31. Menyachikhin, A.: Spectral-linear and spectral-difference methods for generating cryptographically strong S-Boxes. In: Pre-proceedings of CTCrypt 2016, Yaroslavl, Russia, pp. 232–252 (2016)

32. Millan, W.: How to improve the nonlinearity of bijective S-boxes. In: Boyd, C., Dawson, E. (eds.) ACISP 1998. LNCS, vol. 1438, pp. 181–192. Springer, Heidelberg (1998). https://doi.org/10.1007/BFb0053732

33. Millan, W., Burnett, L., Carter, G., Clark, A., Dawson, E.: Evolutionary heuristics for finding cryptographically strong S-boxes. In: Varadharajan, V., Mu, Y. (eds.) ICICS 1999. LNCS, vol. 1726, pp. 263–274. Springer, Heidelberg (1999). https://doi.org/10.1007/978-3-540-47942-0_22

34. Millan, W.: Low order approximation of cipher functions. In: Dawson, E., Golić, J. (eds.) CPA 1995. LNCS, vol. 1029, pp. 144–155. Springer, Heidelberg (1996). https://doi.org/10.1007/BFb0032354

35. NIST: Advanced Encryption Standard. Federal Information Processing Standard (FIPS) 197, November 2001

36. Nyberg, K.: Differentially uniform mappings for cryptography. In: Helleseth, T. (ed.) EUROCRYPT 1993. LNCS, vol. 765, pp. 55–64. Springer, Heidelberg (1994). https://doi.org/10.1007/3-540-48285-7_6

37. Ohkuma, K., Muratani, H., Sano, F., Kawamura, S.: The block cipher hierocrypt. In: Stinson, D.R., Tavares, S. (eds.) SAC 2000. LNCS, vol. 2012, pp. 72–88. Springer, Heidelberg (2001). https://doi.org/10.1007/3-540-44983-3_6

38. Oliynykov R., et al.: DSTU 7624:2014. National Standard of Ukraine. Information technologies. Cryptographic data security. Symmetric block transformation algorithm. Ministry of Economical Development and Trade of Ukraine (2015)

39. Prouff, E.: DPA attacks and S-boxes. In: Gilbert, H., Handschuh, H. (eds.) FSE 2005. LNCS, vol. 3557, pp. 424–441. Springer, Heidelberg (2005). https://doi.org/10.1007/11502760_29

40. Qu, L., Tan, Y., Li, C., Gong, G.: More constructions of differentially 4-uniform permutations on $\mathbb{F}_{2^{2k}}$. arxiv.org/pdf/1309.7423 (2013)

41. Qu, L., Tan, Y., Tan, C., Li, C.: Constructing differentially 4-uniform permutations over $\mathbb{F}_{2^{2k}}$ via the switching method. IEEE Trans. Inform. Theory **59**(7), 4675–4686 (2013)

42. Leander, G., Poschmann, A.: On the classification of 4 bit S-boxes. In: Carlet, C., Sunar, B. (eds.) WAIFI 2007. LNCS, vol. 4547, pp. 159–176. Springer, Heidelberg (2007). https://doi.org/10.1007/978-3-540-73074-3_13

43. Lidl, R., Niederreiter, H.: Finite Fields, Volume 20 of Encyclopedia of Mathematics and Its Applications. Cambridge University Press, Cambridge (1997)

44. Sage Mathematics Software (Version 7.2) (2016). http://www.sagemath.org

45. Saarinen, M.J.O.: STRIBOB: Authenticated encryption from GOST R 34.11-2012 LPS permutation. In: Mathematical Aspects of Cryptography, vol. 6, no. 2, pp. 67–78. Steklov Mathematical Institute of Russian Academy of Sciences (2015)

46. Seberry, J., Zhang, X.M., Zheng, Y.: Systematic generation of cryptographically robust S-boxes. In: Proceedings of the First ACM Conference on Computer and Communications Security, The Association for Computing Machinery, Fairfax, VA, pp. 171–182 (1993)

47. Standaert, F.-X., Piret, G., Rouvroy, G., Quisquater, J.-J., Legat, J.-D.: ICE-BERG: an involutional cipher efficient for block encryption in reconfigurable hardware. In: Roy, B., Meier, W. (eds.) FSE 2004. LNCS, vol. 3017, pp. 279–298. Springer, Heidelberg (2004). https://doi.org/10.1007/978-3-540-25937-4_18

48. STB 34.101.31-2011 Information technologies. Information security. Cryptographic algorithms of enciphering and continuity test. Minsk, Gosstandart (2011)

49. Shirai, T., Shibutani, K., Akishita, T., Moriai, S., Iwata, T.: The 128-bit blockcipher CLEFIA (extended abstract). In: Biryukov, A. (ed.) FSE 2007. LNCS, vol. 4593, pp. 181–195. Springer, Heidelberg (2007). https://doi.org/10.1007/978-3-540-74619-5_12

50. Tesař, P.: A new method for generating high non-linearity S-boxes. Radioengineering 19(1), 23–26 (2010)

XHX – A Framework for Optimally Secure Tweakable Block Ciphers from Classical Block Ciphers and Universal Hashing

Ashwin Jha[1(✉)], Eik List[2(✉)], Kazuhiko Minematsu[3(✉)], Sweta Mishra[4(✉)], and Mridul Nandi[1(✉)]

[1] Indian Statistical Institute, Kolkata, India
{ashwin_r,mridul}@isical.ac.in
[2] Bauhaus-Universität Weimar, Weimar, Germany
eik.list@uni-weimar.de
[3] NEC Corporation, Kawasaki, Japan
k-minematsu@ah.jp.nec.com
[4] National Institute of Standards and Technology, Gaithersburg, USA
email.sweta@gmail.com

Abstract. Tweakable block ciphers are important primitives for designing cryptographic schemes with high security. In the absence of a standardized tweakable block cipher, constructions built from classical block ciphers remain an interesting research topic in both theory and practice. Motivated by Mennink's $\widetilde{F}[2]$ publication from 2015, Wang et al. proposed 32 optimally secure constructions at ASIACRYPT'16, all of which employ two calls to a classical block cipher each. Yet, those constructions were still limited to n-bit keys and n-bit tweaks. Thus, applications with more general key or tweak lengths still lack support. This work proposes the XHX family of tweakable block ciphers from a classical block cipher and a family of universal hash functions, which generalizes the constructions by Wang et al. First, we detail the generic XHX construction with three independently keyed calls to the hash function. Second, we show that we can derive the hash keys in efficient manner from the block cipher, where we generalize the constructions by Wang et al.; finally, we propose efficient instantiations for the used hash functions.

Keywords: Provable security · Ideal-cipher model · Tweakable block cipher

1 Introduction

Tweakable Block Ciphers. In addition to the usual key and plaintext inputs of classical block ciphers, tweakable block ciphers (TBCs, for short) are cryptographic transform that adds an additional public parameter called *tweak*. So, a

© Springer Nature Switzerland AG 2019
T. Lange and O. Dunkelman (Eds.): LATINCRYPT 2017, LNCS 11368, pp. 207–227, 2019.
https://doi.org/10.1007/978-3-030-25283-0_12

tweakable block cipher $\widetilde{E} : \mathcal{K} \times \mathcal{T} \times \mathcal{M} \to \mathcal{M}$ is a permutation on the plaintext/ciphertext space $\mathcal{M}$ for every combination of key $K \in \mathcal{K}$ and tweak $T \in \mathcal{T}$, where $\mathcal{K}$, $\mathcal{T}$, and $\mathcal{M}$ are assumed to be non-empty sets. Their first use in literature was due to Schroeppel and Orman in the Hasty Pudding Cipher, where the tweak still was called *Spice* [18]. Liskov, Rivest, and Wagner [11] have formalized the concept then in 2002.

In the recent past, the status of tweakable block ciphers has become more prominent, last but not least due to the advent of efficient dedicated constructions, such as Deoxys-BC or Joltik-BC that were proposed alongside the TWEAKEY framework [6], or e.g., SKINNY [1]. However, in the absence of a standard, tweakable block ciphers based on classical ones remain a highly interesting topic.

Blockcipher-Based Constructions. Liskov et al. [11] had described two constructions, known as LRW1 and LRW2. Rogaway [17] proposed XE and XEX as refinements of LRW2 for updating tweaks efficiently and reducing the number of keys. These schemes are efficient in the sense that they need one call to the block cipher plus one call to a universal hash function. Both XE and XEX are provably secure in the standard model, i.e., assuming the block cipher is a (strong) pseudorandom permutation, they are secure up to $O(2^{n/2})$ queries, when using an n-bit block cipher. Since this bound results from the birthday paradox on input collisions, the security of those constructions is inherently limited by the birthday bound (BB-secure).

Constructions with Stronger Security. Constructions with beyond-birthday-bound (BBB) security have been an interesting research topic. In [13], Minematsu proposed introduced a rekeying-based construction. Landecker, Shrimpton and Terashima [9] analyzed the cascade of two independent LRW2 instances, called CLRW2. Both constructions are secure up to $O(2^{2n/3})$ queries, however, at the price of requiring two block-cipher calls per block plus per-tweak rekeying or plus two calls to a universal hash function, respectively.

For settings that demand stronger security, Lampe and Seurin [8] proved that the chained cascade of more instances of LRW2 could asymptotically approach a security of up to $O(2^n)$ queries, i.e. full n-bit security. However, the disadvantage is drastically decreased performance. An alternative direction has been initiated by Mennink [12], who also proposed TBC constructions from classical block ciphers, but proved the security in the ideal-cipher model. Mennink's constructions could achieve full n-bit security quite efficiently when both input and key are n bits. In particular, his $\widetilde{F}[2]$ construction required only two block-cipher calls.

Following Mennink's work, Wang et al. [20] proposed 32 constructions of optimally secure tweakable block ciphers from classical block ciphers. Their designs share an n-bit key, n-bit tweak and n-bit plaintext, and linearly mix tweak, key, and the result of a second offline call to the block cipher. Their constructions have the desirable property of allowing to cache the result of the first block-cipher call; moreover, given a-priori known tweaks, some of their constructions allow further to precompute the result of the key schedule.

All constructions by Wang et al. were restricted to n-bit keys and tweaks. While this limit was reasonable, it did not address tweakable block ciphers with tweaks longer than n bit. Such constructions, however, are useful in applications with increased security needs such as for authenticated encryption or variable-input-length ciphers (e.g., [19]). Moreover, disk-encryption schemes are typically based on wide-block tweakable ciphers, where the physical location on disk (e.g., the sector ID) is used as tweak, which can be arbitrarily long.

In general, extending the key length in the ideal-cipher model is far from trivial (see, e.g., [2,5,10]), and the key size in this model does not necessarily match the required tweak length. Moreover, many ciphers, like the AES-192 or AES-256, possess key and block lengths for which the constructions in [12,20] are inapplicable. In general, the tweak represents additional data accompanying the plaintext/ciphertext block, and no general reason exists why tweaks must be limited to the block length.

Before proving the security of a construction, we have to specify the employed model. The standard model is well-established in the cryptographic community despite the fact that proofs base on few unproven assumptions, such as that a block cipher is a PRP, or ignore practical side-channel attacks. In the standard model, the adversary is given access only to either the *real construction* $\widetilde{E}$ or an *ideal construction* $\widetilde{\pi}$. In contrast, the ideal-cipher model assumes an ideal primitive—in our case the classical ideal block cipher E which is used in $\widetilde{E}$—which the adversary has also access to in both worlds. Although a proof in the ideal-cipher model is not an unexceptional guarantee that no attacks may exist when instantiated in practice [3], for us, it allows to capture away the details of the primitive for the sake of focusing on the security of the construction.

A good example for TBCs proven in the standard model is XTX [14] by Minematsu and Iwata. XTX extended the tweak domain of a given tweakable block cipher $\widetilde{E} : \{0,1\}^k \times \{0,1\}^t \times \{0,1\}^n \rightarrow \{0,1\}^n$ by hashing the arbitrary-length tweak to an $(n+t)$-bit value. The first t bits serve as tweak and the latter n bits are XORed to both input and output of $\widetilde{E}$. Given an ϵ-AXU family of hash functions and an ideal tweakable cipher, XTX is secure for up to $O(2^{(n+t)/2})$ queries in the standard model. However, no alternative to XTX exists in the ideal-cipher model yet.

Contribution. This work proposes the XHX family of tweakable block ciphers from a classical block cipher and a family of universal hash functions, which generalizes the constructions by Wang et al. [20]. Like them, the present work also uses the ideal-cipher model for its security analysis. As the major difference to their work, our proposal allows arbitrary tweak lengths and works for any block cipher of n-bit block and k-bit key. The security is guaranteed for up to $O(2^{(n+k)/2})$ queries, which yields n-bit security when $k \geq n$.

Our contributions in the remainder of this work are threefold: First, we detail the generic XHX construction with three independently keyed calls to the hash function. Second, we show that we can derive the hash keys in an efficient manner from the block cipher, generalizing the constructions by Wang et al. finally, we propose efficient instantiations for the employed hash functions for concreteness.

Remark 1. Recently, Naito [15] proposed the XKX framework of beyond-birthday-secure tweakable block ciphers, which shares similarities to the proposal in the present work. He proposed two instances, the birthday-secure $\mathrm{XKX}^{(1)}$ and the beyond-birthday-secure $\mathrm{XKX}^{(2)}$. More detailed, the nonce is processed by a block-cipher-based PRF which yields the block-cipher key for the current message; the counter is hashed with a universal hash function under a second, independent key to mask the input. In contrast to other proposals including ours, Naito's construction demands both a counter plus a nonce as parameters to overcome the birthday bound; as a standalone construction, its security reduces to $n/2$ bits if an adversary could use the same "nonce" value for all queries. Hence, $\mathrm{XKX}^{(2)}$ is tailored only to certain domains, e.g., modes of operation in nonce-based authenticated encryption schemes. Our proposal differs from XKX in four aspects: (1) we do not pose limitations on the reuse of input parameters; moreover, (2) we do not require a minimum key length of $n + k$ bits; (3) we do not use several independent keys, but employ the block cipher to derive hashing keys; (4) finally, Naito's construction is proved in the standard model, whereas we consider the ideal-cipher model (Table 1).

Table 1. Comparison of XHX to earlier highly secure TBCs built upon classical block ciphers. $\mathrm{ICM}(n, k)$ denotes the ideal-cipher model for a block cipher with n-bit block and k-bit key; $\mathrm{BC}(n, k)$ and $\mathrm{TBC}(n, t, k)$ denote the standard-model (tweakable) block cipher of n-bit block, t-bit tweak, and k-bit key. #Enc. = #calls to the (tweakable) block cipher, and #Mult. = #multiplications over $\mathrm{GF}(2^n)$. $a(b) = b$ out of a calls can be precomputed with the secret key; we define $s = \lceil k/n \rceil$.

Scheme	Model	Tweak	Key	Security	Efficiency		Reference
		Length in bit		In bit	#Enc.	#Mult.	
$\widetilde{F}[2]$	$\mathrm{ICM}(n, n)$	n	n	n	2		[12]
$\widetilde{\mathrm{E1}}, \ldots, \widetilde{\mathrm{E32}}$	$\mathrm{ICM}(n, n)$	n	n	n	2 (1)		[20]
XTX	$\mathrm{TBC}(n, t, k)$	any ℓ	$k + 2n$	$(n + t)/2$	1	$2\lceil \ell/n \rceil$	[14]
$\mathrm{XKX}^{(2)}$	$\mathrm{BC}(n, k)$	$-^*$	$k + n$	$\min\{n, k/2\}$	1	1	[15]
XHX	$\mathrm{ICM}(n, k)$	any ℓ	k	$(n + k)/2$	$s + 1$ (s)	$s\lceil \ell/n \rceil$	This work
XHX	$\mathrm{ICM}(n, k)$	$2n$	k	n	$s + 1$ (s)	s	This work

* $\mathrm{XKX}^{(2)}$ employs a counter as tweak.

The remainder is structured as follows: Sect. 2 briefly gives the preliminaries necessary for the rest of this work. Section 3 then defines the general construction, that we call GXHX for simplicity, which hashes the tweak to three outputs. Section 4 continues with the definition and analysis of XHX, which derives the hashing keys from the block cipher. Section 5 describes and analyzes efficient instantiations for our hash functions depending on the tweak length. In particular, we propose instantiations for $2n$-bit and arbitrary-length tweaks.

2   Preliminaries

General Notation. We use lowercase letters x for indices and integers, uppercase letters X, Y for binary strings and functions, and calligraphic uppercase
letters $\mathcal{X}, \mathcal{Y}$ for sets. We denote the concatenation of binary strings X and Y
by $X \parallel Y$ and the result of their bitwise XOR by $X \oplus Y$. For tuples of bit
strings $(X_1, \dots, X_x), (Y_1, \dots, Y_x)$ of equal domain, we denote by $(X_1, \dots, X_x) \oplus$
$(Y_1, \dots, Y_x)$ the element-wise XOR, i.e., $(X_1 \oplus Y_1, \dots, X_x \oplus Y_x)$. We indicate the
length of X in bits by $|X|$ and write X_i for the i-th block. Furthermore, we denote
by $X \twoheadleftarrow \mathcal{X}$ that X is chosen uniformly at random from the set $\mathcal{X}$. We define
three sets of particular interest: $\mathsf{Func}(\mathcal{X}, \mathcal{Y})$ be the set of all functions $F : \mathcal{X} \to \mathcal{Y}$,
$\mathsf{Perm}(\mathcal{X})$ the set of all permutations $\pi : \mathcal{X} \to \mathcal{X}$, and $\mathsf{TPerm}(\mathcal{T}, \mathcal{X})$ for the set of
tweaked permutations over $\mathcal{X}$ with associated tweak space $\mathcal{T}$. $(X_1, \dots, X_x) \xleftarrow{n} X$
denotes that X is split into n-bit blocks i.e., $X_1 \parallel \dots \parallel X_x = X$, and $|X_i| = n$ for
$1 \le i \le x - 1$, and $|X_x| \le n$. Moreover, we define $\langle X \rangle_n$ to denote the encoding
of a non-negative integer X into its n-bit representation. Given a integer $x \in \mathbb{N}$,
we define the function $\mathrm{TRUNC}_x : \{0,1\}^* \to \{0,1\}^x$ to return the leftmost x bits
of the input if its length is $\ge x$, and returns the input otherwise. For two sets $\mathcal{X}$
and $\mathcal{Y}$, a uniform random function $\rho : \mathcal{X} \to \mathcal{Y}$ maps inputs $X \in \mathcal{X}$ independently
from other inputs and uniformly at random to outputs $Y \in \mathcal{Y}$. For an event E,
we denote by $\Pr[E]$ the probability of E. For positive integers n and k, we denote
the falling factorial as $(n)_k := \frac{n!}{k!}$.

Adversaries. An adversary $\mathbf{A}$ is an efficient Turing machine that interacts with
a given set of oracles that appear as black boxes to $\mathbf{A}$. We denote by $\mathbf{A}^{\mathcal{O}}$ the
output of $\mathbf{A}$ after interacting with some oracle $\mathcal{O}$. We write $\Delta_{\mathbf{A}}(\mathcal{O}^1; \mathcal{O}^2) :=$
$|\Pr[\mathbf{A}^{\mathcal{O}^1} \Rightarrow 1] - \Pr[\mathbf{A}^{\mathcal{O}^2} \Rightarrow 1]|$ for the advantage of $\mathbf{A}$ to distinguish between
oracles $\mathcal{O}^1$ and $\mathcal{O}^2$. All probabilities are defined over the random coins of the
oracles and those of the adversary, if any. W.l.o.g., we assume that $\mathbf{A}$ never asks
queries to which it already knows the answer.

A block cipher E with associated key space $\mathcal{K}$ and message space $\mathcal{M}$ is a
mapping $E : \mathcal{K} \times \mathcal{M} \to \mathcal{M}$ such that for every key $K \in \mathcal{K}$, it holds that
$E(K, \cdot)$ is a permutation over $\mathcal{M}$. We define $\mathsf{Block}(\mathcal{K}, \mathcal{M})$ as the set of all block
ciphers with key space $\mathcal{K}$ and message space $\mathcal{M}$. A tweakable block cipher $\widetilde{E}$
with associated key space $\mathcal{K}$, tweak space $\mathcal{T}$, and message space $\mathcal{M}$ is a mapping
$\widetilde{E} : \mathcal{K} \times \mathcal{T} \times \mathcal{M} \to \mathcal{M}$ such that for every key $K \in \mathcal{K}$ and tweak $T \in \mathcal{T}$, it holds
that $\widetilde{E}(K, T, \cdot)$ is a permutation over $\mathcal{M}$. We also write $\widetilde{E}_K^T(\cdot)$ as short form in
the remainder.

The STPRP security of $\widetilde{E}$ is defined via upper bounding the advantage of
a distinguishing adversary $\mathbf{A}$ in a game, where we consider the ideal-cipher
model throughout this work. There, $\mathbf{A}$ has access to oracles $(\mathcal{O}, E^{\pm})$, where
$E^{\pm}$ is the usual notation for access to the encryption oracle E and to the
decryption oracle E^{-1}. $\mathcal{O}$ is called construction oracle, and is either the real
construction $\widetilde{E}_K^{\pm}(\cdot, \cdot)$, or $\widetilde{\pi}^{\pm}(\cdot, \cdot)$ for $\widetilde{\pi} \twoheadleftarrow \mathsf{TPerm}(\mathcal{T}, \mathcal{M})$. $E^{\pm} \twoheadleftarrow \mathsf{Perm}(\mathcal{M})$ is
an ideal block cipher underneath $\widetilde{E}$. The STPRP advantage of $\mathbf{A}$ is defined
as $\Delta_{\mathbf{A}}(\widetilde{E}_K^{\pm}(\cdot, \cdot), E^{\pm}(\cdot, \cdot); \widetilde{\pi}^{\pm}(\cdot, \cdot), E^{\pm}(\cdot, \cdot))$, where the probabilities are taken over

random and independent choice of K, E, $\widetilde{\pi}$, and the coins of $\mathbf{A}$ if any. For the remainder, we say that $\mathbf{A}$ is a (q_C, q_P)-distinguisher if it asks at most q_C queries to its construction oracle and at most q_P queries to its primitive oracle.

Definition 1 (Almost-Uniform Hash Function). Let $\mathcal{H} : \mathcal{K} \times \mathcal{X} \to \mathcal{Y}$ be a family of keyed hash functions. We call $\mathcal{H}$ ϵ-almost-uniform (ϵ-AUniform) if, for $K \leftarrow \mathcal{K}$ and all $X \in \mathcal{X}$ and $Y \in \mathcal{Y}$, it holds that $\Pr_{K \leftarrow \mathcal{K}} [\mathcal{H}(K, X) = Y] \leq \epsilon$.

Definition 2 (Almost-XOR-Universal Hash Function). Let $\mathcal{H} : \mathcal{K} \times \mathcal{X} \to \mathcal{Y}$ be a family of keyed hash functions with $\mathcal{Y} \subseteq \{0,1\}^*$. We say that $\mathcal{H}$ is ϵ-almost-XOR-universal (ϵ-AXU) if, for $K \leftarrow \mathcal{K}$, and for all distinct $X, X' \in \mathcal{X}$ and any $\Delta \in \mathcal{Y}$, it holds that $\Pr_{K \leftarrow \mathcal{K}} [\mathcal{H}(K, X) \oplus \mathcal{H}(K, X') = \Delta] \leq \epsilon$.

Minematsu and Iwata [14] defined partial-almost-XOR-universality to capture the probability of partial output collisions.

Definition 3 (Partial-AXU Hash Function). Let $\mathcal{H} : \mathcal{K} \times \mathcal{X} \to \{0,1\}^n \times \{0,1\}^k$ be a family of hash functions. We say that $\mathcal{H}$ is (n, k, ϵ)-partial-AXU $((n, k, \epsilon)$-pAXU$)$ if, for $K \leftarrow \mathcal{K}$, and for all distinct $X, X' \in \mathcal{X}$ and all $\Delta \in \{0,1\}^n$, it holds that $\Pr_{K \leftarrow \mathcal{K}} [\mathcal{H}(K, X) \oplus \mathcal{H}(K, X') = (\Delta, 0^k)] \leq \epsilon$.

The H-Coefficient Technique. The H-coefficients technique is a method due to Patarin [4,16]. It assumes the results of the interaction of an adversary $\mathbf{A}$ with its oracles are collected in a transcript τ. The task of $\mathbf{A}$ is to distinguish the real world $\mathcal{O}_{\text{real}}$ from the ideal world $\mathcal{O}_{\text{ideal}}$. A transcript τ is called *attainable* if the probability to obtain τ in the ideal world is non-zero. One assumes that $\mathbf{A}$ does not ask duplicate queries or queries prohibited by the game or to which it already knows the answer. Denote by Θ_{real} and Θ_{ideal} the distribution of transcripts in the real and the ideal world, respectively. Then, the fundamental Lemma of the H-coefficients technique states:

Lemma 1 (Fundamental Lemma of the H-coefficient Technique [16]). Assume, the set of attainable transcripts is partitioned into two disjoint sets GOODT and BADT. Further assume, there exist $\epsilon_1, \epsilon_2 \geq 0$ such that for any transcript $\tau \in$ GOODT, it holds that

$$\frac{\Pr[\Theta_{\text{real}} = \tau]}{\Pr[\Theta_{\text{ideal}} = \tau]} \geq 1 - \epsilon_1, \quad \text{and} \quad \Pr[\Theta_{\text{ideal}} \in \text{BADT}] \leq \epsilon_2.$$

Then, for all adversaries $\mathbf{A}$, it holds that $\Delta_{\mathbf{A}} (\mathcal{O}_{\text{real}}; \mathcal{O}_{\text{ideal}}) \leq \epsilon_1 + \epsilon_2$.

The proof is given in [4,16].

3   The Generic GXHX Construction

Let $n, k, \ell \geq 1$ be integers and $\mathcal{K} = \{0,1\}^k$, $\mathcal{L} = \{0,1\}^\ell$, and $\mathcal{T} \subseteq \{0,1\}^*$. Let $E : \mathcal{K} \times \{0,1\}^n \to \{0,1\}^n$ be a block cipher and $\mathcal{H} : \mathcal{L} \times \mathcal{T} \to \{0,1\}^n \times \mathcal{K} \times \{0,1\}^n$

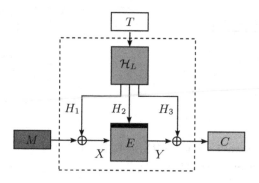

Fig. 1. Schematic illustration of the encryption process of a message M and a tweak T with the general GXHX$[E, \mathcal{H}]$ tweakable block cipher. $E : \mathcal{K} \times \{0,1\}^n \to \{0,1\}^n$ is a keyed permutation and $\mathcal{H} : \mathcal{L} \times \mathcal{T} \to \{0,1\}^n \times \mathcal{K} \times \{0,1\}^n$ a keyed universal hash function.

Algorithm 1. Encryption and decryption algorithms of the general GXHX$[E, \mathcal{H}]$ construction.

11: **function** GXHX$[E, \mathcal{H}]_L(T, M)$	21: **function** GXHX$[E, \mathcal{H}]_L^{-1}(T, C)$
12: $(H_1, H_2, H_3) \leftarrow \mathcal{H}(L, T)$	22: $(H_1, H_2, H_3) \leftarrow \mathcal{H}(L, T)$
13: $C \leftarrow E_{H_2}(M \oplus H_1) \oplus H_3$	23: $M \leftarrow E_{H_2}^{-1}(C \oplus H_3) \oplus H_1$
14: **return** C	24: **return** M

---

be a family of hash functions. Then, we define by GXHX$[E, \mathcal{H}] : \mathcal{L} \times \mathcal{T} \times \{0,1\}^n \to \{0,1\}^n$ the tweakable block cipher instantiated with E and $\mathcal{H}$ that, for given key $L \in \mathcal{L}$, tweak $T \in \mathcal{T}$, and message $M \in \{0,1\}^n$, computes the ciphertext C, as shown on the left side of Algorithm 1. Likewise, given key $L \in \mathcal{L}$, tweak $T \in \mathcal{T}$, and ciphertext $C \in \{0,1\}^n$, the plaintext M is computed by $M \leftarrow$ GXHX$[E, \mathcal{H}]_L^{-1}(T, C)$, as shown on the right side of Algorithm 1. Clearly, GXHX$[E, \mathcal{H}]$ is a correct and tidy tweakable permutation, i.e., for all keys $L \in \mathcal{L}$, all tweak-plaintext inputs $(T, M) \in \mathcal{T} \times \{0,1\}^n$, and all tweak-ciphertext inputs $(T, C) \in \mathcal{T} \times \{0,1\}^n$, it holds that

$$\text{GXHX}[E, \mathcal{H}]_L^{-1}(T, \text{GXHX}[E, \mathcal{H}]_L(T, M)) = M \text{ and}$$
$$\text{GXHX}[E, \mathcal{H}]_L(T, \text{GXHX}[E, \mathcal{H}]_L^{-1}(T, C)) = C.$$

Figure 1 illustrates the encryption process schematically.

4   XHX: Deriving the Hash Keys from the Block Cipher

In the following, we adapt the general GXHX construction to XHX. which differs from the former in two aspects: first, XHX splits the hash function into three functions $\mathcal{H}_1$, $\mathcal{H}_2$, and $\mathcal{H}_3$; second, since we need at least $n + k$ bit of key material for the hash functions, it derives the hash-function key from a key K using the block cipher E. We denote by $s \geq 0$ the number of derived hash-function keys L_i and collect them together with the user-given key $K \in \{0,1\}^k$

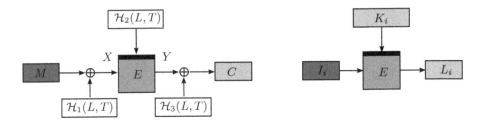

Fig. 2. Schematic illustration of the XHX$[E, \mathcal{H}]$ construction where we derive the hash-function keys L_i from the block cipher E.

Algorithm 2. Encryption and decryption algorithms of XHX where the keys are derived from the block cipher. We define $\mathcal{H} := (\mathcal{H}_1, \mathcal{H}_2, \mathcal{H}_3)$. Note that the exact definitions of I_i and K_i are usecase-specific.

11: **function** XHX$[E, \mathcal{H}]$.KEYSETUP(K)	21: **function** $\mathcal{H}(L, T)$
12: **for** $i \leftarrow 1$ to s **do**	22: $H_1 \leftarrow \mathcal{H}_1(L, T)$
13: $L_i \leftarrow E_{K_i}(I_i)$	23: $H_2 \leftarrow \mathcal{H}_2(L, T)$
14: $L \leftarrow (K, L_1, \ldots, L_s)$	24: $H_3 \leftarrow \mathcal{H}_3(L, T)$
15: **return** L	25: **return** (H_1, H_2, H_3)
31: **function** XHX$[E, \mathcal{H}]_K(T, M)$	41: **function** XHX$[E, \mathcal{H}]_K^{-1}(T, C)$
32: $L \leftarrow$ XHX$[E, \mathcal{H}]$.KEYSETUP(K)	42: $L \leftarrow$ XHX$[E, \mathcal{H}]$.KEYSETUP(K)
33: $(H_1, H_2, H_3) \leftarrow \mathcal{H}(L, T)$	43: $(H_1, H_2, H_3) \leftarrow \mathcal{H}(L, T)$
34: $C \leftarrow E_{H_2}(M \oplus H_1) \oplus H_3$	44: $M \leftarrow E_{H_2}^{-1}(C \oplus H_3) \oplus H_1$
35: **return** C	45: **return** M

---

into a vector $L := (K, L_1, \ldots, L_s)$. Moreover, we define a set of variables I_i and K_i, for $1 \leq i \leq s$, which denote input and key to the block cipher E for computing: $L_i := E_{K_i}(I_i)$. We allow flexible, usecase-specific definitions for the values I_i and K_i as long as they fulfill certain properties that will be listed in Sect. 4.1. We redefine the key space of the hash functions to $\mathcal{L} \subseteq \{0, 1\}^k \times (\{0, 1\}^n)^s$. Note, the values L_i are equal for all encryptions and decryptions and hence, can be precomputed and stored for all encryptions under the same key.

The Constructions by Wang et al. The 32 constructions $\widetilde{\mathbb{E}}[2]$ by Wang et al. are a special case of our construction with the parameters $s = 1$, key length $k = n$, with the inputs $I_i, K_i \in \{0^n, K\}$, and the option $(I_i, K_i) = (0^n, 0^n)$ excluded. Their constructions compute exactly one value L_1 by $L_1 := E_{K_1}(I_1)$. One can easily describe their constructions in the terms of the XHX framework, with three variables $X_1, X_2, X_3 \in \{K, L_1, K \oplus L_1\}$ for which holds that $X_1 \neq X_2$ and $X_3 \neq X_2$, and which are used in XHX as follows:

$$\mathcal{H}_1(L, T) := X_1,$$
$$\mathcal{H}_2(L, T) := X_2 \oplus T,$$
$$\mathcal{H}_3(L, T) := X_3.$$

4.1   Security Proof of XHX

This section concerns the security of the XHX construction in the ideal-cipher model where the hash-function keys are derived by the (ideal) block cipher E.

Properties of $\mathcal{H}$. For our security analysis, we list a set of properties that we require for $\mathcal{H}$. We assume that L is sampled uniformly at random from $\mathcal{L}$. To address parts of the output of $\mathcal{H}$, we also use the notion $\mathcal{H}_i : \mathcal{L} \times \mathcal{T} \rightarrow \{0,1\}^{o_i}$ to refer to the function that computes the i-th output of $\mathcal{H}(L,T)$, for $1 \leq i \leq 3$, with $o_1 := n$, $o_2 := k$, and $o_3 := n$. Moreover, we define $\mathcal{H}_{1,2}(T) := (\mathcal{H}_1(L,T), \mathcal{H}_2(L,T))$, and $\mathcal{H}_{3,2}(T) := (\mathcal{H}_3(L,T), \mathcal{H}_2(L,T))$.

Property P1. For all distinct $T, T' \in \mathcal{T}$ and all $\Delta \in \{0,1\}^n$, it holds that

$$\max_{i \in \{1,3\}} \Pr_{L \leftarrow \mathcal{L}} \left[\mathcal{H}_{i,2}(T) \oplus \mathcal{H}_{i,2}(T') = (\Delta, 0^k) \right] \leq \epsilon_1.$$

Property P2. For all $T \in \mathcal{T}$ and all $(c_1, c_2) \in \{0,1\}^n \times \{0,1\}^k$, it holds that

$$\max_{i \in \{1,3\}} \Pr_{L \leftarrow \mathcal{L}} \left[\mathcal{H}_{i,2}(T) = (c_1, c_2) \right] \leq \epsilon_2.$$

Note that Property P1 is equivalent to saying $\mathcal{H}_{1,2}$ and $\mathcal{H}_{3,2}$ are (n, k, ϵ_1)-pAXU; Property P2 is equivalent to the statement that $\mathcal{H}_{1,2}$ and $\mathcal{H}_{3,2}$ are ϵ_2-AUniform. Clearly, it must hold that $\epsilon_1, \epsilon_2 \geq 2^{-(n+k)}$.

Property P3. For all $T \in \mathcal{T}$, all chosen I_i, K_i, for $1 \leq i \leq s$, and all $\Delta \in \{0,1\}^n$, it holds that

$$\Pr_{L \leftarrow \mathcal{L}} \left[\mathcal{H}_{1,2}(T) \oplus (I_i, K_i) = (\Delta, 0^k) \right] \leq \epsilon_3.$$

Property P4. For all $T \in \mathcal{T}$, all chosen K_i, L_i, for $1 \leq i \leq s$, and all $\Delta \in \{0,1\}^n$, it holds that

$$\Pr_{L \leftarrow \mathcal{L}} \left[\mathcal{H}_{3,2}(T) \oplus (L_i, K_i) = (\Delta, 0^k) \right] \leq \epsilon_4.$$

Properties P3 and P4 represent the probabilities that an adversary's query hits the inputs that have been chosen for computing a hash-function key. We list a further property which gives the probability that a set of constants chosen by the adversary can hit the values I_i and K_i from generating the keys L_i:

Property P5. For $1 \leq i \leq s$, and all $(c_1, c_2) \in \{0,1\}^n \times \{0,1\}^k$, it holds that

$$\Pr_{K \leftarrow \mathcal{K}} \left[(I_i, K_i) = (c_1, c_2) \right] \leq \epsilon_5.$$

In other words, the tuples (I_i, K_i) contain a sufficient amount of close to n bit entropy, and cannot be predicted by an adversary with greater probability, i.e., ϵ_5 should not be larger than a small multiple of $1/2^n$. From Property 5 and the fact that the values L_i are computed from $E_{K_i}(I_i)$ with an ideal permutation E, it follows that for $1 \leq i \leq s$ and all $(c_1, c_2) \in \{0,1\}^n \times \{0,1\}^k$

$$\Pr_{K \leftarrow \mathcal{K}} \left[(L_i, K_i) = (c_1, c_2) \right] \leq \epsilon_5.$$

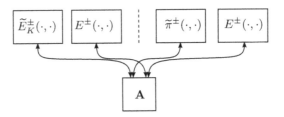

Fig. 3. Schematic illustration of the oracles available to **A**.

Theorem 1. Let $E \leftarrow \mathsf{Block}(\mathcal{K}, \{0,1\}^n)$ be an ideal cipher. Further, let $\mathcal{H}_i : \mathcal{L} \times \mathcal{T} \rightarrow \{0,1\}^{o_i}$, for $1 \leq i \leq 3$ be families of hash functions for which Properties P1 through P4 hold, and let $K \leftarrow \mathcal{K}$. Moreover, let Property P5 hold for the choice of all I_i and K_i. Let s denote the number of keys L_i, $1 \leq i \leq s$. Let **A** be a (q_C, q_P)-distinguisher on $\mathrm{XHX}[E, \mathcal{H}]_K$. Then

$$\underset{\mathbf{A}}{\Delta} \left(\mathrm{XHX}[E, \mathcal{H}], E^{\pm}; \widetilde{\pi}^{\pm}, E^{\pm}\right) \leq q_C^2 \epsilon_1 + 2q_P q_C \epsilon_2 + q_C s(\epsilon_3 + \epsilon_4) + 2q_P s \epsilon_5 + \frac{s^2}{2^{n+1}}.$$

Proof Sketch. The proof of Theorem 1 follows from Lemmas 1, 2, and 3. For the sake of space limitations, the proofs of Lemmas 2 and 3 are deferred to the full version of this work [7].

Let $\widetilde{E}$ denote the $\mathrm{XHX}[E, \mathcal{H}]$ construction and $\widetilde{\pi} \leftarrow \mathsf{TPerm}(\mathcal{T}, \{0,1\}^n)$ in the remainder. Figure 3 illustrates the oracles available to **A**. The queries by **A** are collected in a transcript τ. We will define a series of bad events that can happen during the interaction of **A** with its oracles. The proof will then bound the probability of these events to occur in the transcript in Lemma 2. We define a transcript as bad if it satisfies at least one such bad event, and define BADT as the set of all attainable bad transcripts.

We define that τ is composed of two disjoint sets of queries τ_C and τ_P and L, $\tau = \tau_C \cup \tau_P \cup \{L\}$, where $\tau_C := \{(M^i, C^i, T^i, H_1^i, H_2^i, H_3^i, X^i, Y^i, d^i)\}_{1 \leq i \leq q_C}$ contains exactly the queries by **A** to the construction oracle plus internal variables H_1^i, H_2^i, H_3^i (i.e., the outputs of $\mathcal{H}_1$, $\mathcal{H}_2$, and $\mathcal{H}_3$, respectively), X^i, and Y^i (where $X^i \leftarrow H_1^i \oplus M^i$ and $Y^i \leftarrow H_3^i \oplus C^i$, respectively). The set $\tau_P := \{(\widehat{K}^i, \widehat{X}^i, \widehat{Y}^i, d^i)\}_{1 \leq i \leq q_P}$ contains exactly the queries to the primitive oracle; both sets store also binary variables d^i that indicate the direction of the i-th query, where $d^i = 1$ represents the fact that the i-th query is an encryption query, and $d^i = 0$ that it is a decryption query. The internal variables for one call to XHX are named analogously to those given in Algorithm 2 and Fig. 2.

We apply a common strategy for handling bad events from both worlds: in the real world, all secrets (i.e., the hash-function key L) are revealed to the **A** *after* it finished its interaction with the available oracles, but before it has output its decision bit regarding which world it interacted with. Similarly, in the ideal world, the oracle samples the hash-function key independently from the choice of E and $\widetilde{\pi}$ uniformly at random, $L \leftarrow \mathcal{L}$, and also reveals L to **A** *after* the adversary finished its interaction and before has output its decision bit. The internal variables in construction queries – H_1^i, H_2^i, H_3^i, X^i, Y^i – can then be computed and added to the transcript also in the ideal world using the oracle inputs and outputs T^i, M^i, C^i, H_1^i, H_2^i, and H_3^i.

Let $i, j \in \{1, \ldots, q\}$ where $i \neq j$. We define that an attainable transcript τ is bad, i.e., $\tau \in \mathrm{BADT}$, if at least one of the following conditions is met:

- bad_1: There exist $i \neq j$ s.t. $(H_2^i, X^i) = (H_2^j, X^j)$.
- bad_2: There exist $i \neq j$ s.t. $(H_2^i, Y^i) = (H_2^j, Y^j)$.
- bad_3: There exist $i \neq j$ s.t. $(H_2^i, X^i) = (\widehat{K}^j, \widehat{X}^j)$.
- bad_4: There exist $i \neq j$ s.t. $(H_2^i, Y^i) = (\widehat{K}^j, \widehat{Y}^j)$.
- bad_5: There exist $i \neq j$ s.t. $(\widehat{K}^i, \widehat{X}^i) = (\widehat{K}^j, \widehat{X}^j)$.
- bad_6: There exist $i \neq j$ s.t. $(\widehat{K}^i, \widehat{Y}^i) = (\widehat{K}^j, \widehat{Y}^j)$.
- bad_7: There exist $i \in \{1, \ldots, s\}$ and $j \in \{1, \ldots, q_C\}$ s.t. $(X^j, H_2^j) = (I_i, K_i)$ and $d^j = 1$.
- bad_8: There exist $i \in \{1, \ldots, s\}$ and $j \in \{1, \ldots, q_C\}$ s.t. $(Y^j, H_2^j) = (L_i, K_i)$ and $d^j = 0$.
- bad_9: There exist $i \in \{1, \ldots, s\}$ and $j \in \{1, \ldots, q_P\}$ s.t. $(\widehat{X}^j, \widehat{K}^j) = (I_i, K_i)$.
- bad_{10}: There exist $i \in \{1, \ldots, s\}$ and $j \in \{1, \ldots, q_P\}$ s.t. $(\widehat{Y}^j, \widehat{K}^j) = (L_i, K_i)$.
- bad_{11}: There exist $i, j \in \{1, \ldots, s\}$ and $i \neq j$ s.t. $(K_i, L_i) = (K_j, L_j)$ but $I_i \neq I_j$.

The events

- bad_1 and bad_2 consider collisions between two construction queries,
- bad_3 and bad_4 consider collisions between primitive and construction queries,
- bad_5 and bad_6 consider collisions between two primitive queries, and
- bad_7 through bad_{10} address the case that the adversary may could find an input-key tuple in either a primitive or construction query that has been used to derive some of the subkeys L_i.
- bad_{11} addresses the event that the ideal oracle produces a collision while sampling the hash-function keys independently uniformly at random.

Note that bad_5 and bad_6 are listed only for the sake of completeness and can never occur.

Lemma 2. It holds that

$$\Pr\left[\Theta_{\mathrm{ideal}} \in \mathrm{BADT}\right] \leq q_C^2 \epsilon_1 + 2 q_P q_C \epsilon_2 + q_C s(\epsilon_3 + \epsilon_4) + 2 q_P s \epsilon_5 + \frac{s^2}{2^{n+1}}.$$

The proof can be found in the full version [7].

Good Transcripts. Above, we have considered bad events. In contrast, we define GOODT as the set of all good transcripts, i.e., all attainable transcripts that are *not* bad.

Lemma 3. Let $\tau \in \mathrm{GOODT}$ be a good transcript. Then

$$\Pr\left[\Theta_{\mathrm{real}} = \tau\right] \geq \Pr\left[\Theta_{\mathrm{ideal}} = \tau\right].$$

In the following, we sketch the concept of our proof. The full proof can be found in the full version [7].

Proof Sketch. Assume a good transcript τ. In both worlds, the secret key is sampled uniformly from random: $\Pr[K \twoheadleftarrow \mathcal{K} : K] = 1/|\mathcal{K}|$. For our claim in Lemma 3, we have to show that the probability of outputs in the real world is greater or equal than their probability in the ideal world:

$$\Pr_{\forall i, \forall j, \forall g} \left[\widetilde{E}_L(T^i, M^i) = C^i, \, E(\widehat{K}^j, \widehat{X}^j) = Y^j, \, E(K_g, I_g) = L_g \right] \tag{1}$$

$$\geq \Pr_{\forall i} \left[\widetilde{\pi}(T^i, M^i) = C^i \right] \cdot \Pr_{\forall j} \left[E(\widehat{K}^j, \widehat{X}^j) = Y^j \right] \cdot \prod_{g=1}^{s} \Pr\left[L_g \twoheadleftarrow \{0,1\}^n : L_g \right].$$

We reindex the keys used in primitive queries to $\widehat{\mathsf{K}}^1, \ldots, \widehat{\mathsf{K}}^\ell$ to eliminate duplicates and group all primitive queries into sets $\widehat{\mathcal{K}}^j$, for $1 \leq j \leq \ell$, s.t. all sets $\widehat{\mathcal{K}}^j$ are distinct and each set $\widehat{\mathcal{K}}^j$ contains exactly only the primitive queries with key $\widehat{\mathsf{K}}^j$. We denote by $\widehat{k}^j = |\widehat{\mathcal{K}}^j|$ the number of queries with key $\widehat{\mathsf{K}}^j$. Clearly, it holds that $\ell \leq q_P$ and $\sum_{j=1}^{\ell} \widehat{k}^j = q_P$. Moreover, we also re-index the tweaks of the construction queries to $\mathsf{T}^1, \ldots, \mathsf{T}^r$ for the purpose of eliminating duplicates. Given these new indices, we group all construction queries into sets $\mathcal{T}^j$, for $1 \leq j \leq r$, s.t. all sets are distinct and each set $\mathcal{T}^j$ contains exactly only all construction queries with the tweak T^j. We denote by $t^j = |\mathcal{T}^j|$ the number of queries with tweak T^j. It holds that $r \leq q_C$ and $\sum_{j=1}^{r} t^j = q_C$.

In the ideal world, all keys $L_1, \ldots, L_s$ are sampled independently uniformly at random from $\{0,1\}^n$: $\prod_{g=1}^{s} \Pr[L_g \twoheadleftarrow \{0,1\}^n : L_g] = 1/(2^n)^s$. Recall that every $\widetilde{\pi}(\mathsf{T}^j, \cdot)$ and $\widetilde{\pi}^{-1}(\mathsf{T}^j, \cdot)$ is a permutation, and the assumption that $\mathbf{A}$ does not ask duplicate queries or such to which it already knows the answer. So, all queries are pairwise distinct. The probability to obtain the outputs of the transcript τ, for some fixed tweak T^j, is given by $1/(2^n)_{t^j}$. The same applies for the outputs of the primitive queries in our transcript for some fixed key $\widehat{\mathsf{K}}^j$: $1/(2^n)_{\widehat{k}^j}$. The outputs of construction and primitive queries are independent from each other in the ideal world. Over all disjoint key and tweak sets, the probability for obtaining τ in the ideal world is therefore given by

$$\Pr[\Theta_{\mathrm{ideal}} = \tau] = \left(\prod_{i=1}^{r} \frac{1}{(2^n)_{t^j}} \right) \cdot \left(\prod_{j=1}^{\ell} \frac{1}{(2^n)_{\widehat{k}^j}} \right) \cdot \frac{1}{(2^n)^s} \cdot \frac{1}{|\mathcal{K}|}. \tag{2}$$

In the real world, not only query pairs with equal tweak inputs $T^i = T^j$, but also queries with distinct tweaks whose corresponding hash values collide, $H_2^i = H_2^j$, target the same permutation. Moreover, there can be values H_2^i from construction queries that were equal to keys $\widehat{K}^j$ in primitive queries. Finally, the derived keys L_i are also constructed from the same block cipher E; so, the inputs K_i may also use the same permutation as primitive and construction queries.

Again, we reindex the keys in all primitive queries into sets to $\widehat{\mathsf{K}}^1, \ldots, \widehat{\mathsf{K}}^\ell$, and also reindex the hash values H_2^j to $\mathsf{H}_2^1, \ldots, \mathsf{H}_2^u$ for duplicate elimination, and group the construction queries into sets $\mathcal{H}_2^j$ s.t. each set $\mathcal{H}_2^j$ contains exactly the construction queries with $\mathcal{H}_2(L, T^i) = \mathsf{H}_2^j$. We unify and reindex the values H_2^j, $\widehat{\mathsf{K}}^j$, and K^j to values $\mathsf{P}^1, \ldots, \mathsf{P}^v$ (using P for permutation). We group all queries into sets $\mathcal{P}^j$, for $1 \leq j \leq v$, s.t. all sets are distinct and each set $\mathcal{P}^j$ consists of exactly the union of all construction queries with the hash value $\mathsf{H}_2 = \mathsf{P}^j$, all primitive queries with $\widehat{\mathsf{K}} = \mathsf{P}^j$, and all key-generating tuples with $\mathsf{K} = \mathsf{P}^j$:

$$\mathcal{P}^j := \left\{ \mathcal{H}_2^i : \mathsf{H}_2^i = \mathsf{P}^j \right\} \cup \left\{ \widehat{\mathcal{K}}^i : \widehat{\mathsf{K}}^i = \mathsf{P}^j \right\} \cup \left\{ \mathcal{K}^i : \mathsf{K}^i = \mathsf{P}^j \right\}.$$

We denote by $p^j = |\mathcal{P}^j|$ the number of queries that use the same permutation. It holds that $\sum_{j=1}^{v} p^j = q_P + q_C + s$. Recall that $\mathsf{Block}(k, n)$ denotes the set of all k-bit key, n-bit block ciphers. We call a block cipher E *compatible* with τ iff

1. For all $1 \leq i \leq q_C$, it holds that $C^i = E_{H_2^i}\left(M^i \oplus H_1^i\right) \oplus H_3^i$, where $H_1^i = \mathcal{H}_1(L, T^i)$, $H_2^i = \mathcal{H}_2(L, T^i)$, and $H_3^i = \mathcal{H}_3(L, T^i)$, and
2. for all $1 \leq j \leq q_P$, it holds that $\widehat{Y}^j = E_{\widehat{K}^j}(\widehat{X}^j)$,
3. and for all $1 \leq g \leq s$, it holds that $L_i = E_{K_i}(I_i)$.

Let $\mathsf{Comp}(\tau)$ denote the set of all block ciphers E compatible with τ. Then,

$$\Pr\left[\Theta_{\text{real}} = \tau\right] = \Pr\left[E \leftarrow \mathsf{Block}\,(k, n) : E \in \mathsf{Comp}(\tau)\right] \cdot \Pr\left[K | \Theta_{\text{real}} = \tau\right]. \quad (3)$$

The rightmost term is given by $1/|\mathcal{K}|$ also in the real world, and we can focus on the first factor on the right-hand side. Since we assume that no bad events have occurred, the fraction of compatible block ciphers is given by

$$\Pr\left[E \leftarrow \mathsf{Block}\,(k, n) : E \in \mathsf{Comp}(\tau)\right] = \prod_{i=1}^{v} \frac{1}{(2^n)_{p^i}}.$$

Using a variable substitution, we can show in the full proof that this is larger or equal than the probability to obtain τ in the ideal world:

$$\prod_{i=1}^{v} \frac{1}{(2^n)_{p^i}} \geq \left(\prod_{j=1}^{\ell} \frac{1}{(2^n)_{\widehat{k}^j}}\right) \cdot \left(\prod_{j=1}^{r} \frac{1}{(2^n)_{t^j}}\right) \cdot \frac{1}{(2^n)_s}, \quad (4)$$

which yields our claim in Lemma 3.

5   Efficient Instantiations

The hash function for XHX needs to satisfy multiple conditions for the construction to be secure. This section provides concrete instantiations of hash functions which satisfy those conditions. While it is rather straight-forward to design hash functions in the case of independent keys by using two independent n-bit AXU and AUniform hash functions, the additional conditions for XHX require deeper analysis. We present two instantiations depending on the maximum tweak length.

Algorithm 3. The universal hash function $\mathcal{H}^*$.

11: **function** $\mathcal{H}_L^*(T)$	21: **function** $\mathcal{F}_K(T)$
12: $(K, L_1, \ldots, L_s) \leftarrow L$	22: $p \leftarrow |T| \bmod n$
13: $K' \leftarrow \text{TRUNC}_n(K)$	23: **if** $p \neq 0$ **then**
14: $H_1 \leftarrow \mathcal{F}_{K'}(T)$	24: $T \leftarrow T \| 0^{n-p}$
15: $H_2 \leftarrow \text{TRUNC}_k (\mathcal{F}_{L_1}(T) \| \cdots \| \mathcal{F}_{L_s}(T))$	25: Parse $T_1, \ldots, T_m \xleftarrow{n} T$
16: $H_3 \leftarrow \mathcal{F}_{K'}(T)$	26: $T_{m+1} \leftarrow \langle |T| \rangle_n$
17: **return** (H_1, H_2, H_3)	27: $Y \leftarrow 0$
	28: **for** $i \leftarrow 1$ **to** $m + 1$ **do**
	29: $Y \leftarrow (Y \oplus T_i) \cdot K$
	30: **return** $(Y \cdot K) \oplus K$

While the case of n-bit tweaks has already been covered by Wang et al., the general important case of having a variable-length tweak remained still open and is addressed here with the instantiation $\mathcal{H}^*$. Additionally, we also present a second hash function $\mathcal{H}^2$ that is more efficient for $2n$-bit tweaks. Both our proposals use field multiplications over $\mathbb{GF}(2^n)$ and need $(k + n)$ bits of key material, where the ideal cipher E is used for key derivation. We define $K_i := K$ and $I_i := \langle i \rangle$, for $1 \leq i \leq s$, i.e., we compute the subkeys L_i as $L_i \leftarrow E_K(\langle i \rangle)$.

$\mathcal{H}^*$ – **A Hash Function for Variable-Length Tweaks.** We propose a first instantiation $\mathcal{H}^*$ for variable-length tweaks. $\mathcal{H}^*$ uses two universal hash functions keyed by K and L_1, and takes T as input. Assume k and n be positive integers and $s \leq 2^{k-1}$. More specifically, let $\mathcal{F} := \{F \mid F : \{0,1\}^n \times \{0,1\}^* \rightarrow \{0,1\}^n\}$ denote an $\epsilon(m)$-AXU and $\rho(m)$-AUniform family of hash functions. Here, $\epsilon(m)$ and $\rho(m)$ denote the maximum AXU and AUniform biases for any input (pair) of at most $m \geq \lceil |T|/n \rceil$ n-bit blocks. $\mathcal{H}^* : \mathcal{L} \times \{0,1\}^* \rightarrow \{0,1\}^n \times \{0,1\}^k \times \{0,1\}^n$ is defined in Algorithm 3. We suggest a polynomial hash for $\mathcal{F}_K(\cdot)$ with a minimum degree of one; this means, it holds that $\mathcal{F}_K(\varepsilon) = K$ for the empty string ε to avoid fixed points. For simplicity, $\mathcal{H}^*$ conducts all computations in the same field $\mathbb{GF}(2^n)$ in all calls to $\mathcal{F}$. In general, we have to consider three potential cases for the relation of state size and key lengths:

- **Case $k = n$.** In this case, the hash values H_1, H_2, and H_3 are the results of polynomial hash functions $\mathcal{F}$. In this case, $\mathcal{H}^*$ employs K directly as hashing key to generate H_1 and H_3, and a derived key L_1 to compute H_2. Hence, it holds that $s = 1$ in this case.
- **Case $k < n$.** In this case, we could simply truncate H_2 from n to k bits. Theoretically, we could derive a longer key from K for the computation of H_1 and H_3; however, we disregard this case since ciphers with smaller key size than state length are very uncommon.
- **Case $k > n$.** In the third case, we truncate the hash key K for the computation of H_1 and H_3 to n bits. Moreover, we derive s hashing keys $L_1, \ldots, L_s$ from the block cipher E. For H_2 and we concatenate the output of s instances of $\mathcal{F}$. This construction is well-known to be $\epsilon^s(m)$-pAXU if $\mathcal{F}$ is $\epsilon(m)$-pAXU. Finally, we truncate the result to k bits if necessary.

Lemma 4. $\mathcal{H}^*$ is $2^{sn-k}\epsilon^{s+1}(m)$-pAXU and $2^{sn-k}\rho^{s+1}(m)$-Uniform. Moreover, it satisfies Properties P3 and P4 with probability $2^{sn-k}\rho^{s+1}(m)$ each, and Property P5 with $\epsilon_5 \leq 2/2^k$ for our choice of the values I_i and K_i.

Remark 2. The term 2^{sn-k} results from the potential truncation of H_2 if the key length k of the block cipher is no multiple of the state size n. H_2 is computed by concatenating the results of multiple independent invocations of a polynomial hash function $\mathcal{F}$ in $\mathrm{GF}(2^n)$ under assumed independent keys. Clearly, if $\mathcal{F}$ is ϵ-AXU, then their sn-bit concatenation is ϵ^s-AXU. However, after truncating sn to k bits, we may lose information, which results in the factor of 2^{sn-k}. For the case $k = n$, it follows that $s = 1$, and the terms $2^{sn-k}\epsilon^{s+1}(m)$ and $2^{sn-k}\rho^{s+1}(m)$ simplify to $\epsilon^2(m)$ and $\rho^2(m)$, respectively.

Our instantiation of $\mathcal{F}$ has $\epsilon(m) = \rho(m) = (m+2)/2^n$. Before we prove Lemma 4, we derive from it the following corollary for XHX when instantiated with $\mathcal{H}^*$.

Corollary 1. *Let E and $\mathrm{XHX}[E, \mathcal{H}^*]$ be defined as in Theorem 1, where the maximum length of any tweak is limited by at most m n-bit blocks. Moreover, let $K \twoheadleftarrow \mathcal{K}$. Let $\mathbf{A}$ be a (q_C, q_P)-distinguisher on $\mathrm{XHX}[E, \mathcal{H}^*]$. Then*

$$\underset{\mathbf{A}}{\Delta}\left(\mathrm{XHX}[E, \mathcal{H}^*], E^{\pm}; \tilde{\pi}^{\pm}, E^{\pm}\right) \leq \frac{(q_C^2 + 2q_Cq_P + 2q_Cs)(m+2)^{s+1}}{2^{n+k}} + \frac{4q_Ps}{2^k} + \frac{s^2}{2^{n+1}}.$$

The proof of the corollary stems from the combination of Lemma 4 with Theorem 1 and can be omitted.

Proof of Lemma 4. In the following, we assume that $T, T' \in \{0,1\}^*$ are distinct tweaks of at most m blocks each. Again, we consider the pAXU property first.

Partial Almost-XOR-Universality. This is the probability that for any $\Delta \in \{0,1\}^n$:

$$\underset{L\twoheadleftarrow\mathcal{L}}{\Pr}\left[(\mathcal{F}_{K'}(T), \mathcal{F}_{L_1,\ldots,L_s}(T)) \oplus (\mathcal{F}_{K'}(T'), \mathcal{F}_{L_1,\ldots,L_s}(T')) = (\Delta, 0^n)\right]$$

$$= \underset{L\twoheadleftarrow\mathcal{L}}{\Pr}\left[\mathcal{F}_{K'}(T) \oplus \mathcal{F}_{K'}(T') = \Delta, \mathcal{F}_{L_1,\ldots,L_s}(T) \oplus \mathcal{F}_{L_1,\ldots,L_s}(T') = 0^n\right]$$

$$\leq 2^{sn-k} \cdot \epsilon^{s+1}(m).$$

We assume independent hashing keys $K', L_1, \ldots, L_s$ here. When $k = n$, it holds that $s = 1$, and this probability is upper bounded by $\epsilon^2(m)$ since $\mathcal{F}$ is $\epsilon(m)$-AXU. In the case $k > n$, we compute s words of H_2 that are concatenated and truncated to k bits. Hence, $\mathcal{F}_{L_1,\ldots,L_s}$ is $2^{sn-k} \cdot \epsilon^s(m)$-AXU. In combination with the AXU bound for $\mathcal{F}_{K'}$, we obtain the pAXU bound for $\mathcal{H}^*$ above.

Almost-Uniformity. Here, for any $(\Delta_1, \Delta_2) \in \{0,1\}^n \times \{0,1\}^k$, it shall hold

$$\underset{L\twoheadleftarrow\mathcal{L}}{\Pr}\left[(\mathcal{F}_{K'}(T), \mathcal{F}_{L_1,\ldots,L_s}(T)) = (\Delta_1, \Delta_2)\right] = \underset{L\twoheadleftarrow\mathcal{L}}{\Pr}\left[\mathcal{F}_{K'}(T) = \Delta_1, \mathcal{F}_{L_1,\ldots,L_s}(T) = \Delta_2\right]$$

$$\leq 2^{sn-k} \cdot \rho^{s+1}(m)$$

since $\mathcal{F}$ is $\rho(m)$-AUniform, and using a similar argumentation for the cases $k = n$ and $k > n$ as for partial-almost-XOR universality.

Property P3. For all $T \in \mathcal{T}$ and $\Delta \in \{0,1\}^n$, Property P3 is equivalent to

$$\Pr_{L \twoheadleftarrow \mathcal{L}} \left[\mathcal{F}_{K'}(T) = (\Delta \oplus I_i), \mathcal{F}_{L_1,\ldots,L_s}(T) = K \right]$$

for a fixed $1 \leq i \leq s$. Here, this property is equivalent to almost uniformity; hence, the probability for the latter equality is at most $2^{sn-k} \cdot \rho^s(m)$. The probability for the former equality is at most $\rho(m)$ since the property considers a fixed i. Since we assume independence of K and $L_1, \ldots, L_s$, it holds that $\epsilon_3 \leq 2^{sn-k} \cdot \rho^{s+1}(m)$.

Property P4. For all $T \in \mathcal{T}$ and $\Delta \in \{0,1\}^n$, Property P4 is equivalent to

$$\Pr_{L \twoheadleftarrow \mathcal{L}} \left[\mathcal{F}_{K'}(T) = (\Delta \oplus L_i), \mathcal{F}_{L_1,\ldots,L_s}(T) = K \right]$$

for a fixed $1 \leq i \leq s$. Using a similar argumentation as for Property P3, the probability is upper bounded by $\epsilon_4 \leq 2^{sn-k} \cdot \rho^{s+1}(m)$.

Property P5. We derive the hashing keys L_i with the help of E and the secret key K. So, in the simple case that $s = 1$, the probability that the adversary can guess any tuple (I_i, K_i), for $1 \leq i \leq s$, that is used to derive the hashing keys L_i, or guess any tuple (L_i, K_i) is at most $1/2^k$. Under the reasonable assumption $s < 2^{k-1}$, the probability becomes for fixed i in the general case:

$$\Pr_{K \twoheadleftarrow \mathcal{K}} \left[(I_i, K_i) = (c_1, c_2) \right] \leq \frac{1}{2^k - s} \leq \frac{2}{2^k}.$$

A similar argument holds that the adversary can guess any tuple (L_i, K_i), for $1 \leq i \leq s$. Hence, it holds for $\mathcal{H}^*$ that $\epsilon_5 \leq 2/2^k$.

$\epsilon(m)$ **and** $\rho(m)$. It remains to determine $\epsilon(m)$ and $\rho(m)$ for our instantiation of $\mathcal{F}_K(\cdot)$. It maps tweaks $T = T_1, \ldots, T_m$ to the result of

$$\left(\bigoplus_{i=1}^{m} T_i \cdot K^{m+3-i} \right) \oplus \langle |T| \rangle_n \cdot K \oplus K.$$

This is a polynomial of degree at most $m+2$, which is $(m+2)/2^n$-AXU. Moreover, over $L \in \mathcal{L}$, it lacks fixed points but for every $\Delta \in \{0,1\}^n$, and any fixed subset of m blocks of $T_1, \ldots, T_m$, there are at most $m+2$ out of 2^n values for the block T_{m+1} that fulfill $\mathcal{F}_K(T) = \Delta$. Hence, $\mathcal{F}$ is also $(m+2)/2^n$-AUniform.   □

$\mathcal{H}^*$ is a general construction which supports arbitrary tweak lengths. Though, if we used $\mathcal{H}^*$ for $2n$-bit tweaks, we would need four Galois-Field multiplications. However, we can hash more efficiently, even optimal in terms of the number of multiplications in this case. For this purpose, we define $\mathcal{H}^2$.

$\mathcal{H}^2$ – A Hash Function for $2n$-bit Tweaks. Naively, for two-block tweaks $|T| = 2n$, an ϵ-pAXU construction with $\epsilon \approx 1/2^{2n}$ could be achieved by simply multiplying the tweak with some key $L \in \mathbb{GF}(2^{2n})$ sampled uniformly over

Algorithm 4. The universal hash function $\mathcal{H}^2$.

11: **function** $\mathcal{H}^2_L(T)$	21: **function** $\mathcal{F}_{L_i}(T_1 \| T_2)$
12: $(K, L_1, \ldots, L_s) \leftarrow L$	22: **return** $(T_1 \boxdot L_i) \oplus T_2$
13: $(T_1, T_2) \overset{n}{\leftarrow} T$	
14: $K' \leftarrow \mathrm{TRUNC}_n(K)$	
15: $H_1 \leftarrow T_1 \boxdot K'$	
16: $H_2 \leftarrow \mathrm{TRUNC}_k (\mathcal{F}_{L_1}(T) \| \cdots \| \mathcal{F}_{L_s}(T))$	
17: $H_3 \leftarrow T_1 \boxdot K'$	
18: **return** (H_1, H_2, H_3)	

$\mathrm{GF}(2^{2n})$. However, we can realize a similarly secure construction more efficiently by using two multiplications over the smaller field $\mathrm{GF}(2^n)$. Additional conditions, such as uniformity, are satisfied by introducing squaring in the field to avoid fixed points in multiplication-based universal hash function. Following the notations from the previous sections, let $L = (K, L_1)$ be the $2n$-bit key of our hash function. For $X, Y \in \mathrm{GF}(2^n)$, we define the operation $\boxdot : \mathrm{GF}(2^n) \times \mathrm{GF}(2^n) \to \mathrm{GF}(2^n)$ as

$$X \boxdot Y := \begin{cases} X \cdot Y & \text{if } X \neq 0 \\ Y^2 & \text{otherwise.} \end{cases}$$

We assume a common encoding between the bit space and $\mathrm{GF}(2^n)$, i.e. a polynomial in the field is represented as its coefficient vector, e. g., the all-zero vector denotes the zero element 0, and the bit string $(0\ldots01)$ denotes the identity element. Hereafter, we write X interchangeably as an element of $\mathrm{GF}(2^n)$ or of $\{0,1\}^n$. For $\mathcal{L} = (\{0,1\}^n)^2$, $\mathcal{X} = (\{0,1\}^n)^2$ and $\mathcal{Y} = \{0,1\}^n \times \{0,1\}^k \times \{0,1\}^n$, the construction $\mathcal{H}^2 : \mathcal{L} \times \mathcal{X} \to \mathcal{Y}$ is defined in Algorithm 4. We note that the usage of keys has been chosen carefully, e.g., a swap of K and L_1 in $\mathcal{H}^2$ would invalidate Property P4.

Lemma 5. $\mathcal{H}^2$ is $2^{s+1}/2^{n+k}$-pAXU, $2^s/2^{n+k}$-AUniform, satisfies Properties P3 and P4 with probability $2/2^{n+k}$ each, and Property P5 with $\epsilon_5 = s/2^n$ for our choices of I_i and K_i, for $1 \leq i \leq s$.

Before proving Lemma 5, we derive from it the following corollary for XHX when instantiated with $\mathcal{H}^2$.

Corollary 2. *Let E and $\mathrm{XHX}[E, \mathcal{H}^2]$ be defined as in Theorem 1. Moreover, let $K \twoheadleftarrow \mathcal{K}$. Let $\mathbf{A}$ be a (q_C, q_P)-distinguisher on $\mathrm{XHX}[E, \mathcal{H}^2]_K$. Then*

$$\underset{\mathbf{A}}{\Delta} \left(\mathrm{XHX}[E, \mathcal{H}^2], E^\pm; \widetilde{\pi}^\pm, E^\pm \right) \leq \frac{2^{s+2} q_C^2 + 2^{s+1} q_C q_P + 4 q_C s}{2^{n+k}} + \frac{2 q_P s^2}{2^n} + \frac{s^2}{2^{n+1}}.$$

Again, the proof of the corollary stems from the combination of Lemma 5 with Theorem 1 and can be omitted.

Proof of Lemma 5 Since H_1 and H_3 are computed identically, we can restrict the analysis of the properties of $\mathcal{H}^2$ to only the outputs (H_1, H_2). Note that K

and L_1 are independent. In the following, we denote the hash-function results for some tweak T as H_1, H_2, H_3, and those for some tweak $T' \neq T$ as H_1', H_2', H_3'. Moreover, we denote the n-bit words of H_2 as $(H_2^1, \ldots, H_2^s)$, and those of H_2' as $(H_2'^1, \ldots, H_2'^s)$.

Partial Almost-XOR-Universality. First, let us consider the pAXU property. It holds that $H_1 := T_1 \boxdot K'$ and $H_2 := \mathrm{TRUNC}_k(\mathcal{F}_{L_1}(T), \ldots, \mathcal{F}_{L_s}(T))$. Considering H_1, it must hold that $H_1' = H_1 \oplus \Delta$, with

$$\Delta = (T_1' \boxdot K') \oplus (T_1 \boxdot K').$$

For any $X \neq 0^n$, it is well-known that $X \boxdot Y$ is $1/2^n$-AXU. So, for any fixed T_1 and fixed $\Delta \in \{0,1\}^n$, there is exactly one value T_1' that fulfills the equation if $H_1' \neq K' \boxdot K'$, and exactly two values if $H_1' = K' \boxdot K'$, namely $T_1' \in \{0^n, K'\}$. So

$$\Pr_{K \leftarrow \{0,1\}^k} [(T_1 \boxdot K') \oplus (T_1' \boxdot K') = \Delta] \leq 2/2^n.$$

The argumentation for H_2 is similar. The probability that any $L_i = 0^n$, for fixed $1 \leq i \leq s$, is at most $1/(2^n - s + 1)$, which will be smaller than the probability of $H_2^i = H_2'^i$. So, in the remainder, we can concentrate on the case that all $L_i \neq 0^n$. W.l.o.g., we focus for now on the first word of H_2, H_2^1, in the following. For fixed (T_1, T_2), H_2^1, and T_2', there is exactly one value T_1' s.t. $H_2^1 = H_2'^1$ if $H_2'^1 \neq L_1 \boxdot (L_1 \oplus T_2')$, namely $T_1' := T_1 \oplus (T_2 \oplus T_2') \boxdot L_1^{-1}$. There exist exactly two values T_1' if $H_2'^1 = L_1 \boxdot L_1 \oplus T_2'$, namely $T_1' \in \{0^n, L_1\}$. Hence, it holds that

$$\Pr_{L_1 \leftarrow \mathcal{L}} \left[H_2^1 = H_2'^1\right] \leq 2/2^n.$$

The same argumentation follows for $H_2^i = H_2'^i$, for $2 \leq i \leq s$ since the keys L_i are pairwise independent. Since the sn bits of H_2^s and $H_2'^s$ are truncated if k is not a multiple of n, the bound has to be multiplied with 2^{sn-k}. With the factor of $2/2^n$ for H_1, it follows for fixed $\Delta \in \{0,1\}^n$ that $\mathcal{H}^2$ is ϵ-pAXU for ϵ upper bounded by

$$\frac{2}{2^n} \cdot 2^{sn-k} \cdot \left(\frac{2}{2^n}\right)^s = \frac{2^{s+1}}{2^{n+k}}.$$

Almost-Uniformity. Here, we concern the probability for any H_1 and H_2:

$$\Pr_{L \leftarrow \mathcal{L}} [T_1 \boxdot K' = H_1, \mathrm{TRUNC}_k(\mathcal{F}_{L_1}(T), \ldots, \mathcal{F}_{L_s}(T)) = H_2].$$

If $K' = 0^n$ and $H_1 = 0^n$, then the first equation may be fulfilled for any T_1. Though, the probability for $K' = 0^n$ is $1/2^n$. So, we can assume $K' \neq 0^n$ in the remainder. Next, we focus again on the first word of H_2, i.e., H_2^1. For fixed L_1 and H_2^1, there exist at most two values (T_1, T_2) to fulfill $(T_1 \boxdot L_1) \oplus T_2 = H_2^1$. In the case $H_1 \neq K' \boxdot K'$, there is exactly one value $T_1 := H_1 \boxdot K'^{-1}$ that yields H_1.

Then, T_1, L_1, and H_2^1 determine $T_2 := H_2^1 \oplus (T_1 \boxdot L_1)$ uniquely. In the opposite case that $H_1 = K' \boxdot K'$, there exist exactly two values (T_1, T_1') that yield H_1, namely 0^n and K'. Each of those determines T_2 uniquely. The probability that the so-fixed values T_1, T_2 yield also H_2^2, ..., H_2^s is at most $(2/2^n)^{s-1}$ if k is a multiple of n since the keys L_i are pairwise independent; if k is not a multiple of n, we have again an additional factor of 2^{sn-k} from the truncation. So, $\mathcal{H}^2$ is ϵ-AUniform for ϵ at most

$$2^{sn-k} \cdot \left(\frac{2}{2^n}\right)^s = \frac{2^s}{2^{n+k}}.$$

Property P3. Given $I_i = \langle i - 1 \rangle$ and $K_i = K$, for $1 \leq i \leq s$, ϵ_3 is equivalent to the probability that a chosen (T_1, T_2) yields $\Pr[T_1 \boxdot K' = \Delta \oplus \langle i - 1 \rangle$, $\text{TRUNC}_k(\mathcal{F}_{L_1}(T), \ldots, \mathcal{F}_{L_s}(T)) = K]$, for some i. This can be rewritten to

$$\Pr[T_1 \boxdot K' = \Delta \oplus \langle i - 1 \rangle]$$
$$\cdot \Pr[\text{TRUNC}_k(\mathcal{F}_{L_1}(T), \ldots, \mathcal{F}_{L_s}(T)) = K \,|\, T_1 \boxdot K' = \Delta \oplus \langle i - 1 \rangle].$$

For fixed $\Delta \neq K' \boxdot K'$, there is exactly one value T_1 that satisfies the first part of the equation; otherwise, there are exactly two values T_1 if $\Delta = K' \boxdot K'$. Moreover, K' is secret; so, the values T_1 require that the adversary guesses K' correctly. Given fixed T_1, Δ, and K', there is exactly one value T_2 that matches the first n bits of K; $T_2 := (T_1 \boxdot L_1) \oplus K[k - 1..k - n]$. The remaining bits of K are matched with probability $2^{sn-k}/2^{(s-1)n}$, assuming that the keys L_i are independent. Hence, it holds that ϵ_3 is at most

$$\frac{2}{2^n} \cdot \frac{2^{sn-k}}{2^{sn}} = \frac{2}{2^{n+k}}.$$

Property P4. This argument follows from a similar argumentation as Property P3. Hence, it holds that $\epsilon_4 \leq 2/2^{n+k}$. $\qquad \square$

Acknowledgments. This work was initiated during the group sessions of the 6th Asian Workshop on Symmetric Cryptography (ASK 2016) held in Nagoya. We thank the anonymous reviewers of the ToSC 2017 and Latincrypt 2017 for their fruitful comments.

References

1. Beierle, C., et al.: The SKINNY family of block ciphers and its low-latency variant MANTIS. In: Robshaw, M., Katz, J. (eds.) CRYPTO 2016. LNCS, vol. 9815, pp. 123–153. Springer, Heidelberg (2016). https://doi.org/10.1007/978-3-662-53008-5_5
2. Bellare, M., Rogaway, P.: The security of triple encryption and a framework for code-based game-playing proofs. In: Vaudenay, S. (ed.) EUROCRYPT 2006. LNCS, vol. 4004, pp. 409–426. Springer, Heidelberg (2006). https://doi.org/10.1007/11761679_25
3. Black, J.: The ideal-cipher model, revisited: an uninstantiable blockcipher-based hash function. In: Robshaw, M. (ed.) FSE 2006. LNCS, vol. 4047, pp. 328–340. Springer, Heidelberg (2006). https://doi.org/10.1007/11799313_21

4. Chen, S., Steinberger, J.: Tight security bounds for key-alternating ciphers. In: Nguyen, P.Q., Oswald, E. (eds.) EUROCRYPT 2014. LNCS, vol. 8441, pp. 327–350. Springer, Heidelberg (2014). https://doi.org/10.1007/978-3-642-55220-5_19

5. Gaži, P., Maurer, U.: Cascade encryption revisited. In: Matsui, M. (ed.) ASIACRYPT 2009. LNCS, vol. 5912, pp. 37–51. Springer, Heidelberg (2009). https://doi.org/10.1007/978-3-642-10366-7_3

6. Jean, J., Nikolić, I., Peyrin, T.: Tweaks and keys for block ciphers: the TWEAKEY framework. In: Sarkar, P., Iwata, T. (eds.) ASIACRYPT 2014. LNCS, vol. 8874, pp. 274–288. Springer, Heidelberg (2014). https://doi.org/10.1007/978-3-662-45608-8_15

7. Jha, A., List, E., Minematsu, K., Mishra, S., Nandi, M.: XHX - a framework for optimally secure tweakable block ciphers from classical block ciphers and universal hashing. IACR Cryptology ePrint Archive 2017:1075 (2017)

8. Lampe, R., Seurin, Y.: Tweakable blockciphers with asymptotically optimal security. In: Moriai, S. (ed.) FSE 2013. LNCS, vol. 8424, pp. 133–151. Springer, Heidelberg (2014). https://doi.org/10.1007/978-3-662-43933-3_8

9. Landecker, W., Shrimpton, T., Terashima, R.S.: Tweakable blockciphers with beyond birthday-bound security. In: Safavi-Naini, R., Canetti, R. (eds.) CRYPTO 2012. LNCS, vol. 7417, pp. 14–30. Springer, Heidelberg (2012). https://doi.org/10.1007/978-3-642-32009-5_2

10. Lee, J.: Towards key-length extension with optimal security: cascade encryption and Xor-cascade encryption. In: Johansson, T., Nguyen, P.Q. (eds.) EUROCRYPT 2013. LNCS, vol. 7881, pp. 405–425. Springer, Heidelberg (2013). https://doi.org/10.1007/978-3-642-38348-9_25

11. Liskov, M., Rivest, R.L., Wagner, D.: Tweakable block ciphers. In: Yung, M. (ed.) CRYPTO 2002. LNCS, vol. 2442, pp. 31–46. Springer, Heidelberg (2002). https://doi.org/10.1007/3-540-45708-9_3

12. Mennink, B.: Optimally secure tweakable blockciphers. In: Leander, G. (ed.) FSE 2015. LNCS, vol. 9054, pp. 428–448. Springer, Heidelberg (2015). https://doi.org/10.1007/978-3-662-48116-5_21

13. Minematsu, K.: Beyond-birthday-bound security based on tweakable block cipher. In: Dunkelman, O. (ed.) FSE 2009. LNCS, vol. 5665, pp. 308–326. Springer, Heidelberg (2009). https://doi.org/10.1007/978-3-642-03317-9_19

14. Minematsu, K., Iwata, T.: Tweak-length extension for tweakable blockciphers. In: Groth, J. (ed.) IMACC 2015. LNCS, vol. 9496, pp. 77–93. Springer, Cham (2015). https://doi.org/10.1007/978-3-319-27239-9_5

15. Naito, Y.: Tweakable blockciphers for efficient authenticated encryptions with beyond the birthday-bound security. IACR Trans. Symmetric Cryptol. **2017**(2), 1–26 (2017)

16. Patarin, J.: The "Coefficients H" technique. In: Avanzi, R.M., Keliher, L., Sica, F. (eds.) SAC 2008. LNCS, vol. 5381, pp. 328–345. Springer, Heidelberg (2009). https://doi.org/10.1007/978-3-642-04159-4_21

17. Rogaway, P.: Efficient instantiations of tweakable blockciphers and refinements to modes OCB and PMAC. In: Lee, P.J. (ed.) ASIACRYPT 2004. LNCS, vol. 3329, pp. 16–31. Springer, Heidelberg (2004). https://doi.org/10.1007/978-3-540-30539-2_2

18. Schroeppel, R., Orman, H.: The Hasty Pudding Cipher. AES candidate submitted to NIST (1998)

19. Shrimpton, T., Terashima, R.S.: A modular framework for building variable-input-length tweakable ciphers. In: Sako, K., Sarkar, P. (eds.) ASIACRYPT 2013. LNCS, vol. 8269, pp. 405–423. Springer, Heidelberg (2013). https://doi.org/10.1007/978-3-642-42033-7_21

20. Wang, L., Guo, J., Zhang, G., Zhao, J., Gu, D.: How to build fully secure tweakable blockciphers from classical blockciphers. In: Cheon, J.H., Takagi, T. (eds.) ASIACRYPT 2016. LNCS, vol. 10031, pp. 455–483. Springer, Heidelberg (2016). https://doi.org/10.1007/978-3-662-53887-6_17

Improved XKX-Based AEAD Scheme: Removing the Birthday Terms

Yusuke Naito[✉]

Mitsubishi Electric Corporation, Kamakura, Kanagawa, Japan
Naito.Yusuke@ce.MitsubishiElectric.co.jp

Abstract. Naito [ToSC 2017, Issue 2] proposed XKX, a tweakable block-cipher (TBC) based on a blockcipher (BC). It offers efficient authenticated encryption with associated data (AEAD) schemes with beyond-birthday-bound (BBB) security, by combining with efficient TBC-based AEAD schemes such as ΘCB3. In the resultant schemes, for each data block, a BC is called once. The security bound is roughly $\ell^2 q/2^n + \sigma_A^2/2^n + \sigma_D^2/2^n$, where n is the block size of the BC in bits, ℓ is the number of BC calls by a query, q is the number of queries, σ_A is the number of BC calls handing associated data by encryption queries, and σ_D is the number of BC calls by decryption queries. Hence, assuming $\ell, \sigma_A, \sigma_D \ll 2^{n/2}$, the AEAD schemes achieve BBB security. However, the birthday terms $\sigma_A^2/2^n$, $\sigma_D^2/2^n$ might become dominant, for example, when n is small such as $n = 64$ and when DoS attacks are performed. The birthday terms are introduced due to the modular proof via the XKX's security proof.

In this paper, in order to remove the birthday terms, we slightly modify ΘCB3 called ΘCB3†, and directly prove the security of ΘCB3† with XKX. We show that the security bound becomes roughly $\ell^2 q/2^n$.

Keywords: Blockcipher · Tweakable blockcipher · Efficient authenticated encryption · Beyond-birthday-bound security

1 Introduction

Background.[1] Confidentiality and authenticity of data are the most important properties to securely communicate over an insecure channel. In the symmetric-key setting, an authenticated encryption with associated data (AEAD) scheme ensures jointly these properties. AEAD schemes have been mainly designed from a blockcipher (BC). In AEAD research, designing an efficient AEAD scheme is a main theme. In efficient AEAD schemes such as OCB schemes [13, 24–26] and OTR [20], a BC is called once for each data block[2] (for associated data or a plaintext).

---

[1] Our result is an extension of the result in [21], and thus several parts of the background are reused from [21].

[2] The data block is equal to the block size of the underlying BC.

© Springer Nature Switzerland AG 2019
T. Lange and O. Dunkelman (Eds.): LATINCRYPT 2017, LNCS 11368, pp. 228–246, 2019.
https://doi.org/10.1007/978-3-030-25283-0_13

Efficient BC-based AEAD schemes have been designed by incorporating an efficient BC-based TBC into an efficient tweakable-BC(TBC)-based AEAD scheme: in efficient TBC-based AEAD schemes such as ΘCB3 [13] and $\mathbb{OTR}$ [20], a TBC is called once for each data block; in efficient BC-based TBCs such as LRW2-type TBCs [13,16,25], a BC is called once for each query. Since the efficient BC-based TBCs have birthday-bound security, i.e., security up to $2^{n/2}$ BC calls, so are the combined schemes, where n is the block size in bits. However, birthday-bound security sometimes becomes unreliable; for example, when a lightweight BC is used, when large amounts of data are processed, or when a large number of connections need to be kept secure. Hence, designing an AEAD scheme with *beyond-birthday-bound* (BBB) security is also important.

Landecker et al. [15] proposed a TBC called Chained LRW2 (CLRW2) with security up to $2^{2n/3}$ BC calls, where LRW2 is iterated twice. Lampe and Seurin [14] considered a more general scheme called r-CLRW with security up to $2^{rn/(r+2)}$ BC calls, where LRW2 is iterated r times. Using the TBCs, BC-based AEAD schemes with BBB security can be obtained. Iwata [8] proposed an AEAD scheme with security up to $2^{2n/3}$ BC calls. In the default setting of the AEAD scheme, for each 4 data blocks, it requires 6 BC calls, and for each data block, it requires one multiplication. Iwata and Yasuda [11,12] pointed out that a combination of the xor of BCs [17] and the Feistel network with six rounds [22] offers BBB-secure AEAD schemes. However, the resultant AEAD schemes require 6 BC calls for each data block. Iwata and Minematsu [10] proposed AEAD schemes with security up to $2^{rn/(r+1)}$ BC calls, where for each data block, a BC is called r times, and a tag is generated by using r almost XOR universal hash functions. These AEAD schemes have BBB security but are not efficient.

Recently, Naito [21] proposed XKX, a BC-based TBC that offers efficient nonce-based AEAD schemes with BBB security, by combining with ΘCB3 or $\mathbb{OTR}$. XKX is a combination of Minematsu's TBC Min [19] and LRW2, where a BC's key is defined by using a pseudorandom function (PRF) whose input is a nonce, and then a data block is encrypted by LRW2 with the nonce dependent key.[3] In XKX-based ΘCB3 (or $\mathbb{OTR}$), for each query, after the nonce dependent key is defined, a BC is called once for each data block. The security bounds of the XKX based AEAD schemes are roughly $\ell^2 q/2^n + \sigma_A^2/2^n + \sigma_D^2/2^n$, where ℓ is the number of BC calls by a query, q is the number of queries, σ_A is the number of BC calls handing associated data by encryption queries, and σ_D is the number of BC calls by decryption queries.[4] Hence, if $\ell, \sigma_A, \sigma_D \ll 2^{n/2}$, the AEAD schemes have BBB security.

---

[3] He gave BC-based instantiations of the PRF; the XOR of BCs and the concatenation. The PRF advantage of the XOR is roughly $q/2^n$. The PRF advantage of the concatenation is roughly $q^2/2^n$. Using these instantiations, these terms are introduced in the security bounds of the XKX-based AEAD schemes.

[4] More precisely, (the PRF-security advantage) and $q\times$ (the strong pseudo-random permutation advantage) are defined in the security bound. For simplicity, assume that these terms are negligible.

Motivation. The birthday terms $\sigma_A^2/2^n, \sigma_D^2/2^n$ might become dominant, when n is small e.g., $n = 64$. Security bounds define a span of changing a key, and if the threshold is e.g., $1/2^{20}$ (a key is changed when a security bound reaches the threshold), the security bound reaches the threshold when $\sigma_A = 2^{22}$ or $\sigma_D = 2^{22}$, which might cause frequent key updates due to DoS attacks.

The reason why the birthday terms are introduced is the modular proof, which is a combination of the security proofs of ΘCB3 (or $\mathbb{OTR}$) and of XKX. In the security bound of XKX, the term $\nu^2/2^n$ is defined, where ν is the number of BC calls with the same key. Hence, the birthday term $\sigma_A^2/2^n$ is introduced, since in the AEAD schemes, the same BC's key is used for every associated data block. The birthday term $\sigma_D^2/2^n$ is introduced, since an adversary can make decryption queries with the same nonce (i.e, the corresponding BC's keys are the same).

Instead of the modular proof, the birthday terms might be removed by directly proving the security of the AEAD scheme. However, it might be hard. In XKX-based ΘCB3, the checksum of plaintext blocks is encrypted, associated data is hashed, and the tag is defined by XOR-ing the encrypted checksum with the hash value. For this construction, an adversary can make decryption queries where the encrypted checksums are the same, and thus the randomnesses of the tags depend on the hash values. Since the BC's key to handle associated data (to define hash values) is fixed, the birthday term regarding associated data by decryption queries might remain in the security bound due to the PRF-PRP switch for the BC's outputs.

Our Result. In order to remove the birthday terms, we slightly modify XKX-based ΘCB3 called ΘCB3†, and then directly prove the security of ΘCB3†. In this modification, the hash value is XOR-ed with the checksum (instead of the encrypted checksum). Hence, one does not need to consider the randomnesses of hash values. We show that the birthday terms can be removed, that is, the security bound becomes roughly $\ell^2 q/2^n$. Note that in this modification, since one does not need to keep a hash value when generating a tag, the memory size can be reduced by the hash value.

Related Works. Mennink [18] proposed two TBCs with BBB security in the ideal cipher model (ICM). Wang et al. [27] generalized his TBCs and gave 32 TBCs with BBB security in the ICM, where some of the TBCs offer efficient AEAD schemes with BBB security in the ICM. Note that our target scheme is an efficient AEAD scheme with BBB security in the standard model.

Organization. In Sect. 2, we start by giving notations and security definitions. In Sect. 3, we give the previous result for XKX, where the specifications of XKX schemes and the security results are given. In Sect. 4, we give our result, where the specification of ΘCB3† with XKX, the security bounds, and the proofs are given. In Sect. 5, we give how to realize ΘCB3† with XKX from only a BC with respect to the PRF (in Min) and the almost XOR universal hash function (in LRW2). Finally, in Sect. 6, we give a conclusion of this paper.

2   Preliminaries

2.1   Notations

$\{0,1\}^*$ denotes the set of all bit strings, and λ denotes the empty string. For a natural integer n, $\{0,1\}^n$ denotes the set of n-bit strings, and 0^n denotes the bit string of n-bit zeroes. We write $[i] := \{1, 2, \ldots, i\}$ for a positive integer i. For a finite set $\mathcal{X}$, $x \xleftarrow{\$} \mathcal{X}$ means that an element is randomly drawn from $\mathcal{X}$ and is assigned to x. For a bit string x and a set $\mathcal{X}$, $|x|$ and $|\mathcal{X}|$ denote the bit length of x and the number of elements in $\mathcal{X}$, respectively. For a bit string x and an integer $i \leq |x|$, $[x]^i$ denotes the first i-bit string of x. For a bit string M, $M_1, \ldots, M_m, M_* \xleftarrow{n} M$ means that M is partitioned into n-bit strings $M_1, \ldots, M_m$ and $(|M| - mn)$-bit string M_* such that $|M_*| < n$ and $M = M_1 \| \ldots \| M_m \| M_*$. Let $\mathsf{Perm}(\mathcal{B})$ be the set of all permutations over a non-empty set $\mathcal{B}$. A random permutation over $\mathcal{B}$ is defined as $P \xleftarrow{\$} \mathsf{Perm}(\mathcal{B})$. The inverse is denoted by P^{-1}. For an adversary $\mathbf{A}$ with oracle access to $\mathcal{O}$, its output is denoted by $\mathbf{A}^{\mathcal{O}}$. In this paper, an adversary is a computationally bounded algorithm and the resource is measured in terms of time and query complexities.

2.2   Definitions of (Tweakable) Blockciphers

Blockcipher (BC). A BC $E : \mathcal{K} \times \mathcal{B} \to \mathcal{B}$ is a family of permutations over the set of blocks $\mathcal{B}$ indexed by the set of keys $\mathcal{K}$. $E_K(\cdot)$ denotes the encryption function E having a key $K \in \mathcal{K}$. The decryption function is denoted by E^{-1}, and E_K^{-1} denotes E^{-1} having a key $K \in \mathcal{K}$, and becomes the inverse permutation of E_K. $\mathsf{BC}(\mathcal{K}, \mathcal{B})$ denotes the set of all encryptions of BCs.

We consider Strong-Pseudo-Random Permutation (SPRP) security. The advantage function of an sprp-adversary $\mathbf{A}$ that outputs a bit are defined as

$$\mathbf{Adv}_E^{\mathsf{sprp}}(\mathbf{A}) = \Pr[K \xleftarrow{\$} \mathcal{K}; \mathbf{A}^{E_K, E_K^{-1}} = 1] - \Pr[P \xleftarrow{\$} \mathsf{Perm}(\mathcal{B}); \mathbf{A}^{P, P^{-1}} = 1] ,$$

where the probabilities are taken over $\mathbf{A}$, K and P. We say $\mathbf{A}$ is a (q, t)-sprp-adversary if $\mathbf{A}$ makes q queries and runs in time t.

Tweakable Blockcipher (TBC). A TBC $\widetilde{E} : \mathcal{K} \times \mathcal{TW} \times \mathcal{B} \to \mathcal{B}$ is a family of permutations over the set of blocks $\mathcal{B}$ indexed by the set of keys $\mathcal{K}$ and the set of tweaks $\mathcal{TW}$. $\widetilde{E}_K(tw, \cdot)$ denotes the encryption of $\widetilde{E}$ having a key $K \in \mathcal{K}$ and a tweak $tw \in \mathcal{TW}$. The decryption function is denoted by $\widetilde{E}^{-1}$, and $\widetilde{E}_K^{-1}(tw, \cdot)$ is the inverse permutation of $\widetilde{E}_K(tw, \cdot)$.

We consider Tweakable-Strong-Pseudo-Random Permutation (TSPRP) security. Let $\widetilde{\mathsf{Perm}}(\mathcal{TW}, \mathcal{B})$ be the set of all tweakable permutations with the sets of tweaks $\mathcal{TW}$ and of blocks $\mathcal{B}$, where $\widetilde{P} \in \widetilde{\mathsf{Perm}}(\mathcal{TW}, \mathcal{B})$ is a family of permutations over $\mathcal{B}$ indexed by $\mathcal{TW}$, and a tweakable RP (TRP) is defined as

$\widetilde{P} \overset{\$}{\leftarrow} \widetilde{\mathsf{Perm}}(\mathcal{TW}, \mathcal{B})$. The inverse is denoted by $\widetilde{P}^{-1}$. The advantage function of a tsprp-adversary $\mathbf{A}$ that outputs a bit is defined as

$$\mathbf{Adv}_{\widetilde{E}}^{\mathsf{sprp}}(\mathbf{A}) = \Pr\left[K \overset{\$}{\leftarrow} \mathcal{K}; \mathbf{A}^{\widetilde{E}_K, \widetilde{E}_K^{-1}} = 1\right] - \Pr\left[\widetilde{P} \overset{\$}{\leftarrow} \widetilde{\mathsf{Perm}}(\mathcal{TW}, \mathcal{B}); \mathbf{A}^{\widetilde{P}, \widetilde{P}^{-1}} = 1\right] ,$$

where the probabilities are taken over $\mathbf{A}$, K and $\widetilde{P}$. We say $\mathbf{A}$ is a (q, t)-tsprp-adversary if $\mathbf{A}$ makes at most q queries and runs in time t.

2.3   Definition of Pseudo-Random Function

Let $\mathsf{Func}(\mathcal{X}, \mathcal{Y})$ be the set of all functions from a set $\mathcal{X}$ to a set $\mathcal{Y}$. Let $\mathcal{F} \subseteq \mathsf{Func}(\mathcal{X}, \mathcal{Y})$ be a family of functions that maps $\mathcal{X}$ to $\mathcal{Y}$. We consider Pseudo-Random-Function (PRF) security of $\mathcal{F}$ that is indistinguishability from a random function (RF), where an RF is defined as $f \overset{\$}{\leftarrow} \mathsf{Func}(\mathcal{X}, \mathcal{Y})$. The advantage function of a prf-adversary $\mathbf{A}$ that outputs a bit is defined as

$$\mathbf{Adv}_{\mathcal{F}}^{\mathsf{prf}}(\mathbf{A}) = \Pr[F \overset{\$}{\leftarrow} \mathcal{F}; \mathbf{A}^F = 1] - \Pr[f \overset{\$}{\leftarrow} \mathsf{Func}(\mathcal{X}, \mathcal{Y}); \mathbf{A}^f = 1] ,$$

where the probabilities are taken over $\mathbf{A}$, F and f. We say $\mathbf{A}$ is a (q, t)-prf-adversary if $\mathbf{A}$ makes at most q queries and runs in time t.

2.4   Definition of Nonce-Based Authenticated Encryption with Associated Data

In this paper, we consider nonce-based authenticated encryption with associated data (nAEAD) schemes. The syntax and the definition of nAEAD schemes are given below.

An nAEAD scheme Π is a pair of encryption and decryption algorithms $\Pi = (\Pi.\mathsf{Enc}, \Pi.\mathsf{Dec})$. $\mathcal{K}, \mathcal{N}, \mathcal{M}, \mathcal{C}, \mathcal{A}$ and $\mathcal{T}$ are the sets of keys, nonces, messages, ciphertexts, associated data and tags of the nAEAD scheme. The encryption algorithm with a key $K \in \mathcal{K}$, $\Pi.\mathsf{Enc}_K$, takes a nonce $N \in \mathcal{N}$, associated data $A \in \mathcal{A}$, and a plaintext $M \in \mathcal{M}$. $\Pi.\mathsf{Enc}_K(N, A, M)$ returns, deterministically, a pair of a ciphertext $C \in \mathcal{C}$ and a tag $T \in \mathcal{T}$. The decryption algorithm with a key $K \in \mathcal{K}$, $\Pi.\mathsf{Dec}_K$, takes a tuple $(N, A, C, T) \in \mathcal{N} \times \mathcal{A} \times \mathcal{C} \times \mathcal{T}$. $\Pi.\mathsf{Dec}_K(N, A, C, T)$ returns, deterministically, either the distinguished invalid symbol $\bot$ or a plaintext $M \in \mathcal{M}$. We require $|\Pi.\mathsf{Enc}_K(N, A, M)| = |\Pi.\mathsf{Enc}_K(N, A, M')|$ when $|M| = |M'|$.

We follow the security definition in [1,24] that considers privacy and authenticity of an nAEAD scheme Π. The privacy advantage of an adversary $\mathbf{A}$ that outputs a bit is defined as

$$\mathbf{Adv}_{\Pi}^{\mathsf{priv}}(\mathbf{A}) = \Pr[K \overset{\$}{\leftarrow} \mathcal{K}; \mathbf{A}^{\Pi.\mathsf{Enc}_K} = 1] - \Pr[\mathbf{A}^{\$} = 1] ,$$

where a random-bits oracle \$ has the same interface as $\Pi.\mathsf{Enc}_K$, and for query (N, A, M) returns a random bit string of length $|\Pi.\mathsf{Enc}_K(N, A, M)|$. The authenticity advantage of an adversary $\mathbf{A}$ is defined as

$$\mathbf{Adv}_{\Pi}^{\mathsf{auth}}(\mathbf{A}) = \Pr[K \overset{\$}{\leftarrow} \mathcal{K}; \mathbf{A}^{\Pi.\mathsf{Enc}_K, \Pi.\mathsf{Dec}_K} \text{ forges}] ,$$

where "$\mathbf{A}^{\Pi.\mathrm{Enc}_K, \Pi.\mathrm{Dec}_K}$ forges" means that $\mathbf{A}$ makes a query to $\Pi.\mathrm{Dec}_K$ whose response is not $\perp$. We call queries to $\Pi.\mathrm{Enc}_K$ "encryption queries," and those to $\Pi.\mathrm{Dec}_K$ "decryption queries." We demand that $\mathbf{A}$ is nonce-respecting, namely, never asks two encryption queries with the same nonce, that $\mathbf{A}$ never asks a decryption query (N, A, C, T) such that there is no prior encryption query with $(C, T) = \Pi.\mathrm{Enc}_K(N, A, M)$, and that $\mathbf{A}$ never repeats a query.

2.5 Definition of Almost XOR Universal Hash Function

We will need a class of non-cryptographic functions called universal hash functions [4] defined as follows.

Definition 1. *Let $\mathcal{H}$ be a family of functions from (some set) $\mathcal{TW}_{ctr}$ to $\{0,1\}^n$ indexed by the set of keys $\mathcal{K}$. $\mathcal{H}$ is said to be (ϵ, δ)-almost XOR universal $((\epsilon, \delta)$-AXU) if for any $c \in \{0,1\}^n$ and $ctr, ctr' \in \mathcal{TW}_{ctr}$ with $ctr \neq ctr'$, $\Pr[H \xleftarrow{\$} \mathcal{H} : H(ctr) \oplus H(ctr') = c] \leq \epsilon$ and $\Pr[H \xleftarrow{\$} \mathcal{H} : H(ctr) = c] \leq \delta$.*

3 XK and XKX [21]

3.1 Specification

XK and XKX are a combination of Minematsu's TBC Min [19] and Liskov et al.'s TBC LRW2 [16]. Let n and k be positive integers, and $\mathcal{TW}_N$ and $\mathcal{TW}_{ctr}$ non-empty sets. Let $\mathcal{F} \subseteq \mathsf{Func}(\mathcal{TW}_N, \{0,1\}^k)$ and $\mathcal{H} \subseteq \mathsf{Func}(\mathcal{TW}_{ctr}, \{0,1\}^n)$ be families of functions used in XK and XKX. Let $E \in \mathsf{BC}(\{0,1\}^k, \{0,1\}^n)$, $F \in \mathcal{F}$ and $H \in \mathcal{H}$. For a tweak $tw \in \mathcal{TW}_N$ and a plaintext block $M \in \{0,1\}^n$, the encryption of Minematsu's TBC is defined as

$$\mathtt{Min}[E, F](N, M) = E_{K_N}(M) \text{ where } K_N = F(N) \ .$$

For tweaks $(N, ctr) \in \mathcal{TW}_N \times \mathcal{TW}_{ctr}$ and a plaintext $M \in \{0,1\}^n$, the encryption of XK is defined as

$$\mathtt{XK}[E, F, h]((N, ctr), M) := \mathtt{Min}[E, F](\Delta \oplus M) \text{ where } \Delta := H(ctr) \ ,$$

and the encryption of XKX is defined as

$$\mathtt{XKX}[E, F, h]((N, ctr), M) := \Delta \oplus \mathtt{Min}[E, F](\Delta \oplus M) \text{ where } \Delta := H(ctr) \ .$$

Hereafter, F is called a first tweak function, and H is called a second tweak function. N is called a first tweak, and ctr is called a second tweak. Note that using XK and XKX in a scheme, the second tweak spaces of XK and of XKX should not be overlapped with each other. The combination of XK and XKX is denoted by XKX*.

3.2 Security of XKX*

XKX* is a secure TSPRP [21] as long as E is a secure SPRP, $\mathcal{F}$ is a secure PRF, $\mathcal{H}$ is AXU, an adversary does not make a decryption query to XK and does not make queries to XKX* such that the second tweak spaces of XK and of XKX are not overlapped with each other. The security bound is given below.

Theorem 1 (TSPRP Security of XKX* [21]). *Assume that $\mathcal{H}$ is (ϵ, δ)-AXU. Let $\mathbf{A}$ be a (σ, t)-tsprp-adversary that does not make a decryption query to XK. Here, q is the number of distinct first tweaks, and ℓ_N is the number of queries with first tweak $N \in \mathcal{TW}_N$. Then, there exist a $(\sigma, t + O(\sigma))$-sprp-adversary $\mathbf{A}_E$ and $(q, t + O(\sigma))$-prf-adversary $\mathbf{A}_F$ such that*

$$\mathbf{Adv}^{\widetilde{\mathsf{sprp}}}_{\mathsf{XKX}^*}(\mathbf{A}) \leq q \cdot \mathbf{Adv}^{\mathsf{sprp}}_E(\mathbf{A}_E) + \mathbf{Adv}^{\mathsf{prf}}_{\mathcal{F}}(\mathbf{A}_F) + \sum_{N \in \mathcal{N}} \ell_N^2 \cdot \max\{\epsilon, \delta\} \ .$$

3.3 XKX*-Based AEAD Schemes

In [21], XKX* is applied to TBC-based nAEAD schemes such as ΘCB3 [13] and $\mathbb{OTR}$ [20]. Consider ΘCB3 with XKX*. In ΘCB3, each plaintext block is encrypted by the TBC, where a nonce and a counter are inputted as a tweak, and then the checksum of the plaintext blocks are encrypted. Each associated data block is encrypted by the TBC, where a counter is inputted as a tweak, and then a hash value is defined as the xor of the encrypted values. Finally, a tag is defined as the xor of the encrypted checksum and the hash value. In [21], the security bounds of ΘCB3 with XKX* are given by using Theorem 1. Here, we assume that an adversary makes $q_{\mathcal{E}}$ encryption queries and q queries such that the number of BC calls of handing associated data by encryption queries is σ_A and the number of BC calls by decryption queries is σ_D. For simplicity, we fix ℓ the number of BC calls by a query, and use the optimal parameters for $\mathcal{H}$: $\epsilon = \delta = 1/2^n$. Regarding the privacy, for each query to ΘCB3 with XKX*, the BC's key to take plaintext blocks and the checksum is changed, whereas the BC's key to handle associated data is fixed. Hence, using Theorem 1, the privacy bound becomes roughly $\ell^2 q_{\mathcal{E}}/2^n + \sigma_A^2/2^n$. Regarding the authenticity, when an adversary can make decryption queries with the same nonce, the BC's keys to take ciphertext blocks and the checksums by decryption queries are the same. Hence, using Theorem 1, the term $\sigma_D^2/2^n$ is introduced in addition to $\ell^2 q_{\mathcal{E}}/2^n + \sigma_A^2/2^n$, that is, the authenticity bound becomes roughly $\ell^2 q/2^n + (\sigma_A^2 + \sigma_D^2)/2^n$. Note that we assume that the terms $q \cdot \mathbf{Adv}^{\mathsf{sprp}}_E(\mathbf{A}_E)$ and $\mathbf{Adv}^{\mathsf{prf}}_{\mathcal{F}}(\mathbf{A}_F)$ are negligible compared with other terms.

4 Our Result: Improved Security Bound of XKX*-Based nAEAD Scheme

In stead of the modular proof via XKX's result (Theorem 1), the birthday terms $\sigma_A^2/2^n$ and $\sigma_D^2/2^n$ might be removed by directly proving the security of the

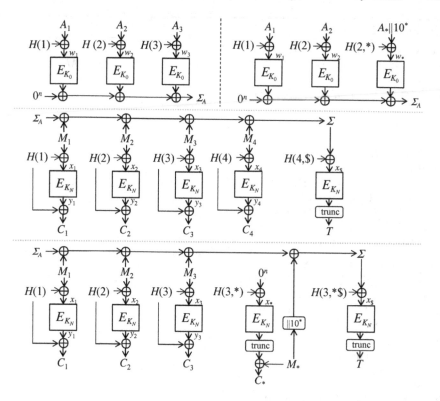

Fig. 1. $\Theta CB3^{\dagger}$.Enc where $K_0 \leftarrow F(0)$ and $K_N \leftarrow F(N)$.

XKX*-based nAEAD scheme. However, as mentioned in Sect. 1, it might be hard. When an adversary makes decryption queries with the same nonce, the encrypted checksums are the same. Thus, the randomnesses of the tags depend on the hash values of associated data. Since the BC's key to handle associated data is fixed, the birthday term regarding associated data by decryption queries might be introduced due to the PRF-PRP switch for the BC's outputs.

In this paper, in order to remove the birthday terms, we modify $\Theta CB3$, where the has value is XOR-ed with the checksum (instead of the encrypted checksum). We call the variant $\Theta CB3^{\dagger}$. Note that by this modification, the memory size is reduced by the hash value, since one does not keep a hash value of associated data when the checksum is encrypted.

4.1   Specification of XKX*-Based $\Theta CB3^{\dagger}$

We give the specification of $\Theta CB3^{\dagger}$ with XKX* by following the notations in [13]. For simplicity, we call it $\Theta CB3^{\dagger}$. Let $\mathcal{N}$ be the set of nonces of $\Theta CB3^{\dagger}$ such that $0 \notin \mathcal{N}$. The sets of first tweaks and of second tweaks of XKX* are defined as

---

Algorithm 1. $\Theta CB3^{\dagger}$

Encryption $\Theta CB3^{\dagger}.\mathtt{Enc}(N, A, M)$

1: $\Sigma \leftarrow \Theta CB3^{\dagger}.\mathtt{Hash}(A); \; K_N \leftarrow F(N); \; C_* \leftarrow \lambda; \; M_1, \ldots, M_m, M_* \xleftarrow{n} M$
2: **for** $i = 1$ **to** m **do**
3: $\quad C_i \leftarrow E_{K_N}(M_i \oplus H(i)) \oplus H(i)$ $\qquad\qquad\qquad\qquad\qquad\qquad$ ▷ XKX
4: $\quad \Sigma \leftarrow \Sigma \oplus M_i$
5: **end for**
6: **if** $M_* = \lambda$ **then**
7: $\quad T \leftarrow [E_{K_N}(\Sigma \oplus H(m, \$))]^{\tau}$ $\qquad\qquad\qquad\qquad\qquad\qquad\qquad$ ▷ XK
8: **else**
9: $\quad \mathrm{Pad} \leftarrow E_{K_N}(0^n \oplus H(m, *))$ $\qquad\qquad\qquad\qquad\qquad\qquad$ ▷ XK
10: $\quad C_* \leftarrow [\mathrm{Pad}]^{|M_*|} \oplus M_*; \; \Sigma \leftarrow \Sigma \oplus M_* \| 10^*$
11: $\quad T \leftarrow [E_{K_N}(\Sigma \oplus H(m, *\$))]^{\tau}$ $\qquad\qquad\qquad\qquad\qquad\qquad$ ▷ XK
12: **end if**
13: **return** $(C_1 \| \cdots \| C_m \| C_*, T)$

Decryption $\Theta CB3^{\dagger}.\mathtt{Dec}(N, A, M, T)$

1: $\Sigma \leftarrow \Theta CB3^{\dagger}.\mathtt{Hash}(A); \; K_N \leftarrow F(N); \; M_* \leftarrow \lambda; \; C_1, \ldots, C_m, C_* \xleftarrow{n} C$
2: **for** $i = 1$ **to** m **do**
3: $\quad M_i \leftarrow E_{K_N}^{-1}(C_i \oplus H(i)) \oplus H(i)$ $\qquad\qquad\qquad\qquad\qquad\qquad$ ▷ XKX
4: $\quad \Sigma \leftarrow \Sigma \oplus M_i$
5: **end for**
6: **if** $M_* = \lambda$ **then**
7: $\quad T^* \leftarrow [E_{K_N}(\Sigma \oplus H(m, \$))]^{\tau}$ $\qquad\qquad\qquad\qquad\qquad\qquad$ ▷ XK
8: **else**
9: $\quad \mathrm{Pad} \leftarrow E_{K_N}(0^n \oplus H(m, *))$ $\qquad\qquad\qquad\qquad\qquad\qquad$ ▷ XK
10: $\quad C_* \leftarrow [\mathrm{Pad}]^{|M_*|} \oplus M_*; \; \Sigma \leftarrow \Sigma \oplus M_* \| 10^*$
11: $\quad T^* \leftarrow [E_{K_N}(\Sigma \oplus H(m, *\$))]^{\tau}$ $\qquad\qquad\qquad\qquad\qquad\qquad$ ▷ XK
12: **end if**
13: **if** $T^* = T$ **then return** $M_1 \| \cdots \| M_m \| M_*$
14: **if** $T^* \neq T$ **then return** $\perp$

Subroutine $\Theta CB3^{\dagger}.\mathtt{Hash}(A)$

1: $K_0 \leftarrow F(0); \; \Sigma_A \leftarrow 0^n; \; A_1, \ldots, A_a, A_* \xleftarrow{n} A$
2: **for** $i = 1$ **to** a **do** $\Sigma_A \leftarrow \Sigma_A \oplus E_{K_0}(A_i \oplus H(i))$ $\qquad\qquad$ ▷ XK
3: **if** $A_* \neq \lambda$ **then** $\Sigma_A \leftarrow \Sigma_A \oplus E_{K_0}(A_* \| 10^* \oplus H(i, *))$ $\quad$ ▷ XK
4: **return** Σ_A

$$\mathcal{TW}_N := \mathcal{N} \cup \{0\}$$
$$\mathcal{TW}_{ctr} := \mathbb{N}_1 \cup (\mathbb{N}_0 \times \{*\}) \cup (\mathbb{N}_0 \times \{\$\}) \cup (\mathbb{N}_0 \times \{*\$\}) \cup \mathbb{N}_1 \cup (\mathbb{N}_0 \times \{*\})$$

where $\mathbb{N}_1$ and $\mathbb{N}_0$ are positive and nonnegative integers, respectively. "0" is used to define a BC's key to handle associated data. Hence, $\Theta CB3^{\dagger}$ uses six types of permutations with tweaks (N, i), $(N, i, *)$, $(N, i, \$)$, $(N, i, *\$)$, (i), and $(i, *)$. The first two permutations are used to encrypt plaintext blocks. The next two permutations are used to generate a tag. The last two permutations are used to handle associated data. In each procedure, the latter permutation is used to avoid an additional permutation call by the padding. The sets of keys, associated data, plaintexts and ciphertexts of ΘCB3† is defined as $\mathcal{K} := \{0,1\}^k$, $\mathcal{A} := \{0,1\}^*$, $\mathcal{M} := \{0,1\}^*$ and $\mathcal{C} := \{0,1\}^*$. In ΘCB3†, plaintext blocks are encrypted by XKX, and other data blocks (a checksum and associated data blocks) are encrypted by XK. In ΘCB3, a one-zero padding 10^* is used, where $X\|10^*$ is a bit string that 1 is appended to the bit string X and an appropriate number of bits 0 is appended so that the bit length becomes n. ΘCB3† is specified in Algorithm 1 and is illustrated in Fig. 1.

4.2 Security Bounds of ΘCB3†

The adversarial parameters are defined as follows.

- $q_\mathcal{E}$: the number of encryption queries.
- $q_\mathcal{D}$: the number of decryption queries.
- $q = q_\mathcal{E} + q_\mathcal{D}$.
- $\sigma_\mathcal{E}$: the number of BC calls by encryption queries.
- σ: the number of BC calls by all queries.
- $\ell_{\mathsf{H},\alpha}$: the number of BC calls in ΘCB3†.Hash at the α-th encryption query, where $\alpha \in [q_\mathcal{E}]$.
- $\ell_{\mathsf{H},\beta}$: the number of BC calls in ΘCB3†.Hash at the β-th decryption query, where $\beta \in [q_\mathcal{D}]$.
- $\ell_{\mathsf{E},\alpha}$: the number of BC calls except for those in ΘCB3†.Hash at the α-th encryption query, where $\alpha \in [q_\mathcal{E}]$.
- $l_{\mathsf{D},\beta}$: the number of BC calls except for those in ΘCB3†.Hash at the β-th decryption query, where $\beta \in [q_\mathcal{D}]$.
- $l_{\mathcal{D},\beta} := l_{\mathsf{H},\beta} + l_{\mathsf{D},\beta}$, where $\beta \in [q_\mathcal{D}]$.
- $\ell_\mathsf{E} := \max\{\ell_{\mathsf{E},\alpha}|\alpha \in [q_\mathcal{E}]\}$.
- $l_\mathsf{D} := \max\{l_{\mathsf{D},\beta}|\beta \in [q_\mathcal{D}]\}$.
- $\ell_\mathcal{E} := \max\{\ell_{\mathsf{E},\alpha} + \ell_{\mathsf{H},\alpha}|\alpha \in [q_\mathcal{E}]\}$.
- $l_\mathcal{D} := \max\{l_{\mathsf{D},\beta} + l_{\mathsf{H},\beta}|\beta \in [q_\mathcal{D}]\}$.

Theorem 2 (Privacy of ΘCB3†). *Assume that $\mathcal{H}$ is (ϵ,δ)-AXU. Let $\mathbf{A}$ be a priv-adversary that runs in time t. Then, there exist a $(\sigma_\mathcal{E}, t + O(\sigma_\mathcal{E}))$-sprp-adversary $\mathbf{A}_E$ and $(q_\mathcal{E}, t + O(\sigma_\mathcal{E}))$-prf-adversary $\mathbf{A}_F$ such that*

$$\mathbf{Adv}^{\mathrm{priv}}_{\Theta\mathrm{CB3}^\dagger}(\mathbf{A}) \leq q_\mathcal{E} \cdot \mathbf{Adv}^{\mathrm{sprp}}_E(\mathbf{A}_E) + \mathbf{Adv}^{\mathrm{prf}}_\mathcal{F}(\mathbf{A}_F) + \sum_{\alpha=1}^{q_\mathcal{E}} \ell^2_{\mathsf{E},\alpha} \cdot \max\{\epsilon,\delta\} \ .$$

Theorem 3 (Authenticity of ΘCB3†). *Assume that $\mathcal{H}$ is (ϵ,δ)-AXU. Let $\mathbf{A}$ be a auth-adversary that runs in time t. Then, there exist a $(\sigma, t + O(\sigma))$-sprp-adversary $\mathbf{A}_E$ and $(q, t + O(\sigma))$-prf-adversary $\mathbf{A}_F$ such that*

$$\mathbf{Adv}^{\mathrm{auth}}_{\Theta\mathrm{CB3}^\dagger} \leq (q+1) \cdot \mathbf{Adv}^{\mathrm{sprp}}_E(\mathbf{A}_E) + \mathbf{Adv}^{\mathrm{prf}}_\mathcal{F}(\mathbf{A}_F)$$
$$+ \frac{q_\mathcal{D}(2^{n-\tau} + 2)}{2^n - (\ell_\mathcal{E} + l_\mathcal{D})} + (\ell_\mathsf{E} + \ell^2_\mathsf{H}) \cdot q_\mathcal{D} \cdot \epsilon + \sum_{\beta=1}^{q_\mathcal{D}} 2l^2_{\mathcal{D},\beta} \cdot \epsilon \ .$$

Before giving the security proofs, we study the security bounds. Assume that the SPRP-security and PRF-security terms are negligible, which can be achieved by using a BC with a long-size key such as $k = 2n$ (See Section 6 in [21] for the detail). For simplicity, we fix ℓ the number of blockcipher calls by a query, and use the optimal parameters for $\mathcal{H}$: $\epsilon = \delta = 1/2^n$. Then, the privacy bound becomes roughly $\ell^2 q_{\mathcal{E}}/2^n$, since $\ell_{\mathsf{E},\alpha} \leq \ell$. Regarding the authenticity bound, the term $\frac{q_{\mathcal{D}}(2^{n-\tau}+2)}{2^n - (\ell_{\mathcal{E}} + l_{\mathcal{D}})}$ becomes roughly $q/2^\tau$ and the terms $(\ell_{\mathsf{E}} + \ell_{\mathsf{H}}^2) \cdot q_{\mathcal{D}} \cdot \epsilon + \sum_{\beta=1}^{q_{\mathcal{D}}} 2l_{\mathcal{D},\beta}^2 \cdot \epsilon$ become roughly $\ell^2 q_{\mathcal{D}}/2^n$, since $\ell_{\mathsf{E}}, \ell_{\mathsf{H}}, l_{\mathcal{D},\beta} \leq \ell$. Hence, the authenticity bound becomes roughly $q/2^\tau + \ell^2 q_{\mathcal{D}}/2^n$, and assuming $q/2^\tau \ll \ell^2 q_{\mathcal{D}}/2^n$, it is roughly $\ell^2 q_{\mathcal{D}}/2^n$. Hence the birthday terms $\sigma_A^2/2^n, \sigma_{\mathcal{D}}^2/2^n$ are absent in the security bounds.

4.3   Proof of Theorem 2

Firstly, XKX^* except for XK in $\Theta\mathsf{CB3}^\dagger.\mathsf{Hash}$ are replaced with a TRP $\widetilde{P} \xleftarrow{\$} \widetilde{\mathsf{Perm}}(\mathcal{TW}_N \times \mathcal{TW}_{ctr}, \{0,1\}^n)$. In this replacement, from Theorem 1, the following terms are introduced.

$$q_{\mathcal{E}} \cdot \mathbf{Adv}_E^{\mathsf{sprp}}(\mathbf{A}_E) + \mathbf{Adv}_{\mathcal{F}}^{\mathsf{prf}}(\mathbf{A}_F) + \sum_{\alpha=1}^{q_{\mathcal{E}}} \ell_{\mathsf{E},\alpha}^2 \cdot \max\{\epsilon, \delta\}$$

In the modified $\Theta\mathsf{CB3}^\dagger$, for each encryption query, the output blocks are defined by $\widetilde{P}$, and for each $\widetilde{P}$ call, a distinct tweak is used. Thereby, all outputs are randomly drawn (regardless of outputs of $\Theta\mathsf{CB3}^\dagger.\mathsf{Hash}$). Hence, the upper-bound in Theorem 2 is obtained.

4.4   Proof of Theorem 3

Let $\Pi_0 := \Theta\mathsf{CB3}^\dagger$, and

$$\mathsf{Game0} := \left(F \xleftarrow{\$} \mathcal{F}; H \xleftarrow{\$} \mathcal{H}; \mathbf{A}^{\Pi_0} \text{ forges} \right) .$$

This game is called Game 0.

We next consider Game 1. From Game 0 to Game 1, Minematsu's TBC, Min, is replaced with a TRP. $\Pi_1 := (\Pi_1.\mathsf{Enc}, \Pi_1.\mathsf{Dec})$ denotes the resultant scheme using a TRP $\widetilde{P} \xleftarrow{\$} \widetilde{\mathsf{Perm}}(\mathcal{TW}_N, \{0,1\}^n)$, which is defined in Algorithm 2, where $\widetilde{P}_N(\cdot) := \widetilde{P}(N, \cdot)$. In Game 1, the following event is considered.

$$\mathsf{Game1} := \left(\widetilde{P} \xleftarrow{\$} \widetilde{\mathsf{Perm}}(\mathcal{TW}_N, \{0,1\}^n); H \xleftarrow{\$} \mathcal{H}; \mathbf{A}^{\Pi_1} \text{ forges} \right) .$$

$\Pr[\mathsf{Game0}] - \Pr[\mathsf{Game1}]$ can be upper-bounded by using the following lemma.

Lemma 1 (TSPRP-Security of Min [19]). *Let $\mathbf{A}$ be a (μ, t)-tsprp-adversary whose queries include ν distinct tweaks in $\mathcal{TW}_N$. Then there exist a $(\mu, t+O(\mu))$-sprp-adversary $\mathbf{A}_E$ and a $(\nu, t + O(\mu))$-prf-adversary $\mathbf{A}_F$ such that*

$$\mathbf{Adv}_{\mathsf{Min}}^{\widetilde{\mathsf{sprp}}}(\mathbf{A}) \leq \nu \cdot \mathbf{Adv}_E^{\mathsf{sprp}}(\mathbf{A}_E) + \mathbf{Adv}_{\mathcal{F}}^{\mathsf{prf}}(\mathbf{A}_F) .$$

Algorithm 2. Scheme Π_1

Encryption $\Pi_1.\text{Enc}(N, A, M)$

1: $\Sigma \leftarrow \Pi_1.\text{Hash}(A); C_* \leftarrow \lambda; M_1, \ldots, M_m, M_* \xleftarrow{n} M$
2: **for** $i = 1$ to m **do** $C_i \leftarrow \widetilde{P}_N(M_i \oplus H(i)) \oplus H(i); \Sigma \leftarrow \Sigma \oplus M_i$
3: **if** $M_* = \lambda$ **then**
4:     $T \leftarrow \left[\widetilde{P}_N(\Sigma \oplus H(m, \$)) \right]^\tau$
5: **else**
6:     $\text{Pad} \leftarrow \widetilde{P}_N(0^n \oplus H(m, *))$
7:     $C_* \leftarrow [\text{Pad}]^{|M_*|} \oplus M_*; \Sigma \leftarrow \Sigma \oplus M_* \| 10^*$
8:     $T \leftarrow \left[\widetilde{P}_N(\Sigma \oplus H(m, *\$)) \right]^\tau$
9: **end if**
10: **return** $(C_1 \| \cdots \| C_m \| C_*, T)$

Decryption $\Pi_1.\text{Dec}(N, A, M, T)$

1: $\Sigma \leftarrow \Pi_1.\text{Hash}(A); M_* \leftarrow \lambda; C_1, \ldots, C_m, C_* \xleftarrow{n} C$
2: **for** $i = 1$ to m **do** $M_i \leftarrow \widetilde{P}_N^{-1}(C_i \oplus H(i)) \oplus H(i); \Sigma \leftarrow \Sigma \oplus M_i$
3: **if** $M_* = \lambda$ **then**
4:     $T^* \leftarrow \left[\widetilde{P}_N(\Sigma \oplus H(m, \$)) \right]^\tau$
5: **else**
6:     $\text{Pad} \leftarrow \widetilde{P}_N(0^n \oplus H(m, *));$
7:     $C_* \leftarrow [\text{Pad}]^{|M_*|} \oplus M_*; \Sigma \leftarrow \Sigma \oplus M_* \| 10^*$
8:     $T^* \leftarrow \left[\widetilde{P}_N(\Sigma \oplus H(m, *\$)) \right]^\tau$
9: **end if**
10: **if** $T^* = T$ **then return** M
11: **if** $T^* \neq T$ **then return** $\perp$

Subroutine $\Pi_1.\text{Hash}(A)$

1: $\Sigma \leftarrow 0^n; A_1, \ldots, A_a, A_* \xleftarrow{n} A$
2: **for** $i = 1$ to a **do** $\Sigma \leftarrow \Sigma \oplus \widetilde{P}_0(A_i \oplus H(i))$
3: **if** $A_* \neq \lambda$ **then** $\Sigma \leftarrow \Sigma \oplus \widetilde{P}_0(A_* \| 10^* \oplus H(i, *))$
4: **return** Σ

Hence, Min can be replaced with a TRP $\widetilde{P} \xleftarrow{\$} \widetilde{\text{Perm}}(\mathcal{TW}_N, \{0, 1\}^n)$ with the above security loss where $\nu = q + 1$ and $\mu = \sigma$, that is,

$$\Pr[\text{Game0}] - \Pr[\text{Game1}] \leq (q + 1) \cdot \mathbf{Adv}_E^{\text{sprp}}(\mathbf{A}_E) + \mathbf{Adv}_{\mathcal{F}}^{\text{prf}}(\mathbf{A}_F) . \quad (1)$$

Next, $\Pr[\text{Game1}]$ is upper-bounded. The probability can be upper-bounded by the similar analysis as PMAC [3] that considers a collision in inputs to $\widetilde{P}_N$ that define tags. If no such collision occurs, all tags are randomly drawn from roughly 2^n values, thereby the probability that $\mathbf{A}$ forgers is roughly $q_\mathcal{D}/2^n$. In the following, the detailed analysis of $\Pr[\text{Game1}]$ is given.

Analysis of Game1. Let $x_i := M_i \oplus H(i)$, $y_i := C_i \oplus H(i)$, $x_* := H(j, *)$, $x_\$:= \Sigma \oplus H(m, \$)$ (if $M_* = \lambda$); $x_\$:= \Sigma \oplus H(m, *\$)$ (if $M_* \neq \lambda$), $w_i := A_i \oplus H(i)$, and $w_* := A_* \| 10^* \oplus H(a, *)$. See also Fig. 1 for these notations. Note that x_* is absent if $M_* = \lambda$. We first consider the case where **A** forges at the β-th decryption query where $\beta \in [q_D]$. The event is denoted by $\mathsf{Forge}[\beta]$. Hereafter, a value v defined at the β-th decryption query is denoted by $\hat{v}$. Then the following cases are considered.

- Case 1: $\hat{N}$ is new, i.e., $\hat{N}$ is distinct from all nonces defined at the previous encryption queries. In this case, the following cases are considered.

— Subcase 1-1: $\hat{x}_\$ \notin \{\hat{x}_1, \hat{x}_2, \ldots, \hat{x}_{\hat{m}}, \hat{x}_*\}$. Since $\hat{x}_\$$ is a new input to $\widetilde{P}_N$, the output $\hat{T}$ is randomly drawn from at least $2^n - l_D$ values, thereby we have $\Pr[\mathsf{Forge}[\beta]] \leq 1/(2^n - l_D)$.

— Subcase 1-2: $\hat{x}_\$ \in \{\hat{x}_1, \hat{x}_2, \ldots, \hat{x}_{\hat{m}}, \hat{x}_*\}$. In this case, $\Pr[\mathsf{Forge}[\beta]]$ is upper-bounded by the probability that Subase 1-2 occurs. Assume that $\hat{x}_\$ = \hat{x}_i$ where $\hat{x}_i \in \{\hat{x}_1, \hat{x}_2, \ldots, \hat{x}_{\hat{m}}, \hat{x}_*\}$. $\hat{x}_\$$ has the form $\hat{x}_\$ = \hat{\Sigma} \oplus H(\hat{tw}_\$)$, and $\hat{x}_i$ has the form $\hat{x}_i = \hat{M}_i \oplus H(\hat{tw}_i)$ where $\hat{tw}_\$ \neq \hat{tw}_i$. $\hat{x}_\$ = \hat{x}_i$ implies that

$$\hat{\Sigma} \oplus H(\hat{tw}_\$) = \hat{M}_i \oplus H(\hat{tw}_i) \Rightarrow H(\hat{tw}_\$) \oplus H(\hat{tw}_i) = \hat{\Sigma} \oplus \hat{M}_i,$$

Since $\mathcal{H}$ is ϵ-AXU, the probability that Subcase 1-2 occurs is at most $l_{D,\beta} \cdot \epsilon$.

- Case 2: $\hat{N}$ is not new. In this case, the following cases are considered. Assume that the nonce defined at the α-th encryption query equals $\hat{N}$, where $\alpha \in [q_\mathcal{E}]$. Note that since **A** is nonce-respecting, the number of encryption queries whose nonces equal $\hat{N}$ is at most 1. Hereafter, a value v defined at the α-th encryption query is denoted by $\bar{v}$.

— Subcase 2-1: $\hat{x}_\$ \notin \{\hat{x}_1, \hat{x}_2, \ldots, \hat{x}_{\hat{m}}, \hat{x}_*, \bar{x}_1, \bar{x}_2, \ldots, \bar{x}_{\bar{m}}, \bar{x}_*, \bar{x}_\$\}$. Since $\hat{x}_\$$ is a new input to $P_{\hat{N}}$, the output is randomly drawn from at least $2^n - (\ell_E + l_D)$, thereby $\Pr[\mathsf{Forge}[\beta]] \leq 2^{n-\tau}/(2^n - (\ell_E + l_D))$.

— Subcase 2-2: $\hat{x}_\$ \in \{\hat{x}_1, \hat{x}_2, \ldots, \hat{x}_{\hat{m}}, \hat{x}_*, \bar{x}_1, \bar{x}_2, \ldots, \bar{x}_{\bar{m}}, \bar{x}_*\}$. Assume that $\hat{x}_\$ = x'$ where $x' \in \{\hat{x}_1, \hat{x}_2, \ldots, \hat{x}_{\hat{m}}, \hat{x}_*, \bar{x}_1, \bar{x}_2, \ldots, \bar{x}_{\bar{m}}, \bar{x}_*\}$. $\hat{x}_\$$ has the form $\hat{x}_\$ = \hat{\Sigma} \oplus H(\hat{tw}_\$)$, and x' has the form $x' = X' \oplus H(tw')$ for some n-bit value X' such that $\hat{tw}_* \neq tw'$. $\hat{x}_\$ = x'$ implies that

$$\hat{\Sigma} \oplus H(\hat{tw}_\$) = X' \oplus H(tw') \Rightarrow H(\hat{tw}_\$) \oplus H(tw') = \hat{\Sigma} \oplus X' .$$

$\Pr[\mathsf{Forge}[\beta]]$ is upper-bounded by the collision probability. Since $\mathcal{H}$ is (ϵ, δ)-AXU, the collision probability is at most $(\ell_{E,\alpha} + l_{D,\beta} - 2) \cdot \epsilon$.

— Subcase 2-3: $\hat{x}_\$ = \bar{x}_\$$ and $\hat{tw}_\$ \neq \bar{tw}_\$$. $\hat{x}_*$ has the form $\hat{x}_* = \hat{\Sigma} \oplus H(\hat{tw}_\$)$, and $\bar{x}_*$ has the form $\bar{x}_* = \bar{\Sigma} \oplus H(\bar{tw}_\$)$. $\hat{x}_* = \bar{x}_*$ implies that

$$\hat{\Sigma} \oplus H(\hat{tw}_\$) = \bar{\Sigma} \oplus H(\bar{tw}_\$) \Rightarrow H(\hat{tw}_\$) \oplus H(\bar{tw}_\$) = \hat{\Sigma} \oplus \bar{\Sigma}.$$

$\Pr[\mathsf{Forge}[\beta]]$ is upper-bounded by the collision probability. Since $\mathcal{H}$ is (ϵ, δ)-AXU, the collision probability is at most ϵ.

— Subcase 2-4: $\hat{x}_\$ = \bar{x}_\$$ and $\hat{tw}_\$ = \bar{tw}_\$$ and $\hat{A} = \bar{A}$. In this case, $\hat{\Sigma} = \bar{\Sigma}$, and by $\hat{tw}_\$ = \bar{tw}_\$$, $\hat{m} = \bar{m}$ and $\ell_{\mathsf{E},\alpha} = l_{\mathsf{D},\beta}$ are satisfied. Let $I := \{1, 2, \ldots, \hat{m}\}$. We remove trivial induces from I, i.e., induces $i \in I$ such that $\hat{M}_i = \bar{M}_i$ are removed. The resultant subset is denoted by I'. Then

$$\hat{\Sigma} = \bar{\Sigma} \Leftrightarrow \left(\bigoplus_{i=1}^{\hat{m}} \hat{M}_i \right) \oplus \hat{P} \oplus \Pi_1.\mathsf{Hash}(\hat{A}) = \left(\bigoplus_{i=1}^{\bar{m}} \bar{M}_i \right) \oplus \bar{P} \oplus \Pi_1.\mathsf{Hash}(\bar{A})$$

$$\Leftrightarrow \left(\bigoplus_{i \in I'} \hat{M}_i \oplus \bar{M}_i \right) = \hat{P} \oplus \bar{P} \tag{2}$$

where $\hat{P} = \hat{M}_* \| 10^*$ or 0^n, and $\bar{P} = \bar{M}_* \| 10^*$ or 0^n. $\Pr[\mathsf{Forge}[\beta]]$ is upper-bounded by $\Pr[(2)]$ (the probability that (2) is satisfied).

$\Pr[(2)]$ is upper-bounded. By $\hat{A} = \bar{A}$, $\hat{C} \neq \bar{C}$ is satisfied, and thus $I' \neq \emptyset$ is satisfied. Let $\hat{\mathcal{Y}} := \{\hat{y}_i | i \in I'\}$ and $\mathcal{Y} := \{\hat{y}_i, \bar{y}_i | i \in I'\}$ be multisets for I'. The following cases are considered.

– The first case is $\exists \hat{y}^\dagger \in \hat{\mathcal{Y}}, y^\ddagger \in \mathcal{Y} \setminus \{\hat{y}^\dagger\}$ s.t. $\hat{y}^\dagger = y^\ddagger$. In this case, $\Pr[(2)]$ is upper-bounded by the probability that $\hat{y}^\dagger = y^\ddagger$. $\hat{y}^\dagger$ has the form $\hat{y}^\dagger = \hat{C}^\dagger \oplus H(\hat{tw}^\dagger)$, and $y^\ddagger$ has the form $y^\ddagger = C^\ddagger \oplus H(\bar{tw}^\ddagger)$, where $\hat{tw}^\dagger \neq \bar{tw}^\ddagger$. $\hat{y}^\dagger = y^\ddagger$ implies that

$$\hat{C}^\dagger \oplus H(\hat{tw}^\dagger) = C^\ddagger \oplus H(\bar{tw}^\ddagger) \Leftrightarrow H(\hat{tw}^\dagger) \oplus H(tw^\ddagger) = \hat{C}^\dagger \oplus C^\ddagger .$$

Since $|\hat{\mathcal{Y}}| \leq l_{\mathsf{D},\beta} - 1$, $|\mathcal{Y}| \leq 2l_{\mathsf{D},\beta} - 3$ and $\mathcal{H}$ is (ϵ, δ)-AXU, in this case, $\Pr[(2)] \leq (l_{\mathsf{D},\beta} - 1)(2l_{\mathsf{D},\beta} - 3) \cdot \epsilon$.

– The second case is $\forall \hat{y}^\dagger \in \hat{\mathcal{Y}}, y^\ddagger \in \mathcal{Y} \setminus \{\hat{y}^\dagger\} : \hat{y}^\dagger \neq y^\ddagger$. In this case, $\hat{y}^\dagger \in \hat{\mathcal{Y}}$ is a new input to $P_{\hat{N}}^{-1}$, and thus the output is randomly drawn from at least $2^n - l_{\mathsf{D}}$ values. Hence, in this case, $\Pr[(2)] \leq 1/(2^n - l_{\mathsf{D}})$.

— Subcase 2-5: $\hat{x}_\$ = \bar{x}_\$$ and $\hat{tw}_\$ = \bar{tw}_\$$ and $\hat{A} \neq \bar{A}$. In this case, $\hat{\Sigma} = \bar{\Sigma}$ and $\hat{m} = \bar{m}$ are satisfied. Let $I := \{1, 2, \ldots, \max\{\hat{a}, \bar{a}\}, *\}$ be the set of induces for associated data blocks. We first remove trivial induces from I, i.e., induces $i \in I$ s.t. $\hat{A}_i = \bar{A}_i$ are removed. The resultant subset is denoted by I'. By $\hat{A} \neq \bar{A}$, $I' \neq \emptyset$ is satisfied. Then

$$\hat{\Sigma} = \bar{\Sigma} \Leftrightarrow \left(\bigoplus_{i=1}^{\hat{m}} \hat{M}_i \right) \oplus \hat{P} \oplus \Pi_1.\mathsf{Hash}(\hat{A}) = \left(\bigoplus_{i=1}^{\bar{m}} \bar{M}_i \right) \oplus \bar{P} \oplus \Pi_1.\mathsf{Hash}(\bar{A})$$

$$\Leftrightarrow \Pi_1.\mathsf{Hash}(\hat{A}) \oplus \Pi_1.\mathsf{Hash}(\bar{A}) = \left(\bigoplus_{i=1}^{\hat{m}} \hat{M}_i \oplus \bar{M}_i \right) \oplus \hat{P} \oplus \bar{P} \tag{3}$$

where $\hat{P} = \hat{M}_* \| 10^*$ or 0^n, and $\bar{P} = \bar{M}_* \| 10^*$ or 0^n. Hence, $\Pr[\mathsf{Forge}[\beta]]$ is upper-bounded by $\Pr[(3)]$ (the probability that (3) is satisfied), and similar to Subcase 2-4, the probability can be upper-bounded by considering a collision in inputs to $\widetilde{P}_0$. The detail is given below. Let $\mathcal{W} := \{\hat{w}_i, \bar{w}_i | i \in I'\}$ be the multiset of inputs to $\widetilde{P}_0$ in $\Pi_1.\mathsf{Hash}$ with respect to induces I'. Then the following cases are considered.

- The first case is $\exists w^\dagger, w^\ddagger \in \mathcal{W}$ s.t. $w^\dagger = w^\ddagger$. This case is a collision in inputs to $\widetilde{P}_0$. $w^\dagger$ has the form $w^\dagger = A^\dagger \oplus H(tw^\dagger)$, and $w^\ddagger$ has the form $w^\ddagger = A^\ddagger \oplus H(tw^\ddagger)$, where $tw^\dagger \neq tw^\ddagger$. $w^\dagger = w^\ddagger$ implies that

$$A^\dagger \oplus H(tw^\dagger) = A^\ddagger \oplus H(tw^\ddagger) \Leftrightarrow H(tw^\dagger) \oplus H(tw^\ddagger) = A^\dagger \oplus A^\ddagger .$$

  In this case, $\Pr[(3)]$ is upper-bounded by the collision probability. Since $\mathcal{H}$ is ϵ-AXU, the collision probability is at most $\binom{\ell_{\mathsf{H},\alpha} + \ell_{\mathsf{H},\beta}}{2} \cdot \epsilon \leq 0.5(\ell_{\mathsf{H},\alpha} + \ell_{\mathsf{H},\beta})^2 \cdot \epsilon$.
- The second case is $\forall w^\dagger, w^\ddagger \in \mathcal{W} : w^\dagger \neq w^\ddagger$. In this case, for $w^\dagger \in \mathcal{W}$, $P_0(w^\dagger)$ is not canceled out and is randomly drawn from at least $2^n - (\ell_{\mathsf{H}} + l_{\mathsf{H}})$ values, since $|\mathcal{W}| \leq \ell_{\mathsf{H},\alpha} + l_{\mathsf{H},\beta} \leq \ell_{\mathsf{H}} + l_{\mathsf{H}}$. We thus have $\Pr[(3)] \leq 1/(2^n - (\ell_{\mathsf{H}} + l_{\mathsf{H}}))$.

Conclusion of the Proof. From the above analyses,

$$\Pr[\mathsf{Forge}[\beta] \wedge \mathsf{Case\ 1}] \leq \frac{1}{2^n - l_\mathsf{D}} + l_{\mathsf{D},\beta} \cdot \epsilon$$

$$\Pr[\mathsf{Forge}[\beta] \wedge \mathsf{Case\ 2}] \leq \frac{2^{n-\tau}}{2^n - (\ell_\mathsf{E} + l_\mathsf{D})} + (\ell_{\mathsf{E},\alpha} + l_{\mathsf{D},\beta} - 2) \cdot \epsilon + \epsilon$$

$$+ (l_{\mathsf{D},\beta} - 1)(2l_{\mathsf{D},\beta} - 3) \cdot \epsilon + \frac{1}{2^n - l_\mathsf{D}}$$

$$+ 0.5(\ell_{\mathsf{H},\alpha} + l_{\mathsf{H},\beta})^2 \cdot \epsilon + \frac{1}{2^n - (\ell_\mathsf{H} + l_\mathsf{H})}$$

$$\leq \frac{2^{n-\tau} + 2}{2^n - (\ell_\mathcal{E} + l_\mathcal{D})} + (\ell_{\mathsf{E},\alpha} + 2l_{\mathsf{D},\beta}^2 + \ell_{\mathsf{H},\alpha}^2 + l_{\mathsf{H},\beta}^2) \cdot \epsilon$$

$$\leq \frac{2^{n-\tau} + 2}{2^n - (\ell_\mathcal{E} + l_\mathcal{D})} + (\ell_\mathsf{E} + \ell_\mathsf{H}^2 + 2l_{\mathcal{D},\beta}^2) \cdot \epsilon .$$

Summing the above bounds gives

$$\Pr[\mathsf{Game1}] \leq \sum_{\beta=1}^{q_\mathcal{D}} \Pr[\mathsf{Forge}[\beta]]$$

$$\leq \sum_{\beta=1}^{q_\mathcal{D}} \max\{\Pr[\mathsf{Forge}[\beta] \wedge \mathsf{Case\ 1}], \Pr[\mathsf{Forge}[\beta] \wedge \mathsf{Case\ 2}]\}$$

$$\leq \sum_{\beta=1}^{q_\mathcal{D}} \Pr[\mathsf{Forge}[\beta] \wedge \mathsf{Case\ 2}]$$

$$\leq \frac{q_\mathcal{D}(2^{n-\tau} + 2)}{2^n - (\ell_\mathcal{E} + l_\mathcal{D})} + (\ell_\mathsf{E} + \ell_\mathsf{H}^2) \cdot q_\mathcal{D} \cdot \epsilon + \sum_{\beta=1}^{q_\mathcal{D}} 2l_{\mathcal{D},\beta}^2 \cdot \epsilon . \qquad (4)$$

Finally, the upper-bound in Theorem 3 is obtained by (1) and (4)

5   BC-Based Instantiations

BC-Based Instantiations of F. As mentioned in [21], F can be instantiated from a BC. Let $w_0, w_1, \ldots, w_{\lfloor k/n \rfloor} \in \{0,1\}^c$ be distinct bit strings for a non-negative integer c. The first tweak space is defined as $\mathcal{TW}_N := \{0,1\}^{n-c}$. Then the instantiations are given below.

- $F_K^{(1)}(N) = \left[Y_0 \| Y_1 \| \cdots \| Y_{\lfloor k/n \rfloor - 1} \right]^k$ where $Y_i = E_K(w_i \| N)$.
- $F_K^{(2)}(N) = \left[(Y_0 \oplus Y_1) \| (Y_0 \oplus Y_2) \| \cdots \| (Y_0 \oplus Y_{\lfloor k/n \rfloor}) \right]^k$ where $Y_i = E_K(w_i \| N)$.

Incorporating the above function into $\Theta CB3^\dagger$, "0" is defined as some bit string $const_0 \in \{0,1\}^{n-c}$ and $\mathcal{N} := \{0,1\}^{n-c} \setminus \{const_0\}$. Note that $2^c \geq \lfloor k/n \rfloor$ for $F^{(1)}$, and $2^c - 1 \geq \lfloor k/n \rfloor$ for $F^{(2)}$.

As mentioned in [21], the security bound of $F^{(1)}$ is obtained by the PRP-PRF switch [2], and that of $F^{(2)}$ is obtained by the security result of CENC [7,9,23].

Lemma 2 (PRF Security of $F^{(1)}$ [2]). *For any (q,t)-prf-adversary $\mathbf{A}$, there exists a $(\lfloor k/n \rfloor \cdot q, t + O(q))$-prp-adversary $\mathbf{A}_E$ such that*

$$\mathbf{Adv}_{F^{(1)}}^{\mathsf{prf}}(\mathbf{A}) \leq \mathbf{Adv}_E^{\mathsf{prp}}(\mathbf{A}_E) + \frac{\lfloor k/n \rfloor \cdot q^2}{2^{n+1}} \ .$$

Lemma 3 (PRF Security of $F^{(2)}$ [7,9,23]). *For any (q,t)-prf-adversary $\mathbf{A}$ such that $q \leq 2^n/134$, there exists a $((\lfloor k/n \rfloor + 1)q, t + O(q))$-prp-adversary $\mathbf{A}_E$ such that*

$$\mathbf{Adv}_{F^{(2)}}^{\mathsf{prf}}(\mathbf{A}) \leq \mathbf{Adv}_E^{\mathsf{prp}}(\mathbf{A}_E) + \frac{(\lfloor k/n \rfloor)^2 \cdot q}{2^n} \ .$$

Hence, incorporating these PRFs into XKX*, these terms are introduced into the security bounds.

BC-Based Instantiations of H. The function H in XKX* can be instantiated from a BC by the powering-up scheme [25], the gray-code-based scheme [13, 26], or the LFSR-based scheme [5,6]. Consider the powering-up scheme. It uses the multiplications by $2, 3$ and 7 over $GF(2^n)$. H is realized as follow. Define $L = E_K(const_H)$ for some constant $const_H \in \{0,1\}^n$. Then, for a non-negative integer i, $H(i) := 2^i \cdot L$, $H(i,*) := 2^i \cdot 3 \cdot L$, $H(i,\$) := 2^i \cdot 7 \cdot L$, and $H(i,*\$) := 2^i \cdot 3 \cdot 7 \cdot L$. Note that the instantiation is defined so that for any two distinct input x, y, $H(x) \neq H(y)$, and we can also choose other instantiations with this condition, e.g., "7" is repaced with "3^2", i.e., $H(i,\$) := 2^i \cdot 3^2 \cdot L$ and $H(i,*\$) := 2^i \cdot 3^3 \cdot L$. Regarding the probabilities ϵ and δ, first E_K is replaced with a random permutation, then since L is randomly drawn from $\{0,1\}^n$, $\epsilon = \delta = 1/2^n$ is satisfied.

Remark. Using the above instantiation of F and the powering-up scheme together, $const_H$ should be distinct from all inputs to the BC in F, i.e., $const_H \neq w_i \| N$ for $\forall i \in \{0, 1, \ldots, \lfloor k/n \rfloor\}, N \in \mathcal{TW}_N$.

6   Conclusion

In this paper, we improved the security bounds of the XKX*-based AEAD scheme. The previous security bounds were given by the modular proof, which are roughly $\ell^2 q/2^n + \sigma_A^2/2^n + \sigma_D^2/2^n$, where ℓ is the number of BC calls by a query, q is the number of queries, σ_A is the number of BC calls to handle associated data by encryption queries, and σ_D is the number of BC calls by decryption queries. The birthday terms $\sigma_A^2/2^n, \sigma_D^2/2^n$ might become dominant, for example, when n is small and when DoS attacks are performed. In this paper, in order to remove the birthday terms, we modified ΘCB3 called ΘCB3†, and proved that for ΘCB3† with XKX*, the birthday terms can be removed, i.e., the security bounds become roughly $\ell^2 q/2^n$.

Acknowledgments. We would like to thank Atul Luykx for his comments and suggestions.

References

1. Bellare, M., Namprempre, C.: Authenticated encryption: relations among notions and analysis of the generic composition paradigm. J. Cryptol. **21**(4), 469–491 (2008)
2. Bellare, M., Rogaway, P.: Code-based game-playing proofs and the security of triple encryption. IACR Cryptology ePrint Archive 2004, 331 (2004)
3. Black, J., Rogaway, P.: A block-cipher mode of operation for parallelizable message authentication. In: Knudsen, L.R. (ed.) EUROCRYPT 2002. LNCS, vol. 2332, pp. 384–397. Springer, Heidelberg (2002). https://doi.org/10.1007/3-540-46035-7_25
4. Carter, L., Wegman, M.N.: Universal classes of hash functions. J. Comput. Syst. Sci. **18**(2), 143–154 (1979)
5. Chakraborty, D., Sarkar, P.: A general construction of tweakable block ciphers and different modes of operations. IEEE Trans. Inf. Theory **54**(5), 1991–2006 (2008)
6. Granger, R., Jovanovic, P., Mennink, B., Neves, S.: Improved masking for tweakable blockciphers with applications to authenticated encryption. In: Fischlin, M., Coron, J.-S. (eds.) EUROCRYPT 2016, Part I. LNCS, vol. 9665, pp. 263–293. Springer, Heidelberg (2016). https://doi.org/10.1007/978-3-662-49890-3_11
7. Iwata, T.: New blockcipher modes of operation with beyond the birthday bound security. In: Robshaw, M. (ed.) FSE 2006. LNCS, vol. 4047, pp. 310–327. Springer, Heidelberg (2006). https://doi.org/10.1007/11799313_20
8. Iwata, T.: Authenticated encryption mode for beyond the birthday bound security. In: Vaudenay, S. (ed.) AFRICACRYPT 2008. LNCS, vol. 5023, pp. 125–142. Springer, Heidelberg (2008). https://doi.org/10.1007/978-3-540-68164-9_9
9. Iwata, T., Mennink, B., Vizár, D.: CENC is optimally secure. IACR Cryptology ePrint Archive 2016, 1087 (2016)
10. Iwata, T., Minematsu, K.: Stronger security variants of GCM-SIV. IACR Trans. Symmetric Cryptol. 2016(1), 134–157 (2016)
11. Iwata, T., Yasuda, K.: BTM: a single-key, inverse-cipher-free mode for deterministic authenticated encryption. In: Jacobson, M.J., Rijmen, V., Safavi-Naini, R. (eds.) SAC 2009. LNCS, vol. 5867, pp. 313–330. Springer, Heidelberg (2009). https://doi.org/10.1007/978-3-642-05445-7_20

12. Iwata, T., Yasuda, K.: HBS: a single-key mode of operation for deterministic authenticated encryption. In: Dunkelman, O. (ed.) FSE 2009. LNCS, vol. 5665, pp. 394–415. Springer, Heidelberg (2009). https://doi.org/10.1007/978-3-642-03317-9_24

13. Krovetz, T., Rogaway, P.: The software performance of authenticated-encryption modes. In: Joux, A. (ed.) FSE 2011. LNCS, vol. 6733, pp. 306–327. Springer, Heidelberg (2011). https://doi.org/10.1007/978-3-642-21702-9_18

14. Lampe, R., Seurin, Y.: Tweakable blockciphers with asymptotically optimal security. In: Moriai, S. (ed.) FSE 2013. LNCS, vol. 8424, pp. 133–151. Springer, Heidelberg (2014). https://doi.org/10.1007/978-3-662-43933-3_8

15. Landecker, W., Shrimpton, T., Terashima, R.S.: Tweakable blockciphers with beyond birthday-bound security. In: Safavi-Naini, R., Canetti, R. (eds.) CRYPTO 2012. LNCS, vol. 7417, pp. 14–30. Springer, Heidelberg (2012). https://doi.org/10.1007/978-3-642-32009-5_2

16. Liskov, M., Rivest, R.L., Wagner, D.: Tweakable block ciphers. In: Yung, M. (ed.) CRYPTO 2002. LNCS, vol. 2442, pp. 31–46. Springer, Heidelberg (2002). https://doi.org/10.1007/3-540-45708-9_3

17. Lucks, S.: The sum of PRPs is a secure PRF. In: Preneel, B. (ed.) EUROCRYPT 2000. LNCS, vol. 1807, pp. 470–484. Springer, Heidelberg (2000). https://doi.org/10.1007/3-540-45539-6_34

18. Mennink, B., Reyhanitabar, R., Vizár, D.: Security of full-state keyed sponge and duplex: applications to authenticated encryption. In: Iwata, T., Cheon, J.H. (eds.) ASIACRYPT 2015, Part II. LNCS, vol. 9453, pp. 465–489. Springer, Heidelberg (2015). https://doi.org/10.1007/978-3-662-48800-3_19

19. Minematsu, K.: Beyond-birthday-bound security based on tweakable block cipher. In: Dunkelman, O. (ed.) FSE 2009. LNCS, vol. 5665, pp. 308–326. Springer, Heidelberg (2009). https://doi.org/10.1007/978-3-642-03317-9_19

20. Minematsu, K.: Parallelizable rate-1 authenticated encryption from pseudorandom functions. In: Nguyen, P.Q., Oswald, E. (eds.) EUROCRYPT 2014. LNCS, vol. 8441, pp. 275–292. Springer, Heidelberg (2014). https://doi.org/10.1007/978-3-642-55220-5_16

21. Naito, Y.: Tweakable blockciphers for efficient authenticated encryptions with beyond the birthday-bound security. ePrint 2017/466 and IACR Trans. Symmetric Cryptol. 2017(2), 1–26 (2017)

22. Patarin, J.: Security of random Feistel schemes with 5 or more rounds. In: Franklin, M. (ed.) CRYPTO 2004. LNCS, vol. 3152, pp. 106–122. Springer, Heidelberg (2004). https://doi.org/10.1007/978-3-540-28628-8_7

23. Patarin, J.: Introduction to mirror theory: analysis of systems of linear equalities and linear non equalities for cryptography. IACR Cryptology ePrint Archive 2010, 287 (2010)

24. Rogaway, P.: Authenticated-encryption with associated-data. In: Proceedings of the 9th ACM Conference on Computer and Communications Security, CCS 2002, Washington, DC, USA, 18–22 November 2002, pp. 98–107 (2002)

25. Rogaway, P.: Efficient instantiations of tweakable blockciphers and refinements to modes OCB and PMAC. In: Lee, P.J. (ed.) ASIACRYPT 2004. LNCS, vol. 3329, pp. 16–31. Springer, Heidelberg (2004). https://doi.org/10.1007/978-3-540-30539-2_2

26. Rogaway, P., Bellare, M., Black, J., Krovetz, T.: OCB: a block-cipher mode of operation for efficient authenticated encryption. In: Proceedings of the 8th ACM Conference on Computer and Communications Security CCS 2001, Philadelphia, Pennsylvania, USA, 6–8 November 2001, pp. 196–205 (2001)
27. Wang, L., Guo, J., Zhang, G., Zhao, J., Gu, D.: How to build fully secure tweakable blockciphers from classical blockciphers. In: Cheon, J.H., Takagi, T. (eds.) ASIACRYPT 2016, Part I. LNCS, vol. 10031, pp. 455–483. Springer, Heidelberg (2016). https://doi.org/10.1007/978-3-662-53887-6_17

Multiparty Computation and Privacy

Aggregation of Time-Series Data Under Differential Privacy

Filipp Valovich[(✉)]

Horst Görtz Institute for IT Security, Faculty of Mathematics,
Ruhr-Universität Bochum, Universitätsstraße 150, 44801 Bochum, Germany
filipp.valovich@rub.de

Abstract. In this work, we investigate the problem of statistical data analysis while preserving user privacy in the distributed and semi-honest setting. Particularly, we study properties of Private Stream Aggregation (PSA) schemes, first introduced by Shi et al. in 2011. A PSA scheme is a secure multiparty protocol for the aggregation of time-series data in a distributed network with a minimal communication cost. We show that in the non-adaptive query model, secure PSA schemes can be built upon any key-homomorphic weak pseudo-random function (PRF) and we provide a tighter security reduction. In contrast to the aforementioned work, this means that our security definition can be achieved in the standard model. In addition, we give two computationally efficient instantiations of this theoretic result. The security of the first instantiation comes from a key-homomorphic weak PRF based on the Decisional Diffie-Hellman problem and the security of the second one comes from a weak PRF based on the Decisional Learning with Errors problem. Moreover, due to the use of discrete Gaussian noise, the second construction inherently maintains a mechanism that preserves (ϵ, δ)-differential privacy in the final data-aggregate. A consequent feature of the constructed protocol is the use of the same noise for security and for differential privacy. As a result, we obtain an efficient prospective post-quantum PSA scheme for differentially private data analysis in the distributed model.

Keywords: Aggregator Obliviousness · Post-quantum cryptography · Differential privacy

1 Introduction

In recent years, *differential privacy* has become one of the most important paradigms for privacy-preserving statistical analyses. Generally, the notion of differential privacy is considered in the centralised setting where we assume the existence of a *trusted curator* (see [4,7,9,16]) who collects data in the clear, aggregates and perturbs it properly (e.g. by adding Laplace-distributed noise) and publishes it. In this way, the output statistics are not significantly influenced

The research was supported by the DFG Research Training Group GRK 1817/1.

© Springer Nature Switzerland AG 2019
T. Lange and O. Dunkelman (Eds.): LATINCRYPT 2017, LNCS 11368, pp. 249–270, 2019.
https://doi.org/10.1007/978-3-030-25283-0_14

by the presence (resp. absence) of a particular record in the database and simultaneously high accuracy of the analysis is maintained. In this work, we study how to preserve differential privacy when we cannot rely on a trusted curator. In this *distributed setting*, the users have to send their own data to an untrusted aggregator. Preserving differential privacy and achieving high accuracy in the distributed setting is of course harder than in the centralised setting, since the users have to execute a perturbation mechanism on their own. To this end, a Private Stream Aggregation (PSA) scheme can be deployed. A PSA scheme is a cryptographic protocol enabling each user of the network to securely send encrypted time-series data to an untrusted aggregator requiring each user to send exactly one message per time-step. The aggregator is then able to decrypt the aggregate of all data in each time-step, but cannot retrieve any further information about the individual data. Using such a protocol, the task of perturbation can be split among the users, such that the differential privacy of the final aggregate is preserved *and* high accuracy is guaranteed. In this framework, the results of this work are as follows: first we show that a secure PSA scheme can be built upon any *key-homomorphic weak pseudo-random function*. From this result, we construct a PSA scheme based on the *Decisional Diffie-Hellman* (DDH) assumption. Moreover, we construct a PSA scheme based on the *Decisional Learning with Errors* (DLWE) assumption that is prospectively secure in the post-quantum world and automatically provides differential privacy to users.

Related Work. The concept of PSA was introduced by Shi et al. [24], where a PSA scheme for sum-queries was provided and shown to be secure under the DDH assumption. However, this instantiation has some limitations. First, the security only holds in the random oracle model. Second, its decryption algorithm requires the solution of the discrete logarithm in a given range, which can be very time-consuming, if the number of users and the plaintext space are large. In contrast, our schemes are secure in the *standard model* and can efficiently decrypt the aggregate, even if the users' data consist of large numbers. In [12], a PSA scheme was provided that is secure in the random oracle model based on the Decisional Composite Residuosity (DCR) assumption. As a result, a factor which is cubic in the number of users can be removed in the security reduction. However, this scheme involves a semi-trusted party for setting some public parameters. In our work, we provide instantiations of our *generic* PSA construction which rely on the DDH assumption and on the DLWE assumption. While in our generic security reduction we cannot avoid a *linear* factor in the number of users, our construction *does not* involve any trusted party and has security guarantees in the standard model. In a subsequent work [3], a generalisation of the scheme from [12] is obtained based on smooth projective hash functions [6]. This allows the construction of secure protocols based on various hardness assumptions (such as the k-LIN assumption). However, the dependencies on a semi-trusted party (for most of the instantiations) and on a random oracle remain.

2   Preliminaries

2.1   Model

We consider a distributed network of users with sensitive data stored in a database. In a distributed network, the users perform computations on their own and do not trust other users or other parties outside the network. More specifically, we assume the existence of an aggregator with the aim to analyse the data in the database. The users are asked to participate in some statistical analyses but do not trust the data aggregator (or analyst), who is assumed to be honest but curious and therefore *corrupted*. In this so-called *semi-honest* model, the users do not provide their own sensitive data in the clear, since they want to preserve the privacy of their data. On the other hand, the untrusted analyst wants to compute some (pre-defined) statistics over these data sets and more-over will use any auxiliary obtained information in order to deduce some more information about the individual users' data. Despite that, and opposed to the *malicious* model, where the corrupted parties may execute *any* behaviour, the analyst will honestly follow the rules of the network.

Moreover, the users perform computations independently and communicate solely and independently with the untrusted analyst. We also assume that the analyst may corrupt users of the network in order to compromise the privacy of the other participants. Uncorrupted users honestly follow the rules of the network and want to release useful information about their data (with respect to particular statistical database queries by the analyst), while preserving the privacy of their data. The remaining users are assumed to be corrupted and following the rules of the network but aiming at violating the privacy of uncorrupted users. For that purpose, these users form a coalition with the analyst and send auxiliary information to the analyst, e.g. their own data in the clear. Therefore, the members of the coalition are allowed to communicate among each other and with the analyst at any time.

We consider all parties to have only limited computational resources, i.e. we consider only algorithms with a running time that is polynomial in some complexity parameter.

The untrusted data analyst wants to analyse the users' data by means of time-series queries and aims at obtaining answers as accurate as possible. More specifically, assume that the users have a series of data items belonging to a data universe $\mathcal{D}$. For a sequence of time-steps $t \in T$, where T is a discrete time period, the analyst sends queries which are answered by the users in a distributed manner. Each query is modelled as a function $f : \mathcal{D}^n \to \mathcal{O}$ for a finite or countably infinite set of possible outputs (i.e. answers to the query) $\mathcal{O}$. We consider only sum-queries in this work.

For computing the answers to the aggregator's queries, a special crypto-graphic protocol, the Private Stream Aggregation (PSA) scheme, is executed by *all* users. In contrast to common secure multi-party techniques (see [11] and [14]), this protocol requires each user to send only one message per time-series query to the analyst.

2.2 Cryptographic Hardness Assumptions and Pseudo-random Functions

In the following, we describe some cryptographic hardness assumptions that will be the basis for two weak pseudo-random functions that we will use for the construction of secure PSA schemes.

The Decisional Diffie-Hellman Assumption. The Decisional Diffie-Hellman (DDH) assumption underlies one of our constructions. It is related to the discrete logarithm (dlog) assumption: it says that no probabilistic polynomial time (ppt) algorithm is able to find $x \in \mathbb{Z}_q$ given g^x for a generator g of a finite cyclic group of order q. Under the DDH assumption, a ppt algorithm cannot distinguish g^{xy} from a random element in the group. The DDH assumption implies the dlog assumption, since by solving the discrete logarithm one can easily distinguish g^z from g^{xy}.

The Learning with Errors Assumption. As an instance of the Learning with Errors (LWE) problem, we are given a uniformly distributed matrix $\mathbf{A} \in \mathbb{Z}_q^{\lambda \times \kappa}$ and a noisy codeword $\mathbf{y} = \mathbf{Ax} + \mathbf{e} \in \mathbb{Z}_q^\lambda$ with an error term $\mathbf{e} \in \mathbb{Z}_q^\lambda$ sampled according to a proper known probability distribution χ^λ and an unknown uniform $\mathbf{x} \in \mathbb{Z}_q^\kappa$. The task is to find the correct vector $\mathbf{x}$. Without the error term, the task would simply be to find the solution to a system of linear equations. Thus, the error term is crucial for the hardness of this problem. In the decisional version of this problem (DLWE problem), we are given $(\mathbf{A}, \mathbf{y})$ and have to decide whether $\mathbf{y} = \mathbf{Ax} + \mathbf{e}$ or $\mathbf{y}$ is a uniformly distributed vector in $\mathbb{Z}_q^\lambda$.

Regev [22] established the average-case-hardness of the search problem by the construction of an efficient quantum algorithm for worst-case lattice problems using an efficient solver for LWE, if the errors follow a *discrete Gaussian* distribution $D(\nu)$, where $X \sim D(\nu)$ iff $\Pr[X = x] = (1/c_\nu) \cdot \exp(-x^2/(2\nu))$ with $c_\nu = \sum_x \exp(-x^2/(2\nu))$.

Theorem 1 (Worst-to-Average Case [22]). *Let κ be a security parameter and let $q = q(\kappa)$ be a modulus, let $\alpha = \alpha(\kappa) \in (0,1)$ be such that $\alpha q > 2\sqrt{\kappa}$. If there exists a ppt algorithm solving the LWE problem with errors distributed according to $D((\alpha q)^2/(2\pi))$ with more than negligible probability, then there exists an efficient quantum algorithm that approximates the decisional shortest vector problem (GapSVP) and the shortest independent vectors problem (SIVP) to within $\tilde{O}(\kappa/\alpha)$ in the worst case.*

Opposed to this quantum reduction, Peikert [21] provided a classical reduction. However, Regev's result suffices for our purposes. Micciancio and Mol [17] provided a sample preserving search-to-decision reduction that works for any error distribution χ, showing the equivalence in the average case.

Theorem 2 (Search-to-Decision [17]). *Let κ be a security parameter, $q = q(\kappa) = \text{poly}(\kappa)$ a prime modulus and let χ be any distribution on $\mathbb{Z}_q$.*

Assume there exists a ppt distinguisher that solves the DLWE problem with more than negligible success-probability, then there exists a ppt adversary that solves the LWE problem with more than negligible success-probability (both with error distribution χ).

Pseudo-Random Functions. A PRF family is a collection of efficiently computable functions that cannot be distinguished from random functions on *arbitrarily* distributed input by any ppt algorithm with black-box access to the function and with more than negligible probability. Constructing a PRF is possible e.g. by assuming the existence of a random oracle, i.e. a random black-box function that obtains an arbitrarily distributed input and outputs something uniformly random (but always the same for the same input). If the range of the random oracle is large enough, each input will have a unique (random) output with overwhelming probability. Then the output of the random oracle serves as input to a *weak* PRF, i.e. a function that takes *uniformly distributed* values as input and outputs pseudo-random values.

Definition 1 ((Weak) PRF [20]). *Let κ be a security parameter. Let A, B, C be sets with sizes parameterised by κ. A family of functions $\mathcal{F} = \{F_a \mid F_a : B \to C\}_{a \in A}$ is called a (respectively weak) pseudo-random function (PRF) family, if for all ppt algorithms $\mathcal{D}_{PRF}^{\mathcal{O}(\cdot)}$ with oracle access to $\mathcal{O}(\cdot) \in \{F_a(\cdot), \mathrm{rand}(\cdot)\}$, on any polynomial number of arbitrarily chosen (respectively uniform and given) inputs, we have $|\Pr[\mathcal{D}_{PRF}^{F_a(\cdot)}(\kappa) = 1] - \Pr[\mathcal{D}_{PRF}^{\mathrm{rand}(\cdot)}(\kappa) = 1]| \leq \mathrm{neg}(\kappa)$, where $a \leftarrow \mathcal{U}(A)$ and $\mathrm{rand} \in \{f \mid f : B \to C\}$ is a random mapping from B to C.*

2.3 Private Stream Aggregation

In this section, we define Private Stream Aggregation (PSA) and provide two security definitions. The notion of PSA was introduced by Shi et al. [24].

The Definition of Private Stream Aggregation. A PSA scheme is a protocol for safe distributed time-series data transfer which enables the receiver (here: the untrusted analyst) to learn nothing else than the sums $\sum_{i=1}^{n} x_{i,j}$ for $j = 1, 2, \ldots$, where $x_{i,j}$ is the value of the ith participant in time-step j and n is the number of participants (or users). Such a scheme needs a key exchange protocol for all n users together with the analyst as a precomputation (e.g. using multi-party techniques), and requires each user to send exactly one message in each time-step $j = 1, 2, \ldots$.

Definition 2 (Private Stream Aggregation [24]). *Let κ be a security parameter, $\mathcal{D}$ a set and $n = poly(\kappa)$, $\lambda = poly(\kappa)$. A Private Stream Aggregation (PSA) scheme $\Sigma = (\mathsf{Setup}, \mathsf{PSAEnc}, \mathsf{PSADec})$ is defined by three ppt algorithms:*

Setup: $(\mathsf{pp}, T, s_0, s_1, \ldots, s_n) \leftarrow \mathsf{Setup}(1^\kappa)$ *with public parameters* pp, $T = \{t_1, \ldots, t_\lambda\}$ *and secret keys s_i for all $i = 1, \ldots, n$.*

PSAEnc: *For $t_j \in T$ and all $i = 1, \ldots, n$: $c_{i,j} \leftarrow \text{PSAEnc}_{s_i}(t_j, x_{i,j})$ for $x_{i,j} \in \mathcal{D}$.*
PSADec: *Compute $\sum_{i=1}^{n} x'_{i,j} = \text{PSADec}_{s_0}(t_j, c_{1,j}, \ldots, c_{n,j})$ for $t_j \in T$ and ciphers $c_{1,j}, \ldots, c_{n,j}$. For all $t_j \in T$ and $x_{1,j}, \ldots, x_{n,j} \in \mathcal{D}$ the following holds:*

$$\text{PSADec}_{s_0}(t_j, \text{PSAEnc}_{s_1}(t_j, x_{1,j}), \ldots, \text{PSAEnc}_{s_n}(t_j, x_{n,j})) = \sum_{i=1}^{n} x_{i,j}.$$

The system parameters pp are public and constant for all t_j with the implicit understanding that they are used in Σ. Every user encrypts her values $x_{i,j}$ with her own secret key s_i and sends the ciphertext to the untrusted analyst. If the analyst receives the ciphertexts of *all* users for some t_j, it can compute the aggregate of the users' data using the decryption key s_0.

Security of Private Stream Aggregation. Our model allows an attacker to corrupt users. It can obtain auxiliary information about the values of users or their secret keys. Even then a secure PSA scheme should release no more information than the aggregates of the uncorrupted users' values. The difference between the following two security definitions is whether the attacker can corrupt users adaptively or not.

Definition 3 (Adaptive (resp. non-adaptive) Aggregator Obliviousness). *Let κ be a security parameter. Let $\mathcal{T}$ be a ppt adversary for a PSA scheme $\Sigma = (\text{Setup}, \text{PSAEnc}, \text{PSADec})$ and let $\mathcal{D}$ be a set. We define a security game between a challenger and the adversary $\mathcal{T}$.*

Setup. The challenger runs the Setup algorithm on input security parameter κ and returns public parameters pp, public encryption parameters T with $|T| = \lambda = poly(\kappa)$ and secret keys $s_0, s_1, \ldots, s_n$. It sends κ, pp, T, s_0 to $\mathcal{T}$.

Queries. $\mathcal{T}$ is allowed to query $(i, t_j, x_{i,j})$ with $i \in \{1, \ldots, n\}, t_j \in T, x_{i,j} \in \mathcal{D}$ and the challenger returns $c_{i,j} \leftarrow \text{PSAEnc}_{s_i}(t_j, x_{i,j})$. Moreover, $\mathcal{T}$ is allowed to make compromise queries $i \in \{1, \ldots, n\}$ and the challenger returns s_i.

Challenge. $\mathcal{T}$ chooses $U \subseteq \{1, \ldots, n\}$ such that no compromise query for $i \in U$ was made and sends U to the challenger. $\mathcal{T}$ chooses $t_{j^*} \in T$ such that no encryption query with t_{j^*} was made. (If there is no such t_{j^*} then the challenger simply aborts.) $\mathcal{T}$ queries two different tuples $(x_{i,j^*}^{[0]})_{i \in U}, (x_{i,j^*}^{[1]})_{i \in U}$ with $\sum_{i \in U} x_{i,j^*}^{[0]} = \sum_{i \in U} x_{i,j^*}^{[1]}$. The challenger flips a random bit $b \leftarrow_R \{0,1\}$. For all $i \in U$ the challenger returns $c_{i,j^*} \leftarrow \text{PSAEnc}_{s_i}(t_{j^*}, x_{i,j^*}^{[b]})$.

Queries. $\mathcal{T}$ is allowed to make the same type of queries as before restricted to encryption queries with $t_j \neq t_{j^*}$ and compromise queries for $i \notin U$.

Guess. $\mathcal{T}$ outputs a guess about b.

The adversary's probability to win the game (i.e. to guess b correctly) is $1/2 + \nu(\kappa)$. A PSA scheme is adaptively aggregator oblivious *or achieves* adaptive Aggregator Obliviousness *(AO2) if there is no ppt adversary $\mathcal{T}$ with more than negligible advantage $\nu(\kappa) > \text{neg}(\kappa)$ in winning the above game. A PSA scheme is* non-adaptively aggregator oblivious *or achieves* non-adaptive

Aggregator Obliviousness (AO1), if there is no ppt adversary $\mathcal{T}$ with advantage $\nu(\kappa) > \mathsf{neg}(\kappa)$ in winning a modified game, where the set U is already specified by $\mathcal{T}$ in the end of the Setup phase, compromise queries are made for all $i \notin U$ and encryption queries can only be made for $i \in U$. A PSA scheme is secure if it achieves either AO2 or AO1.

Encryption queries are made only for $i \in U$, since knowing the secret key for all $i \notin U$ the adversary can encrypt a value autonomously. If encryption queries in time-step t_{j*} were allowed, then no deterministic scheme would be secure. The adversary $\mathcal{T}$ can determine the original data of all $i \notin U$, since it knows $(s_i)_{i \notin U}$. Then $\mathcal{T}$ can compute the sum $\sum_{i \in U} x_{i,j} = \mathsf{PSADec}_{s_0}(t_j, c_{1,j}, \ldots, c_{n,j}) - \sum_{i \notin U} x_{i,j}$ of the uncorrupted users' values. If there is a user's cipher which $\mathcal{T}$ does not receive, then it cannot compute the sum for the corresponding t_j. AO1 differs from AO2 in that the first one requires the adversary to specify the set U of uncorrupted users before making any query, i.e. it does not allow the adversary to determine U adaptively. The notion of AO2 was introduced in [24].

Feasibility of AO2. In the random oracle model, we can achieve the stronger notion AO2 for some constructions. For example, in [24] the following PSA scheme for sum-queries was proposed. It achieves AO2 based on the DDH assumption.

Example 1 ([24]).

Setup: The public parameters are a prime p, some generator $g \in \mathbb{Z}_p^*$ and a hash function $H : T \to \mathbb{Z}_p^*$ modelled as a random oracle. The secret keys are $s_0, \ldots, s_n \leftarrow \mathcal{U}(\mathbb{Z}_p)$ with $\sum_{i=0}^{n} s_i \equiv 0 \bmod p - 1$.

PSAEnc: For $t_j \in T$ and all $i = 1, \ldots, n$, encrypt $x_{i,j} \in \mathbb{Z}_p$ by $c_{i,j} \leftarrow g^{x_{i,j}} \cdot H(t_j)^{s_i}$.

PSADec: For $t_j \in T$ and ciphers $c_{1,j}, \ldots, c_{n,j}$, compute the discrete logarithm of $V_j \leftarrow H(t_j)^{s_0} \cdot \prod_{i=1}^{n} c_{i,j}$. If the $c_{i,j}$ are encryptions of the $x_{i,j}$, then $V_j = g^{\sum_{i=1}^{n} x_{i,j}}$ and computing the discrete logarithm of V_j to the base g yields the desired output.

Note that the computation of the discrete logarithm may be inefficient, if the range to search in is super-polynomially large in the security parameter. In Sect. 4.1, we provide our DDH-based example of a PSA scheme that achieves AO2 in the random oracle model and AO1 in the standard model and has an efficient decryption algorithm even if the plaintext space is super-polynomially large.

2.4   Differential Privacy

We consider a database as an element $D \in \mathcal{D}^n$ with data universe $\mathcal{D}$ and number of users n. We will always assume that a privacy-preserving mechanism for analysing D is applied in the distributed setting. Differential privacy is a well-established notion for privacy-preserving statistical analyses. We recall that a randomised mechanism preserves differential privacy, if its application on two adjacent databases (databases differing in one entry only) leads to close distributions of the outputs.

Definition 4 (Differential Privacy [9]**).** *Let $\mathcal{R}$ be a set and let $n \in \mathbb{N}$. A randomised mechanism $\mathcal{A} : \mathcal{D}^n \to \mathcal{R}$ preserves (ϵ, δ)-differential privacy (short: DP), if for all adjacent databases $D_0, D_1 \in \mathcal{D}^n$ and all measurable $R \subseteq \mathcal{R}$:*

$$\Pr[\mathcal{A}(D_0) \in R] \leqslant e^{\epsilon} \cdot \Pr[\mathcal{A}(D_1) \in R] + \delta.$$

The probability space is defined over the randomness of $\mathcal{A}$.

Thus, the presence or absence of a single user does not affect the probability of any outcome by too much. The aim of the analyst is to obtain information from the database. Therefore it processes queries to the database which are answered while preserving DP. In the literature, there are well-established mechanisms for preserving DP (see [9] and [16]).[1] In order to privately evaluate a query, these mechanisms draw error terms according to some distribution depending on the query's global sensitivity. For any $D \in \mathcal{D}^n$, the global sensitivity $S(f)$ of a query $f : \mathcal{D}^n \to \mathbb{R}$ is defined as the maximum change (in terms of the L_1-norm) of $f(D)$, which can be produced by a change of one entry (i.e. the absence of one user) in D. In particular, we will consider sum-queries $f_{\mathcal{D}} : \mathcal{D}^n \to \mathbb{Z}$ or $f_{\mathcal{D}} : \mathcal{D}^n \to [-m', m']$ for some integer m' defined as $f_{\mathcal{D}}(D) := \sum_{i=1}^{n} d_i$, for $D = (d_1, \ldots, d_n) \in \mathcal{D}^n$ and $\mathcal{D} \subseteq \mathbb{Z}$. If the entries in D are bounded by m, then $S(f_{\mathcal{D}}) \leqslant m$. For measuring how well the output of a mechanism $\mathcal{A}$ estimates the real data with respect to a particular query f (mapping into a metric space), we use the notion of (α, β)-accuracy, defined as $\Pr[|\mathcal{A}(D) - f(D)| \leqslant \alpha] \geqslant 1 - \beta$.

The introduction of differential privacy in 2006 was due to the incapability of cryptography to handle data secrecy and analysability at the same time. It is a mathematically well-founded notion for *privacy-preserving data analysis*. Before that, notions of *syntactic anonymity* for *privacy-preserving data publishing*, like k-anonymity [23], were considered by researchers, where the published anonymised data can be used for data analysis tasks. This model asks that every published record is indistinguishable from $k - 1$ other records. Its extensions like l-diversity [15] or t-closeness [13] gain more privacy (at the cost of loss in data management effectiveness) by introducing equivalence classes for data and attributes (to also prevent attribute disclosure) and thus reducing the representation granularity. However, this model is vulnerable to certain attacks, that extract *belief probabilities* from the published data. Moreover, applying this model on high-dimensional data leads to a *degradation of data quality*. As noticed in [25], although these issues are not unsolvable, they led to a stronger research focus towards differential privacy. Indeed, also differential privacy suffers from some (practical) limitations, like the difficulty to determine a privacy-budget and to compute the exact global sensitivity of the performed data analysis in

---

[1] These mechanisms work in the centralised setting, where a *trusted curator* sees the full database in the clear and perturbs it properly.

advance. This leads to excessive perturbation of the correct analysis. Opposed to syntactic anonymity, in differential privacy the true and the perturbed analyses are *probabilistically* correlated, which leads to high uncertainty. Moreover the application of differential privacy makes the assumption of independent data owners, which is not necessary in syntactic anonymity. Therefore the influence of a single individual on the other database participants may be underestimated.

Hence, we see that both approaches and their extensions have advantages and disadvantages while being applied in different tasks and leading to interesting and relevant research challenges.

3   Feasibility of **AO1**

In this section, we show that a PSA scheme achieving AO2 can be built upon a key-homomorphic weak PRF.

Theorem 3 (Weak PRF gives secure PSA scheme). *Let κ be a security parameter, and $m, n \in \mathbb{N}$ with $\log(m) = \mathsf{poly}(\kappa), n = \mathsf{poly}(\kappa)$. Let $(G, \cdot), (S, *)$ be finite groups and $G' \subseteq G$. For some finite set M, let $\mathcal{F} = \{F_s \,|\, F_s : M \to G'\}_{s \in S}$ be a (possibly randomised) weak PRF family and let $\varphi : \{-mn, \ldots, mn\} \to G$ be a mapping. Then the following PSA scheme $\Sigma = (\mathsf{Setup}, \mathsf{PSAEnc}, \mathsf{PSADec})$ achieves* AO1:

Setup: $(\mathsf{pp}, T, s_0, s_1, \ldots, s_n) \leftarrow \mathsf{Setup}(1^\kappa)$, *where* pp *are parameters of* $G, G', S,$ $M, \mathcal{F}, \varphi$. *The keys are* $s_i \leftarrow \mathcal{U}(S)$ *for all* $i \in [n]$ *with* $s_0 = (*_{i=1}^{n} s_i)^{-1}$ *and* $T \subset M$ *such that all* $t_j \in T$ *are chosen uniformly at random from* M, $j = 1, \ldots, \lambda = \mathsf{poly}(\kappa)$.
PSAEnc: *Compute* $c_{i,j} = F_{s_i}(t_j) \cdot \varphi(x_{i,j})$ *in* G *for* $x_{i,j} \in \widehat{\mathcal{D}} = \{-m, \ldots, m\}$ *and public parameter* $t_j \in T$.
PSADec: *Compute* $V_j = \varphi^{-1}(S_j)$ *(if possible) with* $S_j = F_{s_0}(t_j) \cdot c_{1,j} \cdot \ldots \cdot c_{n,j}$.

Moreover, if $\mathcal{F}$ *contains only deterministic functions that are homomorphic over* S, *if* φ *is homomorphic and injective over* $\{-mn, \ldots, mn\}$ *and if the* $c_{i,j}$ *are encryptions of the* $x_{i,j}$, *then* $V_j = \sum_{i=1}^{n} x_{i,j}$, *i.e. then* **PSADec** *correctly decrypts* $\sum_{i=1}^{n} x_{i,j}$.

The reason for not including the correctness property in the main statement is that in Sect. 4.2, we will provide an example of a secure PSA scheme based on the DLWE problem that does not have a fully correct decryption algorithm, but a noisy one. This noise is necessary for establishing the security of the protocol and will be also used for preserving the differential privacy of the decryption output.

Hence, we need a key-homomorphic weak PRF and a mapping which homomorphically aggregates all users' data. Since every data value is at most m, the scheme correctly retrieves the aggregate, which is at most $m \cdot n$. Importantly, the product of all pseudo-random values $F_{s_0}(t_j), F_{s_1}(t_j), \ldots, F_{s_n}(t_j)$ is the neutral element in the group G for all $t_j \in T$. Note that the secret keys can be pre-generated using a secure multi-party protocol and hence, no trusted party is required. Since the values in T are uniformly distributed in M, it is enough to require that $\mathcal{F}$ is a *weak* PRF family. Thus, the statement of Theorem 3 does not require a random oracle.

3.1   Security Proof

Let **game 1** be the AO1 game from Definition 3 instantiated for the PSA scheme of Theorem 3. We need to show that the advantage $\nu_1(\kappa)$ of a ppt adversary $\mathcal{T}_1$ in winning this game is negligible in the security parameter κ. We define the following intermediate **game 2** for a ppt adversary $\mathcal{T}_2$ and then show that winning **game 1** is at least as hard as winning **game 2**.

Setup. The challenger runs the Setup algorithm on input security parameter κ and returns public parameters pp, time-steps T and secret keys $s_0, s_1, \ldots, s_n$ with $s_0 = (\ast_{i=1}^{n} s_i)^{-1}$. It sends κ, pp, T, s_0 to $\mathcal{T}_2$. The challenger flips a random bit $b \leftarrow_R \{0,1\}$. $\mathcal{T}_2$ chooses $U = \{i_1, \ldots, i_u\} \subseteq [n]$ and sends it to the challenger which returns $(s_i)_{i \in [n] \setminus U}$.

Queries. $\mathcal{T}_2$ is allowed to query $(i, t_j, x_{i,j})$ with $i \in U, t_j \in T, x_{i,j} \in \widehat{\mathcal{D}}$ and the challenger returns the following: if $b = 0$, it sends $\mathsf{F}_{s_i}(t_j) \cdot \varphi(x_{i,j})$ to $\mathcal{T}_2$; if $b = 1$, it chooses

$$h_{1,j}, \ldots, h_{u-1,j} \leftarrow \mathcal{U}(G'),\ h_{u,j} := \prod_{i'=1}^{u} \mathsf{F}_{s_{i_{i'}}}(t_j) \cdot \left(\prod_{i'=1}^{u-1} h_{i',j} \right)^{-1}$$

and sends $h_{i,j} \cdot \varphi(x_{i,j})$ to $\mathcal{T}_2$.

Challenge. $\mathcal{T}_2$ chooses $t_{j^*} \in T$ such that no encryption query at t_{j^*} was made and queries a tuple $(x_{i,j^*})_{i \in U}$. If $b = 0$, the challenger sends $(\mathsf{F}_{s_i}(t_{j^*}) \cdot \varphi(x_{i,j^*}))_{i \in U}$ to $\mathcal{T}_2$; if $b = 1$, it chooses

$$h_{1,j^*}, \ldots, h_{u-1,j^*} \leftarrow \mathcal{U}(G'),\ h_{u,j^*} := \prod_{i'=1}^{u} \mathsf{F}_{s_{i_{i'}}}(t_{j^*}) \cdot \left(\prod_{i'=1}^{u-1} h_{i',j^*} \right)^{-1}$$

and sends $(h_{i,j^*} \cdot \varphi(x_{i,j^*}))_{i \in U}$ to $\mathcal{T}_2$.

Queries. $\mathcal{T}_2$ is allowed to make the same type of queries as before with the restriction that no encryption query at t_{j^*} can be made.

Guess. $\mathcal{T}_2$ outputs a guess about b.

The adversary wins the game, if it correctly guesses b.

Lemma 4. *For a security parameter κ, let $\mathcal{T}_1$ be an adversary in* **game 1** *with advantage $\nu_1(\kappa) > \mathsf{neg}(\kappa)$. Then there exists an adversary $\mathcal{T}_2$ in* **game 2** *with advantage $\nu_2(\kappa) > \mathsf{neg}(\kappa)$.*

Proof. Given a successful adversary $\mathcal{T}_1$ in **game 1** we construct a successful adversary $\mathcal{T}_2$ in **game 2** as follows:

Setup. Receive $\kappa, \mathsf{pp}, T, s_0$ from the **game 2**-challenger and send it to T_1. Flip a random bit $b' \leftarrow_R \{0,1\}$. Receive $U = \{i_1, \ldots, i_u\} \subseteq [n]$ from T_1 and send it to the challenger. Forward the obtained response $(s_i)_{i \in [n] \setminus U}$ to T_1.

Queries. Forward T_1's queries $(i, t_j, x_{i,j})$ with $i \in U, t_j \in T, x_{i,j} \in \widehat{\mathcal{D}}$ to the challenger and forward the obtained response $c_{i,j}$ to T_1.

Challenge. T_1 chooses $t_{j^*} \in T$ such that no encryption query at t_{j^*} was made and queries two different tuples $(x_{i,j^*}^{[0]})_{i \in U}, (x_{i,j^*}^{[1]})_{i \in U}$ with $\sum_{i \in U} x_{i,j^*}^{[0]} = \sum_{i \in U} x_{i,j^*}^{[1]}$. Query $(x_{i,j^*}^{[b']})_{i \in U}$ to the challenger. Receive back $(c_{i,j^*})_{i \in U}$ and forward it to T_1.

Queries. T_1 can make the same type of queries as before with the restriction that no encryption query at t_{j^*} can be made.

Guess. T_1 gives a guess about b'. If it is correct, then output 0; if not, output 1.

If T_1 has output the correct guess about b', then T_2 can say with high confidence that the challenge ciphertexts were generated using a weak PRF and therefore outputs 0. On the other hand, if T_1's guess was not correct, then T_2 can say with high confidence that the challenge ciphertexts were generated using random values and it outputs 1.

Case 1. Let $(c_{i,j^*})_{i \in U} = (F_{s_i}(t_{j^*}) \cdot \varphi(x_{i,j^*}^{[b']}))_{i \in U}$. Then also the queries were answered using pseudo-random values and thus, T_2 perfectly simulates **game 1** for T_1 and the distribution of the ciphertexts is the same as in **game 1**:

$$\Pr[T_2 \text{ outputs } 0] = \frac{1}{2}(\Pr[T_1 \text{ outputs } 0 \mid b' = 0] + \Pr[T_1 \text{ outputs } 1 \mid b' = 1])$$
$$= \Pr[T_1 \text{ wins } \textbf{game 1}]$$
$$= \frac{1}{2} + \nu_1(\kappa).$$

Case 2. Let $(c_{i,j^*})_{i \in U} = (h_{i,j^*} \cdot \varphi(x_{i,j^*}^{[b']}))_{i \in U}$. Then also the queries were answered using random values. The ciphertexts are random with $\prod_{i \in U} c_{i,j^*} = \prod_{i \in U} F_{s_i}(t_{j^*}) \cdot \varphi(x_{i,j^*}^{[b']})$ such that decryption yields the same sum as in case 1. Because of the perfect security of the one-time pad, the probability that T_1 wins **game 1** is $1/2$ and

$$\Pr[T_2 \text{ outputs } 1] = \frac{1}{2}(\Pr[T_1 \text{ outputs } 1 \mid b' = 0] + \Pr[T_1 \text{ outputs } 0 \mid b' = 1])$$
$$= \Pr[T_1 \text{ loses } \textbf{game 1}]$$
$$= \frac{1}{2}.$$

Thus, the advantage of T_2 in winning **game 2** is $\nu_2(\kappa) = \frac{1}{2}\nu_1(\kappa) > \mathsf{neg}(\kappa)$. $\square$

For a ppt adversary T_3, we define a new intermediate **game 3** out of **game 2** by just cancelling the plaintext dependence in each step of **game 2** i.e. in the encryption queries and in the challenge, instead of $(i, t_j, x_{i,j})$ the adversary T_3

now just queries (i, t_j) and the challenger in **game 3** sends $F_{s_i}(t_j)$, if $b = 0$ and $h_{i,j} \leftarrow \mathcal{U}(G')$, if $b = 1$ to the adversary $\mathcal{T}_3$. The rest remains the same as in **game 2**.

It follows immediately that if there exists a successful adversary in **game 2**, then there is also a successful adversary in **game 3**.

Lemma 5. *For a security parameter κ, let $\mathcal{T}_2$ be an adversary in **game 2** with advantage $\nu_2(\kappa) > \mathsf{neg}(\kappa)$. Then there exists an adversary $\mathcal{T}_3$ in **game 3** with advantage $\nu_3(\kappa) > \mathsf{neg}(\kappa)$.*

Remark 1. *For comparison to the proof of AO2 in [24], we emphasise that in the reduction from AO2 to an intermediate problem (Proof of Theorem 1 in their work), an adversary $\mathcal{B}$ has to compute the ciphertexts $c_{i,j} = g^{x_{i,j}} H(t_j)^{s_i}$ for all users $i \in [n]$ and for all (!) time-steps t_j, since $\mathcal{B}$ does not know in advance for which $i \in [n]$ it will have to use the PRF $H(t_j)^{s_i}$ and for which $i \in [n]$ it will have to use random values. Thus, $\mathcal{B}$ has to program the random oracle H in order to know for all t_j the corresponding random number z_j with $H(t_j) = g^{z_j}$ (where g is a generator) for simulating the original AO2 game. In contrast, in our reduction for AO1, it is not necessary to program such an oracle, since the simulating adversary $\mathcal{T}_2$ knows in advance the set of uncorrupted users and, for all (!) t_j, it can already decide for which $i \in [n]$ it will use the PRF (which in our case is $t_j^{s_i}$ instead of $H(t_j)^{s_i}$) and for which $i \in [n]$ it will use a random value.*

In the next step, the problem of distinguishing the weak PRF family $\mathcal{F} = \{F_s : M \to G'\}_{s \in S}$ from a random function family has to be reduced to the problem of winning **game 3**. We use a hybrid argument.

Lemma 6. *For a security parameter κ, let $\mathcal{T}_3$ be an adversary in **game 3** with advantage $\nu_3(\kappa)$. Then $\nu_3(\kappa) \leqslant \mathsf{neg}(\kappa)$, if $\mathcal{F}$ is a weak PRF family.*

Proof. We define the following sequence of hybrid games, **game 3_l** with $l = 1, \ldots, u - 1$, for a ppt adversary $\mathcal{T}_3$.

Setup. As in **game 2** and **game 3**.
Queries. $\mathcal{T}_3$ is allowed to query multiple (i, t_j) with $i \in U, t_j \in T$ and the challenger returns the following: if $i \notin \{i_1, \ldots, i_{l+b}\}$, it sends $F_{s_i}(t_j)$ to $\mathcal{T}_3$; if $i \in \{i_1, \ldots, i_{l+b}\}$, it chooses

$$h_{1,j}, \ldots, h_{l-(1-b),j} \leftarrow \mathcal{U}(G'), \quad h_{l+b,j} := \prod_{i'=1}^{l+b} F_{s_{i_{i'}}}(t_j) \cdot \left(\prod_{i'=1}^{l-(1-b)} h_{i',j} \right)^{-1}$$

and sends the $h_{i,j}$ to $\mathcal{T}_3$.
Challenge. $\mathcal{T}_3$ chooses $t_{j^*} \in T$ such that no encryption query at t_{j^*} was made. The challenger chooses

$$h_{1,j^*}, \ldots, h_{l-(1-b),j^*} \leftarrow \mathcal{U}(G'), \quad h_{l+b,j^*} := \prod_{i'=1}^{l+b} F_{s_{i_{i'}}}(t_{j^*}) \cdot \left(\prod_{i'=1}^{l-(1-b)} h_{i',j^*} \right)^{-1}$$

and sends the following sequence to $\mathcal{T}_3$:

$$(h_{1,j^*}, \ldots, h_{l+b,j^*}, \mathsf{F}_{s_{i_{l+b+1}}}(t_{j^*}), \ldots, \mathsf{F}_{s_{i_u}}(t_{j^*})).$$

Queries. $\mathcal{T}_3$ can make the same type of queries as before with the restriction that no encryption query at t_{j^*} can be made.
Guess. $\mathcal{T}_3$ outputs a guess about b.

The adversary wins the game, if it correctly guesses b.[2]
It is immediate that **game 3_1** with $b = 0$ corresponds to the case $b = 0$ in **game 3** and **game 3_{u-1}** with $b = 1$ corresponds to the case $b = 1$ in **game 3**. Moreover the ciphertexts in **game 3_l** with $b = 1$ have the same distribution as the ciphertexts in **game 3_{l+1}** with $b = 0$. Therefore

$$\Pr[\mathcal{T}_3 \text{ wins } \mathbf{game } 3_{l+1} \,|\, b = 0] = \Pr[\mathcal{T}_3 \text{ loses } \mathbf{game } 3_l \,|\, b = 1].$$

Using an adversary $\mathcal{T}_3$ in **game 3_l** we construct an efficient ppt distinguisher $\mathcal{D}_{\mathrm{PRF}}$ which has access to an oracle $\mathcal{O}(\cdot) \leftarrow_R \{\mathsf{F}_{s'}(\cdot), \mathrm{rand}(\cdot)\}$, where $s' \leftarrow \mathcal{U}(S)$, $\mathsf{F}_{s'} : M \to G'$ is a weak PRF and $\mathrm{rand} : M \to G'$ is a random function. $\mathcal{D}_{\mathrm{PRF}}$ gets κ as input and proceeds as follows.

1. Choose $s_0 \leftarrow \mathcal{U}(S)$, generate pp and T with $t_j \leftarrow \mathcal{U}(M)$ for all $t_j \in T$. Compute $\mathsf{F}_{s_0}(t_j)$ for all $t_j \in T$.
2. Make oracle queries for t_j and receive $\mathcal{O}(t_j)$ for all $t_j \in T$.
3. Send $\kappa, \mathsf{pp}, T, s_0$ to $\mathcal{T}_3$.
4. Receive $U = \{i_1, \ldots, i_u\} \subseteq [n]$ from $\mathcal{T}_3$. For all $i \in [n] \setminus \{i_l, i_{l+1}\}$ choose $s_i \leftarrow \mathcal{U}(S)$. Send $(s_i)_{i \in [n] \setminus U}$ to $\mathcal{T}_3$.
5. **Queries.** If $\mathcal{T}_3$ queries (i, t_j) with $i \in U, t_j \in T$, then return the following: if $i \notin \{i_1, \ldots, i_{l+1}\}$, send $\mathsf{F}_{s_i}(t_j)$ to $\mathcal{T}_3$; if $i = i_{l+1}$, send $\mathcal{O}(t_j)$ to $\mathcal{T}_3$; if $i \in \{i_1, \ldots, i_l\}$, choose $h_{1,j}, \ldots, h_{l-1,j} \leftarrow \mathcal{U}(G')$ and

$$h_{l,j} := \left(\mathsf{F}_{s_0}(t_j) \cdot \mathcal{O}(t_j) \cdot \prod_{i'=1}^{l-1} h_{i',j} \cdot \prod_{i \in [n] \setminus \{i_1, \ldots, i_{l+1}\}} \mathsf{F}_{s_i}(t_j)\right)^{-1}$$

and send the $h_{i,j}$ to $\mathcal{T}_3$.
6. **Challenge.** $\mathcal{T}_3$ chooses $t_{j^*} \in T$ such that no encryption query at t_{j^*} was made. Choose $h_{1,j^*}, \ldots, h_{l-1,j^*} \leftarrow \mathcal{U}(G')$ and

$$h_{l,j^*} := \left(\mathsf{F}_{s_0}(t_{j^*}) \cdot \mathcal{O}(t_{j^*}) \cdot \prod_{i'=1}^{l-1} h_{i',j^*} \cdot \prod_{i \in [n] \setminus \{i_1, \ldots, i_{l+1}\}} \mathsf{F}_{s_i}(t_{j^*})\right)^{-1}$$

and send the sequence $(h_{1,j^*}, \ldots, h_{l,j^*}, \mathcal{O}(t_{j^*}), \mathsf{F}_{s_{i_{l+2}}}(t_{j^*}), \ldots, \mathsf{F}_{s_{i_u}}(t_{j^*}))$ to $\mathcal{T}_3$.
7. **Queries.** $\mathcal{T}_3$ can make the same type of queries as before with the restriction that no encryption query at t_{j^*} can be made.

---

[2] If u is random, we consider $l' = \min\{l, u - 1\}$ instead of l after the choice of u in the execution of **game 3_l** for all l.

8. **Guess.** $\mathcal{T}_3$ outputs a guess about whether the $l + 1^{\text{th}}$ element is random or pseudo-random. Output the same guess.

If $\mathcal{T}_3$ has output the correct guess about whether the $l + 1^{\text{th}}$ element is random or pseudo-random, then $\mathcal{D}_{\text{PRF}}$ can distinguish between $\mathsf{F}_{s'}(\cdot)$ and $\mathsf{rand}(\cdot)$. Now we prove this result formally and show that **game 3$_l$** is perfectly simulated by $\mathcal{D}_{\text{PRF}}$.

Case 1. Let $\mathcal{O}(\cdot) = \mathsf{F}_{s'}(\cdot)$. Define $s_{i_{l+1}} := s'$. Since S is a group, there exists an element s_{i_l} with $s_{i_l} = (s_0 * \divideontimes_{i \in [n] \backslash \{i_l\}} s_i)^{-1}$ and for all $t_j \in T$:

$$
\left(\mathsf{F}_{s_0}(t_j) \cdot \mathsf{F}_{s'}(t_j) \cdot \prod_{i \in [n] \backslash \{i_1, \ldots, i_{l+1}\}} \mathsf{F}_{s_i}(t_j) \right)^{-1} = \prod_{i'=1}^{l} \mathsf{F}_{s_{i_{i'}}}(t_j).
$$

Then for all $t_j \in T$, the value $h_{l,j}$ is equal to

$$
\left(\mathsf{F}_{s_0}(t_j) \cdot \prod_{i'=1}^{l-1} h_{i',j} \cdot \mathsf{F}_{s'}(t_j) \cdot \prod_{i \in [n] \backslash \{i_1, \ldots, i_{l+1}\}} \mathsf{F}_{s_i}(t_j) \right)^{-1} = \prod_{i'=1}^{l} \mathsf{F}_{s_{i_{i'}}}(t_j) \cdot \left(\prod_{i'=1}^{l-1} h_{i',j} \right)^{-1}.
$$

The distribution of the ciphertexts corresponds to the case in **game 3$_l$** with $b = 0$.

Case 2. Let $\mathcal{O}(\cdot) = \mathsf{rand}(\cdot)$. Define the random elements $h_{l+1,j} := \mathsf{rand}(t_j)$ for all $t_j \in T$. Since S is a group, there exists an element $s' \in S$ with $s' = (s_0 * \divideontimes_{i \in [n] \backslash \{i_l, i_{l+1}\}} s_i)^{-1}$. Let $s_{i_l} \leftarrow \mathcal{U}(S)$ and $s_{i_{l+1}} := s' * s_{i_l}^{-1}$. Then for all $t_j \in T$:

$$
\left(\mathsf{F}_{s_0}(t_j) \cdot \prod_{i \in [n] \backslash \{i_1, \ldots, i_{l+1}\}} \mathsf{F}_{s_i}(t_j) \right)^{-1} = \prod_{i'=1}^{l+1} \mathsf{F}_{s_{i_{i'}}}(t_j)
$$

and the value $h_{l,j}$ is equal to

$$
\left(\mathsf{F}_{s_0}(t_j) \cdot h_{l+1,j} \cdot \prod_{i'=1}^{l-1} h_{i',j} \cdot \prod_{i \in [n] \backslash \{i_1, \ldots, i_{l+1}\}} \mathsf{F}_{s_i}(t_j) \right)^{-1}
$$

and equivalently

$$
h_{l+1,j} = \prod_{i'=1}^{l+1} \mathsf{F}_{s_{i_{i'}}}(t_j) \cdot \left(\prod_{i'=1}^{l} h_{i',j} \right)^{-1}.
$$

The distribution of the ciphertexts corresponds to the case in **game 3$_l$** with $b = 1$.

Without loss of generality, let

$$
\Pr[\mathcal{T}_3 \text{ wins } \textbf{game 3}_l \, | \, b = 0] \geqslant \Pr[\mathcal{T}_3 \text{ loses } \textbf{game 3}_l \, | \, b = 1].
$$

In total we obtain

$$\Pr[\mathcal{T}_3 \text{ wins } \mathbf{game\ 3}_l \,|\, b = 0] - \Pr[\mathcal{T}_3 \text{ loses } \mathbf{game\ 3}_l \,|\, b = 1]$$
$$= \Pr[\mathcal{D}_{\mathsf{PRF}}^{\mathsf{F}_{s'}(\cdot)}(\kappa) = 1] - \Pr[\mathcal{D}_{\mathsf{PRF}}^{\mathsf{rand}(\cdot)}(\kappa) = 1].$$

This expression is negligible by the pseudo-randomness of $\mathsf{F}_{s'}(\cdot)$ on uniformly chosen input. Therefore, the advantage of $\mathcal{T}_3$ in winning **game 3**$_l$ is negligible. Finally, by a hybrid argument we have:

$$\Pr[\mathcal{T}_3 \text{ wins } \mathbf{game\ 3}]$$
$$= \frac{1}{2}(\Pr[\mathcal{T}_3 \text{ wins } \mathbf{game\ 3} \,|\, b = 0] + \Pr[\mathcal{T}_3 \text{ wins } \mathbf{game\ 3} \,|\, b = 1])$$
$$= \frac{1}{2}(\Pr[\mathcal{T}_3 \text{ wins } \mathbf{game\ 3}_1 \,|\, b = 0] + \Pr[\mathcal{T}_3 \text{ wins } \mathbf{game\ 3}_{u-1} \,|\, b = 1])$$
$$= \frac{1}{2} + \frac{1}{2}(\Pr[\mathcal{T}_3 \text{ wins } \mathbf{game\ 3}_1 \,|\, b = 0] - \Pr[\mathcal{T}_3 \text{ loses } \mathbf{game\ 3}_{u-1} \,|\, b = 1])$$
$$= \frac{1}{2} + \frac{1}{2}\sum_{l=1}^{u-1}\Pr[\mathcal{T}_3 \text{ wins } \mathbf{game\ 3}_l \,|\, b = 0] - \Pr[\mathcal{T}_3 \text{ loses } \mathbf{game\ 3}_l \,|\, b = 1]$$
$$= \frac{1}{2} + (u - 1) \cdot \mathsf{neg}(\kappa).$$

$\square$

We can now complete the proof of Theorem 3.

Proof (Proof of Theorem 3). By Lemmas 4–6:
$$\nu_1(\kappa) = 2 \cdot \nu_2(\kappa) = 2 \cdot \nu_3(\kappa) = 2 \cdot (u - 1) \cdot \mathsf{neg}(\kappa) < 2 \cdot n \cdot \mathsf{neg}(\kappa) = \mathsf{neg}(\kappa). \square$$

4 The Constructions

In this section, we provide two different PSA schemes that use a key-homomorphic weak PRF. The first construction is based on the DDH assumption and is a modification of the scheme from [24]. We will compare the practical performances of these schemes. The second construction is based on the DLWE assumption and incorporates a differentially private mechanism with discrete Gaussian noise.

4.1 A DDH-Based PSA Scheme

We provide an instantiation of a secure PSA scheme consisting of efficient algorithms. It is constructed from a DDH-based key-homomorphic weak PRF. Hence, its security is based on the DDH assumption making it comparable to the scheme from [24].

Example 2. *Let $q > m \cdot n$ and $p = 2 \cdot q + 1$ be large primes. Let furthermore $G = \mathbb{Z}_{p^2}^*, S = \mathbb{Z}_p, M = G' = \mathrm{Res}_{p^2}(p-1)$ and $g \in \mathbb{Z}_{p^2}^*$ with $\mathrm{ord}(g) = p$. Then g generates the group $M = G' = \mathrm{Res}_{p^2}(p-1)$ of $(p-1)$th-residues modulo p^2. In this group, we make the assumption that the DDH problem is hard. Then we define*

- *Let $\mathsf{pp} = (g, p)$. Choose keys $s_1, \ldots, s_n \leftarrow \mathcal{U}(\mathbb{Z}_{pq})$ and $s_0 \equiv -\sum_{i=1}^{n} s_i \bmod pq$. Let $T \subset M$ with $|T| = \lambda$, i.e. t_j is a power of g for every $t_j \in T$, $j = 1, \ldots, \lambda$.*
- *$\mathsf{F}_{s_i}(t_j) \equiv t_j^{s_i} \bmod p^2$. This is a weak PRF under the DDH assumption in $\mathrm{Res}_{p^2}(p-1)$ (which can be shown using similar arguments as in [19]).*
- *$\varphi(x_{i_j}) \equiv 1 + p \cdot x_{i,j} \bmod p^2$, where $-m \leqslant x_{i,j} \leqslant m$. (It is immediate that φ is homomorphic and injective over $\{-mn, \ldots, mn\}$.)*

For decryption and aggregation, compute $V_j \in \{1 - p \cdot mn, \ldots, 1 + p \cdot mn\}$ with

$$V_j \equiv \mathsf{F}_{s_0}(t_j) \cdot \prod_{i=1}^{n} \mathsf{F}_{s_i}(t_j) \cdot \varphi(x_{i,j}) \equiv \prod_{i=1}^{n}(1 + p \cdot x_{i,j})$$

$$\equiv 1 + p \cdot \sum_{i=1}^{n} x_{i,j} + p^2 \cdot \sum_{i,i' \in [n], i' \neq i} x_{i,j} x_{i',j} + \ldots + p^n \cdot \prod_{i=1}^{n} x_{i,j}$$

$$\equiv 1 + p \cdot \sum_{i=1}^{n} x_{i,j} \bmod p^2$$

and decrypt $\sum_{i=1}^{n} x_{i,j} = \frac{1}{p}(V_j - 1)$ over the integers.

Remark 2. *We argue that the DDH assumption is reasonable in the group $\mathrm{Res}_{p^2}(p-1)$. The order of this group is p and it is cyclic. In this group, all elements taken modulo p are 1. I.e. a possible computation of the discrete logarithm modulo p will always yield 0 and thus not provide any chance to decide whether $w \equiv g^{xy} \bmod p^2$ or $w \equiv g^z \bmod p^2$ given a generator g and g^x, g^y, w. Also the simple Legendre attack, i.e. decide whether $w \equiv g^{xy} \bmod p^2$ or $w \equiv g^z \bmod p^2$ by computing and comparing the Legendre symbols of g^x, g^y, w over p^2, does not work here, since $p - 1 = 2q$ and hence, all elements in $\mathrm{Res}_{p^2}(p-1)$ are also quadratic residues. Thus, the Legendre symbol of g^v over p^2 is 1 for all v and this attack does not provide any way to distinguish g^{xy} from g^z.*

Remark 3. *In the random oracle model, the construction shown in Example 2 achieves the stronger notion of AO2. For details, see the proof in Section A of the appendix in [24]. The same proof can be applied to our instantiation by simply replacing the map φ involved and using a strong version of the PRF F.*

Differential Privacy. In connection with a differentially private mechanism, a PSA scheme assures that the analyst is only able to learn a noisy aggregate of users' data (as close as possible to the real answer) and nothing else. More specifically, for preserving differential privacy, it would be sufficient to add a single copy of (properly distributed) noise Y to the aggregated statistics. Since we deal with a distributed setting, the noise cannot be added, once the aggregate has been computed. Hence, the users themselves have to generate and add noise to their original data in such a way that the sum of the errors has the same distribution as Y. For this purpose, we see two different approaches. In the first one, with small probability, a user adds noise sufficient to preserve the privacy of the entire statistics. This probability is calibrated in such a way only one of the n users is actually expected to add noise at all. Shi et al. [24] investigate this method using the geometric mechanism by Ghosh et al. [10]. In the second approach, each user generates noise of small variance, such that the sum of all noisy terms suffices to preserve differential privacy of the aggregate.[3] To achieve this goal, we need a *discrete* probability distribution which is *closed under convolution* and is known to provide differential privacy. The binomial mechanism by Dwork et al. [8] and the discrete Gaussian mechanism introduced in the next subsection serve these purposes.[4] Note that due to the use of a computationally secure protocol, we achieve differential privacy also only against ppt adversaries. For this case, the notion of computational differential privacy was introduced in [18]. We can prove a composition theorem showing that the use of a differentially private mechanism within a secure PSA scheme preserves computational differential privacy. This is left for a follow-up work.

Comparison of DDH-Based Schemes. Whereas the PRF in Example 1 is similar to the one used in Example 2 (the underlying group G is $\mathbb{Z}_p^*$ rather than $\mathbb{Z}_{p^2}^*$), the aggregational function is defined by $\varphi(x_{i,j}) = g^{x_{i,j}} \bmod p$, which requires to solve the discrete logarithm modulo p for decrypting. In contrast, our efficient construction only requires a subtraction and a division over the integers. Note that for a given p, the running time of the decryption in our scheme does not depend on m, so it provides a small running time, even if m is super-polynomially large.

We compare the practical running times for encryption and decryption of the scheme from [24] with the algorithms of our scheme in Tables 1a and b, respectively. Here, let m denote the size of the plaintext space. Encryption is compared at different security levels with $m = 1$. For comparing the decryption time, we fix the security level and the number of users and let m be variable.

All algorithms are executed on an Intel Core i5, 64-bit CPU at 2.67 GHz. We compare the schemes at the same security level, assuming that the DDH problem modulo p is as hard as modulo p^2, i.e. we use the same value for p in both schemes. For different bit-lengths of p, we observe that the encryption of our scheme is roughly 4 times slower than the encryption of the scheme from [24]. The running time of our decryption algorithm is widely dominated by the

---

[3] One can assume that corrupted users will not add any noise to their data in order to help the analyst to compromise the privacy of the remaining users. For simplicity, we ignore this issue here.

[4] Due to the use of a cryptographic protocol, the plaintexts have to be discrete. This is the reason why we use discrete distributions for generating noise.

Table 1. Time measurements of the schemes for different parameters

(a) Encryption			
Length of p	1024-bit	2048-bit	4096-bit
[24]	1.1 ms	7.5 ms	57.0 ms
This work	3.9 ms	29.4 ms	225.0 ms

(b) Decryption (2048 bit, $n = 1000$)			
m	10^1	10^2	10^3
[24], brute-force	0.24 s	2.67 s	28.97 s
This work	0.08 s	0.08 s	0.09 s

aggregation phase. Therefore it is clear, that it linearly depends on n. The same holds for the brute-force decryption of the scheme in [24], since the range for the discrete logarithm also linearly grows with n. Using a 2048-bit prime and fixing $n = 1000$, the running time of the decryption in our scheme is less than $0.1\,\mathrm{s}$ for varying values of m. In contrast, the time for brute-force decryption in [24] grows roughly linearly in m.

4.2 A DLWE-Based PSA Scheme

We construct a secure PSA scheme from a weak PRF construction based on Theorem 2 that automatically preserves DP. We analyse the privacy and accuracy guarantees of this scheme and also the trade-off between security and accuracy.

Example 3. *We can build an instantiation of Theorem 3 (without correct decryption) based on the DLWE problem as follows. Set $S = M = \mathbb{Z}_q^\kappa, G = \mathbb{Z}_q$, choose $s_i \leftarrow \mathcal{U}(\mathbb{Z}_q^\kappa)$ for all $i = 1, \ldots, n$ and $s_0 = -\sum_{i=1}^n s_i$, set $\mathsf{F}_{s_i}(t_j) = \langle t_j, s_i \rangle + e_{i,j}$, such that $e_{i,j} \leftarrow D(\nu/n)$ with parameter $\nu/n = 2\kappa/\pi$ (by Theorems 1 and 2, this is a so-called randomised weak pseudo-random function as described in [1] and in [2]), and let φ be the identity function. Therefore $\langle t_j, s_i \rangle + e_{i,j} + d_{i,j} = c_{i,j} \leftarrow \mathsf{PSAEnc}_{s_i}(t_j, d_{i,j})$ for data value $d_{i,j} \in \mathbb{Z}_q$, $i = 1, \ldots, n$. The decryption function is defined by*

$$\mathsf{PSADec}_{s_0}(t_j, c_{1,j}, \ldots, c_{n,j}) = \langle t_j, s_0 \rangle + \sum_{i=1}^n c_{i,j} = \langle t_j, s_0 \rangle + \sum_{i=1}^n \mathsf{F}_{s_i}(t_j) + d_{i,j}$$

$$= \sum_{i=1}^n d_{i,j} + \sum_{i=1}^n e_{i,j}.$$

Thus, the decryption is not perfectly correct anymore, but yields a noisy aggregate. The associated DLWE problem is hard and the above scheme is secure.

Remark 4. *The original result by Regev [22] states that the LWE problem is hard in the set $\mathbb{T} = \mathbb{R}/\mathbb{Z}$ when the noise is distributed according to the continuous Gaussian distribution modulo 1. Although the continuous Gaussian distribution is reproducible as well, it does not seem to fit well for a DLWE-based PSA scheme. For data processing reasons, the values would have to be discretised. Therefore the resulting noise would follow a distribution which is not reproducible* *in general. However, in [5] it was shown that the sum of n discrete Gaussians each with parameter σ^2 is statistically close to a discrete Gaussian with parameter $\nu = n\sigma^2$, if $\sigma > \sqrt{n}\eta_\varepsilon(\mathcal{L})$ for some smoothing parameter $\eta_\varepsilon(\mathcal{L})$ of the underlying lattice $\mathcal{L}$.*

Differential Privacy. We show that for the final aggregate $\sum_{i=1}^{n} d_{i,j} + e_{i,j}$ in Example 3, (ϵ, δ)-DP is preserved. First, assume due to Remark 4 that $\sum_{i=1}^{n} e_{i,j}$ is distributed according to $D(\nu)$ if the $e_{i,j}$ are i.i.d. according to $D(\nu/n)$.

Theorem 7 (Discrete Gaussian Mechanism). *Let $0 < \epsilon \leqslant 2, \delta < 1$. For all databases $D \in \mathcal{D}^n$, the randomised mechanism $\mathcal{A}(D) := f(D) + Y$ preserves (ϵ, δ)-DP with respect to any query f with sensitivity $S(f)$, if Y is distributed according to $D(\nu)$ with*

$$\nu = \frac{2S(f)^2}{\epsilon^2} \cdot \left(\log\left(\frac{2S(f)}{\epsilon\delta} \right) + \frac{\epsilon}{2} \right).$$

Proof. Let $D_0, D_1 \in \mathcal{D}^n$ be adjacent databases with $|f(D_0) - f(D_1)| \leqslant S(f)$. The largest ratio between $\Pr[\mathcal{A}(D_0) = R]$ and $\Pr[\mathcal{A}(D_1) = R]$ is reached when $k := R - f(D_1) - S(f) = R - f(D_0) \geqslant 0$, where R is any possible output of $\mathcal{A}$. Then for all possible outputs R of $\mathcal{A}$:

$$\frac{\Pr[\mathcal{A}(D_0) = R]}{\Pr[\mathcal{A}(D_1) = R]} = \frac{\Pr[Y = k]}{\Pr[Y = k + S(f)]} = \frac{\exp(-k^2/(2\nu))}{\exp(-(k + S(f))^2/(2\nu))}$$

$$= \exp(((k + S(f))^2 - k^2)/(2\nu)) = \exp((2kS(f) + S(f)^2)/(2\nu))$$

which is $\leqslant \exp(\epsilon)$ if $k \leqslant (\epsilon\nu)/S(f) - S(f)/2 =: B$. We can bound the ratio ν/B by $2S(f)/\epsilon$. Now we bound the complementary probability:

$$\Pr[Y > B] = \frac{1}{c_\nu} \cdot \sum_{x=B+1}^{\infty} \exp(-x^2/(2\nu)) \leqslant \frac{\nu}{B \cdot c_\nu} \cdot \int_B^{\infty} \frac{x}{\nu} \cdot \exp(-x^2/(2\nu)) dx$$

$$< \frac{\nu}{B} \cdot \exp(-B^2/(2\nu)) < \frac{2S(f)}{\epsilon} \cdot \exp(-\epsilon^2\nu/(2S(f)^2) + \epsilon/2),$$

since $c_\nu > 1$. This expression is equal δ for $\nu = 2S(f)^2(\log(2S(f)/(\epsilon\delta)) + \epsilon/2)/\epsilon^2$. □

We compute the (α, β)-accuracy of the discrete Gaussian mechanism as $\beta = \Pr[|E| > \alpha] < 2 \cdot \frac{\nu}{\alpha} \cdot \exp(-\alpha^2/(2\nu)) \leqslant \nu \cdot \exp(-\alpha^2/(2\nu))$ for $\alpha \geqslant 2$ and therefore $\alpha \leqslant \sqrt{2\nu \log(\nu/\beta)} = \tilde{O}(S(f)/\epsilon)$.

This bound is similar to standard solutions (e.g. [8,9]), especially to the binomial mechanism, that would be a standard solution for (ϵ, δ)-DP in the distributed setting.

Hence, we have two bounds on ν: one for security and one for (ϵ, δ)-DP. Assume all users generate their noise according to the required security level as in Example 3. We can compute the level of (ϵ, δ)-DP that is thus preserved. Therefore we set the two bounds on ν to be equal and solve for ϵ:

$$2n\kappa/\pi = 2S(f)^2(\log(2S(f)/(\epsilon\delta)) + \epsilon/2)/\epsilon^2$$
$$\Leftrightarrow \epsilon = \epsilon(\kappa) \leqslant S(f)\pi\sqrt{(\log(2S(f)/\delta^2) + 1)/(n\kappa)}$$

for $\delta \leqslant \epsilon \leqslant 2$. In addition to a privacy/accuracy trade-off, there is also a security/accuracy trade-off depending on κ and n, since $\alpha = \tilde{O}(S(f)/\epsilon) = \tilde{O}(\sqrt{n\kappa})$.[5]

5 Conclusion

We investigated cryptographic methods for privacy-preserving data analysis in the distributed setting and showed, that a secure PSA scheme for time-series data can be built upon any key-homomorphic weak PRF. Opposed to previous work, our proof works in the standard model and our security reduction is tighter. We provided two instantiations of this result. The first PSA scheme is based on the DDH assumption and has an efficient decryption algorithm even for a super-polynomially large data universe, as opposed to previous work. The other PSA scheme is based on the DLWE assumption with an inherent differentially private mechanism, leading to the first lattice-based secure PSA scheme. An open challenge is to prove that the composition of a PSA scheme with a differentially private mechanism provides computational differential privacy. Another interesting challenge is the following: due to Remark 4, in our DLWE-based scheme, we need $\nu > n^2\eta_\varepsilon(\mathcal{L})^2$ for reproducibility of the error distribution which is in turn necessary for differential privacy. Thus, ν depends on n^2. It is desirable to construct a lattice-based PSA scheme, where the application of a differentially private mechanism is independent of the number of users.

References

1. Applebaum, B., Cash, D., Peikert, C., Sahai, A.: Fast cryptographic primitives and circular-secure encryption based on hard learning problems. In: Halevi, S. (ed.) CRYPTO 2009. LNCS, vol. 5677, pp. 595–618. Springer, Heidelberg (2009). https://doi.org/10.1007/978-3-642-03356-8_35
2. Banerjee, A., Peikert, C., Rosen, A.: Pseudorandom functions and lattices. In: Pointcheval, D., Johansson, T. (eds.) EUROCRYPT 2012. LNCS, vol. 7237, pp. 719–737. Springer, Heidelberg (2012). https://doi.org/10.1007/978-3-642-29011-4_42
3. Benhamouda, F., Joye, M., Libert, B.: A new framework for privacy-preserving aggregation of time-series data. ACM Trans. Inf. Syst. Secur. 18(3), 21 (2016)
4. Blum, A., Ligett, K., Roth, A.: A learning theory approach to non-interactive database privacy. In: Proceedings of STOC 2008, pp. 609–618 (2008)
5. Boneh, D., Freeman, D.M.: Linearly homomorphic signatures over binary fields and new tools for lattice-based signatures. In: Catalano, D., Fazio, N., Gennaro, R., Nicolosi, A. (eds.) PKC 2011. LNCS, vol. 6571, pp. 1–16. Springer, Heidelberg (2011). https://doi.org/10.1007/978-3-642-19379-8_1

---

[5] For sake of comparability, we disregard here the condition for reproducibility of $D(\nu)$.

6. Cramer, R., Shoup, V.: Universal hash proofs and a paradigm for adaptive chosen ciphertext secure public-key encryption. In: Knudsen, L.R. (ed.) EUROCRYPT 2002. LNCS, vol. 2332, pp. 45–64. Springer, Heidelberg (2002). https://doi.org/10.1007/3-540-46035-7_4

7. Dwork, C.: Differential privacy: a survey of results. In: Agrawal, M., Du, D., Duan, Z., Li, A. (eds.) TAMC 2008. LNCS, vol. 4978, pp. 1–19. Springer, Heidelberg (2008). https://doi.org/10.1007/978-3-540-79228-4_1

8. Dwork, C., Kenthapadi, K., McSherry, F., Mironov, I., Naor, M.: Our data, ourselves: privacy via distributed noise generation. In: Vaudenay, S. (ed.) EUROCRYPT 2006. LNCS, vol. 4004, pp. 486–503. Springer, Heidelberg (2006). https://doi.org/10.1007/11761679_29

9. Dwork, C., McSherry, F., Nissim, K., Smith, A.: Calibrating noise to sensitivity in private data analysis. In: Halevi, S., Rabin, T. (eds.) TCC 2006. LNCS, vol. 3876, pp. 265–284. Springer, Heidelberg (2006). https://doi.org/10.1007/11681878_14

10. Ghosh, A., Roughgarden, T., Sundararajan, M.: Universally utility-maximizing privacy mechanisms. In: Proceedings of STOC 2009, pp. 351–360 (2009)

11. Goldreich, O., Goldwasser, S., Micali, S.: How to construct random functions. J. ACM 33(4), 792–807 (1986)

12. Joye, M., Libert, B.: A scalable scheme for privacy-preserving aggregation of time-series data. In: Sadeghi, A.-R. (ed.) FC 2013. LNCS, vol. 7859, pp. 111–125. Springer, Heidelberg (2013). https://doi.org/10.1007/978-3-642-39884-1_10

13. Li, N., Li, T., Venkatasubramanian, S.: t-closeness: privacy beyond k-anonymity and l-diversity. In: Proceedings of ICDE 2007, pp. 106–115 (2007)

14. Lindell, Y., Pinkas, B.: Secure multiparty computation for privacy-preserving data mining. J. Priv. Confidentiality 1(1), 5 (2009)

15. Machanavajjhala, A., Kifer, D., Gehrke, J., Venkitasubramaniam, M.: L-diversity: privacy beyond k-anonymity. In: Proceedings of Knowledge Discovery Data 2007 (2007)

16. McSherry, F., Talwar, K.: Mechanism design via differential privacy. In: Proceedings of FOCS 2007, pp. 94–103 (2007)

17. Micciancio, D., Mol, P.: Pseudorandom knapsacks and the sample complexity of LWE search-to-decision reductions. In: Rogaway, P. (ed.) CRYPTO 2011. LNCS, vol. 6841, pp. 465–484. Springer, Heidelberg (2011). https://doi.org/10.1007/978-3-642-22792-9_26

18. Mironov, I., Pandey, O., Reingold, O., Vadhan, S.: Computational differential privacy. In: Halevi, S. (ed.) CRYPTO 2009. LNCS, vol. 5677, pp. 126–142. Springer, Heidelberg (2009). https://doi.org/10.1007/978-3-642-03356-8_8

19. Naor, M., Pinkas, B., Reingold, O.: Distributed pseudo-random functions and KDCs. In: Stern, J. (ed.) EUROCRYPT 1999. LNCS, vol. 1592, pp. 327–346. Springer, Heidelberg (1999). https://doi.org/10.1007/3-540-48910-X_23

20. Naor, M., Reingold, O.: Synthesizers and their application to the parallel construction of pseudo-random functions. In: Proceedings of FOCS 1995, pp. 170–181 (1995)

21. Peikert, C.: Public-key cryptosystems from the worst-case shortest vector problem: extended abstract. In: Proceedings of STOC 2009, pp. 333–342 (2009)

22. Regev, O.: On lattices, learning with errors, random linear codes, and cryptography. In: Proceedings of STOC 2005, pp. 84–93 (2005)

23. Samarati, P., Sweeney, L.: Generalizing data to provide anonymity when disclosing information (abstract). In: Proceedings of PODS 1998, p. 188 (1998)
24. Shi, E., Hubert Chan, T.-H., Rieffel, E.G., Chow, R., Song, D.: Privacy-preserving aggregation of time-series data. In: Proceedings of NDSS 2011 (2011)
25. Thiruvenkatachar, V.R., Nanjundiah, T.S.: Inequalities concerning bessel functions and orthogonal polynomials. Proc. Indian Nat. Acad. Part A **33**, 373–384 (1951)

The Oblivious Machine
Or: How to Put the C into MPC

Marcel Keller[(✉)]

Department of Computer Science, University of Bristol, Bristol, UK
mks.keller@gmail.com

Abstract. We present an oblivious machine, a concrete notion for a multiparty random access machine (RAM) computation and a toolchain to allow the efficient execution of general programs written in a subset of C that allows RAM-model computation over the integers. The machine only leaks the list of possible instructions and the running time. Our work is based on the oblivious array for secret-sharing-based multiparty computation by Keller and Scholl (Asiacrypt '14). This means that we only incur a polylogarithmic overhead over the execution on a CPU.

We describe an implementation of our construction using the Clang compiler from the LLVM project and the SPDZ protocol by Damgård et al. (Crypto '12). The latter provides active security against a dishonest majority and works in the preprocessing model. The online phase clock rate of the resulting machine is 41 Hz for a memory size of 1024 64-bit integers and 2.2 Hz for a memory of 2^{20} integers. Both timings have been taken for two parties in a local network. Similar work by other authors has only been in the semi-honest setting.

To further showcase our toolchain, we implemented and benchmarked private regular expression matching. Matching a string of length 1024 against a regular expression with 69270 transitions as a finite state machine takes seven hours online time, of which more than six hours are devoted to loading the reusable program.

Keywords: Multiparty computation · Random-access machine · Oblivious RAM · Compilers · Regular expression matching

1 Introduction

Multiparty computation (MPC) refers to a technique that allows a set of parties to compute on data held by them privately without revealing anything to each other, bar the desired result. The feasibility has been established for some time in two lines of work, Yao's garbled circuits [22] and secret-sharing-based multiparty computation [1,4,11]. The former allow two parties to compute binary circuits, and the latter enables any number of parties to compute arithmetic circuits

Electronic supplementary material The online version of this chapter (https://doi.org/10.1007/978-3-030-25283-0_15) contains supplementary material, which is available to authorized users.

T. Lange and O. Dunkelman (Eds.): LATINCRYPT 2017, LNCS 11368, pp. 271–288, 2019.
https://doi.org/10.1007/978-3-030-25283-0_15

over finite fields or rings. In this paper, we focus on secret-sharing-based MPC. There are various schemes differing in the degree of adversarial power such as the number of corrupted parties or the kind of corruption. However, all of them implement the so-called arithmetic black box.

While circuits are complete in the sense that they allow any computation, they generally incur an overhead over random access machine (RAM) programs. This overhead is related to the fact that, to access an array by a data-dependent index, a circuit needs to access the whole array. In addition, accessing only parts of such an array would reveal possibly sensitive data. A first step to remedy this was taken by Ostrovsky and Shoup [26], who proposed the oblivious random access machine (ORAM) as a mean to hide the access pattern of a memory-restricted client on a server with larger memory. They briefly mention the possibility of using their scheme in the context of secure two-party computation with one party holding the encrypted server memory. Damgård et al. [7] on the other hand suggested to secret share the server memory. However, due to the lack of efficient ORAM schemes, no concrete schemes or implementations emerged.

Only following the proposal of tree-based ORAM by Shi et al. [28], practical instantiations of oblivious data structures for multiparty computation have been proposed, both for Yao's garbled circuits [12,23,34] and secret-sharing based MPC [17]. The former only provide security against a semi-honest adversary, while the latter does so against a malicious adversary. These works essentially provide an implementation of an oblivious array with efficient access, that is, one access to a secret index only incurs polylogarithmic cost (in the size of the array). Based on the oblivious array, the latter work goes on to implement an oblivious priority queue, which is then used for Dijkstra's algorithm, as well as the Gale-Shapley algorithm for stable matching. In the case of Dijkstra's algorithm, it turns out that the algorithm has to be reformulated to be implemented as a circuit with access to oblivious data structures.

On the theoretical side, Gentry et al. [10] proposed garbled RAM, which combines Yao's garbled circuit and ORAM. They present two solutions, one based on identity-based encryption, and the other based on revocable pseudorandom functions. Both approaches do not seem to be as practical because they involve the mentioned cryptographic operations being executed in a garbled circuit. In comparison, the works presented in the previous paragraph use relatively lightweight operations.

1.1   Our Contribution

In this work, we present a practical instantiation of an oblivious machine in the arithmetic black-box model, that is, an actively secure MPC protocol that allows efficient, oblivious computation in the RAM model. By oblivious computation we mean that the sequence of instructions executed is not revealed to the adversary, only the running time is. This enables the compilation of a subset of ANSI C (including conditional expressions, loops, arrays, and structs) and thus the execution of many algorithms in C with only polylogarithmic overhead. To the best of our knowledge, we are the first to implement this. We also present a theoretical model of an oblivious machine.

While previous works [12,23] have introduced the concept of secure RAM-model computation, their notions remain rather abstract. Furthermore, Liu et al. [23] call general secure RAM-model computation "relatively inefficient" because one has to execute the universal next-instruction circuit, which must interpret every possible instruction. By contrast, the motivation of this work is to put a price tag on such general secure RAM-model computation.

Our construction essentially uses the oblivious array by Keller and Scholl [17] for storing data and code, and for every step, it executes all possible instructions in a way that minimizes data accesses. While this incurs some overhead, we believe that it is more efficient than using a one instruction set machine because such a machine will inevitably increase the length of programs and thus the length of memory accesses, which we have found to be the most expensive part in our implementation. Instead, we execute all possible instructions in every computation step and then obliviously select the desired result. Since the number of possible instructions is relatively low, the most efficient oblivious selection simply computes the inner product with a vector that contains 1 in one entry and 0 otherwise.

As an application of our concept, we highlight the case of regular expression matching. Regular expressions can be implemented as finite state machines and thus in the RAM model. Kerschbaum [18] presented two MPC protocols for regular expression matching, a secure one and one with leakage. They have complexity in $O(nml)$ and $O(knm^2 + ln)$ for m states, n symbols, string length l and some security parameter k. The security of our solution lies in between because it only leaks the total running time, which is less than every repetition of a previous state being leaked by Kerschbaum's algorithm. With a complexity in $O(nm \log^3 nm + ln(\log^3 nm + \log^3 l))$, our approach beats the previous work on regular expressions that are complex enough, that is, if $km \gg \log^3 nm$ and $km^2 \gg l(\log^3 nm + \log^3 l)$. Using the same approach using a regular CPU has complexity in $O(nm + ln)$ for loading and executing the program. Launchbury et al. [20] also mention an implementation of regular expression matching with multiparty computation. From their description, we estimate that their protocol is similar to the secure one by Kerschbaum.

With MPC, potentially corrupted parties are involved in any computation. While the oblivious machine obscures the instruction currently executed as well as the data accessed, it is inherent that the adversary learns the amount of computation. In our case, this is the number of instructions being executed. A straightforward way to obscure this to some extent is to define a maximal number of instructions and then execute exactly this many steps. However, this can only increase the computation time. We believe that there still is a use case for oblivious computation leaking the total time, for example, if the same program is not executed enough times to mount a timing attack.

Since our oblivious machine does not reveal information about the code other than the set of possible instructions, and code can also be input in secret, it also suits private function evaluation (PFE). Informally, private function evaluation allows two parties to compute a function known to one party on data known by another party without revealing either input to the other party. Previous work on PFE focuses on circuits, such as the solution by Mohassel et al. [25]. Their solution only incurs a constant overhead for circuits. While our solution for RAM-model computation comes with polylogarithmic overhead, it is the first such proposal to the best of our knowledge.

1.2   Related Work

Keller and Scholl [17], while providing much of the foundation of our work, do not consider general oblivious computation but stick to oblivious data structures and specific applications thereof. As an example, they propose a secure computation of Dijkstra's algorithm involving a manual rewrite of the algorithm. In contrast, our scheme allows to execute any algorithm written in C.

Similarly, SCVM [23] and ObliVM [24] are two-party computation implementations that use ORAM for oblivious arrays, but they do not fully support the RAM model. For example, when branching on secret variables, both branches are executed. This makes these approaches infeasible to use with programs using GOTO statements such as the ones output by the regular expression compiler described in Sect. 4. Furthermore, both SCM and ObliVM do not hide the program being executed.

Wang et al. [34] briefly mention the idea of implementing a universal RAM instruction as a circuit. However, they do not present a more detailed account or experimental figures. In an independent preprint [33], Wang et al. propose a compiler of bytecode for a particular processor (MIPS) to garbled circuits. While their independent work shares some characteristics with ours, there are differences in various aspects: First, they analyze a program to find out at which time in the execution a memory access might be necessary. While this reduces the number of expensive ORAM computations, this is limited to relatively small programs because it requires the computation of every possible execution path of the program. Furthermore, this inhibits private function evaluation. In comparison, our approach works for every program because it allows memory accesses in every step.

Secondly, Wang et al.'s garbled circuit implementation only provides semihonest security compared to malicious security in our case. The latter also explains the offline phase that is about 100 times more expensive than the online phase using the recent improvement [16] to the offline phase of SPDZ.

Songhori et al. [29] propose TinyGarble, a framework for garbled circuit computation. While they claim to provide the first scalable emulation of a general purpose processor, they explicitly do not support ORAM, which incurs a linear overhead in contrast to the polylogarithmic overhead of our construction. Furthermore, the examples they present (sum, Hamming distance, comparison, multiplication, matrix multiplication, AES, and SHA3) do not require branching. Similarly, there are several works presenting compilers from high-level languages to two- or multiparty computation [13,14,19,35,36], none of which consider proper branching on secret values. While the authors of Obliv-C [35] consider ORAM, they present examples (edit distance computation and millionaire's problem) that do not require ORAM.

Our oblivious machine is related to the concept of an oblivious Turing machine, which is a Turing machine where the movement of the head only depends on the time. Pippenger and Fischer [27] showed that any Turing machine can be converted into an oblivious one incurring only logarithmic overhead. However, the best known result for converting a RAM program with running time T to a Turing machine results in a running time in $O(T^2)$ [5]. Hence, this transformation is not suitable to achieve polylogarithmic overhead for RAM programs.

In the area of homomorphic encryption, Gentry et al. [9] have proposed to use ORAM to enable private queries to an encrypted database. They do not target general computation however.

Ben-Sasson et al. [2] proposed TinyRAM, a system for succinct verifiable non-interactive arguments to prove the correct execution of C programs. The setting of verifiable computation differs considerably from multiparty computation. In the former, a server can compute a RAM program using a regular CPU and then has to prove to prove this correctness of the computation. In the setting of MPC, we are concerned with the computation of the RAM program itself.

2   From Oblivious Arrays to Oblivious Computation

In this section, we summarize Appendix B of the full version [15].

Keller and Scholl [17] present an implementation of oblivious arrays for any MPC scheme that provides an arithmetic black box while the security properties of the underlying scheme remain intact. An oblivious array in the context of MPC is an array that can be accessed by a secret index without revealing it. Oblivious RAM allows to implement an oblivious array with polylogarithmic access cost.

Even with the result above, all known basic MPC schemes are data-oblivious but leak which operation is executed. This can be avoided by executing a set of operations in every step of the computation and obliviously selecting the actual result. Storing this private selectors (or instructions) in an oblivious array and having a secret program counter point at the current one, we get the oblivious equivalent of a random access machine because the secret program counter can be changed obliviously as well. We call this the oblivious machine. It allows branching (e.g., "if" statements) on secret data without revealing it except the leakage through the total computation time.

Furthermore, the properties of the oblivious machine allow to implement private function evaluation, where the code is only known to one party. This is possible because it is straightforward to initialize the oblivious array holding the instructions with secret inputs from one party.

Complexity. The amount of communication and computation depends on the cost of accessing the oblivious array. Keller and Scholl [17] report an implementation based on Path ORAM [30] with access complexity in $O(\log^3 N)$ for arrays of length N. Using this, the complexity of initializing the data and the code arrays has cost in $O(n \log^3 n)$, where n denotes the maximal size of the data and code array. Similarly, the cost of running the machine is in $O(T \log^3 n)$ where T denotes the running time of the program if the number of possible instructions is constant.

We have also implemented Circuit ORAM [32], but we found it to be slower in our context than Path ORAM, despite the improved asymptotic complexity. We assume that this is due to the higher number of rounds of multiplications in Circuit ORAM, which translate to communication rounds in secret sharing-based MPC.

3   Our Implementation

In this section, we will describe the details of our implementation. We begin by considering the differences between regular CPUs and our implementation.

Unlike in a regular CPU, there is no reason to have data registers because the memory has to be accessed in every step to maintain obliviousness. In other words, if the memory would not be accessed in a particular step, the adversary would learn some information about the current program counter by ruling out all positions in the program that do not involve a memory access. Over time, the adversary could learn the exact position in the program, which in turn would rule out branching on secret variables. Wang et al. [33] use static analysis to evaluate at which execution no possible branch accesses the memory to avoid accessing in every step. However, this approach prevents private function evaluation, and the cost analysis grows exponentially in the number of branches in the worst case.

Lacking registers, all values are referred to by their addresses in the data array. The only register is the program counter referring the current instruction. Similarly, there is only one integer data type because having several types does not make sense in an oblivious execution. Because all possible instructions are executed at every step, any operation for a smaller integer type implies an operation for the larger type. Therefore, it is cheaper to execute the operation for the larger integer type only. This does not rule out the provision of floating point types. Since floating point operations are much more expensive than integer operations, and since they would have to be executed at every step, we did not implement floating point operations.

We found it more practical to implement a Harvard-like architecture, where the memory for instructions is separated from the data storage, instead of the common Von Neumann architecture, where the two are mixed. First, there is an efficiency gain in ORAM by storing uniform tuples under every address (and the structure of the stored information differs between the program and data memory), and second, the overhead of ORAM implies that two smaller oblivious arrays are cheaper to access than one combined array.

Our implementation only supports static memory allocation and no recursion due to the lack of stack pointer. However, there is no inherent reason for this limitation. The stack pointer could be implemented as another register. In such a scenario however, one has to define how to handle memory overflows. Making it public incurs the risk of leaking data while keeping it secret could lead to wasting time for a long computation on corrupted data.

Given the cost of ORAM accesses, the goal is to minimize the number thereof while still supporting all desired instructions. Three ORAM accesses, two reading and one writing, suffice for the kind of instructions that classical processors support. Every such instruction can be described as a four-tuple consisting of an identification of the instruction and three parameters, which can be an address or constant depending on the instruction. Not all parameters need to have a semantic meaning for an instruction.

Instruction	Description
mov x y 0	Copy the data at address y to address x.
load x 0 z	Copy the data at the address stored at address z to address x.
store 0 y z	Copy the data at address z to the address stored at address y.
store_const x y 0	Store the constant y at address x.
eq_const x y z	Compare the number at address z to the constant y and store 1 at address x in case of equality and 0 otherwise.
add_const x y z	Add the number stored at address z and the constant y, and store the result at address x.
ult_pos_const x y z	Test if the unsigned number at address z is less than the positive constant y and store 1 at address x if yes and 0 otherwise.
ule_pos_const x y z	Test if the unsigned number at address z is less or equal than the positive constant y and store 1 at address x if yes and 0 otherwise.
jmp x 0 0	Jump to the instruction at address x.
jmp_ind 0 0 z	Jump to the instruction at the address stored at x.
br x y z	Jump to the instruction at address x if the number at address z is 1 and to the instruction at address y if the number is 0. Undefined behavior in any other case.

Fig. 1. Instructions used in Figs. 4 and 10 (See supplementary material).

Figure 1 lists all instructions used in the example in Fig. 10 in the supplementary material. The example represents a matching algorithm for the regular expression "ab*[cd]" as explained in Sect. 4. Before, after, and between ORAM accesses, all computation is purely in the form of circuits, obliviously selected as described in the Appendix B of the full version [15]. The circuits not only compute arithmetic operations, they also compute the addresses to be read from the data array and the next program counter of the next instruction.

For example, in add_const, one circuit makes sure that z is read from the memory, one circuit computes the addition with y, one circuit outputs x as the writing address, and the final circuit increments the program counter by one. Similarly, most circuits for load simply redirect addresses and the value read from memory. In addition to that, the last circuit of br set the program counter to $y + x \cdot (z - y)$ where x, y, and z denote the values at addresses x, y, and z.

It is easy to see that all instructions fall in one of the three categories represented by the above descriptions. Binary operations can be implemented similar to add_const by loading the operands and storing the result, indirect memory are similar to load, and conditional and unconditional jumps can be specified similarly to br.

3.1 Compilation

To compile C code, we use Clang from the LLVM project [31]. The LLVM project provides a modular compiler toolchain. Clang parses C code and can compile it to the LLVM internal representation. This representation consists of CPU-like instructions for an abstract CPU with infinitely many registers.

We use a Python script to compile this internal representation for our machine. This allows to compile simple C programs without having to write an LLVM specification of our machine. While the latter might be more elegant, our method seemed more time-efficient considering that our machine shares few characteristics with real CPUs that allow optimizations, e.g., registers.

Since our machine does not support registers, the compiler has to allocate memory space for every register. For simplicity, every register is put in a separate space in memory. One could use static analysis to reduce the amount of space used.

We have implemented and tested the following features of C:

– Integer addition, subtraction, multiplication, comparison, and shifting
– Pointers
– Arrays (also multi-dimensional)
– Structs
– for and while loops
– switch statements
– goto statements
– Functions (without recursion).

On the other hand, we have left out the following features:

– Floating-point operations
– Recursive function calls
– Dynamic memory allocation.

While the omitted features clearly are important for a complete support of C, we argue that the main restrictions of circuit-based computation (branching and array accesses) are entirely overcome by our implementation. Furthermore, note that the missing features are only restricted in our implementation and not by our theoretical model presented in Appendix B of the full version [15].

We will now present a few examples of the compilation process. The first example is a "for" loop populating an array. Figure 2 shows the C code. Compiled to LLVM intermediate representation (Fig. 3), the code is divided in five basic blocks: the code before the loop, the loop condition check, the loop body, the loop increment, and the code after the loop. Shown in Fig. 4, the code for our machine contains less instructions than the LLVM code because the compiler gets rid of unnecessary instructions, such as jumping to the next instruction in the code and loading from memory to register. For the latter case, note that our machine does not support registers. The loop variable i is stored in position 8 in the memory, initialized to 0 and compared to the constant 5 in instruction 2. The result of this comparison goes to position 9 in memory, which is used by the branching instruction in instruction 3. Furthermore, memory position 10 holds the address of the array element accessed in the loop body. The array starts at position 3; hence, instruction 4 adds 3 to the loop variable to determine the address of the array element. The loop variable is then stored in the address by instruction 5. For incrementing, instruction 6 adds 1 to the loop variable and stores the result in position 11, which is then copied to position 8 by instruction 7. The execution then jumps back to the condition check in instruction 2.

```
1  int main() {
2    unsigned long a[5];
3    for (unsigned long i = 0; i < 5; i++)
4      a[i] = i;
5  }
```

Fig. 2. A "for" loop populating an array in C.

Another example can be found in Appendix C of the full version [15].

4   Efficient Private Regular Expression Matching with Minimal Leakage

Consider the problem of two parties wanting to decide whether a string known by one party matches a regular expression known by the other. A regular expression can be modeled by a finite state machine, which in turn can be implemented in C using mainly switch and goto statements. Bumbulis and Cowan [3] provide an implementation of such a compilation. Therefore, the oblivious machine solves the problem by the party holding the regular expression inputting an appropriate program securely. In Appendix C of the full version [15], we show an example of the resulting C, LLVM, and machine code.

4.1   Complexity

Using Path ORAM for the oblivious arrays, loading the code and the input string takes time in $O(n \log^3 n)$ with n denoting the maximum of the code size

M. Keller

```
1   define i32 @main() #0 {
2   entry:
3     %retval = alloca i32, align 4
4     %a = alloca [5 x i64], align 16
5     %i = alloca i64, align 8
6     store i32 0, i32* %retval
7     store i64 0, i64* %i, align 8
8     br label %for.cond
9
10  for.cond:
11    %0 = load i64* %i, align 8
12    %cmp = icmp ult i64 %0, 5
13    br i1 %cmp, label %for.body, label %for.end
14
15  for.body:
16    %1 = load i64* %i, align 8
17    %2 = load i64* %i, align 8
18    %arrayidx = getelementptr inbounds [5 x i64]* %a, i32↩
         0, i64 %2
19    store i64 %1, i64* %arrayidx, align 8
20    br label %for.inc
21
22  for.inc:
23    %3 = load i64* %i, align 8
24    %inc = add i64 %3, 1
25    store i64 %inc, i64* %i, align 8
26    br label %for.cond
27
28  for.end:
29    %4 = load i32* %retval
30    ret i32 %4
31  }
```

Fig. 3. A "for" loop populating an array in the LLVM intermediate representation.

and input size. For the regular expression, this means quasi-linear time in the size of the finite state machine. The main execution then takes time in $O(T(\log^3 n_c + \log^3 n_d))$ for T, n_c, and n_d denoting the running time of the machine, the code size, and the size of the input string, respectively. The running time is dominated the by the comparisons made by the C code. This depends both on the input data and the ordering of the comparison within a switch statement. For example, if it makes a difference whether the next character is 'a', 'b', or anything else, one can first check for 'a' or first check for 'b'. The order of the checks influences the number of checks computed if the next character is 'a' or 'b'. However, T can be upper bounded by $O(n_d n_m)$ where n_m denotes the maximum number of comparisons in a single switch statement, which in turn is less than the number of symbols. From a certain size of switch statements, it is more efficient to use

```
 1  # main()
 2    # entry:
 3      store_const  2  0  0  #  0
 4      store_const  8  0  0  #  1
 5    # for.cond:
 6      ult_pos_const  9  5  8  #  2
 7      br  4  9  9  #  3
 8    # for.body:
 9      add_const  10  3  8  #  4
10      store  0  8  10  #  5
11    # for.inc:
12      add_const  11  1  8  #  6
13      mov  8  11  0  #  7
14      jmp  2  0  0  #  8
15    # for.end:
16      mov  0  2  0  #  9
17      jmp  11  0  0  #  10
```

Fig. 4. A "for" loop populating an array in our machine code.

branch tables instead of consecutive comparisons. For example, if every character of the alphabet is treated differently, one would have to conduct 26 comparisons in order to jump to the right position in the code. A branch table is a list of jump instructions where the first one jumps to the code for 'a', the second one jumps to the code for 'b' etc. To use this table, the preceding code simply computes a jump address by adding the correct base address to the number representing the character and then jumps to the result. Of course the code still needs to conduct two comparisons to check whether the next character is within the bounds of the branch table. In this case, the loading complexity of the particular switch statement is in $O(n_s)$ for n_s being the number of symbols and the execution complexity is constant. We did not follow this avenue in our implementation, but point out that it would be possible using the jmp_ind instruction.

4.2 Security

The oblivious machine leaks the running time T, which is linear in the number of the comparison performed and the size of the input string. The latter is public by the fact that the usage of the oblivious machine reveals the input size.[1] However, the former depends on the regular expression, its precise compilation, and the input string. The party holding the regular expression could modify the switch statements such that they have constant size. This could for example be achieved using the approach with branch tables explained above.

---

[1] While there exist works on size-hiding secure computation [21], we do not think that those approaches are compatible with ours. In particular, they seem to be "one-shot" while ORAM requires continuous computation.

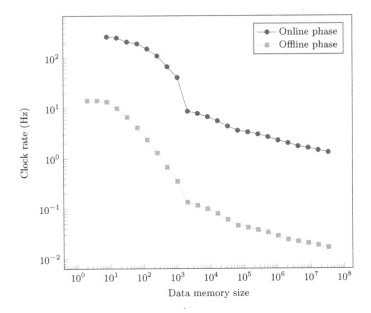

Fig. 5. Clock rate of the machine.

5   Experiments

In order to benchmark our construction, we have implemented it based on the so-called SPDZ scheme by Damgård et al. [8], which provides active security against an adversary corrupting all but one party. It works in the preprocessing model, that is, there is a data-independent offline phase in which correlated randomness is generated. In the case of SPDZ, the online phase requires secret sharings of random multiplicative triples (a, b, ab) in a finite field with some authentication to compute the product of actual inputs.

The original SPDZ protocol used somewhat homomorphic encryption to generate these multiplication triples, but Keller et al. [16] recently found that it is more efficient to use oblivious transfer for the offline phase instead. Therefore, we use their timings in our figures.

In our implementation, we use 64-bit integers as subset of $\mathbb{F}_p$ for a 128-bit prime p. The gap is necessary to accommodate for the statistically secure bit decomposition protocol with security parameter 40. Note that this refers to a 2^{-40} comparison advantage in the security proof, not the possibility of breaking the protocol with 2^{40} complexity.

All experiments were conducted on two off-the-shelf machines with Intel Core i7 processors connected by a 1 GBit/s local network.

Figure 5 shows the online phase clock rate for a minimal program that is executed with varying sizes of the data memory. The offline phase is about in magnitude of a 100 times slower. However, it is highly parallelizable, that is, it can distributed among several machines, which does not hold for the online phase. Furthermore, this cost is due to providing active security, which similar works do not offer. Note that the "bump" at memory size 1000 stems from the fact that for smaller sizes it is more efficient to use linear scanning instead of the more intricate Path ORAM.

Per clock cycle, the complexity ranges from 11 KBytes sent in 40 rounds for memory size 2 to 7.6 MBytes in 2739 rounds for memory size 2^{24}.

5.1 Comparison to Non-oblivious Computation

It is clear that our approach is slower than plain multiparty computation for programs that can be efficiently computed as circuits. In order to compare the performance of the oblivious machine with programs implemented using oblivious arrays directly, we have benchmarked Dijkstra's algorithm using our toolchain. The results in Fig. 6 suggest that using the oblivious machine instead of the implementation by Keller and Scholl is about 100 times slower. However, the comparison is not entirely fair because the previous implementation leaks the algorithm being computed whereas the oblivious machine does not. Furthermore, they have to rewrite the algorithm because its structure with nested variable length loops does not lend itself to oblivious computation. In other words, the price to pay to hide the computation or to avoid manual rewriting is a factor of 100 in this case. We consider this to be representative for algorithms that require the use of oblivious arrays for an efficient implementation. Again, the "bump" in the figure is explained by the change in the implementation of the oblivious array.

5.2 Comparison with Wang et al.'s Secure MIPS Computation

We have compiled and run the set intersection example by Wang et al. [33]. Table 1 shows that our running times are comparable to the unoptimized times by Wang et al. Their optimization involves static analysis of the program, and thus inhibits private function evaluation. Furthermore, note that their implementation uses semi-honest garbled circuits while ours provides active security.

Table 1. Set intersection.

Input size per party	64 inputs	256 inputs	1024 inputs
Wang et al. baseline	58.35 s	324.09 s	3068.19 s
Wang et al. optimized	2.77 s	12.96 s	108.45 s
This work	6.43 s	44.12 s	1346.82 s

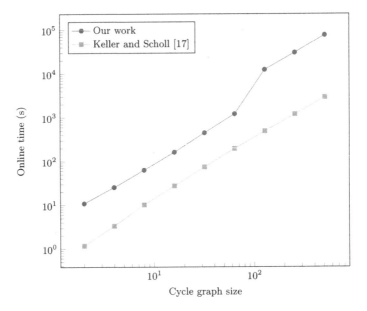

Fig. 6. Dijkstra's algorithm on cycle graphs.

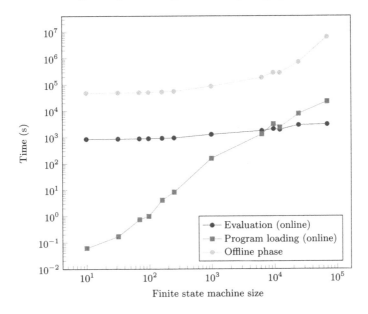

Fig. 7. Regular expression matching timings.

Table 2. Regular expressions used in our experiments.

FSM size	Regular expression
10	[ZrqupR]
32	[aYoNPCI70] [Lxdo] [3jH17]
70	(([x2YUux] | [FEb6o]) ([ssUWGaGuD] ?)?) [nO] [LwhCA] [YOrp6xc] WkaNjg5 M
98	[P] ([zOxwIv48]+) ([IEm] [^isgQn4B]*)
161	([M] | (XP[t]*)) [slUW8XiVe] [iTS2Y 86E] [ykSh9uE] [fAu] 9TOg(Umks(do([^t] | [PEv3e5])+)e62e[iIl]*)

5.3 Regular Expression Matching

We have implemented our protocol for regular expression matching for a string of length 1024 and randomly generated regular expressions of varying complexity. Figure 7 shows our results. We found that the total number of transitions is the most appropriate measure for the complexity of a finite state machine. This coincides with the number of comparisons in the machine code. At more than ten thousand transitions, loading the code becomes the dominant part of the computation. However, if several strings are to be matched to the same regular expression, this is a one-off cost. Table 2 shows the smaller expressions we used for our experiments. We used randomly generated expressions, which explains the irregular increase in the size of the corresponding finite state machines.

6 Conclusion and Future Directions

We have presented a theoretical model for multiparty RAM computation, a concrete protocol, and an implementation as well as an application in the form of private regular expression matching. As future direction we suggest research into quantifying the leakage by the running time of a RAM program. This would allow to navigate the trade-off between the fastest execution of a program with leakage and the overhead by adding padding operations to programs in order to hide the number of comparisons in our regular expression matching scheme for example.

Our experiments have shown that the oblivious machine runs at a few Hertz for larger data memory size, which is about a billion times slower than a regular CPU. Obviously, one cannot hope to achieve a similar speed, but recent ORAM schemes optimized for circuit implementation should allow to improve at least one or two orders of magnitude. Another issue is the round complexity of secret-sharing-based MPC schemes, which is linear in the circuit rounds. Analyzing our implementation, we come to the conclusion that this is the bottleneck. Two-party computation based on Yao's garbled circuits does not suffer from this because it has constant rounds. However, implementations using garbled circuits do not necessarily beat the ones secret sharing [6]. It remains to be seen which approach is more efficient.

Acknowledgments. We would like to thank Peter Scholl for various comments and suggestions. This work has been supported in part by EPSRC via grants EP/I03126X, EP/M012824, and EP/N021940/1.

References

1. Ben-Or, M., Goldwasser, S., Wigderson, A.: Completeness theorems for non-cryptographic fault-tolerant distributed computation (extended abstract). In: 20th ACM STOC, pp. 1–10. ACM Press, May 1988
2. Ben-Sasson, E., Chiesa, A., Genkin, D., Tromer, E., Virza, M.: SNARKs for C: verifying program executions succinctly and in zero knowledge. In: Canetti, R., Garay, J.A. (eds.) CRYPTO 2013, Part II. LNCS, vol. 8043, pp. 90–108. Springer, Heidelberg (2013). https://doi.org/10.1007/978-3-642-40084-1_6
3. Bumbulis, P., Cowan, D.D.: RE2C - a more versatile scanner generator. ACM Lett. Program. Lang. Syst **2**, 70–84 (1994)
4. Chaum, D., Crépeau, C., Damgård, I.: Multiparty unconditionally secure protocols (abstract). In: Pomerance, C. (ed.) CRYPTO 1987. LNCS, vol. 293, p. 462. Springer, Heidelberg (1988). https://doi.org/10.1007/3-540-48184-2_43
5. Cook, S.A., Reckhow, R.A.: Time bounded random access machines. J. Comput. Syst. Sci. **7**(4), 354–375 (1973)
6. Damgård, I., Keller, M., Larraia, E., Miles, C., Smart, N.P.: Implementing AES via an actively/covertly secure dishonest-majority MPC protocol. In: Visconti, I., De Prisco, R. (eds.) SCN 2012. LNCS, vol. 7485, pp. 241–263. Springer, Heidelberg (2012). https://doi.org/10.1007/978-3-642-32928-9_14
7. Damgård, I., Meldgaard, S., Nielsen, J.B.: Perfectly secure oblivious RAM without random oracles. In: Ishai, Y. (ed.) TCC 2011. LNCS, vol. 6597, pp. 144–163. Springer, Heidelberg (2011). https://doi.org/10.1007/978-3-642-19571-6_10
8. Damgård, I., Pastro, V., Smart, N., Zakarias, S.: Multiparty computation from somewhat homomorphic encryption. In: Safavi-Naini, R., Canetti, R. (eds.) CRYPTO 2012. LNCS, vol. 7417, pp. 643–662. Springer, Heidelberg (2012). https://doi.org/10.1007/978-3-642-32009-5_38
9. Gentry, C., Halevi, S., Jutla, C., Raykova, M.: Private database access with HE-over-ORAM architecture. In: Malkin, T., Kolesnikov, V., Lewko, A.B., Polychronakis, M. (eds.) ACNS 2015. LNCS, vol. 9092, pp. 172–191. Springer, Cham (2015). https://doi.org/10.1007/978-3-319-28166-7_9
10. Gentry, C., Halevi, S., Lu, S., Ostrovsky, R., Raykova, M., Wichs, D.: Garbled RAM revisited. In: Nguyen, P.Q., Oswald, E. (eds.) EUROCRYPT 2014. LNCS, vol. 8441, pp. 405–422. Springer, Heidelberg (2014). https://doi.org/10.1007/978-3-642-55220-5_23
11. Goldreich, O., Micali, S., Wigderson, A.: How to play any mental game or a completeness theorem for protocols with honest majority. In: Aho, A. (ed.) 19th ACM STOC, pp. 218–229. ACM Press, May 1987
12. Gordon, S.D., et al.: Secure two-party computation in sublinear (amortized) time. In: Yu, T., Danezis, G., Gligor, V.D. (eds.) ACM CCS 2012, pp. 513–524. ACM Press, October 2012

13. Henecka, W., Kögl, S., Sadeghi, A.-R., Schneider, T., Wehrenberg, I.: TASTY: tool for automating secure two-party computations. In: Al-Shaer, E., Keromytis, A.D., Shmatikov, V. (eds.) ACM CCS 2010, pp. 451–462. ACM Press, October 2010
14. Holzer, A., Franz, M., Katzenbeisser, S., Veith, H.: Secure two-party computations in ANSI C. In: Yu, T., Danezis, G., Gligor, V.D. (eds.) ACM CCS 2012, pp. 772–783. ACM Press, October 2012
15. Keller, M.: The oblivious machine - or: how to put the C into MPC. Cryptology ePrint Archive, Report 2015/467 (2015). http://eprint.iacr.org/2015/467
16. Keller, M., Orsini, E., Scholl, P.: MASCOT: faster malicious arithmetic secure computation with oblivious transfer. In: Weippl, E.R., Katzenbeisser, S., Kruegel, C., Myers, A.C., Halevi, S. (eds.) ACM CCS 2016, pp. 830–842. ACM Press, October 2016
17. Keller, M., Scholl, P.: Efficient, oblivious data structures for MPC. In: Sarkar, P., Iwata, T. (eds.) ASIACRYPT 2014, Part II. LNCS, vol. 8874, pp. 506–525. Springer, Heidelberg (2014). https://doi.org/10.1007/978-3-662-45608-8_27
18. Kerschbaum, F.: Practical private regular expression matching. In: Fischer-Hübner, S., Rannenberg, K., Yngström, L., Lindskog, S. (eds.) SEC 2006. IIFIP, vol. 201, pp. 461–470. Springer, Boston (2006). https://doi.org/10.1007/0-387-33406-8_43
19. Kreuter, B., Shelat, A., Mood, B., Butler, K.R.B.: PCF: a portable circuit format for scalable two-party secure computation. In: Proceedings of the 22th USENIX Security Symposium, pp. 321–336 (2013)
20. Launchbury, J., Archer, D., DuBuisson, T., Mertens, E.: Application-scale secure multiparty computation. In: Shao, Z. (ed.) ESOP 2014. LNCS, vol. 8410, pp. 8–26. Springer, Heidelberg (2014). https://doi.org/10.1007/978-3-642-54833-8_2
21. Lindell, Y., Nissim, K., Orlandi, C.: Hiding the input-size in secure two-party computation. In: Sako, K., Sarkar, P. (eds.) ASIACRYPT 2013, Part II. LNCS, vol. 8270, pp. 421–440. Springer, Heidelberg (2013). https://doi.org/10.1007/978-3-642-42045-0_22
22. Lindell, Y., Pinkas, B.: A proof of security of Yao's protocol for two-party computation. J. Cryptol. 22(2), 161–188 (2009)
23. Liu, C., Huang, Y., Shi, E., Katz, J., Hicks, M.W.: Automating efficient RAM-model secure computation. In: 2014 IEEE Symposium on Security and Privacy, pp. 623–638. IEEE Computer Society Press, May 2014
24. Liu, C., Wang, X.S., Nayak, K., Huang, Y., Shi, E.: ObliVM: a programming framework for secure computation. In: 2015 IEEE Symposium on Security and Privacy, pp. 359–376. IEEE Computer Society Press, May 2015
25. Mohassel, P., Sadeghian, S., Smart, N.P.: Actively secure private function evaluation. In: Sarkar, P., Iwata, T. (eds.) ASIACRYPT 2014, Part II. LNCS, vol. 8874, pp. 486–505. Springer, Heidelberg (2014). https://doi.org/10.1007/978-3-662-45608-8_26
26. Ostrovsky, R., Shoup, V.: Private information storage (extended abstract). In: 29th ACM STOC, pp. 294–303. ACM Press, May 1997
27. Pippenger, N., Fischer, M.J.: Relations among complexity measures. J. ACM 26(2), 361–381 (1979)
28. Shi, E., Chan, T.-H.H., Stefanov, E., Li, M.: Oblivious RAM with $O((\log N)^3)$ worst-case cost. In: Lee, D.H., Wang, X. (eds.) ASIACRYPT 2011. LNCS, vol. 7073, pp. 197–214. Springer, Heidelberg (2011). https://doi.org/10.1007/978-3-642-25385-0_11

29. Songhori, E.M., Hussain, S.U., Sadeghi, A.-R., Schneider, T., Koushanfar, F.: Tiny-Garble: highly compressed and scalable sequential garbled circuits. In: 2015 IEEE Symposium on Security and Privacy, pp. 411–428. IEEE Computer Society Press, May 2015

30. Stefanov, E., et al.: Path ORAM: an extremely simple oblivious RAM protocol. In: Sadeghi, A.-R., Gligor, V.D., Yung, M. (eds.) ACM CCS 2013, pp. 299–310. ACM Press, November 2013

31. The LLVM Project. clang: a C language family frontend for LLVM. http://clang.llvm.org/

32. Wang, X., Chan, T.-H.H., Shi, E.: Circuit ORAM: on tightness of the Goldreich-Ostrovsky lower bound. In: Ray, I., Li, N., Kruegel, C. (eds.) ACM CCS 2015, pp. 850–861. ACM Press, October 2015

33. Wang, X., Gordon, S.D., McIntosh, A., Katz, J.: Secure computation of MIPS machine code. In: Askoxylakis, I., Ioannidis, S., Katsikas, S., Meadows, C. (eds.) ESORICS 2016, Part II. LNCS, vol. 9879, pp. 99–117. Springer, Cham (2016). https://doi.org/10.1007/978-3-319-45741-3_6

34. Wang, X.S., Huang, Y., Chan, T.-H.H., Shelat, A., Shi, E.: SCORAM: oblivious RAM for secure computation. In: Ahn, G.-J., Yung, M., Li, N. (eds.) ACM CCS 2014, pp. 191–202. ACM Press, November 2014

35. Zahur, S., Evans, D.: Obliv-C: a language for extensible data-oblivious computation. Cryptology ePrint Archive, Report 2015/1153 (2015). http://eprint.iacr.org/2015/1153

36. Zhang, Y., Steele, A., Blanton, M.: PICCO: a general-purpose compiler for private distributed computation. In: Sadeghi, A.-R., Gligor, V.D., Yung, M. (eds.) ACM CCS 2013, pp. 813–826. ACM Press, November 2013

Concrete Efficiency Improvements
for Multiparty Garbling
with an Honest Majority

Aner Ben-Efraim[1]([✉]) and Eran Omri[2]

[1] Department of Computer Science, Ben Gurion University of the Negev,
Beer Sheva, Israel
anermosh@post.bgu.ac.il
[2] Department of Computer Science, Ariel University,
Ariel, Israel
omrier@gmail.com

Abstract. Secure multiparty computation is becoming a necessary component in many real-world systems. The efficiency of secure two-party protocols has improved tremendously in the last decade, making such protocols efficient enough for many real-world applications. Recently, much attention is being diverted to making secure *multiparty* computation (for more than two parties) truly practical as well. In particular, the last couple of years saw a resurgence of interest in constant round secure protocols, based on the multiparty garbling paradigm of Beaver et al. (STOC 1990). Such protocols generally offer improved performance in high latency networks, such as the internet.

In this paper we consider the case where a majority of the parties are honest, and construct highly efficient constant round protocols for both the semi-honest setting and the malicious setting. Our protocols in the semi-honest setting significantly improve over the recent multiparty garbling protocols for honest majority of Ben Efraim et al. (ACM CCS 2016), both in asymptotic complexity and in concrete running time.

In the malicious setting, we consider security with abort when assuming more than 2/3 of the parties are honest. We show that by assuming the existence of simple preprocessing primitives, which do not require knowledge of the computed function, we get malicious security at almost the same cost as semi-honest security. I.e., the function dependent preprocessing and the online phase are almost identical to the semi-honest setting.

We ran experiments to measure the effect of our optimizations and to show that our protocols compete with the state-of-the-art constant round protocols.

A. Ben-Efraim—Supported by ISF grants 544/13 and 152/17, by a grant from the BGU Cyber Security Research Center, and by the Frankel Center for Computer Science.
E. Omri—Supported by an Israel Science Foundation grants 544/13 and 152/17, and by a grant from the Israeli Science and Technology ministry.

T. Lange and O. Dunkelman (Eds.): LATINCRYPT 2017, LNCS 11368, pp. 289–308, 2019.
https://doi.org/10.1007/978-3-030-25283-0_16

Keywords: Constant round MPC · Garbled circuits · Concrete efficiency · Honest majority

1 Introduction

Protocols for secure multiparty computation (MPC) enable a set of mutually distrusting parties to carry out a joint computation on private inputs, correctly and without revealing anything but the output. Secure computation was introduced for the 2-party case by Yao [41], who also introduced the notion of *garbled circuits*. These are essentially encrypted versions of the circuit, which can be evaluated without the evaluator learning intermediate wire values. Definitions and protocols for secure multiparty computation soon followed in [21] and [5,11]. Multiparty garbled circuits were introduced by Beaver et al. [1], who constructed a constant round multiparty protocol.

These feasibility results were initially thought to be of theoretical interest only, but since the first 2-party implementation of Fairplay [32], a huge amount of work (e.g., [2,27,28,30,34–37,39,42] to name but a few) has brought down the running time of 2-PC tremendously, making it truly practical today.

The progress for the multiparty case has been somewhat slower, but is quickly catching up. The first implementation of secure *multiparty* computation, FairplayMP [3], was based on the multiparty garbling paradigm. However, since then, most implementations were based on the secret-sharing paradigm, e.g., [7–9,12,15,17,18,26]. In the secret-sharing paradigm, the parties secret-share the values of the input wires of the circuit. Then, for each layer of the circuit, the parties compute shares for the next layer using interaction. Finally, the output wires' values are reconstructed. Thus, the number of rounds depends on the depth of the circuit.

Interestingly, the last couple of years saw a resurgence of interest in constant round protocols based on the multiparty garbling paradigm, e.g., [4,23,29,31,40]. Such protocols generally offer improved performance in high latency networks, such as the internet, as demonstrated in [4].

Our Results and Techniques. We consider the case where a majority of the parties are honest, and construct highly efficient constant round protocols for both the semi-honest setting and the malicious setting. Our protocols in the semi-honest setting significantly improve over the recently published constant round protocols for honest majority of Ben-Efraim et al. [4], both asymptotically and in concrete running time.

We achieve our main improvement by observing that not all values necessary for computing the multiparty garbled circuit need to be secret-shared. This is done in two steps: First, we replace the round reduction technique of [4] with the round reduction technique for BGW presented by Ishai and Kushilevitz [24]. In [24], the last round of BGW is omitted by performing share conversion to (not uniformly random) additive sharing, and then masking with additive shares of zero. Second, we use the fact that the shares are additive to *locally add* the necessary values after the share conversion step. Using this, we manage to bypass the most computationally expensive part of the protocols of [4]. We then optimize further by observing that in the honest majority setting not all parties need to contribute keys. Also, using standard optimizations from the literature, we efficiently compute additive secret-shares of zero locally and distribute the workload in the last round of the offline phase.

We then investigate malicious *security with abort* when assuming that more than 2/3 of the parties are honest. It is well-known that, from a theoretical standpoint, in this scenario full fairness is achievable. However, we relax the security definition, with the aim of obtaining better running times. We present a new 2-round protocol that is secure against malicious adversaries in the linear preprocessing model defined by Damgård and Ishai [16]. The linear preprocessing functionalities can be used before the function is known. Then, the function dependent preprocessing and the online phase in our malicious protocol are almost identical to our protocols in the semi-honest setting.

We ran experiments to measure the effect of our optimizations. For 31 parties, we found that our optimized protocols are more than 70%, and sometimes even more than 85%, faster than the respective protocols in [4]. We also ran experiments comparing our protocol with existing state-of-the-art constant round MPC protocols that use oblivious transfer. We show that in some scenarios, our new protocols outperform all other constant round protocols.

Related Works. Recently, two works have studied constant round MPC based on multiparty garbling in the malicious setting [23,40]. The protocols in these works use oblivious transfer and are secure up to $n - 1$ corrupt parties. Thus, assuming oblivious transfer, they provide a stronger security guarantee, and so are suitable also in scenarios where our protocols are not. Nevertheless, we show that in some scenarios our protocols could be preferred. Furthermore, our protocols do not require OT. Therefore, the results of these works are orthogonal to ours. Previous works for malicious security in constant rounds, such as [16,29,31], provided no implementation, so it is not clear how concretely efficient they are.

Other works, such as [10,13,33], study constant round MPC only in a very restrictive scenario, e.g., only 3 or 5 parties and/or only 1 or 2 corrupt parties. It is not clear if and how the results of [13,33] generalize to an arbitrary number of parties. The extension of [10] to n parties allows only up to $\sqrt{n}$ corrupt parties.

There has also been a significant amount of work done in non-constant round MPC, e.g., [17–19,25,26], but for deep circuits in high latency setting, these protocols have a slow online phase due to the number of rounds. Hence, they are incomparable with our work.

Organization. In Sect. 2, we review multiparty garbling. In Sect. 3, we explain our optimized protocols for the semi-honest setting. In Sect. 4, we present a new protocol that is secure against malicious adversaries, in the linear preprocessing model of Damgård and Ishai [16]. In Sect. 5, we present experimental results, measuring the efficiency of our optimizations and comparing our protocols to state-of-the-art constant round protocols.

2 Preliminaries

In this section, we recall the basic definitions and constructions of multiparty garbling. We assume familiarity with the definitions of secure multiparty computation, with Yao's garbled circuit construction [41], with Shamir secret-sharing [38], and with the BGW protocol and its improvement [5,20].

Conventions and Notations. We list some of the conventions and notations that we will use throughout this paper. We assume the existence of a circular 2-correlation robust PRF, which we denote by $\mathcal{F}^2$. When separating the offline and online phases, we even assume that $\mathcal{F}^2$ is a random oracle.[1] We consider a static adversary $\mathcal{A}$ corrupting a strict minority of the parties (or when stated also less than $1/3$ of the parties). In the malicious setting we consider security with abort, namely, the adversary is allowed to prematurely abort the computation, even after seeing the output. In this case, honest parties that need to output a result should output $\perp$. We denote by $||$ concatenation of strings. The circuit of the function to be computed is denoted by C, and $g \in C$ denotes both the gate and its index. The set of wires is denoted by W, and $\mathcal{W}$ denotes the wires that are *not* outputs of XOR gates. The number of parties in the protocol is n, and t is the bound on the number of corrupt parties. The security parameter will be $\kappa = 128$, and $\oplus$ will denote both XOR of strings and addition in fields of characteristic 2.

Multiparty Garbling. In the multiparty setting, the first proposal for constructing a multiparty garbled circuit was given in [1]. We follow a simplified description for the semi-honest model, given in [4], which also adopts the free-XOR technique of Kolesnikov and Schneider [27].

The protocol consists of two phases. In the first phase, often called the offline phase, the parties collaboratively construct a garbled circuit. Then, in the online phase, the parties exchange masked input values and the corresponding keys. After that, each party locally computes the outputs of the function.

For constructing the garbled circuit, each party P_i chooses, for each wire $\omega \in \mathcal{W}$, two random keys, $k_{\omega,0}^i$ and $k_{\omega,1}^i$. To enable the free-XOR technique [27], the parties need to choose the keys such that $k_{\omega,1}^i = k_{\omega,0}^i \oplus R^i$ for some global offset R^i. A sometimes useful notion is the term "superseed", which refers to the concatenation of the keys of all the parties, for some wire ω and either the zero or the one key, i.e., $k_{\omega,0} \stackrel{\text{def}}{=} k_{\omega,0}^1 || \ldots || k_{\omega,0}^n$ and $k_{\omega,1} \stackrel{\text{def}}{=} k_{\omega,1}^1 || \ldots || k_{\omega,1}^n$.

Each wire ω in the circuit is assigned a random secret permutation bit λ_ω. This bit masks the real values of the wires during the online phase. For an AND gate with input wires $in1, in2$ and output wire out, the garbled gate is the encryptions $\tilde{g}_{\alpha,\beta}^1, \ldots, \tilde{g}_{\alpha,\beta}^n$ for $(\alpha, \beta) \in \{0,1\}^2$, where

---

[1] This is to allow the garbled circuit to be revealed at the end of the offline phase.

$$\tilde{g}^j_{\alpha,\beta} = \left(\bigoplus_{i=1}^{n} \mathcal{F}^2_{k^i_{in1,\alpha}, k^i_{in2,\beta}} (g\|j) \right) \oplus k^j_{out,0} \oplus \left(R^j \cdot ((\lambda_{in1} \oplus \alpha) \cdot (\lambda_{in2} \oplus \beta) \oplus \lambda_{out}) \right).$$

(1)

Notice that all the values are "encrypted" by *all* the parties. XOR gates are computed using the free-XOR technique of Kolesnikov and Schneider [27] – the permutation bit and keys on the output wire are set to be the XOR of those on the input wires; they require no cryptographic operations or communication. For the circuit output wires, the permutation bits are revealed. For input wires of party P_i, the corresponding permutation bits are disclosed to party P_i.

During the online phase, an evaluating party learns at each wire a bit, called the *external* or *public* value, and the corresponding superseed. The external value is the XOR of the real value with the random permutation bit. Since the permutation bit is random and secret, the external value reveals nothing about the real value to the evaluating party. The evaluating party uses the external value and keys to continue the evaluation of the proceeding garbled gates. For the output wires of the circuit, the permutation bit values are revealed, and thus the output is learnt by XORing with the external values.

In the following last part of this section, we explain an abstraction of the general multiparty garbling paradigm. We do this informally and slightly imprecisely for clarity. Precise treatments can be found in [23] and in the full version.

The offline phase can be seen as an invocation of the functionality $\mathcal{F}_{GC}$, given in Fig. 1, which constructs the garbled circuit and assigns the random permutation bits. In the $\mathcal{F}_{GC}$-hybrid model, after invoking the functionality $\mathcal{F}_{GC}$, running the online protocol Π_{online}, given in Fig. 2, securely computes the output of the function in the semi-honest model.

In fact, a much stronger statement is true, as shown in [23]: running the online protocol in the $\mathcal{F}_{GC}$-hybrid model is secure also against malicious adversaries, even if the adversary is allowed to abort (i.e., see the output and hide it from the honest parties). Furthermore, the correctness requirement of $\mathcal{F}_{GC}$ can be weakend – the adversary can choose either to abort or to insert any additive error into the garbled gates *after seeing the garbled circuit*. The intuition is that the adversary cannot base its additive error on the permutation bits, or on the keys and inputs of the honest parties – the attack is only based on the garbled circuit, which appears random to the adversary. Thus, in the online phase, an honest evaluator will either notice the error and output $\perp$, or output the correct result. We denote this modified functionality, introduced in [23], by $\mathcal{F}^{mal}_{GC}$.

3   Optimizations for BGW Based Sub-Protocols

In this section we describe our protocols that are secure in the semi-honest setting. These protocols compute a multiparty garbled circuit using the BGW protocol [5,20]. Our protocols are similar in spirit to the protocols that were presented in [4] for honest majority, specifically to $BGW3$ and $BGW2$. We first present the main ideas of the optimizations in Sects. 3.1 and 3.2. Then, we give

---

Functionality $\mathcal{F}_{GC}$

Computation Course:

1. The functionality assigns[a] a random global offset $R^i \in \{0,1\}^\kappa$ for every party P_i.
2. For each wire $\omega \in \mathcal{W}$, the functionality assigns[a]
   - A random permutation bit $\lambda_\omega \in \{0,1\}$.
   - Random zero keys $k^i_{\omega,0} \in \{0,1\}^\kappa$, and the one keys $k^i_{\omega,1} = k^i_{\omega,0} \oplus R^i$, for each party P_i.
3. For each XOR gate $g \in C$ with input wires $in1, in2$ and output wire out, the functionality computes
   - The permutation bit of the output wire $\lambda_{out} = \lambda_{in1} \oplus \lambda_{in2}$.
   - The zero keys of the output wire, $k^i_{out,0} = k^i_{in1,0} \oplus k^i_{in2,0}$ for each party P_i.
4. The functionality computes the garbled circuit GC. For every AND gate $g \in C$ with input wires $in1, in2$ and output wire out, every $\alpha, \beta \in \{0,1\}$, and every $j \in [n]$, compute:

$$\tilde{g}^j_{\alpha,\beta} = \left(\bigoplus_{i=1}^{n} \mathcal{F}^2_{k^i_{in1,\alpha}, k^i_{in2,\beta}}(g||j) \right) \oplus k^j_{out,0} \oplus \left(R^j \cdot ((\lambda_{in1} \oplus \alpha) \cdot (\lambda_{in2} \oplus \beta) \oplus \lambda_{out}) \right)$$

Outputs:

1. The functionality outputs the garbled gates, $(\tilde{g}^1_{\alpha,\beta} || \cdots || \tilde{g}^n_{\alpha,\beta})$ for every $\alpha, \beta \in \{0,1\}$ and every $g \in C$, to the evaluating party.[b]
2. For output wires of the circuit, the functionality outputs the permutation bits to the evaluating party.[b]
3. The functionality outputs to each party P_i its global difference R^i, its zero key, $k^i_{w,0}$, for each wire $w \in \mathcal{W}$, and the permutation bit of each of its input wires.

---

[a] Unlike [4], we follow [23] and make this functionality inputless.
[b] We slightly divert from [4,23] by having only one evaluating party.

Fig. 1. Functionality $\mathcal{F}_{GC}$ for constructing a multiparty garbled circuit

---

a full description of our protocol with all the optimizations in Sect. 3.3. We state security of our optimized protocol in Sect. 3.4. The proof will appear in the full version.

The protocols we describe in this section are secure against semi-honest adversaries. However, in Sect. 4 we show that our 2-round protocol can be made secure also for malicious adversaries. As often happens, the optimizations presented in this section, in the semi-honest model, carry over also to the malicious model.

Protocol Π_{online}

1. **Send garbled labels associated with inputs:** For every circuit-input wire w:
   (a) Let P_i be the party whose input is associated with wire w and let x_{i_w} be P_i's input bit associated with the wire. Then, P_i sends $e_w = x_{i_w} \oplus \lambda_w$ to all parties. For every wire w, we denote by e_w the XOR of the actual value on the wire (based on the input) and λ_w; we call this the **external value**.
   (b) Each party P_j sends its part k^j_{w,e_w} of the garbled label on w to the evaluating party.
   (c) At this point, the evaluating party holds $k^1_{w,e_w}, \ldots, k^n_{w,e_w}$ for every circuit-input wire.

2. **Local circuit computation:** The evaluating party P_0 locally evaluates the garbled circuit by traversing the circuit in a topological order, computing gate by gate. Let g be the current gate with input wires $in1$, $in2$ and output wire out. Let e_{in1} and e_{in2} be the *extrenal* values on wires $in1$ and $in2$, respectively.
   (a) If g is a XOR gate, then P_0 sets $e_{out} = e_{in1} \oplus e_{in2}$. In addition, for every $j = 1, \ldots, n$, it computes $k^j_{out,e_{out}} = k^j_{in1,e_{in1}} \oplus k^j_{in2,e_{in2}}$.
   (b) If g is an AND gate, then P_0 computes

   $$k^j_{out,e_{out}} = \tilde{g}^j_{\alpha,\beta} \oplus \left(\bigoplus_{i=1}^{n} \mathcal{F}^2_{k^i_{in1,\alpha}, k^i_{in2,\beta}}(g\|j) \right)$$

   for every $j \in [n]$, and for $\alpha = e_{in1}, \beta = e_{in2}$, which are the external values on wires $in1, in2$ as above. Given $k^0_{out,e_{out}}$, the evaluating party P_0 compares it to the garbled labels $k^0_{out,0}, k^0_{out,1}$ that it received in the offline phase on this wire. If it equals $k^0_{out,0}$ then $e_{out} = 0$. If it equals $k^0_{out,1}$ then $e_{out} = 1$. Otherwise, an honest P_0 outputs $\perp$.[a]

3. **Output determination:** For every output wire w, the evaluating party computes the *real* output bit of wire w to be $e_w \oplus \lambda_w$, where e_w is the external value on wire w and λ_w is as received in the offline phase.

---

[a]Note that outputting $\perp$ can only happen in the malicious setting.

Fig. 2. The online phase – circuit evaluation

3.1 Reducing the Computational Complexity

In this section we explain how we reduce the computational complexity of the BGW based protocols described in [4] from being cubic in the number of parties to being quadratic in the number of parties. This involves using techniques suggested in [24, Appendix A]. The idea there was to reduce the number of rounds for computations that use the BGW protocol, by omitting the last degree reduction step. This is done by multiplying the shares by the interpolation constants, to convert the Shamir shares into additive shares, and then masking these with additive shares of 0.[2] Thus, the last round reduction becomes redundant.

In [4], they instead reduced the number of rounds by sharing the PRF values at a higher degree at the onset. Thus, the multiplication of shares were added to the PRF value shares, resulting in legitimate Shamir shares. Therefore, additive shares of 0 were not needed.

The problem with *all* previous *BGW-based* protocols for computing a multi-party garbled circuit, such as in [4], is that the outputs of the PRFs (or PRGs) were secret-shared using Shamir secret-sharing.[3] Since the length of these outputs is linear in the number of parties, and Shamir secret-sharing is computationally quadratic in the number of parties, the total computational complexity of these protocols is cubic in the number of parties.

To overcome this, we show that the PRF values, as well as the keys, do not need to be shared at all! Instead, only the global offset and permutation bits are shared in Shamir secret-sharing. The keys and outputs of the PRFs are instead simply added, after the share-conversion step. Since the result is then masked by additive shares of 0, this is secure. The formal statement is given in Sect. 3.4.

The number of values shared (by each party) using Shamir secret-sharing in the resulting scheme is independent of the number of parties. Therefore, the total complexity of computing these Shamir shares is quadratic in the number of parties. Furthermore, using an observation made in [24], each of these values needs to be shared only *once*. This is regardless of the number of times the value is used. The number of secrets shared additively is linear in the number of parties, but computing additive sharing is also linear in the number of parties. Thus, the total complexity of computing the additive shares is also quadratic in the number of parties.

To summarize, our new protocols have computational complexity $O(|C|\kappa n^2)$ while the computational complexity of previous honest majority protocols, such as those of [4], is $O(|C|\kappa n^3)$. Our protocols also require slightly less communication.

3.2 Further Optimizations

In this section, we describe some further optimizations to our protocol.

Shortening the "Superseed". When assuming an honest majority, or even just a known bound on the number of corrupt parties, the length of the "superseeds" can be shortened. That is, only a subset of the parties need to choose input keys. If the bound on the number of corrupt parties is t, then it is sufficient that $t+1$ parties choose keys, so the length of a "superseed" is $(t+1)\kappa$, where κ is the security parameter.

---

[2] Note that in our protocol, as well as in [24], this "share conversion" is done on multiplication of shares, so the resulting "shares" are not fully random. Nevertheless, they indeed sum to the secret, and the security is maintained by the masking.

[3] An exception is [16] who used the outputs of PRGs for encrypting only, but they instead secret-shared 0's of the same length using Shamir secret-sharing.

Assuming up to $n - 1$ corrupt parties results in the standard "superseed" length. However, when assuming an honest majority, the length of the "superseed" is cut in half. This gives a significant improvement to running time, both in the offline phase and the online phase. To the best of our knowledge, this optimization has not been noticed, or at least not published, in previous works for multiparty garbling with an honest majority, e.g., [1,3,4,16].

This optimization is "for free" when only the evaluating party needs to recover the output. However, when more than one party needs to recover the output, we need to explain how the parties receive the output, because not all the parties can actually perform the evaluation. In the semi-honest model, we can let the evaluating party simply send back the output to all the parties.

In the malicious model, we can solve the issue using a broadcast channel. The evaluating party broadcasts the superseeds of the output wires. Then, each of the $t + 1$ parties that contributed for the superseed broadcasts the external value of the output wires (which they can check by comparing with their key). If any single party aborts or if any two parties broadcast different sets of values, then all honest parties abort. Otherwise, $t + 1$ parties broadcast the same value. Since at least one of these parties is honest, it can be shown that this is the true output – informally, if the adversary can fake the other key for an honest party, then the adversary can recover the global offset of an honest party, which means the adversary already effectively broke security. A formal statement and proof will be given in the full version.

More Efficient Zero Secret Sharing. Assuming the existence of a PRG, there is a standard method to generate additive zero shares locally, and therefore more efficiently in terms of communication, and hence, also in concrete running time. This is done as follows:

Setup: Each party P_i that will need to share 0, sends a private random seed s_i^j to every other party P_j.
Computation: In order for party P_i to additively share 0 among all the parties
  – Each party P_j locally computes its share of desired length by using the PRG with the seed s_i^j.
  – Party P_i locally computes the sum (XOR) of all the above as its share.[4]

Distributing the Last Round. In the last round in our offline protocol, all parties send their shares to the evaluating party. The evaluating party receives the messages from all other parties and sums them together (along with its own shares). This implies that the evaluating party is performing much more work than all other parties. However, in many cases, the computational power and network capabilities of all the parties is approximately equal. Therefore, *in some scenarios*, it is preferable to distribute the workload between all the parties.

To do this, we use a technique known as "hypercube" [6]. The idea is that the 'last round' in the offline phase is done in $\log n$ rounds (instead of 1). At each

---

[4] In fields of characteristic other than 2, party P_i computes the *negation* of the sum.

round, the remaining parties pair up, and at each pair one sends the message to the other, which sums up the shares with its own shares, and proceeds to the next round. It might seem counter-intuitive to go from a constant round protocol to one which has $\log n$ number of rounds, but the idea is to evenly distribute the workload. Notice that the overall amount of information sent over the network remains unchanged.

An example scenario where this optimization could be particularly useful is when the parties are in two far away clusters. Then, all the parties at each cluster can sum their shares together, and only one message needs to be sent over the high latency network. We will see in Sect. 5 that this optimization resulted in significant improvement for the LAN setting. However, we remark that preliminary results for the WAN setting suggest this optimization might not be suitable when there is high latency between *every pair* of parties.

3.3   The Optimized Protocol

In this section, we give the full details of our offline protocols, that include all the above mentioned optimizations. We recall that in the offline phase, the parties securely compute functionality $\mathcal{F}_{GC}$. The online protocol we use, described in Fig. 2, is the same as [4], with the only difference being that here only one party evaluates.

We first give a description of our 3-round protocol, which optimizes $BGW3$ from [4]. We will refer to it as $BGW3_{opt}$.

Protocol Description. All $\tilde{g}^j_{\alpha,\beta}$ values (for all $j = 1,\ldots,t+1$, all $\alpha,\beta \in \{0,1\}$ and all gates) are computed in parallel. Each value is computed as follows (with some of the computations done only once globally, as explained in Sect. 3.1):

Communication round 1: Each party shares a random bit λ^i_ω for every wire $\omega \in \mathcal{W}$, using $(t+1)$-out-of-n Shamir secret sharing, with $t = \lceil n/2 \rceil - 1$. For an input wire, the λ is shared only by the party choosing the input of that wire. Each party P_i, $i \in \{1,\ldots,t+1\}$ also shares its random offset R^i using $(t+1)$-out-of-n Shamir secret sharing. In addition, the first $t+1$ parties share a 0-string of length $4|C|(t+1)\kappa$ in an n-out-of-n additive (XOR) secret-sharing scheme.

Local computation 1: The parties carry out local additions, as required by the circuit (e.g., free-XOR), in order to obtain shares of $\lambda_\omega = \oplus^n_{i=1}\lambda^i_\omega$ for every wire of the circuit. For every AND gate with input wires u,v, the parties locally multiply their shares of λ_u and λ_v. Denote this product by λ_{uv}.

Communication round 2: The parties run the GRR [20] degree reduction step on the product λ_{uv} to recover Shamir shares of $\lambda_u\lambda_v$ of degree t.

Local computation 2: The parties locally compute shares of $(\lambda_u \oplus \alpha)(\lambda_v \oplus \beta) \oplus \lambda_\omega$ by a linear combination of their shares of λ_u, λ_v, λ_w, and $\lambda_u\lambda_v$. Next, the parties locally multiply the result with their share of R^j. The parties next perform a share-conversion step, where each party multiplies the result by the reconstruction constant.[5] Next, each party P_i locally adds $\mathcal{F}^2_{k^i_{u,\alpha},k^i_{v,\beta}}(g||j)$, and party P_j

---

[5] If there are redundant parties for interpolation, then these parties multiply by 0 instead.

also locally adds $k^j_{\omega,0}$, to the result. This is then masked with *a fresh* additive sharing of 0.

Communication round 3: The parties send the above masked values to the evaluator, who sums the received shares to obtain $\tilde{g}^j_{\alpha,\beta}$. As explained in Sect. 3.2, it is sometimes preferable to perform this step in $\log n$ rounds, using the hypercube technique, instead of in one round. In addition, for each circuit output wire ω, each party sends its share of λ_ω to the evaluator, and the evaluator recovers λ_ω.

The above protocol has 3 rounds (or $2 + \log n$ rounds) of interaction. As observed in [4] for their 3-round protocol, if more than 2/3 of the parties are honest, then $3t < n$. Thus, the degree reduction round can be omitted, resulting in the 2-round protocol $BGW2$.

It turns out that also here, if more than 2/3 of the parties are honest, then the degree reduction is unnecessary by setting $t = \lceil n/3 \rceil - 1$. The parties use their local multiplication, λ_{uv}, for the rest of the computations. The reconstruction of the gates works as before. This gives us a two (or $1 + \log n$) round protocol, which we call $BGW2_{opt}$.

3.4 Security

In this section we state the security of the protocols presented in Sect. 3.3 in the semi-honest model. Following [4, Theorem 2.1], if the above protocols securely compute $\mathcal{F}_{GC}$, then there is an efficient constant round MPC protocol secure in the semi-honest setting. Thus, we give our main security statement. The proof is given in the full version.

Theorem 1. *The protocols $BGW3_{opt}$ and $BGW2_{opt}$ securely compute $\mathcal{F}_{GC}$ in the standard model, when there are at most t semi-honest corrupt parties, for $t < \frac{n}{2}$ and $t < \frac{n}{3}$ respectively.*

4 Protocol for the Malicious Model

In this section we describe a new protocol that is secure against malicious adversaries, based on protocol $BGW2_{opt}$. The protocol requires that >2/3 of the parties are honest and allows the adversary to abort prematurely (i.e., learn the output and hide it from the honest parties).

The protocol we describe shares many similarities with the constant round protocol of Damgård and Ishai [16], and uses the same preprocessing functionalities. The protocol of Damgård and Ishai guarantees full security, while ours guarantees only security with abort. However, by allowing the adversary to abort, we gain several efficiency benefits:

- Our online is significantly faster: in [16] they perform error correction and polynomial interpolation for reconstructing the gates in the online phase. In our protocol the interpolation is implicitly achieved using share conversion, in the offline phase. Errors result in abort.

- Our computational complexity and concrete efficiency are better than those of [16]. In particular, allowing abort enables us to use the optimizations described in Sect. 3.
- We can allow a greater number of corrupt parties for a two round MPC protocol in the linear preprocessing model than the two-round protocol of [16] – we require $>2/3$ honest parties whereas they require either $>4/5$ honest parties or more rounds.

The Linear Preprocessing Model. The functionalities we require appear in [16], under the name *the linear preprocessing model*. We did not implement these functionalities, but we note that they are used only independently of the computed function. A suggested implementation appears in [16], but we believe it can be much improved using modern techniques. We leave a fast implementation of these functionalities for future work. We recall the functionalities here:

RandSS(t) – Each party P_i obtains $f(i)$, where f is a random polynomial over $GF(2^\kappa)$ of degree at most t.

RandSS$_0$(t) – Same as **RandSS(t)**, except that f is subject to the restriction that $f(0) = 0$.

RandSS$_{bin}$(t) – Same as **RandSS(t)**, except that f is subject to the restriction that $f(0) \in \{0, 1\}$.

RandSS^{P_i}(t) – Same as **RandSS(t)**, except that party P_i additionally receives the polynomial f.

RandSS$^{P_i}_{bin}$(t) – Same as **RandSS$_{bin}$(t)**, except that party P_i additionally receives the polynomial f.

We further add another simple preprocessing functionality:
AdditiveZeroSharing(AZS) – The parties receive additive (XOR) n-out-of-n shares of 0.

In the semi-honest model, these functionalities are easily achieved, e.g., in **RandSS$_{bin}$(t)** each party shares a random bit using Shamir secret-sharing and the parties sum their received shares. This does not extend to the malicious model, as the parties could share a number not in $\{0, 1\}$, or even inconsistent shares.

In contrast, for the functionality **AZS**, using the semi-honest protocol in which $t+1$ parties additively share 0 and then the parties sum the received shares, suffices for our protocol – an attack on this protocol would be translated to an additive attack on the output of $\mathcal{F}^{mal}_{GC}$, which is allowed. The formal statement and proof will be given in the full version.

Fixing the External Values of the Output Wires. In most descriptions of the BMR protocol, e.g., [1,3,4,23], the evaluating parties receive the hidden permutation bits of the output wires. That way, they can XOR this value with the external value that they recover from the evaluation of the circuit, and thus recover the output.

A possible solution would be to force the parties to commit to their shares of the output wires, as done, e.g., in [23]. However, in order to base our protocol solely on the above preprocessing functionalities, we proceed in a slightly different manner; instead of revealing the hidden output bits of the output wires, they are fixed to be 0. Therefore, the evaluating party can recover the true output value from the output external value, as they are equal.

There are two obvious obstacles. The first is that an output wire may be an output wire of an XOR or XNOR gate.[6] These gates are free in the BMR protocol [4], and this effectively means that the permutation bits of these wires are correlated with permutation bits of the input wires of the gate; the shares of the output wires of XOR gates are computed by XORing the shares of the input wires of the respective gates.

This obstacle can be overcome by changing output "free-XOR" gates to regular garbled XOR gates. But a more efficient solution is to add garbled buffer gates for each output wire which is the output wire of an XOR/XNOR gate. These buffer gates are garbled as follows: for input wire in and output wire out, the garbled rows are

$$\tilde{g}_\alpha^j = \left(\bigoplus_{i=1}^{n} \mathcal{F}_{k_{in,\alpha}^i}^2 (g\|j) \right) \oplus k_{out,0}^j \oplus \left(R^j \cdot ((\lambda_{in} \oplus \alpha) \oplus \lambda_{out}) \right), \qquad (2)$$

for $\alpha \in \{0, 1\}$. Now the permutation bit λ_{out} can be set to 0, simplifying further. Notice that the size of a garbled buffer gate is half the size of a garbled AND gate. Thus, the total size of the garbled circuit is increased by only two garbled rows for every output wire that is the output of an XOR/XNOR gate.

The second obstacle is if the different parties are supposed to recover different outputs. If each wire is supposed to be recovered by either exactly one party or by all parties, then for output wires recovered by party P_i, we could use $\mathbf{RandSS}_{\mathbf{bin}}^{P_i}(t)$ to share its permutation bit. Allowing other types of subsets would require adding another preprocessing functionality, in order to fix the permutation bits on those output wires.

4.1 Protocol Description

In this section we describe our maliciously secure protocol, in the linear preprocessing model.

Upon receiving the circuit, the parties first add to the circuit a buffer gate for each output wire that is an output of a XOR/XNOR gate.[7] These buffer gates will be garbled (cf. Eq. 2). Now the parties follow the protocol $BGW2_{opt}$, with the following changes to the first communication round:

1. For permutation bits, the parties execute $\mathbf{RandSS}_{\mathbf{bin}}(\mathbf{t})$ instead of each party sharing a random bit and then summing the received shares.

---

[6] We ignore NOT gates, as they can be eliminated by modifying the circuit, without enlarging the number of garbled gates.

[7] We again assume that there are no NOT gates in the circuit.

2. For permutation bits of input wires of party P_i, party P_i receives the random permutation bit and all parties receive the shares by executing the functionality $\mathbf{RandSS^{P_i}_{bin}(t)}$.
3. For each required i, each party P_i receives its random offset $R^i \in \mathrm{GF}(2^\kappa)$, and all parties receive Shamir shares of R^i, by executing functionality $\mathbf{RandSS^{P_i}(t)}$.
4. Shares of the permutation bits of the output wires, which are fixed to 0, are received using functionality $\mathbf{RandSS_0(t)}$.
5. Additive shares of 0 are generated using functionality $\mathbf{AZS}$.

The rest of the protocol is identical to $BGW2_{opt}$ (recall that communication round 2 in $BGW3_{opt}$ is omitted in $BGW2_{opt}$), except that the output permutation bit shares are not sent (the output permutation bits are fixed to 0). This implies that the function dependent offline phase of our maliciously secure protocol is almost the same as the function dependent preprocessing of our semi-honest protocol – the only difference is the extra garbled buffer gates sent and that the shares of the output permutation bits are not sent. We call the above protocol $BGW2^{mal}_{opt}$.

Security. We next give the security statement of our protocol. The proof is given in the full version. Using the result of Hazay et al. [23], this suffices to realize an efficient constant round MPC protocol in the malicious setting.

Theorem 2. *Protocol $BGW2^{mal}_{opt}$ securely computes $\mathcal{F}^{mal}_{GC}$ in the linear preprocessing model in the presence of t maliciously corrupt parties, with $t < \frac{n}{3}$.*

5 Experimental Results

In this section we measure the running times of our protocols and compare our results with state-of-the-art constant round protocols.

Implementation and Running Environment. Our code was written in C++; it is publicly available at https://github.com/Aner2005/Protocols. For implementing $\mathcal{F}^2$, we used 128-bit fixed-key AES, as suggested in [2],[8] with pipelined AES-NI. For efficient field multiplications in $\mathrm{GF}(2^{128})$, we used the CLMUL commands [22]. We ran our experiments in a computer cluster comprised of Intel XEON 2.20 GHz machines (E5-2420) with 6 cores running Linux (Ubuntu1404-64-STD), and with a 1 Gb connection and approximately 0.2 ms ping time.

We benchmarked the timing of our protocols for 13 and for 31 parties on both the AES circuit, consisting of 6800 AND gates, and the SHA256 circuit, consisting of 90875 AND gates. All experiment results are the average on 25 protocol timings - 5 runs with 5 repetitions in each run. Synchronization steps were placed before and after each timed phase described below. Following convention, e.g., [23,35,40], we split our timings into the following phases:

---

[8] This gives slightly less than 128 bits of security, see [2].

Function Independent Preprocessing The knowledge required at this phase is only an upper bound on the number of AND gates in the circuit. This part consists of Shamir secret-sharing the permutation bits and offsets, and also of the additive zero-sharing.

Function Dependent Preprocessing This phase requires knowledge of the function to be evaluated. It consists of local multiplication, share conversion and reconstruction of the garbled circuit by the evaluator.[9] In $BGW3$ there is also a degree reduction round performed at this phase.

Online This phase requires the inputs of the parties. It consists of exchanging masked inputs, sending the corresponding input keys to the evaluator, and the evaluation of the garbled circuit by the evaluator.

In addition, there is a short **Setup** phase that is done once regardless of the number of functions/gates evaluated (but requires fixing the parties that will participate throughout). In this phase the parties exchange private keys and precompute the reconstruction constants.

Optimizations Measurements. We tested the effect of our different optimizations with comparison to the original protocols of [4]. We give here the results for 31 parties on the SHA-256 circuit (Table 1). Basic refers to the original sub-protocol of [4] (with only one evaluator). Reduced Complexity is including the optimization described in Sect. 3.1. Short Superseeds, Efficient Zero-Sharing and Hypercube are including the respective optimizations described in Sect. 3.2 (optimizations are aggregated). For 31 parties our optimizations reduced the total time by over 70% in $BGW3$ and over 80%, and in some case over 85%, in $BGW2$!

Table 1. Measuring the effect of our different optimizations on a LAN. Times are average in seconds.

SHA256, 31 parties		Basic	Red. Complexity	Short S.seeds	Eff. Zero-Sharing	Hypercube
BGW3 ($t = 15$)	Ind. Pre	28.006	13.027	6.944	6.094	6.196
	Dep. Pre	6.557	6.427	3.224	3.222	1.092
	Online	1.151	1.153	0.381	0.376	0.401
BGW2 ($t = 10$)	Ind. Pre	27.827	12.710	4.697	4.296	4.26
	Dep. Pre	6.345	6.186	2.088	2.085	0.712
	Online	1.127	1.164	0.27	0.257	0.282

Remark 1. We did not measure the running time of our malicious protocol, as we did not implement the necessary preprocessing functionalities in Sect. 4. However, we note that the running time of the function dependent preprocessing and the running time of the online time should be almost identical to the semi-honest case – the only difference is adding buffer gates to the output wires which are

---

[9] As mentioned, performing the reconstruction of the garbled circuit at the offline phase, before the inputs are given, requires assuming RO for proving security.

output of XOR gates. This corresponds to <1% and <0.2% of the total number of AND gates in the AES and the SHA256 circuits respectively (recall that buffer gates are only half the size of an AND gate). As for the function independent preprocessing, we believe that a fast implementation of the preprocessing functionalities, which would make our malicious protocol truly practical, is possible with today's techniques. We leave this for future work. Furthermore, as noted in [16], if the number of parties is small, then these preprocessing functionalities can be computed locally, by using a one-time setup and share conversion [14] (but this works only for a very small number of parties, as the setup time grows exponentially with the number of parties).

Comparison with the State-of-the-Art. The state-of-the-art, concretely efficient, constant round, secure multiparty (for an arbitrary number of parties) computation protocols are implementations of multiparty garbled circuits using oblivious transfer – the work of [4] for the semi-honest case,[10] and the works of [23] and [40] for the malicious case.

We note that, in contrast to our protocols, these protocols are secure up to $n-1$ corrupt parties. Thus, there are 2 possible comparisons – with respect to the same number of parties or with respect to the same number of *corrupt* parties. For example, for 13 participating parties, if an honest majority is assumed then one could compare running the OT protocols with 13 parties or with 7 parties. If more than 2/3 of the parties are assumed to be honest, one could compare to 13 parties or to 5 parties. We give a comparison of our protocols, for 13 parties, with the BGW and OT protocols of [4] (Table 2).[11]

We see that for the same number of parties, our protocols outperform the protocols of [4]. When comparing the same number of *corrupt* parties, we observe that although our total offline time is slightly slower than that of the OT version of [4], our function dependent preprocessing time is significantly faster. In some scenarios, the function might not be known a long time in advance, and this could therefore be significant. Also, our setup time is faster, because we don't need to perform baseOTs. We remark that since we used the same online protocol as [4], the timing for the same number of *corrupt* parties should be approx. equal, with ours being slightly slower because more parties need to exchange masked inputs.

Unfortunately, at the time of writing, the codes of [23] and of [40] were not yet publicly available. However, as noted in both [23] and [40], their timings are very similar to the timings of the OT protocol of [4] (albeit having a much stronger security guarantee). Thus, following Remark 1, it seems that for the function dependent preprocessing and for the online phase, the comparison of $BGW2_{opt}$ with the OT protocol of [4] is a good indication for the comparison

---

[10] The work of [4] also presented the BGW protocols $BGW2$ and $BGW3$ along with their OT protocol. However, in their work they found that their OT protocol almost always significantly outperforms their BGW protocols for the same number of parties.

[11] For fair comparison, we changed the code of [4] so only one party evaluates the circuit also there.

Table 2. Comparison of our protocols with the protocols of [4]. Times are average in seconds. For the OT protocol, we compare for both the same number of parties and the same number of *corrupt* parties.

		$BGW3_{opt}$	OT protocol of [4]		$BGW3$ of [4]
		13 parties	13 parties	7 parties	13 parties
AES	Ind. Pre	0.115	0.01	0.007	0.315
	Dep. Pre	0.05	0.244	0.102	0.142
	Online	0.021	0.037	0.018	0.033
SHA256	Ind. Pre	1.322	0.125	0.089	3.563
	Dep. Pre	0.448	2.389	1.090	1.154
	Online	0.149	0.303	0.144	0.309
		$BGW2_{opt}$	OT protocol of [4]		$BGW2$ of [4]
		13 parties	13 parties	5 parties	13 parties
AES	Ind. Pre	0.084	0.01	0.006	0.308
	Dep. Pre	0.025	0.244	0.071	0.119
	Online	0.016	0.037	0.011	0.034
SHA256	Ind. Pre	1.005	0.125	0.079	3.514
	Dep. Pre	0.234	2.388	0.802	1.071
	Online	0.1	0.303	0.093	0.303

of $BGW2_{opt}^{mal}$ with the protocols of [23] and [40]. For the function independent preprocessing times, see Remark 1.

To conclude, our protocols are competitive with the state of the art constant round protocols in the semi-honest setting. In the linear preprocessing model, our $BGW2_{opt}^{mal}$ protocol is also competitive in the malicious setting. Thus, in some circumstances, our protocols might be considered as good alternatives.

Acknowledgements. The authors would like to thank Yehuda Lindell, Amos Beimel and Roi Inbar for helpful discussions.

References

1. Beaver, D., Micali, S., Rogaway, P.: The round complexity of secure protocols. In: Proceedings of the Twenty-second Annual ACM Symposium on Theory of Computing, STOC 1990, pp. 503–513. ACM, New York (1990). http://doi.acm.org/10.1145/100216.100287
2. Bellare, M., Hoang, V.T., Keelveedhi, S., Rogaway, P.: Efficient garbling from a fixed-key blockcipher. In: 2013 IEEE Symposium on Security and Privacy, SP 2013, Berkeley, CA, USA, 19–22 May 2013, pp. 478–492 (2013)
3. Ben-David, A., Nisan, N., Pinkas, B.: FairplayMP: a system for secure multi-party computation. In: Proceedings of the 15th ACM Conference on Computer and Communications Security, pp. 257–266. ACM (2008)

4. Ben-Efraim, A., Lindell, Y., Omri, E.: Optimizing semi-honest secure multiparty computation for the internet. In: Proceedings of the 2016 ACM SIGSAC Conference on Computer and Communications Security, Vienna, Austria, 24–28 October 2016, pp. 578–590 (2016)
5. Ben-Or, M., Goldwasser, S., Wigderson, A.: Completeness theorems for noncryptographic fault-tolerant distributed computations. In: Proceedings of the 20th ACM Symposium on the Theory of Computing, pp. 1–10 (1988)
6. Bertsekas, D., Özveren, C., Stamoulis, G., Tseng, P., Tsitsiklis, J.: Optimal communication algorithms for hypercubes. J. Parallel Distrib. Comput. **11**(4), 263–275 (1991). http://www.sciencedirect.com/science/article/pii/0743731591900336
7. Bogdanov, D., Laur, S., Willemson, J.: Sharemind: a framework for fast privacy-preserving computations. In: Jajodia, S., Lopez, J. (eds.) ESORICS 2008. LNCS, vol. 5283, pp. 192–206. Springer, Heidelberg (2008). https://doi.org/10.1007/978-3-540-88313-5_13
8. Bogetoft, P., et al.: Secure multiparty computation goes live. In: Dingledine, R., Golle, P. (eds.) FC 2009. LNCS, vol. 5628, pp. 325–343. Springer, Heidelberg (2009). https://doi.org/10.1007/978-3-642-03549-4_20
9. Burkhart, M., Strasser, M., Many, D., Dimitropoulos, X.: SEPIA: privacy-preserving aggregation of multi-domain network events and statistics. Network **1**, 101101 (2010)
10. Chandran, N., Garay, J., Mohassel, P., Vusirikala, S.: Efficient, constant-round and actively secure MPC: beyond the three-party case. In: 24rd ACM Conference on Computer and Communications Security, CCS 2017. ACM (2017, to appear)
11. Chaum, D., Crépeau, C., Damgård, I.: Multiparty unconditionally secure protocols. In: Proceedings of the 20th ACM Symposium on the Theory of Computing, pp. 11–19 (1988)
12. Choi, S.G., Hwang, K.-W., Katz, J., Malkin, T., Rubenstein, D.: Secure multiparty computation of boolean circuits with applications to privacy in on-line marketplaces. In: Dunkelman, O. (ed.) CT-RSA 2012. LNCS, vol. 7178, pp. 416–432. Springer, Heidelberg (2012). https://doi.org/10.1007/978-3-642-27954-6_26
13. Choi, S.G., Katz, J., Malozemoff, A.J., Zikas, V.: Efficient three-party computation from cut-and-choose. In: Garay, J.A., Gennaro, R. (eds.) CRYPTO 2014. LNCS, vol. 8617, pp. 513–530. Springer, Heidelberg (2014). https://doi.org/10.1007/978-3-662-44381-1_29
14. Cramer, R., Damgård, I., Ishai, Y.: Share conversion, pseudorandom secret-sharing and applications to secure computation. In: Kilian, J. (ed.) TCC 2005. LNCS, vol. 3378, pp. 342–362. Springer, Heidelberg (2005). https://doi.org/10.1007/978-3-540-30576-7_19
15. Damgård, I., Geisler, M., Krøigaard, M., Nielsen, J.B.: Asynchronous multiparty computation: theory and implementation. In: Jarecki, S., Tsudik, G. (eds.) PKC 2009. LNCS, vol. 5443, pp. 160–179. Springer, Heidelberg (2009). https://doi.org/10.1007/978-3-642-00468-1_10
16. Damgård, I., Ishai, Y.: Constant-round multiparty computation using a black-box pseudorandom generator. In: Shoup, V. (ed.) CRYPTO 2005. LNCS, vol. 3621, pp. 378–394. Springer, Heidelberg (2005). https://doi.org/10.1007/11535218_23
17. Damgård, I., Keller, M., Larraia, E., Pastro, V., Scholl, P., Smart, N.P.: Practical covertly secure MPC for dishonest majority – or: breaking the SPDZ limits. In: Crampton, J., Jajodia, S., Mayes, K. (eds.) ESORICS 2013. LNCS, vol. 8134, pp. 1–18. Springer, Heidelberg (2013). https://doi.org/10.1007/978-3-642-40203-6_1

18. Damgård, I., Pastro, V., Smart, N., Zakarias, S.: Multiparty computation from somewhat homomorphic encryption. In: Safavi-Naini, R., Canetti, R. (eds.) CRYPTO 2012. LNCS, vol. 7417, pp. 643–662. Springer, Heidelberg (2012). https://doi.org/10.1007/978-3-642-32009-5_38

19. Furukawa, J., Lindell, Y., Nof, A., Weinstein, O.: High-Throughput secure three-party computation for malicious adversaries and an honest majority. In: Coron, J.-S., Nielsen, J.B. (eds.) EUROCRYPT 2017. LNCS, vol. 10211, pp. 225–255. Springer, Cham (2017). https://doi.org/10.1007/978-3-319-56614-6_8

20. Gennaro, R., Rabin, M.O., Rabin, T.: Simplified VSS and fast-track multiparty computations with applications to threshold cryptography. In: Proceedings of the Seventeenth Annual ACM Symposium on Principles of Distributed Computing, PODC 1998, pp. 101–111. ACM (1998)

21. Goldreich, O., Micali, S., Wigderson, A.: How to play any mental game. In: Proceedings of the 19th ACM Symposium on the Theory of Computing, pp. 218–229 (1987)

22. Gueron, S., Kounavis, M.E.: Efficient implementation of the galois counter mode using a carry-less multiplier and a fast reduction algorithm. Inf. Process. Lett. 110(14–15), 549–553 (2010)

23. Hazay, C., Scholl, P., Soria-Vazquez, E.: Low cost constant round MPC combining BMR and oblivious transfer. In: Takagi, T., Peyrin, T. (eds.) ASIACRYPT 2017. LNCS, vol. 10624, pp. 598–628. Springer, Cham (2017). https://doi.org/10.1007/978-3-319-70694-8_21

24. Ishai, Y., Kushilevitz, E.: Randomizing polynomials: a new representation with applications to round-efficient secure computation. In: Proceedings 41st Annual Symposium on Foundations of Computer Science, pp. 294–304 (2000)

25. Keller, M., Orsini, E., Rotaru, D., Scholl, P., Soria-Vazquez, E., Vivek, S.: Faster secure multi-party computation of AES and DES using lookup tables. In: Gollmann, D., Miyaji, A., Kikuchi, H. (eds.) ACNS 2017. LNCS, vol. 10355, pp. 229–249. Springer, Cham (2017). https://doi.org/10.1007/978-3-319-61204-1_12

26. Keller, M., Orsini, E., Scholl, P.: MASCOT: faster malicious arithmetic secure computation with oblivious transfer. In: Proceedings of the 2016 ACM SIGSAC Conference on Computer and Communications Security, pp. 830–842. ACM (2016)

27. Kolesnikov, V., Schneider, T.: Improved garbled circuit: free XOR gates and applications. In: Aceto, L., Damgård, I., Goldberg, L.A., Halldórsson, M.M., Ingólfsdóttir, A., Walukiewicz, I. (eds.) ICALP 2008. LNCS, vol. 5126, pp. 486–498. Springer, Heidelberg (2008). https://doi.org/10.1007/978-3-540-70583-3_40

28. Kreuter, B., Shelat, A., Shen, C.H.: Billion-gate secure computation with malicious adversaries. In: USENIX Security Symposium, pp. 285–300 (2012)

29. Lindell, Y., Pinkas, B., Smart, N.P., Yanai, A.: Efficient constant round multiparty computation combining BMR and SPDZ. In: Gennaro, R., Robshaw, M. (eds.) CRYPTO 2015, Part II. LNCS, vol. 9216, pp. 319–338. Springer, Heidelberg (2015). https://doi.org/10.1007/978-3-662-48000-7_16

30. Lindell, Y., Riva, B.: Blazing fast 2PC in the offline/online setting with security for malicious adversaries. In: Proceedings of the 22nd ACM SIGSAC Conference on Computer and Communications Security, CCS 2015, pp. 579–590. ACM, New York (2015). http://doi.acm.org/10.1145/2810103.2813666

31. Lindell, Y., Smart, N.P., Soria-Vazquez, E.: More efficient constant-round multiparty computation from BMR and SHE. In: Hirt, M., Smith, A. (eds.) TCC 2016. LNCS, vol. 9985, pp. 554–581. Springer, Heidelberg (2016). https://doi.org/10.1007/978-3-662-53641-4_21

32. Malkhi, D., Nisan, N., Pinkas, B., Sella, Y., et al.: Fairplay-secure two-party computation system. In: USENIX Security Symposium, vol. 4, San Diego, CA, USA (2004)
33. Mohassel, P., Rosulek, M., Zhang, Y.: Fast and secure three-party computation: the garbled circuit approach. In: Proceedings of the 22Nd ACM SIGSAC Conference on Computer and Communications Security, CCS 2015, pp. 591–602. ACM, New York(2015). http://doi.acm.org/10.1145/2810103.2813705
34. Nielsen, J.B., Orlandi, C.: LEGO for two-party secure computation. In: Reingold, O. (ed.) TCC 2009. LNCS, vol. 5444, pp. 368–386. Springer, Heidelberg (2009). https://doi.org/10.1007/978-3-642-00457-5_22
35. Nielsen, J.B., Schneider, T., Trifiletti, R.: Constant round maliciously secure 2PC with function-independent preprocessing using LEGO. In: Network and Distributed System Security Symposium, NDSS (2017)
36. Pinkas, B., Schneider, T., Smart, N.P., Williams, S.C.: Secure two-party computation is practical. In: Matsui, M. (ed.) ASIACRYPT 2009. LNCS, vol. 5912, pp. 250–267. Springer, Heidelberg (2009). https://doi.org/10.1007/978-3-642-10366-7_15
37. Schneider, T., Zohner, M.: GMW vs. Yao? Efficient secure two-party computation with low depth circuits. In: Sadeghi, A.-R. (ed.) FC 2013. LNCS, vol. 7859, pp. 275–292. Springer, Heidelberg (2013). https://doi.org/10.1007/978-3-642-39884-1_23
38. Shamir, A.: How to share a secret. Commun. ACM **22**, 612–613 (1979)
39. Wang, X., Ranellucci, S., Katz, J.: Authenticated garbling and efficient maliciously secure two-party computation. In: 24rd ACM Conference on Computer and Communications Security, CCS 2017. ACM (2017, to appear)
40. Wang, X., Ranellucci, S., Katz, J.: Global-scale secure multiparty computation. In: 24rd ACM Conference on Computer and Communications Security, CCS 2017. ACM (2017, to appear)
41. Yao, A.C.: Protocols for secure computations. In: Proceedings of the 23th IEEE Symposium on Foundations of Computer Science, pp. 160–164 (1982)
42. Zahur, S., Rosulek, M., Evans, D.: Two halves make a whole - reducing data transfer in garbled circuits using half gates. In: Oswald, E., Fischlin, M. (eds.) EUROCRYPT 2015, Part II. LNCS, vol. 9057, pp. 220–250. Springer, Heidelberg (2015). https://doi.org/10.1007/978-3-662-46803-6_8

New Constructions

Homomorphic Rank Sort Using Surrogate Polynomials

Gizem S. Çetin$^{(\boxtimes)}$ and Berk Sunar

Worcester Polytechnic Institute, Worcester, USA
{gscetin,sunar}@wpi.edu

Abstract. In this paper we propose a rank based algorithm for sorting encrypted data using monomials. Greedy Sort is a sorting technique that achieves to minimize the depth of the homomorphic evaluations. It is a costly algorithm due to excessive ciphertext multiplications and its implementation is cumbersome. Another method Direct Sort has a slightly deeper circuit than Greedy Sort, nevertheless it is simpler to implement and scales better with the size of the input array. Our proposed method minimizes both the circuit depth and the number of ciphertext multiplications. In addition to its performance, its simple design makes it more favorable compared to the alternative methods which are hard to parallelize, e.g. not suitable for fast GPU implementations. Furthermore, we improve the performance of homomorphic sorting algorithm by adapting the SIMD operations alongside message slot rotation techniques. This method allow us to pack N integers into a single ciphertext and compute N comparisons at once, thus reducing $\mathcal{O}(N^2)$ comparisons to $\mathcal{O}(N)$.

Keywords: Private computation · Encrypted computing ·
Fully homomorphic encryption · Homomorphic sorting

1 Introduction

Blind sort is basically arranging a set of encrypted integers in order by using a somewhat, leveled or Fully Homomorphic Encryption (FHE) scheme [1–6,9,10, 12–15,18,22,25] without knowledge of neither the plaintext data or the secret key used in encryption. The operations do not require decryption either. The crucial drawback of using FHE schemes in practice is their poor performance in high-level computations due to the high noise growth at the end of deep circuit evaluations. Most recent FHE schemes make use of noise reduction techniques in order to overcome this problem by setting the FHE parameters to evaluate only up to a certain depth. As a result, deep circuits require large parameters and they perform poorly.

In [7], Çetin et al. analyze different sorting algorithms and compare their performances for ordering encrypted data. Their survey include well-known algorithms such as Bubble Sort, Merge Sort and two sorting networks: Bitonic Sort and Odd-Even Merge Sort [20]. Due to the high depths of known algorithms,

© Springer Nature Switzerland AG 2019
T. Lange and O. Dunkelman (Eds.): LATINCRYPT 2017, LNCS 11368, pp. 311–326, 2019.
https://doi.org/10.1007/978-3-030-25283-0_17

the authors propose two new depth-optimized methods: Greedy Sort and Direct Sort. Both of these algorithms require a circuit of depth $\mathcal{O}\left(\log(N) + \log(\ell)\right)$ where N is the number of elements and ℓ is the bit-length of the elements. Other encrypted sorting works in the literature are of Chatterjee et al. [8] and Emmadi et al.'s [11]. In [8], the authors introduce a hybrid technique, i.e. Lazy Sort. This method first uses Bubble Sort to nearly sort the input elements. Then, the list is sorted again by using Insertion Sort. The authors claim that this method has better complexity than the worst case scenario. This is refuted by both [7] and [11]. Emmadi et al. implements and compares Bubble Sort, Insertion Sort, Bitonic Sort and Odd-Even Merge Sort in [11] and their observations are parallel with the analysis of [7]. Recently, Narumanchi et al. compared bitwise and integer-wise encryption within the context of comparison and sorting in [23]. Their analysis shows that it is more efficient to use bitwise encryption in terms of performance. All of the previous works still perform poorly in case of sorting a large data set. In the experiments, the largest N used is around 64.

The main contribution of this work is proposing an alternative way of sorting numbers by computing the Hamming weight of N bits with only N ciphertext multiplications. In comparison to our proposed method with $\mathcal{O}(N)$ multiplications, Direct Sort and Greedy Sort require $\mathcal{O}(N \log N)$ and $\mathcal{O}(2^N)$ multiplications, respectively. Our algorithm implements Direct Sort method with the minimum number of operations. We observe that our proposed method is also a compact implementation of Greedy Sort. Therefore, it both minimizes the circuit depth and the number of homomorphic evaluations. Furthermore, efficient evaluation of the Hamming weight can be used in many other homomorphic applications. In addition to performance improvements, the proposed algorithm is easier to analyze and implement in comparison to previous methods. Even when batching is not applicable, the highly parallelizable nature of the algorithm makes it an efficient candidate for a GPU implementation. Our sorting method is generic and can be implemented with existing software libraries, e.g. HElib [19], SEAL [21].

Our second contribution is adapting Single-Instruction Multiple-Data (SIMD) idea from [24] and permutation technique from [16] to evaluate parallel homomorphic comparisons to sort the elements of a single set. In previous works, batching is used to sort separate number sets simultaneously. This results in not taking advantage of batching when there is only one set to be sorted. We propose placing the set elements into message slots of a single plaintext and using rotation method from [16] when across-slot computation is required. Gentry et al. used this technique to evaluate an AES circuit homomorphically in [17]. This method requires key switching after every rotation. However we are able to reduce the number of comparisons from N^2 to $N/2$.

2   Background

Following a similar notation to [16,17,24], we define the plaintexts with lowercase letters $a \in \mathbb{A}_p$, batched plaintexts with Greek letters $\alpha \in \mathbb{A}_p$ and the ciphertexts with uppercase letters $A \in \mathbb{A}_q$ where $\mathbb{A}_p = \mathbb{Z}_p / \Phi_m(X)$ and $\mathbb{A}_q = \mathbb{Z}_q / \Phi_m(X)$. We use prime p, q in our scheme and $\Phi_m(X)$ is the mth cyclotomic polynomial. Given two ciphertexts A, B that are encrypted under an FHE scheme, computing $A + B$ and $A \times B$ in $\mathbb{A}_q$ gives us encryptions of $a + b$ and $a \times b$ in $\mathbb{A}_p$.

When a number a has k base-p digits, we use an array index notation to represent its digits $[a_0, a_1, \cdots, a_{k-1}]$ and $a = \sum_{i=0}^{k-1} p^i a_i$. An encryption of a would be a vector of ciphertexts with encryptions of its digits, i.e. $[A_0, A_1, \cdots, A_{k-1}]$. When there is a list of numbers, we use the double-indexed positioning with the first one being the number's position and the second one is for the digit's index. For instance, a plaintext $\alpha_{i,j}$ is the jth digit of the ith number and similarly $A_{i,j}$ is an encryption of the jth digit of the ith number.

2.1   Batching and Rotation of the Message Slots

From [24], we know that with specific parameters we can enable batching, a technique that is used for parallel evaluations in the message slots. For example, when we choose the cyclotomic polynomial with m that divides $p^d - 1$ with smallest such d, we have the factorization,

$$\Phi_m(X) = \prod_{i=1}^{\ell} F_i(X) \mod p$$

where F_i's are $\ell = \phi(m)/d$ irreducible polynomials of degree d. Then we have the isomorphism in between the plaintext space and the ℓ copies of $\mathbb{F}_{p^d}$.

$$\mathbb{A}_p \cong \frac{\mathbb{F}_p[X]}{F_1} \otimes \cdots \otimes \frac{\mathbb{F}_p[X]}{F_\ell}$$

We define a vector with ℓ messages $\alpha = \langle \alpha_1, \cdots, \alpha_\ell \rangle$ with each α_i belonging to the field $\mathbb{L}_i = \frac{\mathbb{F}_p[X]}{F_i}$. Applying inverse Chinese Remainder Theorem (CRT), we derive a single message in $\mathbb{A}_p$. We write this as:

$$\alpha = \mathsf{CRT}^{-1}(\langle \alpha_1, \cdots, \alpha_\ell \rangle)$$

with $\alpha_i \in \mathbb{L}_i$ and $\alpha \in \mathbb{A}_p$. We say the plaintext has ℓ message slots and each message is packed in a single slot. Additions and multiplications over CRT plaintexts will be evaluated in each slot due to the natural isomorphism. For example given another plaintext $\beta = \mathsf{CRT}^{-1}(\beta)$, we have

$$\mathsf{CRT}(\alpha + \beta) = \langle \alpha_1 + \beta_1, \cdots, \alpha_\ell + \beta_\ell \rangle$$
$$\mathsf{CRT}(\alpha \times \beta) = \langle \alpha_1 \times \beta_1, \cdots, \alpha_\ell \times \beta_\ell \rangle \ .$$

with $\alpha_i \star \beta_i \in \mathbb{L}_i$ and $\star \in \{+, \times\}$. In some applications, we need to do computation across message slots, i.e. $\alpha_i \star \beta_j$ where $i \neq j$. To this end, we permute the message slots so that message i and message j aligns. Due to the relation in between the factors of the cyclotomic polynomial, the automorphism

$$\kappa_g : \alpha(X) \longmapsto \alpha(x^g) \mod \Phi_m(X)$$

for a g that is not a power of 2 in $(\mathbb{Z}/m\mathbb{Z})^*$ with order ℓ performs a permutation. To see why this works and for the underlying Galois field theory we refer readers to [16].

2.2   Problem Definition and Existing Algorithms

Encrypted Sorting Problem: Given an unordered set of encrypted elements $\{A_0, A_1, \cdots, A_{N-1}\}$, we want to find an ordered set of encrypted elements $\{B_0, B_1 \cdots, B_{N-1}\}$ where the decrypted list $\{b_0, \cdots, b_{N-1}\}$ is a permutation of $\{a_0, \cdots, a_{N-1}\}$ with nondecreasing order, i.e. $b_0 \leq b_1 \leq \cdots \leq b_{N-1}$.

In the following part of this section, we will briefly describe the previously proposed methods to solve the encrypted sorting problem. Before the algorithm descriptions, we shall define a comparator. In order to sort a set of elements, we need to be able to compare two numbers with respect to their magnitude. In [7], where the input elements are bitwise encrypted, this comparison is converted to a binary circuit as follows[1]:

$$A \lessdot B = \sum_{i=0}^{k-1} (A_i \oplus 1) B_i \prod_{j=i+1}^{k-1} (A_j \oplus B_j \oplus 1) \tag{1}$$

where A_i, B_i are the encryptions of ith bit of k bit numbers a and b, respectively. The decryption of $A \lessdot B$ outputs a 1 if $a < b$ and a 0 otherwise.

Greedy Sort. In [7], authors propose Greedy Sort as an alternative method to classical sorting algorithms, due to its low circuit depth. However, due to the algorithm's exhaustive nature, the method is not efficient when implemented without optimizations. In this section, we describe the algorithm and later in Sect. 3, we propose our optimization that minimizes the total number of ciphertext multiplications.

Greedy Sort works by computing every possible permutation of the input set. In order to find the minimum element b_0, one needs to compare each a_i to every other element in the set. If it is smaller than all a_js where $i \neq j$, then we can conclude it is the smallest element and set $b_0 = a_i$. Similarly, in order to find the next smallest element b_1, we need to compare every a_i to every other element and if it is smaller than all but one, then we know that it is the second minimum and set $b_1 = a_i$. We can follow the same idea until the last element of the sorted array b_{n-1} which is the maximum element is found.

---

[1] If the plaintext modulus p is initialized as 2, an XOR "$\oplus$" operation is performed via addition. Otherwise, $A \oplus B = A + B - 2(A \times B)$ and $A \oplus 1 = 1 - A$.

This method requires comparison of every pair in the set, thus the initial step is to build a matrix M that holds the comparison outputs. Entries of this matrix, let them be $M_{i,j}$s are evaluated using the binary circuit given in Eq. 1 such that $M_{i,j} = A_i < A_j$. Here, note that $M_{i,j}$s and $M_{j,i}$s naturally complement each other[2] and $M_{i,i}$s are always zero. Therefore $M_{i,j}$s are only evaluated for $i < j$. Given the comparison matrix, the ordered elements are computed as follows:

$$B_r = \theta_{r,0} A_0 + \cdots + \theta_{r,N-1} A_{N-1} = \sum_{i=0}^{N-1} \theta_{r,i} A_i$$

where

$$\theta_{r,i} = \sum_{\substack{k_1=0 \\ k_1 \neq i}}^{N-r-1} M_{k_1,i} \cdots \sum_{\substack{k_r=k_{r-1}+1 \\ k_r \neq i}}^{N-1} M_{k_r,i} \prod_{\substack{j=0 \\ j \neq i \\ j \neq k_1, \cdots, k_r}}^{N-1} M_{i,j} . \qquad (2)$$

$\theta_{r,i}$ values can be seen as the binary place indicators or a decision flag that indicates whether the input A_i will be mapped to output B_r. In other words, if the input A_i has the rank r, it is an encrypted one. This requires computation of all $\theta_{r,i}$s for $i, r = 0, \cdots, N-1$, thus making the method inefficient. The Greedy Sort algorithm steps can be seen in Appendix C of [7].

Direct Sort. In the same work [7], the authors propose another low-depth method for sorting, i.e. Direct Sort. The algorithm implements Rank Sort in the homomorphic setting. The first step is constructing the same comparison matrix M as in Greedy Sort. Then, it computes the ranks by performing a column-wise summation of the entries of M. Since the elements of M are bits, the summation result gives the Hamming weights of the columns of M. It is implemented using a Wallace Tree of depth $\mathcal{O}(\log_{3/2} N)$. The challenge is having the rank values encrypted after this step. This requires an additional homomorphic equality check to place the elements in the output in an ordered manner. This equality check is performed on rank values which are $\log N$ bit numbers, hence requires a homomorphic evaluation of depth $\log \log N$. The method can be found in Algorithm 1 in [7].

3   Our Proposal: Polynomial Rank Sort

In a nutshell, the idea is to use the rank of an input as the degree of a monomial –which we call a *rank monomial*– and place the input element in the coefficient of the monomial.

Definition. Given an input set $\{a_0, a_1, \cdots, a_{N-1}\}$ with N elements, let r_i be the rank of a_i in the set, we call $\rho_i(x) = x^{r_i}$ the *rank monomial* of integer a_i.

---

[2] $M_{j,i} = M_{i,j} \oplus 1$.

Claim. If we can find the rank monomials $\{x^{r_0}, x^{r_1}, \cdots, x^{r_{N-1}}\}$ of all of the set elements, then we can have an output polynomial with input elements lined up in its coefficients with respect to their rank:

$$b(x) = \sum_{i=0}^{N-1} a_i \rho_i(x) = \sum_{i=0}^{N-1} a_i x^{r_i}$$

$$= b_0 + b_1 x + \cdots + b_{N-1} x^{N-1}$$

with $b_0 \leq b_1 \leq \cdots \leq b_{N-1}$.

Proof Sketch. To see why this works, note that the ranks of the inputs are a permutation of natural numbers in the range $[0, N-1]$. Thus, there is a bijective mapping in between the i and r_i values. The same mapping gives us the ordered permutation of the input elements, i.e. $b_{r_i} = a_i$. Bijection ensures the exclusive positions of each input element in the output polynomial.

Challenge. Implementing this method on private data has two challenges: finding the ranks of encrypted inputs and placing the encrypted rank values in the exponent. In the following section, we propose a solution to this problem.

3.1   Finding Rank Monomials

In order to show how the algorithm works, first we assume that the inputs are not encrypted. After demonstrating the steps of the method, we show how to implement it for encrypted data, i.e. by using only homomorphic operations.

We shortly describe the method as follows: For an N-element input set, we start by finding the zero-based rankings in each 2-subset, being either 0 or 1. We start by constructing surrogate monomials using these ranks. Then, we merge the subsets by performing polynomial multiplication among the surrogates. At the end, this gives us the rank monomials of each input element.

Initially, we consider the base case: an input set with only two elements $\{a, b\}$. We say the rank of a is r_a and rank of b is r_b with the rank monomials defined as:

$$\rho_a(x) = x^{r_a} \quad \text{and} \quad \rho_b(x) = x^{r_b}.$$

If, for instance, the input elements have the relation $a < b$, then we can write $r_a = 0$ and $r_b = 1$ and $\rho_a = 1, \rho_b = x$, respectively.

Now, we include a third element c in the input set. In this case, the first step is to find the ranks in each 2-subset. We look at all two element subsets; $\{a, b\}$, $\{a, c\}$ and $\{b, c\}$ and define the following surrogate monomials:

$$\rho_{ab}(x) = x^{r_{ab}} \qquad\qquad \rho_{ba}(x) = x^{r_{ba}}$$
$$\rho_{ac}(x) = x^{r_{ac}} \qquad\qquad \rho_{ca}(x) = x^{r_{ca}}$$
$$\rho_{bc}(x) = x^{r_{bc}} \qquad\qquad \rho_{cb}(x) = x^{r_{cb}}$$

where r_{ij} is the rank of input i in the 2-subset $\{i, j\}$ and ρ_{ij} is the rank monomial of the same element in the same subset. The next step is merging two subsets to find the final rank monomials. Multiplying two surrogates adjusts the degree of the rank monomial depending on the subset-wise rank values. When we want to find the rank monomial for a particular input, we multiply each surrogate that is pertinent to that element:

$$\rho_a = \rho_{ab} \cdot \rho_{ac} = x^{r_{ab}+r_{ac}}$$
$$\rho_b = \rho_{ba} \cdot \rho_{bc} = x^{r_{ba}+r_{bc}}$$
$$\rho_c = \rho_{ca} \cdot \rho_{cb} = x^{r_{ca}+r_{cb}}$$

Following the previous example with $a < b$, we fix the following relations and the partial rank monomials for the set where $c < a < b$:

$$a < b \Leftrightarrow \rho_{ab}(x) = 1, \; \rho_{ba}(x) = x$$
$$c < a \Leftrightarrow \rho_{ac}(x) = x, \; \rho_{ca}(x) = 1$$
$$c < b \Leftrightarrow \rho_{bc}(x) = x, \; \rho_{cb}(x) = 1$$

Then the rank monomials will be:

$$\rho_a = \rho_{ab} \cdot \rho_{ac} = x$$
$$\rho_b = \rho_{ba} \cdot \rho_{bc} = x^2$$
$$\rho_c = \rho_{ca} \cdot \rho_{cb} = 1 \;.$$

If we examine the degrees of the monomials, we find that the ranks are: $r_a = 1$, $r_b = 2$ and $r_c = 0$ which are consistent with the given relation $c < a < b$.

We now generalize this method to an N-element input set by defining the following surrogate monomials for each input element a_i:

$$\rho_{ij}(x) = x^{r_{ij}} \tag{3}$$

for all 2-subsets $\{a_i, a_j\}$ that contain a_i, i.e. $\forall j \in [0, N-1]$ and $j \neq i$. Then, computing the product of all the surrogates would carry the overall rank of a_i in the power of:

$$\rho_i(x) = \prod_{\substack{j=0 \\ j \neq i}}^{N-1} \rho_{ij}(x) \;. \tag{4}$$

The degree of $\rho_i(x)$ is the rank of a_i in the N-element set. This operation can be viewed as increasing the rank by one whenever an element a_i is larger than another element. In other words, it is counting the number of smaller elements, i.e. the rank of a_i.

Connection to Direct Sort. This method is equivalent to summing the column entries of the comparison matrix M, i.e. computing the Hamming weights, as performed in Direct Sort (see Algorithm 1 in [7]). In order to see this connection, we must first confirm that comparison matrix elements m_{ij} and 2-subset ranks

r_{ij} complement each other. This is because m_{ij} is the Boolean output of the comparison $a_i < a_j$, which is 1 if and only if a_i is smaller than a_j. However r_{ij} is 0 in this case, since it is the smallest element in the same 2-set. Hence, r_{ij} and m_{ij} complement each other and we can assert that $r_{ij} = m_{ji}$. We expand the product as in Eq. 5 and notice that the summation in the exponent is equivalent to the Hamming weight of the columns of M.

$$\rho_i(x) = \prod_{\substack{j=0 \\ j \neq i}}^{N-1} x^{r_{ij}} = x^{\sum_{\substack{j=0 \\ j \neq i}}^{N-1} r_{ij}} = x^{\sum_{\substack{j=0 \\ j \neq i}}^{N-1} m_{ji}} \tag{5}$$

Until now, we have showed that we can find the rank monomials given the base case surrogates by applying polynomial multiplication. In the following section we describe how to apply this method to encrypted input sets.

3.2   Finding Rank Monomials in the Encrypted Domain

In the encrypted domain, we have a set of N encrypted numbers $\{A_0, A_1, \cdots, A_{N-1}\}$ by utilizing an FHE scheme. Recall that the first step of the proposed algorithm constructs the surrogates for all 2-subsets as in Eq. 3. This requires finding the encrypted rank R_{ij} in set $\{A_i, A_j\}$. Hence we use the comparison circuit from Eq. 1 and compute the encrypted rank of a_i as:

$$R_{ij} = 1 - (A_i < A_j)$$

Using this value, we can set the base case surrogate monomial using the following operation that requires arithmetic suitable for homomorphic evaluation:

$$P_{ij}(x) = 1 - R_{ij} + R_{ij} \cdot x \tag{6}$$

Rechecking the base case example with $a < b$, we can confirm that[3];

$$A < B = [\![1]\!] \qquad\qquad B < A = [\![0]\!]$$
$$R_{ab} = [\![0]\!] \qquad\qquad R_{ba} = [\![1]\!]$$
$$P_{ab}(x) = 1 - [\![0]\!] + [\![0]\!]x \qquad P_{ba}(x) = 1 - [\![1]\!] + [\![1]\!]x$$
$$= [\![1]\!] \qquad\qquad = [\![x]\!]$$

What happens when two elements are equal to each other? Then, both $a < b$ and $b < a$ are expected to output a zero. To fix this problem, we always perform only the first comparison and fix the second comparison to its complement. In other words, computing first one of the ranks $R_{ji} = A_i < A_j$ and setting the other $R_{ij} = 1 - R_{ji}$ solves the equality problem by making sure that the ranks always complement each other. Thereby, we also avoid redundant homomorphic comparisons. Note that, in [7], only the upper half of the comparison matrix

---

[3] Here, we use $[\![\,\cdot\,]\!]$ to represent an encryption of a constant value.

M is computed and the lower half entries are set as the complements. This is identical to computing R_{ij} for half of the element pairs.

The next step is to compute the final rank monomials by using Eq. 4. This operation which only includes polynomial multiplication, can simply be evaluated using homomorphic evaluations:

$$P_i(x) = \prod_{\substack{j=0 \\ j\neq i}}^{N-1} P_{ij}(x) .$$

If we multiply each P_i with the corresponding input A_i, i.e. computing P_iA_i, we can place the element in the rank coefficient and since every rank r_i is exclusive to an element, each element will be placed in a distinct coefficient. Thus, we can have an output polynomial B with the ordered elements in its coefficients:

$$B(x) = \sum_{i=0}^{N-1} A_i x^{r_i} = \sum_{j=0}^{N-1} B_j x^j$$

where $b_0 \leq b_1 \leq \cdots \leq b_{N-1}$. The overall algorithm is summarized in Algorithm 1 with given encrypted input set and the set size N. In comparison to intricate Greedy Sort Algorithm given in Appendix C [7], the simplicity and elegance of Algorithm 1 makes it more favorable and convenient to implement and less troublesome to analyze. As we shall see in the next section, we also gain further in efficiency.

Algorithm 1. Polynomial Rank Sort

Input: A, N
Output: $B(x)$
  $B(x) \leftarrow 0$
  for all $A_i \in A$ **do**
    for all $j > i$ **do**
      $M_{ij} \leftarrow A_i < A_j$
      $M_{ji} \leftarrow 1 - M_{ij}$
    end for
    $P_i(x) \leftarrow 1$
    for all $j \neq i$ **do**
      $P_i(x) \leftarrow P_i(x) \times (M_{ij} + M_{ji}x)$
    end for
    $B(x) \leftarrow B(x) + A_i \times P_i(x)$
  end for

Remark. To see the connection to Greedy Sort, note that the coefficients of the product polynomial are the binary place indicator $\theta_{r,i}$ values:

$$
\rho_i(x) = \prod_{\substack{j=0 \\ j \neq i}}^{N-1} \rho_{ij}(x) = \prod_{\substack{j=0 \\ j \neq i}}^{N-1} (m_{i,j} + m_{j,i} x)
$$

$$
= \prod_{\substack{j=0 \\ j \neq i}}^{N-1} m_{i,j} + \left[\sum_{\substack{k=0 \\ k \neq i}}^{N-1} m_{k,i} \prod_{\substack{j=0 \\ j \neq i \\ j \neq k}}^{N-1} m_{i,j} \right] x
$$

$$
+ \cdots + \left[\prod_{\substack{j=0 \\ j \neq i}}^{N-1} m_{j,i} \right] x^{N-1} \tag{7}
$$

3.3   Comparison with the Previous Methods

All three algorithms work by computing the comparison matrix M. Since that is a mutual step for all of the methods, we disregard the cost of constructing M in this analysis. The rest of the operations can be summarized for each method in Table 1.

Table 1. Comparison of the proposed algorithm with the previous methods in terms of number of ciphertext multiplications, multiplicative depth and output size.

	Naïve Greedy	Direct	**Our proposed method**
Ciphertext multiplications	$\mathcal{O}(2^N)$	$\mathcal{O}(N \log N)$	$\mathcal{O}(N)$
Multiplicative depth	$\mathcal{O}(\log N)$	$\mathcal{O}(\log N)$	$\mathcal{O}(\log N)$

The Naïve Greedy implements the Greedy Sort in a straightforward manner, hence the multiplications can be counted in the $\theta_{r,i}$ computations. In order to find the binary place indicators for an arbitrary element X_i, we need to compute $\theta_{0,i}, \theta_{1,i}, \cdots, \theta_{N-1,i}$ as in Eq. 2 with each one contributing

$$
\sum_{k=0}^{N-1} \binom{N-1}{k} = 2^{N-1}
$$

multiplications.

Direct Sort has two steps that involve ciphertext multiplications: summation of columns of M and equality check of the rank values. The first is computed by using a Wallace Tree of N bits for each column. The latter is computed by using the bit-wise equality check circuit for $\log N$ bits for each possible rank, i.e. N times. Therefore, total number of multiplications to find the rank of one element becomes $\mathcal{O}(\log N) + \mathcal{O}(N \log N)$.

Instead, our proposed method requires only a product of $N - 1$ ciphertexts, in order to find a single rank.

4   Batching Input Elements

In this section, we describe how to pack input elements in the plaintexts to evaluate parallel comparisons in the message slots. All previously mentioned sorting algorithms require $\frac{N^2 - N}{2}$ comparisons. By enabling batching, we can reduce it to $N/2$. Finding the rank monomial of one element requires $N - 2$ ciphertext multiplications, thus finding all rank monomials requires $N(N - 2)$ multiplications. We also reduce this number to $N - 2$ with batching. Finally, when we encrypt the input elements, instead of having Nk encryptions, we only have k encryptions when batching is used, where k is the bit-length of the input elements. As a result, we have both a memory and performance gain with a factor of N. However, there is an additional cost of key switching that we need to perform after each rotation. This operation also increases the noise in the ciphertext, thus we try to limit the number of rotations.

For our application, we use the plaintext modulus $p = 2$. Choosing Φ_m with $m | 2^d - 1$, we utilize ℓ message slots defined over $\mathbb{F}_{2^d}$. Next we choose a $g \in (\mathbb{Z}/m\mathbb{Z})^*$ with order ℓ. We fix the first factor $F_1(X)$ and reorder the rest of the factors so that the permutation given by κ_g is a cyclic shift to the left. There is an isomorphism in between the different slot fields, hence we define a mapping in between $\mathbb{L}_1$ and $\mathbb{L}_i$ for each i:

$$\psi_i : \begin{cases} \mathbb{L}_1 \longmapsto \mathbb{L}_i \\ X \longmapsto X^{g^{(1-i)} \mod \ell} \end{cases} \mod F_i(X)$$

Using this mapping we transfer the input elements from $\mathbb{L}_1$ to $\mathbb{L}_i$ and pack them as follows

$$\alpha = \mathsf{CRT}^{-1} \left(\langle \psi_1(\alpha_1), \psi_2(\alpha_2), \cdots, \psi_\ell(\alpha_\ell) \rangle \right)$$

and rotate the slots by computing the automorphism $\gamma = \kappa_g(\alpha)$.

$$\mathsf{CRT}(\gamma) = \langle \kappa_g\left(\psi_2\left(\alpha_2\right)\right), \kappa_g\left(\psi_3\left(\alpha_3\right)\right), \cdots, \kappa_g\left(\psi_\ell\left(\alpha_\ell\right)\right), \kappa_g\left(\psi_1\left(\alpha_1\right)\right) \rangle$$

Using the inverse of the above mappings ψ_i^{-1}, we can retrieve the original message contents after computing $\mathsf{CRT}(\gamma)$:

$$\langle \psi_1^{-1}\left(\kappa_g\left(\psi_2\left(\alpha_2\right)\right)\right), \cdots, \psi_\ell^{-1}\left(\kappa_g\left(\psi_1\left(\alpha_1\right)\right)\right) \rangle = \langle \alpha_2, \cdots, \alpha_1 \rangle \ .$$

Note that, performing a cyclic shift of j is the same as rotating the slots j times, in other words it is equivalent to computing κ_{g^j}. We also define two helpful basic operations to clear out a slot content and to select a slot content. Both can be performed with a logical AND operation by defining a bit-mask vector. If we want to clear the data in the ith slot, we create a vector $\boldsymbol{\zeta}$ with $\zeta_i = 0$ and $\zeta_j = 1$ for all $j \neq i$ and use its batched polynomial, i.e. $\zeta = \mathsf{CRT}^{-1}(\boldsymbol{\zeta})$, to perform a logical AND with the input. Similarly, if we want to select the data in the ith slot, we create a vector $\boldsymbol{\sigma}$ with $\sigma_i = 1$ and $\sigma_j = 0$ for all $j \neq i$, batch it $\sigma = \mathsf{CRT}^{-1}(\boldsymbol{\sigma})$ and multiply it with the input.

$$\mathsf{CRT}(\alpha \times \zeta) = \langle \alpha_1, \cdots, \alpha_{i-1}, 0, \alpha_{i+1}, \cdots, \alpha_{\ell-1} \rangle$$
$$\mathsf{CRT}(\alpha \times \sigma) = \langle 0, \cdots, 0, \alpha_i, 0, \cdots, 0 \rangle$$

Going back to our sorting algorithm, initially we have a set of k-bit elements $\{a_0, a_1, \cdots, a_{N-1}\}$. We declare a vector for each bit,

$$\boldsymbol{\alpha}_0 = \langle a_{0,0}, a_{1,0}, \cdots, a_{N-1,0} \rangle$$
$$\boldsymbol{\alpha}_1 = \langle a_{0,1}, a_{1,1}, \cdots, a_{N-1,1} \rangle$$
$$\vdots$$
$$\boldsymbol{\alpha}_{k-1} = \langle a_{0,k-1}, a_{1,k-1}, \cdots, a_{N-1,k-1} \rangle$$

where the ith slot is reserved for the ith element. Hence, each plaintext corresponding to a bit is batched, i.e. $\alpha_j = \mathsf{CRT}^{-1}(\boldsymbol{\alpha}_j)$, for $j = 0, \cdots, k-1$. Note that, we do not need to apply the mapping ψ_i before batching, when the slot content is an integer. Hence a vector $\boldsymbol{\alpha}$ can be viewed as holding different elements in each slot as,

$$\boldsymbol{\alpha} = \langle a_0, a_1, \cdots, a_{N-1} \rangle$$

for simplicity. Then, $\alpha = \mathsf{CRT}^{-1}(\boldsymbol{\alpha})$ is the batched plaintext with each element in a separate slot. The first step in Algorithm 1 is computing the comparisons $M_{ij} = A_i < A_j$ for all $i < j$. To this end, we apply rotation and obtain the following vectors:

$$
\begin{aligned}
\boldsymbol{\gamma}_0 &= <\ a_0, & a_1, & \cdots, & a_{N-2}, & a_{N-1}\ > \\
\boldsymbol{\gamma}_1 &= <\ a_1, & a_2, & \cdots, & a_{N-1}, & a_0\ > \\
\boldsymbol{\gamma}_2 &= <\ a_2, & a_3, & \cdots, & a_0, & a_1\ > \\
& & & \vdots & & \\
\boldsymbol{\gamma}_{\lfloor \frac{N}{2} \rfloor} &= <\ a_{\lfloor \frac{N}{2} \rfloor}, & a_{\lfloor \frac{N}{2} \rfloor+1}, & \cdots, & a_{\lfloor \frac{N}{2} \rfloor-2}, & a_{\lfloor \frac{N}{2} \rfloor-1}\ >
\end{aligned}
$$

by deploying the cyclic shift as $\gamma_i = \kappa_{g^i}(\alpha)$. We clear second half of the last vector when N is even, i.e. clear slot contents of $\boldsymbol{\gamma}_{\frac{N}{2}}$ in the range $[\frac{N}{2}, \cdots, N-1]$. This is due to the fact that we need exactly $\frac{N(N-1)}{2}$ comparisons. By aligning the elements as above, we can perform parallel comparisons of $M_{ij} = A_i < A_j$ for $0 < j - i \leq \lfloor \frac{N}{2} \rfloor$ and $M_{ji} = A_j < A_i$ where $j - i > \lfloor \frac{N}{2} \rfloor$ by executing the comparison circuit as;

$$\mu_1 = \gamma_0 \lessdot \gamma_1$$
$$\boldsymbol{\mu}_1 = \langle a_0 \lessdot a_1, \cdots, a_{N-2} \lessdot a_{N-1}, a_{N-1} \lessdot a_0 \rangle$$
$$\mu_2 = \gamma_0 \lessdot \gamma_2$$
$$\boldsymbol{\mu}_2 = \langle a_0 \lessdot a_2, \cdots, a_{N-2} \lessdot a_0, a_{N-1} \lessdot a_1 \rangle$$

$$\vdots$$

$$\mu_t = \gamma_0 \lessdot \gamma_{\lfloor \frac{N}{2} \rfloor}$$

$$\boldsymbol{\mu}_t = \begin{cases} \langle a_0 \lessdot a_{\frac{N-1}{2}}, \cdots, a_{N-2} \lessdot a_{\frac{N-1}{2}-2}, a_{N-1} \lessdot a_{\frac{N-1}{2}-1} \rangle, \text{if } N \text{ is odd,} \\ \langle a_0 \lessdot a_{\frac{N}{2}}, \cdots, a_{\frac{N}{2}-1} \lessdot a_{N-1}, 0, \cdots, 0 \rangle, \text{if } N \text{ is even.} \end{cases}$$

Their complements are $\bar{\mu}_i = 1 - \mu_i$ for $i = 1, \cdots, t$. By rotating each complement i times to the right, we successfully align all M_{ij} values with only $N/2$ comparisons and N rotations in total. It is important to remark that even though rotation operation by itself is not expensive it is followed by a key switching operation which is both costly and increasing the noise. Therefore the rotation is not completely free. We define ν_is as follows:

$$\boldsymbol{\mu}_i = \langle m_{0,i}, m_{0,i+1}, \cdots, m_{N-1,i-1} \rangle$$
$$\bar{\mu}_i = 1 - \mu_i$$
$$\bar{\boldsymbol{\mu}}_i = \langle m_{i,0}, m_{i+1,0}, \cdots, m_{i-1,N-1} \rangle$$
$$\nu_i = \kappa_{g-i}(\mu_i)$$
$$\boldsymbol{\nu}_i = \langle m_{0,N-i}, m_{1,N-i+1}, \cdots, m_{i-1,N-1}, m_{i,0}, m_{i+1,0}, \cdots m_{N-1,N-i-1} \rangle$$
$$\bar{\nu}_i = 1 - \nu_i, \qquad\qquad\qquad\qquad\qquad \text{for } i = 1, \cdots, t \,.$$

The vectors, $\boldsymbol{\mu}_1, \cdots, \boldsymbol{\mu}_t, \boldsymbol{\nu}_1, \cdots, \boldsymbol{\nu}_t$ hold all comparison values $m_{i,j}$ for $i \neq j$ in the $(i+1)^{\text{th}}$ slot and $\bar{\boldsymbol{\mu}}_1, \cdots, \bar{\boldsymbol{\nu}}_1, \cdots$ hold their complements, i.e. $m_{j,i} = 1 - m_{i,j}$ in the same slot. Next step of the algorithm is computing the product $\prod_{i \neq j} (M_{ij} + M_{ji}x)$. For multiplication with constant x, we batch an x in each slot and multiply with the complement vectors $\bar{\mu}_i$ and $\bar{\nu}_i$. However, we first need to apply the mapping Ψ_i that is defined in the beginning of this section.

$$\boldsymbol{\chi} = \langle \psi_1(x), \psi_2(x), \cdots, \psi_{N-1}(x) \rangle \text{ and } \chi = \mathsf{CRT}^{-1}(\boldsymbol{\chi})$$

Next, we define the surrogates in the parallel slots as

$$\varphi_i = \mu_i + \chi \bar{\mu}_i$$
$$\varphi_{t+i} = \nu_i + \chi \bar{\nu}_i, \qquad \text{for } i = 1, \cdots, t \,.$$

Finally, the last step is computing the product of the surrogates to find the rank monomials. We write

$$\varphi = \prod_{i=1}^{2t} \varphi_i$$
$$\varphi = \langle \psi_1(\rho_1), \psi_2(\rho_2), \cdots, \psi_{N-1}(\rho_{N-1}) \rangle$$

where ρ_is are the rank monomials of the input elements. The final rotation is performed so that all rank monomials can be summed in the first message slot.

$$\beta = \sigma_i \sum_{i=0}^{N-1} \kappa_{g^i}(\varphi)$$

$$\beta = \langle b, 0, \cdots, 0 \rangle$$

We have the sorted polynomial $b = \sum_{i=0}^{N-1} \rho_i \in \mathbb{L}_1$ in the first message slot.

We give a breakdown of the bandwidth and bottleneck operations in homomorphic evaluation of Polynomial Rank Sort to compare batching with no batching in the Table 2. The cost of a key switching operation depends on the underlying FHE scheme, however it is similar to the relinearization technique and mostly requires $\log q$ multiplications in $\mathbb{A}_q$. A single k-bit comparison circuit requires k ciphertext multiplications. Therefore, the cost of the key switching can exceed the N^2 comparisons, especially with large q. In that case, batching may not be preferable. On the other hand, some new schemes such as GSW [18] and F-NTRU [10] may need to compute $\log q$ multiplications in $\mathbb{A}_q$ for a single ciphertext multiplication. In that case, batching would perform better since the cost of key switching is same as a single ciphertext multiplication.

Table 2. A comparison of the storage and computation with and without batching.

	Inputs	Comparisons	Key switching	Multiplications	Outputs
No Batching	kN	$\frac{N^2-N}{2}$	–	$N^2 - 2N$	k
Batching	k	$\frac{N}{2}$	$2N$	$N - 2$	k

4.1   Choosing m and d

In most recent FHE schemes, the security parameter heavily depends on the degree of $\mathbb{A}_q$, i.e. $\phi(m)$ and it is usually a large number. For instance, in the homomorphic evaluation of AES [17], $(m, d) = (11441, 48)$ is given as an example for a circuit of depth 10. This choice of m and d utilizes $\ell = 224$ message slots. In that scenario, d is chosen to be a multiple of 8 because of the underlying algebra of AES operations. In our case, the only restrictions are:

1. The output of the algorithm is an $N - 1$ degree polynomial, hence we need $d \geq N$.
2. There must be at least N message slots, thus $\ell \geq N$.
3. The depth of the circuit is $\log(N) + \log(k) + 1$ when sorting k-bit numbers.

Thus the parameters depend on the number of elements N. We also have $m | 2^d - 1$ and $\ell = \phi(m)/d$ by definition. For example, when $N \leq 28$, we can use $m = 16385$ and $d = 28$ with ring degree $\phi(m) = 12544$ and $\ell = 448$ message slots. This means that, we can sort $\ell/N = 16$ sets in parallel.

5   Conclusion

In conclusion, our proposed method Polynomial Rank Sort performs significantly better than previous algorithms and provides a depth and cost-optimized circuit for homomorphic sorting. It reduces the number of ciphertext multiplications to $\mathcal{O}(N^2)$ for sorting an array of N elements without packing. Furthermore, it is a refined algorithm suitable for parallelization. When batching is enabled, we sort the whole list with only $N/2$ comparisons and following with only N multiplications. Proposed batching method also reduce the data size from kN to N where k is the bit-length of the input elements. However it requires costly key switching operation in exchange. All of our proposed homomorphic algorithms are generic and can be used with the recent FHE schemes. The performance gain however depends on the choice of the scheme and the trade-off between the cost of key switching and ciphertext multiplication.

Acknowledgment. This work was supported by the US National Science Foundation CNS Award #1561536.

References

1. Brakerski, Z.: Fully homomorphic encryption without modulus switching from classical gapSVP. IACR Cryptology ePrint Archive 2012, 78 (2012)
2. Brakerski, Z., Gentry, C., Vaikuntanathan, V.: Fully homomorphic encryption without bootstrapping. In: Electronic Colloquium on Computational Complexity (ECCC), vol. 18, p. 111 (2011)
3. Brakerski, Z., Gentry, C., Vaikuntanathan, V.: (leveled) fully homomorphic encryption without bootstrapping. In: Proceedings of the 3rd Innovations in Theoretical Computer Science Conference, pp. 309–325. ACM (2012)
4. Brakerski, Z., Vaikuntanathan, V.: Efficient fully homomorphic encryption from (standard) LWE. In: Ostrovsky, R. (ed.) FOCS, pp. 97–106. IEEE (2011)
5. Brakerski, Z., Vaikuntanathan, V.: Fully homomorphic encryption from ring-LWE and security for key dependent messages. In: Rogaway, P. (ed.) CRYPTO 2011. LNCS, vol. 6841, pp. 505–524. Springer, Heidelberg (2011). https://doi.org/10.1007/978-3-642-22792-9_29
6. Brakerski, Z., Vaikuntanathan, V.: Efficient fully homomorphic encryption from (standard) lwe. SIAM J. Comput. **43**(2), 831–871 (2014)
7. Çetin, G.S., Doröz, Y., Sunar, B., Savaş, E.: Low depth circuits for efficient homomorphic sorting. In: LatinCrypt (2015)
8. Chatterjee, A., Kaushal, M., Sengupta, I.: Accelerating sorting of fully homomorphic encrypted data. In: Paul, G., Vaudenay, S. (eds.) INDOCRYPT 2013. LNCS, vol. 8250, pp. 262–273. Springer, Cham (2013). https://doi.org/10.1007/978-3-319-03515-4_17
9. van Dijk, M., Gentry, C., Halevi, S., Vaikuntanathan, V.: Fully homomorphic encryption over the integers. In: Gilbert, H. (ed.) EUROCRYPT 2010. LNCS, vol. 6110, pp. 24–43. Springer, Heidelberg (2010). https://doi.org/10.1007/978-3-642-13190-5_2
10. Doröz, Y., Sunar, B.: Flattening ntru for evaluation key free homomorphic encryption. Cryptology ePrint Archive, Report 2016/315 (2016). http://eprint.iacr.org/2016/315

11. Emmadi, N., Gauravaram, P., Narumanchi, H., Syed, H.: Updates on sorting of fully homomorphic encrypted data. In: 2015 International Conference on Cloud Computing Research and Innovation (ICCCRI), pp. 19–24, October 2015
12. Fan, J., Vercauteren, F.: Somewhat practical fully homomorphic encryption. IACR Cryptology ePrint Archive 2012, 144 (2012)
13. Gentry, C.: A Fully Homomorphic Encryption Scheme. Ph.D. thesis, Stanford University (2009)
14. Gentry, C.: Fully homomorphic encryption using ideal lattices. In: STOC, pp. 169–178 (2009)
15. Gentry, C., Halevi, S.: Fully homomorphic encryption without squashing using depth-3 arithmetic circuits. IACR Cryptology ePrint Archive 2011, 279 (2011)
16. Gentry, C., Halevi, S., Smart, N.P.: Fully homomorphic encryption with polylog overhead. IACR Cryptology ePrint Archive Report 2011/566 (2011). http://eprint.iacr.org/
17. Gentry, C., Halevi, S., Smart, N.P.: Homomorphic evaluation of the AEScircuit. IACR Cryptology ePrint Archive 2012 (2012)
18. Gentry, C., Sahai, A., Waters, B.: Homomorphic encryption from learning with errors: conceptually-simpler, asymptotically-faster, attribute-based. In: Canetti, R., Garay, J.A. (eds.) CRYPTO 2013. LNCS, vol. 8042, pp. 75–92. Springer, Heidelberg (2013). https://doi.org/10.1007/978-3-642-40041-4_5
19. Halevi, S., Shoup, V.: Algorithms in helib. Cryptology ePrint Archive, Report 2014/106 (2014). http://eprint.iacr.org/2014/106
20. Knuth, D.E.: The Art of Computer Programming, Fundamental Algorithms, vol. 1, 3rd edn. Addison Wesley Longman Publishing Co., Inc, Reading (1998)
21. Laine, K., Player, R.: Simple encrypted arithmetic library - seal (v2.0). Technical report, September 2016. https://www.microsoft.com/en-us/research/publication/simple-encrypted-arithmetic-library-seal-v2-0/
22. López-Alt, A., Tromer, E., Vaikuntanathan, V.: On-the-fly multiparty computation on the cloud via multikey fully homomorphic encryption. In: STOC (2012)
23. Narumanchi, H., Goyal, D., Emmadi, N., Gauravaram, P.: Performance analysis of sorting of fhe data: Integer-wise comparison vs bit-wise comparison
24. Smart, N.P., Vercauteren, F.: Fully homomorphic SIMD operations. IACR Cryptology ePrint Archive 2011, 133 (2011)
25. Stehlé, D., Steinfeld, R.: Faster fully homomorphic encryption. Cryptology ePrint Archive 2010/299 (2010)

On Trees, Chains and Fast Transactions in the Blockchain

Aggelos Kiayias and Giorgos Panagiotakos[✉]

School of Informatics, University of Edinburgh, Edinburgh, UK
{akiayias,giorgos.pan}@inf.ed.ac.uk

Abstract. A fundamental open problem in the area of blockchain protocols is whether the Bitcoin protocol is the only solution for building a secure transaction ledger. A recently proposed and widely considered alternative is the GHOST protocol which, notably, was proposed to be at the core of Ethereum as well as other recent proposals for improved Bitcoin-like systems. The GHOST variant is touted as offering superior performance compared to Bitcoin (potentially offering block production speed up by a factor of more than 40) without a security loss. Motivated by this, in this work, we study from a provable security point of view the GHOST protocol.

We introduce a new formal framework for the analysis of blockchain protocols that relies on trees (rather than chains) and we showcase the power of the framework by providing a unified description of the GHOST and Bitcoin protocols, the former of which we extract and formally describe. We then prove that GHOST implements a "robust transaction ledger" (i.e., possesses liveness and persistence) and hence it is a provably secure alternative to Bitcoin; moreover, our bound for the liveness parameter is superior to that proven for the bitcoin backbone in line with the original expectation for GHOST. Our proof follows a novel methodology for establishing that GHOST is a robust transaction ledger compared to previous works, which may be of independent interest and can be applicable to other blockchain variants.

Keywords: GHOST · Provable security · Bitcoin · Blockchain protocols

1 Introduction

The popularity of Bitcoin [17] has lead to a surge in the interest about its core protocol that maintains a distributed data structure called the "blockchain." In [9], the core of the Bitcoin protocol was abstracted under the moniker "Bitcoin Backbone" and it was demonstrated to be a powerful tool for solving consensus, [15,21], in a synchronous, anonymous and Byzantine setting where (unreliable)

Aggelos Kiayias—Research supported by ERC project CODAMODA #25915. Part of this work was based in a technical report published in e-print (https://eprint.iacr.org/2015/1019).

T. Lange and O. Dunkelman (Eds.): LATINCRYPT 2017, LNCS 11368, pp. 327–351, 2019.
https://doi.org/10.1007/978-3-030-25283-0_18

broadcast is the communication operation available to the participants, (a problem first considered in [2,18]). In [9], it was shown that the core protocol provably guarantees two properties: (i) *persistence:* if a transaction is reported as stable by one node, then it will be also reported as such by any other honest node of the system, (ii) *liveness:* all honestly generated transactions that are broadcasted are eventually reported as stable by some honest node. This provides a formal framework for proving the security of systems like Bitcoin, since their security can be reduced to the persistence and liveness of the underlying transaction ledger. Furthermore, it provides a way to argue formally about transaction confirmation time since the liveness property is equipped with a delay parameter that specifies the maximum transaction delay that can be caused by an adversary.

Naturally, implementing a robust transaction ledger may be achieved in various other ways, and it is a fundamental open question of the area whether the Bitcoin protocol itself is an "optimal" implementation of a robust transaction ledger, i.e. whether the parameters of the persistence and liveness properties are optimal. Indeed, many researchers have challenged various aspects of the Bitcoin system and they have proposed modifications in its core operation. Some of the modified systems maintain the protocol structure but modify the hard-coded parameters (like the block generation rate) or the basic primitives, e.g., the way proof of work is performed (a number of alternative proof of work implementations have been proposed using functions like scrypt [22], lyra2 [24] and others). However, more radical modifications are possible that alter the actual operation of the protocol.

One of the most notable such variants is the GHOST protocol, which was suggested by Sompolinsky and Zohar in [25]. After the initial suggestion many cryptocurrencies using variants of the GHOST rule were proposed and implemented. The most popular among them, Ethereum [6] has received substantial research attention [4,11,13,14,19,23]. Ethereum is essentially a Bitcoin-like system where transaction processing is Turing-complete and thus it can be used to implement any public functionality in a distributed way. Bitcoin-NG [7] is another popular Bitcoin-like system relying on GHOST that separates blocks in two categories, namely key blocks and microblocks, reflecting the fact that transaction serialization and leader election may be separated.

Unfortunately, the security analysis of [25] is not as general as [9] (e.g., their attacker does not take advantage of providing conflicting information to different honest parties), while the analysis of [9] does not carry to the setting of GHOST. This is because the GHOST rule is a natural, albeit radical, reformulation of how each miner determines the main chain. In GHOST, miners adopt blocks in the structure of a *tree*. Note that in both Bitcoin and GHOST one can consider parties collecting all mined blocks in a tree data structure. However, while in Bitcoin the miners would choose the most difficult chain as the main chain, in GHOST, they will determine the chain by greedily following the "heaviest observed subtree." This means that for the same subtree, a Bitcoin miner and a GHOST miner may choose a completely different main chain. Furthermore, it means that the

difficulty of the main chain of honest parties does not necessarily increase monotonically (it may decrease at times) and thus a fundamental argument (namely
that blockchains monotonically increase) that made the analysis of [9] possible,
does not hold anymore.

Our Results. We propose a new analysis framework for blockchain protocols
focusing on trees of blocks as opposed to chains as in [9]. Our framework enables
us to argue about random variables on the trees of blocks that are formed by
the participants. In our framework, we can express concepts like a node being
d-dominant, which means that the block corresponding to that node would
be preferred by a margin of d compared to other sibling nodes according to
a specified weight measure. This actually enables us to unify the description of
Bitcoin and GHOST by showing they obey the same rule, but simply for a different
weight measure.

Using our framework we then provide a first formal security proof of the
GHOST rule for blockchain protocols. Specifically, we prove that GHOST is a robust
transaction ledger that satisfies liveness and persistence. We achieve this result,
by a new methodology, that reduces the properties of the robust transaction
ledger to a single lemma, that we call the *fresh block lemma* and is informally
stated as follows.

Fresh Block Lemma. (Informally) At any point of the execution and for
any past sequence of s consecutive rounds, there exists an honest block
mined in these rounds, that is contained in the chain of any honest player
from this point on.

As we will demonstrate, the fresh block lemma is a powerful tool in the presence of an adversary: we show easily that the properties of the robust transaction
ledger reduce to it in a black-box fashion.

In more details our result is as follows. In blockchain protocols there is a predicate parameterized by a security parameter k that determines when a transaction
has been stabilized in the ledger. The "stable" predicate for Bitcoin can be seen
to be true whenever the transaction is at least k blocks deep in the blockchain.
The stable predicate for GHOST is different and is true whenever the block that
the transaction belongs to is the root of a subtree of at least k blocks. We prove
the following.

Persistence: if in a certain round an honest player reports a transaction
tx as stable, then when an honest party reports tx transaction as stable
tx will be in the same position in the ledger.
Liveness: if a transaction is given as input to all honest players continuously for $u = \Theta(k)$ rounds then all of them will report it as stable.

The above properties will depend on the parameter k of the stable predicate of GHOST; we prove them to hold with a probability of error which drops
exponentially in k over all executions of the protocol.

Our proof strategy for persistence and liveness utilizes the fresh block lemma
in the following (black-box) manner.

In the case of persistence, it is sufficient to ensure that reporting the transaction as stable by any honest player implies that a sufficient amount of time has passed so that the fresh block lemma is applicable and has produced a block that is a descendant of the block that contains the transaction. Using the moderate hardness of proofs of work (specifically that they are *hard enough*) it is easy to translate from number of blocks in a subtree to actual running time in terms of rounds. It follows that the fresh block lemma applies and all honest parties will be mining on a subtree rooted at this fresh block for the remaining of the execution. As a result, the transaction will always be reported as stable since it belongs to the heaviest observed path for all of the honest parties.

In the case of liveness, we proceed in two steps. First, for our choice of u, in a time window lasting $\Theta(k)$ rounds, it will be ensured that the fresh block lemma can be applied once implying that all honest parties will mine blocks in a subtree rooted by a common block that includes the transaction. Then, after another $\Theta(k)$ rounds, the honest parties will have accumulated enough honest blocks in this subtree to pronounce this transaction as stable. This latter statement requires again the moderate hardness of proofs of work but from the opposite perspective, i.e., that they are *easy enough*.

The above strategy provides an alternative proof methodology for establishing the properties of a robust transaction ledger compared to previous works that analyzed blockchain protocols, [9,12] and [20] who reduced the properties of the robust transaction ledger to three other properties called common prefix, chain quality and chain growth. As such, the proof strategy itself may be of independent interest as it could be applicable to other blockchain variants, especially those that are using trees of blocks instead of chains of blocks as in bitcoin in their chain selection rule.

Our results align with the original expectation that GHOST performs better than bitcoin in terms of liveness, since our proven liveness parameter is superior to the liveness parameter for bitcoin proven in [9].

On the Generality of the Adversarial Model. The adversarial model we adopt in this work is the one proposed by Garay et al. [9]. This model is quite general in the sense that, it can captures many attack models that were proposed in the literature. For example, it captures the double spending attacker of [17], the block withholding attacker of [8] (which can be simulated because the adversary can change the order in which messages arrive for each honest player) and the eclipse attacker of [5] where the communication of a portion of the honest nodes in the network is completely controlled (eclipsed) by the adversary (this can be simulated by simply considering the eclipsed nodes to be controlled by the adversary and having the adversary honestly execute their program while dropping their incoming messages). For a quantitative analysis of these attacks the reader is referred to [10].

Limitations and Directions for Future Research. Our analysis is in the standard Byzantine model where parties fall into two categories, those that are honest (and follow the protocol) and those that are dishonest and may deviate in an arbitrary (and coordinated) fashion as dictated by the adversary. It is an interesting direction for future work to consider the rational setting where all parties wish to optimize a certain utility function. Designing suitable incentive mechanisms, for instance see [16] for a suggestion related to the GHOST protocol, or examining the requirements for setup assumptions, cf. [1], are related important considerations. Our analysis is in the static setting, i.e., we do not take into account the fact that parties change dynamically and that the protocol calibrates the difficulty of the POW instances to account for that; we note that this may open the possibility for additional attacks, say [3], and hence it is an important point for consideration and future work. Finally, it is interesting to consider our results in more general models such as the semi-synchronous model of [20].

Organization. In Sect. 2 we overview the model that we use for expressing the protocols and the theorems regarding the security properties. In Sect. 3 we introduce our new tree-based framework. Then, in Sect. 4 we present our security analysis of an abstraction of the GHOST protocol that demonstrates it is a robust transaction ledger in the static setting.

2   Preliminaries and the GHOST Backbone protocol

2.1   Model

For our model we adopt the abstraction proposed in [9]. Specifically, in their setting, called the q-bounded setting, synchronous communication is assumed and each party is allowed q queries to a random oracle. The network supports an anonymous message diffusion mechanism that is guaranteed to deliver the messages of all honest parties in each round. The delivery of all messages occurs at the start of the next round. Note that the diffusion mechanism is not reliable, i.e. the adversary may send messages only to a portion of the parties in the network. Moreover, the adversary is rushing and adaptive. Rushing here means that in any given round he gets to see all honest players' messages before deciding on his own strategy. In addition, he has complete control of the order that messages arrive to each player. The model is "flat" in terms of computational power in the sense that all honest parties are assumed to have the same computational power while the adversary has computational power proportional to the number of players that it controls.

The total number of parties is n and the adversary is assumed to control t of them (honest parties don't know any of these parameters). Obtaining a new block is achieved by finding a hash value that is smaller than a difficulty parameter D. The success probability that a single hashing query produces a solution is $p = \frac{D}{2^\kappa}$ where κ is the length of the hash. The total hashing power of the honest players is $\alpha = pq(n - t)$, the hashing power of the adversary is $\beta = pqt$ and the total hashing power is $f = \alpha + \beta$. A number of definitions that will be used extensively are listed below.

Definition 1. *A round is called:*

- *successful if at least one honest player computes a solution in this round.*
- *uniquely successful if exactly one honest player computes a solution in this round.*

Definition 2. *In an execution blocks are called:*

- *honest, if mined by an honest party.*
- *adversarial, if mined by the adversary.*

Definition 3. *Some chain notation:*

- *By $C^{\lceil k}$ we denote the chain that results by dropping the last k blocks of C.*
- *We will say that a chain C' extends another chain C if a non-empty prefix of C' is a suffix of C.*

In [9], a lower bound to the probabilities of two events, that a round is successful or that is uniquely successful (defined above), was established and denoted by $\gamma_u = \alpha - \alpha^2$. While this bound is sufficient for the setting of small f, here we will need to use a better lower bound to the probability of those events, denoted by γ, and with value approximately $\alpha e^{-\alpha}$ (see Appendix). Observe that $\gamma > \gamma_u$.

2.2   The GHOST Backbone Protocol

In order to study the properties of the core Bitcoin protocol, the term *Backbone Protocol* was introduced in [9]. At this level of abstraction we are only interested in properties of the blockchain, independently from the data stored inside the blocks. The main idea of the Bitcoin Backbone is that honest players, at every round, receive new chains from the network and pick the longest valid one to mine. Then, if they obtain a new block (by finding a small hash), they broadcast their chain at the end of the round.

The same level of abstraction can also be used to express the GHOST protocol. The GHOST Backbone protocol, as presented in [25], is based on the principle that blocks that do not end up in the main chain, should also matter in the chain selection process. In order to achieve this, players store a tree of all mined blocks they have received, and then using the greedy heaviest observed subtree (GHOST) rule, they pick which chain to mine.

At every round, players update their tree by adding valid[1] blocks sent by other players. The same principle as Bitcoin applies; for a block to be added to the tree, it suffices to be a valid child of some other tree block. The adversary can add blocks anywhere he wants in the tree, as long as they are valid. Again, as in Bitcoin, players try to extend the chains they choose by one or more blocks. Finally, in the main function, a tree of blocks is stored and updated at every round. If a player updates his tree, he broadcasts it to all other players.

---

[1] As in [9], a block $B = \langle s, x, ctr \rangle$ is valid if it satisfies two conditions: $H(ctr, G(s, x)) < D$ and $ctr \leq q$, where D is the block's difficulty level and H, G are cryptographic hash functions.

Algorithm 1. The chain selection algorithm. The input is a block tree $\mathcal{T}$. The $|\cdot|$ operator corresponds to the number of nodes of a tree. By $C_1||C_2$ we denote the concatenation of chains C_1, C_2.

```
1: function GHOST(T)
2:     B ← root(T)
3:     if children_T(B) = ∅ then
4:         return B
5:     else
6:         B ← argmax_{B'∈children_T(B)} |subtree_T(B')|
7:         return B||GHOST(subtree_T(B))
8:     end if
9: end function
```

The protocol is also parameterized by three external functions $V(\cdot)$, $I(\cdot)$, $R(\cdot)$ which are called: the input validation predicate, the input contribution function, and the chain reading function, respectively. $V(\cdot)$ dictates the structure of the information stored in each block, $I(\cdot)$ determines the data that players put in the block they mine, $R(\cdot)$ specifies how the data in the blocks should be interpreted depending on the application.

Algorithm 2. The GHOST backbone protocol, parameterized by the *input contribution function* $I(\cdot)$ and the *reading function* $R(\cdot)$. $\mathbf{x}_C$ is the vector of inputs of all block in chain C.

```
1: T ← GenesisBlock                                              ▷ T is a tree.
2: state ← ε
3: round ← 0
4: while TRUE do
5:     T_new ← update(T, blocks found in RECEIVE())
6:     C̃ ← GHOST(T_new)
7:     ⟨state, x⟩ ← I(state, C̃, round, INPUT(), RECEIVE())
8:     C_new ← pow(x, C̃)
9:     if C̃ ≠ C_new or T ≠ T_new then
10:        T ← update(T_new, head(C_new))
11:        BROADCAST(head(C_new))
12:    end if
13:    round ← round + 1
14:    if INPUT() contains READ then
15:        write R(x_C) to OUTPUT()
16:    end if
17: end while
```

Next, for completeness we present the remaining procedures of the GHOST backbone protocol. Function pow (see Algorithm 3), which has to do with block mining and is the same as the one defined in the Bitcoin Backbone and function update (see Algorithm 4) which refers to the way the block tree is updated.

Algorithm 3. The *proof of work* function, parameterized by q, D and hash functions $H(\cdot), G(\cdot)$. The input is $(x, \mathcal{C})$.

```
 1: function pow(x, C)
 2:     if C = ε then                              ▷ Determine proof of work instance
 3:         s ← 0
 4:     else
 5:         ⟨s', x', ctr'⟩ ← head(C)
 6:         s ← H(ctr', G(s', x'))
 7:     end if
 8:     ctr ← 1
 9:     B ← ε
10:     h ← G(s, x)
11:     while (ctr ≤ q) do
12:         if (H(ctr, h) < D) then
13:             B ← ⟨s, x, ctr⟩
14:             break
15:         end if
16:         ctr ← ctr + 1
17:     end while
18:     C ← CB                                      ▷ Extend chain
19:     return C
20: end function
```

2.3 Security Properties

In [9, Definitions 2&3] two crucial security properties of the Bitcoin backbone protocol were considered, the common prefix and the chain quality property. The common prefix property ensures that two honest players have the same view of the blockchain if they prune a small number of blocks from the tail. On the other hand the chain quality property ensures that honest players' chains do not contain long sequences of adversarial blocks. These properties are defined as predicates over the random variable formed by the concatenation of all parties' views denoted by $\text{VIEW}_{\Pi,\mathcal{A},\mathcal{Z}}^{H(\cdot)}(\kappa, q, z)$.

Definition 4 (Common Prefix Property). *The common prefix property Q_{cp} with parameter $k \in \mathbb{N}$ states that for any pair of honest players P_1, P_2 maintaining the chains $\mathcal{C}_1, \mathcal{C}_2$ in $\text{VIEW}_{\Pi,\mathcal{A},\mathcal{Z}}^{H(\cdot)}(\kappa, q, z)$, it holds that*

$$\mathcal{C}_1^{\lceil k} \preceq \mathcal{C}_2 \text{ and } \mathcal{C}_2^{\lceil k} \preceq \mathcal{C}_1.$$

Definition 5 (Chain Quality Property). *The chain quality property Q_{cq} with parameters $\mu \in \mathbb{R}$ and $\ell \in \mathbb{N}$ states that for any honest party P with chain $\mathcal{C}$ in $\text{VIEW}_{\Pi,\mathcal{A},\mathcal{Z}}^{H(\cdot)}(\kappa, q, z)$, it holds that for any ℓ consecutive blocks of $\mathcal{C}$ the ratio of adversarial blocks is at most μ.*

Algorithm 4. The tree update function, parameterized by q, D and hash functions $H(\cdot), G(\cdot)$. The inputs are a block tree $\mathcal{T}$ and an array of blocks.

```
1: function update(T,B)
2:     foreach ⟨s, x, ctr⟩ in T
3:         foreach ⟨s′, x′, ctr′⟩ in B
4:             if ((s′ = H(ctr, G(s, x))) ∧ (H(ctr′, G(x′, ctr′)) < D)) then
5:                 children_T(⟨s, x, ctr⟩) = children_T(⟨s, x, ctr⟩) ∪ ⟨s′, x′, ctr′⟩   ▷ Add to the
       tree.
6:         end if
7:     return T
8: end function
```

These two properties were shown to hold for the Bitcoin backbone protocol. Formally, in [9, Theorems 9&10] the following were proved:

Theorem 1. *Assume $f < 1$ and $\gamma_u \geq (1 + \delta)\lambda\beta$, for some real $\delta \in (0, 1)$ and $\lambda \geq 1$ such that $\lambda^2 - f\lambda - 1 \geq 0$. Let S be the set of the chains of the honest parties at a given round of the backbone protocol. Then the probability that S does not satisfy the common-prefix property with parameter k is at most $e^{-\Omega(\delta^3 k)}$.*

Theorem 2. *Assume $f < 1$ and $\gamma_u \geq (1 + \delta)\lambda\beta$ for some $\delta \in (0, 1)$. Suppose $\mathcal{C}$ belongs to an honest party and consider any ℓ consecutive blocks of $\mathcal{C}$. The probability that the adversary has contributed more than $(1 - \frac{\delta}{3})\frac{1}{\lambda}\ell$ of these blocks is less than $e^{-\Omega(\delta^2 \ell)}$.*

Robust Public Transaction Ledger. In [9] the robust public transaction ledger primitive was presented. It tries to capture the notion of a book where transactions are recorded, and it is used to implement Byzantine Agreement in the honest majority setting.

A *public transaction ledger* is defined with respect to a set of valid ledgers $\mathcal{L}$ and a set of valid transactions $\mathcal{T}$, each one possessing an efficient membership test. A ledger $\mathbf{x} \in \mathcal{L}$ is a vector of sequences of transactions $\mathrm{tx} \in \mathcal{T}$. Each transaction tx may be associated with one or more *accounts*. Ledgers correspond to chains in the backbone protocols. In the protocol execution there also exists an oracle Txgen that generates valid transactions. Note, that it may be possible for the adversary to create two transactions that are conflicting; valid ledgers must not contain conflicting transaction. We will assume that the oracle is unambiguous, i.e. the adversary cannot create transactions that come in 'conflict' with the transactions generated by the oracle. Finally, a transaction is called neutral if there does not exist any transactions that comes in conflict with it. For more details we refer to [9].

We slightly alter the definitions of persistence and liveness so that they are relative to the way parties verify transactions. For example, in Bitcoin a transaction is 'stable' with parameter k if it is at least k blocks deep in the chain. On the other hand, in GHOST the subtree rooted at the block containing a transaction must be of size at least k in order for this transaction to be considered 'stable'. Whenever we talk about the persistence or liveness of Bitcoin or GHOST from now on, we will imply the parameterized versions with the respective definitions of stability that we just mentioned.

Definition 6. *A protocol* Π *implements a* robust public transaction ledger *in the q-bounded synchronous setting if it satisfies the following two properties:*

- Persistence: *Parameterized by* $k \in \mathbb{N}$ *(the "depth" parameter), if in a certain round an honest player reports a transaction* tx *as 'stable' with parameter* k, *then whenever an honest party reports it as stable,* tx *will be in the same position in the ledger.*
- Liveness: *Parameterized by* $u, k \in \mathbb{N}$ *(the "wait time" and "depth" parameters, resp.), provided that a transaction either (i) issued by* Txgen, *or (ii) neutral, is given as input to all honest players continuously for* u *consecutive rounds, then all honest parties will report it as 'stable' with parameter* k *from this round on.*

These two properties were shown to hold for the ledger protocol Π_{PL} build on top of the Bitcoin Backbone protocol and appropriate instantiation of the functions V, R and I. Formally, in [9, Lemma 15&16] the following were proved:

Lemma 1 (Persistence). *Suppose* $f < 1$ *and* $\gamma_\mathsf{u} \geq (1 + \delta)\lambda\beta$, *for some real* $\delta \in (0, 1)$ *and* $\lambda \geq 1$ *such that* $\lambda^2 - f\lambda - 1 \geq 0$. *Protocol* Π_{PL} *satisfies Persistence with probability* $1 - e^{-\Omega(\delta^3 k)}$, *where* k *is the depth parameter.*

Lemma 2 (Liveness). *Assume* $f < 1$ *and* $\gamma_\mathsf{u} \geq (1 + \delta)\lambda\beta$, *for some* $\delta \in (0, 1)$, $\lambda \in [1, \infty)$ *and let* $k \in \mathbb{N}$. *Further, assume oracle* Txgen *is unambiguous. Then protocol* Π_{PL} *satisfies Liveness with wait time* $u = 2k/(1 - \delta)\gamma_\mathsf{u}$ *and depth parameter* k *with probability at least* $1 - e^{-\Omega(\delta^2 k)}$.

3   A Unified Description of Bitcoin and GHOST Backbone

Next, we introduce our new analysis framework for backbone protocols that is focusing on trees of blocks and we show how the description of the Bitcoin and GHOST can be unified. In this model, every player stores all blocks he receives on a tree, starting from a pre-shared block called the *Genesis* (or v_{root}) block. This is the model where GHOST was initially described. Bitcoin, and other possible backbone variants, can also be seen in this model and thus a unified language can be built. We first define block trees (or just trees) that capture the knowledge of honest players (regarding the block tree on different moments at every round).

Definition 7. *We denote by $\mathcal{T}_r^P$ (resp. $\mathcal{T}_r$) the tree that is formed from the blocks that player P (resp. at least one honest player) has received up to round r. Similarly, $\hat{\mathcal{T}}_r$ is the tree that contains all blocks of $\mathcal{T}_r$ and all blocks mined by honest players at round r. For any tree T and block $b \in T$, we denote by $T(b)$ the subtree of T rooted on b.*

Notice that, due to the fact that broadcasts of honest players always succeed, blocks in $\hat{\mathcal{T}}_r$ are always in $\mathcal{T}_{r+1}^P$. Thus for every honest player P it holds that:

$$\mathcal{T}_r^P \subseteq \mathcal{T}_r \subseteq \hat{\mathcal{T}}_r \subseteq \mathcal{T}_{r+1}^P$$

Intuitively, heavier trees represent more proof of work. However, there is more than one way to define the weight of a tree. For example, in Bitcoin the heaviest tree is the longest one. On the other hand, for GHOST a heavy tree is one with many nodes. To capture this abstraction we condition our definitions on a norm w that assigns weights on trees. This norm will be responsible for deciding which tree has more proof of work, and thus which tree is favored by the chain selection rule. We choose to omit w from the notation since it will always be clear from the context which norm we use.

Definition 8. *Let w be a norm defined on trees. For any tree $\mathcal{T}$ let $siblings(v)$ denote the set of nodes in $\mathcal{T}$ that share the same parent with v. Then node v is **d-dominant** in $\mathcal{T}$ (denoted by $\mathrm{Dom}_\mathcal{T}(v, d)$) iff*

$$w(\mathcal{T}(v)) \geq d \wedge \forall v' \in siblings(v) : w(\mathcal{T}(v)) \geq w(\mathcal{T}(v')) + d$$

The chain selection rule in the Bitcoin protocol can be described using the notion of the d-dominant node. Let $w(\mathcal{T})$ be the height of some tree $\mathcal{T}$. Each player P, starting from the root of his $\mathcal{T}_r^P$ tree, greedily decides on which block to add on the chain by choosing one of its 0-dominant children and continuing recursively[2] (ties are broken based on time-stamp, or based on which block was received first). Interestingly, the GHOST selection rule can also be described in exactly the same way by setting w to be the number of nodes of the tree. Thus we have a unified way for describing the chain selection rule in both protocols. Building upon this formalism we can describe the paths that fully informed honest players may choose to mine at round r (denoted by HonestPaths(r)) in a quite robust way, thus showcasing the power of our notation.

$$\text{HonestPaths}(r) = \{p = v_{\text{root}}v_1 \ldots v_k | p \text{ is a root-leaf path in } \mathcal{T}_r \text{ and}$$
$$\forall i \in \{1, .., k\}\mathrm{Dom}_{\mathcal{T}_r}(v_i, 0)\}$$

We conclude this section by presenting two crucial properties that both the Bitcoin and GHOST backbones satisfy. The first property states that by broadcasting k blocks the adversary can decrease the dominance of some block at most by k.

---

[2] This is exactly Algorithm 1 with a minor modification. At line 6 the subtree $\mathcal{T}$ that is chosen maximizes $w(\mathcal{T})$.

Intuitively, if the adversary's ability to mine new blocks is limited, then his influence over the block tree is also limited. On the other hand, the second property states that uniquely successful rounds increase the dominance of the nodes in the path from the root to the new block.

We will use the term node and block interchangeably from now on.

Proposition 1. *For the Bitcoin and* GHOST *backbone protocols it holds that:*

- *if the adversary broadcast $k \leq d$ blocks at round $r - 1$ then for every block $v \in \hat{T}_{r-1}$ it holds that $\text{Dom}_{\hat{T}_{r-1}}(v, d)$ implies $\text{Dom}_{T_r}(v, d - k)$.*
- *if r is a uniquely successful round and the newly mined block b extends a path in* HonestPaths(r)*, then $\text{Dom}_{\hat{T}_r}(b, 1)$ and for any block v in the path from v_{root} to b it holds that $\text{Dom}_{T_r}(v, d)$ implies $\text{Dom}_{\hat{T}_r}(v, d + 1)$.*

Proof. The lemma stems from the fact that adding only one block in the tree reduces or increases the dominance of some block by at most 1. For the first bullet, adding k blocks one by one, implies that the dominance of any node will reduce or increase by at most k. For the second bullet, notice that dominance increases only for blocks that get heavier. The only blocks that get heavier in this case are the ones in the path from the root to the newly mined block. Since these blocks are in HonestPaths(r), they are at least 0-dominant and so their dominance will further increase. Furthermore, the newly mined block is 1-dominant since it does not have any siblings.   □

4   Security Analysis and Applications

Next, we prove that the GHOST backbone protocol is sufficient to construct a robust transaction ledger. From now on we assume that $w(T)$ is the total number of nodes of tree T.

4.1   The Fresh Block Lemma

In [9], it was shown that the Bitcoin Backbone satisfies two main properties: common prefix and chain quality. However, another fundamental property needed for their proof, is that the chains of honest players grow at least at the rate of successful rounds. This does not hold for GHOST. The reason is that, if an honest player receives a chain that is heavier than the one he currently has, he will select it, *even if it is shorter*. To reflect these facts, we develop an argument that is a lot more involved and leads to a power lemma that we call the "fresh block lemma".

First, we introduce a new notion, that of a path that all of its nodes are dominant up to a certain value. Intuitively, the more dominant a path is, the harder it gets for the adversary to stop honest players from choosing it.

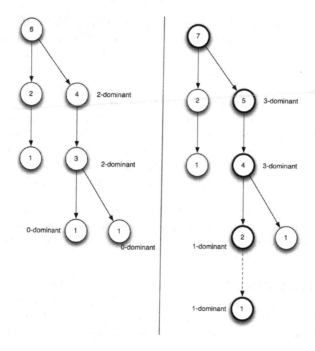

Fig. 1. An example of the change in dominance after a uniquely successful round. The only nodes which increase their dominanceare the ones in the path from the root to the newly mined block as stated in Proposition 1.

Definition 9. *For $d > 0$, $\mathrm{p_{dom}}(r, d)$ is the longest path $p = v_{\mathrm{root}} v_1 \ldots v_k$ in $\hat{\mathcal{T}}_r$ s.t.*

$$p \neq v_{\mathrm{root}} \wedge \forall i \in \{1, \ldots, k\} : \; \mathrm{Dom}_{\hat{\mathcal{T}}_r}(v_i, d)$$

If no such path exists $\mathrm{p_{dom}}(r, d) = \bot$.

Note that the dominant path $\mathrm{p_{dom}}(r, d)$, if it is not $\bot$, will be unique (this stems from the requirement that $d > 0$).

In the next lemma, we show that unless the number of blocks the adversary broadcasts in a round interval is at least as big as the number of uniquely successful rounds that have occurred, an honest block mined in one of these rounds will be deep enough in the chains of honest players. More specifically, for any sequence of m (not necessarily consecutive) uniquely successful rounds starting at some round r', no matter the strategy of the adversary, at round r there will be at least one honest block in $\mathrm{p_{dom}}(r, m - k)$ where k is the number of adversarial blocks that have been released during rounds $[r' - 1, r - 1]$.

Lemma 3. *Let $r_1, .., r_m$ be uniquely successful rounds from round r' until round r. If the adversary broadcasts $k < m$ blocks from round $r' - 1$ until round $r - 1$, then there exists an honest block b, mined in one of the rounds $r_1, .., r_m$ such that b is in $\mathrm{p_{dom}}(r, m - k)$.*

Proof sketch. The proof is based on two observations. Firstly, if the adversary does not broadcast a block in the round before a uniquely successful round s, then the newly mined honest block will be in $p_{dom}(s, 1)$. Secondly, if the adversary broadcasts $k < d$ blocks in the round before a uniquely successful round s, all blocks in $p_{dom}(s - 1, d)$ at round $s - 1$ will also be in $p_{dom}(s, d + 1 - k)$. It follows that for each uniquely successful round, unless the adversary broadcasts a block, an honest block will be introduced in the dominant path and will be maintained there unless the adversary broadcasts more blocks than the number of uniquely successful rounds that follow. As a result, in the period from round r' until round r, our assumption that the adversary broadcasts strictly less than m blocks, implies that at least one block will be maintained in $p_{dom}(r, m - k)$.   □

The fresh block lemma is stated next. Informally, it states that at any point in time, in any past sequence of s consecutive rounds, at least one honest block was mined and is permanently inserted in the chain that every honest player adopts, with overwhelming probability on s.

Lemma 4 (Fresh Block Lemma). *Assume $\gamma \geq (1 + \delta)\beta$, for some real $\delta \in (0, 1)$ and $f < 1$. Then, for all $s \in \mathbb{N}$ and $r \geq s$ it holds that there exists a block mined by an honest player on and after[3] round $r - s$, that is contained in the chain which any honest player adopts on and after round r with probability $1 - e^{-\Omega(\delta^2 s)}$.*

Proof sketch. The difficulty of proving this lemma stems from the fact that in GHOST, the chains of honest players are not always strictly increasing. That is, honest players may switch from a longer to a shorter chain. Monotonicity allows us to prove many useful things; for example that the adversary cannot use very old blocks in order to maintain a fork as in [9].

To overcome this difficulty, we first show that whenever the adversary forces honest players to work on a different branch of the block tree, he has to broadcast as many blocks as the ones that where mined on uniquely successful rounds on this branch of the tree. Hence, it is hard for the adversary to force honest players to change branches all the time, and moreover, after s rounds this will be impossible due to the fact that $\gamma \geq (1 + \delta)\beta$. But if all honest players stay on one branch, the blocks near the root of the branch will permanently enter their chains. We show that at least one of these blocks will be mined by an honest player. By applying this idea in an iterative manner, the lemma follows.   □

For the full proof of the lemma we refer to the Appendix.

4.2 A Robust Public Transaction Ledger

In [9] it is shown how to instantiate the functions V, R, I so that the resulting protocol, denoted by Π_{PL}, built on top of the Bitcoin backbone, implements a

---

[3] Throughout this work, we only consider executions that run for a polynomial number of rounds in the security parameter κ.

robust transaction ledger. In this section we show how we can achieve the same goal, using exactly the same instantiation of V,R,I, but on top of the GHOST backbone. We call the resulting protocol, Π_{PL}^{GHOST}.

Having established that every s rounds a fresh and honest block is inserted permanently in the chain of all players, we are in a position to prove the main properties of a robust transaction ledger. Liveness stems from the fact that after s rounds from the time a transaction was issued, an honest block that contains this transaction will stabilize in the chain. Thus, by waiting for at most s/α more rounds, the honest parties will mine enough block so that this transaction becomes 'stable' with parameter s. Persistence is implied by the fact that when a player reports a transaction as stable for the first time, enough time has passed from the time the block containing the transaction was mined, and thus there exists an honest block descending it that has been permanently added to the chain of all honest parties.

Lemma 5 (Liveness). *Assume $\gamma \geq (1 + \delta)\beta$, for some $\delta \in (0, 1)$ and $f < 1$. Further, assume oracle Txgen is unambiguous. Then for all $k \in \mathbb{N}$ protocol Π_{PL}^{GHOST} satisfies Liveness with wait time $u = k + \frac{k}{(1-\delta)\alpha}$ rounds and depth parameter k with probability at least $1 - e^{-\Omega(\delta^2 k)}$.*

Proof. We prove that assuming all honest players receive as input the transaction tx for at least u rounds, any honest party at round r with chain $\mathcal{C}$ will report tx as 'stable'. By Lemma 4 it follows that with probability $1 - e^{-\Omega(\delta^2 k)}$ there exists an honest block mined during rounds $[r - u, r - u + k]$, such that all honest players have this block in the chains they mine from round $r - u + k$ and onward. Without loss of generality this block contains tx. All blocks that honest players mine during the remaining $\frac{k}{(1-\delta)\alpha}$ rounds will be descendants of this block. By an application of the Chernoff bound, with probability $1 - e^{-\Omega(\delta^2 k)}$, the honest parties will mine at least k blocks in this round interval and thus the lemma follows with the desired probability. $\qquad\square$

Lemma 6 (Persistence). *Suppose $\gamma \geq (1+\delta)\beta$ and $(1+\delta)f \leq 1$, for some real $\delta \in (0, 1)$. Then for all $k \in \mathbb{N}$ protocol Π_{PL}^{GHOST} satisfies Persistence with probability $1 - e^{-\Omega(\delta^2 k)}$, where k is the depth parameter.*

Proof. Let B be the block that contains transaction tx that the honest party P reported as stable at round r. We will argue that B must have been computed before round $r - k$, and thus by Lemma 4 all honest players will report it in the same position in their chains.

Let E_1 be the event where B is computed after round $r - k/((1+\delta)f) < r - k$. The number of descendants of B cannot be greater than the number of solutions Y obtained from the oracle in this amount of rounds. By the Chernoff bound,

$$\Pr\left[Y \geq (1 + \delta)f\frac{k}{(1+\delta)f}\right] = \Pr[Y \geq k] \leq e^{-\delta^2 fs/3}.$$

Since tx is reported as stable, B must have k descendants and thus E_1 implies that Y must be greater or equal to k. Hence, $\Pr[E_1] \leq \Pr[Y \geq k] \leq e^{-\delta^2 fs/3}$.

Let E_2 be the event where Lemma 4 does not hold for round r. This happens with probability at most $e^{-\Omega(\delta^2 k)}$. By the union bound, the event $E_1 \vee E_2$ happens with probability at most $e^{-\Omega(\delta^2 k)}$. Assuming that $E_1 \vee E_2$ does not occur, it follows that there exists an honest block B' mined on and after round $r - k$ that will be in the chains of all honest players from round r and onward. Hence, B must be an ancestor of B' and all honest players will report B and tx at the same position as P from round r and onward. Persistence follows with the desired probability.

Theorem 3. *Assuming $\gamma \geq (1 + \delta)\beta$ and $(1 + \delta)f \leq 1$, for some real $\delta \in (0, 1)$, the protocol $\Pi_{\mathsf{PL}}^{\mathsf{GHOST}}$ implements a robust transaction ledger.*

As a final note, Lemma 4 is sufficient to prove Persistence and Liveness in a black-box way. Compared to the approach of [9], that was further expanded in [12] and [20], only one property, instead of three, of the underlying "backbone" protocol suffices in order to get a robust public transaction ledger in a black-box manner. On the other hand, the three properties described in these works, common-prefix, chain quality and chain growth, also serve as metrics of the efficiency of the underlying mechanism and provide more information than the fresh block lemma.

A   Probability of Uniquely Successful Rounds

In this section we demonstrate a lower bound on the probability of uniquely successful rounds. This bound allows us to argue about the security of GHOST even when f is larger than 1.

Lemma 7. *For $p < 0.1$ and $a \in (p, 2k) : e^{-a-kp} \leq (1-p)^{\frac{a}{p} - k} \leq e^{-a+kp}$*

Proof. The second inequality is well studied and holds for $p > 0$. For the first inequality by solving for a we get $a \leq k \frac{ln(1-p)}{1 + \frac{ln(1-p)}{p}}$ which holds for $p < 0.1$ and $a \in (p, 2k)$. $\qquad\square$

Let γ be a lower bound on the probability of a uniquely successful round (a round where only one block is found). From the event where $(n - t)$ players throw q coins each and exactly one coin toss comes head, the probability of a uniquely successful rounds is at least:

$$(n - t)qp(1 - p)^{q(n-t)-1} \geq \alpha e^{-\alpha - kp}$$

We set $\gamma = ae^{-a-kp}$, for the minimum k that satisfies the relation $\alpha \in (p, 2k)$. This is a substantially better bound that γ_u and is also a lower bound for the event that at a round is successful. The relation of the two bounds is depicted in Fig. 2.

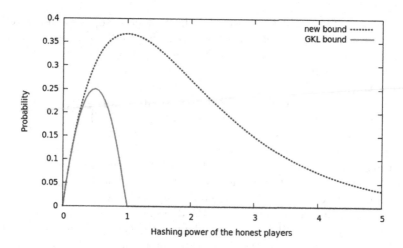

Fig. 2. Comparison of the lower bounds on the probability of a uniquely successful round, γ and γ_u, used respectively in this work and [9]. Notice that γ allows as to argue about security when f is greater than 1.

B   Proofs

B.1   Proof of Lemma 3

Proof. We are first going to prove two preliminary claims that show the effect of a uniquely successful round to p_{dom}. The first claim shows that if a uniquely successful round s is not compensated accordingly by the adversary, a newly mined block will be forced into $p_{dom}(s, 1)$.

Claim 1. Let round s be a uniquely successful round and b be the honest block mined at round s. If the adversary does not broadcast any block at round $s - 1$ then $b \in p_{dom}(s, 1)$.

Proof of Claim. First, notice that since the adversary does not broadcast any block it holds that for any honest player P, $\mathcal{T}_s$ is equal to $\mathcal{T}_s^P$. Therefore, all nodes in the path from v_{root} to the parent of b are at least 0-dominant in $\mathcal{T}_s$ and thus this path is in HonestPaths(s). Since s is uniquely successful, all conditions of the second bullet of Proposition 1 are met, and thus it is implied that all nodes up to the newly mined block in $\hat{\mathcal{T}}_s$ are 1-dominant. It follows that $b \in p_{dom}(s, 1)$.   ⊣

The second claim shows the effect of a uniquely successful round s to an existing $p_{dom}(s - 1, d)$ path. Notice that if the adversary broadcasts less than d blocks the same nodes continue to be at least 1-dominant in the following round.

Claim 2. Let round s be a uniquely successful round, b be the honest block mined at round s and $p_{dom}(s - 1, d) \neq \perp$. If the adversary broadcasts (i) $k < d$ blocks at round $s - 1$ then $p_{dom}(s - 1, d) \subseteq p_{dom}(s, d + 1 - k)$, (ii) $k = d$ blocks at round $s - 1$ then either $b \in p_{dom}(s, 1)$ or $p_{dom}(s - 1, d) \subseteq p_{dom}(s, 1)$ and b is a descendant of the last node in $p_{dom}(s - 1, d)$.

Proof of Claim. There are two cases. In the first case suppose the adversary broadcasts $k < d$ blocks. Then, according to the first bullet of Proposition 1, the adversary can lower the dominance in $\mathcal{T}_s$ of nodes in $\mathrm{p_{dom}}(s-1,d)$ by at most k. Thus $\mathrm{p_{dom}}(s-1,d)$ will be a prefix of all the chains in HonestPaths(s). But because s is a uniquely successful round, the dominance in $\hat{\mathcal{T}}_s$ of all nodes in $\mathrm{p_{dom}}(s-1,d)$ will increase by one. Therefore $\mathrm{p_{dom}}(s-1,d) \subseteq \mathrm{p_{dom}}(s,d+1-k)$ and b will be a descendant of the last node in $\mathrm{p_{dom}}(s-1,d)$.

In the second case suppose the adversary broadcasts $k = d$ blocks. If he does not broadcast all of these blocks to reduce the dominance in $\mathcal{T}_s$ of the nodes in $\mathrm{p_{dom}}(s-1,d)$, then $\mathrm{p_{dom}}(s-1,d)$ will be a prefix of all the chains in HonestPaths(s) and as in the previous case, $\mathrm{p_{dom}}(s-1,d) \subseteq \mathrm{p_{dom}}(s,d+1-k)$ and b will be a descendant of the last node in $\mathrm{p_{dom}}(s-1,d)$.

Otherwise the adversary will reduce the dominance in $\mathcal{T}_s$ of at least one node in $\mathrm{p_{dom}}(s-1,d)$ to zero. If b is a descendant of the last node in $\mathrm{p_{dom}}(s-1,d)$, then all nodes in $\mathrm{p_{dom}}(s-1,d)$ will be 1-dominant in $\hat{\mathcal{T}}_s$ and $\mathrm{p_{dom}}(s-1,d) \subseteq \mathrm{p_{dom}}(s,1) = \mathrm{p_{dom}}(s,d+1-d)$. If b is not a descendant of the last node in $\mathrm{p_{dom}}(s-1,d)$, then for the player P that mined this block it holds that $\mathcal{T}_s^P = \mathcal{T}_s$, because he would have not mined a chain that does not contain $\mathrm{p_{dom}}(s-1,d)$ at round s otherwise. Therefore, P at round s was mining a chain that belonged to HonestPaths(s, v_{root}) and thus all nodes in the chain are at least 0-dominant in $\mathcal{T}_s$. But because s is a uniquely successful round the dominance of all nodes in the chain that b belongs to will increase by one and thus $b \in \mathrm{p_{dom}}(s,1)$.   ⊣

Let b_i denote the honest block mined at round r_i. Let us assume that $r = r_m$. We are going to prove the lemma using induction on the number of uniquely successful rounds m.

For the base case suppose $m = 1$. The adversary does not broadcast any block until round $r_1 - 1$ and from the first claim $b_1 \in \mathrm{p_{dom}}(r_1,1)$. Thus the base case is proved. Suppose the lemma holds for $m - 1$ uniquely successful rounds and let k_1 be the number of blocks that the adversary broadcasts in the round interval $[r'-1, r_{m-1}-1]$. We have two cases.

(First case) $k_1 = m - 1$ and the adversary broadcasts no blocks in the rest of the rounds. From the first claim it follows that $b_m \in \mathrm{p_{dom}}(r_m,1)$.

(Second case) $k_1 < m - 1$ and from the induction hypothesis there exist blocks $b'_1, ..., b'_{m-1-k_1}$ mined by honest players at the uniquely successful rounds $r_1, .., r_{m-1}$ where $b'_i \in \mathrm{p_{dom}}(r_{m-1}, i)$. Let k_2 be the number of blocks that the adversary broadcasts until round $r_m - 2$ and k_3 the number of blocks he broadcasts at round $r_m - 1$. If $k_2 = m - 1$ then again from the first claim it follows that $b_m \in \mathrm{p_{dom}}(r_m, 1)$. If $k_2 < m - 1$ then if $k_3 + k_2 = m - 1$ then from the second claim either $b_m \in \mathrm{p_{dom}}(r_m, 1)$ or $b'_{m-1-k_1} \in \mathrm{p_{dom}}(r_m, 1)$. If $k_3 + k_2 < m - 1$ then again from the second claim at round r_m, $b'_i \in \mathrm{p_{dom}}(r_m - 1, i)$ for i in $\{k_2 + k_3 + 1, .., m - 1 - k_1\}$ and either $b'_{k_2+k_3}$ is in $\mathrm{p_{dom}}(r_m, 1)$ or b_m is in $\mathrm{p_{dom}}(r_m, 1)$. This completes the induction proof.

We proved that if $k_4 < m$ is the number of blocks the adversary broadcasts until round $r_m - 1$, then there exists honest blocks $b'_1, .., b'_{m-k_4}$ s.t. b'_i is in $\mathrm{p_{dom}}(r_m, i)$. Now in the case $r > r_m$, let $k_5 < m - k_4$ be the number of blocks the adversary broadcasts in the remaining rounds. The lemma follows easily from the second claim.

Remark 1. Let $r_1, .., r_m$ be uniquely successful rounds up to round r and the honest block mined at round r_1 be in $\mathrm{p_{dom}}(r_1, 1)$. If the adversary broadcasts $k < m$ blocks from round r_1 until round $r - 1$, then there exists an honest block b mined in one of the rounds $r_1, .., r_m$ such that b in $\mathrm{p_{dom}}(r, m - k)$. (to see why the remark holds notice that blocks that the adversary broadcasts before round r_1 affect only the dominant path at round r_1, and not at the following rounds)   □

B.2   Proof of Lemma 4

Proof. Let random variable Z_{s_1, s_2} (resp. $Z^{bd}_{s_1, s_2}$) denote the number of blocks the adversary computes (resp. broadcasts) from round s_1 until round s_2, and random variable X_{s_1, s_2} denote the number of rounds that are uniquely successful in the same interval.

We are first going to prove two preliminary claims. We show that as long as from some round r and afterwards the adversary broadcasts less blocks than the total number of uniquely successful rounds, the chain that any honest player adopts after round r extends $\mathrm{p_{dom}}(r, X_{1,r} - Z_{1,r})$. More generally we can prove the following claim.

Claim 3. Consider any execution such that for all rounds $s_2 \geq s_1$, for some round s_1, it holds that $Z_{1,s_2} < X_{1,s_2}$. Then, the chain that any honest player adopts after round s_1 extends $\mathrm{p_{dom}}(s_1, X_{1,s_1} - Z_{1,s_1})$.

Proof of Claim. Since $X_{1,s_1} > Z_{1,s_1}$ from Lemma 3 it follows that

$$ p = \mathrm{p_{dom}}(s_1, X_{1,s_1} - Z_{1,s_1-1}) \neq \bot $$

As long as the number of blocks that the adversary broadcasts at round s_2 are less than the dominance of the nodes in p in $\hat{T}_{s_2-1}$, all honest players at round s_2 will adopt chains containing p. Thus uniquely successful rounds will increase the dominance of these nodes. But since from the assumptions made, $Z_{1,s_2} < X_{1,s_2}$, in all rounds after round s_1, the nodes in p are at least 1-dominant in every $T^P_{s_2}$ where P is an honest player; the claim follows.   ⊣

Next we will show that if successive u.s. rounds occur such that the blocks mined are on different branches, then the adversary must broadcast an adequate number of blocks, as specified below.

Claim 4. Consider any execution where $s_1 < s_2 < ... < s_m$ are u.s. rounds and s_k is the first u.s. round such that the honest block mined in this round is not a descendant of the honest block mined in round s_{k-1}, for $k \in \{2, .., m\}$. Then either $Z^{bd}_{s_1-1, s_m-1} > X_{s_1, s_m-1}$ or $Z^{bd}_{s_1-1, s_m-1} = X_{s_1, s_m-1}$ and the honest block mined at round s_m will be in $\mathrm{p_{dom}}(s_m, 1)$.

Proof of Claim. Let $b_1, .., b_m$ denote the honest blocks mined at rounds $s_1, .., s_m$ respectively. We are going to prove the claim for $m = 2$. Suppose, for the sake of contradiction, that $Z^{bd}_{s_1-1,s_2-1} < X_{s_1,s_2-1}$. By the definition of s_2, the honest blocks mined on all u.s. rounds until round $s_2 - 1$ are descendants of b_1. From Lemma 3 at least one honest block b computed in one of the u.s. rounds in $[s_1, s_2-1]$ will be in $\mathrm{p_{dom}}(s_2-1, X_{s_1,s_2-1}-Z^{bd}_{s_1-1,s_2-2})$. Since from our hypothesis the adversary will broadcast less than $Z^{bd}_{s_2-1,s_2-1} < X_{s_1,s_2-1} - Z^{bd}_{s_1-1,s_2-2}$ blocks at round $s_2 - 1$, it is impossible for b_2 not to be a descendant of b and thus of b_1 which is a contradiction. Hence, $Z^{bd}_{s_1-1,s_2-1} \geq X_{s_1,s_2-1}$. If $Z^{bd}_{s_1-1,s_2-1} > X_{s_1,s_2-1}$ the base case follows. Otherwise, $Z^{bd}_{s_1-1,s_2-1} = X_{s_1,s_2-1}$ and we have two cases. In the first case, $X_{s_1,s_2-1} = Z^{bd}_{s_1-1,s_2-2}$ and at round round $s_2 - 1$ the adversary does not broadcast any block. From Claim 1 of Lemma 3, b_2 will be in $\mathrm{p_{dom}}(s_2, 1)$. In the second case, it holds that the adversary broadcasts exactly $X_{s_1,s_2-1} - Z^{bd}_{s_1-1,s_2-2}$ blocks at round $s_2 - 1$. From Claim 2 of Lemma 3, since b_2 cannot be a descendant of the last node of $\mathrm{p_{dom}}(s_2 - 1, 1)$, b_2 will be in $\mathrm{p_{dom}}(s_2, 1)$. Hence, the base case follows.

Suppose the lemma holds until round s_m. By the inductive hypothesis we have two cases. In the first case $Z^{bd}_{s_1-1,s_m-1} > X_{s_1,s_m-1}$, which implies that $Z^{bd}_{s_1-1,s_m-1}$ is greater or equal to X_{s_1,s_m}. If no u.s. round happens during rounds $s_m+1, \ldots, s_{m+1}-1$ then from Claim 1 in the proof of Lemma 3 the claim follows. Otherwise, a u.s. round s' happens during these rounds, where the honest block mined is a descendant of b_m. Then we can make the same argument as for the base case starting from round s' and get that either $Z^{bd}_{s'-1,s_{m+1}-1} > X_{s',s_{m+1}-1}$ or $Z^{bd}_{s'-1,s_{m+1}-1} = X_{s',s_{m+1}-1}$ and the honest block mined at round s_{m+1} will be in $\mathrm{p_{dom}}(s_{m+1}, 1)$. Since $Z^{bd}_{s'-1,s_{m+1}-1} < Z^{bd}_{s_m-1,s_{m+1}-1}$ and $X_{s',s_{m+1}-1}$ is equal to $X_{s_{m+1},s_{m+1}-1}$, by the inequality of the inductive hypothesis the claim follows.

In the second case $Z^{bd}_{s_1-1,s_m-1} = X_{s_1,s_m-1}$ and the honest block b_m mined at round s_m will be in $\mathrm{p_{dom}}(s_m, 1)$. From Remark 1 of the proof of claim Lemma 3, for an application of this Lemma from rounds s_m until $s_{m+1} - 1$ we can count the adversarial blocks starting from round s_m. Thus from the same argument as for the base case starting from round s_m we get that either $Z^{bd}_{s_m,s_{m+1}-1} > X_{s_m,s_{m+1}-1}$ or $Z^{bd}_{s_m,s_{m+1}-1} = X_{s_m,s_{m+1}-1}$ and the honest block mined at round s_m will be in $\mathrm{p_{dom}}(s_m, 1)$. By the equality of the inductive hypothesis the claim follows. $\dashv$

Next, we observe that Lemma 3 as well as Claims 3 and 4 can be applied on a subtree of the block tree, if all honest blocks mined after the round the root of the subtree was mined are on this subtree.

Observation 1. *Let b be an honest block computed at round s_1 that is in the chains adopted by all honest players after round s_2. Also, suppose that all blocks mined at u.s. rounds after round s_1 are descendants of b. Then the following hold:*

1. *Regarding applications of Lemma 3 and Claim 4 on the subtree of the block tree rooted on b after round s_1, we can ignore all blocks that the adversary has mined up to round s_1.*

2. *Regarding applications of Claim 3 after round s_2, we can ignore all blocks that the adversary has mined up to round s_1.*

To see why the observation holds consider the following. Since the adversary receives block b for the first time at round $s_1 + 1$, all blocks that the adversary mines before round $s_1 + 1$ cannot be descendants of b. Regarding the first point, blocks that are not descendants of b do not affect the validity of Lemma 3 and Claim 4 on the subtree of the block tree rooted on b; this is because blocks that are not descendants of b, do not affect the dominance of the nodes of the subtree rooted at b. Regarding the second point, consider the dominant path at round $s_3 > s_2$ in the subtree that is rooted on b. Then, this path can be extended up to the root node, since, by our assumption, b is in the chains adopted by all honest players after round s_2.

We are now ready to prove the lemma. First, we are going to define a set of bad events which we will show that hold with probability exponentially small in s. Assuming these events don't occur we will then show that our lemma is implied, and thus the lemma will follow with overwhelming probability.

Let $BAD(s_1, s_2)$ be the event that $X_{s_1,s_2} \leq Z_{s_1,s_2}$. In [9, Lemma 5], by an application of the Chernoff bounds it was proved that assuming that $\gamma \geq (1+\delta)\beta$ for some $\delta \in (0,1)$, then with probability at least $(1 - e^{-\frac{\beta}{243}\delta^2 s'})(1 - e^{-\frac{\gamma}{128}\delta^2 s'}) \geq 1 - e^{-(\min(\frac{\beta}{243}, \frac{\gamma}{128})\delta^2 s' - \ln(2))}$ for any $r' > 0, s' \geq s$:

$$X_{r',r'+s'-1} > \left(1 + \frac{\delta}{2}\right) Z_{r',r'+s'-1} \tag{1}$$

Thus, there exists an appropriate constant $\epsilon = \delta^2 \min(\frac{\beta}{243}, \frac{\gamma}{128})$, independent of r, such that it holds that for any $r' > 0, s' \geq s$, $BAD(r', r' + s' - 1)$ occurs with probability at most $e^{-\epsilon\delta^2 s' + \ln 2}$. From an application of the union bound, we get that for the function $g(s) = \epsilon\delta^2 s - \ln 2 + \ln(1 - e^{-\epsilon\delta^2})$, the probability that $\bigvee_{r' \geq s} BAD(s_1 + 1, s_1 + r')$ happens is:

$$\Pr\left[\bigvee_{r' \geq s} BAD(s_1 + 1, s_1 + r')\right] \leq \sum_{r' \geq s} e^{-\epsilon\delta^2 r' + \ln 2}$$

$$\leq e^{\ln 2} \sum_{r' \geq s} e^{-\epsilon\delta^2 r'}$$

$$\leq e^{\ln 2} \frac{e^{-\epsilon\delta^2 s}}{1 - e^{-\epsilon\delta^2}}$$

$$\leq e^{-g(s)}$$

Until now we have assumed that the execution we are studying is collision-free; no two queries in the oracle return the same value for different inputs. Let COL denote the event where a collision occurs in our execution. The probability of COL in a polynomial number of rounds, is exponentially small on κ.

$$\Pr[COL] \leq (f\kappa^c)^2 / 2^{\kappa+1} = e^{-\Omega(\kappa)} \leq e^{-\Omega(s)}$$

Let $BAD(s_1)$ denote the event where $\bigvee_{r' \geq s} BAD(s_1 + 1, s_1 + r')$ or COL happens. From the union bound the probability that $BAD(s_1)$ happens, for any s_1 is negligible.

$$\Pr[BAD(s_1)] \leq e^{-g(s)} + e^{-\Omega(s)} \leq e^{-\Omega(s)}$$

We are going to show next that, conditioning on the negation of this event the statement of the lemma follows.

We will use the convention that block b_i is mined at round r_i. Let b_1 be the most recent honest block that is in the chains that all honest players have adopted on and after round r, such that the blocks mined at all u.s. rounds after round r_1 are descendants of b_1. This block is well defined, since in the worst case it is the genesis block. If r_1 is greater or equal to $r - s$, then the lemma follows for block b_1 with probability 1.

Suppose round r_1 is before round $r - s$ and that $BAD(r_1)$ does not happen. The negation of $BAD(r_1)$ implies that $X_{r_1+1, r-1+c} > Z_{r_1+1, r-1+c}$, for $c \geq 0$. By Lemma 3 and Claim 3 there exists at least one honest block b_2, mined in a u.s. round and contained in the chains of all honest players on and after round r. W.l.o.g. let b_2 be the most recently mined such block. By the definition of b_1, b_2 is a descendant of b_1. If r_2 is greater or equal to $r - s$ then the lemma follows, since b_2 is an honest block mined on and after round $r - s$ that satisfies the conditions of the lemma.

Suppose round r_2 is before round $r - s$. Let r_3 be the earliest u.s. round, such that b_3 and the blocks mined at all u.s. rounds afterwards are descendants of b_2. Since b_2 will be in the chains of all honest players after round r, round r_3 is well defined. Also let $s_1 < \ldots < s_m < \ldots$ be the sequence of u.s. rounds after round r_1 that satisfy the conditions of Claim 4. That is, s_k is the first u.s. round such that the honest block mined in this round is not a descendant of the honest block mined in round s_{k-1}, for $k \in \{2, .., m\}$. The first u.s. round after round r_1 corresponds to s_1.

We will argue that r_3 is equal to some $s_i > s_1$ in the aforementioned sequence. Suppose, for the sake of contradiction that it does not. This implies that the honest block mined at round r_3 (denoted by b_3) is a descendant of the honest block mined at some round s_i of the sequence. W.l.o.g. suppose that s_i is the largest such round that is before round r_3. There are three cases. In the first case, $r_2 < s_i < r_3$. By the definition of s_i and r_3, the block mined at round s_i is an ancestor of b_3 and also a descendant of b_2. Hence, s_i satisfies the definition of r_3 which is a contradiction (there is an earlier round than r_3 with the same property). In the second case, $s_i = r_4$, where b_4 is a descendant of b_1 and either $b_2 = b_4$ or b_4 is an ancestor of b_2. Then b_4 is a block that satisfies the definition of b_1, and is more recent, which is a contradiction. In the third case, $r_1 < s_i < r_2$ and the block mined at round s_i is not an ancestor of b_2. By the definition of s_i, the honest block mined at round s_i is an ancestor of b_3, that has been mined before round r_2. But this is contradictory, since no honest block can be an ancestor of b_3, mined before round r_2, but not be an ancestor of b_2.

Since we proved that r_3 is equal to some s_i we can apply Claim 4 from round $r_1 + 1$ until round r_3. Again, from Observation 1, regarding applications of

Claim 4 after round r_1 we can ignore blocks that were mined before round r_1+1. Then either $Z_{r_1+1,r_3-1} \geq Z_{r_1+1,r_3-1}^{bd} > X_{r_1+1,r_3-1}$ or $Z_{r_1+1,r_3-1} \geq Z_{r_1+1,r_3-1}^{bd} = X_{r_1+1,r_3-1}$ and the honest block mined at round r_3 will be in $p_{dom}(r_3,1)$.

Suppose, for the sake of contradiction, that round r_3 is after round $r_2 + s$. Then $(r_3-1)-(r_1+1) \geq s$ and $Z_{r_1+1,r_3-1} \geq X_{r_1+1,r_3-1}$. This is a contradiction, since in this case $\neg BAD(r_1)$ implies $Z_{r_1+1,r_3-1} < X_{r_1+1,r_3-1}$. Therefore, $r_3 \leq r_2 + s < r$. In addition, notice that $\neg BAD(r_1)$ also implies

$$X_{r_1+1,r_2+s} > Z_{r_1+1,r_2+s} \tag{2}$$

We are going to apply Lemma 3 and Observation 1 from round r_3 until round $r_2 + s$ in the subtree rooted at b_2. According to the analysis we made previously there are two cases. In the first case, $Z_{r_1+1,r_3-1}^{bd} > X_{r_1+1,r_3-1}$ or equivalently $Z_{r_1+1,r_3-1}^{bd} \geq X_{r_1+1,r_3}$. Suppose, for the sake of contradiction, that $r_3 = r_2 + s$. Then $Z_{r_1+1,r_2+s-1} \geq X_{r_1+1,r_2+s}$. But this is a contradiction, since $\neg BAD(r_1)$ implies Inequality 2. Therefore, $r_3 < r_2 + s$. From Inequality 2:

$$X_{r_3+1,r_2+s} \geq X_{r_1+1,r_2+s} - X_{r_1+1,r_3} > Z_{r_1+1,r_k+s} - Z_{r_1+1,r_3-1}^{bd} \geq Z_{r_3,r_2+s}^{bd}$$

The last inequality, stems from two facts: that we can ignore blocks that were mined before round $r_1 + 1$ regarding applications of Lemma 3 and also that the blocks that the adversary broadcasts at distinct rounds are different (adversaries that broadcast the same block multiple times can be ignored without loss of generality).

In the second case, $Z_{r_1+1,r_3-1}^{bd} = X_{r_1+1,r_3-1}$ and the honest block mined at round r_3 will be in $p_{dom}(r_3,1)$. Again from Inequality 2:

$$X_{r_3,r_2+s} = X_{r_1+1,r_2+s} - X_{r_1+1,r_3-1} > Z_{r_1+1,r_k+s} - Z_{r_1+1,r_3-1}^{bd} \geq Z_{r_3,r_2+s}^{bd}$$

The same analysis holds for all rounds after $r_2 + s$. By an application of Claim 3, an honest block b, computed in one of the u.s. rounds after round r_2 and before round r, will be in the chains that honest players adopt on and after round r. Since b_2 is the most recently mined block, before round $r - s$, included in the chain of all honest players, b must have been mined on and after round $r - s$ (since $r_3 > r_2$). Let A be the event that there exists a block mined by an honest player on and after round $r - s$, that is contained in the chain which any honest player adopts after round r. We have proved that $(\neg BAD(r_1))$ implies A. Then:

$$\begin{aligned} Pr[A] &= Pr[A \wedge BAD(r_1)] + Pr[A \wedge \neg BAD(r_1)] \\ &\geq Pr[A \wedge \neg BAD(r_1)] \\ &= Pr[A|\neg BAD(r_1)]Pr[\neg BAD(r_1)] \\ &= Pr[\neg BAD(r_1)] \\ &\geq 1 - e^{-g(s)} \end{aligned}$$

Hence, the lemma holds with probability at least $1 - e^{-g(s)}$. $\qquad\square$

References

1. Andrychowicz, M., Dziembowski, S.: PoW-based distributed cryptography with no trusted setup. In: Gennaro, R., Robshaw, M. (eds.) CRYPTO 2015. LNCS, vol. 9216, pp. 379–399. Springer, Heidelberg (2015). https://doi.org/10.1007/978-3-662-48000-7_19

2. Aspnes, J., Jackson, C., Krishnamurthy, A.: Exposing Computationally-Challenged Byzantine Impostors. Department of Computer Science, Yale University, New Haven, CT, Technical Report (2005)

3. Bahack, L.: Theoretical bitcoin attacks with less than half of the computational power (draft). Cryptology ePrint Archive, Report 2013/868 (2013). http://eprint.iacr.org/

4. Bonneau, J.: Ethiks: Using ethereum to audit a coniks key transparency log

5. Ethan Heilman, S.G., Kendler, A., Zohar, A.: Eclipse attacks on bitcoin's peer-to-peer network. Cryptology ePrint Archive, Report 2015/263 (2015).http://eprint.iacr.org/

6. ethereum/wiki. A next-generation smart contract and decentralized application platform, October 2015. https://github.com/ethereum/wiki/wiki/White-Paper/

7. Eyal, I., Gencer, A.E., Sirer, E.G., van Renesse, R.: Bitcoin-ng: a scalable blockchain protocol. CoRR, abs/1510.02037 (2015)

8. Eyal, I., Sirer, E.G.: Majority is not enough: bitcoin mining is vulnerable. In: Financial Cryptography (2014)

9. Garay, J., Kiayias, A., Leonardos, N.: The bitcoin backbone protocol: analysis and applications. In: Oswald, E., Fischlin, M. (eds.) EUROCRYPT 2015. LNCS, vol. 9057, pp. 281–310. Springer, Heidelberg (2015). https://doi.org/10.1007/978-3-662-46803-6_10

10. Gervais, A., Karame, G.O., Wüst, K., Glykantzis, V., Ritzdorf, H., Capkun, S.: On the security and performance of proof of work blockchains. Cryptology ePrint Archive, Report 2016/555 (2016). http://eprint.iacr.org/2016/555

11. Juels, A., Kosba, A., Shi, E.: The ring of gyges: Using smart contracts for crime. aries, 40:54 (2015)

12. Kiayias, A., Panagiotakos, G.: Speed-security tradeoffs in blockchain protocols. Technical report, IACR: Cryptology ePrint Archive (2015)

13. Kiayias, A., Zhou, H.-S., Zikas, V.: Fair and robust multi-party computation using a global transaction ledger (2015)

14. Kosba, A., Miller, A., Shi, E., Wen, Z., Papamanthou, C.: Hawk: the blockchain model of cryptography and privacy-preserving smart contracts. Technical report, Cryptology ePrint Archive, Report 2015/675 (2015). http://eprint.iacr.org

15. Lamport, L., Shostak, R.E., Pease, M.C.: The byzantine generals problem. ACM Trans. Program. Lang. Syst. 4(3), 382–401 (1982)

16. Lerner, S.D.: Even faster block-chains with the decor protocol. Cryptology ePrint Archive, Report 2013/881, May 2014. https://bitslog.wordpress.com/2014/05/02/decor/

17. Nakamoto, S.: Bitcoin: a peer-to-peer electronic cash system (2008). http://bitcoin.org/bitcoin.pdf

18. Okun, M.: Agreement among unacquainted byzantine generals. In: Fraigniaud, P. (ed.) DISC 2005. LNCS, vol. 3724, pp. 499–500. Springer, Heidelberg (2005). https://doi.org/10.1007/11561927_40

19. Omohundro, S.: Cryptocurrencies, smart contracts, and artificial intelligence. AI Matters 1(2), 19–21 (2014)

20. Pass, R., Seeman, L., Shelat, A.: Analysis of the blockchain protocol in asynchronous networks. Cryptology ePrint Archive, Report 2016/454, 2016. http://eprint.iacr.org/
21. Pease, M.C., Shostak, R.E., Lamport, L.: Reaching agreement in the presence of faults. J. ACM **27**(2), 228–234 (1980)
22. Percival, C.: Stronger key derivation via sequential memory-hard functions. Self-published, pp. 1–16 (2009)
23. Peterson, J., Krug, J.: Augur: a decentralized, open-source platform for prediction markets. arXiv preprint arXiv:1501.01042 (2015)
24. Simplicio Jr., M.A., Almeida, L.C., Andrade, E.R., dos Santos, P.C., Barreto, P.S.: The lyra2 reference guide. Technical report, version 2.3. 2. Technical report (2014)
25. Sompolinsky, Y., Zohar, A.: Secure high-rate transaction processing in bitcoin. In: Böhme, R., Okamoto, T. (eds.) FC 2015. LNCS, vol. 8975, pp. 507–527. Springer, Heidelberg (2015). https://doi.org/10.1007/978-3-662-47854-7_32

Using Level-1 Homomorphic Encryption to Improve Threshold DSA Signatures for Bitcoin Wallet Security

Dan Boneh[1], Rosario Gennaro[2], and Steven Goldfeder[3]([✉])

[1] Stanford University, Stanford, USA
dabo@cs.stanford.edu
[2] City College, City University of New York, New York, USA
rosario@cs.ccny.cuny.edu
[3] Princeton University, Princeton, USA
stevenag@cs.princeton.edu

Abstract. Recently Gennaro et al. (ACNS '16) presented a threshold-optimal signature algorithm for DSA. Threshold-optimality means that if security is set so that it is required to have $t + 1$ servers to cooperate to sign, then it is sufficient to have $n = t + 1$ honest servers in the network. Obviously threshold optimality compromises robustness since if $n = t + 1$, a single corrupted player can prevent the group from signing. Still, in their protocol, up to t corrupted players cannot produce valid signatures. Their protocol requires six rounds which is already an improvement over the eight rounds of the classic threshold DSA of Gennaro et al. (Eurocrypt '99) (which is not threshold optimal since $n \geq 3t + 1$ if robust and $n \geq 2t + 1$ if not).

We present a new and improved threshold-optimal DSA signature scheme, which cuts the round complexity to **four** rounds. Our protocol is based on the observation that given an encryption of the secret key, the encryption of a DSA signature can be computed in only four rounds if using a level-1 Fully Homomorphic Encryption scheme (i.e. a scheme that supports at least one multiplication), and we instantiate it with the very efficient level-1 FHE scheme of Catalano and Fiore (CCS '15).

As noted in Gennaro et al. (ACNS '16), the schemes have very compelling application in securing Bitcoin wallets from thefts happening due to DSA secret key exposure. Given that network latency can be a major bottleneck in an interactive protocol, a scheme with reduced round complexity is highly desirable. We implement and benchmark our scheme and find it to be very efficient in practice.

1 Introduction

In a threshold signature scheme, the ability to sign a message is shared among n servers such that any group of size $t + 1$ can sign, but t or less servers cannot. The immediate consequence is that if a network adversary corrupts up to t servers (we call this a t-*adversary*), it will still not be able to sign a message.

© Springer Nature Switzerland AG 2019
T. Lange and O. Dunkelman (Eds.): LATINCRYPT 2017, LNCS 11368, pp. 352–377, 2019.
https://doi.org/10.1007/978-3-030-25283-0_19

A scheme is said to be *threshold-optimal* if we can set $n = t + 1$ and still prevent a t-adversary from forging signatures. Note that if one sets $n = t + 1$, a t-adversary can always mount a *denial-of-service* attack by refusing to cooperate, leaving the lone honest server unable to sign (actually for $n = t + 1$ even a 1-adversary can mount such an attack). A scheme is said to be *robust* if a t-adversary cannot prevent the group from signing. Clearly robustness requires $n \geq 2t + 1$ so that there always are at least $t + 1$ honest servers in the network.

Much research has been devoted to building secure and efficient threshold signature protocols for a variety of signature schemes. Threshold signatures provide increased security in the presence of break-ins that can compromise one's secret key. By sharing the key among n servers, a user forces the adversary to compromise many of them (a security level parametrized by t) possibly even in a short period of time (by using so-called *proactive* schemes [14]).

THRESHOLD DSA. Threshold scheme for the Digital Signature Algorithm (DSA) were presented in many works. We focus on the protocols described in [26,27, 35,36]. The "classic" protocol in [26,27] requires 8 communication rounds to complete and also $n \geq 3t + 1$ if desiring robustness, and $n \geq 2t + 1$ without. Note that the protocol is not threshold-optimal.

In particular this protocol rules out the simple $n = 2, t = 1$ case (e.g. 2-out-of-2, where two servers have to cooperate to sign). That case was discussed and solved in [36] using techniques that inform much of the work in [25] and this paper. Lindell recently presented an improved version of [36] that achieves much faster speeds by eliminating many of the costly zero-knowledge proofs, but that protocol is also exclusively for the 2-party case, whereas we are interested in the general case.

THE THRESHOLD DSA SCHEME IN [25]. Gennaro et al. solve the above problem by presenting a threshold DSA scheme which is threshold optimal, with a constant (6) number of rounds, and constant local long-term storage [25].

The main idea of the paper comes from [36]: to use a threshold cryptosystem to provide players with shares of the DSA secret key. A threshold cryptosystem achieves the same notion of threshold security but for encryption rather than signatures. The ability to decrypt a ciphertext is shared among n servers in such a way that any group of size $t + 1$ can decrypt, but t or less servers cannot. If the servers are provided with $\alpha = E(x)$ for such a threshold cryptosystem E, then this implicitly constitutes a secret sharing of the value x.

Following [36], Gennaro et al. show that if $x = sk_{DSA}$ (i.e. the secret key of a DSA signature scheme), and E is an additively homomorphic threshold encryption scheme[1] then we can build a threshold DSA scheme with the above properties.

As shown by the implementation presented in [25] their scheme is reasonably practical and efficient, and the response from the Bitcoin community to the work

---

[1] i.e. a scheme where given $c = E(m)$ and $c' = E(m')$ it is possible to compute $\hat{c} = E(m + m')$ where $+$ is a group operation over the message space, e.g. [41] and its threshold version in [31].

was overwhelmingly positive. It seems however that the limiting factor in the deployment of the [25] protocol is its round complexity, since network latency is a big problem in practice that was not considered by [25]. This leaves open the question if a better (ideally non-interactive) protocol can be found.

1.1   Our Contribution

We present a new threshold signature protocol for DSA with only four rounds of interaction. We make several improvements to the security proof of the best previous scheme, and also answer a previously open question about non-malleable commitments. In particular:

- We present a new threshold-optimal DSA scheme with only *four (4)* rounds, whereas the best protocol until now used six (6) rounds. The reduction in the number of rounds will reduce the slowdown caused by network latency.
- We achieve a better reduction than the proof of [25], and thus our proof enables the use shorter keys in practice.
- The proof of [25] requires, among other things, the use of *independent commitments* [28], but we are able to reduce it to the more standard notion of *non-malleable commitments* [20,22]. In the process, we prove a result of general interest – we answer the question that was left open by [28] and show that *non-malleability* does indeed imply *independence*. We show that they are equivalent, which may be useful in future works as the independence definition is often easier to work with when writing security proofs.
- We implement our signature generation scheme and benchmark our results. We find that our scheme is more parallelizable than that of [25] and will have better runtimes in practice for sufficiently large threshold sets.
- Aside from the implementation of our own scheme, we also provide the only public implementation of the L1FHE scheme of Catalano and Fiore [16]. We built our software modularly so that the two components are completely decoupled, and the FHE software is fully re-usable for other applications.

While the scheme of [25] has received much positive press in the Bitcoin community, it has yet to be adopted by any commercial Bitcoin wallet. Our scheme is less interactive and less complex to code (as we significantly reduce the number of zero knowledge proofs). We therefore believe that it will be our scheme and not the one from [25] that will be adopted in practice.

1.2   Our Solution in a Nutshell

The protocol in [25] starts by encrypting the secret key x of the DSA scheme with an additively homomorphic encryption scheme E. If the matching decryption key is shared using a threshold cryptosystem for E then this is a secret sharing of x and the protocols in [25,36] show how to leverage this to obtain a threshold DSA signature.

Our starting observation is that if one uses a threshold *fully homomorphic encryption* scheme then *any* signature scheme can be turned into a *non-interactive* threshold one. Conceptually the idea is simple: if $\alpha = \mathsf{FHE}(x)$ is an encryption of the secret key for a signature scheme, then by using the homomorphic properties of FHE the parties are able to locally compute.

$E(\sigma)$ where σ is the signature on any message M. This idea can be seen actually as a special case of the non-interactive multiparty computation protocol based on threshold FHE in [39].

We then turned to optimize the above idea for the specific case of DSA. Recall how (a generic form of) DSA works – given a cyclic group $\mathcal{G}$ of prime order q generated by an element g, a hash function H defined from arbitrary strings into Z_q, and another hash function H' defined from $\mathcal{G}$ to Z_q we define:

- **Secret Key** x chosen uniformly at random in Z_q.
- **Public Key** $y = g^x$ computed in $\mathcal{G}$.
- **Signing Algorithm** on input an arbitrary message M, we compute $m = H(M) \in Z_q$. Then the signer chooses k uniformly at random in Z_q and computes $R = g^k$ in $\mathcal{G}$ and $r = H'(R) \in Z_q$. Then she computes $s = k^{-1}(m + xr) \bmod q$. The signature on M is the pair (r, s).
- **Verification Algorithm** on input $M, (r, s)$ and y, the receiver checks that $r, s \in Z_q$ and computes

$$R' = g^{ms^{-1} \bmod q} y^{rs^{-1} \bmod q} \text{ in } \mathcal{G}$$

and accepts if $H'(R') = r$.

A straightforward application of the above FHE-based approach would result in a relatively inefficient protocol due to the current state of affairs for FHE. Indeed we can see that a circuit computing a DSA signatures from encryptions of x and k is quite deep since it must compute $R = g^k$ and k^{-1}.

We use the same techniques as [25] for the computation of R: basically each player reveals a "share" of R together with a zero-knowledge proof of its correctness (that can be checked against the encrypted values).

Where we diverge from [25] is in the computation of k^{-1} and s. We assume that our encryption scheme E is level-1 HE. This means that given $E(x)$ it is possible to compute $E(F(x))$ for any function F that can be expressed by an arithmetic circuit of multiplicative depth 1. In other words one can perform an unlimited number of additions over encrypted values but only 1 multiplication.

Given $c_k = E(k)$ for such an encryption E, the parties use a variation of Beaver's inversion protocol [4]. First they generate an encryption $c_\rho = E(\rho)$ for a random value ρ, then using the level-1 property they compute $c_{\rho k} = E(\rho k)$ and decrypt it using the threshold decryption property. Now they have a public value $\eta = \rho k$ which reveals no information about k, but allows them to compute an encryption of k^{-1} as follows. First compute η^{-1} and then use the additive homomorphism to compute $c_{k^{-1}} = \eta^{-1} \times c_\rho = E(\eta^{-1}\rho) = E(k^{-1})$.

EFFICIENT LEVEL-1 HE INSTANTIATION. There are various possible choices to instantiate the Level-1 HE in our protocol. We chose to use the construction recently presented in [16] where it is shown that any additively homomorphic encryption scheme can be turned into a level-1 HE with small computational overhead. By implementing the underlying additively homomorphic encryption with Paillier's scheme [41] we are able to "recycle" all the other components of the [25] protocol: (i) all the zero-knowledge proofs that show some type of consistency property for public values vs. encrypted values and (ii) the threshold encryption based on [31].

1.3   Improvements to the Proof of [25]

A Tighter Reduction. Aside from the improvements in the protocol, our security proof is also significantly improved. In the proof of [25], if there exists an adversary $\mathcal{A}$ that forges with probability $O\epsilon$ in the centralized DSA scheme, then we can build a forger $\mathcal{F}$ that succeeds with probability $O\epsilon^3$ in the threshold scheme. In terms of concrete security, this means that in order to get an equivalent level of security, one would have to use keys three times as long when using the threshold version of the scheme.

While our simulation of the distributed key generation protocol maintains the $O\epsilon^3$ probability, we get a tighter reduction for the threshold signature generation protocol: $O(\epsilon^2)$. This leads to a smaller key size in practice when we use our threshold protocol together with a centralized dealer. We note that this use case is very practical in the Bitcoin application: when one wants to add threshold security to an existing Bitcoin address (i.e. an address that was generated using the centralized DSA key generation scheme), one will deal shares of the existing secret to multiple servers only use the threshold protocol for subsequent signature generation.

Non-malleable vs. Independent Commitments. The proof of [25] relies on independent commitments [28] rather than the more standard notion of non-malleable commitments [20,22]. While [28] showed that independence implies non-malleability, the converse was hitherto unknown. Thus, the use of independence of their paper was a stronger assumption than the use of non-malleability.

We improved their proof by using non-malleable commitments instead of independent commitments, but in the process we were able to prove a more general and interesting lemma: that independence implies non-malleability, and that the two notions are therefore equivalent.

1.4   Results of Implementation

We implemented the Level-1 FHE scheme from [16] as well as our signature generation protocol. We also optimized the code from [25], and achieve much better runtimes than reported in that paper.

We found that the runtime of our protocol was comparable but slightly slower than that of [25]. However, when we parallelized the verification of the zero-knowledge proofs of both protocols and ran it on a four-core machine, we found that our protocol was more parallelizable and outperformed that of [25] for thresholds greater than or equal to 13.

Moreover, we argue that the raw-computation time metric only tells a partial story as it does not account for network latency. In a real network setting, the slightly slower runtime of the serial version of our protocol will be amply compensated by the network savings due to the reduction of rounds.

1.5 Motivation: Bitcoin Wallet Security

Following [25] we now present the main motivation of our work: distributed signing for Bitcoin transactions. Bitcoin is the most widely used electronic currency. In Bitcoin users are identified by *addresses* which can be thought simply as DSA public keys[2]. A user with address pk_1 transfers Bitcoins to another user with address pk_2 simply by digitally signing a statement to that extent using sk_1. Consensus on who owns what is achieved via a distributed public ledger (with which we are not going to concern ourselves). We focus on the issue that a user's Bitcoins are as secure as the secret key of its address. If the secret key is compromised, the adversary can easily steal all the Bitcoins associated with the matching public key by simply transferring the coins to itself.

The suggestion to use the classic threshold DSA protocol in [26,27] to achieve transparent splitting of signature keys, was rejected by Bitcoin practitioners for various reasons. First of all the protocol in [26,27] was considered to be too computationally heavy, particularly in the number of rounds. Even more seriously, the lack of threshold optimality would force a user to put online a high number of signing servers (e.g. for a security threshold of $t = 3$ a user would have to deploy $n = 7$ or $n = 10$ servers depending if robustness is required or not) with a substantial operating cost, and higher number of possible infection targets. As discussed in [25] it was quite clear the Bitcoin community would much prefer a threshold optimal scheme with $n = t + 1$ even if that meant compromising robustness and allowing denial-of-service attacks[3].

While the protocol in [36] achieves threshold-optimality, it is limited to the case of $(n = 2, t = 1)$ and does not allow for flexible[4] choices of n, t.

---

[2] Bitcoin uses ECDSA, the DSA scheme implemented over a group of points of an elliptic curve. As in [25] we ignore this fact since our results hold for a generic version of DSA which is independent of the underlying group where the scheme is implemented (provided the group is of prime order and DSA is obviously unforgeable in this implementation.).

[3] The rationale for that is that provided a bad server in a denial-of-service attack can be easily identified – that is the case in both our protocol and the protocol of [25] – then the corrupted server can be rebooted, restarted from a trusted basis, and the adversary eliminated.

[4] A preliminary version of [25] provided a simple extension of [36] to the n-out-of-n case which however required $O(n)$ rounds to complete. The same version also uses a standard combinatorial construction to go from n-out-of-n to the generic n, t case, but that requires $O(n^t)$ local long-term storage by each server.

2   Model, Definitions and Tools

In this section we introduce our communication model and provide definitions
of secure threshold signature schemes.

COMMUNICATION MODEL. We assume that our computation model is composed
of a set of n *players* $P_1, \ldots, P_n$ connected by a complete network of point-to-point
channels and a broadcast channel.

THE ADVERSARY. We assume that an adversary, $\mathcal{A}$, can corrupt up to t of the
n players in the network. $\mathcal{A}$ learns all the information stored at the corrupted
nodes, and hears all broadcasted messages. We consider two type of adversaries:

- *honest-but-curious:* the corrupted players follow the protocol but try to learn
  information about secret values;
- *malicious:* corrupted players to divert from the specified protocol in *any* (possibly malicious) way.

We assume the network is "partially synchronous", meaning the adversary
speaks last in every communication round (also known as a *rushing* adversary.)
The adversary is modeled by a probabilistic polynomial time Turing machine.

Adversaries can also be categorized as *static* or *adaptive*. A static adversary
chooses the corrupted players at the beginning of the protocol, while an adaptive
one chooses them during the computation. In the following, for simplicity, we
assume the adversary to be static, though the techniques from [15,32] can be
used to extend our result to the adaptive adversary case.

Given a protocol $\mathcal{P}$, the *view* of the adversary, denoted by $\mathcal{VIEW}_\mathcal{A}(\mathcal{P})$, is
defined as the probability distribution (induced by the random coins of the play-
ers) on the knowledge of the adversary, namely, the computational and memory
history of all the corrupted players, and the public communications and output
of the protocol.

SIGNATURE SCHEME. A signature scheme $\mathcal{S}$ is a triple of efficient randomized
algorithms (Key-Gen, Sig, Ver). Key-Gen is the *key generator* algorithm: on input
the security parameter 1^λ, it outputs a pair (y, x), such that y is the *public key*
and x is the *secret key* of the signature scheme. Sig is the *signing* algorithm:
on input a message m and the secret key x, it outputs sig, a signature of the
message m. Since Sig can be a randomized algorithm there might be several valid
signatures sig of a message m under the key x; with $\mathsf{Sig}(m, x)$ we will denote
the set of such signatures. Ver is the *verification* algorithm. On input a message
m, the public key y, and a string sig, it checks whether sig is a proper signature
of m, i.e. if $sig \in \mathsf{Sig}(m, x)$.

The notion of security for signature schemes was formally defined in [29] in
various flavors. The following definition captures the strongest of these notions:
existential unforgeability against adaptively chosen message attack.

Definition 1. *We say that a signature scheme* $\mathcal{S}$ = (Key-Gen,Sig,Ver) *is*
unforgeable *if no adversary who is given the public key* y *generated by* Key-Gen,

and the signatures of k messages $m_1, \ldots, m_k$ adaptively chosen, can produce the signature on a new message m (i.e., $m \notin \{m_1, \ldots, m_k\}$) with non-negligible (in λ) probability.

THRESHOLD SECRET SHARING. Given a secret value x we say that the values $(x_1, \ldots, x_n)$ constitute a (t, n)-threshold secret sharing of x if t (or less) of these values reveal no information about x, and if there is an efficient algorithm that outputs x having $t + 1$ of the values x_i as inputs.

THRESHOLD SIGNATURE SCHEMES. Let $\mathcal{S} = (\text{Key-Gen, Sig, Ver})$ be a signature scheme. A (t, n)-threshold signature scheme $\mathcal{TS}$ for $\mathcal{S}$ is a pair of protocols (Thresh-Key-Gen, Thresh-Sig) for the set of players $P_1, \ldots, P_n$.

Thresh-Key-Gen is a distributed key generation protocol used to jointly generate a pair (y, x) of public/private keys on input a security parameter 1^λ. At the end of the protocol, the private output of P_i is a value x_i such that the values $(x_1, \ldots, x_n)$ form a (t, n)-threshold secret sharing of x. The public output of the protocol contains the public key y. Public/private key pairs (y, x) are produced by Thresh-Key-Gen with the same probability distribution as if they were generated by the Key-Gen protocol of the regular signature scheme $\mathcal{S}$. In some cases it is acceptable to have a *centralized* key generation protocol, in which a trusted dealer runs Key-Gen to obtain (x, y) and the shares x among the n players.

Thresh-Sig is the distributed signature protocol. The private input of P_i is the value x_i. The public inputs consist of a message m and the public key y. The output of the protocol is a value $sig \in \text{Sig}(m, x)$.

The verification algorithm for a threshold signature scheme is, therefore, the same as in the regular centralized signature scheme $\mathcal{S}$.

Definition 2. *We say that a (t, n)-threshold signature scheme $\mathcal{TS} = $ (Thresh-Key-Gen, Thresh-Sig) is unforgeable, if no malicious adversary who corrupts at most t players can produce, with non-negligible (in λ) probability, the signature on any new (i.e., previously unsigned) message m, given the view of the protocol Thresh-Key-Gen and of the protocol Thresh-Sig on input messages $m_1, \ldots, m_k$ which the adversary adaptively chose.*

This is analogous to the notion of existential unforgeability under chosen message attack as defined by Goldwasser, Micali, and Rivest [29]. Notice that now the adversary does not just see the signatures of k messages adaptively chosen, but also the internal state of the corrupted players and the public communication of the protocols. Following [29] one can also define weaker notions of unforgeability.

In order to prove unforgeability, we use the concept of *simulatable adversary view* [13,30]. Intuitively, this means that the adversary who sees all the information of the corrupted players and the signature of m, could generate by itself all the other public information produced by the protocol Thresh-Sig. This ensures that the run of the protocol provides no useful information to the adversary other than the final signature on m.

Definition 3. *A threshold signature scheme $\mathcal{TS} = $ (Thresh-Key-Gen, Thresh-Sig) is simulatable if the following properties hold:*

1. *The protocol* Thresh-Key-Gen *is simulatable. That is, there exists a simulator* SIM_1 *that, on input a public key* y, *can simulate the view of the adversary on an execution of* Thresh-Key-Gen *that results in* y *as the public output.*
2. *The protocol* Thresh-Sig *is simulatable. That is, there exists a simulator* SIM_2 *that, on input the public input of* Thresh-Sig *(in particular the public key* y *and the message* m*),* t *shares* $x_{i_1}, \ldots, x_{i_t}$*, and a signature sig of* m*, can simulate the view of the adversary on an execution of* Thresh-Sig *that generates sig as an output.*

THRESHOLD OPTIMALITY. As in [25], we are interested in a *threshold-optimal* scheme. Given a (t, n)-threshold signature scheme, obviously $t + 1$ honest players are necessary to generate signatures. A scheme is *threshold-optimal* if $t + 1$ honest players also suffice [25].

If we consider an honest-but-curious adversary, then it will suffice to have $n = t + 1$ players in the network to generate signatures (since all players will behave honestly, even the corrupted ones). But in the presence of a malicious adversary one needs at least $n = 2t + 1$ players in total to guarantee *robustness*, i.e. the ability to generate signatures even in the presence of malicious faults. But as we discussed in the introduction, we want to minimize the number of servers, and keep it at $n = t + 1$ even in the presence of malicious faults. In this case we give up on robustness, meaning that we cannot guarantee anymore that signatures will be provided. But we can still prove that our scheme is unforgeable. In other words an adversary that corrupts almost all the players in the network can only create a denial-of-service attack, but not forge signatures.

2.1 Level-1 Homomorphic Encryption

We now define the notion of a Level-1 Homomorphic Encryption scheme. An encryption scheme E defined as usual by a key generation, encryption and decryption algorithms is Level-1 Homomorphic if the following conditions hold:

- The message space is integers modulo a given (large) integer N;
- The ciphertext space $\mathcal{C}$ is partitioned into two disjoint sets $\mathcal{C}_0, \mathcal{C}_1$. We say that a ciphertext that belongs to $\mathcal{C}_i$ is a ciphertext at *level* i;
- The encryption algorithm for E always outputs ciphertexts at level 0;
- There is an efficiently computable operation $+_E$ over the ciphertext space such that, if $\alpha = Enc(a), \beta = Enc(b) \in \mathcal{C}_i$, where $a, b \in Z_N$, then

$$\gamma = \alpha +_E \beta = E(a + b \bmod N) \in \mathcal{C}_i$$

- There is an efficiently computable operation $\times_E$ over the ciphertext space such that, if $\alpha = Enc(a), \beta = Enc(b) \in \mathcal{C}_0$, where $a, b \in Z_N$, then

$$\gamma = \alpha \times_E \beta = E(ab \bmod N) \in \mathcal{C}_1$$

INSTANTIATION. We use the level-1 homomorphic encryption scheme from [16] which is built in a "black-box" manner from any additively homomorphic encryption scheme (i.e. a scheme for which only the $+_E$ operation exists). For the latter we follow [25] and use Paillier's encryption scheme (described below). This choice allows us to use unchanged many of the other components of the [25] protocol: (i) all the zero-knowledge proofs that show some type of consistency property for public values vs. encrypted values and (ii) the threshold Paillier's cryptosystem from [31].

PAILLIER'S CRYPTOSYSTEM

- Key Generation: generate two large primes P, Q of equal length. and set $N = PQ$. Let $\lambda(N) = lcm(P - 1, Q - 1)$ be the Carmichael function of N. Finally choose $\Gamma \in Z_{N^2}^*$ such that its order is a multiple of N. The public key is (N, Γ) and the secret key is $\lambda(N)$.
- Encryption: to encrypt a message $m \in Z_N$, select $x \in_R Z_N^*$ and return $c = \Gamma^m x^N \bmod N^2$.
- Decryption: to decrypt a ciphertext $c \in Z_{N^2}$, let L be a function defined over the set $\{u \in Z_{N^2} : u = 1 \bmod N\}$ computed as $L(u) = (u - 1)/N$. Then the decryption of c is computed as $L(c^{\lambda(N)})/L(\Gamma^{\lambda(N)}) \bmod N$.
- Homomorphic Properties: Given two ciphertexts $c_1, c_2 \in Z_{N^2}$ define $c_1 +_E c_2 = c_1 c_2 \bmod N^2$. If $c_i = E(m_i)$ then $c_1 +_E c_2 = E(m_1 + m_2 \bmod N)$. Similarly, given a ciphertext $c = E(m) \in Z_{N^2}$ and a number $a \in Z_n$ we have that $a \times_E c = c^a \bmod N^2 = E(am \bmod N)$.

CATALANO-FIORE LEVEL 1 HOMOMORPHIC ENCRYPTION. Here we briefly recall the level-1 homomorphic encryption in [16]. Let E be any additively homomorphic encryption scheme. Level-0 ciphertexts are then constructed as follows

$$\mathsf{Enc}(m) = [m - b, E(b)] \quad \text{for} \quad b \in_R Z_N$$

Obviously, component-wise addition of these ciphertexts results in the encryption of the addition of the messages. If $[\alpha_i, \beta_i] = \mathsf{Enc}(m_i)$ then

$$[\alpha_1, \beta_1] +_{\mathsf{Enc}} [\alpha_2, \beta_2] = [\alpha_1 + \alpha_2 \bmod N, \beta_1 +_E \beta_2] = \mathsf{Enc}(m_1 + m_2 \bmod N)$$

Level-1 ciphertexts are created by the multiplication homomorphism

$$[\alpha_1, \beta_1] \times_{\mathsf{Enc}} [\alpha_2, \beta_2] = [\alpha, \beta_1, \beta_2]$$

where

$$\alpha = E(\alpha_1 \alpha_2 \bmod N) +_E \alpha_2 \odot_E \beta_1 +_E \alpha_1 \odot_E \beta_2$$

where with $\odot_E$ we denote the operation of multiplication of a ciphertext by a scalar: if ψ is an integer and $\beta = E(b)$ is a ciphertext, then

$$\psi \odot_E \beta = E(\psi b \bmod N)$$

Addition of level-1 ciphertexts is done by using the $+_E$ operator on the first component and concatenating all the other components (notice that addition of level-1 ciphertexts is not length-preserving).

$$[\alpha, \beta_1, \beta_2] +_{\mathsf{Enc}} [\hat{\alpha}, \hat{\beta}_1, \hat{\beta}_2] = [\alpha +_E \hat{\alpha}, \beta_1, \beta_2, \hat{\beta}_1, \hat{\beta}_2]$$

2.2   Threshold Cryptosystems

In a (t, n)-threshold cryptosystem, there is a public key pk with a matching secret key sk which is shared among n players with a (t, n)-secret sharing. When a message m is encrypted under pk, $t+1$ players can decrypt it via a communication protocol that does not expose the secret key.

More formally, a public key cryptosystem $\mathcal{E}$ is defined by three efficient algorithms:

- key generation Enc-Key-Gen that takes as input a security parameter λ, and outputs a public key pk and a secret key sk.
- An encryption algorithm Enc that takes as input the public key pk and a message m, and outputs a ciphertext c. Since Enc is a randomized algorithm, there will be several valid encryptions of a message m under the key pk; with $\mathsf{Enc}(m, pk)$ we will denote the set of such ciphertexts.
- and a decryption algorithm Dec which is run on input c, sk and outputs m, such that $c \in \mathsf{Enc}(m, pk)$.

We say that $\mathcal{E}$ is semantically secure if for any two messages m_0, m_1 we have that the probability distributions $\mathsf{Enc}(m_0)$ and $\mathsf{Enc}(m_1)$ are computationally indistinguishable.

A (t, n) threshold cryptosystem $\mathcal{TE}$, consists of the following protocols for n players $P_1, \ldots, P_n$.

- A key generation protocol TEnc-Key-Gen that takes as input a security parameter λ, and the parameter t, n, and it outputs a public key pk and a vector of secret keys $(sk_1, \ldots, sk_n)$ where sk_i is private to player P_i. This protocol could be obtained by having a trusted party run Enc-Key-Gen and sharing sk among the players.
- A threshold decryption protocol TDec, which is run on public input a ciphertext c and private input the share sk_i. The output is m, such that $c \in \mathsf{Enc}(m, pk)$.

We point out that threshold variations of Paillier's scheme have been presented in the literature [2,18,19,31]. In order to instantiate our dealerless protocol, we use the scheme from [31] as it includes a dealerless key generation protocol that does not require $n \geq 2t + 1$.

2.3   Non-malleable Trapdoor Commitments

TRAPDOOR COMMITMENTS. A trapdoor commitment scheme allows a sender to commit to a message with information-theoretic privacy. i.e., given the transcript of the commitment phase, the receiver, even with infinite computing power, cannot guess the committed message better than at random. On the other hand when it comes to opening the message, the sender is only computationally bound to the committed message. Indeed the scheme admits a *trapdoor* whose knowledge allows opening a commitment in any possible way (we will refer to this as *equivocate* the commitment). The trapdoor should be hard to compute efficiently.

Formally a (non-interactive) trapdoor commitment scheme consists of four algorithms KG, Com, Ver, Equiv with the following properties:

- KG is the key generation algorithm, on input the security parameter it outputs a pair pk, tk where pk is the public key associated with the commitment scheme, and tk is called the *trapdoor*.
- Com is the commitment algorithm. On input pk and a message M it outputs $[C(M), D(M)] = \mathsf{Com}(\mathsf{pk}, M, R)$ where r are the coin tosses. $C(M)$ is the commitment string, while $D(M)$ is the decommitment string which is kept secret until opening time.
- Ver is the verification algorithm. On input C, D and pk it either outputs a message M or $\perp$.
- Equiv is the algorithm that opens a commitment in any possible way given the trapdoor information. It takes as input pk, strings M, R with $[C(M), D(M)] = \mathsf{Com}(\mathsf{pk}, M, R)$, a message $M' \neq M$ and a string T. If $T = \mathsf{tk}$ then Equiv outputs D' such that $\mathsf{Ver}(\mathsf{pk}, C(M), D') = M'$.

We note that if the sender refuses to open a commitment we can set $D = \perp$ and $\mathsf{Ver}(\mathsf{pk}, C, \perp) = \perp$. Trapdoor commitments must satisfy the following properties

Correctness. If $[C(M), D(M)] = \mathsf{Com}(\mathsf{pk}, M, R)$ then $\mathsf{Ver}(\mathsf{pk}, C(M), D(M)) = M$.

Information Theoretic Security. For every message pair M, M' the distributions $C(M)$ and $C(M')$ are statistically close.

Secure Binding. We say that an adversary $\mathcal{A}$ wins if it outputs C, D, D' such that $\mathsf{Ver}(\mathsf{pk}, C, D) = M$, $\mathsf{Ver}(\mathsf{pk}, C, D') = M'$ and $M \neq M'$. We require that for all efficient algorithms $\mathcal{A}$, the probability that $\mathcal{A}$ wins is negligible in the security parameter.

NON-MALLEABLE TRAPDOOR COMMITMENTS. To define non-malleability [22], think of the following game. The adversary, after seeing a tuple of commitments produced by honest parties, outputs his own tuple of committed values. At this point the honest parties decommit their values and now the adversary tries to decommit his values in a way that his messages are related to the honest parties' ones[5]. Intuitively, we say that a commitment scheme is non-malleable if the adversary fails at this game.

However the adversary could succeed by pure chance, or because he has some a priori information on the distribution of the messages committed by the

---

[5] We are considering *non-malleability with respect to opening* [20] in which the adversary is allowed to see the decommitted values, and is required to produce a related decommitment. A stronger security definition *(non-malleability with respect to commitment)* simply requires that the adversary cannot produce a commitment to a related message after being given just the committed values of the honest parties. However for information-theoretic commitments (like the ones considered in this paper) the latter definition does not make sense. Indeed information-theoretic secrecy implies that given a commitment, *any* message could be a potential decommitment. What specifies the meaning of the commitment is a valid opening of it.

honest parties. So when we formally define non-malleability for commitments we need to focus on ruling out that the adversary receives any help from seeing the committed values. This can be achieved by comparing the behavior of the adversary in the above game, to the one of an adversary in a game in which the honest parties' messages are not committed to and the adversary must try to output related messages without any information about them.

We now give the formal definition of non-malleability from [17]. We have a publicly known distribution $\mathcal{M}$ on the message space and a randomly chosen public key pk (chosen according to the distribution induced by KG).

Define Game 1 (the real game) as follows. We think of the adversary $\mathcal{A}$ as two separate efficient algorithms $\mathcal{A}_1, \mathcal{A}_2$. We choose t messages according to the distribution $\mathcal{M}$, compute the corresponding commitments and feed them to the adversary $\mathcal{A}_1$. The adversary $\mathcal{A}_1$ outputs a vector of u commitments, with the only restriction that he cannot copy any of the commitments presented to him. $\mathcal{A}_1$ also transfers some internal state to $\mathcal{A}_2$. We now open our commitments and run $\mathcal{A}_2$, who will open the u commitments prepared by $\mathcal{A}$ (if $\mathcal{A}_2$ refuses to open some commitment we replace the opening with $\perp$). We then invoke a distinguisher $\mathcal{D}$ on the two vectors of messages. $\mathcal{D}$ will decide if the two vectors are related or not (i.e. $\mathcal{D}$ outputs 1 if the messages are indeed related). We denote with $\mathsf{Succ1}_{\mathcal{D},\mathcal{A},\mathcal{M}}$ the probability that $\mathcal{D}$ outputs 1 in this game, i.e.

$$\mathsf{Succ1}_{\mathcal{D},\mathcal{A},\mathcal{M}}(k) = Prob \left[\begin{array}{c} \mathsf{pk}, \mathsf{tk} \leftarrow \mathsf{KG}(1^k) \; ; \; m_1, \ldots, m_t \leftarrow \mathcal{M} \; ; \\ r_1, \ldots, r_t \leftarrow \{0,1\}^k \; ; \; [c_i, d_i] \leftarrow \mathsf{Com}(\mathsf{pk}, m_i, r_i) \; ; \\ (\omega, \hat{c}_1, \ldots, \hat{c}_u) \leftarrow \mathcal{A}_1(\mathsf{pk}, c_1, \ldots, c_t) \text{ with } \hat{c}_j \neq c_i \forall i, j \; ; \\ (\hat{d}_1, \ldots, \hat{d}_u) \leftarrow \mathcal{A}_2(\mathsf{pk}, \omega, d_1, \ldots, d_t) \; ; \\ \hat{m}_i \leftarrow \mathsf{Ver}(\mathsf{pk}, \hat{c}_i, \hat{d}_i) \; : \\ \mathcal{D}(m_1, \ldots, m_t, \hat{m}_1, \ldots, \hat{m}_u) = 1 \end{array} \right]$$

Define now Game 2 as follows. We still select t messages according to $\mathcal{M}$ but this time feed nothing to the adversary $\mathcal{A}$. The adversary now has to come up with u messages on its own. Again we feed the two vectors of messages to $\mathcal{D}$ and look at the output. We denote with $\mathsf{Succ2}_{\mathcal{D},\mathcal{A}}$ the probability that $\mathcal{D}$ outputs 1 in this game, i.e.

$$\mathsf{Succ2}_{\mathcal{D},\mathcal{A},\mathcal{M}}(k) = Prob \left[\begin{array}{c} \mathsf{pk}, \mathsf{tk} \leftarrow \mathsf{KG}(1^k) \; ; \; m_1, \ldots, m_t \leftarrow \mathcal{M} \; ; \\ (\hat{m}_1, \ldots, \hat{m}_u) \leftarrow \mathcal{A}(\mathsf{pk}) \; ; \\ \text{s.t. } \hat{m}_i \in \mathcal{M} \cup \{\perp\} \; : \\ \mathcal{D}(m_1, \ldots, m_t, \hat{m}_1, \ldots, \hat{m}_u) = 1 \end{array} \right]$$

Finally we say that a distinguisher $\mathcal{D}$ is admissible, if for any input $(m_1, \ldots, m_t, \hat{m}_1, \ldots, \hat{m}_u)$, its probability of outputting 1 does not increase if we change any message $\hat{m}_i$ into $\perp$. This prevents the adversary from artificially "winning" the game by refusing to open its commitments.

We say that the commitment scheme is (t, u) ϵ-non-malleable if for every message space distribution $\mathcal{M}$, every efficient admissible distinguisher $\mathcal{D}$, every $0 < \epsilon < 1$, and for every efficient adversary $\mathcal{A}$, there is an efficient adversary $\mathcal{A}'$ (whose running time is polynomial in ϵ^{-1}) such that

$$|\mathsf{Succ1}_{D,\mathcal{A},\mathcal{M}}(k) - \mathsf{Succ2}_{D,\mathcal{A}',\mathcal{M}}(k)| \leq \epsilon$$

In other words $\mathcal{A}'$ fares almost as well as $\mathcal{A}$ in outputting related messages.

2.4   Independent Trapdoor Commitments

Following [25], our proof uses *independent* commitments as introduced in [28]. Consider the following scenario: an honest party produces a commitment C and the adversary, after seeing C, will produce another commitment C' (which we to require to be different from C in order to prevent the adversary from simply copying the behavior of the honest party and outputting an identical committed value). At this point the value committed by the adversary should be *fixed*, i.e. no matter how the honest party opens his commitment, the adversary will always open in a unique way.

A formal definition is presented below. In [28] the authors proved that independence implies non-malleability, therefore establishing it as a stronger property. Here, however, we show that the two notions are actually equivalent, and therefore we show that both our proof and the one in [25] hold under the more standard (and natural) definition of non-malleability.

The following definition takes into account that the adversary may see and output many commitments [17].

Independence. For any adversary $\mathcal{A} = (\mathcal{A}_1, \mathcal{A}_2)$ the following probability is negligible in k:

$$Prob \left[\begin{array}{c} \mathsf{pk}, \mathsf{tk} \leftarrow \mathsf{KG}(1^k) \; ; \; m_1, \ldots, m_t \leftarrow \mathcal{M} \\ r_1, \ldots, r_t \leftarrow \{0,1\}^k \; ; \; [c_i, d_i] \leftarrow \mathsf{Com}(\mathsf{pk}, m_i, r_i) \\ (\omega, \hat{c}_1, \ldots, \hat{c}_u) \leftarrow \mathcal{A}_1(\mathsf{pk}, c_1, \ldots, c_t) \text{ with } \hat{c}_j \neq c_i \forall i, j \\ m'_1, \ldots, m'_t \leftarrow \mathcal{M} \; ; \; d'_i \leftarrow \mathsf{Equiv}(\mathsf{pk}, \mathsf{tk}, m_i, r_i, m'_i) \\ (\hat{d}_1, \ldots, \hat{d}_u) \leftarrow \mathcal{A}_2(\mathsf{pk}, \omega, d_1, \ldots, d_t) \\ (\hat{d}'_1, \ldots, \hat{d}'_u) \leftarrow \mathcal{A}_2(\mathsf{pk}, \omega, d'_1, \ldots, d'_t) \\ \exists i : \bot \neq \hat{m}_i = \mathsf{Ver}(\mathsf{pk}, \hat{m}_i, \hat{c}_i, \hat{d}_i) \neq \mathsf{Ver}(\mathsf{pk}, \hat{m}'_i, \hat{c}_i, \hat{d}'_i) = \hat{m}'_i \neq \bot \end{array} \right]$$

In other words even if the honest parties open their commitments in different ways using the trapdoor, the adversary cannot change the way he opens his commitments $\hat{C}_j$ based on the honest parties' opening.

EQUIVALENCE OF NON-MALLEABILITY AND INDEPENDENCE. In [28] it was shown that independence implies non-malleability, therefore establishing it as a stronger property. Here, however, we show that the two notions are actually equivalent, and therefore we show that both our proof and the one in [25] hold under the more standard (and natural) definition of non-malleability.

Lemma 1. *Let* KG, Com, Ver, Equiv *be a non-malleable commitment. Then* KG, Com, Ver, Equiv *s also an independent commitment.*

Proof. Assume by contradiction that the commitment is not independent, that is there exists an adversary $\mathcal{A}$ that is able to open its commitment in different ways depending on the opening of its input commitments. Then construct the following distinguisher $\mathcal{D}$ in the definition of non-malleable commitments: given the messages $m_1, \ldots, m_t$ and the messages $\mu_1, \ldots, \mu_u$ output by $\mathcal{A}$, we have that $\mathcal{D}(m_1, \ldots, m_t, \mu_1, \ldots, \mu_u) = 1$ if the μ_i are indeed the messages that $\mathcal{A}$ reveals when the m_i are opened. So $\mathcal{D}$ always outputs 1 with adversary $\mathcal{A}$.

Now another adversary $\mathcal{A}'$ who does *not* see any information about the m_i except for the message distribution $\mathcal{M}$, will only be able to guess the correct μ_i with probability substantially bounded away from 1 (the probability that m_i appears as the message tuple in $\mathcal{M}$, which is definitely bounded away from 1 by a non-negligible quantity – at least the probability that m'_i is selected).

2.5   Candidate Non-malleable/Independent Trapdoor Commitments

The non-malleable commitment schemes in [20,21] are not suitable for our purpose because they are not "concurrently" secure, in the sense that the security definition holds only for $t = 1$ (i.e. the adversary sees only 1 commitment).

The stronger concurrent security notion of non-malleability for $t > 1$ is achieved by the schemes presented in [17,24,37]). Therefore for the purpose of our threshold DSA scheme, we can use any of the schemes in [17,24,37]).

3   The New Scheme

We start by giving an informal description of the initialization phase and the key generation protocol which are identical to the ones in [25]. Readers are referred to [25] for details. We will then get into the details of our new signature generation protocol and how it differs from the one in [25].

INITIALIZATION PHASE. As in [25] a common reference string containing the public information pk for a non-malleable[6] trapdoor commitment KG, Com, Ver, Equiv is selected and published. This could be accomplished by a trusted third party, who can be assumed to erase any secret information (i.e. the trapdoor of the commitment) after selection or via some publicly verifiable method that generates the public information, without the trapdoor being known.

KEY GENERATION. The parties run the key generation protocol from [31] to generate a public key E for the Paillier's encryption scheme, together with a sharing of its matching secret key. The value N for Paillier's scheme is chosen such that $N > q^8$. Then as in [25] a value x is generated, and encrypted with E, with the value $\alpha = E(x)$ made public. This is an implicit (t, n) secret sharing of x, since the decryption key of E is shared among the players. We use non-malleable commitments KG, Com, Ver, Equiv to enforce the independence

---

[6] In [25] they require an independent commitment scheme, but following our Lemma 1 it suffices that the scheme is non-malleable.

of the values contributed by each player to the selection of x. Note that the resulting distribution of public DSA keys generated by the protocol is not necessarily uniform, but as proven in [25] it has sufficiently high entropy to guarantee unforgeability.

3.1   Signature Generation

We now describe our new signature generation protocol, which is run on input m (the hash of the message M being signed).

In the following with $\bigoplus_{i=1}^{t+1} \alpha_i$ we denote the summation over the addition operation $+_E$ of the encryption scheme: i.e. $\bigoplus_{i=1}^{t+1} \alpha_i = \alpha_1 +_E \ldots +_E \alpha_{t+1}$. Similarly with $\odot_E$ we denote the operation of multiplication of a ciphertext by a scalar: if ψ is an integer and $\alpha = E(a)$ is a ciphertext, then

$$\psi \odot_E \alpha = \bigoplus_{i=1}^{\psi} \alpha = E(\psi a \bmod N)$$

Moreover in the protocol below we assume that if any commitment opens to $\bot$ or if any of the ZK proofs fails, the protocol outputs $\bot$.

- Round 1
  Each player P_i
    - chooses $\rho_i, k_i \in_R Z_q$ and $c_i \in_R [-q^6, q^6]$
    - computes $r_i = g^{k_i}$
    - computes $u_i = E(\rho_i)$, $v_i = E(k_i)$ and $w_i = E(c_i)$
    - computes $[C_i, D_i] = \mathsf{Com}([r_i, u_i, v_i, w_i])$ and broadcasts C_i
- Round 2
  Each player P_i broadcasts
    - D_i. This allows everybody to compute $[r_i, u_i, v_i, w_i] = \mathsf{Ver}(C_i, D_i)$
    - a zero-knowledge argument $\Pi_{(i)}$ which states
      $\exists \nu_1, \nu_2 \in [-q^3, q^3]$ and $\nu_3 \in [-q^6, q^6]$:
        * $g^{\nu_1} = r_i$
        * $D(v_i) = \nu_1$
        * $D(u_i) = \nu_2$
        * $D(w_i) = \nu_3$
- Round 3
  Each player P_i
    - verifies the ZKPs of all other players
    - computes $R = \Pi_1^{t+1} r_i = g^k$ and $r = H'(R) \in Z_q$
    - computes $u = \bigoplus_{i=1}^{t+1} u_i = E(\rho)$, $v = \bigoplus_{i=1}^{t+1} v_i = E(k)$ and $w = \bigoplus_{i=1}^{t+1} w_i = E(c)$ where $\rho = \sum_{i=1}^{t+1} \rho_i$, $k = \sum_{i=1}^{t+1} k_i$ and $c = \sum_{i=1}^{t+1} c_i$ (all over the integers)
    - computes $z = E(k\rho + cq) = (v \times_E u) +_E (q \odot_E w)$
    - jointly decrypt z using TDec to learn the value $\eta = D(z) \bmod q = k\rho \bmod q$

- Round 4
  Each player P_i
    • computes $\psi = \eta^{-1} \bmod q$
    • computes $\hat{v} = E(k^{-1}) = \psi \odot_E u$
    • computes

$$\sigma = \hat{v} \times_E [(E(m) +_E (r \odot \alpha)]$$
$$= E(k^{-1}(m + xr))$$
$$= E(s)$$

The players invoke distributed decryption protocol TDec over the ciphertext σ. Let $s = D(\sigma) \bmod q$. The players output (r, s) as the signature for m.

THE SIZE OF THE MODULUS N. We note that since $N > q^8$ all the plaintext operations induced by the ciphertext operations $+_E, \times_E, \odot_E$ are over the integers. In turns this implies that the reduction modulo q are correct.

THE ZERO-KNOWLEDGE ARGUMENTS. The ZK arguments invoked by our protocol are nearly identical to the ones in [25] due to the fact that we are using Paillier's scheme to implement our level-1 homomorphic encryption (and we only require a subset of the proofs needed in that protocol). As in [25,36] the proofs require an auxiliary RSA modulus $\tilde{N}$ to construct the "range proofs" via [23]. Moreover the security of the arguments require the strong RSA assumption on the modulus $\tilde{N}$. For details readers are referred to [25,36].

Our protocol only requires zero-knowledge proofs on level-0 ciphertexts. Since the proofs that we use are a subset of the ones used in [25], we can recycle their proofs with one simple modification. Recall that when we instantiate the cryptosystem of [16] using Paillier as the underlying scheme, the level-0 ciphertexts are of the form
$$\mathsf{Enc}(m) = [m - b, E(b)] \quad \text{for} \quad b \in_R Z_N$$

where $E(b)$ is a Paillier encryption of b. In order to directly utilize the proofs of [25], however, we need $E(m)$, a Paillier encryption of m. We can obtain a Paillier encryption of m by deterministically encrypting $m - b$, and computing the sum of these ciphertexts using the addition operator of Paillier. In particular, let $E(b) = \Gamma^b x^N \bmod N^2$ for some $x \in Z_N^*$. Then

$$E(m) = E(b) \times [\Gamma^{m-b} 1^N \bmod N^2] \bmod N^2 = \Gamma^m x^N \bmod N^2$$

The prover now has an encryption of m and can use the zero knowledge proofs from [25] directly. Moreover, because the encryption of $m - b$ is deterministic, the verifier can perform the operation himself, and thus be convinced that the ciphertexts being used for the proofs is a Pallier encryption of the same value as the original level-0 ciphertext.

THE HOMOMORPHISM OF THE ENCRYPTION E. Note that the scheme performs two multiplications of ciphertexts, but in each case the ciphertexts are of level 0. So level-1 homomorphism suffices.

4 Security Proof

We prove the following Theorem:

Theorem 1. *Assuming that*

- *The DSA signature scheme is unforgeable;*
- *E is a semantically secure, additively homomorphic encryption scheme;*
- KG, Com, Ver, Equiv *is a non-malleable trapdoor commitment;*
- *the Strong RSA Assumption holds;*

then our threshold DSA scheme in the previous section is unforgeable.

The proof follows from a standard simulation: if there is an adversary $\mathcal{A}$ that forges in the threshold scheme with a significant probability, then there exists a forger $\mathcal{F}$ that forges in the centralized DSA scheme also with a significant probability. The adversary $\mathcal{A}$ will be run in a simulated environment by the forger $\mathcal{F}$ which will use the forgery produced by $\mathcal{A}$ as its own forgery.

The forger $\mathcal{F}$ runs on input a public key y for DSA. Its first task is to run a simulation for $\mathcal{A}$ that terminates with y as the public key of the threshold signature scheme. We refer to [25] for a simulation of the key generation protocol[7].

As discussed in [25] we cannot simulate an exact distribution for the public keys generated by the key generation protocol, but we can only generate keys at random over a sufficiently large subset of all possible keys. This is still enough to prove unforgeability (in other words our $\mathcal{F}$ will only work on a polynomially large fraction of public keys which is still a contradiction to the unforgeability of DSA). For those subset of keys, the view of the adversary during the simulated protocol is indistinguishable from its view during a real execution.

Now whenever $\mathcal{A}$ requests the signature of a message m_i, the forger $\mathcal{F}$ can obtain the real signature (r_i, s_i) from its signature oracle. It will then simulate an execution of the threshold signature protocol which is indistinguishable from the real one (in particular on input m_i it will output $\perp$ or a correct signature with essentially the same probability as in the real case – when the protocol terminates with a signature, the output will be (r_i, s_i).).

Because these simulations are indistinguishable from the real protocol for $\mathcal{A}$, the adversary will output a forgery with the same probability as in real life. Such a forgery m, r, s is a signature on a message that was never queried by $\mathcal{F}$ to its signature oracle and therefore a valid forgery for $\mathcal{F}$ as well.

We now present some more details about the simulation of the signature generation protocol.

4.1 Signature Generation Simulation

During this simulation the forger $\mathcal{F}$ will handle signature queries issued by the adversary $\mathcal{A}$. We recall that during the simulation we assume that

---

[7] Again, in [25] the proof requires independent commitments but thanks to our Lemma 1 we can relax that assumption to non-malleable commitments.

- $\mathcal{F}$ controls the lone honest player, and that without loss of generality this player is P_1 and it always speaks first at each round;
- $\mathcal{F}$ can equivocate any of the commitment produced by P_1 during the simulation, since $\mathcal{F}$ sets up the CRS for the adversary during the initialization phase, and can do so with knowledge of the trapdoor for the commitment scheme.

During the simulation $\mathcal{F}$ has access to a signing oracle that produces DSA signatures under the public key $y = g^x$ issued earlier to $\mathcal{F}$. However the ciphertext α that in the real execution contains an encryption of x, during the simulation contains the encryption of a different value τ known to $\mathcal{F}$.

As in the real case in the simulation below, we assume that if any commitment opens to $\perp$ or if any of the ZK proofs fails, the simulation aborts.

When $\mathcal{A}$ requests to sign a message M, such that $m = H(M)$, the forger $\mathcal{F}$ obtains a signature (r, s) from its signature oracle. $\mathcal{F}$ first computes $R = g^{ms^{-1} \bmod q} y^{rs^{-1} \bmod q} \in \mathcal{G}$. Note that $H'(R) = r \in Z_q$ due to the fact that the signature is valid. Also $\mathcal{F}$ chooses a random value $\eta \in_R [-q^7, q^7]$ such that $\eta^{-1}(m + r\tau) = s \bmod q$

The simulation then proceeds as follows:

- Round 1
  Each player P_i
  • chooses $\rho_i, k_i \in_R Z_q$ and $c_i \in_R [-q^6, q^6]$
  • computes $r_i = g^{k_i}$
  • computes $u_i = E(\rho_i)$, $v_i = E(k_i)$ and $w_i = E(c_i)$
  • computes $[C_i, D_i] = \mathsf{Com}([r_i, u_i, v_i, w_i])$ and broadcasts C_i
- Round 2
  Each player P_i broadcasts
  • D_i. This allows everybody to compute $[r_i, u_i, v_i, w_i] = \mathsf{Ver}(C_i, D_i)$
  • the zero-knowledge argument $\Pi_{(i)}$
  At this point $\mathcal{F}$ rewinds the adversary to the beginning of the round and changes the opening of P_1 to $[r'_1, u'_1, v'_1, w'_1]$ such that:
  • $r'_1 = R \cdot \Pi_{j=2}^{t+1} r_j$
  • $u'_1 = E(\rho'_1)$, such that $\rho'_1 + \sum_{i=2}^{t+1} \rho_i = 1$;
  • $v'_1 = E(k'_1)$ such that

$$(k'_1 + \sum_{i=2}^{t+1} k_i) + q \sum_{i=1}^{t+1} c_i = \eta$$

and simulates the appropriate ZK proof for P_1. If after the rewinding any player P_i changes the opening of its commitment to $D'_i \neq D_i$ then the forger $\mathcal{F}$ aborts.
- Round 3
  Each player P_i
  • verifies the ZKPs of all other players
  • computes $R = \Pi_1^{t+1} r_i = g^k$ and $r = H'(R) \in Z_q$

- computes $u = \bigoplus_{i=1}^{t+1} u_i = E(1)$, $v = \bigoplus_{i=1}^{t+1} v_i$ and $w = \bigoplus_{i=1}^{t+1} w_i$
- computes $z = (v \times_E u) +_E (q \odot_E w) = E(\eta)$
- jointly decrypt z using TDec to learn the value η

- Round 4

Each player P_i

- computes $\psi = \eta^{-1} \bmod q$
- computes $\hat{v} = E(\eta^{-1}) = \psi \odot_E u$ since $u = E(1)$
- computes

$$\begin{aligned}
\sigma &= \hat{v} \times_E [(E(m) +_E (r \odot \alpha)] \\
&= E(\eta^{-1}(m + r\tau)) \\
&= E(s)
\end{aligned}$$

The players invoke distributed decryption protocol TDec over the ciphertext σ. Let $s = D(\sigma) \bmod q$. The players output (r, s) as the signature for m.

Lemma 2. *On any input M the simulation terminates with $\mathcal{F}$ aborting only with negligible probability.*

Proof (of Lemma 2). $\mathcal{F}$ aborts only if the adversary changes its opening of the commitments after the rewinding in Round 2. This is obviously ruled out by the independence property of the commitment scheme that we use in the protocol. More precisely, due to Lemma 1 the non-malleable commitment scheme that we use in the protocol is also independent. The independence property guarantees that the adversary can change its opening only with negligible probability.

Lemma 3. *The simulation terminates in polynomial time and is indistinguishable from the real protocol.*

Proof (of Lemma 3). The only differences between the real and the simulated views are

- in the simulated view the forger $\mathcal{F}$ might abort, but as proven in Lemma 2, this only happens with negligible probability;
- in the simulated view, the plaintexts encrypted in the ciphertexts published by $\mathcal{F}$ do not satisfy the same properties that they would in the protocol when they were produced by a real player P_1. It is not hard to see that in order to distinguish between the two views one must be able to break the semantic security of the encryption scheme.
- $\mathcal{F}$ runs simulated ZK proofs instead of real ones that would prove those properties. But the simulations are statistically indistinguishable from the real proofs.
- The distribution of the value η. In the real protocol, η is a fixed value $k\rho$ (which we know is bounded by q^6 at most because of the ZK proofs), masked by a random value in the range of q^7. In our protocol, η is a random value in the range of q^7. It is not hard to see that the two distributions are statistically indistinguishable.

4.2   Concrete Analysis

Assuming the our adversary $\mathcal{A}$ forges with probability ϵ, the concrete analysis in [25] shows that $\mathcal{F}$ has a roughly ϵ^3 probability of forging. In [25] this bound applies to both the simulation of the key generation and signature protocol. When simulating both protocols, our proof achieves the same bound, since our simulation of the key generation protocol is basically identical to the one in [25].

However, our simulation of the signature generation protocol is substantially different than the one in [25] since we do not require every single protocol to successfully complete with a correct signature. Indeed in order to guarantee that $\mathcal{F}$ forges, it is not necessary that every single message M queried by the adversary is correctly signed. It is sufficient that the protocol execution on input M is indistinguishable from the real one, even if the input is $\perp^8$. This results in a better reduction, where the success probability of $\mathcal{F}$ is approximately ϵ^2.

The practical implication is that in application where the key generation does not have to be simulated (e.g. where the key has already been chosen and it is then shared, or the key generation and sharing is done by a trusted party), our proof yields a reduction with better parameters.

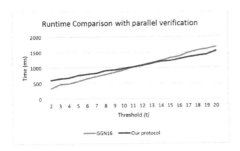

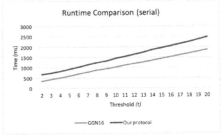

Fig. 1. Runtime comparison between our scheme and that of [25] on a four core machine when we parallelize the ZKP verification.

Fig. 2. Runtime comparison between our scheme and that of [25] running on a single core.

5   Implementation Report

We provide an open-source Java implemented of our signature scheme, and compare it to the runtimes of [25]. All benchmarks were done on an Ubuntu desktop with an Intel® quad-core i7-6700 CPU @ 3.40 GHz and 64 GB of RAM.

We implemented our code in Java to be consistent with the implementation in [25] so that we could get an accurate comparison of the runtime. We re-used

---

^{8} This is not possible in the key generation part, since $\mathcal{F}$ must "hit" the target public key y in order to subsequently forge.

the code from their paper when possible, and thus also used the independent trapdoor commitment scheme from [24] using the Jpair library.

We were able to make improvements to the code of [25] that sped up the runtime significantly. Firstly, rather than using Java's built-in BigInteger class for modular exponentiation and inversion, we used Square's jna-gmp[9] instead. In Fig. 3, we show the effects of making this switch. Secondly, considering that for sufficiently large thresholds, the signature generation time is dominating by verifying other players' proofs, we added some parallelization support for the zero-knowledge proof verification. In order to make sure that the benchmark comparison was accurate, we made all improvements both to our code as well as to the code from [25].

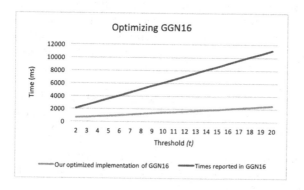

Fig. 3. Comparison between the runtime reported in GGN16 and the runtime that we achieved by using jna-gmp. We note that the benchmark machine was not the same and worse in their case, and thus this speedup is mostly but not entirely due to our optimizations. All benchmarks were done on a single core.

For the underlying Paillier scheme, we modified the Java implementation of threshold Paillier in [42]. We fixed an undocumented overflow error in the library that caused decryption to fail for threshold values greater than or equal to 15.

We did not know of any Java implementation (or any open source implementation) of the Level-1 FHE scheme from [16], so we implemented that as well, and this may be of independent interest.

As is the case with the scheme of [25], the cost of verifying commitments and zero-knowledge proofs will dominate the base proving time for most threshold parameters. As the proof verification contains multiple checks that are highly parallelizable, we added parallelization support to both our implementation as well as that of [25].

In Fig. 1, we compare the performance of our scheme to the scheme of [25] for threshold sets of up to size 20. We found that for thresholds of 13 players or more, our scheme outperformed the one of [25] when run on our four-core

---

[9] https://github.com/square/jna-gmp.

benchmark machine. In all of these parameter sets, our scheme is highly efficient and finished in under 2 s. We stress that the benchmarks only depend on t, the threshold, and not on n, the total number of players in the scheme.

In Fig. 2, we compare the runtime of our scheme to that of [25] when we turn off parallelization. The runtimes are comparable, but ours are somewhat slower. It emerges that while our scheme is slower on a single thread, it is more parallelizable. Intuitively, this makes sense as we are condensing the computation into fewer rounds, and thus there is more room for parallelization.

We stress that both Figs. 1 and 2 reflect the computation time of a single player, which will be the computation time of the protocol as all players can run in parallel. However these benchmarks do not take network communication time into effect. Even for the serial implementation, in a real network setting, the slight loss of performance of our protocol will be amply compensated for by the reduction of two rounds of communication. This is particularly true when the number of players increases as we cannot proceed to the next round until all players have received the output from every player in the previous round and posted their output for the current round.

Acknowledgements. This work was supported by NSF, DARPA, a grant from ONR, and the Simons Foundation. Opinions, findings and conclusions or recommendations expressed in this material are those of the authors and do not necessarily reflect the views of DARPA.

Rosario Gennaro is supported by NSF Grant 1565403. Steven Goldfeder is supported by the NSF Graduate Research Fellowship under grant number DGE 1148900 and NSF award CNS-1651938.

References

1. Andresen, G.: Github: Shared Wallets Design. https://gist.github.com/gavinandresen/4039433. Accessed 20 Mar 2014
2. Baudron, O., Fouque, P.-A., Pointcheval, D., Poupard, G., Stern, J.: Practical multi-candidate election system. In: PODC 2001 (2001)
3. Barić, N., Pfitzmann, B.: Collision-free accumulators and fail-stop signature schemes without trees. In: Fumy, W. (ed.) EUROCRYPT 1997. LNCS, vol. 1233, pp. 480–494. Springer, Heidelberg (1997). https://doi.org/10.1007/3-540-69053-0_33
4. Bar-Ilan, J., Beaver, D.: Non-cryptographic fault-tolerant computing in constant number of rounds of interaction. In: PODC, pp. 201–209 (1989)
5. Bitcoin Forum member dree12. List of Bitcoin Heists (2013). https://bitcointalk.org/index.php?topic=83794.0
6. Bitcoin Forum member gmaxwell. List of Bitcoin Heists (2013). https://bitcointalk.org/index.php?topic=279249.0
7. Bitcoin wiki: Transactions. https://en.bitcoin.it/wiki/Transactions. Accessed 11 Feb 2014
8. Bitcoin wiki: Elliptic Curve Digital Signature Algorithm. https://en.bitcoin.it/wiki/Elliptic_Curve_Digital_Signature_Algorithm. Accessed 11 feb 2014
9. Bitcoin wiki: Elliptic Curve Digital Signature Algorithm. https://en.bitcoin.it/w/index.php?title=Secp256k1&oldid=51490. Accessed 11 Feb 2014

10. Bonneau, J., Narayanan, A., Miller, A., Clark, J., Kroll, J.A., Felten, E.W.: Mixcoin: anonymity for bitcoin with accountable mixes. In: Christin, N., Safavi-Naini, R. (eds.) FC 2014. LNCS, vol. 8437, pp. 486–504. Springer, Heidelberg (2014). https://doi.org/10.1007/978-3-662-45472-5_31

11. Camenisch, J., Kiayias, A., Yung, M.: On the portability of generalized schnorr proofs. In: Joux, A. (ed.) EUROCRYPT 2009. LNCS, vol. 5479, pp. 425–442. Springer, Heidelberg (2009). https://doi.org/10.1007/978-3-642-01001-9_25

12. Camenisch, J., Krenn, S., Shoup, V.: A framework for practical universally composable zero-knowledge protocols. In: Lee, D.H., Wang, X. (eds.) ASIACRYPT 2011. LNCS, vol. 7073, pp. 449–467. Springer, Heidelberg (2011). https://doi.org/10.1007/978-3-642-25385-0_24

13. Canetti, R.: Universally composable security: a new paradigm for cryptographic protocols. In: Proceedings of 42nd IEEE Symposium on Foundations of Computer Science, FOCS 2001, pp. 136–145 (2001)

14. Canetti, R., Gennaro, R., Herzberg, A., Naor, D.: Proactive security: Long-term protection against break-ins. RSA Laboratories' CryptoBytes 3(1), 1–8 (1997)

15. Canetti, R., Gennaro, R., Jarecki, S., Krawczyk, H., Rabin, T.: Adaptive security for threshold cryptosystems. In: Wiener, M. (ed.) CRYPTO 1999. LNCS, vol. 1666, pp. 98–116. Springer, Heidelberg (1999). https://doi.org/10.1007/3-540-48405-1_7

16. Catalano, D., Fiore, D.: Using linearly-homomorphic encryption to evaluate degree-2 functions on encrypted data. In: ACM Conference on Computer and Communications Security, pp. 1518–1529 (2015)

17. Damgård, I., Groth, J.: Non-interactive and reusable non-malleable commitment schemes. In: Proceedings of 35th ACM Symposium on Theory of Computing, STOC 2003, pp. 426–437 (2003)

18. Damgård, I., Jurik, M.: A generalisation, a simplification and some applications of Paillier's probabilistic public-key system. In: Kim, K. (ed.) PKC 2001. LNCS, vol. 1992, pp. 119–136. Springer, Heidelberg (2001). https://doi.org/10.1007/3-540-44586-2_9

19. Damgård, I., Koprowski, M.: Practical threshold RSA signatures without a trusted dealer. In: Pfitzmann, B. (ed.) EUROCRYPT 2001. LNCS, vol. 2045, pp. 152–165. Springer, Heidelberg (2001). https://doi.org/10.1007/3-540-44987-6_10

20. Di Crescenzo, G., Ishai, Y., Ostrovsky, R.: Non-interactive and non-malleable commitment. In: Proceedings of 30th ACM Symposium on Theory of Computing, STOC 1998, pp. 141–150 (1998)

21. Di Crescenzo, G., Katz, J., Ostrovsky, R., Smith, A.: Efficient and non-interactive non-malleable commitment. In: Pfitzmann, B. (ed.) EUROCRYPT 2001. LNCS, vol. 2045, pp. 40–59. Springer, Heidelberg (2001). https://doi.org/10.1007/3-540-44987-6_4

22. Dolev, D., Dwork, C., Naor, M.: Non-malleable cryptography. SIAM J. Comp. 30(2), 391–437 (2000)

23. Fujisaki, E., Okamoto, T.: Statistical zero knowledge protocols to prove modular polynomial relations. In: Kaliski, B.S. (ed.) CRYPTO 1997. LNCS, vol. 1294, pp. 16–30. Springer, Heidelberg (1997). https://doi.org/10.1007/BFb0052225

24. Gennaro, R.: Multi-trapdoor commitments and their applications to proofs of knowledge secure under concurrent man-in-the-middle attacks. In: Franklin, M. (ed.) CRYPTO 2004. LNCS, vol. 3152, pp. 220–236. Springer, Heidelberg (2004). https://doi.org/10.1007/978-3-540-28628-8_14

25. Gennaro, R., Goldfeder, S., Narayanan, A.: Threshold-optimal DSA/ECDSA signatures and an application to bitcoin wallet security. In: Manulis, M., Sadeghi, A.-R., Schneider, S. (eds.) ACNS 2016. LNCS, vol. 9696, pp. 156–174. Springer, Cham (2016). https://doi.org/10.1007/978-3-319-39555-5_9

26. Gennaro, R., Jarecki, S., Krawczyk, H., Rabin, T.: Robust threshold DSS signatures. In: Maurer, U. (ed.) EUROCRYPT 1996. LNCS, vol. 1070, pp. 354–371. Springer, Heidelberg (1996). https://doi.org/10.1007/3-540-68339-9_31

27. Gennaro, R., Jarecki, S., Krawczyk, H., Rabin, T.: Secure distributed key generation for discrete-log based cryptosystems. In: Stern, J. (ed.) EUROCRYPT 1999. LNCS, vol. 1592, pp. 295–310. Springer, Heidelberg (1999). https://doi.org/10.1007/3-540-48910-X_21

28. Gennaro, R., Micali, S.: Independent zero-knowledge sets. In: Bugliesi, M., Preneel, B., Sassone, V., Wegener, I. (eds.) ICALP 2006. LNCS, vol. 4052, pp. 34–45. Springer, Heidelberg (2006). https://doi.org/10.1007/11787006_4

29. Goldwasser, S., Micali, S., Rivest, R.L.: A digital signature scheme secure against adaptive chosen-message attacks. SIAM J. Comput. **17**(2), 281–308 (1988)

30. Goldwasser, S., Micali, S., Rackoff, C.: The knowledge complexity of interactive proof-systems. SIAM J. Comput. **18**(1), 186–208 (1989)

31. Hazay, C., Mikkelsen, G.L., Rabin, T., Toft, T., Nicolosi, A.A.: Efficient RSA key generation and threshold Paillier in the two-party setting

32. Jarecki, S., Lysyanskaya, A.: Adaptively secure threshold cryptography: introducing concurrency, removing erasures. In: Preneel, B. (ed.) EUROCRYPT 2000. LNCS, vol. 1807, pp. 221–242. Springer, Heidelberg (2000). https://doi.org/10.1007/3-540-45539-6_16

33. Johnson, D., Menezes, A., Vanstone, S.: The elliptic curve digital signature algorithm (ECDSA). Int. J. Inf. Secur. **1**(1), 36–63 (2001)

34. Kaspersky Labs. Financial cyber threats in 2013. Part 2: malware (2013). http://securelist.com/analysis/kaspersky-security-bulletin/59414/financial-cyber-threats-in-2013-part-2-malware/

35. Lindell, Y.: Fast Secure Two-Party ECDSA Signing. IACR Cryptology ePrint Archive 2017: 552 (2017)

36. MacKenzie, P., Reiter, M.: Two-party generation of DSA signatures. Int. J. Inf. Secur. **2**, 218–239 (2004)

37. MacKenzie, P., Yang, K.: On simulation-sound trapdoor commitments. In: Cachin, C., Camenisch, J.L. (eds.) EUROCRYPT 2004. LNCS, vol. 3027, pp. 382–400. Springer, Heidelberg (2004). https://doi.org/10.1007/978-3-540-24676-3_23

38. Meiklejohn, S., et al.: A fistful of bitcoins: characterizing payments among men with no names. In: Proceedings of the 2013 Conference on Internet Measurement Conference, pp. 127–140. ACM (2013)

39. Mukherjee, P., Wichs, D.: Two round multiparty computation via multi-key FHE. In: Fischlin, M., Coron, J.-S. (eds.) EUROCRYPT 2016. LNCS, vol. 9666, pp. 735–763. Springer, Heidelberg (2016). https://doi.org/10.1007/978-3-662-49896-5_26

40. Nakamoto, S.: Bitcoin: a peer-to-peer electronic cash system. Consulted **1**, 2012 (2008)

41. Paillier, P.: Public-key cryptosystems based on composite degree residuosity classes. In: Stern, J. (ed.) EUROCRYPT 1999. LNCS, vol. 1592, pp. 223–238. Springer, Heidelberg (1999). https://doi.org/10.1007/3-540-48910-X_16

42. Paillier Threshold Encryption Toolbox. http://cs.utdallas.edu/dspl/cgi-bin/pailliertoolbox/manual.pdf

43. Pedersen, T.P.: Distributed provers with applications to undeniable signatures. In: Davies, D.W. (ed.) EUROCRYPT 1991. LNCS, vol. 547, pp. 221–242. Springer, Heidelberg (1991). https://doi.org/10.1007/3-540-46416-6_20
44. Rivest, R., Shamir, A., Adelman, L.: A method for obtaining digital signature and public key cryptosystems. Commun. ACM **21**, 120–126 (1978)
45. Shamir, A.: How to share a secret. Commun. ACM **22**, 612–613 (1979)

Adversarial Cryptography

Environmental Authentication in Malware

Jeremy Blackthorne[1], Benjamin Kaiser[2], Benjamin Fuller[3(✉)],
and Bülent Yener[4]

[1] Boston Cybernetics Institute, Cambridge, MA 02138, USA
jblackthorne@bostoncybernetics.org
[2] Princeton University, Princeton, NY 08544, USA
bkaiser@princeton.edu
[3] University of Connecticut, Storrs, CT 06269, USA
benjamin.fuller@uconn.edu
[4] Rensselaer Polytechnic Institute, Troy, NY 12151, USA
byener@rpi.edu

Abstract. Malware needs to execute on a target machine while simultaneously keeping its payload confidential from a malware analyst. Standard encryption can be used to ensure the confidentiality, but it does not address the problem of hiding the key. Any analyst can find the decryption key if it is stored in the malware or derived in plain view.

One approach is to derive the key from a part of the environment which changes when the analyst is present. Such malware derives a key from the environment and encrypts its true functionality under this key.

In this paper, we present a formal framework for *environmental authentication*. We formalize the interaction between malware and analyst in three settings: (1) blind: in which the analyst does not have access to the target environment, (2) basic: where the analyst can load a single analysis toolkit on an effected target, and (3) resettable: where the analyst can create multiple copies of an infected environment. We show necessary and sufficient conditions for malware security in the blind and basic games and show that even under mild conditions, the analyst can always win in the resettable scenario.

Keywords: Environmental keying · Environmental authentication · Malware

1 Introduction

In many settings, programs try to prevent observers from learning their behavior. These settings vary from legitimate software protecting its intellectual property through digital rights management to malware hiding from analysts to extend the life of a criminal endeavor.

We focus on malware hiding from an analyst, but our discussion applies to the other scenarios as well. Our goal is to improve the understanding of current

© Springer Nature Switzerland AG 2019
T. Lange and O. Dunkelman (Eds.): LATINCRYPT 2017, LNCS 11368, pp. 381–400, 2019.
https://doi.org/10.1007/978-3-030-25283-0_20

and future malware techniques. Our work proceeds from the point of view of the malware hiding from an adversarial analyst. Thus, our discussion reverses roles: the malware designer is the party trying to ensure security and the analyst acts as the adversary.

Malware follows two approaches to hiding its behavior: (1) making the observed program unintelligible, i.e. *obfuscation* [CTL97,BGI+01,GGH+13], and (2) preventing observation from even occurring when executing in the wrong environment, i.e. *environmental authentication* [RS98,SRL12].

Obfuscation is the subject of informal [CTL97] and formal [BGI+01] treatments. Obfuscation works as follows: an obfuscator function $\mathcal{O}(.)$ takes some program P as input and creates P' such that P' is input-output equivalent to P but is implemented differently. The implementation is changed with the goal of confusing an analyst which tries to understand the program. But even the strongest obfuscation scheme cannot hide important aspects of the program including input/output behavior. Some functions can be recovered by just observing a polynomial number of input-output pairs [SWP08]. Such functions are known as learnable. For malware, the desire is to hide the effects on the target computer system, the inner workings of the algorithm are a secondary concern. For this stronger level of protection, malware attempts to prevent observation from occurring. Malware achieves this by distinguishing environments in which it is being observed from environments which it is not. This distinguishing of environments we call *environmental authentication.*

Environmentally authenticating malware targets a particular computer (or set of computers) and learns as much as possible about this *target* environment. It then creates (at least) two distinct behaviors: one for the target environment and another for non-target or observed environments. At runtime, the malware determines its current executing environment and executes the appropriate behavior [BCK+10a]. Environmental authentication can be subdivided into two approaches: (1) environmental sensitivity and (2) environmental keying.

Environmental Sensitivity. Environmentally sensitive malware reads system state and incorporates this state into program control flow [BKY16]. As an example, the Windows API includes a function IsDebuggerPresent which allows a program to detect if a user level debugger is instrumenting their program. Many pieces of malware change their behavior based on the value of this call. This approach makes a binary and observable decision on how the environment affects control flow. This means that an analyst can run a debugger, create a breakpoint at this system call, and manually overwrite the return to be true. This corresponds to a weak form of authentication (also known as binary matching [ICF+15]).

This has lead to an arms race between malware trying to sense the presence of analysis techniques and analysis techniques trying to create small and unobservable changes in the system state. Malware authors created techniques to detect debuggers [CAM+08,Fer11,SH12], virtual machines [Fer07,SH12], and system emulators [KYH+09, PMRB09]. All environmental sensing techniques make binary decisions based on the environment.

Environmental Keying. Environmental keying replaces the binary decision of environmental sensing with key derivation. This approach is performed in three stages:

1. The malware author targets a computer (or class of computers). Information about the target computer is observed and recorded in the malware. In addition, the author gathers information about other configurations which can be considered as invalid or under *observation.*
2. The author derives cryptographic keys from the target environment and observed environments.[1]
3. The author encrypts different program behaviors under each of these keys and adds a key derivation process to switch between these behaviors.

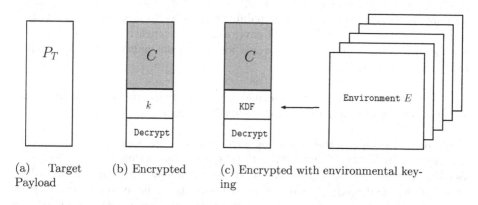

(a) Target Payload
(b) Encrypted
(c) Encrypted with environmental keying

Fig. 1. A plaintext payload P_T is shown in (a) as a baseline. In (b) we see the same payload P_T transformed into an encrypted version C. The encrypted payload must include an unencrypted key and a decryption function. In (c) we see the same encrypted payload from (b) with k replaced with the KDF function. KDF takes the environment E as an input and derives k as output. In this figure the alternate payload P_O is removed for clarity.

At run time, the malware measures the environment and derives a key from this environment. Environmentally keyed malware is split into three functionalities: a key derivation function (KDF) and encrypted payloads P_T and P_O

---

[1] Extractors [NZ96] and fuzzy extractors [DRS04] can be used to derive keys in non-noisy and noisy environments, respectively. See the works of Nisan and Ta-Sha [NTS99] and Dodis et al. [DRS08] respectively for more information. Throughout this work we assume that the key derivation techniques are implemented properly and the only weakness that can be targeted is guessing a valid input to the key derivation process.

corresponding to the desired behavior in the target and observed environments respectively. When deployed, the malware first derives a key from the environment and then try to decrypt each payload. This process of unlocking functionality is shown in Fig. 1. For example, the malware Gauss derives a key from its environment by computing an MD5 hash 10,000 times over a combination of the %PATH% variable and the directory names in %PROGRAMFILES% [RT12]. To the best of our knowledge, Gauss' target behavior has not been decrypted.

Encryption prevents an analyst from reasoning about the target payload P_T. There is no binary decision that can be flipped by an analyst to force the malware to decrypt the payload in an incorrect environment. There are two main questions in this setting, (1) can the malware designer find high entropy sources for key derivation, (2) can the analyst observe the malware without disturbing these sources.

Obfuscation has a long history in both the systems and theoretical computer science communities. Environmental authentication, on the other hand, is known in the systems community but unexplored from a theoretical perspective. The malware community is rapidly adopting new techniques, forcing analysts to scramble to develop new analysis capabilities in order to keep up. The development of a theoretical foundation for environmental authentication will empower analysts to develop more effective tools for analyzing malware that uses environment authentication.

Our Contribution. We put forth a formal model for environmental authentication and evaluate three common malware analysis settings:

Section 3. An analyst that does not have access to the target environment to which the malware is keyed. We call this the *blind* setting.
Section 4. The analyst has access to the environment after the malware has infected it and cannot create an offline backup of the system. This setting represents an analyst performing incident response on a critical system. For example, a controller at a power plant cannot be taken offline. We call this the *basic* setting.
Section 5. The analyst is able to snapshot an infected system. They are able to create multiple copies and install different analysis tools on each copy. We call this the *resettable* setting.

In all settings a piece of malware M interacts with the environment E through a series of decision algorithms, $\mathcal{D}_1, ..., \mathcal{D}_n$, which read subsets of the environment to determine the execution path. Recalling the stages of environmental keying: the decision algorithms represent measuring the environment, deriving a key, and attempting to decrypt the next section of the program. We do not allow the analyst observe the code of the current decision algorithm or beyond so (1) our results hold in the presence of obfuscation and (2) because any code beyond the decision procedure may be encrypted. The analyst's primary means of interacting with the malware is by providing inputs to the decision algorithms, which represents altering the environment (as the input to each decision algorithm is a reading of the environment). The (informal) goal of M is to satisfy correctness and soundness:

Correctness. M achieves correctness if it reaches the payload stage P_T in the target environment.

Soundness. M achieves soundness if it never reaches the payload stage P_T when the analyst A is present in the environment.

We provide necessary and sufficient conditions for M to be secure in the blind and basic games. In the resettable game, we show that under very mild assumptions, the analyst always wins.

Our results for the blind game are intuitive: for M to be secure, it is necessary that a decision procedure rarely outputs 1 in a random environment. It is sufficient that there does not exist a "worst case" environment that can cause a random decision procedure to regularly output 1. This means that in practice, decision procedures must be precisely keyed to their target environment.

Our results for the basic game are more complicated. In this setting, the analyst may read the target environment but first has to load an analysis technique. This process of loading can overwrite some critical part of the environment. A necessary condition for security is for the analysis technique to be likely to overwrite a large subset of the environment that will be used in some decision procedure. A sufficient condition for security is that this subset is likely to be "entropic", i.e., there are few values for it that cause a decision procedure to accept. The first condition is intuitive, but the second conflicts somewhat with our understanding of computers, for although we don't know the distribution of all aspects of a computer system, it seems unlikely to be large for all subsets.

For the resettable game, we provide a simple proof that the analyst can learn the entire target environment, and thus environmental keying provides little security. Our results for the blind and basic settings are summarized in Table 1. We note our results are information-theoretic as we assume that the A only has oracle access to decision procedures.

Table 1. Summary of results. Necessary and sufficient conditions are from the point of view of the malware designer. The resettable setting is omitted as M security is not possible in this setting.

	Necessary	Sufficient
Blind	Theorem 2: Some $\mathcal{D}_i$ outputs 1 with **negl** probability on random inputs	Theorem 3: Some $\mathcal{D}_i$ outputs 1 with **negl** probability on best case inputs
Basic	Theorem 4: Decision procedure and analyst likely to overlap	Theorem 5: Most of environment is entropic

1.1   Other Related Work

Protecting programs by depending on the environment has been studied under many names, including environmental key generation [RS98], secure triggers [FKSW06], host-based fingerprinting [KLZS12], environment-sensitive malware [LKMC11,SRL12], host-identity based encryption [SRL12], environment-targeted malware [XZGL14], malware with split personalities [BCK+10b], and environmental keying [Moo15,Bau14]. We use the term *environmental authentication* to describe any technique that creates a dependence on a specific environment or type of environment for the purposes of preventing observation or analysis.

Transparent analysis analyzes programs while minimizing detectable environmental changes [Yan13]. Dinaburg et al. present a formalization for transparent malware analysis in [DRSL08] and describe the requirements for transparent analysis. Their requirements are higher privilege, the absence of side-channels, transparent exception handling, and identical timings. Kang et al. also formulate the problem of transparent malware analysis within emulators [KYH+09].

Key derivation is a sub-field of cryptography that studies ways to extract uniformly random strings from high-entropy, non-uniform sources [Kra10]. Deriving keys in the presence of noise is often necessary for real-world applications and is achieved by fuzzy extractors [DRS04]. Throughout this work we assume that key derivation is ideal, a resulting key is secure if it results from super-logarithmic min-entropy. In the noise-free setting, this is sufficient in the random oracle model [BR93]. This may not be sufficient in the noisy case, a more precise notion is fuzzy min-entropy [FRS16], we ignore these losses in this work.

Organization. The rest of the paper is organized as follows: in Sect. 2, we provide the necessary background information, notation, and preliminary definitions, including the formal definition of environmental authentication. In Sects. 3, 4 and 5, we describe the blind, basic, and resettable settings respectively.

2   Definitions

Functions are written in the typewriter font, e.g. `Function`, distributions using script font and a single letter, e.g. $\mathcal{D}$, and scalar values using math font with a single lowercase letter, e.g. k. If k is sampled from a distribution $\mathcal{D}$, we say $k \leftarrow \mathcal{D}$. If k is an element in a set K, we say $k \in K$.

2.1   Modeling Computer Systems

Computer systems are complex, as programs can read state from a variety of sources: memory, hard drive, cache, side-channels, operating system calls, registers, installed devices, network interfaces, and more. Turing machines and interactive Turing machines do not capture all of this interaction, particularly for two programs operating in the same system.

The goals of malware are (1) *correctness*: detecting if they are resident on a target set of machines and (2) *soundness*: discerning if the system is being analyzed. These goals can be modeled by abstracting various device state into a single array E which we call the environment. The two goals can be stated as:

Correctness. The malware should read enough of E to be sure it is on a targeted machine. In particular, it should read features that vary between devices. During targeting it is necessary for the designer to learn the relevant features of the target set.

Soundness. The malware should read parts of the array that are likely to change under observation. As mentioned in the introduction, parts of the array that change under observation include IsDebuggerPresent (which is easy to hide) and timing side-channels (which are harder to hide).

The goal of the analyst is to understand both E and the malware M without causing changes to E. In pursuing this goal, we assume that the analyst has two main capabilities

1. They are able to create (representative) computer systems and read all of E.
2. If the analyst has access to the target computer they can read from the environment after being loaded on the system. This action may cause detectable and irreversible changes to E.

We now formalize the correctness goal of malware. We defer soundness to the following sections as we consider it with regards to multiple analysis postures.

Model. A computer system is a one-dimensional array E of length ℓ ($E \in \{0,1\}^{\ell}$). We denote by $\mathcal{E}$ the distribution of possible system environments and a single computer system E is sampled from $\mathcal{E}$ ($E \leftarrow \mathcal{E}$). Either the malware author or analyst may have more information about the target environment or the overall distribution of computer systems. For instance, the malware designer may be targeting an English language system while this is unknown to the analysts. Our model should extend to this setting but we leave this formalization as future work.

All algorithms are executed in the environment but must be loaded into E via the Load function. This (irreversibly) changes the environment E into E'. Only after being loaded can an algorithm read from or write to the environment. When M is loaded onto E, denoted Load(M, E), its goal is to authenticate the environment using a sequence of decision algorithms $\mathcal{D}_i$ and sensors S_i. A sensor S_i is a subset of $[1..\ell]$. The corresponding decision algorithm $\mathcal{D}_i(E'_{S_i})$ takes as input the environment at the set of locations $\{E_j | j \in S_i\}$. $\mathcal{D}_i$ outputs 1 to indicate the environment matches the target environment (i.e. continue on a execution path that allows it to deliver its target payload) and 0 otherwise.

We assume this payload is of minimal size in comparison to the environment and thus we do not include it in the model. The analyst wins if they pass all decision procedures. Authentication decisions may be implicit through the use of cryptographic authentication, thus we only allow an analyst to provide inputs to $\mathcal{D}_i$ in a black-box manner and decision algorithms output a binary decision. There is no way to force the decision procedure to output a 1.

Limitations of our Model. Computer systems change over time. We do not model time for an analyst because a determined analyst can control the system environment and essentially stop time. In real computer systems, the malware can only read a single address at a time which is either 32 or 64 bits. Several of our results will depend on the size of memory that M can read in a single decision algorithm, we call this parameter readsize or α. We assume that α is substantially larger than a single memory location. It is an interesting open problem to extend our results to a setting where a decision procedure cannot read all of its input in a single timestep.

Correctness. For malware to authenticate its environment it must be *correct*, meaning that it executes its payload in its intended environment, and *sound*, meaning that it does not reveal its payload in an observed environment. We present a definition for correctness here and define three soundness definitions in the following sections. First, however, we must describe precisely how sensitive a piece of malware with both correctness and soundness is against an analysis technique A. We capture this property in the following definition.

We define correctness with the following game:

$$\textbf{Experiment Exp}_{M,E}^{\text{cor}}:$$
$$(\mathcal{D}_1, S_1, ..., \mathcal{D}_n, S_n) \leftarrow M(\cdot)$$
$$E' \leftarrow \mathsf{Load}(M, E)$$
$$\text{If } \forall i, [\mathcal{D}_i(E'_{S_i}) = 1] \text{ return } 1$$
$$\text{Else return } 0.$$

Denote by the parameter n the number of decision algorithms and α the maximum size of S_i. We assume that each $\mathcal{D}_i$ is deterministic and the probability is over the coins of M and Load.

Definition 1. *A piece of malware M is δ-correct on E if* $\Pr[\textbf{Exp}_{M,E}^{\text{per}}(\cdot) = 1] = \delta$.

Environment Samplability. We assume the analyst is able to read the state of representative computers and may be able to load on the targeted computer with the malware present. We now formalize this first capability:

Assumption 1. *There exists a randomized algorithm Sam_E running in time $t_{\mathcal{E}}$ such that $\mathsf{Sam}_E(\cdot) \overset{d}{=} \mathcal{E}$.*

If the malware accepts frequently on random computers there is no need for the analyst to understand the target environment. That is, access to the target environment is not necessary if the decision procedures output 1 frequently on random computers:

Definition 2. *Define the* accepting probability *of M over n possible environments, denoted* $\mathsf{Accept}(M, \mathcal{E})$, *as*

$$\mathsf{Accept}(M, \mathcal{E}) = \min_{1 \leq i \leq n} \left(\mathbb{E}_{E \leftarrow \mathcal{E}} \left(\Pr_{\mathcal{D}_i, S_i \leftarrow M} [\mathcal{D}_i(E_{S_i}) = 1] \right) \right).$$

Accepting probability captures how frequently the malware succeeds on a random computer system. However, it may be possible for an analyst to learn more information by observing the behavior of the previous decisions procedures. To capture this notion we present the following (information-theoretic) definition:

Definition 3. *Define the* adaptive guessing probability *of M over n possible environments, denoted as*
$\mathtt{AGuess}(M, \mathcal{E})$, *as*

$$\mathtt{AGuess}(M, \mathcal{E}) = \min_{1 \leq i \leq n} \left(\max_{E' \in \mathcal{E}} \left(\Pr_{\mathcal{D}_i, S_i \leftarrow M} [\mathcal{D}_i(E'_{S_i}) = 1 | \mathcal{D}_1, ..., \mathcal{D}_{i-1}] \right) \right).$$

where $\mathcal{D}_i$ is the entire truth table of $\mathcal{D}_i$.

These definitions capture security against an analyst trying random computer systems and an analyst finding the best computer system respectively. They can be thought of as analogues of Shannon and min-entropy respectively [Rén61]. We do not condition on the previous decision algorithms in Definition 2 as this does not change the expectation but this could be included without affecting $\mathtt{Accept}$.

Definition 4. *M is (β, γ)-environmentally authenticating if:*

- $\mathtt{Accept}(M, \mathcal{E}) \geq 2^{-\beta}$.
- $\mathtt{AGuess}(M, \mathcal{E}) \leq 2^{-\gamma}$.

Proposition 1. $\mathtt{AGuess}(M, i, \mathcal{E}) \geq \mathtt{Accept}(M, i, \mathcal{E})$ *and thus for any (β, γ)-environmentally authenticating malware $\gamma \leq \beta$.*

With these definitions we can formalize the notion of environmental sensitivity and environmental keying described in the introduction.

Definition 5. *Let λ be a security parameter. If M is (β, γ) environmentally authenticating for $\beta = O(\log \lambda)$ then M is* environmentally sensing.

Definition 6. *Let λ be a security parameter. If M is (β, γ) environmentally authenticating for $\gamma = \omega(\log \lambda)$ then M is* environmentally keying.

By Proposition 1 $\gamma \leq \beta$, thus malware cannot be both environmentally sensing and environmentally keying. There is malware that is neither environmentally sensing nor environmentally keying.

3   Blind Scenario

The first adversarial scenario models malware being found in the wild separate from its target environment. This is common in real malware, which may spread widely and infect many machines beyond its target, if it even has a specific target. This separation of malware and target environment is important when attempting to understand malware with environmental authentication. In this scenario, the analyst does not know or have access to the target environment, we also assumes that the analyst cannot determine the target environment by reverse engineering the malware; this scenario is demonstrated in practice by the malware Gauss, for which a target environment has not been found despite significant effort by the analysis community [RT12].

We define blind soundness using the following game:

$$\textbf{Experiment Exp}_{M,E,A}^{\text{bli-sou}}:$$
$$(\mathcal{D}_1, S_1, ..., \mathcal{D}_n, S_n) \leftarrow M$$
$$\text{For } i = 1 \text{ to } n$$
$$\quad \texttt{Guess}_i = A^{\mathcal{D}_i(\cdot)}(S_i, \mathcal{D}_{i-1}, S_{i-1}, ..., \mathcal{D}_1, S_1).$$
$$\text{If } \forall i, \ \mathcal{D}_i(\texttt{Guess}_i) = 1 \text{ return } 1$$
$$\text{Else return } 0.$$

In this game, A receives a complete description of all prior decision algorithms and the current sensor readings. They also have oracle access to the current decision procedure. We denote by t_{oracle} the time needed to make an oracle call and assume this time is consistent across decision procedures.

Definition 7. M *is ϵ-blind sound against A if* $\Pr[\textbf{Exp}_{M,E,A}^{\text{bli-sou}}(\cdot) = 1] < \epsilon$.

Our results in the blind game are intuitive. A necessary condition for soundness is that Accept accepts with negligible probability on random inputs. A sufficient condition for soundness is that AGuess accepts with negligible probability on worst case inputs.

Theorem 2. *For any (β, γ)-environmentally authenticating malware $\mathcal{M}$ with n decision procedures that is at most $1 - \delta$ correct, for any $0 < \epsilon < 1$ there exists A such that M is at most $(\epsilon + \delta)$-blind sound where A runs in time*

$$t_A = 2^{\beta} n (t_E + t_{oracle}) \ln \left(\frac{n}{1 - \epsilon} \right)$$

The proof of this theorem can be found Appendix A.1. At a high level, the A can sample environments randomly until each decision procedure accepts. The result implies that environmentally sensitive malware is not sound in the blind game:

Corollary 1. *Let λ be a security parameter, if M is environmentally sensing (i.e. $2^{\beta} = \texttt{poly}(\lambda)$) and $1 - \delta$ correct, and $n, t_{oracle}, t_E = \texttt{poly}(\lambda)$ for any $\epsilon \leq 1 - 2^{-\texttt{poly}(\lambda)}$, there exists an A that runs in time $\texttt{poly}(\lambda)$ such that M is at most $\epsilon + \delta$ sound.*

We further show having a high γ suffices for security in the blind game.

Theorem 3. *For any (β, γ, n)-environmentally authenticating malware $\mathcal{M}$ that is $1 - \delta$-correct, let A be a block-box algorithm that makes at most t calls to the decision oracles, then M is at least ϵ-sound for $\epsilon = (t + 1)\frac{2^{-\gamma}}{1 - t2^{-\gamma}}$.*

The proof of this theorem can be found in Appendix A.2. At a high level, since a decision procedure has a negligible probability of accepting, even with a polynomial number of guesses the overall acceptance probability remains negligible in the security parameter. The result implies that all environmentally keyed systems are secure in the Blind game:

Corollary 2. *Let λ be a security parameter, if M is environmentally keying, then for any black-box A making $t = \texttt{poly}(\lambda)$ oracle calls, $\epsilon = \texttt{negl}(\lambda)$.*

Proof. The proof proceeds by noting that for $t = \texttt{poly}(\lambda)$ and $2^{-\gamma} = \texttt{negl}(\lambda)$ then $1 - t2^{-\gamma} \geq 1/2$ and thus $\epsilon \leq 2(t+1)2^{-\gamma} = \texttt{negl}(\lambda)$.

Without access to the intended environment E, the blind adversary is at a significant disadvantage. As long as the key has sufficient entropy, the scheme is sound. We see a real example of this in the malware Gauss. Almost four years after Gauss was first reported [RT12], we see that there still have been no public success in deciphering its payload. There has even been developed an open source, distributed cracker developed to harness global computing power to solve the mystery without success [Jst16].

4   Basic Scenario

The next adversary represents a common scenario for malware analysts: incident response. This refers to the situation in which an analyst is called to assess the damage achieved by a piece of malware that has already infected a computer and currently still running on it [CMGS12]. In this scenario, the targeted computer is part of critical infrastructure which cannot be taken offline: e.g., a power control system. The analyst does not have an image of the computer that contains the uninfected state and must perform analysis on the infected image without being detected by the malware. That is, the analyst has access to E where M has already been loaded. However, they can gain no information about E without loading themselves, which changes E.

Basic Soundness. We define the *basic soundness* game as follows:

> **Experiment $\mathbf{Exp}^{\mathrm{sou}}_{M,E,A,\mathrm{Load}}$:**
> $(\mathcal{D}_1, S_1, ..., \mathcal{D}_n, S_n) \leftarrow \mathcal{M}(E)$
> $E_M \leftarrow \mathrm{Load}(M, E)$
> $E_{M,A} \leftarrow \mathrm{Load}(A, E_M)$
> For $i = 1$ to n
> $\mathsf{Guess}_i = A^{\mathcal{D}_i(\cdot)}(E_{M,A}, S_i, \mathcal{D}_{i-1}, S_{i-1}, ..., \mathcal{D}_1, S_1)$.
> If $\forall i, \mathcal{D}_i(\mathsf{Guess}_i) = 1$
>   return 1
> Else
>   return 0.

Definition 8. *Let* Load *be a program loading module. A program* M *is* ϵ-*sound for the target* E *(drawn from* $\mathcal{E}$*) with respect to* A *if*

$$\Pr[\mathbf{Exp}^{\mathrm{sou}}_{M,E,A,\mathsf{Load}}(\cdot) = 1] > 1 - \epsilon.$$

Our results in this model are slightly more complicated than those in the Blind game. By our earlier-stated assumption, the analyst loading their tools causes some change in E. For the malware to successfully evade, this change must be large enough such that the analyst cannot easily guess values that will make D_i accept. If the analyst only overwrites a few bits, for example, they can trivially guess the correct sequence. We will formalize this notion, noting where our model differs from reality.

First, we assume for convenience that loading A changes a random subset of locations of size ν. This differs somewhat from reality, in which changes will be limited to certain subsets of the environment (such as the filesystem or registry). However, in both cases, portions of E that would not be overwritten by A can be ignored by both M and A.[2] We further assume that the locations of $E_{M,A}$ that are changed are known to A and they are set to values independent of the values in E_M. We also assume that the M is always able to execute with A loaded. This requires that loading A never overwrites M's functionality; in practice, analysts avoid overwriting the program they are analyzing, so this assumption holds.

Theorem 4. *Let* M *be a* (β, γ)-*authenticating piece of malware with* n *decision procedures and maximum read size* α *where* $n \cdot \alpha = \ell^c$ *for some* $0 < c < 1$. *Furthermore, suppose that* M *is* δ *correct on all* $E_M \leftarrow$ Load(M, E). *Let* $c' > 0$ *be some parameter. If there exists some* A *with artifact size* $\nu = \ell^{1-c}$, *then by making at most* $2^{c'+2}$ *oracle queries* M *is at most* $(e^{-1/4\ell^{1-c}} + \delta + e^{-2/3c'^2})$-*basic sound.*

The proof of this theorem can be found in Appendix A.3. Roughly, when the product of the read size of the malware and the size of the analyst is at most the total size of the environment ℓ we expect the malware read locations and the analyst to collide in a small (logarithmic) number of positions. The analyst is then able to exhaustively search over the relevant locations that were erased. We simplify the theorem for common parameter settings:

Corollary 3. *Let* λ *be a security parameter where* $\ell =$ poly(λ). *Let* M *be a* (β, γ)-*authenticating piece of malware with* n *decision procedures and maximum read size* α *where* $n \cdot \alpha = \ell^c$ *for some* $0 < c < 1$. *Furthermore, suppose that* M *is* δ *correct on all* $E_M \leftarrow$ Load(M, E). *If there exists some* A *with artifact size* $\nu = O(\ell^{1-c})$, *then by making at most* poly(λ) *oracle queries* M *is at most* $(\delta + 1/$poly$(\lambda))$-*basic sound.*

The above statement says that if the product of the size of the sensed positions and the analyst size is less than the total environment length then it is

---

[2] In reality, we expect certain portions of E to be more likely to be overwritten by different A. Our results extend to that model.

possible for the A to evade the malware and force the decision procedures to output 1.

We now proceed to show a sufficient condition for security. The necessary condition requires that the intersection between S_i and A is large. However, it also requires that A is not able to come up with valid guesses for the missing parts of the E. Creating a simple definition for this condition is complicated by two factors:

1. The malware, M, does not know ahead of time where A will be loaded. If A can load in a location S_i whose values, E_{S_i} are easy to predict, it is impossible for M to provide security.
2. Once loaded, the A has access to the rest of E. This means that any redundancies or observable patterns or structures in E can be used to increase A's probability of guessing successfully.

Combining these two requirements, M should sense from as much of the environment as possible and E at sensed locations has to be hard to predict even knowing the rest of the environment. It is unlikely that computer systems satisfy these requirements. Environments have known structures and patterns – OS structures, filesystem contents, common libraries, etc. – and there are areas that have very low entropy. To codify the difficulty of satisfying these requirements, we present an analogue of Definition 3 and a corresponding sufficient condition for security. However, our condition should be seen as a largely negative result, as it only applies under unrealistic conditions on E and M.

Definition 9. *Let λ be a security parameter. A piece of M is μ-entropic sensing if for every subset $E_{sub} \subset E$ such that $|E_{sub}| \geq \mu$, then*

$$\min_{1 \leq i \leq n} \left(\max_{E' \in \mathcal{E}} \left(\Pr_{\substack{E \leftarrow \mathcal{E} \wedge \mathcal{D}_i, \\ S_i \leftarrow M(E)}} [\mathcal{D}_i(E'_{S_i}) = 1 | \mathcal{D}_1, S_1, ..., \mathcal{D}_{i-1}, S_{i-1}, E \backslash E_{sub}] \right) \right)$$

$$= \mathtt{negl}(\lambda)$$

where $\mathcal{D}_i$ is the entire truth table of $\mathcal{D}_i$ and $E \backslash E_{sub}$ is the portion of E which is not contained in E_{sub}.

Definition 9 imposes a constraint both on the malware and on the environmental distribution $\mathcal{E}$ itself. This implicitly requires that all large subsets of $\mathcal{E}$ have super-logarithmic min-entropy conditioned on the rest of the environment.

Theorem 5. *Let λ be a security parameter. Let M be a μ-entropic sensing with n decision procedures. If all A have artifact size at least μ, then any black-box A making at most $\mathtt{poly}(\lambda)$ oracle queries then M is at least $(1 - \mathtt{negl}(\lambda))$-basic sound.*

The proof of this theorem can be found in Appendix A.4. Most of the complexity of the proof is contained in Definition 9 which implies that the analyst's first guess on some decision procedure succeeds with negligible probability. Standard arguments show that even with a polynomial number of guesses their overall success remains negligible.

Note: It is possible to weaken Definition 9 to be probabilistic. That is, there is a good chance that the set overwritten by the A will make it difficult to provide good inputs to some $\mathcal{D}_{i^*}$. However, this does not fundamentally change the character of the result which says that all large subsets of E must be entropic and that M must read all subsets of E with good probability.

5 Resettable Adversary

Finally, we turn to our least setting which we call the *resettable* adversary. In this setting A is allowed access to the malware M and the environment E while they are still separated. They are allowed to Load in the environment E multiple times and reset. Not surprisingly, our results in this model are negative. As long as there are multiple analysis techniques that are disjoint it is always possible for the analyst to acquire the state of the environment that exists without the analyst being present. This allows the analyst to present the pristine environment to the malware, thus unlocking it. We begin by formalizing the interaction.

Resettable Soundness. We define the *resettable soundness* game as follows:

> **Experiment $\mathbf{Exp}_{M,E,A,\mathrm{Load},\psi}^{\mathrm{res-sou}}(\cdot)$:**
> $(\mathcal{D}_1, S_1, ..., \mathcal{D}_n, S_n) \leftarrow M(E)$
> $E_M \leftarrow \mathrm{Load}(M, E)$
> $state =\perp$
> For $i = 1$ to ψ
> $\quad A_i \leftarrow A(\mathcal{D}_1, S_1, ..., \mathcal{D}_{i-1}, S_{i-1}, \mathcal{D}_i, S_i, state)$
> $\quad E_i \leftarrow \mathrm{Load}(A_i, E)$
> $\quad (\mathrm{Guess}_i, f, state) = A_i(E_i, \mathcal{D}_i, S_i).$
> $\quad$ if $f = 1$ break
> If $\forall i,\ D_i(E_i) = 1$ return 1
> Else return 0.

Definition 10. *Let* Load *be a program loading module and let λ be a security parameter. A program M is ϵ-resettable sound for the target E (drawn from $\mathcal{E}$) with respect to A if for all $\psi = \mathrm{poly}(\lambda)$,*

$$\Pr[\mathbf{Exp}_{M,E,A,\mathrm{Load},\psi}^{\mathrm{sou}}(\cdot) = 1] > 1 - \epsilon.$$

Theorem 6. *If there exists multiple analysis techniques A_1, A_2 such that the locations overwritten by A_1, A_2 are disjoint, then all M that is δ-correct is at most δ-resettable sound.*

Proof (Sketch). The analyst A proceeds in three stages. First, they load some tool A_1 and output all non overwritten parts of E as state. They then load A_2 that does the same. Finally, they create an A_3 that encodes a copy of the entire environment as it exists without any tools present. This A_3 recreates the proper inputs to the decision procedures and only fails when M fails to authenticate in the legitimate environment.

In the above proof sketch we assume that A_3 is able to encode the entire target environment E in an analysis module. In reality, once the analyst has recovered the environment, they can produce an module that only includes the relevant information which is read in by M. The only requirement for the analyst is to be able to encode the entire environment and their guessing logic on the target machine. One could imagine that the loaded module could communicate with outside storage for pieces of the environment but this is out of scope for our model.

The resettable analyst A can forge the pristine environment and thus unlock the malware. With the ability to reset the environment and malware, the analyst can understand the entire target environment with the same precision as the malware making security impossible.

A   Proofs

A.1   Proof of Theorem 2

Proof (of Theorem 2). We show a stronger statement, we show a single algorithm A that works for any (β, γ)-environmentally authenticating malware. Let $t = 2^\beta \ln\left(\frac{n}{1-\epsilon}\right)$. Define A as follows for decision procedure i:

1. Input $\mathcal{D}_i, S_i, \mathcal{D}_{i-1}, S_{i-1}, ..., \mathcal{D}_1, S_1$.
2. For $j = 1$ to t
   (a) Sample $E_j \leftarrow \mathsf{Sam}_{\mathcal{E}}$.
   (b) If $D_i(E_{j,S_i}) = 1$ output $\mathtt{Guess}_i = E_j$.
3. Output $\bot$.

This procedure is repeated for each decision procedure. A wins if all decision procedures output 1. We first note that the probability that some decision procedure is incorrect is bounded by at most δ. We now bound the probability that A outputs $\bot$ for any iteration conditioned on the malware being correct. We first consider a single iteration. By Definition 4 and Assumption 1, $\mathbb{E}_{E_j \in \mathcal{E}}(\Pr[D_i(E_{j,S_i}) = 1]) \geq 2^{-\beta}$. That means that

$$\Pr[A \text{ outputs } \bot \text{ on } D_i] = \forall j, \Pr[D_i(E_{j,S_i}) = 0]$$
$$= (\mathbb{E}_{E \in \mathcal{E}} \Pr[D_i(E_{S_i}) = 0])^t$$
$$= (1 - \mathtt{Accept}(M, i, \mathcal{E}))^t$$
$$\leq \left(1 - 2^{-\beta}\right)^t$$

$$\leq \left(\left(1 - 2^{-\beta} \right)^{2^{\beta}} \right)^{\left(t/2^{\beta} \right)}$$

$$\leq \left(\frac{1}{e} \right)^{\left(\frac{t}{2^{\beta}} \right)} \leq e^{-t/2^{\beta}}. \tag{1}$$

Then across all iterations by union bound and Eq. 1: $\Pr[A \text{ outputs } \bot \text{ on any } \mathcal{D}_i]$ $\leq ne^{-t/2^{\beta}}$. That is,

$$\Pr[\mathbf{Exp}_{M,\mathcal{E},A}^{\text{bli}-\text{sou}}(\cdot) = 1] \geq 1 - ne^{-t/2^{\beta}} = 1 - ne^{-\ln(n/(1-\epsilon))} = 1 - n\left(\frac{1-\epsilon}{n} \right) = \epsilon.$$

Note that the overall running time of A is at most $t_A = n(t_E + t_{oracle}) \cdot t$ as required. The statement of the theorem is achieved by adding the probability δ that the malware is incorrect.

A.2   Proof of Theorem 3

Proof (of Theorem 3). Let A be a black box algorithm that only provide inputs to the current decision algorithm. Since the entire decision procedure is revealed once a "true" input is found there is no reason to query a previous decision algorithm. Consider some decision algorithm i^* that minimizes the probability in Definition 3. We bound the probability that A can make $\mathcal{D}_{i^*}$ output 1 as this bounds the probability of all algorithms outputting 1 (it may be that only a single decision algorithm outputs 0 on some inputs). The only information about values E that cause $\mathcal{D}_i$ to output 1 are contained in the query responses. Since the adversary wins if they get a single 1 response we can assume that A makes t deterministic queries and if none of those responses is 1 their guess will also be a deterministic value. Denote by $g_1, ..., g_{t+1}$ these values. Then we bound:

$$\sum_{j=1}^{t+1} \Pr_{D_i, S_i \leftarrow M}[D_{i^*}(g_j) = 1] \leq \Pr[D_{i^*}(g_1) = 1] + \Pr[D_{i^*}(g_2) = 1 | g_1 = 0] + ...$$

$$+ \Pr[D_{i^*}(g_{t+1}) = 1 | D_{i^*}(g_1) = 0 \wedge ... \wedge D_{i^*}(g_t) = 0]$$

$$\leq 2^{-\gamma} + \frac{\Pr[D_{i^*}(g_2) = 1 \wedge D_{i^*}(g_1) = 0]]}{\Pr[D_{i^*}(g_1) = 0]} + ...$$

$$+ \frac{\Pr[D_{i^*}(g_{t+1}) = 1 \wedge D_{i^*}(g_1) = 0 \wedge ... \wedge D_{i^*}(g_t) = 0]}{\Pr[D_{i^*}(g_1) = 0 \wedge ... \wedge D_{i^*}(g_t) = 0]}$$

$$\leq 2^{-\gamma} + \frac{\Pr[D_{i^*}(g_2) = 1]}{\Pr[D_{i^*}(g_1) = 0]} + ... + \frac{\Pr[D_{i^*}(g_{t+1}) = 1]}{\Pr[D_{i^*}(g_1) = 0 \wedge ... \wedge D_{i^*}(g_t) = 0]}$$

$$\leq 2^{-\gamma} + \frac{\Pr[D_{i^*}(g_2) = 1]}{1 - 2^{-\gamma}} + ... + \frac{\Pr[D_{i^*}(g_{t+1}) = 1]}{1 - t2^{-\gamma}}$$

$$\leq (t+1)\frac{2^{-\gamma}}{1 - t2^{-\gamma}}$$

A.3   Proof of Theorem 4

Proof (of Theorem 4). The adversary A does not know where in E that the malware M exists, A runs the risk of overwriting the sensors positions S_i. As stated above, we assume that M is operable after A has been loaded. The total size of M's reads from E are of size at most $n \cdot \alpha$. We define a single A that works for all M. Let A overwrite a random set of ν locations. However, rather than considering this A we instead consider some A' that overwrites each element of E_M with probability $2\nu/\ell$. Note that,

$$\Pr[||A'| < \nu] = \Pr\left[|A'| < (1 - \frac{1}{2})\mathbb{E}|A'|\right] = e^{-1/8\mathbb{E}|A'|} = e^{-1/4\nu} = e^{-1/4\ell^{1-c}}$$

using the multiplicative version of the Chernoff bound. Assume that A' simply outputs $\bot$ in this setting. Thus, all of A' success occurs when it overwrites at least ν positions and the job of A' to provide inputs to $\mathcal{D}_i$ is at least as difficult as A. For the reminder of the proof we consider A'.

We now bound the size of the intersection between the locations read by M and the locations overwritten by $\mathsf{Load}(A', E_M)$. Denote by E_{bad} the locations overwritten by $\mathsf{Load}(A', E_M)$ conditioned on the event that A' overwrites at least ν locations.

To bound the success probability of A', we care about the size of the intersection between the locations read by M and overwritten by E_{bad}. Since E_{bad} represents ν random locations the intersection between $(\cup_i S_i) \cap E_{bad}$ is distributed as a Binomial distribution, which we denote as X, with parameters $B(n\alpha, 2\nu/\ell)$. Then one has that,

$$\mathbb{E}[X] = \frac{2\nu n\alpha}{\ell} = \frac{2\ell^c \ell^{1-c}}{\ell} = 2.$$

Let $c' > 0$ be a constant. By a second application of the Chernoff bound one has that:

$$\Pr[X > 2 + c'] = e^{-2/3c'^2}.$$

For an intersection of size κ the correct E_M can be found using 2^κ oracle queries. Note that this is an upper bound, in the setting where a decision algorithm takes a smaller number of corrupted bits, these bits can be recovered in parts. Here we assume that all corrupted bits are necessary for a single decision algorithm. The statement of the theorem follows by using an A' that exhaustively searches over corrupted bits when the size of the corrupted bits is at most $c' + 2$ and aborts otherwise.

A.4   Proof of Theorem 5

Proof (of Theorem 5). Consider some A with artifact size at least μ. Let A be a black box algorithm that only provide inputs to the current decision algorithm.

Since the entire decision procedure is revealed once a "true" input is found there is no reason to query a previous decision algorithm. Denote by E_{sub} the subset of size at least μ that is overwritten by $\texttt{Load}(A, E_M)$, Then by Definition 9. There exists some i^* such that

$$\left(\max_{E' \in \mathcal{E}} \left(\Pr_{E \leftarrow \mathcal{E} \wedge \mathcal{D}_i, S_i \leftarrow M(E)} [\mathcal{D}_i(E'_{S_{i^*}}) = 1 | \mathcal{D}_1, ..., \mathcal{D}_{i^*-1}, S_1, ..., S_{i^*-1}, E \backslash E_{sub}] \right) \right)$$
$$= \texttt{negl}(\lambda).$$

We bound the probability that A can make $\mathcal{D}_{i^*}$ output 1 as this bounds the probability of all algorithms outputting 1 (it may be that only a single decision algorithm outputs 0 some fraction of the time). The only information about values E that cause $\mathcal{D}_{i^*}$ to output 1 are contained in the query responses. Since the adversary wins if they get a single 1 response we can assume that A makes $t = \texttt{poly}(\lambda)$ deterministic queries and if none of those responses is 1 their guess will also be a deterministic value. Denote by $g_1, ..., g_{t+1}$ these values. Then we bound:

$$\sum_{j=1}^{t+1} \Pr_{D_i, S_i \leftarrow M} [D_{i^*}(g_j) = 1] \le \Pr[D_{i^*}(g_1) = 1] + \Pr[D_{i^*}(g_2) = 1 | g_1 = 0] + ...$$
$$+ \Pr[D_{i^*}(g_{t+1}) = 1 | D_{i^*}(g_1) = 0 \wedge ... \wedge D_{i^*}(g_t) = 0]$$
$$\le \texttt{negl}(\lambda) + \frac{\Pr[D_{i^*}(g_2) = 1 \wedge D_{i^*}(g_1) = 0]]}{\Pr[D_{i^*}(g_1) = 0]} + ...$$
$$+ \frac{\Pr[D_{i^*}(g_{t+1}) = 1 \wedge D_{i^*}(g_1) = 0 \wedge ... \wedge D_{i^*}(g_t) = 0]}{\Pr[D_{i^*}(g_1) = 0 \wedge ... \wedge D_{i^*}(g_t) = 0]}$$
$$\le \texttt{negl}(\lambda) + \frac{\Pr[D_{i^*}(g_2) = 1]}{\Pr[D_{i^*}(g_1) = 0]} + ... + \frac{\Pr[D_{i^*}(g_{t+1}) = 1]}{\Pr[D_{i^*}(g_1) = 0 \wedge ... \wedge D_{i^*}(g_t) = 0]}$$
$$\le \texttt{negl}(\lambda) + \frac{\Pr[D_{i^*}(g_2) = 1]}{1 - \texttt{negl}(\lambda)} + ... + \frac{\Pr[D_{i^*}(g_{t+1}) = 1]}{1 - t\texttt{negl}(\lambda)}$$
$$\le (t+1) \frac{\texttt{negl}(\lambda)}{1 - t\texttt{negl}(\lambda)} = \texttt{negl}(\lambda)$$

References

[Bau14] Bauer, C.: ReMASTering Applications by Obfuscating during Compilation. blog post, August 2014

[BCK+10a] Balzarotti, D., Cova, M., Karlberger, C., Kirda, E., Kruegel, C., Vigna, G.: Efficient detection of split personalities in malware. In: NDSS, Citeseer (2010)

[BCK+10b] Balzarotti, D., Cova, M., Karlberger, C., Kruegel, C., Kirda, E., Vigna, G.: Efficient detection of split personalities in Malware. In: Proceedings of the Symposium on Network and Distributed System Security (NDSS) (2010)

[BGI+01] Barak, B., et al.: On the (im)possibility of obfuscating programs. In: Kilian, J. (ed.) CRYPTO 2001. LNCS, vol. 2139, pp. 1–18. Springer, Heidelberg (2001). https://doi.org/10.1007/3-540-44647-8_1

[BKY16] Blackthorne, J., Kaiser, B., Yener, B.: A formal framework for environmentally sensitive malware. In: Monrose, F., Dacier, M., Blanc, G., Garcia-Alfaro, J. (eds.) RAID 2016. LNCS, vol. 9854, pp. 211–229. Springer, Cham (2016). https://doi.org/10.1007/978-3-319-45719-2_10

[BR93] Bellare, M., Rogaway, P.: Random oracles are practical: a paradigm for designing efficient protocols. In: Proceedings of the 1st ACM Conference on Computer and Communications Security, pp. 62–73. ACM (1993)

[CAM+08] Chen, X., Andersen, J., Mao, Z.M., Bailey, M., Nazario, J.: Towards an understanding of anti-virtualization and anti-debugging behavior in modern malware. In: IEEE International Conference on Dependable Systems and Networks With FTCS and DCC, 2008. DSN 2008, pp. 177–186, June 2008

[CMGS12] Cichonski, P., Millar, T., Grance, T., Scarfone, K.: Computer Security Incident Handling Guide: Recommendations of the National Institute of Standards and Technology, 800–61. Revision 2. NIST Special Publication, 800–61:79 (2012)

[CTL97] Collberg, C., Thomborson, C., Low, D.: A Taxonomy of Obfuscating Transformations (1997)

[DRS04] Dodis, Y., Reyzin, L., Smith, A.: Fuzzy extractors: how to generate strong keys from biometrics and other noisy data. In: Cachin, C., Camenisch, J.L. (eds.) EUROCRYPT 2004. LNCS, vol. 3027, pp. 523–540. Springer, Heidelberg (2004). https://doi.org/10.1007/978-3-540-24676-3_31

[DRS08] Dodis, Y., Reyzin, L., Smith, A.: Fuzzy extractors-a brief survey of results from 2004 to 2006. In: Security with Noisy Data. Citeseer (2008)

[DRSL08] Dinaburg, A., Royal, P., Sharif, M., Lee, W.: Ether: malware analysis via hardware virtualization extensions. In: CCS 2008 Proceedings of the 15th ACM Conference on Computer and Communications Security, pp. 51–62 (2008)

[Fer07] Ferrie, P.: Attacks on More Virtual Machine Emulators. Technical report, Symantec Advanced Threat Research (2007)

[Fer11] Ferrie, P.: The Ultimate Anti-Debugging Reference, May 2011. http://pferrie.host22.com/papers/antidebug.pdf. Accessed 6 Apr 2015

[FKSW06] Futoransky, A., Kargieman, E., Sarraute, C., Waissbein, A.: Foundations and applications for secure triggers. In: ACM Transactions of Information Systems Security, p. 2006 (2006)

[FRS16] Fuller, B., Reyzin, L., Smith, A.: When are fuzzy extractors possible? In: Cheon, J.H., Takagi, T. (eds.) ASIACRYPT 2016. LNCS, vol. 10031, pp. 277–306. Springer, Heidelberg (2016). https://doi.org/10.1007/978-3-662-53887-6_10

[GGH+13] Garg, S., Gentry, C., Halevi, S., Raykova, M., Sahai, A., Waters, B.: Candidate indistinguishability obfuscation and functional encryption for all circuits. In: FOCS, pp. 40–49. IEEE Computer Society (2013)

[ICF+15] Itkis, G., Chandar, V., Fuller, B.W., Campbell, J.P., Cunningham, R.K.: Iris biometric security challenges and possible solutions: for your eyes only? Using the iris as a key. IEEE Signal Process. Mag. 32(5), 42–53 (2015)

[Jst16] Jsteube. oclGaussCrack (2016)

[KLZS12] Kolbitsch, C., Livshits, B., Zorn, B., Seifert, C.: Rozzle: de-cloaking internet malware. In: Proceedings of the 2012 IEEE Symposium on Security and Privacy. SP 2012, pp. 443–457. IEEE Computer Society, Washington (2012)

[Kra10] Krawczyk, H.: Cryptographic extraction and key derivation: the HKDF scheme. In: Rabin, T. (ed.) CRYPTO 2010. LNCS, vol. 6223, pp. 631–648. Springer, Heidelberg (2010). https://doi.org/10.1007/978-3-642-14623-7_34

[KYH+09] Kang, M.G., Yin, H., Hanna, S., McCamant, S., Song, D.: Emulating emulation-resistant malware. In: Proceedings of the 1st ACM Workshop on Virtual Machine Security, VMSec 2009, pp. 11–22. ACM, New York (2009)

[LKMC11] Lindorfer, M., Kolbitsch, C., Milani Comparetti, P.: Detecting environment-sensitive malware. In: Sommer, R., Balzarotti, D., Maier, G. (eds.) RAID 2011. LNCS, vol. 6961, pp. 338–357. Springer, Heidelberg (2011). https://doi.org/10.1007/978-3-642-23644-0_18

[Moo15] Moon, P.: The Use of Packers, Obfuscators and Encryptors in Modern Malware. Technical report, Information Security Group, Royal Holloway University of London (2015)

[NTS99] Nisan, N., Ta-Shma, A.: Extracting randomness: a survey and new constructions. J. Comput. Syst. Sci. **58**(1), 148–173 (1999)

[NZ96] Nisan, N., Zuckerman, D.: Randomness is linear in space. J. Comput. Syst. Sci. **52**(1), 43–52 (1996)

[PMRB09] Paleari, R., Martignoni, L., Roglia, G.F., Bruschi, D.: A fistful of red-pills: how to automatically generate procedures to detect CPU emulators. In: Proceedings of the 3rd USENIX Conference on Offensive Technologies. WOOT 2009, p. 2. USENIX Association, Berkeley (2009)

[Rén61] Rényi, A.: On measures of entropy and information. In: Proceedings of the fourth Berkeley Symposium on Mathematical Statistics and Probability, vol. 1, pp. 547–561 (1961)

[RS98] Riordan, J., Schneier, B.: Environmental key generation towards clueless agents. In: Vigna, G. (ed.) Mobile Agents and Security. LNCS, vol. 1419, pp. 15–24. Springer, Heidelberg (1998). https://doi.org/10.1007/3-540-68671-1_2

[RT12] Kaspersky Lab Global Research and Analysis Team: Gauss: Abnormal Distribution. Technical report, Kaspersky Lab (2012)

[SH12] Sikorski, M., Honig, A.: Practical Malware Analysis: The Hands-On Guide to Dissecting Malicious Software, 1st edn. No Starch Press, San Francisco (2012)

[SRL12] Song, C., Royal, P., Lee, W.: Impeding automated malware analysis with environment-sensitive malware. In: Hotsec (2012)

[SWP08] Saxena, A., Wyseur, B., Preneel, B.: White-box cryptography: formal notions and (im) possibility results (2008). IACR Cryptology ePrint Archive, 2008, 2008:273

[XZGL14] Xu, Z., Zhang, J., Gu, G., Lin, Z.: GOLDENEYE: efficiently and effectively unveiling malware's targeted environment. In: Stavrou, A., Bos, H., Portokalidis, G. (eds.) RAID 2014. LNCS, vol. 8688, pp. 22–45. Springer, Cham (2014). https://doi.org/10.1007/978-3-319-11379-1_2

[Yan13] Yan, L.K.: Transparent and precise malware analysis using virtualization: from theory to practice (2013). https://surface.syr.edu/cgi/viewcontent.cgi?referer=https://scholar.google.com/&httpsredir=1&article=1336&context=eecs_etd

Threshold Kleptographic Attacks on Discrete Logarithm Based Signatures

George Teşeleanu[✉]

Department of Computer Science, "Al.I.Cuza" University of Iaşi,
700506 Iaşi, Romania
george.teseleanu@info.uaic.ro

Abstract. In an ℓ out of n *threshold scheme*, ℓ out of n members must cooperate to recover a secret. A *kleptographic attack* is a backdoor which can be implemented in an algorithm and further used to retrieve a user's secret key. We combine the notions of *threshold scheme* and *kleptographic attack* to construct the first ℓ out of n threshold kleptographic attack on discrete logarithm based digital signatures and prove its security in the standard and random oracle models.

1 Introduction

Simmons [30,31] was the first to study the use of digital signatures as a channel to convey information (subliminal channels). Later on, Young and Yung [34–38] combined subliminal channels and public key cryptography to leak a user's private key or a message (SETUP attacks). Young and Yung assumed a black-box environment[1], while mentioning the existence of other scenarios. These attacks need a malicious device manufacturer[2] to work. The input and output distributions of a device with SETUP should not be distinguishable from the regular distribution. However, if the device is reverse engineered, the deployed mechanism may be detectable.

Although SETUP attacks were considered far-fetched by some cryptographers, recent events [5,25] suggest otherwise. As a consequence, this research area seems to have been revived [4,6,15,21,26]. In [7], SETUP attacks implemented in symmetric encryption schemes are referred to as *algorithmic substitution attacks* (ASA). The authors of [7] point out that the sheer complexity of open-source software (*e.g.* OpenSSL) and the small number of experts who review them make ASAs plausible not only in the black-box model. ASAs in the symmetric setting are further studied in [6,13] and, in the case of hash functions, in [3].

A practical example of leaking user keys is the Dual-EC generator. As pointed out in [9], using the Dual-EC generator facilitates a third party to recover a user's

---

[1] A black-box is a device, process or system, whose inputs and outputs are known, but its internal structure or working is not known or accessible to the user (*e.g.* tamper proof devices).

[2] that implements the mechanisms to recover the secrets.

© Springer Nature Switzerland AG 2019
T. Lange and O. Dunkelman (Eds.): LATINCRYPT 2017, LNCS 11368, pp. 401–414, 2019.
https://doi.org/10.1007/978-3-030-25283-0_21

private key. Such an attack is a natural application of Young and Yung's work. Some real world SETUP attack examples may be found in [10,11]. Building on the earlier work of [33] and influenced by the Dual-EC incident, [14,15] provide the readers with a formal treatment of backdoored pseudorandom generators (PRNG).

A more general model entitled *subversion attacks* is considered in [4]. This model includes SETUP attacks and ASAs, but generic malware and virus attacks are also included. The authors provide subversion resilient signature schemes in the proposed model. Their work is further extended in [26,27], where subversion resistant solutions for one-way functions, signature schemes and PRNGs are provided. In [26], the authors point out that the model from [4] assumes the system parameters are honestly generated (but this is not always the case). In the discrete logarithm case, examples of algorithms for generating trapdoored prime numbers may be found in [18,20].

A different method for protecting users from subversion attacks are *cryptographic reverse firewalls* (RF). RFs represent external trusted devices that sanitize the outputs of infected machines. The concept was introduced in [16,23]. A reverse firewall for signature schemes is provided in [4].

In this paper, we extend the SETUP attacks of Young and Yung on digital signatures. We introduce the first SETUP mechanism that leaks a user's secret key, only if ℓ out of n malicious parties decide to do this. We assume that the signature schemes are implemented in a black-box equipped with a volatile memory, erased whenever someone tampers with it.

In the following we give a few examples where a threshold kleptographic signature may be useful.

Since digitally signed documents are just as binding as signatures on paper, if a recipient receives a document signed by A he will act according to A's instructions. Finding A's private key, can aid a law enforcement agency into collecting additional informations about A and his entourage. In order to protect citizens from abuse, a warrant must be issued by a legal commission before starting surveillance. To aid the commission and to prevent abuse, the manufacturer of A's device can implement an ℓ out of n threshold SETUP mechanism. Thus, A's key can be recovered only if there is a quorum in favor of issuing the warrant.

Digital currencies (*e.g.* Bitcoin) have become a popular alternative to physical currencies. Transactions between users are based on digital signatures. When a transaction is conducted, the recipient's public key is linked to the transfered money. Only the owner of the secret key can now spend the money. To protect his secret keys, a user can choose to store them in a tamper proof device, called a hardware wallet. Let's assume that a group of malicious entities manages to infect some hardware wallets and they implement an ℓ out of n threshold SETUP mechanism. When ℓ members decide, they can transfer the money from the infected wallets without the owner's knowledge. If $\ell - 1$ parties are arrested, the mechanism remains undetectable as long as the devices are not reverse engineered.

Structure of the Paper. We introduce notations and definitions used throughout the paper in Sect. 2. In order to mount the SETUP attacks, we use a variant of the Generalized ElGamal encryption scheme [22] that is described in Sect. 3. In Sect. 4 we describe a SETUP attack on the Generalized ElGamal signature [22], extended in Sect. 5. We conclude in Sect. 6.

Full Version. A full version of this extended abstract is available on the Cryptology ePrint archive [32].

2   Preliminaries

Notations. Throughout the paper, λ will denote a security parameter. The action of selecting a uniformly random element x from a sample space X is denoted by $x \xleftarrow{\$} X$. We also denote by $x \leftarrow y$ the assignment of value y to variable x. The probability that event E happens is denoted by $Pr[E]$. The action of choosing a random element from an entropy smoothing[3] (ES) family $\mathcal{H}$ is further referred to as "H is ES". Encryption of message m with key k using the AES algorithm[4] is denoted by $AES_k(m)$.

2.1   Diffie-Hellman Assumptions

Definition 1 (Computational Diffie-Hellman - CDH). *Let $\mathbb{G}$ be a cyclic group of order q, g a generator of $\mathbb{G}$ and let A be a probabilistic polynomial-time algorithm (PPT algorithm) that returns an element from $\mathbb{G}$. We define the advantage*

$$ADV_{\mathbb{G},g}^{CDH}(A) = Pr[A(g^x, g^y) = g^{xy} | x, y \xleftarrow{\$} \mathbb{Z}_q^*].$$

If $ADV_{\mathbb{G},g}^{CDH}(A)$ is negligible for any PPT algorithm A, we say that the Computational Diffie-Hellman problem is hard in $\mathbb{G}$.

Definition 2 (Decisional Diffie-Hellman - DDH). *Let $\mathbb{G}$ be a cyclic group of order q, g a generator of $\mathbb{G}$. Let A be a PPT algorithm which returns 1 on input (g^x, g^y, g^z) if $g^{xy} = g^z$. We define the advantage*

$$ADV_{\mathbb{G},g}^{DDH}(A) = |Pr[A(g^x, g^y, g^z) = 1 | x, y \xleftarrow{\$} \mathbb{Z}_q^*, z \leftarrow xy]$$

$$- Pr[A(g^x, g^y, g^z) = 1 | x, y, z \xleftarrow{\$} \mathbb{Z}_q^*]|.$$

If $ADV_{\mathbb{G},g}^{DDH}(A)$ is negligible for any PPT algorithm A, we say that the Decisional Diffie-Hellman problem is hard in $\mathbb{G}$.

---

[3] We refer the reader to [29].
[4] We refer the reader to [12] for a description of AES.

Definition 3 (Hash Diffie-Hellman - HDH). *Let* $\mathbb{G}$ *be a cyclic group of order* q, g *a generator of* $\mathbb{G}$ *and* $H : \mathbb{G} \to \mathbb{Z}_q^*$ *a hash function. Let A be a PPT algorithm which returns 1 on input* (g^x, g^y, z) *if* $H(g^{xy}) = z$. *We define the advantage*

$$ADV_{\mathbb{G},g,H}^{\text{HDH}}(A) = |Pr[A(g^x, g^y, H(g^{xy})) = 1 | x, y \xleftarrow{\$} \mathbb{Z}_q^*]$$
$$- Pr[A(g^x, g^y, z) = 1 | x, y, z \xleftarrow{\$} \mathbb{Z}_q^*]|.$$

If $ADV_{\mathbb{G},g,H}^{\text{HDH}}(A)$ *is negligible for any PPT algorithm A, we say that the Hash Diffie-Hellman problem is hard in* $\mathbb{G}$.

Remark 1. The two first assumptions (CDH and DDH) are standard and are included for completeness. The HDH assumption was formally introduced in [1,2], although it was informally introduced as a composite assumption in [8,39]. According to [8], the HDH assumption is equivalent with the CDH assumption in ROM. If the DDH assumption is hard in $\mathbb{G}$ and H is ES, then the HDH assumption is hard in $\mathbb{G}$ [1,24,29]. In [19], the authors show that the HDH assumption holds, even if the DDH assumption is relaxed to the following assumption: $\mathbb{G}$ contains a large enough group in which DDH holds. One particular interesting group is $\mathbb{Z}_p^*$, where p is a "large"[5] prime. According to [19], it is conjectured that if $\mathbb{G}$ is generated by an element $g \in \mathbb{Z}_p^*$ of order q, where q is a "large"[6] prime that divides $p - 1$, then the DDH assumption holds. The analysis conducted in [19] provides the reader with solid arguments to support the hypothesis that HDH holds in the subgroup $\mathbb{G} \subset \mathbb{Z}_p^*$.

2.2   Definitions and Security Models

Definition 4 (Signature Scheme). *A Signature Scheme consists of three PPT algorithms: KeyGen, Sign and Verification. The first one takes as input a security parameter and outputs the system parameters, the public key and the matching secret key. The secret key together with the Sign algorithm is used to generate a signature σ for a message m. Using the public key, the last algorithm verifies if a signature σ for a message m is generated using the matching secret key.*

Definition 5 (Public Key Encryption - PKE). *A Public Key Encryption (PKE) scheme consists of three PPT algorithms: KeyGen, Encrypt and Decrypt. The first one takes as input a security parameter and outputs the system parameters, the public key and the matching secret key. The public key together with the Encrypt algorithm is used to encrypt a message m. Using the secret key, the last algorithm decrypts any ciphertext encrypted using the matching public key.*

---

[5] at least 2048 bits, better 3072 bits.
[6] at least 192 bits, better 256 bits.

Remark 2. For simplicity, public parameters will be implicit when describing an algorithm.

Definition 6 (Indistinguishability from Random Bits - INDS).
The security model of indistinguishability from random bits for a PKE scheme $\mathcal{AE}$ is captured in the following game:

KeyGen(λ): The challenger C generates the public key, sends it to adversary A and keeps the matching secret key to himself.

Query: Adversary A sends C a message m. The challenger encrypts m and obtains the ciphertext c_0. Let c_1 be a randomly chosen element from the same set as c_0. The challenger flips a coin $b \in \{0, 1\}$ and returns c_b to the adversary.

Guess: In this phase, the adversary outputs a guess $b' \in \{0, 1\}$. He wins the game, if $b' = b$.

The advantage of an adversary A attacking a PKE scheme is defined as

$$ADV_{\mathcal{AE}}^{\text{IND\$}}(A) = |2Pr[b = b'] - 1|,$$

where the probability is computed over the random bits used by C and A. A PKE scheme is INDS secure, if for any PPT adversary A the advantage $ADV_{\mathcal{AE}}^{\text{IND\$}}(A)$ is negligible.

Definition 7 (Anonymity under Chosen Plaintext Attacks - ANO-CPA).
The security model against anonymity under chosen plaintext attacks for a PKE scheme $\mathcal{AE}$ is captured in the following game:

KeyGen(λ): The challenger C generates two public keys pk_0 and pk_1, sends them to adversary A and keeps the matching secret keys to himself.

Query: Adversary A sends C a message m. The challenger flips a coin $b \in \{0, 1\}$ and encrypts m using pk_b. The resulting ciphertext c is sent to the adversary.

Guess: In this phase, the adversary outputs a guess $b' \in \{0, 1\}$. He wins the game, if $b' = b$.

The advantage of an adversary A attacking a PKE scheme is defined as

$$ADV_{\mathcal{AE}}^{\text{ANO-CPA}}(A) = |2Pr[b = b'] - 1|,$$

where the probability is computed over the random bits used by C and A. A PKE scheme is ANO-CPA secure, if for any PPT adversary A the advantage $ADV_{\mathcal{AE}}^{\text{ANO-CPA}}(A)$ is negligible.

Definition 8 (Secretly Embedded Trapdoor with Universal Protection - SETUP).
A Secretly Embedded Trapdoor with Universal Protection (SETUP) is an algorithm that can be inserted in a system such that it leaks encrypted private key information to an attacker through the system's outputs. Encryption of the private key is performed using an asymmetric encryption scheme. It is assumed that the decryption function is accessible only to the attacker.

Remark 3. We consider that the attacks presented from now on are implemented in a device D that digitally signs messages. The owner of the device is denoted by V and his public key by pk_V. We assume that his secret key sk_V is stored only in D's volatile memory.[7] The victim V thinks that D signs messages using the signature scheme described in Sect. 2.3. We stress that *KeyGen* and *Verification* algorithms are identical to the ones from Sect. 2.3. Thus, *KeyGen* and *Verification* are omitted when presenting the attacks.

Throughout the paper, when presenting the SETUP mechanisms, we make use of the following algorithms

- *Malicious Party(s) KeyGen* – used by the attacker(s) to generate his (their) parameters;
- *Recovering* – used by the attacker(s) to recover V's secret key.

The algorithms above are not implemented in D.

2.3 Generalized ElGamal Signature

Originally described in [17], the ElGamal digital signature scheme can easily be generalized to any finite cyclic group $\mathbb{G}$. We shortly describe the algorithms of the generalized ElGamal signature scheme, as presented in [22].

KeyGen(λ): Generate a large prime number q, such that $q \geq 2^\lambda$. Choose a cyclic group $\mathbb{G}$ of order q and let g be a generator of the group. Let $h : \mathbb{G} \to \mathbb{Z}_q$ be a hash function. Choose $a \xleftarrow{\$} \mathbb{Z}_q^*$ and compute $y \leftarrow g^a$. Output the system parameters $pp = (q, g, \mathbb{G}, h)$ and the public key $pk_V = y$. The secret key is $sk_V = a$.

Sign(m, sk_V): To sign a message $m \in \mathbb{G}$, first generate a random number $k \xleftarrow{\$} \mathbb{Z}_q^*$. Then compute the values $r \leftarrow g^k$ and $s \leftarrow k^{-1}[h(m) - a \cdot h(r)] \bmod q$. Output the signature (r, s).

Verification(m, r, s, pk_V): To verify the signature (r, s) of message m, compute $v_1 \leftarrow y_V^{h(r)} \cdot r^s$ and $v_2 \leftarrow g^{h(m)}$. Output **true** if and only if $v_1 = v_2$. Else output **false**.

2.4 Young-Yung SETUP Attack on the Generalized ElGamal Signature

In [34–37], the authors propose a kleptographic version of ElGamal signatures and prove it secure in the standard model under the HDH assumption. The Young-Yung SETUP mechanism can be easily adapted to the generalized ElGamal signature, while maintaining its security. The algorithms of the generalized version are shortly described below. We assume that user V is the victim of a malicious user M. After D signs at least two messages, M can recover V's secret key and thus impersonate V.

---

[7] If V knows his secret key, he is able to detect a SETUP mechanism using its description and parameters (found by means of reverse engineering a black-box, for example).

Malicious Party KeyGen(pp): Let $H : \mathbb{G} \to \mathbb{Z}_q^*$ be a hash function. Choose $x_M \xleftarrow{\$} \mathbb{Z}_q^*$ and compute $y_M \leftarrow g^{x_M}$. Output the public key $pk_M = y_M$. The public key pk_M and H will be stored in D's volatile memory. The secret key is $sk_M = x_M$; it will only be known by M and will not be stored in the black-box.

Signing Sessions: The possible signing sessions performed by D are described below. Let $i \geq 1$.

Session$_0$(m_0, sk_V): To sign message $m_0 \in \mathbb{G}$, D does the following

$$k_0 \xleftarrow{\$} \mathbb{Z}_q^*, r_0 \leftarrow g^{k_0}, s_0 \leftarrow k_0^{-1}[h(m_0) - a \cdot h(r_0)] \bmod q.$$

The value k_0 is stored in D's volatile memory until the end of *Session$_1$*. Output the signature (r_0, s_0).

Session$_i$(m_i, sk_V, pk_M): To sign message $m_i \in \mathbb{G}$, D does the following

$$z_i \leftarrow y_M^{k_{i-1}}, k_i \leftarrow H(z_i), r_i \leftarrow g^{k_i}, s_i \leftarrow k_i^{-1}[h(m_i) - a \cdot h(r_i)].$$

The value k_i is stored in D's volatile memory until the end of *Session$_{i+1}$*. Output the signature (r_i, s_i).

Recovering($m_i, r_{i-1}, r_i, s_i, sk_M$): Compute $\alpha \leftarrow r_{i-1}^{x_M}$ and $k_i \leftarrow H(\alpha)$. Recover a by computing

$$a \leftarrow h(r_i)^{-1}[h(m_i) - k_i \cdot s_i)].$$

3   Multiplicative ElGamal Encryption

The ElGamal encryption scheme was first described in [17]. The underlying group of the scheme is $\mathbb{Z}_p$, where p is a prime number. The scheme can easily be generalized to any finite cyclic group $\mathbb{G}$. The description of the generalized ElGamal can be found in [22]. Based on this description, we propose a new version of the ElGamal encryption scheme, which will later be used to deploy our SETUP mechanisms. We prove that the scheme is secure and that it preserves anonymity.

3.1   Scheme Description

KeyGen(λ): Generate a large prime number q, such that $q \geq 2^\lambda$. Choose a cyclic group $\mathbb{G}$ of order q and let g be a generator of the group. Let $H : \mathbb{G} \to \mathbb{Z}_q^*$ be a hash function. Choose $x \xleftarrow{\$} \mathbb{Z}_q^*$ and compute $y \leftarrow g^x$. Output the system parameters $pp = (q, g, \mathbb{G}, H)$ and the public key $pk = y$. The secret key is $sk = x$.

Encryption(m, pk): To encrypt a message $m \in \mathbb{Z}_q^*$, first generate a random number $k \xleftarrow{\$} \mathbb{Z}_q^*$. Then compute the values $\alpha \leftarrow g^k, \beta \leftarrow y^k, \gamma \leftarrow H(\beta)$ and $\delta \leftarrow m \cdot \gamma$. Output the pair (α, δ).

Decryption(α, δ, sk): To decrypt ciphertext (α, δ), compute $\epsilon \leftarrow \alpha^x$, $\zeta \leftarrow H(\epsilon)$. Recover the original message by computing $m \leftarrow \delta \cdot \zeta^{-1}$.

We need to prove that the scheme is sound. If the pair (α, δ) is generated according to the scheme, it is easy to see that $\delta \cdot \zeta^{-1} \equiv m \cdot H(y^k) \cdot [H(\alpha^x)]^{-1} \equiv m \cdot H((g^x)^k) \cdot [H((g^k)^x)]^{-1} \equiv m$.

Remark 4. In the original ElGamal encryption we have $m \in \mathbb{G}$ and $\delta \leftarrow m \cdot \beta$, but in modern use of Diffie-Hellman we have $\delta \leftarrow AES_\gamma(m)$.

3.2   Security Analysis

Theorems 1 and 2 are proven in the full version of the paper [32] as sequences of games. We denote by $\mathcal{MEG}$ the Multiplicative ElGamal scheme.

Theorem 1. *If* HDH *is hard in* $\mathbb{G}$ *then* $\mathcal{MEG}$ *is* IND\$ *secure in the standard model. Formally, let A be an efficient PPT* IND\$ *adversary. There exists an efficient algorithm B such that*

$$ADV^{\text{IND\$}}_{\mathcal{MEG}}(A) \leq 2ADV^{\text{HDH}}_{\mathbb{G},g,H}(B).$$

Theorem 2. *If* HDH *is hard in* $\mathbb{G}$ *then* $\mathcal{MEG}$ *is* ANO-CPA *secure in the standard model. Formally, let A be an efficient PPT* ANO-CPA *adversary. There exists an efficient algorithm B such that*

$$ADV^{\text{ANO-CPA}}_{\mathcal{MEG}}(A) \leq 4ADV^{\text{HDH}}_{\mathbb{G},g,H}(B).$$

4   A SETUP Attack on the Generalized ElGamal Signature

We further introduce a new SETUP mechanism. Compared to Young-Yung's attack, it is very easy to modify our mechanism to allow ℓ out of n malicious parties to recover V's secret key.[8] The best we were able to do, using Young-Yung's mechanism, was to devise an ℓ out of ℓ threshold scheme.[9] We point out, that like Young-Yung's mechanism, our proposed mechanism can be modified to leak data continuously to the attacker.

To implement the attack, M works in almost the same environment as in Sect. 2.4. Thus, we only mention the differences between the two environments.

Signing Sessions: The possible signing sessions performed by D are described below. Let $i \geq 2$.

Session$_0$ (m_0, sk_V): To sign message $m_0 \in \mathbb{G}$, D does the following

$$k_0 \xleftarrow{\$} \mathbb{Z}_q^*, r_0 \leftarrow g^{k_0}, s_0 \leftarrow k_0^{-1}[h(m_0) - a \cdot h(r_0)] \bmod q.$$

---

[8] We refer the reader to Sect. 5.
[9] We refer the reader to the full version of the paper [32].

The value k_0 is stored in D's volatile memory until the end of $Session_1$. Output the signature (r_0, s_0).

$Session_1(m_1, sk_V, pk_M)$: To sign message $m_1 \in \mathbb{G}$, D does the following

$$k_1 \leftarrow k_0 \cdot H(y_M^{k_0}), r_1 \leftarrow g^{k_1}, s_1 \leftarrow k_1^{-1}[h(m_1) - a \cdot h(r_1)] \bmod q.$$

We remark that s_1 is used as a data carrier for M. Output the signature (r_1, s_1).

$Session_i(m_i, sk_V)$: To sign message $m_i \in \mathbb{G}$, D does the following

$$k_i \xleftarrow{\$} \mathbb{Z}_q^*, r_i \leftarrow g^{k_i}, s_i \leftarrow k_i^{-1}[h(m_i) - a \cdot h(r_i)] \bmod q.$$

$Recovering(m_0, m_1, r_0, r_1, s_0, s_1, sk_M)$: Compute $\alpha \leftarrow [s_1 \cdot H(r_0^{x_M})]^{-1}$. Recover a by computing

$$a \leftarrow \left(\alpha \cdot h(m_1) - s_0^{-1} \cdot h(m_0)\right) \cdot \left(\alpha \cdot h(r_1) - s_0^{-1} \cdot h(r_0)\right)^{-1} \bmod q.$$

The correctness of the $Recovering$ algorithm can be obtained as follows. From $Session_0$ and $Session_1$, we obtain the value of k_0

$$k_0 \equiv s_0^{-1}[h(m_0) - a \cdot h(r_0)] \quad \bmod q \tag{1}$$
$$k_0 \equiv [s_1 \cdot H(y_M^{k_0})]^{-1} \cdot [h(m_1) - a \cdot h(r_1)] \quad \bmod q. \tag{2}$$

From equalities (1) and (2) we obtain

$$a \cdot \left(\alpha \cdot h(r_1) - s_0^{-1} \cdot h(r_0)\right) \equiv \alpha \cdot h(m_1) - s_0^{-1} \cdot h(m_0) \bmod q.$$

Using the above equality and the fact that $y_M^{k_0} = r_0^{x_M}$, we obtain the correctness of the $Recovering$ algorithm.

5   A Threshold SETUP Attack on the Generalized ElGamal Signature

In this section we introduce an ℓ out of n threshold SETUP attack, based on $\mathcal{N} - \mathcal{GEGS}$. In this secret sharing scenario, user V is the victim of n malicious parties (denoted by $\{M_i\}_{1 \leq i \leq n}$) that somehow convince the manufacturer of D to implement the described SETUP mechanism. After D signs $n + 1$ messages, any coalition of ℓ participants M_i can recover V's secret key. Once the key is obtained, V can be impersonated. We remark that starting from signature $\ell + 1$ some coalitions of M_i can impersonate V.

To ease description, we assume without loss of generality, that the first ℓ participants M_i decide to recover V's secret key and denote by $M = \{m_i\}_{0 \leq i \leq \ell}$, $R = \{r_i\}_{0 \leq i \leq \ell}$, $S = \{s_i\}_{0 \leq i \leq \ell}$, $SK_M = \{sk_i\}_{1 \leq i \leq \ell}$. We present our proposed threshold SETUP scheme below.

$Malicious\ Parties\ KeyGen(pp)$: Let $H : \mathbb{G} \to \mathbb{Z}_q^*$ be a hash function. For each $M_i, 1 \leq i \leq n$, choose $x_i \xleftarrow{\$} \mathbb{Z}_q^*$ and compute $y_i \leftarrow g^{x_i}$. Output the public keys

$pk_i = y_i$. The public keys pk_i and H will be stored in D's volatile memory. The secret keys are $sk_i = x_i$; they will only be known by the respective M_i and will not be stored in the black-box.

Signing Sessions: The possible signing sessions performed by D are described below. Let $1 \le i \le n$ and $j > n$.

Session$_0$(m_0, sk_V): To sign message $m_0 \in \mathbb{G}$, D does the following

$$k_0 \xleftarrow{\$} \mathbb{Z}_q^*, r_0 \leftarrow g^{k_0}, s_0 \leftarrow k_0^{-1}[h(m_0) - a \cdot h(r_0)] \bmod q.$$

The device also chooses $\{f_j\}_{1 \le j < \ell}$ at random from $\mathbb{Z}_q^*$ and forms the polynomial $f(z) = k_0 + f_1 \cdot z + \ldots + f_{\ell-1} \cdot z^{\ell-1}$. The polynomial $f(z)$ is stored in D's volatile memory until the end of *Session$_n$*. Output the signature (r_0, s_0).

Session$_i$(m_i, sk_V, pk_i): To sign message $m_i \in \mathbb{G}$, D does the following

$$k_i \leftarrow f(i) \cdot H(y_i^{k_0}), \; if \; f(i) \not\equiv 0 \bmod q;$$
$$k_i \xleftarrow{\$} \mathbb{Z}_q^*, \; otherwise;$$
$$r_i \leftarrow g^{k_i}, s_i \leftarrow k_i^{-1}[h(m_i) - a \cdot h(r_i)] \bmod q.$$

We remark that s_i is used as a data carrier for M_i. Output the signature (r_i, s_i).

Session$_j$(m_j, sk_V): To sign message $m_j \in \mathbb{G}$, D does the following

$$k_j \xleftarrow{\$} \mathbb{Z}_q^*, r_j \leftarrow g^{k_j}, s_j \leftarrow k_j^{-1}[h(m_j) - a \cdot h(r_j)] \bmod q.$$

Output the signature (r_j, s_j).

Recovering(M, R, S, SK_M): Compute $\alpha_i \leftarrow [s_i \cdot H(r_0^{x_i})]^{-1}$ and $\Delta_i \leftarrow \prod_{j \neq i} \frac{j}{j-i}$, $i, j \le \ell$. Recover a by computing

$$a \leftarrow \left(\sum_{i=1}^{\ell} \alpha_i h(m_i) \Delta_i - s_0^{-1} h(m_0) \right) \left(\sum_{i=1}^{\ell} \alpha_i h(r_i) \Delta_i - s_0^{-1} h(r_0) \right)^{-1} \bmod q. \quad (3)$$

The correctness of the *Recovering* algorithm can be obtained as follows. From *Session$_0$*, we obtain the value of k_0

$$k_0 \equiv s_0^{-1}[h(m_0) - a \cdot h(r_0)] \quad \bmod q. \quad (4)$$

From *Sessions$_i$*, we obtain M_i's share

$$f(i) \equiv [s_i \cdot H(y_i^{k_0})]^{-1} \cdot [h(m_i) - a \cdot h(r_i)] \quad \bmod q.$$

Using Lagrange interpolation we use the shares $f(i)$, $1 \le i \le \ell$ to recover k_0

$$k_0 \equiv \sum_{i=1}^{\ell} [s_i \cdot H(y_i^{k_0})]^{-1} \cdot [h(m_i) - a \cdot h(r_i)] \cdot \Delta_i \quad \bmod q. \quad (5)$$

From equalities (4) and (5) we obtain

$$a \cdot \left(\sum_{i=1}^{\ell} \alpha_i \cdot h(r_i) \cdot \Delta_i - s_0^{-1} \cdot h(r_0) \right) \equiv \sum_{i=1}^{\ell} \alpha_i \cdot h(m_i) \cdot \Delta_i - s_0^{-1} \cdot h(m_0) \bmod q.$$

Using the above equality and the fact that $y_i^{k_0} = r_0^{x_i}$, we obtain the correctness of the *Recovering* algorithm.

Remark 5. The probability that key recovery is not possible due to failure is $\epsilon = 1 - \left(1 - \frac{1}{q} \right)^{n-\ell+1}$. Since q is a large prime number, we have that $\epsilon \simeq 0$.

Remark 6. When all n participants are required to recover V's secret key, the ℓ out of ℓ scheme described in the full version of the paper [32] requires two infected signatures, while the above scheme requires n infected signatures. Thus, the scheme described in this section is less efficient in this case. Unfortunately, we could not devise a method to extend the ℓ out of ℓ scheme to an ℓ out of n threshold scheme.

Remark 7. The mechanism described in this section requires the malicious parties to directly compute V's secret key. In some cases this raises security concerns. For example, if the mechanism is used for surveillance purposes and a warrant is issued, if V's secret key is directly computed, when the warrant expires V can still be impersonated. In the full version of the paper [32] we present a two party protocol extension of our scheme in order to mitigate this issue. We could not find an extension for the ℓ out of ℓ scheme described in [32].

Remark 8. In the scheme described above, D plays the role of a trusted dealer, that leaks the shares using a subliminal channel to the n participants. This design choice was made in order to minimize communication between the malicious parties. The only moment when the participants communicate is when ℓ of them want to recover V's secret key.

Another possible scenario, was to use a secret sharing protocol with or without a trusted dealer between the n parties. After the participants agree on a shared public key $y_M = g^{x_M}$, the manufacturer implements, for example, the mechanism described in Sect. 2.4.[10] Note that this approach works without any modifications to the SETUP mechanism.

6   Conclusions

In this paper we introduced two threshold SETUP mechanisms that allow a group of malicious parties to recover a user's secret key. We adapted Shamir's secret sharing scheme [28] and the Hashed ElGamal encryption scheme [29] in order to infect the Generalized ElGamal signature scheme [22].

As an application of the devised threshold SETUP methods, in the full version of the paper [32] we present other schemes that can be modified in order to

---

[10] that uses y_M.

recover a user's secret key. We, also provide countermeasures for the mechanisms described in Sect. 5 and cover PRNGs based on the schemes described in Sects. 4 and 5.

Future Work. An interesting area of research would consist in finding a method to extend SETUP attacks applied to encryption schemes to threshold SETUP attacks. Also, it would be interesting to see if one can mount a successful SETUP attack or threshold SETUP attack if threshold signature schemes are used.

In [32] we describe an ℓ out of ℓ threshold SETUP mechanism that uses only two sessions in order to recover V's secret key. An extension to ℓ out of n may be more efficient than the approach from Sect. 5.

Acknowledgments. The author would like to thank Adrian Atanasiu, Alejandro Hevia, Tanja Lange, Diana Maimuţ and Ferucio Laurenţiu Ţiplea, and the anonymous reviewers for their helpful comments.

References

1. Abdalla, M., Bellare, M., Rogaway, P.: DHAES: an encryption scheme based on the diffie-hellman problem. IACR Cryptology ePrint Archive 1999/7 (1999)
2. Abdalla, M., Bellare, M., Rogaway, P.: The oracle diffie-hellman assumptions and an analysis of DHIES. In: Naccache, D. (ed.) CT-RSA 2001. LNCS, vol. 2020, pp. 143–158. Springer, Heidelberg (2001). https://doi.org/10.1007/3-540-45353-9_12
3. Albertini, A., Aumasson, J.-P., Eichlseder, M., Mendel, F., Schläffer, M.: Malicious hashing: eve's variant of SHA-1. In: Joux, A., Youssef, A. (eds.) SAC 2014. LNCS, vol. 8781, pp. 1–19. Springer, Cham (2014). https://doi.org/10.1007/978-3-319-13051-4_1
4. Ateniese, G., Magri, B., Venturi, D.: Subversion-resilient signature schemes. In: ACM-CCS 2015, pp. 364–375. ACM (2015)
5. Ball, J., Borger, J., Greenwald, G.: Revealed: how US and UK spy agencies defeat internet privacy and security, 5 September 2013. https://www.theguardian.com/world/2013/sep/05/nsa-gchq-encryption-codes-security
6. Bellare, M., Jaeger, J., Kane, D.: Mass-surveillance without the state: strongly undetectable algorithm-substitution attacks. In: ACM-CCS 2015, pp. 1431–1440. ACM (2015)
7. Bellare, M., Paterson, K.G., Rogaway, P.: Security of symmetric encryption against mass surveillance. In: Garay, J.A., Gennaro, R. (eds.) CRYPTO 2014. LNCS, vol. 8616, pp. 1–19. Springer, Heidelberg (2014). https://doi.org/10.1007/978-3-662-44371-2_1
8. Bellare, M., Rogaway, P.: Minimizing the use of random oracles in authenticated encryption schemes. In: Han, Y., Okamoto, T., Qing, S. (eds.) ICICS 1997. LNCS, vol. 1334, pp. 1–16. Springer, Heidelberg (1997). https://doi.org/10.1007/BFb0028457
9. Bernstein, D.J., Lange, T., Niederhagen, R.: Dual EC: a standardized back door. In: Ryan, P.Y.A., Naccache, D., Quisquater, J.-J. (eds.) The New Codebreakers. LNCS, vol. 9100, pp. 256–281. Springer, Heidelberg (2016). https://doi.org/10.1007/978-3-662-49301-4_17

10. Checkoway, S., et al.: A systematic analysis of the juniper dual EC incident. In: ACM-CCS 2016, pp. 468–479. ACM (2016)
11. Checkoway, S., et al.: On the practical exploitability of dual EC in TLS implementations. In: USENIX Security Symposium, pp. 319–335. USENIX Association (2014)
12. Daemen, J., Rijmen, V.: The Design of Rijndael: AES - The Advanced Encryption Standard. Springer, Heidelberg (2013). https://doi.org/10.1007/978-3-662-04722-4
13. Degabriele, J.P., Farshim, P., Poettering, B.: A more cautious approach to security against mass surveillance. In: Leander, G. (ed.) FSE 2015. LNCS, vol. 9054, pp. 579–598. Springer, Heidelberg (2015). https://doi.org/10.1007/978-3-662-48116-5_28
14. Degabriele, J.P., Paterson, K.G., Schuldt, J.C.N., Woodage, J.: Backdoors in pseudorandom number generators: possibility and impossibility results. In: Robshaw, M., Katz, J. (eds.) CRYPTO 2016. LNCS, vol. 9814, pp. 403–432. Springer, Heidelberg (2016). https://doi.org/10.1007/978-3-662-53018-4_15
15. Dodis, Y., Ganesh, C., Golovnev, A., Juels, A., Ristenpart, T.: A formal treatment of backdoored pseudorandom generators. In: Oswald, E., Fischlin, M. (eds.) EUROCRYPT 2015. LNCS, vol. 9056, pp. 101–126. Springer, Heidelberg (2015). https://doi.org/10.1007/978-3-662-46800-5_5
16. Dodis, Y., Mironov, I., Stephens-Davidowitz, N.: Message transmission with reverse firewalls—secure communication on corrupted machines. In: Robshaw, M., Katz, J. (eds.) CRYPTO 2016. LNCS, vol. 9814, pp. 341–372. Springer, Heidelberg (2016). https://doi.org/10.1007/978-3-662-53018-4_13
17. ElGamal, T.: A public key cryptosystem and a signature scheme based on discrete logarithms. IEEE Trans. Inf. Theory **31**(4), 469–472 (1985)
18. Fried, J., Gaudry, P., Heninger, N., Thomé, E.: A kilobit hidden SNFS discrete logarithm computation. In: Coron, J.-S., Nielsen, J.B. (eds.) EUROCRYPT 2017. LNCS, vol. 10210, pp. 202–231. Springer, Cham (2017). https://doi.org/10.1007/978-3-319-56620-7_8
19. Gennaro, R., Krawczyk, H., Rabin, T.: Secure hashed diffie-hellman over Non-DDH groups. In: Cachin, C., Camenisch, J.L. (eds.) EUROCRYPT 2004. LNCS, vol. 3027, pp. 361–381. Springer, Heidelberg (2004). https://doi.org/10.1007/978-3-540-24676-3_22
20. Gordon, D.M.: Designing and detecting trapdoors for discrete log cryptosystems. In: Brickell, E.F. (ed.) CRYPTO 1992. LNCS, vol. 740, pp. 66–75. Springer, Heidelberg (1993). https://doi.org/10.1007/3-540-48071-4_5
21. Maimuţ, D., Teşeleanu, G.: Secretly embedding trapdoors into contract signing protocols. In: Farshim, P., Simion, E. (eds.) SecITC 2017. LNCS, vol. 10543, pp. 166–186. Springer, Cham (2017). https://doi.org/10.1007/978-3-319-69284-5_12
22. Menezes, A.J., Van Oorschot, P.C., Vanstone, S.A.: Handbook of Applied Cryptography. CRC Press, Boca Raton (1996)
23. Mironov, I., Stephens-Davidowitz, N.: Cryptographic reverse firewalls. In: Oswald, E., Fischlin, M. (eds.) EUROCRYPT 2015. LNCS, vol. 9057, pp. 657–686. Springer, Heidelberg (2015). https://doi.org/10.1007/978-3-662-46803-6_22
24. Naor, M., Reingold, O.: Number-theoretic constructions of efficient pseudo-random functions. J. ACM (JACM) **51**(2), 231–262 (2004)
25. Perlroth, N., Larson, J., Shane, S.: NSA able to foil basic safeguards of privacy on web, 5 September 2013. https://www.nytimes.com/2013/09/06/us/nsa-foils-much-internet-encryption.html

26. Russell, A., Tang, Q., Yung, M., Zhou, H.-S.: Cliptography: clipping the power of kleptographic attacks. In: Cheon, J.H., Takagi, T. (eds.) ASIACRYPT 2016. LNCS, vol. 10032, pp. 34–64. Springer, Heidelberg (2016). https://doi.org/10.1007/978-3-662-53890-6_2

27. Russell, A., Tang, Q., Yung, M., Zhou, H.S.: Destroying steganography via amalgamation: kleptographically CPA secure public key encryption. IACR Cryptology ePrint Archive 2016/530 (2016)

28. Shamir, A.: How to share a secret. Commun. ACM **22**(11), 612–613 (1979)

29. Shoup, V.: Sequences of games: a tool for taming complexity in security proofs. IACR Cryptology ePrint Archive 2004/332 (2004)

30. Simmons, G.J.: The subliminal channel and digital signatures. In: Beth, T., Cot, N., Ingemarsson, I. (eds.) EUROCRYPT 1984. LNCS, vol. 209, pp. 364–378. Springer, Heidelberg (1985). https://doi.org/10.1007/3-540-39757-4_25

31. Simmons, G.J.: Subliminal communication is easy using the DSA. In: Helleseth, T. (ed.) EUROCRYPT 1993. LNCS, vol. 765, pp. 218–232. Springer, Heidelberg (1994). https://doi.org/10.1007/3-540-48285-7_18

32. Teşeleanu, G.: Threshold kleptographic attacks on discrete logarithm based signatures. IACR Cryptology ePrint Archive 2017/953 (2017)

33. Vazirani, U.V., Vazirani, V.V.: Trapdoor pseudo-random number generators, with applications to protocol design. In: FOCS 1983, pp. 23–30. IEEE (1983)

34. Young, A., Yung, M.: The dark side of "Black-Box" cryptography or: should we trust capstone? In: Koblitz, N. (ed.) CRYPTO 1996. LNCS, vol. 1109, pp. 89–103. Springer, Heidelberg (1996). https://doi.org/10.1007/3-540-68697-5_8

35. Young, A., Yung, M.: Kleptography: using cryptography against cryptography. In: Fumy, W. (ed.) EUROCRYPT 1997. LNCS, vol. 1233, pp. 62–74. Springer, Heidelberg (1997). https://doi.org/10.1007/3-540-69053-0_6

36. Young, A., Yung, M.: The prevalence of kleptographic attacks on discrete-log based cryptosystems. In: Kaliski, B.S. (ed.) CRYPTO 1997. LNCS, vol. 1294, pp. 264–276. Springer, Heidelberg (1997). https://doi.org/10.1007/BFb0052241

37. Young, A., Yung, M.: Malicious Cryptography: Exposing Cryptovirology. Wiley, Hoboken (2004)

38. Young, A., Yung, M.: Malicious cryptography: kleptographic aspects. In: Menezes, A. (ed.) CT-RSA 2005. LNCS, vol. 3376, pp. 7–18. Springer, Heidelberg (2005). https://doi.org/10.1007/978-3-540-30574-3_2

39. Zheng, Y., Seberry, J.: Immunizing public key cryptosystems against chosen ciphertext attacks. IEEE J. Sel. Areas Commun. **11**(5), 715–724 (1993)

Author Index

Printed in the United States
By Bookmasters